A CONTEMPORARY
INTRODUCTION TO THE BIBLE

A CONTEMPORARY INTRODUCTION TO THE BIBLE

SECOND EDITION

SACRED TEXTS AND IMPERIAL CONTEXTS

Colleen M. Conway and David M. Carr

WILEY Blackwell

Registered Offices
John Wiley & Sons, Inc., 111 River Street, Hoboken, NJ 07030, USA
John Wiley & Sons Ltd, The Atrium, Southern Gate, Chichester, West Sussex, PO19 8SQ, UK

Editorial Office
The Atrium, Southern Gate, Chichester, West Sussex, PO19 8SQ, UK

For details of our global editorial offices, customer services, and more information about Wiley products visit us at www.wiley.com.

Wiley also publishes its books in a variety of electronic formats and by print-on-demand. Some content that appears in standard print versions of this book may not be available in other formats.

Library of Congress Cataloging-in-Publication Data
A catalogue record for this book is available from the Library of Congress

Paperback ISBN: 9781119637059; ePub ISBN: 9781119636991; ePDF ISBN: 9781119637028.

Cover image: © Joseph Calev/Shutterstock
Cover design by Wiley

Set in 9.5/12pt STIX Two Text by Integra Software Services Pvt. Ltd, Pondicherry, India

10 9 8 7 6 5 4 3 2 1

CONTENTS

14 THE GOSPEL OF JOHN AND THE JOHANNINE LETTERS: TURNING INWARD AS A STRATEGY FOR LIFE IN THE EMPIRE   343

15 FOLLOWING CHRIST IN THE EMPIRE: DIVERSE APPROACHES IN THE NEW TESTAMENT   363

FIGURES

Maps

Main Discussions/Outlines of Biblical Books

Where to Find Basic Information on Biblical Books (Basics Boxes and More)

Below is a list of where you can find basic discussions of books (or major parts of books) in the Hebrew scriptures, with the books listed here in the order that they appear in the Jewish Tanakh (//Hebrew Bible). The page given in **bold number(s)** indicates where you can find a "Basics Box" that provides major information about a biblical book. This includes an outline, information about the time(s) in which the book was written, and (usually) a discussion of a major issue in interpretation of the book or text. In addition, some other pages are provided where you can find more information on different biblical books.

Genesis	48–51, 172–6, 184–5, **202–203**
Exodus	51–4, 179–89, **203–4**
Leviticus	**183**
Numbers	**204**
Deuteronomy	134–8, **135**
Joshua	42–5, **138–40**
Judges	**140–1**
1–2 Samuel	**142**, see also 62–5.
1–2 Kings	**143**
Isaiah	118–23, 167–71, **169**, 200, 209–11
Jeremiah	145–**149**
Ezekiel	164–7, **166**
Hosea	108–15, **111**
Amos	106–**108**
Jonah	199–200
Micah	115–18, **117**
Nahum	128–**129**
Zephaniah	**129**
Haggai	**195**
Zechariah	**196**
Psalms	69–75, **73**, 206–8, **207**
Job	**207**
Proverbs	78–82, **79**

BOXES

WHAT IS A MORE ON METHOD BOX?

These boxes give a brief introduction to methods used to interpret the Hebrew Bible. They detail the sorts of questions that each method attempts to answer, give an example of how the method has been applied, and include a reference to an article or book with more information about the method under discussion.

What Is in Special Topics Boxes?

These boxes offer extra information relevant to the broader discussion. Some pull together relevant dates for a period, while others show parallels between texts, or summarize information on a theme or question that relates to the topic at hand. This information is not optional or superfluous. Instead, these boxes highlight topics that are worth focused attention.

PREFACE

This book introduces students to the books of the Bible as shaped in the crucible of the history of Israel and the early church. A prominent theme throughout is the way the books of the Bible reflect quite different sorts of interaction with empires that dominated the ancient Near East and Mediterranean. At first some students and professors may find this approach unusual, since we do not begin with Genesis and do not proceed through biblical books in order. The group of texts introduced early on in this textbook is quite different from the Bible they now know. So why have we chosen this approach? There are many advantages. On the basis of our experience with using this approach we have seen that the picture of the Bible's development comes into focus as the narrative of its formation unfolds. By the end, students should find meaning in aspects of the Bible that they once overlooked, even as they also understand that much of the power of the Bible has been its capability to transcend the original contexts in which it was written. Moreover, through discussion of the history of Jewish and Christian interpretation of focus texts toward the end of many chapters, students will gain a taste of how faith communities have used the Bible in creative, inspired, and sometimes death-dealing ways to guide and make sense of their lives. Given the already large scope of this *Introduction*, we have focused on texts included in the Old and New Testaments, with a particular emphasis – in the case of the Hebrew Bible/Old Testament – on books included in the scriptures of Judaism and various forms of Christianity. This meant that we could not give sustained attention to apocryphal/deuterocanonical books of the Old Testament, or to the range of non-canonical early Christian works that did not end up being included in the Christian Bible.

The date framework given in this textbook follows that of Anson Rainey and Steven Notley's *The Sacred Bridge: Carta's Atlas of the Biblical World* (Jerusalem: Carta, 2005). In many cases specific dates are uncertain, but Rainey and Notley provide a recent, solid framework to start from on an introductory level. Unless otherwise indicated, the translations from Hebrew and Greek are our own.

As with any such textbook there is always room for improvement. We know that there are multiple ways in which virtually everything that is written here could be footnoted, qualified, and balanced with other perspectives. What this introduction provides is one general outline of a historical approach to the Bible that students can then supplement, correct, and balance in their future studies. We certainly invite all possible suggestions for correction and improvement of future editions of this textbook.

We have been helped by many people in writing this textbook. In particular, a diverse set of colleagues – Charles Carter, Thomas Dozeman, Esther Hamori, Mahri Leonard-Fleckman, Benjamin Sommer, Kent Reynolds, Robert Rezetko, Adele Reinhartz, Jerusha Rhodes, William Schniedewind,

Mark Smith, and Marvin Sweeney – generously reviewed portions of chapters on the Hebrew Bible and/or offered advice on revisions and corrections for the first edition or this second edition. In addition, students at Union Theological Seminary and Seton Hall University have read chapter drafts and suggested corrections, and we received some further helpful suggestions from anonymous reviewers recruited by Wiley Blackwell. Some students and teaching assistants who have offered a particularly large volume of helpful corrections are Mary Ellen Kris, Candice Olson, Lizzie Berne-DeGear, Laurel Koepf-Taylor, Meagan Manas, and Todd Kennedy. Maia Kotrosits provided timely assistance with the glossary and web materials. Our thanks to all for their generous help in this project.

Finally, with love we dedicate this volume to our parents, James and Patricia Conway, John (now departed) and Adrienne Carr, whose love of teaching and care for their students helped inspire this book.

Colleen M. Conway and David M. Carr

ACKNOWLEDGMENTS

The author and publisher gratefully acknowledge the permission granted to reproduce the copyrighted material in this book:

Figure 0.1	Biblia Hebraica Stuttgartensia, edited by Karl Elliger and Wilhelm Rudolph, Fifth Revised Edition, edited by Adrian Schenker, © 1977 and 1997 Deutsche Bibelgesellschaft, Stuttgart. Used by permission.
Figure 0.2	Israel Talby/Israel images/Alamy Stock Photo
Figure 1.1	FALKENSTEINFOTO/Alamy Stock Photo
Figure 2.1	Zev Radovan/BibleLandPictures/Alamy Stock Photo
Figure 2.3	bpk/Vorderasiatisches Museum, SMB/Gudrun Stenzel
Figure 2.4	Jürgen Liepe
Figure 3.1	Lloyd K. Townsend
Figure 3.2	William Schniedewind
Figure 3.3	akg-images/Erich Lessing
Figure 3.4	Courtesy of R. E. Tappy and The Zeitah Excavations Photograph by B. Zuckerman and M. Lundberg, overlay by P. K. McCarter, Jr.
Figure 3.5	Zev Radovan/BibleLandPictures/Alamy Stock Photo
Figure 3.6	© The Trustees of the British Museum. All rights reserved
Figure 3.7	www.BibleLandPictures.com/Alamy Stock Photo
Figure 3.8	Francis G. Mayer/Getty Images
Figure 4.1	Zev Radovan/BibleLandPictures/Alamy Stock Photo
Figure 4.2	akg-images/Erich Lessing
Figure 4.3	Zev Radovan/BibleLandPictures/Alamy Stock Photo
Figure 4.4	AP Images/NAM Y HUH
Figure 4.5	akg-images/Fototeca Gilardi
Figure 4.6	Stiftung BIBEL+ORIENT
Figure 4.7	Stiftung BIBEL+ORIENT
Figure 5.1	Stiftung BIBEL+ORIENT
Figure 6.1	Zev Radovan/BibleLandPictures/Alamy Stock Photo
Figure 6.2	akg-images/Erich Lessing
Figure 6.3	Puddingstone/Natural History Museum, London, UK/Bridgeman Images
Figure 7.1	Prisma by Dukas Presseagentur GmbH/Alamy Stock Photo
Figure 7.2	akg-images/Erich Lessing
Figure 8.1	Photo © The Israel Museum, Jerusalem
Figure 8.2	Courtesy of Carta, Jerusalem
Figure 9.1	Todd Bolen/BiblePlaces.com
Figure 9.2	Bojan Brecelj/Getty Images
Figure 9.3	Berthold Werner, Image taken from https://commons.wiki-media.org/wiki/File:Jerusalem_Modell_BW_2.JPG

Figure 9.4	Hulton Archive/Getty Images
Figure 9.5	https://commons.wikimedia.org/wiki/File:Sbs-0008_028r_Jesus_macht_die_Tonv%C3%B6gelchen_lebendig.TIF
Figure 9.6	The Picture Art Collection/Alamy Stock Photo
Figure 10.1	Todd Bolen/BiblePlaces.com
Figure 10.2	DEA/G. DAGLI ORTI/De Agostini/Getty Images
Figure 10.3	akg-images/Electa
Figure 10.4	DEA/G. DAGLI ORTI/De Agostini/Getty Images
Figure 10.5	Mary Evans Picture Library/Alinari
Figure 11.1	Courtesy of the American Numismatic Society
Figure 11.2	GRANGER COLLECTION (RDA)/Bridgeman Images
Figure 11.3	Courtesy of the Hecht Museum, University of Haifa, Israel
Figure 12.2	Richard Beacham (2005),The Emperor as Impresario: Producing the Pageantry of Power, pp 151-174. DOI: https://doi.org/10.1017/CCOL0521807964.008 reproduced by Cambridge University Press
Figure 13.1	Deutsches Archäologisches Institut Rome, D-DAI-ROM 1975.1289/photo Rossa
Figure 13.2	Photo Scala, Florence
Figure 13.3	© The Trustees of the British Museum. All rights reserved
Figure 14.1	Reproduced by courtesy of the University Librarian and Director, The John Rylands University Library, The University of Manchester
Figure 14.2	Web Gallery of Art, Image taken from https://commons.wikimedia.org/wiki/File:13th-century_unknown_painters_-_Crucifixion_with_Two_Roundels_-_WGA23753.jpg
Figure 15.1	akg-images/Pirozzi
Figure 15.2	William Blake, Image taken from https://commons.wikimedia.org/wiki/File:Whore-of-babylon-blake-1809.jpg
Figure 16.1	Andre Nantel/Shutterstock.com
Figure 16.2	Granger, NYC./Granger Historical Picture Archive/Alamy Stock Photo

Chapter opener photo © Joseph Chalev/Shutterstock.com

The Pharaoh Merneptah hymn in Chapter 3, page 64, and the Cyrus cylinder text in Chapter 7, page 187: Pritchard, James; *Ancient Near Eastern Texts Relating to the Old Testament – Third Edition with Supplement*. © 1950, 1955, 1969, renewed 1978 by Princeton University Press. Reprinted by permission of Princeton University Press.

At points throughout the book extracts have been used from the Revised Standard Version of the Bible: Revised Standard Version of the Bible, copyright 1952 (2nd edition, 1971) by the Division of Christian Education of the National Council of the Churches of Christ in the United States of America. Used by permission. All rights reserved.

The publisher apologizes for any errors or omissions in the above list and would be grateful if notified of any corrections that should be incorporated in future reprints or editions of this book.

ABBREVIATIONS

ANET	James Pritchard (ed.), *Ancient Near Eastern Texts Relating to the Old Testament with Supplement*. Princeton: Princeton University Press, 1969.
George	Andrew George, *The Babylonian Gilgamesh Epic: Introduction, Critical Edition and Cuneiform Texts*. New York: Oxford University Press, 2003.
Livingstone	Alasdair Livingstone (ed.), *Court Poetry and Literary Miscellanea*. State Archives of Assyria, 3. Helsinki: Helsinki University Press, 1989.
NJPS	*The New Jewish Publication Society Tanakh Translation*. Philadelphia: Jewish Publication Society, 1985.
NRSV	*The New Revised Standard Version of the Bible*. New York: National Council of Churches, 1989.
NT	New Testament
OT	Old Testament
OT Parallels	Victor Matthews and Don Benjamin, *Old Testament Parallels: Laws and Stories from the Ancient Near East* (3rd revised and expanded edition). Mahwah, NJ: Paulist Press, 2007.

For Bible abbreviations, see the Prologue, "Bible Abbreviations, Chapters and Verses."

Asterisks after Bible citations, e.g. "Genesis 12–50*," indicate that only parts of the cited texts are included.

//indicate that the texts before and after the slashes are parallel to each other.

OVERVIEW OF THE HISTORICAL PERIOD

This shows major periods and corresponding texts covered in this book.

DATES	1250–1000 BCE (13th–11th centuries)	1000–930 (10th century)	930–800 (10th–9th centuries)	800–700 (8th century)	700–586 (7th and early 6th centuries)	586–538 (6th century)	538–332 (6th–4th centuries)	332–63 (4th–1st centuries)	63 BCE–100 CE (1st century BCE to 1st century CE)
Chapter	2	3	4	4	5	6	7	8	9–15
MAJOR EVENTS (IN CHRON-OLOGI-CAL ORDER)	Spread of villages in hill country Tribal "Israel" emerges Saul's chieftain-ship	Formation of Davidic monarchy Jerusalem taken as capital of Judah/Israel David and Solomon	Formation of northern kingdom of "Israel" Rise and fall of Omride dynasty	Domi-nation and destruc-tion of northern "Israel" by Assyria Domi-nation of Judah by Assyria	Eventual decline of Assyrian power Enact-ment of Josiah's "reform" Decline of Judah into dom-ination by Babylon First wave of exile	Destruc-tion of Jeru-salem and its Temple Second and third waves of exile of elites to Babylon	Persian victory, waves of return, rebuilding of Temple Nehe-miah's rebuilding of the wall Divorce of foreign wives under Ezra and elevation of Torah	Hellenistic rule Hellenizing crisis Hasmo-nean kingdom	Roman rule
MAJOR WRIT-INGS (AND ORAL TRADI-TIONS)	(No writings, but oral traditions about exodus, trickster ancestors)	Royal and Zion psalms Proverbs (early forms of other texts like the non-P primeval history)	Jacob narrative Joseph narrative Exodus – wilder-ness story Song of Deborah	Prophecy to the north by Amos and Hosea Prophecy to the south by Micah and Isaiah	Formation of Deuteron-omy and following historical books (Joshua–2 Kings) Nahum and Zepha-niah Early proph-ecies from Jeremiah	Exilic additions to biblical books Lamen-tations Ezekiel and Second Isaiah Non-P (L) narrative of early Israel P coun-ter-narrative of early Israel	Haggai Zechariah Nehemiah memoir Temple rebuilding Ezra narrative Third Isaiah Combined L/P Pentateuch Psalter	Early parts of Enoch Ben Sira Ezra–Nehe-miah Esther 1–2 Chronicles Daniel 1–2 Maccabees Judith	Most of the New Testa-ment
MAJOR NEW IDEAS AND THEMES	Election theology	Royal/Zion theology			Exclusive devotion to Yahweh enforced (briefly) by Josiah	Mono-theism	Dual Temple – Torah focus	Judaism Resur-rection	Emer-gent belief in Jesus as messiah and Son of God

TIMELINE

Important texts are noted in **bold**.

BCE	SOUTH (Judah)	NORTH ("Israel" in narrower sense)
1300	(Waning Egyptian domination of Canaan)	
		Spread of villages in Israelite hill country
1200		Merneptah Stela
		(Assorted battles, e.g. Deborah, of hill-country Israelites with neighbors)
		Oral exodus traditions
		Oral ancestral traditions
1100		**Oral victory traditions**
	Saul's "chieftainship"	
	David (Hebron; 1010–1002)	
1000	David (Jerusalem; 1002–970)	
	Royal psalms, Zion psalms	
	Solomon (Jerusalem; 970–930)	
	Proverb collections (early form??) **Non-P primeval history**	
	Rehoboam (Jerusalem)	Jeroboam founds northern monarchy
900		(early written forms of) **Jacob narrative, Joseph novella exodus-Moses narrative, and Song of Deborah**
		Omride dynasty (880–841)
800		Jehu's coup (841)
		Jeroboam II (782–753)
	Isaiah (start of collection)	**Amos**
	Syro-Ephraimite war (735–734)	
	Assyrian domination of Israel begins (745–)	
		Hosea
		Assyrian domination of Judah begins (734–)
		Isaiah (continued), **Micah**
	Hezekiah (715–686)	Assyrian destruction of Israel (722)
		Hezekiah's rebellion and reform (705)

700   Sennacherib's attack and mysterious withdrawal (701)
        Manasseh (697–642)
        Amon (642–640)   (Waning of Assyrian power)
        Josiah (640–609)
                        Zephaniah
                        Josiah's reform (623)
                        Josianic edition of Deuteronomy, 2 Kings, etc
                                    (Fall of Nineveh, Assyria's capital)
                        Nahum
                        Jeremiah
        Domination of Judah by Babylonia
600   First wave of exiles (597)
                                    Ezekiel's early prophecy

        Destruction of Jerusalem
        and second wave of exiles
        (586)
                                    Lamentations and Psalm 137
                                    Ezekiel's later prophecy

        Third wave of exiles (582)
                                    Exilic additions to Deuteronomy,
                                    2 Kings, and other books
                                    Non-P/L Pentateuchal Source
                                    (incorporating exilic-modified
                                    forms of older non-P primeval his-
                                    tory, Jacob–Joseph story,
                                    exodus-Moses story, and
                                    Deuteronomy)
                                    Priestly Pentateuchal Source
                                    Second Isaiah
        Persian conquering of
        Babylonian empire (539)
                                    First wave of returnees (538)
                                    Another wave, beginning of Temple
        restoration (532)

                                    Another wave with Zerubbabel,
                                    completion of Temple rebuilding
                                    (520–515)
500   **Haggai and Zechariah (1–9)**
        Nehemiah's return and governorships (445–425)
        (rebuilding wall, purification of priesthood)
        Nehemiah memoir
400   Return with Ezra, divorce of foreign wives, elevation of Torah (397–)
        Combined (P and non-P/L) Pentateuch
        Narratives of Temple-rebuilding and Ezra
        Third Isaiah
        Psalter (final, Torah-oriented version of the book)
        Greek conquering of Persian empire (332)

300	(Shifting domination of Palestine by Greek Ptolemies [Egypt] and Seleucids [Mesopotamia]; 332–142) **Early parts of Enoch** **1–2 Chronicles** **Wisdom of Ben Sira**
200	Jason purchase of high priesthood, attempt to Hellenize Jerusalem (174) Menelaus purchase of high priesthood (171) and Judean rebellion against him **Daniel** Antiochus Epiphanes IV campaign to eradicate observant Judaism and beginning of Hasmonean-led rebellion against Hellenistic rule (167–) Purification and rededication of Temple (164) Hasmonean independence and rule (142–63) **Ezra–Nehemiah, Esther** **1–2 Maccabees, Judith**
100	Roman takeover of Palestine (63) Rule of Herod in Palestine (40–4) Beginning of Roman empire with reign of Caesar Augustus (Octavian) (27) Birth of Jesus (4?)
CE	**Paul's letters (50s)** Jewish War (first Jewish revolt) (66–70) Destruction of the Temple (70)

Gospel of Mark
Gospels of Matthew and Luke
Acts of the Apostles
Revelation of John
Gospel of John
Pastoral Epistles

Second Jewish revolt (132–5)

MAP 0.1

The ancient Near East. Redrawn from Adrian Curtis (ed.), *Oxford Bible Atlas* (4th edition). Oxford, New York: Oxford University Press, 2007, page 67.

Orientation to Multiple Bibles and Multiple Translations

Chapter Outline

Chapter Overview

This prologue helps you learn the basic characteristics and background of the Bible that you will use across the course. As you will see, not all Bibles are the same. Judaism and different forms of Christianity include different books in their Bibles. Also, ancient manuscripts of the Bible diverge from one another, and contemporary translations follow different manuscript readings and translation practices. By the end of this chapter you should know the differences between the bibles of Judaism and Christianity, as well as the relationship of the Islamic Qur'an to both sets of scriptures. You will also learn how the study of different readings of ancient manuscripts of the Bible, "textual criticism," and advances in knowledge of ancient languages have led to major progress in translation of the Bible since the King James Version was completed in 1611. Finally, you will learn some basic things to keep in mind in choosing and using an up-to-date English translation of the Bible.

A Contemporary Introduction to the Bible: Sacred Texts and Imperial Contexts, Second Edition. Colleen M. Conway and David M. Carr.
© 2021 Colleen M. Conway and David M. Carr. Published 2021 by John Wiley & Sons Ltd.

EXERCISES

1. Using the parallels provided at the end of the chapter in Appendix 1, compare the translations of (and paraphrase) Isa 52:13–15. What differences do you notice?
2. Take a look at two pages of a biblical book in your Bible. Make a list of *all* types of elements on those pages aside from the actual text of the Bible. Using the discussions in this chapter, identify where those elements came from.

The Bible as a Complex Product of Many Hands

We start here with your Bible – the book that you hold in your hands. A major aim of this chapter, and this *Introduction* as a whole, is to give you a deeper appreciation of the way this seeming simple book is actually the complex product of centuries of human work. The last stages of that work are already obvious when you take a closer look at the Bible you hold in your hands. Notice the type of cover it is packaged in (unless you are working with a digital copy!). Look at the typeface used for the biblical text and various aids that are provided for you as a reader (depending on your particular Bible): paragraph divisions, headings for different Bible passages, and maybe some cross-references to other Bible passages or brief explanatory notes. None of these aspects come from ancient manuscripts. They are aids that the publisher of your Bible provides to you as a reader.

These parts of your Bible, however, are just the first set of ways that your Bible has been worked into the form you have it now. Take, for example, the chapter and verse numbers in your Bible. None appear in ancient manuscripts. They were added to the text over a thousand years after it was written. Or consider the translation in your Bible. The biblical texts were originally written in Hebrew, Aramaic (an ancient language similar to Hebrew), and Greek. We will see in this prologue how every translation of these ancient texts involves significant style decisions, reasoned guesses, and compromises. In addition, we have multiple, handwritten copies of ancient biblical manuscripts. These ancient copies disagree with each other. As a result, a translator must not just decide how to translate a given biblical verse. She or he also must choose which manuscript reading to translate in the first place. And all this does not even get into the centuries-long process that produced these ancient Hebrew, Aramaic, and Greek biblical texts, or how they were collected into specific scriptural collections by Jews and Christians. That long process will be the focus of much of the rest of this *Introduction*.

For now we are focusing on some of the elements that were added to those texts in the Bible before you, many of which distinguish one Bible that you might find from another. These include what books are included and in what order, what kind of translation is used, and how translators chose, for a given phrase or word, to follow a reading in one ancient manuscript versus another.

This prologue discusses these elements in turn, aiming to help you be a more informed user of your Bible.

The Different Scriptures of Judaism and Christianity

To begin, it is important to recognize that the Bibles of different faith communities contain somewhat different books, put those books in different order, and call their Bibles different things. Your Bible reflects one of those collections or a mix of them. These are often referred to as different "canons" of the Bible, with "**canon**" meaning a collection of books that are recognized as a divinely inspired scripture by a given religious community. Such books are recognized as "**canonical**."

The Jewish people calls its Scriptures the "**TaNaK**" (or "**Tanakh**," with the kh pronounced like the ch in Bach). Tanakh is a word formed out of the Hebrew names of the three main parts of the Jewish Bible: **Torah** (Genesis, Exodus, Leviticus, Numbers, and Deuteronomy), *Neviim* ("prophets"), and *Ketuvim* ("writings"). See the box on "Contents of the Hebrew Bible/Tanakh/Old Testament" for an overview of the contents of each of these three parts. Judaism focuses particularly on the Torah, otherwise known as the **Pentateuch**, with most synagogues reading the Torah's five books all across the year, starting with Genesis at the outset of the Fall (the Jewish New Year) and concluding with Deuteronomy twelve months later. Jews certainly read other parts of the Tanakh, for example singing psalms (part of the "Writings") and reading portions of the "Prophets" to accompany the Torah reading. Nevertheless, the Torah takes pride of place within the Jewish Bible, while other parts of the Tanakh are often seen as a commentary on it. In accordance with an emphasis in Judaism on temple and purity, the overall Tanakh concludes on a hopeful note, as 2 Chronicles anticipates a new rebuilding of the Temple (2 Chr 36:22–3).

The Christian version of these scriptures, the "**Old Testament**" (OT), is part of a two-part Bible that also includes specifically Christian scriptures, the **New Testament** (NT). Later in this *Introduction* (starting in Chapter 9) we will look more closely at the writings in the New Testament. For now, we focus on similarities and differences between the Christian Old Testament and the Jewish Tanakh. Most importantly, these similar sets of scriptures are organized differently. Though both the Tanakh and the Christian Old Testament start with the biblical narrative-historical books of Genesis to 2 Kings, the Christian Old Testament then goes straight to the parallel narration of that history in Chronicles, Ezra, and Nehemiah. It then sequences the other biblical books in the order of their traditional authors, starting with the book of Job (an early Edomite sage), and moving through Psalms (David as traditional author), Proverbs, Ecclesiastes, and Song of Songs (Solomon as traditional author), and on to the major (Isaiah, Jeremiah, Ezekiel) and minor (Hosea, etc.) prophets. As in the case of the Jewish Tanakh, the ending of the Christian Old Testament is revealing. It concludes with the last chapter of Malachi, a prediction of the second coming of Elijah (Mal 4:5). This ending leads nicely into the first book

Contents of the Hebrew Bible/Tanakh/Old Testament			
Jewish Tanakh	Protestant OT	Roman Catholic OT (*italics* = not in Tanakh)	Eastern Orthodox OT (*italics* = not in Tanakh)
Torah	**(Pentateuch)**	**(Pentateuch)**	**(Pentateuch)**
Genesis, Exodus, Leviticus, Numbers, Deuteronomy	Genesis, Exodus, Leviticus, Numbers, Deuteronomy	Genesis, Exodus, Leviticus, Numbers, Deuteronomy	Genesis, Exodus, Leviticus, Numbers, Deuteronomy
Prophets (Neviim)	**(Historical Books)**	**(Historical Books)**	**(Historical Books)**
Former prophets			
Joshua, Judges	Joshua, Judges	Joshua, Judges	Joshua, Judges
	Ruth	Ruth	Ruth
1–2 Samuel	1–2 Samuel	1–2 Samuel	1–2 Samuel
1–2 Kings	1–2 Kings	1–2 Kings	1–2 Kings
	1–2 Chronicles	1–2 Chronicles	1–2 Chronicles
Latter prophets	Ezra–Nehemiah	Ezra–Nehemiah	Ezra–Nehemiah
			1 Esdras (2 Esdras in
Major prophets			*Russian Orthodox)*
		Tobit	*Tobit*
Isaiah		*Judith*	*Judith*
Jeremiah	Esther	Esther (*with additions*)	Esther (*with additions*)
Ezekiel		*1–2 Maccabees*	*1–3 Maccabees*
Minor prophets/	**(Poetical Books)**	**(Poetical Books)**	**(Poetical Books)**
book of the twelve			
	Job	Job	Job
Hosea, Joel, Amos,	Psalms	Psalms	Psalms (with Psalm 151)
Obadiah, Jonah,	Proverbs	Proverbs	Proverbs
Micah, Nahum,	Ecclesiastes	Ecclesiastes	Ecclesiastes
Habakkuk,	Song of solomon	Song of solomon	Song of solomon
Zephaniah, Haggai,		*Wisdom of Solomon*	*Wisdom of Solomon*
Zechariah, Malachi		*Sirach*	*Sirach*
Writings (Ketuvim)	**(Prophets)**	**(Prophets)**	**(Prophets)**
Psalms	Isaiah	Isaiah	Isaiah
Proverbs	Jeremiah	Jeremiah	Jeremiah
Job	Lamentations	Lamentations	Lamentations
		Baruch	*Baruch*
Five festal scrolls		*Letter of Jeremiah*	*Letter of Jeremiah*
Song of Songs	Ezekiel	Ezekiel	Ezekiel
Ruth	Daniel	Daniel (*with additions*)	Daniel (*with additions*)
Lamentations	Hosea, Joel, Amos,	Hosea, Joel, Amos,	Hosea, Joel, Amos,
Ecclesiastes	Obadiah, Jonah,	Obadiah, Jonah,	Obadiah, Jonah,
Esther	Micah, Nahum,	Micah, Nahum,	Micah, Nahum,
	Habakkuk,	Habakkuk,	Habakkuk,
Daniel	Zephaniah, Haggai,	Zephaniah, Haggai,	Zephaniah, Haggai,
Ezra–Nehemiah	Zechariah, Malachi	Zechariah, Malachi	Zechariah, Malachi
1–2 Chronicles			*4 Maccabees* (appendix)

of the New Testament, the Gospel of Matthew, which describes the coming of John the Baptist, who is clothed like Elijah, and prophesies the coming of Jesus (Matt 3:1–6).

You should also know that there are differences between the books included in different Christian Old Testament collections. The Protestant Old Testament contains the same books as the Jewish Tanakh, though in the above-noted different order leading up to the New Testament. The Roman Catholic Old Testament includes some additional books such as 1 and 2 Maccabees, Sirach, and the Wisdom of Solomon. The Ethiopic church recognizes the book of Enoch as part of its Old Testament, and various forms of Orthodox Christianity likewise recognize slightly different groups of additional books. For Roman Catholics, such additional books (not in the Jewish Tanakh) are "**deuterocanonical**," which means that they belong to a "second canon." For Protestants, such books not in the Jewish Tanakh are not considered true scripture, but "**apocrypha**," which means "books hidden away." We will not hide such books away in this textbook, but neither will we be able to discuss them at length. Instead, in Chapter 8 of this *Introduction*, we will briefly discuss a sampling of them: Ben Sira/Sirach, Enoch, and Judith. In addition, we will discuss how Jewish and Christian communities ended up with these slightly different collections of scriptural books.

"**Hebrew Bible**" is yet another term that is often used to designate the scriptures shared by Jews and Christians. Many people prefer the expression "Hebrew Bible" because it avoids the pejorative connotations that the term "Old Testament" has assumed in many Christian circles. The terms "Old" and "New Testament" derive from Greek and Latin terms that have been used by Christians to contrast an old covenant (with Israel) and new covenant through Jesus Christ. Often this has been part of a Christian **supersessionist** assumption that God's covenant with the world through Christ superseded any prior covenant that God made with Israel. For Christians who subscribe to this idea, the Old Testament is often treated as the *Old* and superseded Testament. It is seen as the outdated book of the "law," as opposed to the New Testament, which is understood to be the truly scriptural word about Jesus, love, and grace. Such views reflect a lack of close reading of both the Old and the New Testament, but they are widespread and influential. This is why many people avoid the term "Old Testament," with its possible implications of **supersessionism**, and use terms such as "Hebrew Bible" or "First Testament" instead. Others, however, find these terms odd and/ or inaccurate (for example, several chapters in the Tanakh/Old Testament are not in Hebrew, but Aramaic). They prefer sticking with the Christian term "Old Testament," at least within specifically Christian contexts, but emphasize the more ancient understanding of "Old" as implying something good, rather than the more contemporary idea of "Old" being something that is outdated.

The important thing for academic study of the Bible is to understand the meanings of these different terms for the Tanakh/Old Testament/Hebrew scriptures and the slight differences in contents and order of these otherwise similar collections. These differences reflect the fact that these scriptures have come to belong to multiple faith communities. In addition, the Islamic tradition sees the scriptures of Judaism and Christianity as possessing a secondary authority to that of its central text, the **Qur'an**. From the Islamic perspective, the Qur'an represents the final part of a long line of divine revelations to human communities, including the Jewish Tanakh and Christian Old and New Testaments.. This Qur'an is quite different in contents from the Tanakh/Old Testament, containing 114 chapters (surahs) of primarily ethical and theological exhortations that were communicated by the prophet Muhammad. It is not a parallel "Old Testament" or "Tanakh." Nevertheless, parts of the Qur'an reflect post-biblical Jewish traditions about history up to Moses (e.g. about Abraham, Ishmael, Mary) and other Muslim traditions (e.g. the biography and example of the prophet Muhammad).

From this discussion, we can see that there is no one "Bible," not even one "Hebrew Bible," shared by Judaism and Christianity, let alone Islam. Even if we focus on the overlapping contents of the Jewish Tanakh and Christian Old

Testament, there are significant differences in order and (occasionally) content as well. This is an initial indicator of the quite different readings that Christians and Jews give to the texts they hold in common. We will see others along the way. Moreover, this diversity of Jewish and Christian Bibles is preceded by a diversity of perspectives and voices found within the Hebrew scriptures themselves. In the following chapters, we will see this diversity in texts written at different times and even in texts offering different perspectives on the same time.

Basics on Bible Translations

Since most students do not know Hebrew, Aramaic, or Greek, they can only read a Bible in translation. There are several things that every user of such Bible translations should know about them in order to be an informed user.

First, every translation involves many decisions by the translator about the Hebrew, Greek, or (in a few cases) Aramaic text. Scholars are still not sure about the meanings of some words, and the biblical languages do not translate precisely into English (or other modern languages). In addition, we have no original manuscript of any biblical book, and the existing biblical manuscripts disagree with each other at many points. This means that scholars must use **textual criticism** to decide the best Hebrew, Aramaic, or Greek text in each case where the manuscripts disagree with each other. Luckily, over the last several centuries much progress has been made in uncovering ancient manuscripts and learning to identify copying errors and other changes in such manuscripts. In addition, there has been a huge growth in knowledge about the biblical languages.

More on Method: Textual Criticism

As indicated in the text, "textual criticism" is not a general study of a text. Instead, textual criticism studies the diverse *ancient manuscript copies* of biblical texts, analyzing their development and providing data that can be used to choose which reading of a biblical text to follow. Over the centuries scribes have introduced tens of thousands of minor changes into biblical texts as they have copied them by hand. Some changes were introduced by accident, as when a scribe might accidentally copy a given line twice or confuse letters. Other changes seem more intentional, where a scribe seems to have added a clarification of a place name or a theological correction or expansion. The ancient copies are often termed **manuscript witnesses** because they "witness" to diverse forms of these hand-copied texts.

Deciding which reading to follow A translator or translation committee often needs to decide word by word whether to follow a reading in one manuscript tradition or another. To do this, most scholars use "critical editions" prepared by textual critics that gather and compare the readings found in ancient biblical manuscripts (see Figure 0.1 on p. 8). For the Hebrew Bible, the usual comparison point is the **Masoretic text (MT)**, the authoritative version of the Hebrew/Aramaic text that was produced by Jewish scribes in the medieval period. Most critical editions feature a high-quality version of the Masoretic text as the main section of each page. Notes in the critical edition then provide an overview of variant readings from other important manuscript witnesses for the Hebrew Bible, such as the biblical manuscripts found at the Dead Sea (Qumran), the Pentateuch preserved by the Samaritan community (around Samaria in the north), and very early translations of early Hebrew manuscripts, especially the **Septuagint (LXX)**, an ancient set of translations of various biblical books into Greek.

Drawing on this data, a translator must then decide on which ancient manuscript reading to follow and translate, often determining that some ancient readings are errors, while other manuscripts witness to an earlier, better reading, at least for a given verse or phrase. On occasion, a biblical scholar may judge that all of the manuscript witnesses preserve an error. In such cases, that scholar may propose a reading that is not preserved in any manuscript. This second method of correction is called **conjectural emendation**.

These advances in knowledge about the text and language of the Bible mean that academic study of the Bible requires use of up-to-date translations of the biblical text. The **King James Version** (also known as the KJV or "Authorized Version"), though beautiful and cherished by many, is not an up-to-date translation. It was done four hundred years ago. Scholars then knew far less about biblical languages than they do now. Moreover, the KJV translation is based on unusually corrupt manuscripts with more errors and expansions than higher-quality biblical manuscripts used today. Therefore, the King James Version should not be used for readings in a twenty-first-century academic course on the Bible.

Translations also vary in religious perspective. The New Jewish Publication Society (NJPS) translation obviously comes out of a tradition of Jewish interpretation of the Tanakh. The New Jerusalem Bible (NJB) and New American Bible (NAB) were produced by Catholic scholars. The New Revised Standard Version (NRSV; preceded by the Revised Standard Version – RSV) aims to be an ecumenical translation, but it is part of a line of Protestant revisions of the King James Version. The New International Version (NIV; now available in updated form as Today's New International Version) is also Protestant and was conceived as an evangelical alternative to the RSV/NRSV.

Translations also vary in style: whether they aim to stay as close to the biblical languages as possible or whether they aim for maximum readability. **Formal correspondence** translations, while still containing interpretation on the part of translators, aim to stay as close as possible to word-for-word translation of the Hebrew, Aramaic, or Greek text. This can make them good tools for study, but it also makes them more difficult to understand. Translations that tend toward formal correspondence include the NRSV, NIV, and New American Standard Bible (NASB). Other translations tend toward **dynamic equivalence**, which aims for equivalent meaning, but not a word-for-word translation. This results in translations that are more readable, but also may contain

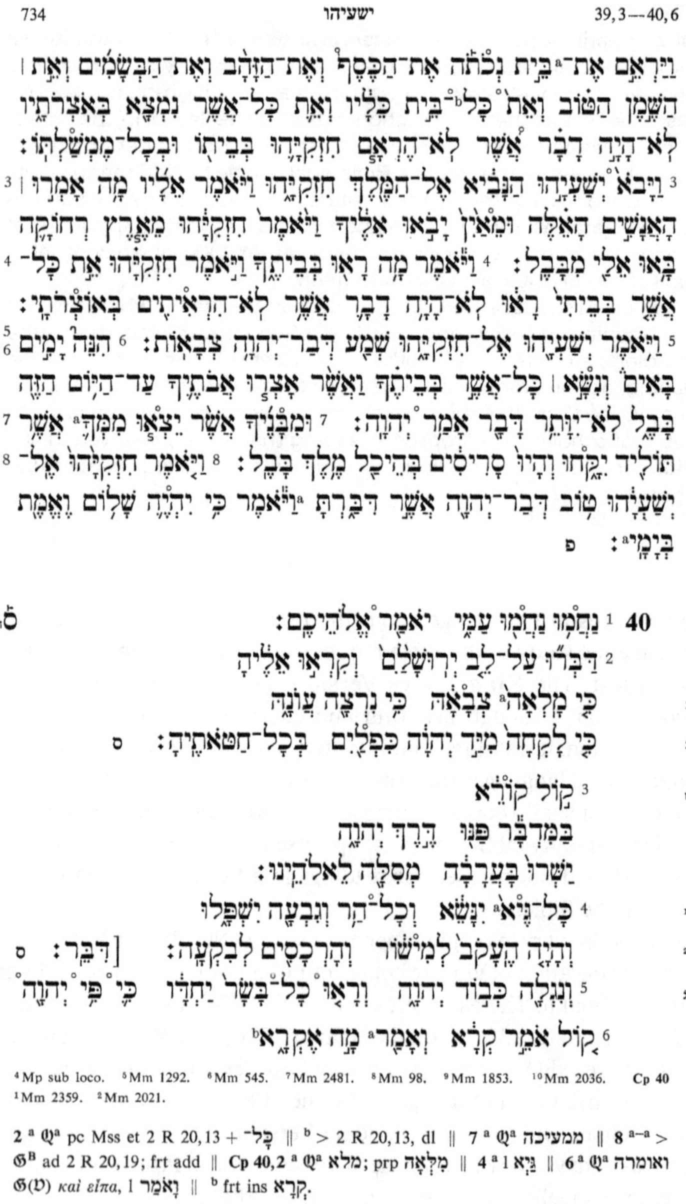

734   ישעיהו   39,3—40,6

וַיַּרְאֵם אֶת־כׇּל־בֵּית נְכֹתֹה אֶת־הַכֶּסֶף וְאֶת־הַזָּהָב וְאֶת־הַבְּשָׂמִים וְאֵת |

הַשֶּׁמֶן הַטּוֹב וְאֵת כׇּל־בֵּית כֵּלָיו וְאֵת כׇּל־אֲשֶׁר נִמְצָא בְּאֹצְרֹתָיו

לֹא־הָיָה דָבָר אֲשֶׁר לֹא־הֶרְאָם חִזְקִיָּהוּ בְּבֵיתוֹ וּבְכׇל־מֶמְשַׁלְתּוֹ:

3 וַיָּבֹא יְשַׁעְיָהוּ הַנָּבִיא אֶל־הַמֶּלֶךְ חִזְקִיָּהוּ וַיֹּאמֶר אֵלָיו מָה אָמְרוּ |

הָאֲנָשִׁים הָאֵלֶּה וּמֵאַיִן יָבֹאוּ אֵלֶיךָ וַיֹּאמֶר חִזְקִיָּהוּ מֵאֶרֶץ רְחוֹקָה

בָּאוּ אֵלַי מִבָּבֶל: 4 וַיֹּאמֶר מָה רָאוּ בְּבֵיתֶךָ וַיֹּאמֶר חִזְקִיָּהוּ אֵת כׇּל־

אֲשֶׁר בְּבֵיתִי רָאוּ לֹא־הָיָה דָבָר אֲשֶׁר לֹא־הִרְאִיתִים בְּאוֹצְרֹתָי:

5 וַיֹּאמֶר יְשַׁעְיָהוּ אֶל־חִזְקִיָּהוּ שְׁמַע דְּבַר־יְהוָה צְבָאוֹת: 6 הִנֵּה יָמִים

בָּאִים | וְנִשָּׂא כׇּל־אֲשֶׁר בְּבֵיתֶךָ וַאֲשֶׁר אָצְרוּ אֲבֹתֶיךָ עַד־הַיּוֹם הַזֶּה

בָּבֶל לֹא־יִוָּתֵר דָּבָר אָמַר יְהוָה: 7 וּמִבָּנֶיךָ אֲשֶׁר יֵצְאוּ מִמְּךָ אֲשֶׁר

תּוֹלִיד יִקָּחוּ וְהָיוּ סָרִיסִים בְּהֵיכַל מֶלֶךְ בָּבֶל: 8 וַיֹּאמֶר חִזְקִיָּהוּ אֶל־

יְשַׁעְיָהוּ טוֹב דְּבַר־יְהוָה אֲשֶׁר דִּבַּרְתָּ וַיֹּאמֶר כִּי יִהְיֶה שָׁלוֹם וֶאֱמֶת

בְּיָמָי: פ

1 **40** נַחֲמוּ נַחֲמוּ עַמִּי יֹאמַר אֱלֹהֵיכֶם:

2 דַּבְּרוּ עַל־לֵב יְרוּשָׁלַ͏ִם וְקִרְאוּ אֵלֶיהָ

כִּי מָלְאָה צְבָאָהּ כִּי נִרְצָה עֲוֺנָהּ

כִּי לָקְחָה מִיַּד יְהוָה כִּפְלַיִם בְּכׇל־חַטֹּאתֶיהָ: ס

3 קוֹל קוֹרֵא

בַּמִּדְבָּר פַּנּוּ דֶּרֶךְ יְהוָה

יַשְּׁרוּ בָּעֲרָבָה מְסִלָּה לֵאלֹהֵינוּ:

4 כׇּל־גֶּיא יִנָּשֵׂא וְכׇל־הַר וְגִבְעָה יִשְׁפָּלוּ

וְהָיָה הֶעָקֹב לְמִישׁוֹר וְהָרְכָסִים לְבִקְעָה: [דָּבֵּר: ס

5 וְנִגְלָה כְּבוֹד יְהוָה וְרָאוּ כׇל־בָּשָׂר יַחְדָּו כִּי פִּי יְהוָה

6 קוֹל אֹמֵר קְרָא וְאָמַר מָה אֶקְרָא

---

4 Mp sub loco.   5 Mm 1292.   6 Mm 545.   7 Mm 2481.   8 Mm 98.   9 Mm 1853.   10 Mm 2036.   **Cp 40**
1 Mm 2359.   2 Mm 2021.

2 a 𝔔ᵃ pc Mss et 2 R 20,13 + כׇּל־ ‖ b > 2 R 20,13, dl ‖ 7 a 𝔔ᵃ ממעיכה ‖ 8 ᵃ⁻ᵃ >
𝔊ᴮ ad 2 R 20,19; frt add ‖ **Cp 40,**2 ᵃ 𝔔ᵃ מלא; prp מִלְאָה ‖ 4 ᵃ 1 גַּיְא ‖ 6 ᵃ 𝔔ᵃ
ואומרה ‖ 𝔊(𝔙) καὶ εἶπα, l וָאֹמַר ‖ b frt ins קְרָא.

FIGURE 0.1
Scholarly edition of the same text as in figure 0.2 below. In contrast to that early manuscript, the edition seen here has chapter and verse numbers along with scholarly notes at the bottom about alternative Hebrew readings to the ones given in the body of the text.

further interpretation on the part of translators. Examples of translations that tend toward dynamic equivalence include the NJB, NEB, and several other translations produced by Protestant groups, such as the Good News Translation (GNT; also known as the "Good News Bible" and TEV – Today's English

Version) and the Contemporary English Version (CEV). These translations should be distinguished from resources such as the Living Bible or the Amplified Bible. The latter are not direct translations of the Hebrew and Greek texts, but paraphrases or expansions of other translations. For example, the Living Bible is a paraphrase of the nineteenth-century American Standard Version. Such paraphrase subtly adds yet another level of interpretation between the reader and the Hebrew or Greek text and is not helpful for academic work on the Bible. This becomes evident, for example, in cases like the one given at the end of this chapter in Appendix 1, where the Living Bible adds a long section to Isa 52:15 (anticipating Jesus) that has no parallel in the Hebrew text.

One more way that contemporary Bible translations vary is in the extent to which they aim to use gender-neutral language, such as "humanity" instead of "mankind." Though older writing conventions endorsed the use of "man" for "human" or "he" for "he or she," many now argue that general use of such male-focused language reinforces male domination of women. This has led to two levels of revision of older translations that used such male-specific language. In some cases, past English translators had used male-specific words to translate Hebrew or Greek expressions that were gender neutral. The recent revision of the NIV translation, Today's New International Version (TNIV), aims to correct such mistranslations to what are termed "gender-accurate" English expressions. For example, where the King James Version and some other versions render the first part of Gen 1:26 as "Let us make man in our image," versions like the TNIV more accurately reflect the gender neutrality of the Hebrew word for "humanity" that is used here, e.g. "let us make human beings in our image."

Some other translations go yet further, revising other references to human beings toward gender-neutral English terms, even in cases where the original biblical languages use masculine nouns. Examples of such translations include the NRSV, NJB, and the Contemporary Torah, a "gender-sensitive" revision of the NJPS. We generally follow that policy in this textbook, using "God" rather than "he" or "him" and preferring gender-neutral references to human beings. Nevertheless, the Bible was formed in a culture that privileged masculinity and conceived its God in largely masculine terms, and this is reflected at points in the translations included in this textbook.

Finally, readers should recognize that all these translations are published in different editions, each with its own perspective and added resources. For example, the *New Oxford Annotated Bible with Apocrypha* and the *HarperCollins Study Bible* are not different translations, but different editions of the NRSV. Each one has a different introductory essay, introductions to the biblical books, and brief commentary on the biblical text written by biblical scholars commissioned by the publisher. Indeed, whenever you use a given translation, it usually includes many other elements that were added by the publisher of that particular edition: headings for different sections of the biblical text, marginal references to other biblical passages, maps, and other additions. These can be helpful resources. Nevertheless, users of such editions should be aware of how these additional elements – none of which is actually part of the Bible per se – can subtly influence how one reads a given biblical passage. They should be used critically.

In the end, there is no one contemporary translation that scholars agree is decisively best. Arguments can be made for a variety of the contemporary translations that are listed in Appendix 2 of this chapter. Also, if your work focuses on a particular passage, you can get a good sense of particular translation issues in it by comparing multiple up-to-date translations with each other. Some like to use online resources for this, such as Bible Study Tools (www.biblestudytools.com\compare-translations) or the Bible Gateway (www.bible gateway.com). It should be noted, however, that these resources contain a number of out-of-date translations and often neglect Jewish translations (e.g. the New Jewish Publication Society [NJPS] version). If you use these sites, be sure to select up-to-date translations on the Christian comparison sites (e.g. NRSV, NIV) and compare those with the Jewish NJPS translation, which can be purchased in book form or accessed online at www.sefaria.org. Alternatively, you can greatly benefit from using a Bible software tool (such as Accordance) and purchasing multiple, recent Christian (e.g. NRSV, NJV) and Jewish (e.g. NJPS) translations for it that you then can compare with each other. Such comparison can reveal major differences between translations, and the more one finds such differences, the more one wonders how to decide between the alternatives. This is ideally solved by learning biblical languages! Many students, however, lack time and/or interest in going that far with biblical studies. For those lacking knowledge of biblical languages it is important to know where a given translation is only one possible rendering in English of a phrase in Hebrew, Aramaic, or Greek that could also be rendered, perhaps better, in another way. Comparison of Bible translations shows this.

Bible Abbreviations, Chapters and Verses

When books and articles cite biblical passages by chapter and verse, they usually follow this order: abbreviation for the biblical book, followed by the chapter number, a colon (:), followed by the verse. An example is Isa 44:28 (chapter 44, verse 28). If more than one verse is cited, dashes and commas can be used: Isa 44:20, 28 or Isa 44:10–13, 28. When scholars want to refer to the bulk of a passage without detailing specific verses left out, they will add an asterisk to indicate that some verses are not meant to be included in the reference, e.g. Genesis 28*. Occasionally, you will also see scholars refer to half-verses, e.g. 2:4a or 2:4b, following accent divisions found in their Hebrew Bibles. Such notations will be used in this book only to label citations that begin or end in a half-verse.

Here are some standard abbreviations for biblical books shared by Jewish and Christian Bibles (given in the order followed by most Christian Bibles). Sometimes these are further shortened by just giving the first two letters (e.g. Ex instead of Exod) or removing a vowel (e.g. Jdg for Judges):

Gen = Genesis	Esther = Esther	Hos = Hosea
Exod = Exodus	Job = Job	Joel = Joel
Lev = Leviticus	Ps or Pss = Psalms	Amos = Amos

Num = Numbers

Deut = Deuteronomy

Josh = Joshua

Judg = Judges

Ruth = Ruth

Sam = Samuel

Kgs = Kings

Chr = Chronicles

Ezra = Ezra

Neh = Nehemiah

Prov = Proverbs

Eccl = Ecclesiastes

Song = Song of Songs

(also known as Canticles,

and Song of Solomon)

Isa = Isaiah

Jer = Jeremiah

Lam = Lamentations

Ezek = Ezekiel

Dan = Daniel

Ob = Obadiah

Jon = Jonah

Micah = Micah

Nah = Nahum

Hab = Habakkuk

Zeph = Zephaniah

Hag = Haggai

Zech = Zechariah

Here are the abbreviations for books in the New Testament:

Matt = Matthew

Mark = Mark

Luke = Luke

John = John

Acts = Acts

Rom = Romans

1–2 Cor = 1–2 Corinthians

Gal = Galatians

Eph = Ephesians

Phil = Philippians

Col = Colossians

1–2 Thess = 1–2

Thessalonians

1–2 Tim = 1–2 Timothy

Titus = Titus

Phlm = Philemon

Heb = Hebrews

Jas = James

1–2 Pet = 1–2 Peter

1–2–3 John = 1–2–3 John

Jude = Jude

Rev = Revelation

The Origins of Chapters and Verses

The earliest Hebrew and Greek manuscripts of the Bible lack any chapter or verse numbering (see Figure 0.2). The Hebrew Bible was divided into sections for reading in the synagogue, and the Greek New Testament was divided into sections as well, but there were no numbers in these early manuscripts. Verse divisions were first added into the Hebrew Bible (without numbers) by the Masoretes, a group of Jewish scholars who worked in the seventh to tenth centuries CE and produced the standard edition of the Hebrew Bible now used in Judaism. The chapter divisions we now have were developed in 1205 by Stephen Langton, a professor in Paris and eventually an archbishop of the Church of England. He introduced them into

his edition of the Latin Vulgate translation of the Bible, and these divisions were later adopted by Jewish scholars as they became popular means to refer to biblical passages.

The first Old Testament and New Testament Bible with numbered verses was produced in 1555 by a Parisian book seller, Robert Estienne (also known as Stephanus). He is reported to have divided a copy of his New Testament into the present 7,959 verses while riding on horseback from Paris to Lyon. He also numbered the chapters and verses of both the Old and New Testament. Now these verses are found in scholarly editions of the Hebrew Bible (see Figure 0.1 on p. 8) and in translations of the Bible.

Conclusion on Critically Analyzing a Page of Your Own Bible

This chapter just starts to indicate how every page of your Bible, whether a Jewish Tanakh or a particular Christian Bible, is the product of an intense process of textual criticism, analysis of the original language of biblical passages, and packaging of the particular translation of such passages through elements like chapter and verse numbers. Ancient manuscripts were often divided into longer, unnumbered reading sections (for use in worship and study), and they sometimes included marginal comments or additional verses here or there (see Figure 0.2 below). Nevertheless, they did not have the numbering, headings, or reader guides now in the Bible before you. Take note of every element on a given page of your contemporary Bible that helps frame the biblical text and present it to you. Your first step as a critical reader of the Bible is become more conscious of these elements and more familiar with their characteristics.

FIGURE 0.2
One of our earliest manuscripts of the book of Isaiah, dated to the early first century BCE. Note how the letters are hung from lines on the parchment and a scribe has added a verse into the middle.

PROLOGUE REVIEW

1 Know the meaning and significance of the following terms discussed in this chapter:

- apocrypha
- canon and canonical
- conjectural emendation
- deuterocanonical books
- dynamic equivalence translation
- formal correspondence translation
- Hebrew Bible
- King James Version
- LXX
- manuscript witness

- Masoretic text (MT)
- Old Testament
- Qur'an
- Pentateuch
- Septuagint
- supersessionism
- Tanakh or TaNaK
- textual criticism
- Torah

2 What are the main differences between the Christian Old Testament and the Jewish Tanakh?

3 How is the Islamic Qur'an related to the Jewish and Christian Bibles?

RESOURCES FOR FURTHER STUDY

Editions of Translations

The New Jerusalem Bible. New York: Doubleday, 1985. This is the NJB.

The New Oxford Annotated Bible with Apocrypha (5th edition), eds. Michael Coogan et al. New York: Oxford University Press, 2018. This contains the NRSV.

The Jewish Study Bible, eds. A. Berlin et al. New York: Oxford University Press, 2004. This contains the NJPS.

The HarperCollins Study Bible (fully revised and updated), eds. Harold W. Attridge et al. San Francisco, CA: Harper-SanFrancisco, 2006. This contains the NRSV.

One-Volume Commentaries

Mays, James L., ed. *HarperCollin's Bible Commentary* (revised edition). San Francisco, CA: Harper & Row, 2000.

Newsom, Carol A., and Ringe, Sharon H. *The Women's Bible Commentary* (3rd edition). Louisville, KY: Westminster John Knox Press, 2012.

Technological Resources

Bible Software: Accordance Bible Software. It is recommended that you purchase the NRSV, NJB, or other up-to-date translation. As of the writing of this *Introduction*, you are given the King James Version (outdated for academic study of the Bible) as part of the initial package.

You can also obtain free software for searching and reading the Bible at www.crosswire.org.

Useful Websites for Translation Comparison

The Bible Gateway (mostly Christian translations) – www.biblegateway.com

Bible Study Tools (mostly Christian translations) – https://www.biblestudytools.com/compare-translations

Sefaria (access to the New Jewish Publication Society version and other Jewish texts) – www.sefaria.org

APPENDIX 1: TRANSLATION AND PARAPHRASE COMPARISON OF ISA 52:13–15

Isaiah Chapter and Verse	Revised Standard Version	New American Standard Version	New International Version	Today's English Version (Good News Bible)
52:13	Behold my servant shall prosper, he shall be exalted and lifted up, and shall be very high.	Behold my servant will prosper, He will be high and lifted up, and greatly exalted.	See, my servant will act wisely; he will be raised and lifted up and highly exalted.	The Lord says, My servant will succeed in his task; he will be highly honored.
52:14	As many were astonished at him – his appearance was so marred, beyond human semblance, and his form beyond that of the sons of men –	Just as many were astonished at you, *My People*, so His appearance was marred more than any man, And his form more than the sons of men.	Just as there were many who were appalled at him – his appearance was so disfigured beyond that of any man and his form marred beyond human likeness –	Many people were shocked when they saw him; he was so disfigured that he hardly looked human.
52:15	so shall he startle many nations; kings shall shut their mouths because of him;	Thus he will sprinkle many nations, Kings will shut their mouths on account of Him;	so will he sprinkle many nations, and kings will shut their mouths because of him.	But now many nations will marvel at him, and kings will be speechless with amazement.
	for that which has not been told them they shall see, and that which they have not heard they shall understand.	For what had not been told them they will see, And what they had not heard they will understand.	For what they were not told, they will see, and what they have not heard, they will understand.	They will see and understand something they had never known.

Isaiah Chapter and Verse	New English Bible	Living Bible	Tanakh	New Jerusalem Bible
52:13	Behold, my servant shall prosper, he shall be lifted up, exalted to the heights.	See, my Servant shall prosper; he shall be highly exalted.	Indeed, My servant shall prosper, be exalted and raised to great heights.	Look, my servant will prosper, will grow great, will rise to great heights.
52:14	Time was when many were aghast at you, my people;	Yet many shall be amazed when they see him – yes, even far-off foreign nations and their kings; (See the end of 52:15 for the rest)	Just as the many were appalled at him – So marred was his appearance, unlike that of man, His form, beyond human semblance –	As many people were aghast at him – he was so inhumanly disfigured that he no longer looked like a man –
52:15	… so now many nations recoil at the sight of him, and kings curl their lips in disgust. For they see what they had never been told and things unheard before fill their thoughts.	… they shall stand dumbfounded, speechless in his presence. For they shall see and understand what they had not been told before. They shall see my Servant beaten and bloodied, so disfigured one would scarcely know it was a person standing there. So shall he cleanse many nations.	Just so he shall startle many nations. Kings shall be silenced because of him, For they shall see what has not been told them, Shall behold what they never have heard.	so many nations will be astonished and kings will stay tightlipped before him, seeing what had never been told them, learning what they had not heard before.

APPENDIX 2: CHARACTERISTICS OF SELECT ENGLISH TRANSLATIONS OF THE BIBLE

Translation	Background	Style	Use of MT (Masoretic text, with translation of Isa 7:14 as indicator of theological leanings)	Gender language
NJPS (1985)	Jewish Publication Society	Formal correspondence, colloquial	No deviation from MT and uses Jewish chapter/verse numbering	Aims at "gender accuracy" (Note: 2006 JPS *Contemporary Torah* with more changes)
NRSV (1989)	Protestant, National Council of Churches	Formal correspondence, literary	Some deviation from MT in light of Dead Sea Scrolls and LXX	Modest move toward inclusive language
NIV (1978)	Protestant Evangelical, International Bible Society	Formal correspondence, literary	Very modest deviation from MT, mostly in notes. Modifies Hebrew of Isa 7:14 to match Matthew	
Today's NIV (TNIV) (2005)	Protestant Evangelical, International Bible Society	Formal correspondence, literary	Very modest deviation from MT, mostly in notes. Modifies Hebrew of Isa 7:14 to match Matthew	Modest move toward "gender-accurate" language
NASB (1971)	Protestant Evangelical, Lockman Foundation	Formal correspondence, quite literal and often awkward	Little revision of MT. Modifies Hebrew of Isa 7:14 to match Matthew	
GNT (formerly TEV) (1992)	Protestant, American Bible Society (particularly for missionaries)	Dynamic equivalence, colloquial and simple vocabulary	Little deviation from MT	Includes revisions toward gender-inclusive language
CEV (1999)	Protestant, American Bible Society	Dynamic equivalence, colloquial, yet more simple vocabulary and syntax	Little deviation from MT. Modifies Hebrew of Isa 7:14 to match Matthew	Moves toward gender-inclusive language for humans

Translation	Background	Style	Use of MT (Masoretic text, with translation of Isa 7:14 as indicator of theological leanings)	Gender language
REB (1989), revision of NEB (1970)	British Protestant and Roman Catholic churches	Dynamic equivalence, literary	Substantial deviations from MT	Moves in 1989 revision toward gender-inclusive language
NJB (1985)	European Roman Catholic	Dynamic equivalence, literary	Some substantial deviations from the MT	Very modest moves toward gender-inclusive language
NAB (1991)	United States Roman Catholic	Mix of dynamic equivalence and formal correspondence (the latter especially in NT)	Some substantial deviations from the MT. Modifies Hebrew of Isa 7:14 to match Matthew	Modest moves toward gender-inclusive language in NT and Psalms

Studying the Bible in Its Ancient Context(s)

1

Chapter Overview

This chapter introduces the basic orientation of the textbook and sets the stage for what follows with three overviews: geographical, historical, and methodological. The beginning of the chapter answers the questions "What makes academic study of the Bible different from typical 'bible study'?" and "Why is such academic study important?" We will briefly compare the general outline of the biblical story with the history of Israel that will structure this textbook. Next you gain a bird's-eye view of the major regions of the land of Israel, the periods of Israel's history, and methods used by scholars to analyze the Bible. Your future study will be helped in particular by learning the location of the two major regions of ancient Israel – the heartland of tribal Israel to the north and the area of David's clan, Judah, to the south (with the famous city of Jerusalem between these two areas) – and by memorizing the dates of the major periods in the history of Israel and beginnings of Judaism and Christianity (see also the appendix to this chapter).

A Contemporary Introduction to the Bible: Sacred Texts and Imperial Contexts, Second Edition. Colleen M. Conway and David M. Carr.
© 2021 Colleen M. Conway and David M. Carr. Published 2021 by John Wiley & Sons Ltd.

EXERCISE

Write a half-page to one-page statement or mini-autobiography of your past encounters with the Bible. Which parts of it have been most central in such encounters? Have you studied the Bible in an academic context before? Have you had unusually positive or negative experiences with the Bible or people citing it?

Why History Is Important in Studying the Bible

At first glance, the Bible is one of the most familiar of books. Many families own a copy. Every weekend, Jews and Christians read from it at worship. There are echoes of the Bible in all kinds of music, from Handel's *Messiah* to reggae and hip hop. Popular expressions, such as "Thou shalt not" or "Love thy neighbor as thyself," come from the Bible. Movies are often filled with biblical allusions. And you can still find a copy of the Bible, or at least the New Testament and Psalms, in many hotels.

AD, BC, BCE, and CE

The older expressions for dates, BC and AD, are explicitly Christian in orientation. BC comes from "Before Christ," and AD comes from the Latin *anno Domini*, which means "in the year of the Lord."

Over the past decades scholarly works have tended to use the more neutral terms BCE and CE, which refer to "Before the Common Era" and "Common Era," respectively. The year references are the same, but the labels are not specifically Christian.

This *Introduction* uses the standard scholarly BCE and CE abbreviations.

At second glance, the Bible is one of the most foreign of books. Its language, even in English translation, is often difficult to understand, especially if you are reading the King James Translation (1611), with its beautiful, but often obscure, seventeenth-century cadences and words. The biblical texts that are translated in the King James and other versions are still older. The New Testament was written in Greek, and its texts date from about two thousand years ago (50–200 CE). The Hebrew Bible/Old Testament was mostly written in Hebrew (a handful of chapters are in a related language, Aramaic), and some of its parts date as far back as three thousand years (1000–164 BCE). Both testaments reflect their ancient origins in many ways. They use ancient literary forms and images that are not common now. They come out of religious contexts much different from contemporary Judaism or Christianity. And they are addressed to historical struggles and circumstances that most readers of the Bible do not know.

The ancient aspects of the Bible are part of what give it its holy aura, but they also make biblical texts difficult to understand. If someone sees a reference to "Cyrus" in Isa 44:28 and 45:1, that person will likely have few associations with who "Cyrus" was and what he meant to the writer of this text. Most readers have even fewer associations with places and empires mentioned in the Bible, such as "Ephraim" or "Assyria." Usually, their only acquaintance with "Egypt" or "Babylonia" is a brief discussion in a world history class. Furthermore, certain types of writing mean little or nothing to contemporary readers, for example, the long genealogies of Genesis or the detailed instructions for sacrificing animals in Leviticus. As a result of all this unfamiliarity, few people who try to read the Bible from beginning to end actually get very far, and those who do often fail to make much sense out of what they have read.

The goal of this book is to give you keys to understand the Bible, including its more obscure parts. Names (e.g. Cyrus), events (e.g. the liberation from Babylonian captivity), and general perspectives in the Bible that previously you might have skipped past or not noticed should come into focus and make sense. For many, the experience of reading the Bible in historical context is much like finally getting to see a movie in color that beforehand had only been available in black and white. It is not at all that the meaning of the Bible can or should be limited to the settings in which it was originally composed. On the contrary: along the way we will see how the Bible is an important document now, thanks to the fact that it has been radically reinterpreted over centuries, first by successive communities of ancient Israelites and later by Jewish and Christian communities who cherished the Bible. Still, learning to see scriptures in relation to ancient history and culture can make previously bland or puzzling biblical texts come alive.

To pursue this historical approach, we will *not* read the Bible from beginning to end. Instead, we will look at biblical texts in relationship to when they were written. This means that, rather than starting with the creation stories of Genesis 1–3, this book starts with remnants of Israel's earliest oral traditions. These are songs and sagas from the time when Israel had no cities and was still a purely tribal people. Our next stop will be texts from the rise of Israel's first monarchies, particularly certain "royal" psalms that celebrate God's choice of Jerusalem and anointing of kings there. When we move to the New Testament, it will mean beginning with Paul's letters, all of which were written before the gospels. Overall, as we move through Israelite and early Christian history, we will see how biblical texts reflect the very different influences of successive world empires: the Mesopotamian empires of Assyria and Babylonia, and then the Persian, Hellenistic (Greek), and Roman empires. The common thread will be historical, and this will mean starting most chapters with some discussion of the historical and cultural context of the biblical texts to be discussed there.

Overview: Order of Main Discussions of Biblical Books

Steps in the Bible's own story	This textbook's discussion of biblical texts and traditions in the order they were created
Creation, flood, and other materials about the origins of the world (Genesis 1–11)	See below
Stories of Israel's patriarchs and matriarchs (e.g. Abraham and Sarah, Jacob, and Joseph; Genesis 12–50)	See below
The growth of the people of Israel and their exodus from Egypt (Exodus 1–15)	See below
Forty years in the wilderness, and gift of law at Sinai (Exodus 16–40; Leviticus, Numbers, Deuteronomy)	
Israel's conquest of Canaan (Joshua) Tribal life under various leaders (Judges)	*Period of the Judges: Chapter 2.* Oral traditions in Genesis 12–35, Exodus, and Judges 5.
The establishment of Saul and then David's monarchy (1–2 Samuel)	*Early monarchy/David and Solomon: Chapter 3.* Royal and Zion Psalms, books associated with Solomon (Song of Songs, Ecclesiastes, and Proverbs), and parts of Genesis 1–11. The text group here in Chapter 3 gathers a set of texts from various periods – many associated with David and Solomon – that show adaptation of older ancient Near Eastern traditions.
The kings of Jerusalem and Israel (1–2 Kings 17 and also 1 Chronicles 10–2 Chronicles 28) The later kingship in Jerusalem (after destruction of the kingdom of Israel) (2 Kings 18–25//2 Chronicles 29–36)	*Later northern and southern monarchies: Chapter 4.* Amos, Hosea, Micah, and early parts of Isaiah (along with possible early traditions in Exodus 1–15, Genesis 25–35, etc.). *Twilight of the monarchy in Jerusalem: Chapter 5.* Deuteronomy through 2 Kings, Jeremiah, Nahum, and Zephaniah.
(The Bible lacks narratives directly of this time [the book of Daniel is a much later legend])	*Exile of Judeans to Babylonia: Chapter 6.* Lamentations, Ezekiel, Isaiah 40–55, and major parts of Genesis through Numbers (especially the Abraham story in Genesis 12–25 and the book of Leviticus).
Rebuilding of a temple-focused community under Persian rulership (Ezra–Nehemiah)	*Return of exiles and rebuilding: Chapter 7.* Haggai, Zechariah, Isaiah 56–66, Jonah, Ruth, Job, and the book of Psalms (along with parts of Ezra–Nehemiah and Genesis through Numbers).
Deuterocanonical/Apocryphal books of (e.g. 1–4 Maccabees)	*The Hellenistic empires and crisis: Chapter 8.* Sirach, Enoch, Daniel, Ezra–Nehemiah, 1–2 Chronicles, Esther, Judith, and questions about the final formation of the Hebrew Bible (along with some of Ecclesiastes and Song of Songs).
Gospel stories of Jesus (Matthew, Mark, Luke, and John)	*The Roman empire: Chapters 9–15.* The books of the New Testament, starting with Paul and then moving to the gospels and select other writings. Treated later in the textbook, Chapters 11–14

Steps in the Bible's own story	This textbook's discussion of biblical texts and traditions in the order they were created
The emergence of the early church (Acts)	Discussed in part of Chapter 14 on Luke–Acts
Paul's missionary work (Acts and Paul's letters)	Preliminary reflections on the New Testament's setting, Chapter 9
	Discussed in Chapter 10 (Hebrews treated in Chapter 15)
Letters attributed to other Apostles: Peter and John	Discussed in Chapter 15
The Book of Revelation	Discussed in Chapter 15

At first this approach may be disorienting, since it involves placing familiar biblical texts in a different order and in new contexts. Take the example of the story of creation in Gen 1:1–2:3. It seems straightforward enough as it is. Why wait to talk much about this opening story of the Bible until Chapter 6 of this *Introduction*? As we will see, one reason is that reading Gen 1:1–2:3 in relation to the Judeans' experience of forced exile in Babylonia (the focus of Chapter 6) explains the major emphasis in this text on the Sabbath. This is an aspect of the text that many people, especially non-Jews, completely miss, since it has little meaning for them. But the whole seven-day structure of the story is meant to lead up to one thing: God's rest on the seventh day and blessing of it (Gen 2:1–3). Reading this text in relation to the Babylonian exile highlights this important feature and makes sense of other aspects of the creation story as well.

This is just one way in which academic study of the Bible is quite a different thing from study of the Bible in Sunday school or even high school religion classes in parochial schools. Many people come to a university or seminary class on the Bible expecting a summary of the contents of the Bible or indoctrination into biblical theologies or values. Others expect a devotional approach that they have learned in church Bible studies where the Bible is often read as a lesson book for life. All these approaches have their value and place, but they differ from the academic approach of a college or seminary course. Moreover, they are misleading indicators of what to expect from such a course. Where a student might expect to work hard in a history or organic chemistry class, study of the "Bible" – especially if it's imagined on the basis of earlier experience with religious education – promises to be easy. Yet an *academic* course on the Bible offers its own set of challenges, somewhat similar to those of a good course in history or English literature. Indeed, some students find academic study of the Bible especially difficult because it offers alternatives to their past interpretations of biblical texts that they cherish. These students not only must learn the course material about the Bible, but must integrate this knowledge with their beliefs and values.

The benefits of such study are substantial. Familiar texts offer new meanings. Difficult biblical texts start to make better sense when placed in their original historical contexts. Where once the Bible might have seemed a monolithic, ancient set of rules, it becomes a rich variety of different perspectives that have stood the test of time. We encourage you to be open to this approach. *Frequently* consult the historical timeline and overview charts at the outset of the *Introduction* to orient yourself (see pp. xxvii–xxx), and learn for yourself what this way of studying the Bible has to offer.

The Geography and Major Characters of the Biblical Drama

We start by setting the scene for the drama of biblical history, looking at the geography of the biblical world, major nations, and major historical periods. This information is important, because it will orient you to the quite different world in which the Bible was created.

Asked to picture the land of Israel, many would conjure up images from TV specials or popular movies where biblical events occur amidst sand dunes, palm trees, and small villages. The reality is that the area of Israel encompasses sharp contrasts in topography, rainfall, and vegetation. Imagine Map 1.1 as divided into four narrow strips running up and down. The strip to the left is the *coastal plain* along the Mediterranean Sea. It is low, flat, and fertile and receives relatively regular rainfall. Non-Israelites lived here through most of Israelite history, and it was ruled from Jerusalem only for short periods. The next strip is the *central hill country* and runs down the middle of the map, encompassing the hill country of Judah, hill country of Ephraim (Israel), and Galilee. This is an area of rocky hills that eventually rise up to 3000 feet. This hill country is where most of Israelite history took place. It is drier and less accessible than the coastal plain to the west. The third strip is the *Jordan Valley*, encompassing the Dead Sea, Jordan River, and Sea of Galilee (from south to north). This is one of the lowest places on earth, about 1000 feet below sea level, and – aside from some oases – it is very dry and barren. The fourth strip is the *Transjordanian Plateau*, including Edom, Moab, Ammon, and the Gilead region (where Israelites settled). This plateau, now in the contemporary nation of Jordan, has similar characteristics to the central highlands of Israel. To the east of it (and off the map) lies the desert.

As you start your study of the Bible, it is particularly important to get an understanding of the different parts of the land of Israel and the peoples who lived there. Though people often apply the term "Israel" to this entire area, this term often refers more narrowly to the peoples who settled in the *northern* highlands described above ("Hill Country of Ephraim/Israel" on Map 1.1, with Shechem at its center) along with parts of the Gilead of the Transjordan. For much of biblical history, this area and this people are to be distinguished from "Judah," which is located in the *southern* highlands of the map ("Hill Country of Judah"; Hebron is a Judean city). Note that Jerusalem lay between Israel and Judah and was not "Israelite"/"Judean" until David conquered it by stealth at the outset of his monarchy. This distinction between "Judah" in the south and "Israel" in the north is important for much of Israel's early history. Later on, the term "Israel" came to encompass Judah as well, and the narratives of the Hebrew Bible – many of them written later – project that picture onto the earliest history of the people. Therefore, the word **"Israel"** has at least two major meanings in the Bible: a narrow sense referring to the ancient tribal groups settled in the northern highlands and a broader sense referring to Judah along with those other tribal groups. When people refer to the "land of Israel" or the "people of Israel," they are usually using the word "Israel" in the broader sense, but there will be numerous times in this *Introduction* when it will be important to remember the narrower sense of "Israel" (in the north) as opposed to "Judah" (in the south).

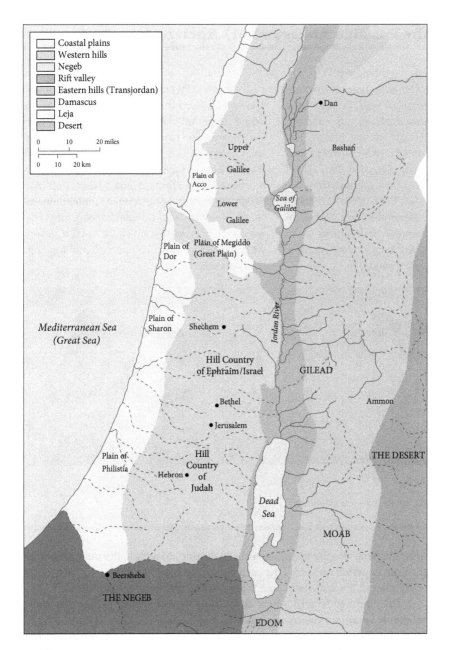

MAP 1.1
The land of Israel and its surroundings. Redrawn from Adrian Curtis (ed.), *Oxford Bible Atlas*
(4th edition). Oxford, New York: Oxford University Press, 2007.

Those are the scholarly terms for the region and its inhabitants. As we
move forward, it is important to distinguish such terms from contemporary des-
ignations for the land. In particular, it is important not to confuse the word
"Israelite," which refers to ancient inhabitants of the land of Israel, and the word
"Israeli," which is a modern term referring to citizens of the contemporary state

Visualizing (the Possible Ancestors of) Ancient Israelites

These ancient Israelites were different in important ways from all contemporary peoples, including Israelis. Unfortunately we do not have contemporary representations of ancient Israelites. The best we can do are images like Figure 1.1 (a relief painting from an official's tomb at Beni Hasan), which is an Egyptian depiction of visitors to Egypt from the east, perhaps from the region of Canaan. As we will see in the next chapter, the Israelites likely descended from Canaanite peoples, and so this representation gives us an image of what the ancestors of ancient Israelites (or their near-neighbors) looked like.

On the far right of the picture there is a clean-shaven Egyptian with darker brown skin. The visitors from the east (Canaan?) are the six figures to the left of him. They have lighter brown skin, beards, and some colorful tunics. One thing such images make clear is that the people who dwelled east of Egypt looked more like the contemporary inhabitants of the Middle East and Africa than the light-skinned inhabitants of North America and Europe. Indeed, not only were ancient Israelites non-white, but the ancient world lacked an exact correlate to modern concepts of race.

FIGURE 1.1
Ancient visitors to Egypt from the East (Canaanites?).

of Israel. Note also the use of the term "Palestine" to refer to the same area from the Roman period onward. This term is now used by Palestinians and many others to refer to the same land area that Jews and others refer to as "Israel."

The "land of Israel," where most biblical events took place, is actually relatively small. As you can see on Map 1.1, the Sea of Galilee is only 30 miles from the Mediterranean Sea, and the Dead Sea is only 60 miles away. The distance from the area around Shechem in the north to Beersheba in the south is about 90 miles. This means that the main setting of biblical history, the area of the central highlands (thus excluding the non-Israelite coastal plains), is about 40 miles by 90 miles – not much bigger than many large metropolitan areas. This tiny area is the site where texts and religious ideas were formed that would change world history. Notably, this highland area also encompasses many areas most in dispute in the contemporary Middle East, areas that are variously designated as "the West Bank," "occupied

MAP 1.2
The major routes of the ancient Near East. Note how the major routes move from Egypt on the left through Judah/Israel near the Mediterranean to Syria and Mesopotamia to the northeast and east. Redrawn from Yohanan Aharoni and Michael Avi-Yonah (eds.), *The Macmillan Bible Atlas* (revised edition). New York, Macmillan, 1977, map 9.

territories," and "Judea and Samaria." Before 1967 these regions were not part of the modern nation of Israel, but they were seized by Israel from Jordan during the 1967 war, and their status is one major issue in the ongoing Middle East conflict.

This conflict is the latest chapter in thousands of years of struggles between different groups for control of this narrow strip of land. In ancient times, the land of Israel occupied a strategic location along the "Fertile Crescent" extending from Egypt in the southwest to the Mesopotamian empires of Assyria and Babylonia in the northeast. Because much of the area east of Israel was impassable desert, the major roads between Egypt and Mesopotamia had to cross the narrow strip of land between the Mediterranean Sea and the desert (see Map 1.2). Israel lay right along those roads and was often run over by the armies of its more powerful neighbors. The various empires of the ancient Near East were almost always laying claim to Israel and the surrounding areas, and the peoples of Israel were caught in the middle.

Major Periods in the Biblical Drama

The major turns in biblical history can be seen in this context. The Egyptian empire dominated the area of ancient Israel from around 1450 to 1200 BCE, the years when many scholars think the biblical exodus may have happened. Then a series of catastrophes ended Egyptian rule over the area and inaugurated a power vacuum in the land of Israel. This is when we first see identifiable archaeological evidence of a "people of Israel." This people settled in small villages in the hill country of Judah and Israel during the **pre-state tribal period** (1250–1000 BCE, including the time of the chieftain, Saul). At the outset of the first millennium (BCE), David and Solomon established what might be termed a proto-monarchy in Jerusalem that ruled the Israelite tribes for several decades (around 1000–930 BCE). In the later ninth century, the tribes of Israel formed a monarchy of their own and we see a period of **neighboring monarchies**, where there are two kingdoms in broader Israel: a kingdom of Israel in the north and a kingdom of Judah in the south (930–722 BCE).

This window of freedom from imperial domination, however, was not to last. Especially in the late eighth century (745 BCE and onward), the Assyrian empire, based in what is now northern Iraq, gained control of both Israel and (later) Judah (see Map 1.3). This empire completely destroyed the kingdom of Israel in 722 BCE and dominated the kingdom of Judah for decades. Indeed, from 745 to 586 BCE, Israel and Judah were dominated by a series of brutal empires – Assyria, Egypt (for a couple of years), and Babylonia (based in middle Iraq). Though Judah enjoyed brief independence between domination by the Assyrians and Egyptians, the nation was dominated and eventually destroyed by the Babylonian empire, which reduced Jerusalem, along with its Temple, to rubble in 586 BCE (**destruction of Jerusalem**, ending a period of "Judah alone," 722–586 BCE). Thus began one of the most important periods of biblical history, the **Babylonian exile** (586–538 BCE). At the outset of this period, most of the elite who had lived in Judah were forcibly deported to Babylon, and in many cases neither they nor their children ever returned. The Hebrew Bible is a collection of documents from the perspective of these deportees and their children, such that biblical history is now usually defined (from their point of view) in terms of "pre-exile" and "exile."

The story of Israel and empires, however, was not over. Just decades later, the Persian ruler, Cyrus, conquered the Babylonian empire, ushering in a period of Persian rule of Judah that lasted from 538 to 332 BCE (the **Persian period**, the beginning of the **post-exilic period** starting in 538 BCE). The Bible records a number of ways in which Cyrus and his successors helped former exiles in Babylonia rebuild the temple and rebuild their community. Later, Alexander the Great conquered the area in 333 BCE, beginning a period of Hellenistic rule, and it appears that he and his successors generally continued the Persian policies of support of Jerusalem and its leadership during

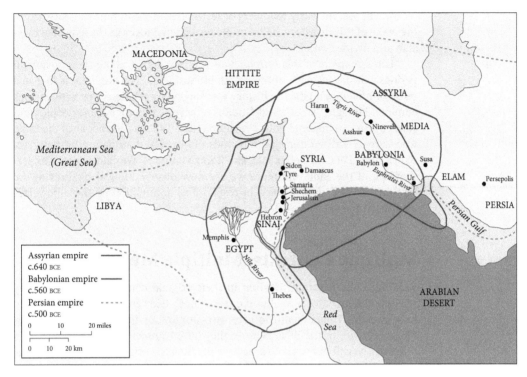

MAP 1.3
The reach of three of the major empires that dominated Israel and/or Judah: the Assyrian, Babylonian, and Persian empires. Redrawn from www.bible.ca, Abingdon Press, 1994.

their rule of Judah and Jerusalem (**Hellenistic period**, 332–167 BCE). Nevertheless, in the late second century (starting in 167 BCE), there was a major crisis in Judah, precipitated by the efforts of some elite Judeans to turn the city of Jerusalem into a Greek city. This crisis eventually led to the formation, for a brief period, of another monarchy in Judah, this one led by a priestly family called the **Hasmoneans** (also known as the **Maccabees**). This **Hasmonean monarchy** continued from 142 to 63 BCE, when the Romans took control of the area, which they named "Palestine" and put under control of a series of governors. The year 63 BCE represents the beginning of the **Roman period** in Palestine.

With this, "Palestine" joined much of the surrounding world as part of the Roman empire. This is the time when Jesus lived, the early church formed in the wake of his crucifixion by the Romans, and the Christian movement spread across the Mediterranean Sea to cities around the Roman empire. This was also the time of multiple Judean revolts against Roman control that eventually led to the destruction in 70 CE of the Jerusalem Temple (**destruction of the Second Temple** [earlier rebuilt under the Persians]) and the complete destruction of Jewish Jerusalem in 135 CE. Thus the Jewish temple state was completely destroyed. The main form of Jewish life to survive this catastrophe was rabbinic Judaism, which grew out of the Torah-centered scholarship and leadership of the earlier, popular movement of the Pharisees.

As we will see, the early followers of Jesus offered a different way forward in the wake of this disaster – belief in the resurrected Jesus as the expected messiah and divine Son of God.

Later chapters of this *Introduction* will give details about these historical periods, correlating each of them with biblical texts. The aim here is to give a sense of how much Israelite history was shaped by relationships with various empires. Though "Israel" (and "Judah") emerged as recognizable peoples and states during an imperial power vacuum (1200–745 BCE), the books of the Bible were largely written during the periods of imperial domination by Assyrian, Babylonian, Persian, Hellenistic, and Roman empires. We gain a deeper understanding of the Bible the more we see how diverse biblical pictures of the "empire of God" were formed in response to domination by these powerful empires in the ancient world.

Multiple Contexts, Multiple Methods

Reading biblical texts in relation to their original contexts can make many aspects of them come alive, but the reason such texts are read now is that they have remained meaningful to diverse communities in much later contexts. These texts are in the Bible because they have transcended their origins. This *Introduction* will discuss both aspects of the Bible: its origins in the ancient Near East and its later interpretation by Jewish and Christian communities today. Knowing more about the Bible's early contexts gives some perspective on contemporary differences in interpretation. The more you know about the antiquity of the Bible, the more you may appreciate both the care and the creativity with which it has been read and reread over time by different communities.

This can be illustrated through a brief look at how different methods of biblical criticism might look at Israel's "exodus," the story of **Yahweh**'s (see the Special Topics Box on "The Name of Israel's God: Yahweh/the LORD") liberation of the people from Egypt that is now found in the first chapters of the book of Exodus (Exodus 1–15). To start, some scholars try to reconstruct whether and when this exodus actually happened. Such academic study of the history of Israel uses biblical texts as one among multiple sources for the reconstruction of "what probably happened." So far, the results of such study have been inconclusive. On the one hand, many scholars believe some sort of exodus out of Egypt happened, probably during the centuries just before the emergence of the people of "Israel" as a distinct group in the highlands of Canaan. On the other hand, most academic scholars of the Bible also believe that the written texts of the Bible are so far removed from the events that they describe that they are not useful for precise retelling of what actually happened back then: who said what, how many and who were involved, etc. The biblical texts are not reliable for such details because they have been filtered by centuries of oral retelling and written expansions by later Israelites. Imagine a game of "telephone" where hundreds of people over a period of five hundred years retell stories about an event important to them (e.g. of the exodus from Egypt), continually adapting such stories for new situations and audiences, and then imagine trying to use the end result of this complex process for historical analysis. Because biblical texts are so shaped by time, scholars studying the history of Israel attempt to reconstruct what happened through analyzing them and comparing them – where possible – with archaeological records and non-biblical historical sources.

The Name of Israel's God: Yahweh/the LORD

The name of Israel's God in Hebrew is Yahweh, but you will not see this name written out in most English translations of the Bible. Instead, most translations have "the LORD" where the Hebrew manuscripts have a strange combination of the consonants for Yahweh (YHWH) and the vowels for the Hebrew word "lord." Why this combination?

The consonants are earlier, since the earliest Hebrew Bible manuscripts were written in all consonants. When Jewish scholars started producing manuscripts with vowels, the divine name Yahweh had become so holy that they did not pronounce it out loud. (This is still true for many Jews.) Therefore, they added the vowels for "lord" in every place where the consonants for Yahweh occurred so that readers would say "lord" rather than the holy name. English translations reflect this combination when they put "lord" in all capital letters (LORD), indicating that this particular "lord" is Yahweh. (Note "Jehovah" is the word that is produced when you simply pronounce the consonants of YHWH with the vowels for the Hebrew word for "lord.")

We will be focusing here on the state of the Bible before such prohibitions on pronouncing the divine name existed. So there will be occasions where it will be helpful to refer to Israel's God by the name Yahweh.

Historical criticism is a family of historical methods that analyzes how and where the biblical texts (and oral traditions in them) were composed. "Criticism" in this case does not mean that historical critics find fault with the biblical texts that they study, but that they use academically critical analysis to arrive at their conclusions rather than starting on the basis of faith assumptions. Through **tradition criticism**, for example, biblical scholars attempt to identify early oral traditions standing behind the biblical text. For example, past tradition critics have supposed that the following song of Miriam may be one of the earliest traditions in the Bible to speak of the defeat of the Egyptian army at the Red Sea:

> Sing to Yahweh, for he has been victorious
> Horse and rider, he has thrown into the sea. (Exod 15:21)

The next chapter will discuss places where other texts of the Bible, though being later written texts, still reflect the general outlines of earlier oral traditions.

Many scholars, however, focus not on how the Bible was formed, but on what it means and has meant to generations of readers of the Bible. For example, **literary criticism** has drawn on methods in the study of modern literature to study the plot, characterization, pacing, and shape of biblical texts. Scholars employing such criticism have examined Exodus 1–15 as if it were a novel, looking at *how* the story is artfully told: how is Moses introduced and characterized? How does this contrast with the characterization of the Egyptians and their leaders? What does the reader expect and learn as the narrative unfolds? Such study of the poetic and narrative dynamics of biblical texts is distinct from study of how such texts have been interpreted by later readers, which is the **history of interpretation**. Historians of interpretation study how the story of the exodus became central to Judaism and Christianity in different ways. For example, the exodus story is the centerpiece of the Jewish celebration of Passover and is a founding story for the Christian practices of baptism and Eucharist.

Finally, various forms of **ideological criticism** analyze ways that the exodus story can be, has been, and should be read in the midst of systemic structures of power. For example, early **feminist criticism** lifted up the importance of the story of the midwives in the lead-up to the exodus (Exod 1:15–21), and later feminist critics have raised questions about the male (androcentric) focus of the exodus story and most other parts of the Bible.

This is just a sampling of some of the different types of academic research that are used to investigate the Bible and its readings. Across this *Introduction* numerous other forms of biblical criticism will be introduced.

Looking Forward to the Big Picture

This chapter has given an overview, which will be filled in by the following chapters. It may be disorienting to encounter so many terms and dates at once. Nevertheless, it is important to get this larger picture in order to understand the details of what follows. The next seven chapters of this *Introduction* will unfold the story of the creation of the Hebrew Bible/Old Testament. This story moves from discussion of oral traditions in pre-literate Israel all the way through to the writing of the latest books of the Hebrew Bible during the Hellenistic (and Hasmonean) period. Though the first chapters will uncover a strange and different ancient Israel unfamiliar to many readers, this historical approach will illuminate many aspects of the Bible that otherwise make little sense. In addition, it will provide a starting point for engaging other scholarly methods of looking at biblical texts in new ways. Similarly, Chapters 9–15 will trace the development of the New Testament writings, beginning with a discussion of the earliest oral traditions about Jesus.

Of course, the analysis of the formation of the Bible and its texts is always in flux. Within the space of this brief *Introduction* we will only be able to touch on a few of the major debates. Nevertheless, scholars have been doing this kind of historical analysis of the Bible for about three hundred years, and these efforts have produced some interesting and important results. This textbook draws on the breadth of that scholarship in giving a historical orientation to the Bible that can be a starting point for further study, questioning, and correction. For now, use this textbook as your initial guide, rather than doing internet searches on Bible-related topics (internet sites are particularly variable in quality). Each chapter concludes with recommended written resources, and this chapter concludes with websites that also provide high-quality resources for further study.

CHAPTER ONE REVIEW

1 Know the meaning and significance of the following terms discussed in this chapter:
- Israel (two meanings)
- Israelite (know the difference from "Israeli")
- Yahweh
- literary criticism
- tradition criticism
- historical criticism

2. Be able to identify the following areas on a map and describe their general characteristics:
- coastal plain
- central hill country
- Jordan Valley
- Judah
- Transjordan

3. Know the dates and basic significance of the following overall periods of history:
- pre-state tribal period

- proto-monarchy
- neighboring monarchies
- Judah alone
- destruction of Jerusalem
- Babylonian exile
- Persian period
- post-exilic period
- Hellenistic period
- Hasmonean (Maccabean) monarchy
- beginning of the Roman period
- destruction of the Second Temple

4. Know the order in which the following empires dominated Israel and Judah:
- Assyrian
- Babylonian
- Persian
- Hellenistic (or Greek)
- Roman

RESOURCES FOR FURTHER STUDY

Overviews of the History of Israel

Miller, J. Maxwell. *The History of Israel: An Essential Guide.* Nashville, TN: Abingdon, 1997.

Schipper, Bernd. *A Concise History of Ancient Israel: From the Beginnings Through the Hellenistic Era.* Translated by Michael J. Lesley. University Park, PA: Eisenbrauns, 2019.

Shanks, Hershel. *Ancient Israel: From Abraham to the Roman Destruction of the Temple* (2nd edition). Washington, DC: Biblical Archaeology Society, 1999.

Geography of Lands and Places Featured in the Bible

Atlas of the Bible Lands (revised edition). Maplewood, NJ: Hammond, 1990.

Rainey, Anson F., and Notley, R. Steven. *The Sacred Bridge: Carta's Atlas of the Biblical World.* Jerusalem: Carta, 2006. Detailed. Much focus on reconstructing history.

Rogerson, John. *The New Atlas of the Bible.* London: McDonald, 1985. Organized not by historical periods, but by regions. Excellent photographs and art.

Discussions of Methods in Biblical Interpretation

McKenzie, Steven L., and Haynes, Stephen R. *To Each Its Own Meaning: An Introduction to Biblical Criticisms and Their Application* (2nd edition). Louisville, KY: Westminster John Knox Press, 1999.

McKenzie, Steven L., and Haynes, Stephen R. *New Meanings for Ancient Texts: Recent Approaches to Biblical Criticisms and Their Applications.* Louisville, KY: Westminster John Knox Press, 2013.

Especially Good Internet Resources

The Bible Odyssey (by the Society of Biblical Literature): www.bibleodyssey.org. This website offers a collection of short articles by biblical scholars on people, places, and things related to the Bible.

www.TheTorah.com. A non-profit website run by Jewish scholars with accessible articles on Tanakh/Bible

APPENDIX: ISRAEL'S HISTORY AND EMPIRES

(Prehistory of Israel: domination of Canaan by Egypt, 1450–1200 BCE)

Emergence of "Israel" in imperial power vacuum

    Appearance of Israelite villages in unsettled hill country (approximately 1250–1000 BCE)

    David and Solomon's proto-monarchy in Jerusalem (approximately 1000–930 BCE)

    Neighboring monarchies: southern Judah and northern Israel (from approximately 930 to 722 BCE)

Oppression by successive empires: Assyria, Egypt, and Babylonia (745–586 BCE)

    Fall of northern kingdom (722 BCE)

    Destruction of Jerusalem and exile of its leadership (586 BCE; also other waves of exile)

Imperial sponsorship of (formerly exiled) Judeans: post-exilic period (starting 538 BCE)

    Persian-sponsored rebuilding and rule of Judah (538–332 BCE)

    Hellenistic continuation of Persian policies until Hellenistic crisis (332–167 BCE)

    Hellenistic crisis and emergence of Hasmonean/Maccabean monarchy (167–63 BCE)

Roman rule (starting 63 BCE with different end dates)

    Destruction of the Second Temple (70 CE)

    Total destruction of Jerusalem (135 CE)

The Emergence of Ancient Israel and Its First Oral Traditions

2

Chapter Overview

This chapter addresses the questions "How did the earliest Israelites live?" and "What were some of Israel's most ancient traditions?" You will learn about ancient Israelite tribal life and how that form of social organization is distinguished from two other forms of social life important in later chapters of Israel's history: the monarchal city-state and the empire. The chapter discusses some unique characteristics of the kind of oral tradition typical of such tribal groups, and it finds evidence of such oral traditions embedded in biblical texts about Jacob, the exodus from Egypt, and Deborah's victory over the armies of Hazor. In their early oral form (no longer available to us), these stories and poems, often celebrating devious "tricksters" who triumph over all odds, formed part of a "collective memory" that helped distinguish the tribal-culture Israelites from the Canaanites surrounding them. At the same time, despite these differences in social organization and tribal tradition, you will also discover in this chapter ways that early Israel was more "Canaanite" in its religion and culture than you previously thought. Read both for ways ancient Israel was different from its neighbors and for ways it was similar.

A Contemporary Introduction to the Bible: Sacred Texts and Imperial Contexts, Second Edition.
Colleen M. Conway and David M. Carr.
© 2021 Colleen M. Conway and David M. Carr. Published 2021 by John Wiley & Sons Ltd.

Imagining Early Israel

We begin with a look at the stories and songs treasured by Israel at the outset of its history. More than anywhere else in this book this requires a lot of imagination, since we have no Israelite writings from this period. Therefore, we must piece together a picture of Israel based on a combination of archaeology, some material from neighboring cultures, and distant echoes of early Israel in the much later writings now found in our Bible.

So we start with imagination – a creative reconstruction of the kind of village where Israel's first oral traditions might have developed. It is a journey back to the time described in the Bible in the books of Joshua and Judges. Nevertheless, there are major contrasts between what these books say about this "period of the Judges" and what historians reconstruct of it. Later, in Chapter 5 of this *Introduction*, we will discuss the later writing of Joshua and Judges. For now, however, the focus is not on the written books of the Bible, but on the oral culture that produced Israel's first traditions. Here is a picture based on archaeology and careful analysis of the Bible and non-biblical texts.

If we were to take a time machine back to Israel's beginnings, the journey would probably take us to one of the hilltop villages in the hill country that existed in the late second millennium (1250–1000 BCE) between the coastal plains and Jordan valley (see Figure 2.1). The early Israelites in the **village** lived on a subsistence level, surviving largely on the crops that they grew. Generally there were two main seasons, a dry summer–fall season and a rainy

FIGURE 2.1
Part of the hill country of central Israel. Notice the ancient terraces cut into the limestone hills to help in farming them.

winter–spring season culminating in the harvest of barley, then wheat and other crops. The rain on which they depended was fickle. They would store water from the rainy season in sealed underground holes, "cisterns." They used large pottery jars to store food produced from the harvest. Nevertheless, about every three or four years there would be too little rain for crops. Life would be especially hard then, with families struggling to keep from starving until another year, a better rainy season, and the first harvests from that next year's crop. In such times they might sacrifice and eat one of their precious animals in order to survive. Otherwise, animals were primarily sources of milk and clothing (wool or skins).

Our village would have only a few homes, housing a handful of clans, settled in separate households where extended families lived together (see figure 2.2 for an image of a typical house): grandparents, their sons and sons'

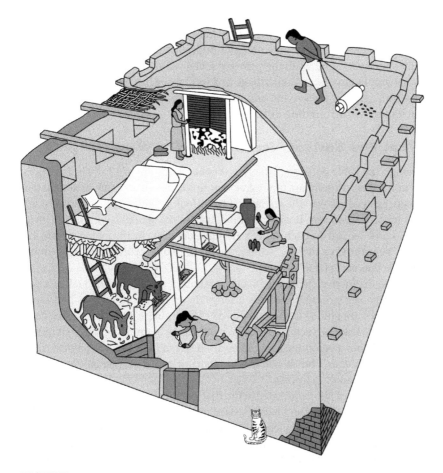

FIGURE 2.2

Typical pillared house of the Israelites. The bottom floor had stables for animals, cistern for water, and areas for cooking and food preparation. The top floor was where the family slept, dined, and entertained. Redrawn from Philip J. King and Lawrence E. Stager, *Life in Biblical Israel*. Louisville, KY: Westminster John Knox Press, 2001, page 29.

wives, unmarried daughters, and dependents. Only about 50–200 people would have lived in each such village, and their lives were short and hard (as everywhere else in the ancient world). Though a few lucky individuals lived much longer, most males who survived early childhood typically lived into their mid-thirties, while most women died as early as their late twenties, half of them in childbirth. They were vulnerable to starvation, diseases, warfare, and (for women) the hazards of childbirth.

Because a village lacked a wall or many men of fighting age, it was vulnerable to raids from other areas or attacks by the organized armies of the city-states in the coastal areas and lowlands. Their only hope of defense was divine help, along with assistance from banding together with other villages in their tribe (e.g. Ephraim, Manasseh, Asher). In times of particular crisis, the villages of multiple tribes might join together in a temporary military alliance led by a charismatic individual. As we will see in the Song of Deborah, it was not always easy to pull together these scattered tribes and villages into a coordinated defense. Such texts show that – contrary to some other biblical portrayals – earliest "Israel" was a very loosely organized whole. Villages and tribes bonded together to counter the unpredictabilities of military or agricultural catastrophe. Still, the primary social reality for most people in early Israel would have been their village and its clans. They would have spent the vast bulk of their lives living and working within the confines of the village itself and the surrounding hills.

What Was Earliest "Israel" and Who Were "Judges"?

Though the Bible portrays "Israel" as a coherent group of 12 tribes descended from Jacob, most scholars now agree that this is not an accurate historical portrayal. Instead, as we will see later (in our look at Judges 5), earliest "Israel" was loosely organized. It was a group of tribes who shared a way of life (in villages) and helped in each other's military defense. Anthropologists use the term "**segmentary society**" to describe the kind of decentralized social grouping that was early Israel.

One distinctive element of such segmentary societies is the lack of a permanent power structure, such as a kingship. Instead, the villages and larger groupings were guided in their day-to-day life by elders. In times of great need, charismatic leaders, such as Deborah, would arise to unite the different groups of "Israel" into a common army. They are referred to in English biblical translations as "judges," but a better – though awkward – translation probably would be "temporary leaders."

This way of life contrasted with that of non-Israelite **monarchal city-states** near Israel. Ancient Near Eastern city-states were territories controlled by a city, generally cities ruled by kings. Such cities could amass resources and achieve levels of organization that were impossible in more decentralized systems such as tribal Israel. The walls around cities gave them immense defensive advantages over forces attacking with superior numbers. City-states often had a professional army, whose training and equipment gave them an advantage over more disorganized voluntary forces like those of Israel. Their greater military power and social organization allowed them to dominate surrounding areas, requiring peasants under their domination to help build fortifications in the city and provide regular deliveries of a certain amount of their produce. Even though the stories of the book of Judges come from a later time, we can read between the lines to see signs of struggle by Israelites against the attempts of surrounding city-states (e.g. Hazor) to dominate them. These threats, along

FIGURE 2.3

Tablet containing a letter from Abdi-heba, the ruler of Jerusalem while it was still a Jebusite city, before David captured it. In it the ruler reports on the area to his overlords in Egypt.

with raids from groups such as the Midianites and Amalekites, created the need for charismatic leaders in crisis, "judges" such as Deborah or Samson, to rally disparate villages and tribes together, pooling their resources to repel a common enemy.

One enemy these Israelites did not have to face – in stark contrast to later periods in the history of Israel – was the might of a major ancient Near Eastern **empire** such as Egypt or Babylonia. The most this village culture would have known of such superpowers would have been distant echoes of Egyptian influence in some of the cities against which the villages had to fight for survival. Before the Israelite settlements emerged, Egypt had dominated the area for about two hundred years, subduing and demanding allegiance from the rulers of its major cities. Eventually, Egypt lost control of the area. Nevertheless, Egyptian influence continued for centuries in major coastal cities such as Byblos, and elsewhere in Palestine.

Unfortunately, we lack written texts from the Israelites of this period. Like other peoples of small villages across the Near East, the early Israelites almost certainly did not have time or need to learn to read and write extensive literary texts. We know from both comparative and archaeological evidence that writing – when it occurs – is primarily connected to centralized and hierarchical urban forms of social organization (e.g. Jerusalem). Nevertheless, like other small groups throughout time, our early Israelite villagers would have had a rich and varied cultural life. Rather than writing texts, they passed on traditions orally from one generation to another. These traditions would have included genealogical trees organizing clans and villages into tribal groups and subgroups, stories of cultural heroes such as Jacob, and songs of deliverance about the exodus or the victory under Deborah.

History and the Books of Joshua and Judges

At this point we are discussing Israel's earliest history in the land. This is the time when Israel lived in villages and did not yet have a king, a period described in the biblical books of Joshua and Judges. These books, however, date from around 600 BCE at the earliest, at least five hundred years after the events they describe. They are different from each other, and each builds on diverse oral and written traditions to tell its stories. For example, the books tell up to three different stories of the conquest of several cities: e.g. Hebron in Josh 10:36–7, 15:13–14, and Judg 1:10 or Debir in Josh 10:38–9, 15:15–17, and Judg 1:11. Because of problems like these historians of ancient Israel are ever more careful about how they use information from Joshua and Judges. Also, the discipline of archaeology has provided an important control for helping such historians evaluate the historical usefulness of biblical traditions. Later in this *Introduction* we will return to look at the books of Joshua and Judges as theological texts addressed to the people of the seventh century.

These **oral traditions** were in flux, as they were sung and told from year to year amidst constantly cycling generations. At one time scholars used to think that nonliterate cultures, such as the early Israelites, had unusual powers of memory that allowed them to memorize and precisely recite oral traditions over hundreds of years. Careful study of such cultures, however, has revealed that people who memorize traditions through purely oral means change those traditions constantly and substantially. To be sure, some elements may be preserved because they are anchored in a name, topographical feature, or ongoing cultural practice. Nevertheless, the singers of oral cultures regularly adapt the traditions they receive – telling versions of the same story about different figures and/or in different settings, revising what those figures say, conforming the story over time to certain broader types of tales (e.g. adding trickster themes), etc.

This means that the early traditions of ancient Israel, whatever they were, evolved in their journey across the centuries of the late second and early first millennia, passing from one set of lips to another. A name such as "Moses" might stick, even the name of a long-abandoned Egyptian city – "Rameses" – but the story of the Israelites' exodus out of Egypt would evolve as they faced new enemies and challenges in later centuries. In the process of oral telling and retelling, the "Moses" of the story might start to resemble leaders or liberators at the time of retelling, and the "Egypt" of the retold story might resemble later enemies. Similarly, the story of Jacob wrestling God at the Jabbok (now in Gen 32:22–32) explains the place name "Penuel," and because the place name implies a divine encounter (Penuel is interpreted as Hebrew for "face of God"), that part of the story may have stayed stable over time while other details changed in the retelling process.

MORE ON METHOD: TRADITION HISTORY AND TRANSMISSION HISTORY

Though traditions can be written as well as oral, many scholars use the term **"tradition history"** to refer to the history of oral traditions that existed before and alongside the written texts now in the Bible. Different versions of an oral tradition can be recognized by the combination of thematic or plot parallels on the one hand and variation in characters, setting, and especially wording on the other. Take the example of the parallel stories of Abraham and Sarah at Philistine Gerar with King Abimelech (Gen 20:1–18, 21:22–34) and Isaac and Rebekah at the same place and with the same king (Gen 26:6–33). Look at the similarities and differences! Though the two sets of stories are remarkably parallel, they diverge enough from each other that many believe them to be oral variants of the same tales. The same is likely true of different versions of the story of Hagar in the wilderness (Gen 16:1–14, 21:8–19) or three different versions of stories where a patriarch (whether Abraham or Isaac) endangers his wife in the process of trying to protect himself (Gen 12:10–20, 20:1–18, 26:6–11).

The more you compare these texts with each other, the more you should realize just how fluid oral tradition really is. This means we need to move away from concepts of verbatim repetition of traditions and toward a focus on the complex process of *transmission* (including revision) of traditions, both oral *and* written! Scholars often use the term **"transmission history"** to refer more broadly to the history of the transmission of oral *and* written biblical traditions. Later in this *Introduction* we will discuss numerous examples of the growth of written texts through the combination or expansion of earlier sources.

One characteristic appears to have been remarkably frequent, particularly in Israel's early traditions: the **trickster** – that is, a character whose ability to survive through trickery and even lawbreaking is celebrated in religion, literature, or another part of culture. As we will see below, the Bible features both male and female versions of such characters, such as the figure of Jacob in Genesis, along with his mother, Rebecca, and his second wife, Rachel. Anthropologists have long noted that many cultures, particularly cultures of more vulnerable groups, celebrate such tricksters who survive against difficult odds through cunning and sometimes deceptive behavior. Figures such as the Plains Indian Coyote demonstrate to their people how one can survive in a hostile environment where the rules are stacked against you. Throughout time people in vulnerable circumstances have celebrated such tricksters, who are often heroes within their own group. In home rituals, agricultural celebrations, weddings and other rites of passage, and other events, they would tell and sing stories of how their ancestors had triumphed against all odds, often tricking and defeating their more powerful opponents. Oral stories about figures like Jacob, Rebecca, and Rachel may have served similar functions in early Israel.

Problems in Reconstructing Early Israel

EXERCISE

Read Joshua 11. What impression do you get from this chapter of the Israelites' military accomplishments? How does this compare with the picture of these as summarized in Judges 1? As indicated in the above discussion of "History and the Books of Joshua and Judges", both these narratives about Israel's origins were written centuries after the events they describe and are historically problematic.

The village imagined above is forever lost for us, if it ever existed in anything like that form. At the most we have fragments of its existence. Archaeological surveys have uncovered the remains of hundreds of settlements in the northern hill country of Israel that suddenly sprang up in unusual numbers around 1250 BCE. Strikingly, this also happens to be around the time when we see the first mention of the name "Israel" in a datable ancient document. A stone monument set up by Pharaoh Merneptah (see Figure 2.4) celebrates his army's victory over cities and other groups in Syria-Palestine, saying:

> Canaan is plundered, Ashkelon is carried off, and Gezer is captured. Yenoam [a town near the sea of Galilee] is made into non-existence; Israel is wasted, its seed [offspring] is no more; and Hurru [a term for Syria] has become a widow because of Egypt. (Translation adapted from that by James Hoffmeier in *Hallo, Context of Scripture*, vol. 2, p. 41)

FIGURE 2.4
Merneptah stela, including a list of Egyptian conquests and dating to around 1200 BCE. It contains the earliest mention of "Israel" outside the Bible.

The stela commemorates an Egyptian campaign carried out sometime around 1220 BCE. Interestingly, the Egyptian writing system clearly indicates that this "Israel" is a tribal people, not a territory. The next securely datable mention of anything specifically Israelite comes four hundred years later. So this mention of a people, "Israel," in the Merneptah stela of 1207 is a precious clue. It helps us interpret the village settlements across the hill country in

1250–1000 BCE as the earliest remains of "Israel," the people who would later create the Hebrew Bible/Old Testament.

The earlier history of this people cannot be recovered. This is as far back as we can go using academic methods of historical reconstruction. Through a combination of archaeological evidence for early hilltop villages and the Merneptah stela, we have good reason to think that some kind of village culture "Israel" already lived in the hill country of Palestine from around 1300 onward (see Map 2.1). Nevertheless, we do not have the kind of secure written or other sources that historians would typically rely on to tell us where these people came from or how they got there.

To be sure, the Bible tells a story of how this people was formed from ancestors of Jacob's sons, who went down into Egypt, emerged in the exodus, and wandered in the wilderness, before entering Canaan through a triumphant military conquest of all of the area and destruction of all its inhabitants. Scholars once thought that archaeological remains confirmed this picture of external origins and total conquest, since there are destruction layers in many Canaanite towns in the late second millennium. Some thought these destruction layers were evidence of an Israelite onslaught. Nevertheless, others have rightly argued that the cities where destruction layers were found are not generally cities mentioned in the Bible. Moreover, their destructions apparently occurred over a period of over one hundred years rather than in a single conquest as related in the book of Joshua. This calls into question the idea that they are the result of a coordinated Israelite conquest of the sort described in Joshua. Instead, many of these cities probably disappeared as part of a more widespread destruction of major urban centers that occurred toward the end of the second millennium, a destruction caused by a combination of environmental catastrophe and invasions of "sea peoples" from the Western Mediterranean. Furthermore, of the nineteen cities mentioned in the Bible as destroyed by the Israelites, only three were clearly destroyed, while the rest either were not destroyed or were abandoned at the times when most scholars think the conquest could have occurred. In sum, the archaeological evidence, if anything, contradicts rather than confirms the picture of total destruction of the Canaanite people given in Joshua. Indeed, it better matches the picture of the coexistence of Israelites and Canaanites in the land given in Judges 1, a biblical text that contrasts with the account of total conquest in Joshua.

So, one might ask, where did the biblical stories in Joshua come from? There are different explanations for individual stories on the one hand and of the broader account of total conquest on the other. For example, many scholars now understand individual stories such as the conquest of Jericho as tales of triumph that were built up to explain ancient ruins. Much later in Israel's history, an Israelite storyteller, unaware that the ruins at Jericho long predated the presence of Israel in the land, told a story that explained those ruins as the remains of a great victory by God when Israel entered the land. This story developed over time until it was included in a broader story of Israel's conquest of the whole land under Joshua. This story of total conquest of the land (Joshua 1–12) in response to God's command (Deuteronomy 7) is even further from

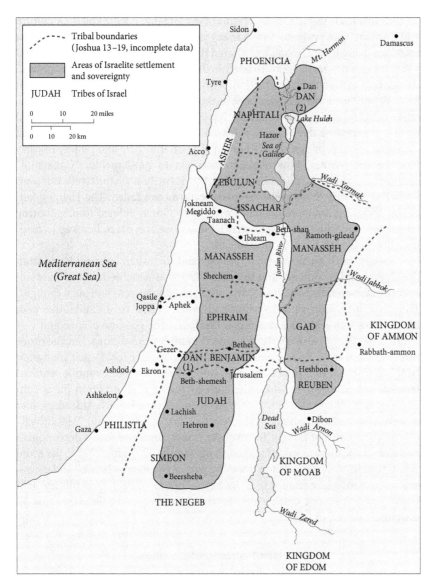

MAP 2.1
Areas of the hill country occupied by the Israelites and Judeans, and where the tribes are said
to have been located in the pre-state period. Redrawn from Norman Gottwald, *The Hebrew
Bible: A Socio-Literary Introduction*. Minneapolis: Fortress, 1985, page 133.

being a photographic reproduction of ancient events. The language and theology of Joshua 1–12 make clear that it was a story composed to empower a
much later Israelite people who had been repeatedly humiliated and oppressed
by the superpowers of their day. Chapter 5 of this textbook will feature more
discussion of the biblical picture of conquest, since it focuses on the time in
which the book of Joshua was written.

All this leads us back to the origins of the Israelite people and their culture – *in* Canaan. Our evidence shows every sign that the vast bulk of the earliest Israelites came from Canaan and shared its language, its material culture, and – to some extent – its religion. To be sure, there may have been a "Moses group," themselves of Canaanite extraction, who experienced slavery and liberation from Egypt, but most scholars believe that such a group – if it existed – was only a small minority in early Israel, even though their story came to be claimed by all. The rest of the early Israelites did not come from outside the land through conquest or gradual settlement. The architecture and pottery of early Israelite settlements show close connections to pre-Israelite, "Canaanite" architecture and pottery. Prior attempts to identify a distinctively different "Israelite" pottery, house type, or other feature have failed. The Hebrew language, including its more ancient forms, is so closely related to neighboring languages that a student who learns Hebrew is well on his or her way to reading Phoenician, Moabite, Ammonite, etc.

Finally, both archaeological remains and the much later evidence from the Hebrew Bible indicate that the oldest forms of Israelite religion were not as distinct from non-Israelite, "Canaanite" religion as scholars once thought. The Canaanites worshipped various gods, such as the creator and father god, **El**, his wife **Asherah**, the storm god **Baal**, and the goddess of love and war **Anat**. Anat is not particularly prominent in biblical traditions, but the other three all appear to have played significant roles in early Israel, alongside Israelite worship of a non-Canaanite God, "Yahweh." For example, ancient Israelites often expressed their theology by giving their children pious sentence names. The Bible records that Saul, one of Israel's earliest leaders, had descendants named "Ishbaal" (Hebrew for "man of Baal") and "Mephibaal" ("from the mouth of Baal"). In this case, these names of Saul's descendants probably indicate reverence for Baal in his family. The name "El" is yet more prominent in biblical tradition, forming part of the name "Isra*el*," and of several important place names (e.g. Bethel – "house of El"). One biblical text even uses a frequent epithet of El, "the Most High," to describe how El assigned Yahweh to Israel:

> When the Most High assigned the nations,
>   when he divided humankind,
> He determined the boundaries of the peoples
>   according to the number of the gods.
> Yahweh's own portion was his people,
>   Jacob was his assigned share. (Deut 32:8–9)

Israel's worship was probably not confined to male deities such as Baal, El, or Yahweh. Archaeologists have found remains in early Israelite settlements both of female figurines and of early Israelite depictions of trees, a frequent symbol in ancient Canaan of female reproductive power (see Figure 2.5). Many scholars think these early images of trees/women were representations of the goddess Asherah, the wife of the creator god El. Worship of Asherah appears to have been widespread in earliest Israel. Each ancient village probably had its

FIGURE 2.5
Animals feeding on trees, an early Israelite reflection of a yet earlier artistic pattern seen in pre-Israelite remains where the same animals were fed by a goddess figure, possibly Asherah. Redrawn from Othmar Keel and Christoph Uehlinger, *Göttinnen, Götter und Gottessymbole: neue Erkenntnisse zur Religionsgeschichte Kanaans und Israels aufgrund bislang unerschlossener ikonographischer Quellen* (Quaestiones disputatae). Freiburg im Breisgau: Herder, 1992, page 134.

own hilltop sanctuary, a raised platform for sacrifice, featuring both a pillar to symbolize male deity and a tree to symbolize divine female power. Asherah, whose symbol is the tree, was the probable focus of the tree symbolism.

The Name "Israel"

The name "Israel," like most ancient Hebrew names, is a sentence. It is formed from the divine name "El," and may mean "El rules" or "May El prove his rulership." It reflects the potential focus in earliest Israel on El's role in helping early tribal groups resist the "rulership" of surrounding cities and their armies.

Traces of the Most Ancient Israelite Oral Traditions in the Bible

Because a tribal society like early Israel did not produce extended literary texts, the Bible does not contain many traditions from this early period. Instead, the Bible, even parts that talk of Israel's early history, is a corpus of texts written down centuries later, long after the conclusion of the tribal period. Nevertheless, these ancient villages had their own oral traditions, passed down by word of mouth from generation to generation. These traditions, constantly evolving to fit the hopes and fears of the performers and their audiences, expressed the deepest values of their community. The following sections of this chapter discuss three sets of biblical texts that are good candidates for providing a view, however blurry and indistinct, of distinctive elements of early Israel's theology and traditions.

The Oral Background of Genesis

READING

Stories of the Endangerment of the Matriarch: compare Gen 12:10–20,
20:1–18, and 26:6–11
Abraham and Lot Cycle of Stories: Genesis 13, 18–19
Stories of Hagar and Ishmael: compare Gen 16:1–14 and 21:8–19
Skim stories about Jacob, his family, and his Journey to Haran: Genesis 27–32.

We turn now to look at how stories in the first book of the Bible, Genesis, are
built on oral traditions, including some trickster elements. Notably, the stories we will discuss here do not come from the first chapters of Genesis, narratives of primeval beginnings (creation, etc.) found in Genesis 1–11. We will
discuss those chapters once we come to the development of writing in later
Israel. Rather, the parts of Genesis that most reflect oral origins are narratives about Israel's ancestors in Genesis 12–50 – Abraham, Isaac, Jacob, and
their families.

Of course the written biblical text contains no such oral tradition in pure
form. The often-repeated idea that people in oral cultures perfectly remember and repeat their traditions was long ago shown to be untrue (see above
pp. 40–41). That said, blurry forms of ancient Israelite traditions can be seen
in biblical texts, especially in ways that those texts feature one or more
accounts of how such figures survived by means of deception and trickery.
Take, for example, the multiple accounts of how a patriarch worked to avoid
being killed by a king because of his beautiful wife by telling the king that she
actually was his sister. The Bible preserves two versions of this story about
Abraham (Gen 12:10–20 and 20:1–18) and one version about Isaac (Gen
26:6–11). At least one biblical author seems to have found Abraham's lying
on this point problematic, since the second version of this story (in Genesis
20) has Abraham claiming that she was his half-sister (Gen 20:12).
Nevertheless, the Bible's own narrative says nothing of the sort about her (see
Gen 11:29–30), and this additional part of Abraham's speech is probably
evidence of the discomfort that some later authors had with the trickster
traditions that they adapted.

As we move to the section of Genesis focused on Jacob (Genesis 25–35), we
see more places where the Bible's written text preserves echoes of earlier trickster traditions. In Genesis 25 Jacob cleverly gets a hungry Esau to sell his birth-
right for a pot of lentil stew. Then, in Genesis 27, Rebekah, Jacob's mother,
develops a tricky ruse to get Jacob's father, Isaac, to give Jacob the superior blessing that he meant to give to Esau. At Rebekah's urging, Jacob flees to escape
Esau's plan to murder him, and he gets a taste of his own medicine in Haran,
where his father-in-law, Laban, gets him to work seven years to marry Rachel,
but then slips Leah into Jacob's marriage bed instead (Genesis 29). Soon Jacob
turns the tables on Laban, using magical means to outwit Laban's plan to deprive
Jacob of his wages in livestock (Genesis 30) and later escaping with Laban's
daughters without Laban's knowledge (Genesis 31). In the process, Rachel

shows her own capacity for trickery, stealing her father's household gods and then preventing him from finding them by sitting on them and then telling her father that she cannot get up because she has her period ("the way of woman is on me"; Gen 31:35). In these ways and others, the story depicts Jacob and his closest family as crafty tricksters, able to survive and flourish in the face of difficult odds. Not only is he himself a trickster, but his mother helped get him started, and he worked 14 years to marry a woman, Rachel, who continues the tradition.

These traditions of trickery are not the sort of thing typically focused on in sermons and Sunday school lessons. Many within dominant cultures are not used to celebrations of such culture heroes – figures who trick and even lie to get their way. Nevertheless, such stories can be encouraging to people who feel that they will inevitably perish if they play by "the rules" of their social context. Whether Native American or ancient Israelite, vulnerable people often gain empowerment through celebrating ancestors who made their way in the world through using cleverness to overcome impossible odds. For people on the top, such trickster stories can appear to be embarrassing elements in an otherwise tidy Bible. For people on the bottom, such stories can be a major way of gaining hope and resisting domination.

That said, none of the texts in the Bible, including Genesis, are transcripts of early oral traditions. Rather these are later literary texts where earlier oral traditions have been radically reshaped to fit into a broader narrative. This means that we must distinguish between the present *written* level of the biblical text and faint outlines of oral traditions standing behind that text. The written text develops a new picture of Abraham as a recipient of God's promises and even adds the idea of God making a covenant with him. This picture of Abraham and focus on God's promise to him and his descendants developed as a response to Israel's trauma under later empires. Meanwhile, another set of stories about Israel's ancestors looms behind this picture: older oral stories of how some of Israel's ancestors successfully fended for themselves.

(Echoes of) earlier oral traditions in Genesis	Elements specific to the present written text of Genesis 12–50
A focus on how both men (e.g. Abraham, Jacob) and women (e.g. Rebekah, Rachel) survived and flourished through their wits	A focus on how God promised the patriarchs of Israel (Abraham, Isaac, Jacob) to make them a great people, bless them, and give them the land of Canaan
Traditions about these figures circulate in one or more cycles of stories about each figure (e.g. Abraham, Isaac, Jacob, Hagar), with some of the same stories told about different figures (e.g. wife endangerment by Abraham in Gen 20:1–18 and 21:22–34; Isaac in Gen 26:6–33)	The reshaping and connection of originally separate traditions so that they are linked with new themes of blessing and promise that spoke to the despair of later Israelites
A celebration of deception if it ensures the success of the underdog trickster	Introduction of divine speeches to early ancestors (Abraham, Jacob, Isaac, and also Hagar) and focus on their need to trust in God's covenant with them and provision for them

Basics on the Written Version of the Ancestral Story (Genesis 12–50)

Though this chapter focuses on reconstructing ancient Israel's oral traditions, it can be helpful to contrast such speculation about now-lost oral traditions with a look at the written text that we actually have. In the case of Israel's ancestors, we start with the written text of Genesis 12–50, one that is thoroughly shaped by the above-noted, later written themes of promise and covenant.

Outline: the three major parts of Genesis 12–50

I   Abraham: God's promises of blessing and land to Abraham and his descendants   11:27–25:11
[Interlude: Genealogy of the descendants of Ishmael   25:12–18]

II   Jacob: Transfer of promises to Isaac and Jacob; also stories of Rebekah, Esau, Rachel   25:19–35:29
[Interlude: Genealogy of the descendants of Esau   36:1–43]

III   Joseph and other sons of Jacob: division among brothers and eventual reconciliation   37–50

Key themes

An overarching theme for this section is God's gift of promises of blessing and land to Abraham (Gen 12:1–7) and covenant with him (Genesis 15 and 17), promises that are then passed on to his heirs Isaac (Gen 26:2–5, 24) and Jacob (Gen 28:13–14; 35:9–15).

Much of the Abraham story is particularly oriented toward these promises. It tells of how Abraham is protected by God in Egypt and in Gerar when he leaves Israel because of famine (Gen 12:10–20; 20:1–18), how God eventually makes covenants with him sealed by sacrifice (Genesis 15) and the sign of male circumcision (Genesis 17), and how God provides him a son through Sarah to inherit the promise, Isaac (Genesis 18; 21:1–7), alongside his son, Ishmael, whom he fathers through Sarah's slave, Hagar (Gen 16; 21:8–21).

The theme of promise continues in the Jacob story (Genesis 25–35), especially in an initial digression focused on Isaac (Gen 26:1–33). Nevertheless, most of this part of Genesis focuses on Jacob's journey away from home, fleeing the wrath of his brother, Esau, caused by Jacob's trickery (Gen 25:29–34; 27:1–45). Jacob travels to stay with Abraham's relatives in Haran and acquires family and flocks there, including fathering the ancestors of the twelve tribes of Israel (Genesis 28–30). The story concludes with Jacob's return to the land, wrestling with God (Gen 32:22–32) just before reconciling with his brother Esau (Genesis 33).

The Joseph story in Genesis 37–50 is even more focused on the theme of division among brothers. Joseph's brothers sell him into slavery at the outset (Genesis 37), but he rises to power in Egypt (Genesis 39–41), and he is then able to provide for his father and brothers when they flee to Egypt because of another famine in Israel (42–50).

Women in Israel's ancestral stories

There are some important stories focusing on women among Israel's ancestors. On the one hand, we see biblical matriarchs exerting a limited form of power in the household sphere, whether through using slaves as sexual surrogates (Sarah using Hagar in Genesis 16; Rachel and Leah using Bilhah and Zilpah in Gen 30:3–13) or using their wits to promote their favored son (Rebekah in Genesis 27) or protect their husband from a vengeful father-in-law (Rachel in Gen 31:26–35). On the other hand, the stories of Dinah and Tamar show the extreme vulnerability of women in the Israelite world. Tamar exposes her body and risks death in the process of trying to secure a lineage for her father-in-law Judah (Genesis 38), and Dinah is raped and revenged amidst a power struggle between her brothers and the inhabitants of Shechem (Genesis 34).

Try reading through Genesis 12–50 now with this background. These are **Further reading**
some of the most famous stories in the Bible, particularly because three
major world faiths – Judaism, Christianity, and Islam – focus on Abraham and
God's promises to him and his heirs. We will return to these texts later in this
Introduction, but this is a good time to initially familiarize yourself with them.

Your reading of texts like Genesis becomes more nuanced when you are
attuned to the fact that it contains such earlier oral traditions. Rather than trying to explain away or excuse strategies like Jacob's tricking of Esau out of his
father's blessing (Genesis 27), you can see such elements as part of the Bible's
complex mix. Not only does the Bible describe God's promises to and covenants with Israel's great patriarchs (e.g. Genesis 15 and 17), but it includes
adaptations of these stories of ancestral trickery and self-reliance.

Finally, it should be stressed that these earlier oral traditions are adaptations themselves of centuries of earlier oral traditions. As stories about
Abraham and Jacob, Rebekah and Rachel were told and retold in the vulnerable unwalled villages of Israel, they were selected and reshaped to encourage
early Israelites. Those Israelites faced challenges in securing their livelihood
and defending themselves against the kings of surrounding city-states.
Generations of Israelite storytellers selected certain stories and reshaped them
for their hearers. Some tales fell by the wayside while others gained new elements. And this complex oral storytelling process produced uncanny elements
in Israel's ancestral narratives that readers often overlook.

The Exodus from Egypt

Exodus 2, 5–10, and the potential early song of Miriam in Exod 15:20–1.

READING

The book of Exodus, like Genesis, is a complex mix. In Chapter 6 of this
Introduction, we will discuss how major parts of Exodus – such as the stories of
God's delay of the exodus to inflict plagues on Egypt – were shaped in relation
to later Israel's experiences of imperial trauma. That does not mean, however,
that later storytellers completely made up the figure of Moses and the exodus
event. Rather, key parts of the exodus story would never have been invented by
later writers, such as Moses having an Egyptian name (consider, for example,
the famous Pharaoh Thut*mose*) or Moses having foreign wives from Midian
(Exodus 2) and Cush (Numbers 12). And these are just two initial indicators
that some kind of story of the exodus circulated in ancient Israel from a very
early period. At the start, such a story may well have been the property of a

subgroup in Israel, perhaps an "exodus group" of prisoners who had escaped from Egypt who then joined others living in hill-country villages and told their story of liberation from Pharaoh under the leadership of Moses.

Yet, even assuming that some sort of exodus from Egypt occurred histori-cally, the story about it would not have survived if it had not also spoken an important new word to the people living in the hill-country villages. And there are good reasons to think it did. For these village-culture Israelites had "pharaohs" of their own day, the rulers of the city-states surrounding them, whom they needed to resist. The Song of Deborah in Judges 5 (and the later accompanying story in Judges 4) vividly describes the kind of threat posed by such cities, with their professional armies and chariots. Furthermore, it is likely that some such formerly Egyptian-dominated cities, such as Jerusalem or Shechem, preserved remnants of the Egyptian culture. At the least, these former outposts of Egyptian domination of Canaan would have been per-ceived by villagers as the closest oppressive counterpart to the Egypt that had once dominated the area.

The story of Yahweh's deliverance of slaves from Egypt would have served as a powerful rallying cry for villagers now fighting for survival against such city-states. The story became the property of all "Israel," not just former slaves and their descendants. We see this sort of community claiming of an older story today, for example, in the way later African Americans have claimed the stories of the Bible for themselves. In his March 2008 speech on race, "A More Perfect Union," Barack Obama drew on his autobiography to describe how he found hope in the merging of biblical stories and contemporary lives in the black church:

> People began to shout, to rise from their seats and clap and cry out, a forceful wind carrying the reverend's voice up into the rafters ... And in that single note – hope! – I heard something else; at the foot of that cross, inside the thousands of churches across the city, I imagined the stories of ordinary black people merg-ing with the stories of David and Goliath, Moses and Pharaoh, the Christians in the lion's den, Ezekiel's field of dry bones. Those stories – of survival, and free-dom, and hope – became our story, my story; the blood that had spilled was our blood, the tears our tears; until this black church, on this bright day, seemed once more a vessel carrying the story of a people into future generations and into a larger world. Our trials and triumphs became at once unique and universal, black and more than black; in chronicling our journey, the stories and songs gave us a means to reclaim memories that we didn't need to feel shame about ... memories that all people might study and cherish – and with which we could start to rebuild.

This claiming of older stories by new groups is hardly limited to the black church. Much as many Americans now claim for themselves the story of the *Mayflower* and the Puritan holiday of thanksgiving, despite the fact that many descend from immigrants of the twentieth century, so also Israelite villagers of varied origins claimed the exodus story as their own. That story celebrated the god, Yahweh, who had liberated "them" from Egypt, and it expressed their confidence that this exodus God would also fight on their behalf against their contemporary "pharaohs," the local city-states.

MORE ON METHOD: AFRICAN AMERICAN BIBLICAL INTERPRETATION

The above-quoted speech by President Obama connects with a complicated history of African Americans and the Bible. On the one hand, African Americans have seen the Bible used against them. In particular, slaveholders reinterpreted the story of Noah's curse of Ham (Gen 9:20–7) as an eternal curse of Africans to slavery, and they noted that slavery is assumed as an ongoing reality in a number of biblical writings (e.g. Lev 25:44–6). On the other hand, African Americans have also found encouragement in the Bible's story of God's liberation of slaves from Egypt, calls for justice in prophets like Amos, and the Bible's picture of Jesus.

African American scholars have engaged in multiple ways with this complicated history. To start, a number of scholars highlighted the presence of African characters in the Bible and countered racist interpretations of stories like the curse of Ham. More recently, a number of studies have analyzed the diverse ways that the Bible, especially elements like the story of exodus from Egyptian slavery, have functioned in African American religion and culture. For one survey of the broader field of critical African American interpretation, see Mitzi J. Smith, *Insights from African American Interpretation* (Minneapolis: Fortress, 2017). We will return to themes of African American interpretation in later chapters, starting with the next chapter's discussion of Afrocentric and womanist interpretation and the biblical Song of Songs.

Yet again we must remember that the exodus story (or stories) that ancient Israelites claimed was not identical with the story found in the Bible in Exodus 1–15. No one would have been writing such texts in the villages of early Israel. Moreover, there are numerous signs – to be discussed elsewhere in this book – that these stories in the book of Exodus were shaped into their present form by much later Israelites rereading the story of exodus in relation to ever new "pharaohs": the "pharaoh" of Solomon and his kingdom, the "pharaoh" of Assyrian and Babylonian superpowers, etc. This process of merging of stories described by Barack Obama has been going on a very long time.

That said, there are some trickster elements in the biblical exodus story that may point to a few early oral elements lying in some form behind the text in Exodus 1–15. Take, for example, the tale of the tricky midwives, Shiphrah and Puah (Exod 1:15–22), who disobey Pharaoh's command to kill all male Israelite babies, claiming "Hebrew women are not like Egyptian women; they are so strong that they give birth before the midwife has a chance to get to them." Later on, fully intending to depart for good, Moses nevertheless tries to get the Israelites free by asking Pharaoh for a three-day vacation in the wilderness so they can fulfill God's command to worship there (Exod 5:1–5). Later, when Pharaoh agrees to let the Israelites have a three-day festival in Egypt rather than going away, Moses claims that they cannot do so because the Israelite sacrifices would be too distasteful to the Egyptians (8:21–3). When the plagues finally persuade Pharaoh to let the male Israelites go on their supposed worship pilgrimage, Moses slyly insists that the men cannot adequately observe this particular festival without all of their families and livestock along (10:7–10). These elements are now found in later, written biblical texts (some composed amidst later contexts of cultural resistance). Nevertheless, these stories about the exodus reflect a tone of trickery particularly characteristic of early oral traditions.

Judges 5 (note that this probable early poem is different from the later account in Judges 4).

READING

FOCUS
TEXT

The Song of Deborah

The Song of Deborah in Judges 5 is the one of the best candidates for being a biblical text that might more closely reflect an ancient village-culture tradition than the (prose) narratives discussed so far. It is a poem celebrating Israel's triumph over the Canaanite king, Sisera, and its poetic – and perhaps sung – form could aid more precise memorization and recitation over the years. In addition, the song contains archaic elements of Hebrew language, and the list of tribes and other groups in Judges 5 only partially overlaps with later lists of tribes that made up early Israel (an example can be found in Numbers 1). Judges 5 does not even mention some of the southern tribes, and it mentions other names not typically found in 12 – tribe lists such as that in Numbers 1 (e.g. Machir = Manasseh; and Meroz). These are among some of our first clues that this text may reflect a very early poem. Open up your Bible to Judges 5 and we will use this text as an evocative window to a time long before texts of our Bible began to be written down.

5:2–5: The song opens with a hymn of praise describing Yahweh's triumphant appearance from the southern desert regions of Seir and Edom (5:4–5). It is one of several potentially early texts that locate Sinai and Yahweh's origins in the desert regions south of Palestine (Deut 33:2; Hab 3:3; Ps 68:7–9). Our ancient text envisions Yahweh as a powerful storm god, whose arrival is marked by earthquakes and torrential floods. Yet there is also a focus here and throughout the poem on the people. The first verse of the poem celebrates the way leaders took the lead and the people responded willingly (5:2), and the second verse (5:3) calls on the powerful "kings and princes" of the world to hear this "song" about the triumph of a kingless group of tribal villagers.

5:6–12: The next section of the poem celebrates the emergence of leadership in this otherwise disorganized group: the rise of Deborah. Beforehand, trails had become unsafe, settlements were defenseless, and the people had no weapons (5:6–7a). But then Deborah arose "as a mother in Israel." The poem then again calls on those who volunteered in the effort to offer praise (5:9), along with other groups (5:10–11), and Deborah and Barak themselves (5:12).

5:13–18 and 5:23: The poem then details which tribal groups answered the call to battle willingly, and which did not. Six tribes came when called: Ephraim, Benjamin, Machir (related to Manasseh; Num 26:29), Zebulun, Issachar, and Naphtali. Four did not: Reuben, Gilead (perhaps in place of Gad in the standard lists of tribes), Dan, and Asher. Two southern tribes are not even mentioned: Judah and Simeon. Apparently at the time the Song was written they were not even envisioned as potential partners in this kind of military effort. Even the northern groups that appear here are clearly not unified. Only six out of ten answered the call to battle. Indeed, from the initial call to praise those who volunteered (5:2) to the contrast of those who volunteered and those who did not (5:13–18), much of Deborah's song seems aimed at encouraging the separate tribes to affirm their common destiny. It calls on villagers to sing praises to God for a victory where six tribes joined together to defeat – with God's help – the mighty forces of Sisera. And it soon calls on them to curse "Meroz," an unknown group who failed to answer the call (5:23).

5:19–22: The actual description of the battle occurs only in these four verses. They move beyond the conflict between Israel and Sisera to juxtapose the "kings of Canaan" with their horses on the one hand with the cosmic powers of Yahweh on the other. The kings may have the superior military technology, but they have no chance against the power of stars fighting from heaven and the force of the Kishon River (5:19–21). Soon the once powerful stallions were fleeing (5:22).

5:24–31: In two scenes, 5:24–7 and 28–30, the poet concludes with vignettes about the aftermath of the battle. The first blesses Jael, of the Kenites, for aiding in the effort by cleverly tricking Sisera into enjoying her hospitality and then killing him with a mallet (5:24–7). Again, there is an element of the trickster here, since hospitality is otherwise celebrated as a profound value, not just in surrounding cultures, but in Israelite traditions as well. Nevertheless, Jael welcomes Sisera into her tent and feeds him, before killing him. Like a slow-motion movie, the poetry uses repetition to focus in on the moment.

> Between her feet he sank, he fell, he lay.
> Between her feet he sank, he fell.
> Where he sank, there he fell, destroyed. (Judg 5:27)

Meanwhile, in 5:28–30 the poet offers another vision featuring a woman, this time, the mother of Sisera, waiting for him to return triumphant from battle, not knowing of his recent death. As she wonders at his delay, her "wise women" speculate that he is probably delayed by dividing spoil: a few Israelite maidens for each warrior and some nice cloth to bring back to the women at home.

In this way, "Deborah's song" uses two scenes involving women to illustrate the contrast between the destinies of Yahweh's friends and enemies. Yahweh's enemies will perish and their women (like Sisera's mother) will mourn, but those who join in the effort to fight, like Jael, will be "like the sun when it rises with all its might" (5:31).

This belief in the triumph of the people that God chooses is an early form of what is often termed **"election theology"** – that is, the idea that God has chosen a particular people to care for and defend. This idea is present in the affirmation of the exodus tradition that Yahweh delivered Israel from Egypt. And it is implicit in the stories of God's protection and provision for Israel's trickster ancestor, Jacob, and his family. In all these traditions, God chooses not a place, nor a territorial nation, but a people, and protects them against seemingly impossible odds. This belief in God's choosing of a particular people, rooted in tribal traditions like the Song of Deborah and the exodus story, is a fundamental bedrock of later Israelite theology, especially in the northern part of Israel. Moreover, this idea of the distinctiveness and chosenness of a *people*, election theology, may have distinguished early Israel from some of the monarchal nation-states that surrounded it. Those states were more focused on how their gods chose a particular city and/or royal-priestly dynasty.

The Creation of "Israel" Through Cultural Memory of Resistance to Domination

All this is a prelude to the gradual creation of the Hebrew Bible. At this point in the history of Israel no books, not even chapters, had been written. "Israel" was only a very loose association of village-tribal groups. These villages shared, however, a common way of life. They aided each other in times of famine, and charismatic leaders such as Deborah rose up in times of crisis to fight common enemies. Whatever their diverse origins, these villagedwellers came to claim a common story of liberation from Egypt. They claimed a common ancestor, Jacob, along with the rest of his trickster family. And through poems like the Song of Deborah, they celebrated those occasions where they joined together to experience Yahweh's deliverance against the more powerful city-states around them.

Some scholars, such as Maurice Halbwachs (*On Collective Memory* [Chicago: University of Chicago Press, 1992]) and Jan Assmann (*Religion and Cultural Memory* [Stanford: University of Stanford Press, 2005]), have argued persuasively that such common memories are what form groups of people. Such **cultural memory** is reinforced through parental teaching, schools, festivals, and other practices in which people in groups recite or act out their common heritage. For example, national holidays, such as July 4 in the United States, are occasions when national identity is reinforced through various festivities, in this case marking the day when the nation was born. New citizens are required to learn the common story before they can become "Americans." Similarly, the worship year in Jewish synagogues and Christian churches continually reminds those communities of their stories, having them relive the events of the Torah (for synagogues) or the life of Jesus (for churches) and reinforce their sense of a particular religious identity. You become a "Jew" or "Christian" partly through learning the story of that group and claiming it as your own.

We do not know exactly how the oral versions of the texts about exodus, Jacob's family, and Deborah's victory were used, but they appear to have served a similar purpose in helping to create and reinforce a sense of common "Israelite" identity out of varied groups. Whether taught to children, recited at clan worship, sung at festivals, or used in some other way, the ancient oral traditions discussed in this chapter helped turn the people living in the hill country of Syria-Palestine into the "Israelites" who would create the later Bible.

The shared oral memories discussed in this chapter made for a particular kind of community: one that celebrated powerful work by God on the one hand and the clever action of tricksters on the other. In the midst of the pluralistic Canaanite religious environment, these traditions praise the liberative work of Yahweh, a god known from the southern deserts. Yet they also celebrate Israelite resourcefulness and wit. In particular, they empower people living on the margins by celebrating clever underdogs such as Jacob or Jael. Women are quite prominent in these traditions, as mothers, tricksters, and even military leaders (Deborah). Meanwhile, "kings" and their representatives are the opponents in these village-culture traditions, whether Pharaoh or Hazor's general Sisera.

Even when Israel developed writing, the stories of these oral traditions – in highly varied forms – continued to be told and sung among Israelites, many of whom never learned to write. We must keep in mind that our written Bible is but the tip of the iceberg of a largely lost oral tradition in ancient Israel. The process started not with writing, but with telling tales of Israelite liberation, survival, and victory.

CHAPTER TWO REVIEW

1. Know the meaning and significance of the following terms discussed in this chapter:
   - Asherah
   - Baal
   - cultural memory
   - El
   - election theology
   - empire
   - monarchal city-state
   - oral traditions
   - segmentary society
   - trickster
   - village

2. Know the main differences between the following three ancient forms of social organization:
   - empire
   - monarchal city-state
   - village

3. What do anthropologists now know about the character of oral traditions? How does this affect their usability for reconstructing early traditions? How specifically are such oral traditions reflected in Genesis 12–25 or Exodus 1–15?

4. List ways that the Bible's picture of Israel's origins (where Israelites came from, what their religion was, ethnic makeup, political unity) contrasts with the picture developed by archaeologically informed historians. Specify at least three such contrasts.

5. What are two specific reasons that led scholars to doubt that ancient Israelites took possession of the land by killing all of the Canaanites in a single conquest?

6. (Focus text: Judges 5) Find three verses in this poem that illustrate three different aspects of earliest Israel. What is each aspect and how does it contrast with the picture of Israel's origins found elsewhere in the Bible like the book of Joshua, or even other parts of Judges like Judges 4? What is your overall impression about earliest Israel and its conception of God based on this poem in Judges 5?

RESOURCES FOR FURTHER STUDY

Commentaries and Other Books on Joshua

Nelson, Richard D. *Joshua*. Louisville, KY: Westminster John Knox Press, 1997.

Commentaries and Other Books on Judges

McCann, J. Clinton. *Judges*. Louisville, KY: Westminster John Knox Press, 2002.

Niditch, Susan. *Judges*. Louisville, KY: Westminster John Knox Press, 2008.

Trible, Phyllis. *Texts of Terror: Literary-Feminist Readings of Biblical Narratives*. Philadelphia, PA: Fortress, 1984. Chapters on the Levite's wife and Jephthah's daughter.

Everyday Life in Ancient Israel

King, Philip J., and Stager, Lawrence E. *Life in Biblical Israel*. Louisville, KY: Westminster John Knox Press, 2001.

The History of Israelite Religion

Keel, Othmar, and Uehlinger, Christoph. *Gods, Goddesses, and Images of God in Ancient Israel*, trans. Allan W. Mahnke. Minneapolis, MN: Fortress, 1997. Difficult, but good.

The Rise of Writing and Echoes of Past Empires in Monarchal Israel

3

Chapter Outline

Chapter Overview

This chapter outlines the huge changes in Israelite culture that led to the writing of the first books of the Hebrew Bible. Up to this point, Israelite village culture had many and varied oral traditions. Texts were something that empires and some smaller city-states had. But starting in the tenth century – the 900s BCE – we see the beginnings of an *Israelite* monarchy in Jerusalem, one ruled by David and his successors. Moreover, this emerging power structure in Israel appears to have modeled itself on the older, non-Israelite empires that preceded it, imitating their state structures and adapting models of writing from them.

A Contemporary Introduction to the Bible: Sacred Texts and Imperial Contexts, Second Edition.
Colleen M. Conway and David M. Carr.
© 2021 Colleen M. Conway and David M. Carr. Published 2021 by John Wiley & Sons Ltd.

This is the time when scribes in early Israel began to develop the very first corpus of written Hebrew texts, often modeling their new compositions on yet older writings from Egypt and Mesopotamia. The scribes created something like a "bible before our Bible." But as we will see, this "bible" was still a far cry from the one we have now. We may even find traces of this shorter, older "bible before our Bible" in several texts now in the Hebrew Bible that "echo" written traditions of more ancient cultures.

Imagining Early Monarchal Israel

Once again, we start with an imaginary reconstruction of the context in which these biblical traditions were formed. Our sources are few, varied, and disputed. Although the Bible describes Israel as a world power at the time of David and Solomon, it is likely that the Bible's picture of their glory is a fictional creation of an Israelite golden age. In developing the *beginnings* of a city-state monarchy David and Solomon imitated foreign models for kingship. The following reconstruction of these monarchal beginnings is based on a combination of archaeological and biblical evidence.

Our journey takes us back to another hilltop in ancient Canaan, this time Mount **Zion**, a hilltop to the south of the heartland of tribal Israel. Generally speaking, "Zion" and the city associated with it, "Jerusalem," are synonymous in the Bible. What is less well known is that Jerusalem had a long history as a city before David conquered it and made it the capital of his kingdom. In Chapter 2, we saw a letter from Abdi-heba, a king of pre-Davidic Jerusalem (Figure 2.3). This letter is but one sign that Jerusalem before David had its own cultural and political traditions. Moreover, David and his successors may have adapted some of the traditions of this ancient city in the process of setting up their fledgling kingdom. For example, the Bible contains a tantalizing suggestion that the pre-Israelite (Jebusite) inhabitants of the city already had a belief in Jerusalem's invulnerability. When David laid siege to Jerusalem, the Jebusites are said to have told David that "you will not come in, even the blind and lame will ward you off" (2 Sam 5:6). Such a claim that Jerusalem was unconquerable parallels later biblical **Zion theology** – that is, theology about Jerusalem's specialness and invulnerability – that we will see in some of Israel's psalms and other literature.

Let us return now to imagining the Jerusalem of both Davidic and later, Solomonic, times. As it turned out, the Jebusites were wrong. David succeeded in conquering Jerusalem by stealth. He conquered it and made it the capital of his kingdom. Located between David's own clan of Judah in the southern hills and the Israelite tribes toward the north, the small stronghold in Jerusalem was well situated to function as the base for David's role now as leader of Israel, and he solidified this function by moving an object sacred to the Israelites, the ark of Yahweh at Shiloh, to Jerusalem (2 Samuel 6). The later Jerusalem of Solomon's time houses this ark in a new temple for Yahweh (see Figure 3.1), one that stands alongside a new palace for the king.

FIGURE 3.1
Artist's reconstruction of Solomon's Jerusalem. The Temple is on the upper right, next down is the palace, and then the citadel of David with a stepped-stone structure supporting it.

King Solomon serves in this city/stronghold as both high priest and commander of the army. Below him is a small but expanding class of priestly, royal, and military officials. This is a new form of leadership, showing an evolution under David from tribal structures to foreign models of monarchy, particularly as seen in Egypt. Solomon's court bears a resemblance to the Egyptian royal court, and many of its positions are filled by the sons of officials who served in David's court. Indeed, one of Solomon's scribes may even have had an Egyptian father, David's scribe "Shisha," whose name is quite similar to the Egyptian word for "scribe." These officials and those under them administered the complex kingdom. They were the glue that held this broad kingdom of varied tribes and territories together.

This fledgling nation developed various provisions for continuity across space and time building on models from the monarchies of surrounding nations. Previously tribal culture had charismatic leaders such as Deborah who galvanized the people in a time of crisis. The development of a monarchy under Solomon and his successors allowed the people to achieve political stability through an ongoing royal dynasty. Where tribal culture depended on tribes volunteering to join others in resisting enemies, this monarchy had a standing army. And where groups in tribal culture shared ever-fluid *oral* traditions, this monarchy resembled other such monarchies in beginning to use *written* texts to reinforce and standardize oral memory. These written texts were not accessible to everyone in a largely non-literate society, but they provided an essential way to educate the new ruling class for this more expansive realm. By memorizing a specific collection of written texts, youths preparing to be leaders learned a common worldview that persisted across space and time. The scribes of Israel's early monarchy are the probable authors of the first such collection of Hebrew, written literary-theological texts.

The Rise of the Israelite Monarchy and Resistance to It

READING

2 Samuel 2–10 and 1 Kings 1–10.

Before looking at the earliest Hebrew texts, we need to appreciate the city-state context in which they were created. In Chapter 2 we saw how Israel emerged as a loose association of villages organized into tribes, settled largely in the northern hill country of Palestine. They were a "people," not a city-state. Their limited resources and social organization made it difficult for them to resist raids by neighboring tribes or attempts to dominate them by nearby city-states. Aside from the rise of temporary leaders in times of crisis, "judges" in the Bible, there were no elite classes. The people shared common access to the orally transmitted "cultural memory" that helped identify them as Israelites.

The book of 1 Samuel, written hundreds of years after the period it narrates, gives many explanations for why this tribal existence under judges came to an end: the people requested a king because Samuel's sons were corrupt, or because they wanted to imitate other nations, or because they wanted a human king instead of Yahweh as king. These explanations say more about the perspective of much later authors than they do about the true dynamics surrounding kingship. Meanwhile, another, unnamed force probably played a much bigger role in the beginnings of the monarchy: the Israelites accepted kingship under David and his successors because it was the only form of social organization that was centralized enough to repel the Philistine invasions into the hill country of central Palestine. The Bible records clashes between Israelites and Philistines in stories about Samson (Judges 14–16), the time of Samuel (1 Sam 4:1–7:1), Saul (1 Samuel 13–31), and David (2 Samuel 5 and 8). Saul, a member of the tribe of Benjamin, was anointed as king to repel the Philistines. Nevertheless, in some respects Saul was little more than a powerful local military leader. He did not develop a city capital or a professional army, and he achieved only limited success before being killed in battle with the Philistines, along with his heir Jonathan (1 Samuel 31//2 Chronicles 10). Saul's leadership was not the sort of "kingship" needed to repel the Philistines. It was really more of a "chieftainship."

We see more characteristics of kingship with David and especially his heir, Solomon. Within biblical texts, David is remembered as a paradoxical mix. On the one hand, several texts depict him as a king "faithful" to Yahweh (e.g. 1 Kgs 3:6). On the other hand, he is flawed enough to seduce an officer's wife, Bathsheba, and send her husband to certain death in order to be able to marry her (2 Samuel 11–12). In the broader scheme of things, however, David appears to have been an extraordinarily gifted military commander who established the groundwork for a monarchy that would last hundreds of years.

David started as an officer in Saul's Israelite army, and he was so militarily successful against the Philistines that he had to flee Saul's jealous wrath (see 1 Samuel 16–29). Later, when Saul died, David ruled his tribe, Judah, for a few years from the Judean town of Hebron, while Saul's son Eshbaal ruled Israel (2 Samuel 2–3). Then, when Eshbaal was assassinated, the Israelite leaders anointed David as king over them, so that David became king of both Judah and Israel (2 Sam 4:1–5:5). One of the first things he did as ruler of both peoples was to start a series of campaigns against the Philistines that permanently ended their threat to Judah and Israel (2 Sam 5:17–25; 8:1; see also 2 Sam 21:15–22).

Yet David did much more than defeat the Philistines. He introduced societal changes associated with kingship: city-based rule, organization of a professional army, and enforcement of taxes on the people to support the fortified city and army. First, David captured the Jebusite city of Jerusalem by stealth, and made it the capital of his new kingdom (2 Sam 5:6–16). This was a politically smart move for a Judean king claiming authority over Israel. Jerusalem was not identified with the southern tribe of Judah the way that Hebron was. Second, David solidified Jerusalem's claim as the capital of "Israel" by bringing into it the ark of the covenant, an object sacred to all the Israelite tribes (2 Samuel 6). Third, he achieved additional military success, in particular over the Philistine tribes that had troubled Israel up through the time of Saul (1 Samuel 5). Fourth and finally, he started to build longer-term city-state structures, solidifying ties with neighboring groups through marriage alliances (2 Sam 3:2–5) and developing an effective army (from 1 Sam 22:1–2 to 2 Sam 23:8–39). He even appears to have followed Egyptian models in developing the beginnings of a royal court, eventually one that also included a position for "forced labor" of his citizens to help with fortifying the country (2 Sam 20:23–6; compare with 2 Sam 8:16–18).

David's successor, Solomon, went yet further in developing the beginnings of a city-state monarchy based in Jerusalem. After being put in power by a virtual coup d'étatimplemented by his mother, Bathsheba (working in concert with several of David's close associates; see 1 Kings 1–2), Solomon started construction projects that would enhance the Jerusalem stronghold's claim to be the center of a Near Eastern city-state, such as building a palace for the king and a temple for Yahweh (1 Kgs 6–8). To do this, Solomon required significant resources. The Bible reports that he established a system of forced labor across Israel to support these construction efforts (1 Kgs 5:27–32), building an infrastructure of twelve administrators over the tribal areas of northern Israel (1 Kgs 4:7–19). Especially since elements like forced labor were seen by some biblical authors as a negative aspect of kingship (see, e.g., the sentiments we see attributed to Samuel in 1 Sam 8:11–17), it is unlikely that later authors created such elements in an effort to build up Israel's glorious past. Instead, Solomon appears to have gone beyond his predecessors in implementing a fuller form of kingship in early Israel, even as his accomplishments, and the regions that he and David were said to rule (see Map 3.1), were much embellished and expanded upon by later authors.

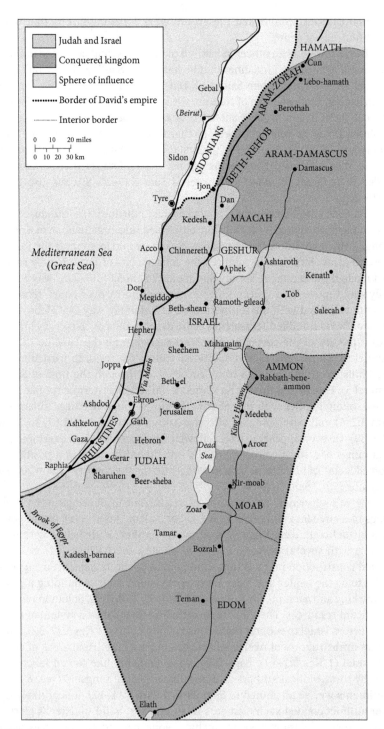

MAP 3.1
Areas ruled and dominated by David and Solomon. Redrawn from Yohanan Aharoni and Michael Avi-Yonah (eds.), *The Macmillan Bible Atlas* (revised edition). New York: Macmillan, 1977, map 104.

Archaeology and Problems of History Surrounding David, Solomon, and the Beginning of the Israelite Monarchy

As noted at the outset of this chapter, the Bible's description of David's and Solomon's monarchy has been thoroughly shaped by later authors into a picture of a golden age. Those authors do not even seem to have known specific dates for the beginning and end of the reigns of these two kings. Instead, these later writers assert that both David and Solomon had forty-year long reigns (1 Kgs 2:11; 11:42). The round number forty was widely used to designate "a very long time." Other aspects of the narrative also seem questionable, such as the idea that Solomon's wisdom was so famous that other kings and queens flocked to Jerusalem with gifts of gold, silver, and other valuables to seek his counsel (1 Kgs 4:29–34 [Hebrew 5:9–14]; 10:1–25). There is actually no mention of Solomon in any preserved texts from other nations of the time, and it is unlikely that a leader in a tiny provincial town like Jerusalem would have attracted such attention. Finally, archaeologists have not succeeded in finding much evidence of major construction in Jerusalem during the overall time that the Bible attributes to their two, supposed forty-year reigns when David supposedly built a place and Solomon a temple (approximately 1010–930 BCE). Together, these sorts of data have led some to doubt that David and Solomon even existed, or if they did, whether they established much of a centralized monarchy. Nevertheless, we do see mention of "the house of David" in a Syrian inscription (the "Tel Dan Stele") written in the century after David and Solomon. Only discovered in 1993, this apparent reference to the dynasty of David suggests that he founded some kind of political structure, even if his and Solomon's kingdoms were not as grand as later biblical authors made them out to be. For more on archaeology, biblical study, and questions surrounding the kingdoms of David and Solomon, see Matthieu Richelle, *The Bible and Archaeology* (trans. Sarah E. Richelle; Peabody, Mass: Hendrickson, 2018).

Not all Israelites were happy with the changes that came with David's and Solomon's rule. Though surely they were glad to see the Philistine threat contained, many perceived David and especially Solomon as Judean versions of the oppressive kings they had just defeated. After all, village-culture Israelites now had a new burden to add to the struggle for everyday existence. Not only did they need to find a way to provide for their kin each year, but they also had to provide substantial resources to the king and his city-state, both a portion of their crops and providing laborers on a rotation for the king's construction projects. The unhappiness of tribal leaders over this led to several rebellions against David's kingship, mainly centered in the north, where people in the heartland of ancient tribal "Israel" were the least happy with being ruled by Judah. One was led by Absalom, David's own son; another was led by Sheba, a leader from the Israelite north; and the final and successful one was led by Jeroboam, who will be discussed more in Chapter 4. What is important for our purposes now is an appreciation that the leaders in this early monarchy had to contend with opponents, particularly those associated with the Israelite north, who doubted the benefits of this new monarchy. The (proto)monarchy was a major new form of communal life, with many foreign elements, that involved many costs as well as benefits.

Influence of Ancient Empires on Early Israel's Monarchy and Writings

David and Solomon did not start from scratch when they began to develop the Israelite monarchy and associated Jerusalemite city-state. They were adopting a more ancient social form that was known elsewhere. After all, city-states had been around in Mesopotamia, Syria, Egypt, and even Palestine from the third millennium onward. Indeed, as we have seen, Jerusalem itself was the site of a small, pre-Israelite, Jebusite stronghold that had once been dominated by Egypt. There are numerous signs that David and Solomon drew on older Egyptian and other models in building the monarchy in Jerusalem: the makeup of their royal court, the models used for construction of temple and palace, etc. These are non-textual "echoes of empire" seen in the emergent Davidic monarchy in Jerusalem.

Yet there is another sort of "echo of empire" to be discussed here, and that is the way some biblical texts appear to reflect pre-Israelite texts that were used in the much older empires of Mesopotamia and Egypt. One thing that distinguished many ancient monarchies from the tribal groups surrounding them was their use of written texts, including the sorts of texts found in the Bible: wisdom sayings, psalms, myths, and stories. These written texts were a form of cultural memory like the oral traditions that continued to exist. Nevertheless, there were important differences. Most importantly, the relative firmness of written traditions made them good tools for shaping elites across time and space. Written texts do not change as readily as oral traditions do. This was important in city-states and empires, which spanned greater distances and joined disparate groups together. An empire or even a centralized city-state could bind together its different parts by making sure that its leaders all learned writing and memorized the same educational texts.

Our best examples of such literary education come from Egypt and Mesopotamia, much larger civilizations whose texts are better preserved (in Egypt because of climate, in Mesopotamia because they used clay tablets). The evidence from Egypt and Mesopotamia shows how students were educated in homes, often learning to read texts from either their own fathers or teachers whom they called "father." Ancient education in Egypt and Mesopotamia followed a similar pattern, a pattern probably common across the ancient world. Students started by learning to write and read basic symbols. The next step was memorizing and reciting basic "wisdom" instructions on how to live, and the final and most advanced stage was internalizing and performing other types of texts, such as royal hymns or stories of creation and flood. Careful analysis of student exercises, such as that seen in Figure 3.3, has allowed scholars to see how students in these cultures were taught to memorize their culture's texts line by line. Only a few in any ancient society had time to acquire such knowledge, but it was an important means by which Egypt, Mesopotamia, and other cultures trained future leaders.

This background from the cultures of Egypt and Mesopotamia is important because their educational-literary systems were used as models for the monarchies of Syria-Palestine in the centuries just before Israel emerged. The

FIGURE 3.2
Scribe standing before the king of a small neighboring kingdom with a scroll in his hand, dating from about a century after David and Solomon. The image shows the prestige attached to scribal writing even in the small kingdoms of the area.

kingdom of David and Solomon was too small to develop its own brand-new counterpart to the massive literatures of those ancient empires. Thus when scribes began writing the first Israelite literary texts in the time of David and Solomon (see Figures 3.4 and 3.5 for possible scribal exercises from that period), it seems that they did *not* focus on creating textual versions of earlier Israelite oral traditions about ancestors, exodus, or the like. Instead, the earliest authors of Hebrew literature were dependent on *foreign* models for literary education and imitated *foreign* texts from Egypt and Mesopotamia. Why? Perhaps because in creating Israel's first written literature these early Judean scribes were most interested in adapting earlier examples of such writings (all of which were foreign) and thus drawing on their prestige to buttress new leadership structures, rather than transforming properly oral traditions from the Israelite tribal north. So they wrote Hebrew versions of the sorts of texts used elsewhere to educate leaders for their emergent monarchy: creation and flood myths, hymns about the king, instructions on proper living, etc.

FIGURE 3.3

Mesopotamian student exercise tablet where the teacher wrote a couple of lines of an educational text on the top half and the student copied below.

FIGURE 3.4

Letters inscribed into the surface of a stone, with an overlay indicating their shape. The stone was found embedded in a wall from the tenth century BCE.

FIGURE 3.5
The "Gezer Calendar." This may be a school exercise from the time of Solomon. It lists what was done in the months of the agricultural year of ancient Canaan.

Echoes of Near Eastern Royal Theology in the Royal and Zion Psalms

Read the following (royal) psalms and make a list of ideas that come up two or more times in them: 2 Sam 23:1–7; Psalms 2, 21, 72, and 110. Include citations in your notes of where each idea occurred. Then read the following (Zion) psalms and list ideas that occur two or more times in them: Pss 9, 15, 46, and 48. These are later psalms that celebrate Zion (//Jerusalem) and articulate what scholars refer to as "Zion theology.".

EXERCISE

We turn now to look at texts that show particularly close links to the monarchy and some reliance on foreign models as well: royal and Zion psalms. Though some of these texts are attributed to David (e.g. 2 Sam 23:1–7; Pss 21 and 110) or Solomon (Psalm 72) none were written by those kings personally, and many probably originate from later periods in the monarchy (see the textbox below on "Labels [e.g. "Psalm of David"]: What They [Don't] Tell Us"). Yet, whether dating from the time of David and Solomon or later, these texts provide another crucial example of how Israel modeled key texts on the traditions of surrounding empires. Comparing Israel's royal psalms with non-biblical hymns can teach us much about how such hymns were used and what made them special.

Labels (e.g. "Psalm of David"): What They (Don't) Tell Us

As noted above, we must be careful about how much weight we put on associations of psalms and other texts with kings like David or Solomon. Ancient texts could be attributed to authors for a variety of reasons – to continue a stream of tradition associated with a given ancient figure, to gain authority through being associated with an ancient figure, etc.

Therefore, when we see a text such as Psalm 110 assigned to David, this may mean that it was written at the time of David by one of David's scribes, or it may just mean that this psalm was seen as part of a longer tradition of Davidic psalms. Similarly, labels that assign the Song of Songs, Ecclesiastes, and most parts of Proverbs to Solomon do not mean that Solomon wrote these texts. Instead, some may have been written at the time of Solomon, while others may just be part of a broader stream of "Solomonic" tradition extending even to apocryphal texts, such as the Wisdom of Solomon.

That said, the Bible's attribution of texts to figures such as David or Solomon can still be significant. For one thing, they are among the first Judean or Israelite figures in the Bible to have whole biblical texts attributed to them. The attributions of texts to David and Solomon may be recollections, preserved in the Bible, that David and Solomon's *time* was the first phase of the development of Israelite literature.

It should be emphasized that there is no usable historical information in the smaller collection of superscriptions that place certain psalms at particular points in David's life. These include, for example, the superscription to Psalm 51 (a confessional psalm) that locates that psalm in David's life just after Nathan had confronted him about having an affair with Bathsheba and murdering her husband, Uriah, by arranging to have him die in battle (story in 2 Sam 11:1–12:23). Such historicizing superscriptions are marked by their language and theology as later additions to the Psalter and represent examples of early biblical interpretation.

One of the main emphases in the literature of ancient empires was the monarchy. For example, Egyptian enthronement texts describe the new king (Pharaoh) receiving a document on which were written his throne names, climaxing with the throne name that marked his status as the only begotten son of the sun god, Re. Temple reliefs show the process by which Re conceived the king, not through intercourse, but through spreading his aroma over the king's mother. By the end of the process Re equipped the king with all he needed to rule the world in Re's place, proclaiming:

> Son of my body, beloved, lord of the righteousness [Maat] of Re, whose body I have made with me in the palace, I give you all life and wellbeing, to appear as the king of Upper and Lower Egypt on the throne of Horus.

Meanwhile, we also have hymns used in Egyptian education that taught students to celebrate the Egyptian king's power to vanquish wrongdoing and establish prosperity. The following one focuses on the Pharaoh Merneptah:

> Be glad of heart, the entire land! The good times have come. A lord – life, prosperity, health – is given in all lands, and normality has returned to its place. The king of Upper and Lower Egypt, the lord of millions of years, great of kingship like Horus ...he who bestows happiness on Egypt, the son of Re, most competent of any king, Merneptah – life, prosperity, health.
>
> All you who are righteous, come that you may see! Right has banished wrong. Evildoers have fallen on their faces. The oppressors are ignored. (ANET 378, adapted)

Similar themes appear in the royal literature of ancient Mesopotamia. For example, we find the following proclamation to the king in an ancient Babylonian coronation ritual:

> May Assur and Ninlil, the lords of your crown, set your crown on your head for a hundred years! May your foot in Ekur and your hands stretched toward the breast of Assur, your God, be pleasing! May your priesthood and the priesthood of your sons be pleasing to Assur, your god! With your straight scepter widen your land! May Assur give you authority, obedience, concord, justice and peace! (Translation: Livingstone, 472)

Royal texts from both ancient Mesopotamia and Egypt emphasized the choosing of the king by the high god of the pantheon, the king's appointment as the highest authority and priest of the land, his overcoming of all enemies in the name of the god, and his bestowing of justice and peace on the land through his rule. Together, these and other themes comprise what is meant here by **royal theology**.

Many elements of Egyptian and Mesopotamian royal theology are common in the **royal psalms** of the Hebrew Bible (Psalms 2, 18, 20, 21, 45, 72, 89, 110, and 144; along with 2 Sam 23:1–7). These poetic texts feature a distinctive focus on the king and his relationship with God. For example, Psalm 110 opens with a call for the king to sit at the right hand of God (Ps 110:1), a common motif in ancient Egyptian royal art. Its picture of the king subduing his enemies (Ps 110:1–3a) is typical of ancient royal literature, whether Egyptian or Mesopotamian. The latter part of verse 3, however, contains an obscure text whose meaning may be clarified when we look back to Egyptian royal ideology. God proclaims to the king: "from the womb of dawn, I fathered you like dew." Recall that the sun god, Re, in Egypt conceived the king through spreading his aroma over the king's mother. The Egyptian word for "aroma" rhymes with the Hebrew word for "dew." In speaking of Yahweh "fathering" the king "like dew before the womb of the dawn," Psalm 110 seems to apply these ideas to the Judean king. The psalm then hearkens back to the pre-Israelite royal traditions of Jerusalem in reporting God's oath to give the king eternal priesthood "according to the order of Melkizedeq" (110:4), a figure remembered elsewhere in the Bible as one of Jerusalem's kings in the time before David (Gen 14:18). Next come pictures of the king destroying his enemies (Ps 110:5–6) that are quite typical of ancient royal literature, before the psalm concludes with a reference to the king's drinking from Jerusalem's spring (Ps 110:7). Apparently the Judean king was anointed near the Gihon spring in Jerusalem (1 Kgs 1:33–4, 38–9). Thus Psalm 110 is a good example of a psalm whose obscure references can be understood when we see how it adapts ancient ideas about kingship recalled from pre-Davidic Jerusalem and the yet older royal theologies of Egypt and Mesopotamia. It does not depend on any specific pre-Israelite text, but in a broader way it contains "echoes of ancient empires."

The same can be said of many other biblical royal psalms. Just as the Egyptian king received a written decree from the gods proclaiming his status as the "son of Re," so Psalm 2 has the king report receiving a similar decree from Yahweh:

> I will proclaim the decree of Yahweh.
> He said to me, "You are my son,
>   I have fathered you today.
> Ask me,
>   and I will give nations as your birthright,
>   The entire world as your possession." (Ps 2:7–8)

This theme of God offering the king whatever he wants, especially military victory (Ps 2:8), is found in other royal psalms as well (Ps 21:2; see also 1 Kgs 3:5), and is a major feature of ancient Egyptian and Mesopotamian royal theology. Over and over again the texts of these ancient empires emphasize that it is the king who is authorized to call on God for military help. The king, and the king alone, is authorized by God to ask for and achieve military success for his people, and one of the main jobs of the king in ancient Egyptian and Mesopotamian royal texts is to destroy the people's enemies.

This emphasis in royal psalms on the king's violent power can seem harsh to contemporary readers, particularly those in Europe or North America who have not personally experienced the direct threat of military attack. To ancient Israelites, however, such words sounded differently. Though many may have been inclined to follow calls such as Absalom's or Sheba's to reject the monarchy, these royal psalms insist that the king was appointed by God and would protect and defend them against any threat like that of the Philistines. In the process, the psalms draw on older Near Eastern royal imagery – e.g. divine "fathering" of the king, setting the king at God's right hand, the grant of the king's wishes – to justify the Jerusalem monarchy to skeptical Israelites.

Basics on the Book of Psalms: Part 1

(For "Book of Psalms: Part 2," see Basics Box on p. 207.)

The book of Psalms was created over a very long period of time. It contains **Multiple levels in** some of Israel's earliest texts. Yet it was still being expanded late into Israel's **the book of Psalms** history. This mix of ancient and later texts in Psalms reflects the fact that these texts were integrally linked to and reflected shifts in the lives of Israelites as they faced ever different individual and national challenges.

It is impossible to be sure whether a given Psalm comes from the pre-exilic **Tracking down the** period, let alone from the time of David and Solomon. Nevertheless, most **earliest psalms** scholars agree that some psalms are good candidates for being among Israel's earliest literature. Some hymns, such as the praise of the storm god in Psalm 29 or the praise of God's power for fertility in Psalm 104, may have originated as pre-Israelite hymns to other gods before being adapted for Israelite use. Some other potentially early psalms mention the king, ark, or Zion, such as the celebration in Psalm 132 of Yahweh's choice of Zion and David's moving of the ark there. It is relatively unlikely that Israelite authors wrote all such references after the destruction of the monarchy and the Zion Temple with its ark.

The psalms discussed above point to the probable existence of early psalms **Other potentially** across the book of Psalms. They stand as potential indicators that *some* of **early psalms?** the other psalms that lack such historical references, such as some psalms of lament or trust, may also originate from Israel's early periods. Such texts about individual suffering or rescue are inherently difficult to date. Luckily, such dating is relatively unimportant for their interpretation.

One other important theme in these royal psalms is the emphasis on the importance to the kingship of "social responsibility" – Hebrew *tsedeqah*. This Hebrew word is usually translated into English as "righteousness," but it refers more specifically to the virtue of fulfilling one's social obligations to others, particularly defending those most vulnerable in ancient society: the orphan, widow, and foreign immigrant (the "stranger" or "alien"). For example, 2 Sam 23:3 notes that the king must rule with such "social solidarity" to dawn on his people like the morning light, and virtually all of Psalm 72, a "psalm of Solomon," is a prayer that God may give the king the power to rule his people with such *tsedeqah*:

> Give the king your justice, O God,
> 	and your social solidarity to the royal son!
> May he judge your people with social solidarity [*tsedeqah*],
> 	and your poor with justice! (Ps 72:1–2)

More on Method: Poetic Analysis

Poetry in the Bible does not have the kind of sound rhymes found in much English-language poetry. Instead, it is characterized by a phenomenon called "**seconding**," where the second line of a poetic **couplet** – or pair of lines – builds on the idea or imagery of the first line, but somehow takes it further. Some poems may have a **triplet** (or more). In triplets the stress is on the final, third line, which builds on and advances the idea(s) or imagery of the first two. Take the example of the following triplet from verse 2 of Psalm 110, a royal psalm:

> The LORD sends out from Zion
>   your mighty scepter
>   *rule in the midst of your foes* (NRSV)

Note how a translation like the NRSV marks a triplet like this through slightly indenting the second and third lines. These indentations of about two spaces indicate where the translators locate the Hebrew line breaks.

The example above uses italics for the third and climactic, seconding, line of the triplet. If you are analyzing a couplet or triplet, it is a good idea to write it out this way and underline or highlight the final line. Look at the parallels and differences between this final line and the two lines that precede it. How do the first two lines prepare for the final line and what is the impact of concluding the triplet this way? Can you identify an emotional impact of this poetic couplet in addition to summarizing it?

Take a Bible with the NRSV and try to find and analyze the poetic units in verse 3 of Psalm 110. (Hint: according to the NRSV, there is a triplet and a couplet here.)

For more see Robert Alter, *The Art of Biblical Poetry* (New York: Basic Books, 1985).

These texts show that Israelite kingship aimed to be an institution that protected the formerly vulnerable peoples of Israel's hill country and provided true justice. As we will see in Chapter 4, the monarchy – like all human institutions – did not always live up to its highest aims, and Israelites rebelled against the monarchy several times. Nevertheless, these psalms show how Israel's kingship was meant to be an institution through which God provided both protection and care for the most vulnerable of God's people.

These same values of justice and social solidarity are also prominent in another group of psalms, often termed "**Zion psalms**" because of their common emphasis on the special significance of Zion/Jerusalem, the capital of the new monarchy. For example, Psalm 9 describes how God who dwells in Zion "judges the peoples with social solidarity" (9:8) and is "a stronghold for the oppressed" (9:9). Psalms 15 and 24 are ancient liturgies for those making a pilgrimage to Zion. These psalms bar from Zion those who cannot affirm that they have "clean hands and a pure heart" (24:4) and do not exploit others through lending practices (15:5). Zion, at the heart of ancient Jerusalem, was the mountain where God dwelt. Those who would come there had to hold themselves to a higher standard of behavior. They were expected to be just as the God of Zion is just. Furthermore, these and other psalms repeatedly assert what will be one of the most important claims of Zion theology: that Jerusalem, the dwelling place of God, is invulnerable to foreign attack. See, for example, the description of Jerusalem/Zion in Psalm 46:

> There is a river whose streams bring joy to the city of God,
>> The holy dwelling of the most high.
> God is in the midst of her [the city], she shall not fall.
>> God will rescue her at the break of day. (46:4–5)

Though at least some of these royal and Zion psalms were written or revised at later points in the history of the Jerusalem monarchy, they stand as excellent examples of how early Israelites – who had lived for hundreds of years in hilltop villages – made theological sense of this new social form: a new monarchy set in a new capital, Jerusalem. Later Jewish and Christian interpreters, of course, have reinterpreted many of these psalms, so that – for example – the king praised in texts such as Psalm 2 or 110 is understood to be the Messiah. Such reinterpretations can be legitimate, since these texts would not have survived and become part of the Hebrew Bible if later readers had understood them only to be relevant to a monarchy that would eventually perish. Yet these texts should also be understood in their historical context. As such, they are a witness to some of Israel's earliest ideas about power and community, ideas that would prove very important to the later writers of prophecies and histories.

Prov 6:20–8:36; 10:1–32; 22:17–29. Ecclesiastes 1:1–3:22 and Song of Songs 1:1–2:7.

READING

Echoes of Texts from Earlier Empires in Writings Attributed to Solomon

Some of the most striking echoes of ancient empires in the entire Bible are found in books associated with Solomon, David's successor: Proverbs, Song of Songs, and Ecclesiastes (hereafter usually referred to by its Hebrew name, Qohelet). This does not, of course, mean that Solomon wrote these books, any more than David was the actual author of the psalms attributed to him (see above, box on p. 70).

And indeed, the form of the Hebrew language found in Song of Songs and Qohelet resembles the Hebrew that was written centuries after the time of Solomon. Nevertheless, whatever their date, these books were attributed to Solomon partly because they reflect the kind of international wisdom for which he was so famous (1 Kgs 5:9–14; 10). We turn to them now as another illustration of how biblical texts associated with David and Solomon echo earlier texts from Egypt and Mesopotamia.

Basics on the Song of Songs

It has proven difficult to find a systematic pattern in the loosely connected love poems that make up the Song of Songs. The following is a rough overview based particularly on the striking set of parallel refrains across the Song (2:7; 3:5; 8:4). These refrains structure a series of love songs spoken by a woman to a man and vice versa, something that is made clear by the distinct male and female pronouns in the original Hebrew of the Song. The student is highly encouraged to consult an English translation that identifies the distinct speeches of these male and female characters.

Outline

I	Introduction of themes	1:1–2:7
	Seeking day/night scenes	2:8–3:5
	Riches and praise	3:6–5:1
	Seeking night scene	5:2–6:3
	Riches and praise	6:4–8:3
II	Concluding statements on themes	8:4–14

Date

Most scholars would date the Song of Songs to the third or fourth centuries BCE, centuries after Solomon, particularly because of late features in its language. A minority see indicators of earlier origins of these materials, such as the way they resemble Egyptian and other early love songs.

Theme: sex, God, and the poetics of the Song

Many readers insist that one must decide that the Song is *either* about human desire *or* about divine–human love. The poetry of the Song, however, is more elusive. The dense metaphors and disconnected dialogues invite readers to build their own images of what is happening. The lack of explicit divine references and other features of the Song suggest that the book was meant to evoke the drama of human love. Still, the poetry allows multiple readings, especially now that the Song stands in a Bible that elsewhere depicts God's love for God's people (e.g. the book of Hosea, to be discussed later in this textbook).

Take, for example, the Song of Songs (otherwise known as Song of Solomon or Canticles), an often overlooked book of passionate love poetry at the heart of the Hebrew Bible. Though early Jewish and Christian communities often read this book as a love dialogue between God and God's beloved community (whether church or synagogue), the book's closest parallels are secular love songs found in Egypt just before the emergence of Israel. Those ancient Egyptian love poems and their parallels in the biblical Song of Songs do not describe the love affairs of gods. The Song of Songs does not ever clearly refer to Yahweh! Instead, like the Egyptian love poetry it most resembles, the Song of Songs is focused on the drama of human physical love: desiring, seeking, losing, and seeking again human passion with one's true love. Moreover, like the love literature that it echoes, the Song of Songs presents a positive, not fearful, picture of female desire. Unlike many other biblical books, the Song foregrounds the words and wishes of a female figure, one who proclaims that she is "black" and "beautiful" (Song 1:4). This woman is a powerful figure, not afraid to ask her lover for what she wants and speaking more than half of the words of the book. Nowhere in the book is she judged for her desire, nor is her lover, even though their love remains frustratingly secret and forbidden (Song 8:1–2).

More on Method: Afrocentric and Womanist Interpretation

Partly because it features a dark-skinned female figure, the Song of Songs has been a focus for a number of African American studies of the Bible. Where the King James version and related translations often translated Song of Songs 1:4 as "I am black, *but* beautiful" (emphasis added), Afrocentric interpreters like Kenneth Waters argued persuasively that the Hebrew of the verse supports an affirmation of Black beauty, "I am black *and* beautiful" ("The Beauty of Blackness," pp. 56–64 in *Afrocentric Sermons: Beauty of Blackness in the Bible* [Valley Forge, PA: Judson, 1993]). Such **Afrocentric interpretation** foregrounds and celebrates African bodies and culture, while a **womanist** approach to interpretation more specifically builds on and foregrounds the experience and wisdom of African American women. In her commentary on the Song of Songs, womanist scholar, Renita Weems, argues that the book was authored by a Black woman whose body and sexuality were stigmatized in a way similar to the experience of contemporary Black women ("Song of Songs" in *The New Interpreter's Bible*, vol. 5 [Nashville: Abingdon, 1997], 361–434). So also Cheryl Anderson's womanist reading of the book lifts up the Song of Songs as an important resource for the Black church confronting the particular impact of the HIV/AIDS epidemic on Black women and men. It offers the church a helpful alternative picture of gender and sexual desire that can counter body-denying, patriarchal constructions drawn from other parts of the Bible. See "A Womanist Reading of the Song of Songs in the Age of AIDS," pp. 73–92 in *The Five Scrolls: Texts@Contexts*, eds. Athalya Brenner-Idan, Gale A. Yee, and Archie C. C. Lee (New York: Bloomsbury, 2018). A broader survey and discussion of womanist readings of the Bible can be found in especially in Gay Byron and Vanessa Lovelace, eds. *Womanist Biblical Interpretation: Expanding the Discourse* (Atlanta: SBL, 2016)).

Scholars are not sure when to date the Song of Songs, though its links to late second millennium Egyptian love poetry might point to some kind of core of early love songs. Ecclesiastes/Qohelet is similarly difficult to date, and it likewise echoes literature from the ancient Near East. The book, attributed to "the teacher, the son of David in Jerusalem," is a combination of skepticism about wisdom and affirmation of life's small joys. Its main idea is the way all values are called into question by the fact that everyone dies and "you can't take it with you." During ancient Israel's history, there was no belief in a heaven or hell where people would be rewarded or punished for their behavior during life. In light of this, the "teacher" of Ecclesiastes ends up deciding that "emptiness, emptiness, all is emptiness" (Eccl 1:2, 14; 2:1; etc.). Since everyone dies sooner or later, both frantic pleasure seeking (Eccl 2:1–11) and excessive wisdom and righteousness (2:12–23) are pointless, "chasing after wind." Rather than getting too attached to any great project, the teacher of this text urges all to enjoy each day's moderate pleasures:

> Go, eat your food with pleasure, and drink your wine with a happy heart; for God has long approved what you do. Let your clothing always be white, do not let oil be lacking on your head. Enjoy life with the woman you love, all the days of your empty life that you are given under the sun. For that is your portion in life and your work which you work under the sun. (Eccl 9:7–9; see also 2:24–5; 5:18–20; 8:15)

This kind of day-to-day living, eating, drinking, and enjoying romantic love, this "imperative of joy" (as one scholar has called it), is the "teacher's" prescription for life lived in a world where "emptiness, emptiness, all is emptiness." Moreover, we find a close parallel to both the concern about death and Ecclesiastes/Qohelet's "imperative of joy" in a very ancient Mesopotamian text, the Epic of Gilgamesh. There Gilgamesh expresses his terror in the face of mortality and is told, "let your belly be full, ... every day make merry ... let your clothes be clean, let your head be washed, ... let a wife enjoy your repeated embrace."

Whenever one dates Ecclesiastes/Qohelet, that book seems to be responding with skepticism to older wisdom of the kind seen in Proverbs, the "Solomonic" book with the best claim to being datable (in part) to the time of David or (more likely) Solomon. Proverbs actually contains multiple collections, many of which are identified by separate headings: "the Proverbs of Solomon, son of David, king of Israel" (Prov 1:1–9:18), "the Proverbs of Solomon" (Prov 10:1–22:16), "the Proverbs of Solomon that were collected by Hezekiah's men" (Prov 25:1ff.), and so on. What we have in Proverbs, then, is a collection of collections of ancient Israel's educational materials.

Basics on Ecclesiastes/Qohelet

Outline: counter-wisdom instruction	I	Introductory royal testament	1:1–2:26
	II	Instruction in skeptical wisdom	3:1–12:8
	III	Epilogue with later affirmations	12:9–14

Major themes: Qohelet's contradictions — The lead themes through most of Ecclesiastes are the emptiness of all human striving (Eccl 1:2, 14; 2:1; etc.) and the benefits of daily pleasures in life (2:24–5; 5:18–20; etc.). Yet the last verses of the book (12:13–14) as well as isolated sections in its midst (e.g. 2:26; 3:17) affirm the more traditional idea that good eventually is rewarded and evil punished. Many would take these more traditional affirmations to be late additions to the book.

Date — Most scholars consider Ecclesiastes/Qohelet to be among the latest books in the Hebrew Bible. The Hebrew in which it is written contains some late features, and many would see the book's perspective to be Greek. Certainly, as noted above, the book in its present form contains multiple, identifiable revisions. Nevertheless, as in the case of the Song of Songs, there are some reasons to think some early form of Ecclesiastes may be older, reasons including its resemblance to the Gilgamesh Epic (see the previous page).

This collection of collections in Proverbs contains some of the clearest echoes of foreign educational texts found in the Bible. For example, we find a collection of "words of the wise" in Proverbs 22:17–24:22 whose "thirty sayings" (Prov 22:20) loosely adapt and echo some of the thirty chapters of the Egyptian Instruction of Amenemope (see Figure 3.6). Both collections begin with a call to memorize the following instruction (Amenemope chapter 1; Prov 22:17–21), and continue with similar instructions not to oppress the poor (Amenemope 2; Prov 22:22–3), not to move boundary stones (Amenemope 6; Prov 22:28), not get tied up in pursuing wealth (Amenemope 7; Prov 23:4–5), to avoid fools (Amenemope 9; Prov 22:24–5), and to take care in eating in front of nobles (Amenemope 23; Prov 23:1–3). To be sure, the author of Proverbs did not translate the ancient Egyptian instruction. The existing parallels between the texts are parallels in general content, and there are many parts of Prov 22:17–24:22 that have no counterpart in the Instruction of Amenemope. Nevertheless, the shared concept of thirty sayings and multiple parallels between these texts are good reasons to conclude that the author of Prov 22:17–24:22 knew of and loosely appropriated parts of the Egyptian Instruction of Amenemope, along with other wisdom traditions, in composing his own version of "thirty" sayings. In this sense Prov 22:17–24:22 is an important "echo of ancient [Egyptian] empire" in the Bible.

Basics on the Book of Proverbs

I	Introductory instruction: seek wisdom!	1:1–9:18	**Outline: treasury**
II	Additional wisdom collections	10:1–31:9	**of ancient Israel-**
III	A good woman as embodiment of wisdom	31:10–31	**ite wisdom**

Most scholars see a great diversity of date in the material of Proverbs. Sections such as Proverbs 1–9 are dated many centuries after Solomon, while parts of other sections, such as Prov 22:17–24:22, are thought to be among the earliest parts of the Bible. A minority of scholars, however, find indicators of early date in sections such as Proverbs 1–9 as well. **Date**

Since Proverbs is a collection of collections, it is particularly difficult to summarize with a single theme or set of themes. Nevertheless, major features of the book include its prominent focus on female figures toward the beginning (Proverbs 1–9) and end (Prov 31:10–31), and its repeated emphasis on the importance of "fear of Yahweh" (Prov 1:7, 29; 2:5; etc.) throughout. **Major themes**

The book of Proverbs also shows the importance of female wisdom in ancient Israel. Proverbs starts and continues with calls for students to attend to

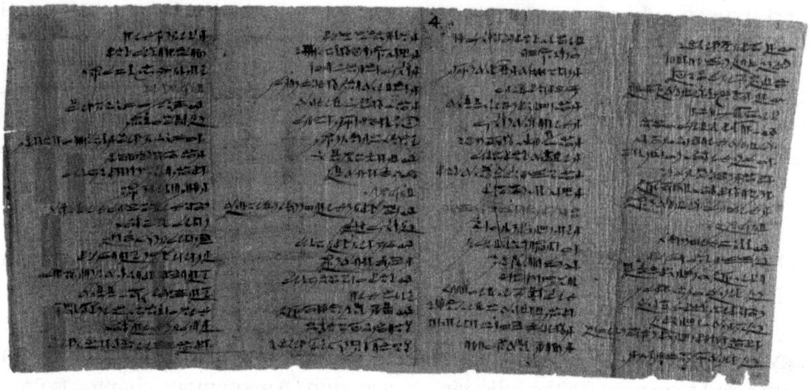

FIGURE 3.6

Copy of the Egyptian Instruction of Amenemope, dated approximately 1200 BCE. The topics of its thirty sayings (cf. Prov 22:20) loosely parallel those found in Prov 22:17–24:22.

both the father's *and* the mother's wisdom (Prov 1:8; 6:20; 23:22). The early chapters of Proverbs feature a powerful depiction of wisdom as a female, semi-divine figure (e.g. Prov 1:20–33; 8:1–36). And Proverbs concludes with an instruction attributed to King Lemuel's *mother* (Prov 31:1–9) and an A–Z praise of the "woman of power" that Jewish men often sing to their wives over the table of the Friday evening Sabbath meal (Prov 31:10–31).

Alongside all this, there also is a religious element. Both the instructions and the proverbs in the book of Proverbs have a distinctive emphasis on the "fear of Yahweh" as crucial to the successful life (Prov 1:7, 29; 14:26–7; 23:17; etc.). Nevertheless, the collections of educational texts in Proverbs offer broader instruction in how to succeed with both god and human beings. Combined with assertions of the importance of fearing Yahweh (e.g. Prov 14:26) are pragmatic sayings such as the affirmation in Prov 17:8 that bribes often work well. Most materials in Proverbs (in contrast to Qohelet) affirm the basic idea of **moral act-consequence**: the idea that good actions and/or fear of God produce good results, while bad behavior leads to disaster. The task of the student is to walk the path toward success, not toward death.

Returning to Qohelet, the vast bulk of the book directly critiques this idea of moral act-consequence. Where the materials in Proverbs affirm the act-consequence idea that evil is punished, and good rewarded, the author of Qohelet observes that, in actuality, righteous people often die in the midst of their uprightness while evil people prosper despite their wickedness (e.g. Eccl 3:16; 4:1–4; 7:15). In light of this, the author constantly repeats the basic refrain on the basic moral incoherence of the universe, beginning and ending his teaching on that note: "emptiness, emptiness, all is emptiness" (Eccl 1:2; 12:8). But some ancient scribes were apparently not satisfied with leaving the matter there. For we find isolated affirmations of the traditional act-consequence idea across the book (e.g. Eccl 2:26; 3:17), and even the following strange "summary" of Qohelet in the last two verses of the book:

The end of the matter is this. Fear God and observe his commandments ... For God will bring every act to judgment, all that is hidden, whether good or bad. (Eccl 12:13–14).

The author who began and concluded his discourse with the affirmation "emptiness, emptiness, all is emptiness" (Eccl 1:2; 12:8) is hardly likely to have summarized his book in this way. Instead, this summary in Eccl 12:13–14, along with similar elements in the book, likely are part of an orthodox revision of an earlier book of Qohelet. It can be quite important to recognize the distinctive character of such later, potential revisionary texts. A reader who gives undue attention to them and them alone can be blinded to the unorthodox counter-wisdom message of the rest of the book.

The Speech of Lady Wisdom in Proverbs 8

FOCUS
TEXT

The speech of wisdom in Proverbs 8 provides an illustration of the complex way that biblical texts creatively appropriate motifs from non-biblical materials. The "lady Wisdom" figure in Proverbs 8 appears partly to be modeled on wise and clever human women, whether clever female trickster types of the sort discussed in the last chapter or the mother-teachers discussed in this one. Yet this female Wisdom is also semi-divine. God created her before making anything else (Prov 8:22–6), and she was present to watch God make the world and delight in the presence of humans (8:27–31). Her presence from the beginning allows Wisdom to claim to provide many benefits – the capacity to rule effectively (8:15–16), material wealth (8:18, 21), and the surpassing benefits of wisdom itself (8:11–14, 19–20). And Wisdom's promises of various benefits, in turn, grounds her call – at the beginning and end of the text (8:4–10, 32–6) – for students to *seek wisdom* and thus gain happiness, life, and success. In sum, personified Wisdom in Proverbs 8 goes far beyond human figures seen elsewhere in Proverbs, even the "father" figure who elsewhere promises similar benefits to those who seek wisdom. She is a superhuman female figure vividly symbolizing the benefits of wisdom to the readership of a wisdom text – Proverbs.

Scholars have long wondered how and why Israelite sages would advertise wisdom in such a way. To be sure, this "Wisdom" in Proverbs 8 is never called a goddess. She is a symbol, created to serve a motivational aim. Nevertheless, the rest of the Bible does not have many good analogies to this remarkable picture of a semi-divine female figure. Moreover, the features of this figure of wisdom do not clearly correspond to earlier goddesses of the area, such as Asherah.

This has led scholars to conclude that parts of this picture may derive from Israelite adaptation of non-Israelite motifs, whether from goddess worship or elsewhere. Some have argued that the Egyptian goddess, Maat, could be a model for Wisdom in Proverbs 8. She personifies the principle of truth, justice, and order, and various Egyptian texts praise her as pre-existing creation, caring for those who love her (cf. Prov 8:17), and providing life and protection to her devotees. Others find the Egyptian goddess, Isis, to be a better analogy, since she is reported to actually give speeches about her early origins and powers that are analogous to that in Proverbs 8. See, for example,

> I, Isis, am ruler of all lands,
> And I was educated by Hermes
> I set down laws for men and legislated that which no one can alter.
> I am the eldest daughter of Kronos.

Later in this text we see some additional elements pertinent to Proverbs 8.

> I have made justice powerful...
> I have made justice more powerful than gold and silver.
> (Translation: Jan Bergman, *Ich bin Isis* [Uppsala: Universitet, 1968], 301)

Yet there are questions about when and how the authors of Proverbs 8 would have been influenced by either Maat or Isis traditions. Only an Egyptian native could have conveyed the kinds of detailed ideas about Maat that are paralleled in Proverbs 8, perhaps an Egyptian scribe in Solomon's court or a later visitor. Meanwhile, speeches of Isis like the one quoted above were not written until a couple of centuries *after* the latest parts of Proverbs were written.

Ultimately, these parallels do not help us date Proverbs 8 in any particular period. Instead, biblical scholars often prefer one parallel or the other, depending on the dating of Proverbs that they decided on for other reasons. Scholars inclined to date this part of Proverbs to the time of Solomon or a bit later may relate Proverbs 8 to Maat traditions. Meanwhile, scholars who date Proverbs 8 to the Persian period or later are most prone to link Proverbs 8 with later Isis traditions. Whatever the dating, the closest parallels so far seem to point to an Egyptian background to the picture of Wisdom in Proverbs 8. In addition, consideration of Proverbs 8 alongside these traditions about Maat and Isis can sensitize us to the ways that the authors of all these ancient texts developed such depictions of symbolic female figures in order to make broader points.

As argued by Carol Newsom in her article "Woman and the Discourse of Patriarchal Wisdom," the depiction of female Wisdom in Proverbs 8 is developed for particular motivational purposes. Within the broader context of the text, the reader is urged to follow the powerful, beneficent figure of female Wisdom while avoiding the seductive lure of the dangerous strange woman described in the previous chapter, Proverbs 7. Proverbs 8 must thus be understood as part of a contrast of "good" and "bad" female figures. On the one side stands semi-divine "Wisdom," symbolizing Proverbs and perhaps modeled in some way on Egyptian female divine figures. On the other side stands the "strange woman," a female figure symbolizing the dangerous attraction of perspectives contrary to Proverbial wisdom.

Echoes of Texts from Past Empires Elsewhere in the Bible

Genesis 2–3 and 6–9.

READING

EXERCISE

Before reading this section, read Gen 6:5–9:17 and note every place where the same or a quite similar event is narrated twice. An example would be God's announcement of the flood both in Gen 6:13 and in 7:4. Another is Noah's multiple entries into the ark in 7:7 and 7:13. Once you have developed a list of such doubly narrated events, see whether "God" or "LORD" is used to refer to God in any of these doublets. Come up with your own theory about how the biblical flood story ended up this way.

So far we have found echoes of texts from earlier empires in entire texts (e.g. royal psalms) or books (e.g. Song of Songs, Proverbs) that are associated in different ways with the time of David and Solomon. Nevertheless, other texts from the Bible also contain strong echoes of ancient Near Eastern literature, and we can learn much about them through comparison. For example, recent scholarship by David Wright (*Inventing God's Law: How the Covenant Code of the Bible Used and Revised the Laws of Hammurabi* [New York: Oxford University Press, 2009]) has identified multiple and specific parallels between the ancient Mesopotamian code of Hammurabi (see figure 3.7) and a collection of biblical laws in Exodus 20:22–23:33 called the "Covenant Code" (see Exod 24:7). For over a century scholars have judged that this "Covenant Code" was one of the earliest collections of laws in the Bible, because its laws about topics such as building altars (Exod 20:24–6) and celebrating festivals (Exod 23:14–17) reflect early practices of offering sacrifices all over the land and not just in Jerusalem. Only recently, however, have scholars seen ways that the Covenant Code may be loosely modeled on parts of the Code of Hammurabi, much as Prov 22:17–24:22 was modeled partially on the Instruction of Amenemope. Indeed, it is likely that many of the purity and ritual regulations of Leviticus and Numbers also had ancient precursors, since we have extensive examples of similar sorts of documents about priestly matters found among the remains of the peoples preceding and surrounding ancient Israel. Law, whether royal decree or priestly instruction, was one of the most important forms of ancient writing.

Perhaps the most famous echoes of texts from the ancient Near East are found at the very beginning of the Bible, in the **primeval narrative** (Genesis 1–11), which tells stories about the whole earth and its peoples. Before looking at these echoes, however, it is important to realize that these chapters of Genesis contain *two* parallel sets of stories about the origins of the world. Lots of things are described twice in these chapters. "God" creates plants, animals, and humans (male and female) in Genesis 1, and then "Yahweh" (LORD in many translations) creates the first man, animals, and then woman in Genesis 2. Genesis 3–4 tell stories about these first humans and their descendants up to the time of Noah, and then Genesis 5 gives a genealogy from Adam to Noah. Then, the flood story of Genesis 6–9 is full of doubly narrated events: two descriptions of God's perception of the problem leading up to the flood (6:5 and 6:12), two assertions that Noah was exceptional in his righteousness (6:8 and 9), and so on. Looking at these duplicate narratives in the flood story and across

FIGURE 3.7

The stela of Hammurabi (c. 1700 BCE). The top image depicts the king showing respect before the enthroned Mesopotamian god of justice, Shamash. The text below describes his appointment by the gods to give justice and then quotes his proclamation of laws that roughly parallel (in topic) parts of the Covenant Code in Exod 20:22–23:33.

Genesis 1–11 more generally, it appears as if an Israelite author had two complete written stories of creation and flood, and that author wove those older written stories, these ancient "sources" of Genesis, together to create the present biblical text. **Source criticism** (see the textbox on p. 85) is a method by which scholars use clues in the biblical text, such as doubled narratives of the same event and shifts in terminology, to reconstruct lost, written sources that were combined into the present Bible.

Over the past two hundred years, source critics have reached a high level of agreement on how to untangle these interwoven creation and flood writings (sources) embedded in Genesis 1–11 and beyond. They call one of these sources "**P**" or the **Priestly source**, because its sequence of stories (Gen 1:1–2:3; 5:1–32; 6:9–22; 7:6, 11, and other parts of the flood up through 9:1–17) links with other parts of the Pentateuch that focus on priests. The other source starts with the Garden of Eden story in Genesis 2:4–3:24, continues with the Cain and Abel story and genealogies of Genesis 4, includes its own flood narrative (Gen 6:1–8; 7:1–5, 10, 12, and other parts up through 8:20–2), and contains an epilogue about Noah and his sons (Gen 9:18–27). In the past this source has been termed the "**J**" or the "**Yahwistic source**" (sometimes spelled "Jahwistic source") since this source uses the holy Hebrew name Yahweh to refer to God. (The German scholars who first discovered the J source two hundred years ago used the letter "j" for their "y" sound and spelled the name Yahwist "Jahwist.") As will be discussed later, in Chapter 6, many scholars see this J source, like P, continuing across the Pentateuch, but there are good reasons to be skeptical of their claims. Instead, any such early "J" source appears to be limited to some portions of the non-P primeval history. In this textbook the term "non-P primeval history" will be used for this source to avoid confusion of it with the longer "J" posited in earlier scholarship.

MORE ON METHOD: SOURCE AND REDACTION CRITICISM

The term "**source criticism**" refers to the scholarly attempt to identify previously existing, separate written sources now embedded in the biblical text. We have no manuscripts of these earlier sources. Instead, scholars must examine the biblical text we now have and look for clues to earlier sources, such as doublets, contradictions, and major shifts in language. Sometimes scholars can achieve substantial consensus in reconstructing hypothetical earlier documents, such as the Priestly/P and non-Priestly sources discussed in this chapter.

In addition, scholars speak of editorial additions to ancient sources as **redaction** and often engage in an attempt to identify layers of editorial additions through use of **redaction criticism.** For example, there are signs that the editors who combined the Priestly and non-Priestly primeval narratives added some redactional texts to connect those sources with each other. In other cases, scribes simply expanded on earlier narratives or prophecies with one or more layers of redaction.

For now, it is just important to recognize the general, centuries-long scholarly consensus on two basic types of material across the Pentateuch – a Priestly source and an earlier source, a non-Priestly one, starting with the above-mentioned Garden of Eden story in Genesis 2–3. This chapter will focus on elements from the earlier, non-Priestly source. We will come back to the Priestly source when we come (in Chapter 6) to the Babylonian exile in which it likely was written.

Contrasts and Parallels Between Biblical and Mesopotamian Flood Narratives

The land of Mesopotamia is prone to floods, especially in the spring. Several Mesopotamian texts describe how the gods of the Mesopotamian pantheon tried to kill humanity through a global flood, but were foiled by a crafty god (Enki or Ea, depending on the version) who told a human of the coming flood and instructed him to build a boat to allow him, his family, and others to survive it. The intertwined biblical flood narratives in Genesis 6–9 merge the roles of these two gods, having the same God bring the flood and instruct the flood hero (Noah) on how he can survive it. Nevertheless, they parallel numerous aspects of the Mesopotamian flood narratives. As indicated in the table below, there is a particularly striking parallel between the biblical scene of Noah sending birds to determine if the flood waters have receded (Gen 8:6–12; part of the non-Priestly flood narrative) and a similar scene in one of the earlier Mesopotamian flood narratives (the Gilgamesh Epic) where the flood hero describes having sent out birds in a similar way.

Gilgamesh, tablet 11:147–56 (translation by A. George)	Non-Priestly flood narrative (Gen 8:6–12)
When the seventh day arrived	**6** At the end of forty days, Noah opened the window of the ark that he had made,
I brought out a dove, setting it free:	**7** and sent the raven out.
Off went the dove…	It went to and fro until the waters dried up from the earth.
No perch was available for it and it came back to me.	
I brought out a swallow, setting it free:	**8** Noah sent the dove out to see if the waters had diminished from the surface of the ground,
Off went the swallow…	**9** but it did not find a resting place for its foot and returned to him into the ark because water was still on the surface of the entire earth. He stretched out his hand, took it, and brought it back to him in the ark.
No perch was available for it and it came back to me.	**10** He waited another seven days and again sent out the dove from the ark.
I brought out a raven, setting it free:	**11** The dove came back in to him at evening time, and a plucked olive leaf was in its mouth.
Off went the raven and it saw the waters receding.	Noah then knew that the water on the earth had diminished.
It was eating, bobbing up and down, it did not come back to me.	**12** He waited another seven days and sent the dove out, but it did not return to him again.

As is evident above, the parallels are not exact, but they are striking enough to suggest some kind of dependence of the non-Priestly flood narrative on its earlier Mesopotamian counterpart. Take a look for yourself at online versions of the Mesopotamian flood story in the Atrahasis and Gilgamesh Epics (see, e.g. "The Epic of Atrahasis" and "The Great Flood" at www.livius.org) and compare them with Genesis 6–9. A close comparison will turn up both a list of similarities and some important ways in which the P and non-P flood narratives both resemble and yet diverge from their Mesopotamian precursors.

We do not know how or when biblical authors accessed those Mesopotamian traditions. Nevertheless, we have good reason to think that they knew them in some form. Israelite authors lived in a highland area not prone to floods, and the extensive parallels to the specific form of flood tradition as it is seen in Mesopotamia is excellent evidence that the P and non-Priestly authors adapted foreign traditions in the process of writing stories of creation and flood. We will see other examples of such appropriation of foreign traditions across this textbook.

The Garden of Eden Story (Gen 2:4–3:24)

FOCUS
TEXT

We turn next to look more closely at the text that opens the earlier, non-Priestly source discussed above: the Garden of Eden story in Gen 2:4–3:24 (here and elsewhere often referred to as Genesis 2–3). Most people approach this text with presuppositions shaped by its history of interpretation. For example, if asked to name the fruit that Adam and Eve ate in the garden, most would instantly reply "an apple." The Genesis text, however, does not say this. Similarly, though many assume that the snake in the garden was "Satan," that is never specified in the Bible. These and other elements were added to the biblical story by later interpreters (see Figure 3.8).

This history of interpretation of the Garden of Eden text has also influenced what people think the whole story is about. For example, many have understood Paul in Rom 5:18–21 to imply that Genesis 2–3 is a tale of how sin entered the world, putting all humans under the curse of death. In the post-Pauline letter of 1 Timothy, this tragedy is blamed on women, who must now pay the price by bearing children:

> For Adam was formed first, then Eve; and Adam was not deceived, but the woman was deceived and became a transgressor. Yet she will be saved through childbearing, provided they continue in faith and love and holiness, with modesty. (1 Tim 2:13–15; translation: NRSV)

Later Christian interpreters expanded on this type of interpretation, with the early theologian Gregory Nazianzen talking of how Eve "beguiled the man by means of pleasure" and Tertullian saying to a group of nuns, "Are not each of you an Eve? ... You are the Devil's gateway." With these and many other interpretations setting the stage for contemporary readings, it is little wonder that many people today assume that this text is an anti-female text blaming Eve for seducing Adam and introducing sin and death into the world.

Yet particularly thanks to groundbreaking work by Phyllis Trible (*God and the Rhetoric of Sexuality* [Philadelphia: Fortress, 1978]) and others in the mid-1970s, scholars have gradually recognized that there is no more basis for that reading in the text itself than there is for the idea that the fruit that the first humans ate was an "apple" (that word never occurs in Genesis 3). Both of these ideas are later interpretations that have been laid on a text that has very different concerns. Trible and others have pointed out that the text actually celebrates the woman as the culmination of creation. "Sin" is never mentioned in it, and the woman and man share responsibility for the garden crime. Moreover, the consequences for this act that come on them are depicted in the text as tragic, not divinely willed elements of creation. Let us now take a new look at this often-interpreted text.

FIGURE 3.8
Titian's painting of Adam and Eve taking the apple from a snake-tailed cherubic Satan. It well illustrates how later interpretation of Genesis 2–3 influenced people's visions of the scene.

More on Method: Feminist Criticism and History of Interpretation/Reception

History of biblical interpretation is the study of how a biblical text has been interpreted over time, often with an emphasis on how it was interpreted in Jewish and/or Christian religious contexts. A similar method, **reception history** (of the Bible), focuses particularly on how biblical texts are represented in other media (e.g. painting, film, music; see Figure 4.4) and/or secular interpretations of biblical texts (e.g. in novels, theater). Study of history of interpretation and reception history of biblical texts can be interesting in itself. In addition, it can help the historical-critical reader of the Bible identify interpretive tendencies that might shape their own, unconscious interpretation of the text. For example, study of the history of interpretation of Genesis 2–3 can highlight the particular background and development of readings of the story as an account of "original sin," helping the reader bracket such approaches and take a new look at the text and see if other approaches to it might yield new insights.

One such newer approach is **feminist biblical criticism**. This chapter already noted Phyllis Trible's groundbreaking work on Genesis 2–3, and this kind of research has been done by many others. For example, Carol Meyers's *Rediscovering Eve: Ancient Israelite Women in Context* (New York: Oxford University Press, 2013 [original 1988]) gathers archaeological and textual evidence to show the prominent role that women played in the ancient Israelite economy. In this light, she raises the possibility that God's pronouncement over the woman's future in Gen 3:16 is not a prediction of her "pain" in pregnancy (as it's often translated), but instead of her future hard work (Hebrew *itzbon*) along with pregnancy, much like similar toil-labor (*itzbon*) is predicted for the man (Gen 3:17–19). Trible's, Meyers's and others' work in **feminist biblical criticism** (academic study that analyzes female characters, imagery, and speech) has offered a corrective to predominantly male perspectives in the earlier history of interpretation of Genesis 2–3 (and other texts as well).

The story is organized into three main parts: a description of God's creation of a deeply connected partnership of men and women working the earth (Gen 2:4–25), a crime scene describing their disobedience of God's one prohibition (3:1–6), and an account of the tragic loss of original connectedness to each other and the earth as a result of the crime (3:7–25). The story opens with God creating the first "human" (Hebrew *Adam*) out of the earth (Hebrew *adamah*), and giving him life through breathing the divine breath into him. God sets him in the garden to work and protect it, and the word play on *Adam/Adamah* (much like "human" and "humus") emphasizes the original connectedness of the human to the earth he was destined to work.

Yet God immediately recognizes that there is a problem with this picture: "It is not good for the human to be alone" (Gen 2:18). God then decides to create a partner "corresponding to him." God creates the animals, and brings each to the human for him to name them, but none truly "corresponds" to him (Gen 2:19–20). So God tries a new approach, anesthetizing the first human by putting him to sleep, removing a rib, and "building" the woman out of it. When the human awakens and sees the woman, he sings the first song of creation, one that emphasizes the connectedness they share:

> This one, at last,
>> is bone from my bones,
>> flesh from my flesh!
> This one will be called "woman" [Hebrew *ishah*]
>> Because from man [Hebrew *ish*]
>> this one was taken. (Gen 2:23)

The text concludes by saying that this is the origin of love and marriage, it is the reason a man leaves his parents and "clings to his wife and they become one flesh." In stark contrast to many other world-creation stories, sex is not initially connected here to having children. Instead, sex is a sign of the original connectedness of the man and the woman created out of a part of him so that they would truly correspond to each other. This is a story of God's will that humans be in close relationship with each other and the earth. In the wake of this creation, both man and woman "were naked and not ashamed" (Gen 2:25). They may work the garden together and eat of its fruit, with one exception: they may not eat of the "tree of knowledge of good and evil" lest they "certainly die" (Gen 2:17).

The scene shifts in Gen 3:1–6 to a new cast of characters, the man, woman, and now a "clever" snake in place of God (Gen 3:1). Again, the history of interpretation has often pictured Satan as the snake, but there is no basis for that in the Hebrew text. Instead, the snake stands as an ancient symbol of wisdom and immortality, and the adjective used to describe him – *arum* ("clever") – is a virtue frequently praised in the wisdom writings of Proverbs. Furthermore, though interpreters have often supposed that the sin of the first humans somehow consisted of sex or desire, there is no hint of that here. As we saw, Genesis 2 already explains the first sexual partnership of humans as the result of God's creation of a woman out of part of a man. Instead, the issue is human acquisition of godlike "wisdom." Not only is the "clever" snake associated with wisdom, but the "tree of knowledge of good and evil" is a symbol of wisdom's fruits. This then is underlined when the snake convinces the woman to consider eating of the tree, and she sees that the "tree was good for food, a delight to the eyes, and good for becoming wise" (Gen 3:6). Performing a role analogous to female wisdom in Proverbs 8, the first woman eats of the fruit of wisdom, gives fruit to her husband; he eats of it as well; and the text says that "the eyes of both were opened" (Gen 3:7). This is a frequent expression for gaining education. Thus Gen 3:1–7 describes the first act of human disobedience as the defiance of God and the gaining of a form of "wisdom" that shows many signs of being associated with the ancient Israelite textual wisdom we have seen in books such as Proverbs.

This then sets in motion a tragic unraveling of much of the connectedness that God had created at the outset. The text already illustrates this when God arrives in the garden, the humans hide, and when questioned about why they are hiding, begin to blame each other. The man blames both the woman and God who made the woman (3:12), and the woman blames the snake (3:13). In response, God proclaims consequences for all three. The snake will now crawl on the ground and be an eternal enemy of humans. The woman will no longer enjoy idyllic life in the garden, but God will "multiply her toilsome pregnancies" (not "increase pangs in childbearing" as often translated). And the idyllic life of the man likewise will come to an end. His "toil" is to work the ground from which he was made until he dies and returns to it. Where once there was mutual desire, now the woman's desire will be for her husband, and where once there was mutuality between corresponding partners, now the husband will "rule" over his wife (3:16). The story goes on to describe the (hu)man's naming of his wife "Eve" (a name made from the Hebrew word for "life") to reflect her new job of producing children (3:20). God gives the human pair clothes (3:21) – a sign of human civilization that is also seen in ancient non-biblical texts such as the Gilgamesh Epic. Finally, God expels them from the garden for fear that they might gain godlike immortality much as they already gained godlike wisdom (Gen 3:22–4). Now, denied the chance to eat of the tree of life, it turns out to be true that the humans will "certainly die" after eating the forbidden fruit of knowledge (see the prohibition in Gen 2:17).

In this way the text accurately depicts the non-ideal world that actual Israelites lived in, but with a twist. Most Israelites still lived lives closely tied to the land, working it by the sweat of their brow until they returned to it. The work was hard, famine was frequent, and death came much sooner than it does for people in the developed world today. Women lived in patriarchal marriages, sustaining the household with their work, while undergoing an endless series of pregnancies, many of which were very dangerous. Analysis of female remains has suggested that as many as half of women eventually died in childbirth. In this sense, the realities described in the latter part of Genesis 3 all held true for the ancient Israelite men and women. Yet what is remarkable about this text is its suggestion that this often harsh and patriarchal reality is not what God originally intended for humans. God originally made humans for fruitful farming, long life, and mutual, truly corresponding life and desire between men and women. It was only with the human step toward godlike wisdom that they emerged into the harsh reality that they experience today. "Wisdom" – not women – is the source of the tragic endless labor, patriarchy, and death that characterize the present.

This kind of narrative about human origins is as timeless as many texts discussed above, but it may also stand as a reflection on what "wisdom" was coming to mean in monarchal Israel. Though most still lived in villages, Judah and Israel gradually became increasingly dominated by urban elites who were educated in new literary traditions modeled on non-biblical sources. As this happened, the leaders of Israel during this period underwent a momentous shift in their collective memory. Before the monarchy, tribal villages all had their oral traditions, such as tales of trickster ancestors, the exodus, or military triumph. But, with kingship developing in Jerusalem and Israel, we start to see the emergence of an Israelite literary tradition recited and memorized from *written* texts: royal psalms, stories of royalty, royal wisdom, and stories of primeval origins. Moreover, many of these written texts were based on educational literature from outside Israel, such as Egyptian wisdom and love songs or Mesopotamian traditions about creation and flood. This growing Israelite literary corpus, so difficult to identify and date, was the means by which a small and growing number of literate Israelites gained "knowledge of good and evil" and had their "eyes" "opened."

Read this way, the Garden of Eden story – itself a highly learned, written text – suggests that wisdom is both an essential part of human growing up and a source of many human ills. On the one hand, it suggests that there is no return to an idyllic life in the garden, munching on fruit and obeying God's one clear command – not to eat of the tree of knowledge of good and evil. On the other hand, this enlightenment, this human journey to mature civilization, has brought many of the ills of adult life with it: endless pregnancies and agricultural work. The marks of original creation persist, such as the way humans are still drawn to "cleave to each other" and "become one flesh." Yet the story recognizes that adult life also has its toil and tragic imperfections. The journey out of the garden has brought a life where humans have work in place of leisure, "wisdom" in place of the single garden command, and male rule over women in place of the connectedness that God originally wished.

Conclusion

As was stressed at the outset of the chapter, this discussion gathers biblical texts of diverse date that have been modeled on earlier Near Eastern texts. These texts illustrate how Israelite scribes, starting with the emergence of kingship in ancient Israel, interacted with earlier Near Eastern myths, laws, and poetry.

Such echoes of non-biblical texts in the Bible can teach us about how ancient Israelites used the sorts of written texts now in the Bible. For example, texts like the Instruction of Amenemope and the Gilgamesh Epic were used in ancient Egyptian or Mesopotamian education (respectively). Mesopotamian and Egyptian leaders were qualified for their jobs by learning to read and memorize such texts. When we turn to similar biblical texts, such as the "words of the wise" in Prov 22:17–24:34 that echo Amenemope, it is logical to hypothesize that such biblical texts likewise were used to educate leaders from the beginnings of the Israelite monarchy. Whatever the original function of earlier oral traditions now embedded in such biblical texts, as *writings* they probably helped educate the leadership elite in such an emergent monarchy.

Meanwhile, the differences between biblical texts and their non-biblical counterparts are as important as the similarities. We can learn much about the particular values and perspectives of biblical authors through comparing the "words of the wise" in Prov 22:17–24:34 with the Instruction of Amenemope, the non-Priestly primeval narrative in Genesis 1–11 with Atrahasis, and so on. Biblical authors did not just copy major texts of Mesopotamia and Egypt. They reframed non-biblical traditions in light of their particular values. There is a major difference, for example, between the biblical story of the flood in Genesis 6–9, where just one god brings the flood and rescues a human from it, and the polytheistic tale in Atrahasis, where most of the gods bring the flood while one god rescues a human from it. In this and other biblical texts discussed here, we see ancient Israelite authors building freely on and yet radically adapting more ancient literary traditions from elsewhere. These unknown authors are responsible for writing the first building blocks of what would later become the Hebrew Bible.

By including some texts that likely mix early and late elements (e.g. Song of Songs, Qohelet) this chapter stepped out of the chronological framework of the rest of the *Introduction*. Nevertheless, it may not be so important to determine in which century such texts were written. After all, texts like Proverbs and the Garden of Eden story reflect on timeless aspects of existence, albeit in distinctly different ways, and it is unclear how much one would learn from dating the love poetry of Song of Songs to one century or another. In this way, the texts discussed here are different from the prophetic texts to be discussed in the next and following chapters. Those prophetic texts were addressed to particular historical crises being experienced by the people of Israel and Judah. We turn to those texts now.

CHAPTER THREE REVIEW

1. Know the meaning and significance of the following terms discussed in this chapter:
   - Afrocentric interpretation
   - couplet
   - feminist biblical interpretation
   - history of (biblical) interpretation
   - J
   - moral act-consequence
   - P
   - Priestly source
   - primeval narrative
   - reception history
   - royal psalms
   - royal theology
   - seconding
   - source criticism
   - triplet
   - *tsedeqah*
   - Womanist interpretation
   - Yahwistic source
   - Zion
   - Zion psalms
   - Zion theology

2. The biblical narratives in 1 Samuel 8–12 describe the people's establishment of Saul as Israel's first king because they were unhappy with Samuel's sons as his successors (1 Sam 8:3–4), they wanted a "king like other nations" (1 Sam 8:5, 20), and they had rejected God as their king (1 Sam 8:7–8). Name two specific ways that this account contrasts with this chapter's historical reconstruction of the emergence of kingship in ancient Israel.

3. What are two different ways in which comparison of a biblical text with an ancient non-biblical text can be useful? Give two examples of such comparison from this chapter.

4. Know the basic character of the following ancient Near Eastern texts and how they are related by scholars to biblical texts that were discussed in this chapter:
   - Atrahasis Epic
   - Egyptian love songs
   - Gilgamesh Epic
   - Instruction of Amenemope

5. (Focus texts: Proverbs 8 and Genesis 2–3) Compare the different depictions of feminine figures associated with wisdom/knowledge in Proverbs 8 (feminine Wisdom) and Genesis 2–3 (Eve). Focus especially on the roles of Wisdom and Eve with respect to knowledge. Why do you think the different authors of Proverbs 8 and Genesis 2–3 chose a feminine figure (rather than a masculine figure) for each role?

RESOURCES FOR FURTHER STUDY

General Introductions to Wisdom Literature

Balentine, Samuel E. *Wisdom Literature*. Nashville, TN: Abingdon, 2018.

Proverbs

Fox, Michael V. *Proverbs*. 2 volumes. New York: Doubleday, 2000, 2009.

Leeuwen, Raymond C. Van. "Proverbs." Pp. 17–264 in Leander Keck (general ed.), vol. 5 of the *New Interpreter's Bible*. Nashville, TN: Abingdon, 1997.

Newsom, Carol A. "Woman and the Discourse of Patriarchal Wisdom: A Study of Proverbs 1–9." Pp. 142–60 in Peggy L. Day (ed.), *Gender and Difference in Ancient Israel*. Philadelphia, PA: Fortress, 1989.

Ecclesiastes

Brown, William. *Ecclesiastes*. Louisville, KY: Westminster John Knox Press, 2000.

Duncan, Julie Ann. *Ecclesiastes*. Nashville, TN: Abingdon, 2016.

Song of Songs

Exum, Cheryl. *Song of Songs*. Louisville, KY: Westminster John Knox Press, 2005.

Weems, Renita. "Song of Songs." Pp. 361–434 in Leander Keck (general ed.), vol. 5 of the *New Interpreter's Bible*. Nashville, TN: Abingdon, 1997.

Genesis 1–11

Gowan, Donald. *From Eden to Babel: A Commentary on the Book of Genesis*. Grand Rapids, MI: Eerdmans, 1988.

O'Connor, Kathleen. *Genesis 1–25A*. Macon, GA: Smyth & Helwys, 2018.

Discussion of Song of Songs, Genesis, and Other Texts Relating to Sexuality

Carr, David M. *The Erotic Word: Sexuality and Spirituality in the Hebrew Bible*. New York: Oxford University Press, 2003.

Narrative and Prophecy Amidst the Rise and Fall of the Northern Kingdom

4

Chapter Overview

Chapter 3 traced echoes of past empires in the Hebrew Bible, while this one focuses on the reverberations of an imperial onslaught. The time to be reviewed here is the ninth and eighth centuries BCE (800s and 700s). The attacking empire was **Assyria**, a Mesopotamian state based in what is now northern Iraq (see Map 1.2 on p. 27). By this point there were two kingdoms in the land of Israel. A kingdom of "Israel" had risen up in the north, while a southern kingdom in Judah was ruled by descendants of David in Jerusalem. Initially, this northern kingdom (Israel) was stronger than its southern counterpart, and it developed its own

A Contemporary Introduction to the Bible: Sacred Texts and Imperial Contexts, Second Edition.
Colleen M. Conway and David M. Carr.
© 2021 Colleen M. Conway and David M. Carr. Published 2021 by John Wiley & Sons Ltd.

corpus of texts that were largely distinct from those used in the south. Yet ultimately the northern kingdom was destroyed by Assyria, and the southern kingdom suffered almost a century of Assyrian domination.

The Hebrew Bible reflects this initial imperial encounter in at least two main ways. First, although the Hebrew Bible is a collection of Judean texts, it preserves some remnants of texts from the destroyed northern kingdom, texts that have been appropriated and adapted by Judean scribes. Second, the Bible's first prophetic books came from this time of imperial encounter. The books of Amos, Hosea, Micah, and Isaiah all contain early prophecies that reflect the crises faced by Judah and Israel leading up to and during the Assyrian onslaught. Knowing more about the origins of these texts – whether northern texts now embedded in the Hebrew Bible (e.g. an early Jacob story) or prophetic writings formed in the crucible of imperial crisis – can help us understand them in new ways.

Setting the Stage: The Rise of the Northern Kingdom of Israel and Its Texts

READING

1 Kings 12; 2 Kgs 14:23–9; 15:17–31; 17:1–6 (from Jeroboam of Israel to the fall of the north).

Our journey toward greater understanding of these texts starts with the story of the emergence of a monarchy in the Israelite north. This monarchy was the ultimate outgrowth of a long process of tribal rebellion. Groups in Israel had tried in the past to gain liberty from the Davidic monarchy, but they did not succeed in breaking free until Solomon's death, around 927 BCE.

According to the description of this event in 1 Kings 12 (//2 Chronicles 10), Solomon's son, Rehoboam, went to the ancient tribal center of Shechem to be anointed by the elders of northern Israel. Instead, they ended up having a confrontation. The elders asked if Rehoboam's "yoke," that is his domination of them, would be as heavy as that of his father. Against the advice of his older advisors, Rehoboam is reported to have said: "I will add to your yoke; my father disciplined you with whips, but I will discipline you with scorpions" (1 Kgs 12:11//2 Chr 10:14). As one might expect, this did not get a good response. The elders called for withdrawal of support of the Davidic monarchy in Jerusalem, saying "To your tents, oh Israel. Look to your own house, David" (1 Kgs 12:16; cf. 2 Sam 20:1). When Rehoboam sent his chief of forced labor to bring the northerners back in line, they stoned him to death (1 Kgs 12:18).

As 1 Kings 12 tells it, the elders of Israel chose a new monarch rather than returning to the loose tribal grouping they had before kingship. In place of Rehoboam, they anointed as king one of their own countrymen, Jeroboam, who was a man from the tribe of Ephraim. Earlier he had worked for Solomon as chief of forced labor, but rebelled and fled to Egypt when Solomon tried to kill him (1 Kgs 11:26–7). As a new king of Israel, Jeroboam first established Shechem

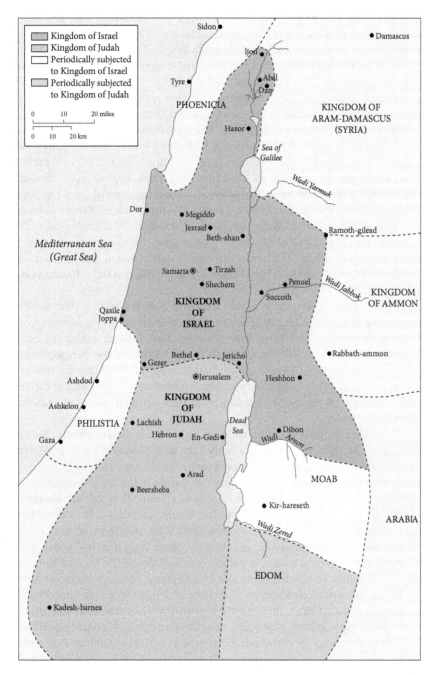

MAP 4.1
The neighboring kingdoms of Israel and Judah. Redrawn from Norman Gottwald, *The Hebrew Bible: A Socio-Literary Introduction*. Minneapolis: Fortress, 1985, page 291.

as his capital, then moved to Penuel, and he established royal sanctuaries at the towns of Bethel (toward the south of Israel) and Dan (in the far north; see Map 4.1). He installed statues of calves at each sanctuary and proclaimed "Here are your gods, oh Israel, who led you out of Egypt" (1 Kgs 12:28).

This narrative in 1 Kings 12 represents a perspective by later southern scribes on how awful it was that Israel in the north broke away from Judah. Its depiction of a northern kingdom extending to Dan and its implicit critique of Jeroboam's calves as idolatry are just a couple of the signs that this story is a later creation by Judean (not northern, Israelite) scribes. At the same time, even this unsympathetic narrative preserves a memory of an Israelite northern monarchy that was different from the Davidic monarchy in the south. Having gained liberty, Jeroboam invokes exodus traditions when he sets up his royal sanctuaries in Bethel and Dan ("Here are your gods ... who led you out of Egypt"). He picks ancient northern cities as bases for his new kingdom, cities such as Shechem and then Penuel. And though Jeroboam's "calves" are viewed negatively in these chapters of the Bible (and in its parallel in the story of Moses, Exodus 32), this critique of them as idols was added by the later (Judean) narrators of the story. Archaeological finds of ancient statues of bulls in Israelite sites suggest that they were one of the most ancient symbols of divinity known in early Israel, and no one in Jeroboam's time would have questioned his use of this revered religious symbol for divinity.

There is one other way in which Jeroboam's scribes and/or other northerners forged a path in founding the northern monarchy: they *appear to have developed a corpus of (northern) Israelite written texts*. Indeed, this corpus even seems to have been a "counter-curriculum" that balanced the perspective of the Jerusalem-centered Zion theology that was central in the Davidic monarchy of the south. This counter-curriculum featured written versions of earlier oral traditions of the north, writings that thus featured northern themes, places, and heroes.

A good example is the story of Jacob found in Genesis (Genesis 25–35). It features Jeroboam's royal sanctuary city of Bethel and early northern capitals such as Penuel (where Jacob wrestles God – Gen 32:22–32). Indeed, the story of Jacob in Genesis counters the claims of the older monarchy in Jerusalem. Where Jerusalem Zion traditions claimed that Yahweh dwelled at Mount Zion (Pss 9:11; 135:21), the Jacob story embedded in Genesis has God (quoted by Jacob) say, "I am the God who dwells in Bethel" (Gen 31:13). These clues suggest that much of the Jacob story now in Genesis was written in the north as a counterpoint to the writings of the Davidic monarchy in the south. To be sure, as we saw in Chapter 2, the Genesis Jacob story builds on more ancient trickster and other oral traditions about Jacob and his family. Nevertheless, most of the *written* story of Jacob probably originates from the northern monarchy of Israel as part of its counter-curriculum. It even seems as if the northern prophet, Hosea, studied this early Jacob story and could refer specifically to it (Hos 12:3–4, 12 [Hebrew and some translations 12:4–5, 13]).

Basics on the Jacob Story

Design: the Jacob story chiasm
  A Encounter Jacob/Esau (25:21–34; 27:1–45)
    B Divine encounter, departure (28:10–22*)
      C Wives acquisition (29:1–30)
        D Fertility: children (29:31–30:24)
        D′ Fertility: flocks (30:25–43)
      C′ Wives extrication (31:1–55)
    B′ Divine encounter, return (32:22–32)
  A′ Encounter Jacob/Esau (33:1–17)

A **chiasm** is a circular literary form that moves through a set of themes to the **Defining "chiasm"**
center (e.g. A, B, C, D) and then goes through similar themes in reverse order
after the center (e.g. D′, C′, B′, A′). Major emphasis is often put on the texts that
occur at the center of a chiasm.

The center of this early Jacob story is the fertility of Jacob's family and flocks **Major themes of**
(Gen 29:31–30:43). This is a major theme of the story, alongside emphasis on his **the Jacob story**
(and his women's) resourcefulness amidst conflict and danger.

MORE ON METHOD: THE JOSEPH STORY AND LITERARY APPROACHES

The Joseph story as a potential early northern text
The Joseph story (Genesis 37–50 minus probable later additions such as Genesis 38, 46, and 48–9) is another good candidate for being a northern text that has been adapted into the present Bible. These chapters tell a tale that starts with a pair of dreams that Joseph has. In one, the sheaves of grain belonging to Joseph's brothers bow down in obedience to Joseph's sheaf. In the other dream, eleven stars and the sun and moon bow down to Joseph. His (eleven) brothers interpret these dreams as claims by Joseph that he will dominate them, and their murderous resentment about these claims results in Joseph being taken into slavery in Egypt (Genesis 37). There he rises to prominence, is able to provide food for his family when they flee a famine in Israel, and is reconciled with his brothers (Genesis 45 and 50).

    Especially since Joseph was seen as an ancestor of Ephraim and Manasseh (Gen 41:50–2, ancestors of the tribes of the heartland of Israel) and thus the ancestor of Jeroboam, an Ephraimite (1 Kgs 11:26), tribal groups of the north could have seen this narrative as an allegory of power. It may have been designed to help them recognize the need for rulers like Jeroboam to rule and provide for "their brothers" much like Joseph's brothers come to recognize his need to rule over and provide for them. As such, an early form of the Joseph narrative that is now embedded in Genesis may have been composed and circulated in Israel (of the northern hill country).

Literary approaches and Joseph
Meanwhile, the Joseph story has been a major focus of literary study of the Bible. No matter when one dates the Joseph story (and there is debate), there is much room for analysis of its characterization of Joseph and his brothers, the contrast between what the storyteller says happened at

points and what different brothers report about what happened, and the move of the plot from brotherly resentment to reconciliation. Literary study of biblical narrative draws on the study of modern literature to reach insights about texts like the Joseph story that are not related to particular theories about dating or social context.

Such literary approaches to biblical narrative have grown ever more varied as study of literature in the humanities itself has evolved. For more on diverse literary approaches to narrative, see David Gunn, "Narrative Criticism," pp. 201–29 in S. McKenzie and S. Haynes (eds.), *To Each Its Own Meaning* (Louisville, KY: Westminster John Knox Press, 1999) and Hugh Pyper, "Postmodernism," pp. 117–36 in S. McKenzie and J. Kaltner (eds.), *New Meanings for Ancient Texts* (Louisville, KY: Westminster John Knox, 2013).

It is difficult to know exactly what other biblical texts were composed in the north, but there are many other chapters of the Hebrew Bible that show strong northern connections. Chapter 2 of this textbook discussed one of those chapters, Deborah's victory song in Judges 5, which focuses exclusively on northern tribes. This early song was probably composed (building on earlier oral tradition) in this northern kingdom of Israel. Some form of the book of Deuteronomy may have started in the north as well. It includes a scene of covenant making on northern mountains (Deut 27:1–13) that almost certainly would not have been composed by later Judean scribes. In addition, it is likely that there was some kind of northern version of the Moses-exodus story, whether oral or written. Not only is Jeroboam described as invoking the god of the exodus as the sponsor of his royal sanctuary (1 Kgs 12:28), but the book of the northern prophet, Hosea, contains an unusual density of references to Moses, the exodus, and wilderness.

It should be no surprise that parts of the Bible would originate from such northern traditions. There is much archaeological evidence that the kingdom of Israel in the north, during its two centuries of existence, was more powerful and prominent than the kingdom of Judah to the south. In particular, Israel reached a zenith of power during the time of King Omri and his son, Ahab (see Figure 4.1). Omri established a massive new capital in Samaria, made a major marriage alliance with Phoenicia (Ahab's wife, Jezebel, was from the major Phoenician city of Sidon), and dominated the smaller, southern kingdom of Judah, which was still ruled by descendants of David. Though the Omride dynasty was eventually brought down through a coup d'état led by a general Jehu (841 BCE), years afterward, Mesopotamian kings would still refer to the whole area as "the house of Omri." The kingdom of Israel could achieve such prominence during this time partly because it had more land and population than the kingdom of Judah and controlled more central trade routes. Indeed, in many respects the kingdom of Israel represents the first clearly recognizable monarchy for the people of Israel, leaving its mark in the form of a number of urban structures and fortifications in the north that archaeologists date to the time of Omri and afterward. Given this, we can surmise that the kingdom of Israel that was based in the north (ultimately Samaria) is a likely context for multiple writings that came to be included in our present Hebrew Bible.

Imperial clouds, however, were on the horizon. In the second half of the eighth century, the Assyrian empire under King Tiglath-Pileser III began

FIGURE 4.1
One of the ivory carvings found in Samaria, the site of Ahab's famous "ivory palace" (1 Kgs 22:39). Originally covered in gold, these objects illustrate the kind of wealth and power possessed by the northern kingdom, particularly under Omri and Ahab.

extending its reach westward to secure access to resources and trade routes in the area of Israel. The Assyrians had long been a major trading power in the Near East, but by this time they had also assembled an extremely efficient army that was the terror of their neighbors. Figure 4.2 on the next page shows an Assyrian depiction of an attack on a Judean city in 701. Other parts of the same set of reliefs show Judean resisters being impaled and inhabitants of the town being led away in chains. Through such attacks, and reports and depictions of them, the Assyrians terrorized the area and enforced their domination. One Assyrian king brags, "Many of the captives ... I took alive; from some of these I cut off their hands to the wrist, from others I cut off their noses, ears, and fingers; I put out the eyes of many of the soldiers." Another reports, "I fixed up a pile of corpses in front of the gate. I flayed the nobles, as many as had rebelled and spread their skins out on the piles of corpses." It was in the face of threats like these that central parts of the biblical tradition were formed.

Facing the prospect of possible Assyrian invasion, many countries voluntarily submitted to Assyria and promised to send regular tribute to the Assyrian king. This happened first in the north, perhaps as early as the ninth century with

FIGURE 4.2

Detail from a wall-sized panorama, in the palace of the Assyrian king Sennacherib, of the defeat of the town of Lachish in Judah. The Assyrians are pushing a siege engine up a ramp to break a hole in the wall of Lachish while the Judean defenders attempt to set the engine on fire by throwing torches down from the wall.

Jehu (as in Figure 4.3), but first in an ongoing way when king Menahem of Israel started paying substantial tribute to Assyria around 738 BCE. But Menahem died, and the kingship was soon taken over around 735 BCE by Pekah, who aimed to join Syria and other nations in rebelling against Assyria and stopping payment of the onerous tribute. In what is called the **Syro-Ephraimite war** (735–734 BCE) this new anti-Assyrian coalition even laid siege to Jerusalem in the south in an attempt to force similar anti-Assyrian policies on Ahaz, who was king of Judah at the time. Ahaz escaped the Israelite and Syrian forces by appealing for Assyrian help, thus defeating those besieging him, but also falling under Assyrian domination himself. Thus began a process by which the northern kingdom was gradually reduced in size and eventually totally destroyed in 722 BCE, while Judah barely survived its period of Assyrian rule.

A few years later Hezekiah, king of Judah, also rebelled. In retaliation, the Assyrians destroyed virtually all the towns of Judah and were poised to destroy Jerusalem as well. Nevertheless, they pulled back – for unknown

FIGURE 4.3
Panel from the Black Obelisk of the Assyrian king Shalmaneser III, depicting the Israelite king Jehu offering tribute to and kissing the ground before the Assyrian king. It documents the brief subservience of the northern kingdom to Assyria about a hundred years before Assyria dominated and eventually destroyed the kingdom of Israel in the late eighth century.

reasons. The account of his attack and withdrawal is found in both an Assyrian version and multiple biblical versions (see the next page for "A View from the Assyrian Imperial Court: The Annals of Sennacherib"). The kingdom of Judah barely survived, and Hezekiah and, later, his son Manasseh ruled for decades as vassals of Assyria over a much reduced kingdom of Judah. Zion theology was apparently affirmed, but Judah was forever wounded.

This whole process decisively affected the formation of the Hebrew Bible. Whatever texts we now have from the northern kingdom were preserved – in tatters and fragments – in the kingdom of Judah, which survived the Assyrian onslaught. Moreover, this drama of Assyrian invasions, anti-Assyrian coalitions, and switching between pro-Assyrian and anti-Assyrian kings forms the backdrop for much of Israel's earliest written prophecy. The prophecies of Hosea, Micah, and Isaiah, in particular, are difficult to understand without a sense of the political turmoil their countries were facing. Even the harsh prophecy of Amos, which was delivered prior to the worst of Israel's encounters with Assyria, became as important as it did as an explanation of the disaster that eventually overtook that kingdom.

In sum, much of the Hebrew Bible was formed in the shadow of Assyria's imperial domination of Israel and Judah. The rich literature of the north was destroyed as such, only to be preserved in fragments strewn across Judah's later Bible. In addition, this Assyrian crisis was the starting point for the development of written prophecy in ancient Israel and Judah. Prophets such as Hosea and Amos, Micah and Isaiah, may not have gotten much of a hearing in

A View from the Assyrian Imperial Court: The Annals of Sennacherib

The following is a quotation from the prism shown in figure 4.4 where Sennacherib, king of Assyria, describes his invasion of Judah and siege of Jerusalem during the reign of king Hezekiah of Judah.

FIGURE 4.4
The Sennacherib prism.

As for Hezekiah of the land Judah, I surrounded and conquered forty-six of his fortified walled cities and smaller settlements in their environs, which were without number by having ramps trodden down and battering rams brought up, the assault of foot soldiers, sapping, breaching and siege engines. I brought out of them 200,150 people, young and old, male and female, horses, mules, donkeys, camels, oxen, sheep, and goats, which were without number, and I counted them as booty. As for him (Hezekiah) I confined him inside the city Jerusalem, his royal city, like a bird in a cage. I set up blockades against him and made him dread exiting his city gate.

I detached from his land the cities of his which I had plundered and I gave (them) to Mitinti, the King of the city Ashdod, and Padi, the King of the city Ekron, (and) to Sillibel, the King of the land Gaza and thereby made his land smaller. To the former tribute, their annual giving, I added the payment (of) gifts (in recognition) of [my] overlordship and imposed (it) upon them.

As for him (Hezekiah), fear of my lordly brilliance overwhelmed him and, after my departure, he had brought into Niniveh, my capital city, the auxiliary forces and his elite troops whom he had brought inside to strengthen the city Jerusalem, his royal city, and who had provided support, along with 30 talents [420 pounds] of gold ... as well as his daughters, his palace women, male (and) female ssinger. Furthermore, he sent a mounted messenger of his to me to deliver this payment and to do obeisance. (Translation adapted from A. Kirk Grayson and Jamie Novotny (eds), *The Royal Inscriptions of Sennacherib, King of Assyria (704-681 BC), Part 1*. Winona Lake, Ind: Eisenbrauns, 2012,,., 65-66)

Exercise

How does this description compare with Isaiah 36–7 (parallel to 2 Kgs 18:13, 17–19:37)? How does it compare to 2 Kgs 18:14–16 (material not found in Isaiah)?

their own day. Nevertheless, the writings attributed to them became important to later generations of Judeans who had to endure yet more catastrophes like the eighth-century Assyrian onslaught. We turn now to look at the phenomenon of such written prophecy.

Ancient Near Eastern Prophecy

Prophecy was a widespread phenomenon in the Near East. The cultures of Egypt, Phoenicia, Syria, and the kingdoms of Mesopotamia all included people, some amateurs and some professionals, who pronounced oracles from the gods. This was part of a broader system by which kings and others tried to predict the future. Much as some people learn to read scrolls, these scholars aimed to learn to "read" clues in the cosmos to the gods' intentions, clues encoded in dreams, omens, parts of special animals sacrificed to divine the future, and other means. Life was unpredictable, and the people of the Near East marshaled every resource they could to understand more about what the gods were doing and what they wished. Verbal prophecies from human mediums were a major way of gaining such information.

Most such prophecies were oral, but sometimes they were written down. The archives at Mari, a Syrian city that became very powerful in the second millennium BCE, contain hundreds of records of prophecies given there, just in case such prophecies might be useful later. Later Mesopotamian archives likewise contain careful records of prophetic oracles and even a few small collections of oracles. Perhaps one of the most interesting written prophecies, however, is a wall inscription found in the Transjordan, just across from Israel, in a crossroads village now known as Deir Alla. This inscription, dated a few decades before those of the biblical prophets to be discussed here, gives the contents of a scroll describing how "Balaam, son of Beor" (a figure known as a seer in Numbers 22–4) received a vision of judgment much like the Hebrew prophets to be discussed below. Together, the Deir Alla text and early prophetic collections in the Hebrew Bible show peoples in the neighborhood of Israel collecting and studying prophetic words of judgment, not just hearing those words preached. Let us turn now for a closer look at the earliest of the prophetic teachings preserved in the Hebrew Bible.

Overview of the Four Eighth-Century Prophets

	Prophecy addressed to Israel (the northern kingdom)	Prophecy addressed to Judah (the southern kingdom)
Prediction of doom	Amos	Micah
Prediction of hope on the other side of painful judgment	Hosea	Isaiah

Amos, a Southern Prophet Preaching Justice and Doom to the North

READING

Amos 1–2 and 7–9.

The prophet Amos may be best known right now – insofar as he is known at all – as a prophet of social justice. No other prophet packs so much social critique into so little space. The book starts and finishes with similar divine critiques of elites of northern Israel taking advantage of their power to exploit the poor:

> For the three crimes of Israel
> > and for four, I will not turn back the punishment.
> Because they sell the innocent for silver
> > And the poor for a pair of sandals.
> They trample the head of the poor into the dust of the earth
> > And push the oppressed out of their way. (Amos 2:6–7; also 8:4–6)

Later, Amos proclaims disaster for the women of the capital city of Samaria, who "oppress the poor and crush the needy" (4:1). He announces disaster for those "who turn justice into wormwood and bring down social solidarity" (5:7). In a passage later echoed by Martin Luther King Jr. and others, he calls for "justice [to] roll down like waters and righteousness like an everflowing stream" (5:24).

This prophecy by Amos does not seem to have been received positively in his own time. To start with, he was an outsider in northern Israel. The Bible records that he came from Judah, having been a shepherd near the small town of Tekoa (Amos 1:1; 7:14). Moreover, most of his prophecies to the north were uncompromisingly harsh, often undermining the ancient traditions most dear to his audience. The Israelites might have thought they were safe because the God of the exodus was on their side, but Amos suggested that this exodus was nothing special:

> Are you not like the Ethiopians
> > to me, O Israel?   Oracle of Yahweh
> Did I not bring Israel
> > out of Egypt
> And the Philistines from Caphtor
> > And the Arameans from Kir?

The Israelites might have thought that God's choosing of them would protect them ("election theology"), but the book of Amos quotes God giving an interesting twist on such northern election theology:

> You only have I known
>> among all the clans of the earth,
> Therefore, I will hold you accountable
>> for all your crimes. (Amos 3:2)

A later story about Amos in Amos 7:10–17 gives a vivid picture of one response to his message. It starts by telling how Amos went to the royal sanctuary at Bethel, and announced that the king of Israel at the time, Jeroboam II, would die by the sword, while his people would go into exile. The high priest at Bethel, Amaziah, sent a message about this to the king and then said to Amos:

> Go away, seer, flee to Judah, eat bread there and prophesy, but don't ever again prophesy at Bethel because it is the king's sanctuary and the temple of the kingdom. (7:12–13)

Amos in this story responds that he is – or was – not a professional prophet just trying to prophesy anywhere. Instead, God called him from his farmwork in Tekoa to go prophesy to "God's people, Israel" (Amos 7:14–15). But now that Amaziah has told him to stop prophesying in Israel, Amos adds to his former prophecy that the priest's wife will become a city prostitute, his sons will die in battle, and he, a priest, will die "in an unclean land" (7:17).

There is no hint in this and many other prophecies that Amos aimed to change the ways of his Israelite audience. To be sure, there are some isolated calls for the people to change in chapter 5 (Amos 5:4, 6, and 14) and some predictions of hope for Judah added to the end of the book (Amos 9:8b, 11–15). These fragments, however, hardly outweigh the book's general tone of doom. It starts with a set of prophecies where God proclaims that "for three crimes and for four" God will not turn back the punishment (Amos 1–2). It ends with a series of four visions: in the first two Amos turns back God's punishment through his pleas on Israel's behalf (Amos 7:1–6), but in the "third" and "fourth" visions God will not turn back the punishment (7:7–9; 8:1–8). Instead, God has a "plumbline of justice" by which God has measured Israel (7:7–9), and it will be struck by a horrible earthquake (8:8; see also 2:13).

As it turns out, Israel was actually hit by an earthquake around the time of Amos. This has been confirmed by a combination of archaeological and geological data. This fulfillment of Amos's prophecy was never forgotten (Amos 1:1). Yet his prophecies of disaster proved to be correct in a broader way as well. As Amos had predicted (Amos 2:13–16; 3:11–15; 6:1–7), the northern kingdom was completely destroyed, though not in a way he envisioned. Amos prophesied in a time before the Assyrians' dominance and does not mention them, but in 722 BCE they invaded, destroyed Israel's sanctuaries and palaces, and carried into exile its surviving leaders.

Basics on the Book of Amos

Outline: Judean prophetic judgment on Israel	I	Sayings against the nations: setting the judgment of Israel in context	1:1–2:16
	II	Elaboration of judgment: the inversion of Israel's election	3:1–9:8a
	III	Final qualification: future for "Israel" in a revived Davidic kingdom	9:8b–15

How Amos was adapted for the south

Most specialists in Amos agree that the book of Amos contains numerous additions that adapted his prophecy to the north so that it could speak to the south as well. For example, the oracle of judgment against Judah in Amos 2:4–5 stands out from the other oracles in 1:3–16 and is probably an addition designed to include Judah among the nations judged by Amos. Likewise, the concluding promise that the "booth of David" will be rebuilt (Amos 9:11–15, also introduced by 8b) was probably added to provide a word of hope for Judah (and "Israel" in the wider sense) in contrast to the word of judgment throughout the rest of the book on the northern kingdom of Israel.

More information: Amos and praise?

The middle of the book is punctuated by three similar praises of Yahweh: 4:13; 5:8–9; 9:5–6. Read them and see the similarities. These late elements of Amos challenge the reader to praise the awesome God who brings such judgment on Israel and set that judgment in the context of God's creation.

By this time Amos had returned to Judah, and his written prophecy was a form of prophetic "teaching" that Judeans could reinterpret – now in relation to the threat (and later reality) of Assyrian domination. Like teachings seen in Proverbs, these sayings by Amos followed a format of "3 and 4" (Prov 30:15–31; cf. Amos 1–2; 7:1–9 and 8:1–8), rhetorical questions (Amos 3:4–6), and riddles (Amos 3:12; 6:12). Yet this written prophetic teaching of Amos consists of quotations of God, not of a sage like Solomon. And the focus of the teaching is on social acts and their national consequences, not the smaller-scale "moral act-consequence" of an individual student emphasized in Proverbs (see Chapter 3 on moral act-consequence). In the end, this written form of Amos's prophecy had a more lasting effect than any oral words that he delivered. Though he was told to go home by the northern high priest Amaziah, Amos's words are still being read more than two and a half thousand years after they were written.

Hosea, the Northern Prophet, Calling for Israel's Devotion to Yahweh Alone

READING

Hosea 1–2 and 11–12.

The book of Hosea was also addressed to the kingdom of Israel around this time, but it is quite different from the prophecy of Amos. Where Amos emphasized judgment for Israel's injustice, Hosea pleaded for his own people to change, to "sow social solidarity" (10:12) and "protect justice" (12:6 [12:7 in some translations]). Where Amos announced irreversible disaster, Hosea predicted restoration on the other side of God's punishment. And where Amos inverted and critiqued his audience's deep belief in their chosenness (ancient "election theology"), Hosea found new ways of describing that chosenness, ways that emphasized God's love for Israel and God's wish for Israel's devotion. For Hosea, Israel's main failing was a lack of devotion to God and a love of false gods instead.

This is most vividly illustrated at the outset of the book with Hosea's image of God's broken marriage to Israel. The book starts with the story of a rather remarkable and personal act of symbolic prophecy – yet one that we will see also has disturbing overtones. Hosea is called by God to marry and have children by a promiscuous woman, giving these children Hebrew sentence-names that symbolize what God plans to do with Israel, such as "not pitied" and "not my people" (Hos 1:2–9). Then, after the brief insertion of a yet later text reversing this prophecy of judgment (Hos 1:10–2:1), we encounter one of the most powerful passages of the whole book: God's agonized speech to Israel in the wake of Israel's spiritual promiscuity (Hos 2:2–15 [2:4–17 in some translations]). In this speech God, not Hosea, is the husband, and the nation of Israel is the wife. God starts with an address to the children of this "Israel," telling them – in effect – that God has divorced their mother:

> Protest to your mother, protest,
> For she is not my wife
> And I am not her husband. (Hos 2:2a)

Yet God in Hosea 2 is not as done with this relationship as first appears. God's speech immediately turns toward a plea for the children to get their "mother," their nation, to end her adulterous ways, lest she be subject to the sort of stripping and shaming that wives suspected of adultery had to endure at the hands of their husbands:

> She must put away her promiscuity,
> and her adultery from between her breasts.
> Lest I strip her naked,
> And display her like the day she was born,
> Make her bare as the desert,
> and make her dry like parched earth,
> And let her die of thirst. (Hos 2:2b–3)

This Israel, this wife of God, is facing the prospect of drought and famine (the "stripping") because she has gone after "other lovers" in search of love gifts. Yet Yahweh in Hosea's speech insists that she was mistaken about who was providing for her. In actuality, it was really Yahweh, her husband, who was giving her the things a man was to give to his wife: food, clothing, and oil (Hos 2:5, 8).

This list of gifts suggests that Hosea sees Yahweh as betrayed by Israel's worship of other gods, such as Baal (Hos 2:13). According to Hosea, the problem is that Israel sought grain and other benefits from these other gods rather than relying on Yahweh alone. Such worship of multiple gods, of course, was quite common in ancient cultures, and we even see signs (discussed in Chapter 2) that people in earliest Israel worshipped other gods alongside Yahweh. Nevertheless, Hosea proclaims to his people that Yahweh is as offended by such worship of other gods as a husband would be by his wife's adultery. Like a good husband, he provided his wife with good things, and she undermined his manhood by giving her love to others who she thought could provide better.

In response, Yahweh says that he will block Israel's way to her lovers so that – like the woman of the Song of Songs – she will "seek" her lovers and not "find" them (Hos 2:6–7; see Song of Songs 3:1–5). Much of the rest of the speech elaborates how Yahweh will devastate the land of Israel for its unfaithfulness. Nevertheless, it concludes not with judgment, but with hope – in this case Yahweh's plan to seduce Israel and bring back the early times when Israel was in the wilderness and fully in love with God:

> Therefore, look, I will entice her,
> > and I will lead her in the desert,
> > And speak tenderly to her.
> I will give her vineyards from there,
> > and the valley of Achor as a gate of hope.
> She will respond there as in her youthful days,
> > As when she came out of the land of Egypt. (Hos 2:14–15)

In this way, Hosea's image of marriage between Yahweh and Israel is meant to depict not just Yahweh's pain at what Hosea saw as Israel's betrayal, not just Yahweh's intent to bring consequences, but also Yahweh's enduring love, a love that means that God cannot bear to let Israel go for good and aims to bring her back into a relationship with him. As if this were not enough, the book further underscores this point through having Hosea himself describe another act of symbolic prophecy. As a symbol of God's intent to take back Israel despite what "she" has done, God tells Hosea to pay a price to hire a woman known for promiscuity and then specify that she not seek any lovers – not even be with Hosea – for a long time (Hos 3:1–5).

The narratives of symbolic prophecy in Hosea 1 and 3 have led many readers to psychologize Hosea's message, believing that his bold new vision of God was prompted by problems in his personal life, perhaps a propensity to end up with the wrong kinds of women. There are clues elsewhere in the book, however, that suggest a more important background: the power politics surrounding Assyrian domination of Israel going all the way back to the time of king Jehu. In Hos 5:8–6:6 we see Hosea's critique of Israel and Judah's lack of steadfast "love" for Yahweh (6:4). Hosea sees this lovelessness proven when Israel (called "Ephraim" here) pursued "futile" plans (5:11) and even sent away to Assyria to save itself (5:13). In Hos 7:3–7 Hosea condemns as "adultery" (7:4) the constant shifting of kings in Israel, largely in response to the Assyrian threat. In Hos 8:7–10 Hosea likens the kingdom's tribute payments to a case where a prostitute is actually paying her clients ("Ephraim hires its lovers," 8:9). Finally, Hos 9:1–6 mixes images of agricultural plenty and international politics. The prophet tells the people at a harvest festival not to rejoice, because they are like a promiscuous woman who has loved her wages for sex at threshing floor and winepress (9:1–2), and who will soon go into exile in Assyria and

Egypt (9:3–6). In these passages, Hosea critiques the multitude of ways that Israel (and Judah) tried to manipulate or buy their way out of oppression by Assyria. According to Hosea, they should have been devoted to and trusted in Yahweh instead of pursuing such power politics.

Basics on the Book of Hosea

I   Introduction of judgment and hope by way of family imagery   1–3

II Elaboration of prophecy of judgment and hope by way of other images   4–14

Outline: prophecy of judgment and hope

Hosea himself may have spoken about Judah in the south (one example is 5:8–15), but there are signs that later Judean scribes adapted Hosea's sayings so that they included Judah in Hosea's judgment (examples are 5:5; 6:4, 11). Still other additions resemble the conclusion to Amos (Amos 9:11–15). Like that conclusion, they see future hope for destroyed "Israel" being located in a broader "Israel" that is centered in Judah and its Davidic monarchy (1:11; 3:5; 11:12).

How Hosea was adapted for the south

This adaptation of Hosea was but the first step in having the book's images speak to new communities that Hosea had not addressed. Whatever personal or cultic background there once was to Hosea's marriage and other imagery, it gained a symbolic life of its own. Within the present form of the book, the marriage imagery of Hosea 1–3 introduces Hosea's prophecy more generally and then fades into the background. Later, Hosea quotes Yahweh as saying that "by the hand of the prophets I gave analogies" (Hos 12:10; probably mistranslated in the NRSV). These analogies in Hosea – marriage, parent, covenant – have been applied and reapplied by centuries of later readers.

Hosea's prophecy for the ages

There may be some critique of Israel's cult practices as well, especially given the frequent references to "Baal" throughout Hosea. The people of Israel had worshipped various gods alongside Yahweh, long before Hosea's time, and apparently continued to do so. Indeed, scholars have not been able to reconstruct an early period when the tribes of Israel did not worship other gods. Ancient tribal and later sites have yielded female statues that many interpret to be goddess figurines (see Figure 4.5). Early Israelites appear to have borne names formed from the names of various deities, including "Baal" and "El." And a couple of early inscriptions from around the time of Hosea feature blessings "by Yahweh and his asherah [or Asherah]" (see Figure 4.6). Though there is debate about how to interpret these blessings, many understand them to imply that Yahweh had taken over Asherah, formerly El's wife, as his own. In all these ways, Hosea faced a much more diverse religious landscape than we often picture for early Israel. What was new was that he argued that this religious diversity, this lack of pure worship of Yahweh, was one reason for Israel's ills. He believed that the religious diversity of his time was a falling away from Israel's past pure devotion to Yahweh in the wilderness. That is how most contemporary readers of the present Bible perceive the matter. Yet his audience probably perceived his calls for pure worship of Yahweh alone as something *new*.

Overall, Hosea's main point seems to be that his people are displaying a massive unfaithfulness – whether in international policy or in religious practice. Such unfaithfulness, for Hosea, is like a wife's unfaithfulness to her husband.

FIGURE 4.5

Pillar figurines of a sort common in archaeological remains of the eighth century. They indicate to many scholars that some kind of goddess worship continued to prevail in the time of Hosea and Amos.

FIGURE 4.6

Drawing and inscription found at a desert trading post called Kuntillet Adjrud used by eighth-century Israelites. Interpretation of the drawings is disputed, but note the figure playing a lyre on the upper right. The inscription toward the top is understood by many to refer to "Yahweh and his Asherah.".

Yahweh's response is a mix of emotions typical of wronged husbands: agony and jealous wrath at his wife's betrayal combined with a wish to have her back again. In this way Hosea suggests to his fellow Israelites oppressed by Assyria that Yahweh did not fail or abandon Israel; rather Israel abandoned Yahweh first.

Readers over the years have responded differently to Hosea's picture of God and Israel. For many, the book stands as a powerful picture of God's longing for steadfast love and his willingness to go to any length to bring the people back. Yet others are disturbed by ominous parallels between God's behavior in Hosea's prophecy and the cycle of spousal abuse: a husband's anger at his wife and/or jealous accusations of adultery, physical beating and/or sexual humiliation of the wife, and wooing of the wife back. Hosea used the image metaphorically. Just as – within his time – a husband was seen as justified in punishing, even killing, an unfaithful wife, so also Hosea depicts God as having the right to punish Israel's spiritual promiscuity, starving and stripping her. Most people now would reject this image of God as a husband depriving and beating his sinful, human wife (before taking her back again). Furthermore, such metaphors can be and have been extended to justify literal spouse abuse. Some husbands and religious professionals have taken Hosea's picture to be a biblical endorsement of the right of human husbands to beat or sexually humiliate wives whom they suspect of adultery or other wrongs. Finally, Hosea's use of the image of a sexually promiscuous woman as an image of sin also had consequences. Even though he was critiquing male leaders as much as or more than females, his particular association of feminine sexuality with sin is echoed in several later prophets, the New Testament, and later traditions as well. In light of these concerns, these images in Hosea and later prophets are too painful to serve for many readers as images of a God of love.

Hosea and the "Book of the Twelve Prophets"

The book of the Twelve Prophets

Hosea is the first in the **book of the Twelve Prophets**, a collection of 12 shorter prophetic books, including the books of Amos and Micah, that is usually placed in bibles after Ezekiel or (Ezekiel and) Daniel. The books are attributed to so-called **"minor prophets"** – Hosea through Malachi. The word "minor" is applied to these prophets not because they are thought to be unimportant, but because the books attributed to them are relatively short. Each of these short books has its own character, but they also show signs of being edited into a larger whole by later scribes.

Hosea 14:9 and prophetic teaching

One possible sign of such editing is the last verse of Hosea, Hos 14:9. It stresses that the "wise" will understand the words of Hosea, and it praises the ways of Yahweh as "right." Such mention of the "wise" is otherwise typical of books such as Proverbs. This verse marks the book of Hosea as a form of prophetic "teaching," much like Solomon's teaching in Proverbs and Ecclesiastes.

At the same time, since Hosea is the first book of the 12 minor prophets, this framing of Hosea's book as a teaching has implications for understanding the eleven books that follow. With this conclusion to Hosea in Hos 14:9, they too stand as prophetic teaching to be understood by the "wise."

There are, however, other images in Hosea that offer alternative ways of envisioning God's agony and passion for reconciliation. Consider, for example, the picture in Hosea 11, where God now is Israel's parent, agonizing over a son's disobedience after God's tender care for him. The chapter starts with God's description of having tenderly cared for Israel as for a child, and Israel's response to such care by sacrificing to other gods and going their own way (Hos 11:1–4). At first God responds by announcing the destruction of Israel (11:5–6), but then God starts to relent:

> How can I give you up, oh Ephraim?
>> How can I surrender you, oh Israel? ...
> I have changed my mind.
>> My compassion has taken hold of me.
> I will not act on my wrath,
>> I will not again destroy Ephraim.
> For I am God,
>> not a man,
> The holy one in your midst.
>> I will not come in anger. (Hos 11:8–9*)

Here Hosea draws on the metaphorical power of the parental relationship, yet clearly distinguishes this picture of God from that of a human "man." God here is deeply hurt by the faithlessness of God's people. Yet God cannot bear to destroy God's own child, Israel. Even if a father could bear to destroy his son, God here is "not a man" (11:9). For Hosea, God's infinite compassion can be imaged, but only partially so, by the powerful compassion a parent feels for his or her child.

Hosea's prophecy proved particularly influential in later biblical writings. We will see elements of his picture of divine–human marriage appear in several other prophets. Moreover, his call for exclusive devotion to Yahweh was foundational for later Israelites. Although the present Bible contains much later narratives that project this call for devotion back into earlier periods of Israel's history (such as Exod 20:1–3), the book of Hosea is our earliest datable witness to this idea, and it probably was not well received at first. Nevertheless, this belief in God's exclusive claims on God's people grew in importance, particularly as Israel and Judah had to grapple with Assyrian and Babylonian oppression, destruction, and exile. The people suffering through these experiences asked themselves what they could learn from them. They looked back to traditions such as Hosea, spoken out of the crucible of imperial oppression, and concluded that they needed to learn to be more faithful to Yahweh and Yahweh alone. They believed they must reject any other lord (human or divine) and choose Yahweh's boundless love instead.

Micah, a Southern Prophet, Predicting Judgment for Judah and Jerusalem

Micah 1–3 and 5–6.

READING

We turn now for a brief look at one of the earliest books containing prophecy from the south, the book of Micah. Here we find, at least in the book's earliest materials (in Micah 1–3), the words of a southern prophet like Amos. Just as Amos spoke to Israel as an outsider from Judah, so Micah spoke to Jerusalem as a Judean refugee coming from an area decimated by Assyria (the town Moresheth). Moreover, both prophets spoke words of judgment to their audiences, attempting to pierce their false sense of security. Yet the differences between these prophets are striking as well, and they point once again to the different traditions held dear by their different audiences. Where Amos undermined northern Israelite ideas of election, Micah attacks southern trust in Zion theology, particularly the idea that Zion/Jerusalem was invulnerable to all attacks, a belief manifest in biblical texts such as Psalm 46: "God is in the midst of the city, it shall not be moved" (Ps 46:5 NRSV).

The book of Micah starts with judgment, as Micah proclaims to the people of Judah that they are not immune from the Assyrian disaster that has hit the north. The first oracle describes an awesome theophany (divine appearance) of Yahweh coming from the Temple (Micah 1:2), yet it quickly becomes clear that this is no cuddly God:

> For, see!, Yahweh is coming out from his place,
> > And he will come down and tread on the sanctuaries of the earth.
> Then the mountains will melt under him,
> > And the valleys will burst open
> Like wax on a fire
> > Like waters cascading down a slope. (Mic 1:3–4)

All this, Micah says, is happening because of the "crime of Jacob and the sins of the house of Israel" (1:5). The reader may ask, "What is this crime?" and the text soon answers that it is the capital cities of Samaria and Jerusalem. In a section that sounds much like Hosea, Micah announces that God is about to destroy Samaria, the capital of the northern kingdom, because of its "idols," which he sees as "wages of a prostitute" (1:6–7). But, lest his country-people think they are immune from this disaster, Micah concludes by saying that Judah will be hit by the same destructive power, with the "wound" even reaching the gate of Jerusalem (1:8–9). The next saying, 1:10–12, makes a similar point – tracing the path of the invading Assyrian army as it moves from Gath, town by town, to the gate of Jerusalem.

Obviously Micah, like Hosea, is speaking in the context of Assyrian invasion, but he insists that the impending destruction at Assyrian hands is actually caused by God's judgment of the inner ills of the people of Judah. In a social critique reminiscent of Amos, he pronounces a lament over those who:

> plan evil
>> and acts of evil on their beds,
> When morning comes, they do it,
>> Because they have the power to do so,
> They covet fields, and seize them
>> Houses, and they take them away.
> They exploit a strong one and home,
>> And individuals and inherited land. (2:1–2)

Such critiques continue, as in Micah's attack on those who make women and children homeless (2:9) or in his quotation of God's vivid judgment on the leaders who "devour my people's flesh, flay the skin off them, the flesh off their bones, and ... breaking their bones to bits, chop them up like soup meat in a pot, like flesh in a caldron" (3:2–3).

Apparently, the powers that be in Micah's time did not like this message. He quotes others as telling him "stop preaching ... that's no way to preach, shame will not overtake us! Is the house of Jacob really condemned? Is God's patience really so short?" (2:6–7). Apparently there were others proclaiming more hopeful messages, and Micah proclaims Yahweh's judgment on those who "cry 'peace' when they have food in their mouths, but launch war on the one who takes food from them" (3:5). In a climactic message, Micah announces an end to all of the leaders who "build Zion with blood and Jerusalem with malice" (3:10):

> [Jerusalem's] leaders administer justice for bribes,
>> Her priests give rulings for a fee,
> And her prophets predict the future for pay.
>> And then they rely on Yahweh, saying,
> "Isn't Yahweh in our midst?
>> No disaster will come on us!" (3:11)

For Micah, these leaders and their trust in ancient Zion theology are bringing about the very disaster they consider unthinkable:

> Therefore, because of you,
>> Zion shall be plowed as a field
> Jerusalem will become heaps of ruins,
>> And the temple mount will be a wooded height. (3:12)

Up to this point, Micah sounds a lot like Amos. He maintains that Jerusalem's corruption is so deep that Yahweh will let the Assyrians destroy it. The book so far explains Judah's oppression by Assyria as a result of its deep-seated iniquity.

Nevertheless, much of the rest of the book, including some of its most famous passages, sounds a much more hopeful note. Micah 4 starts with a famous prophecy (4:1–3), also seen in Isaiah 2:2–4, that God will make Zion/Jerusalem the center of world justice, so that – in a reversal of the usual transformation of farmers into fighters (see Joel 3:10) – nations will "hammer swords into plowshares and spears into pruning hooks" (4:3). The rest of Micah 4–5 contains prophecies of how Yahweh will redeem "daughter Zion," who has endured pain like a woman in labor, bringing her exiles back to her (4:6–7, 8–10). The book goes on to say that when "[Zion] who is in labor has brought forth" (5:3), a powerful ruler will arise from tiny Bethlehem of Ephratah to reign in glory from Jerusalem (5:2–4 [5:1–3 in some translations]). This prophecy, often understood by Christians to be a prophecy of Jesus's birth in Bethlehem, is part of a series of prophecies about how Zion will triumph over the Assyrians and other enemies who dominated her (4:11–5:15).

Basics on the Book of Micah

I Destruction up to the gates of Jerusalem (1:1–2:11) and prediction of the in-gathering of exiles (2:12–13)

II Destruction of Zion (3:1–12) and its restoration along with the Judean monarchy and people (4:1–5:15)

III Judgment of Israel (6:1–7:7) and prophetic prayer for restoration (7:8–20)

Outline: cycles of judgment and salvation – Judah

Whereas the original prophet, Micah, stressed God's impending judgment on Zion, the book now emphasizes salvation on the other side of such judgment. It was addressed to much later Judeans who had experienced many of the disasters that Micah described. The book encouraged them and later communities to have hope for the future. Though God might destroy everything they held dear, God also could restore them.

Theme

Micah's words of judgment were not forgotten. A story in the book of Jeremiah, Jeremiah 26, describes how the later, seventh-century prophet Jeremiah was almost executed for proclaiming the destruction of the temple. At this point, the elders reminded the people of Micah's proclamation of Zion's destruction, a prophecy given a century before the time of Jeremiah (Micah 3:12). In addition, they told a story – not found elsewhere in the Bible – of King Hezekiah listening to Micah's prophecy and repenting (Jer 26:19). Jeremiah's life was spared.

More information

These words of hope for exiles and promise of victory in Micah 4–5 contrast sharply with the proclamation of absolute doom on Zion in Micah 1–3. Chapters 4 and 5 hardly sound like the words of the prophet who announced that "Zion shall be plowed as a field, and Jerusalem will be heaps of ruins" (3:12). Because of this, most scholars believe that much of Micah 4–5, and likely 6–7 as well (along with a word of hope to later exiles in Micah 2:12–13), was added by later – anonymous – prophets to the book of Micah. To copy and expand an earlier work was an ancient way of recognizing its ongoing importance and applying its message to later times. In this case, these prophets had seen Micah's earlier prophecies of destruction come true, had come to treasure his prophecies, and yet addressed an audience in Babylonian exile who needed new words of comfort to balance Micah's words of judgment.

These later prophets declared to their exilic (or post-exilic) audience that Yahweh had a grand future for Zion/Jerusalem and for them. These visionary words of hope – both of a glorious ruler (5:2–4) and of a world where people would not "study war any more" (4:1–3) – have been as important or more important to later communities as the earlier words of judgment on which they were built.

The rest of the book of Micah, however, is not all words of hope. Micah 6:9–16 accuses Jerusalem of succumbing to the same social ills as its northern neighbor: "You have kept the statutes of Omri and the works of the house of Ahab" (6:16). This may be another saying from the same eighth-century prophet (Micah) who proclaimed that the wound of Israel was coming to the gate of Jerusalem (1:9, 12). Most famous of all is the speech in Micah 6:1–8, which responds to people's complaints that God has burdened them (6:3) by saying that God's requirements are simple: "to do justice, love kindness, and walk wisely with your God" (6:8). Soon afterward, the book insists that "it is true wisdom to fear your [God's] name" (6:9), reflecting the fact that the book of Micah, like Amos and Hosea, is prophetic *teaching* or *wisdom*. It is not clear that Micah 6:2–8 came from the same eighth-century prophet who spoke most of Micah 1–3, but it is quite clear that this saying has served for many as a powerful distillation of the long-term significance of the message of the prophets. The sayings in 6:2–8 well exemplify the way the book of Micah has been enriched over time by multiple voices that could be considered "inspired." As a result, the book of Micah is now a powerful mix of Micah's eighth-century words of judgment and later prophetic teachings about hope and God's true wishes for God's people.

Isaiah's Vision of Hope for Jerusalem/Zion Embedded in the Book of Isaiah

Isaiah 1–11 and 28–32.

READING

The book of Isaiah was one of the first places where scholars recognized this kind of mix of earlier prophecy and later expansion. Isaiah starts with a super-scription that identifies what follows as "the vision of Isaiah, son of Amoz, which he saw concerning Judah and Jerusalem during the time of Uzziah, Jotham, Ahaz, and Hezekiah, kings of Judah" (1:1; see also 2:1) – that is, as the revelation given to Isaiah about the southern monarchy during the last few decades of the eighth century. Nevertheless, scholars have found many signs that the book was written over centuries. As early as nine hundred years ago, the Jewish scholar Abraham Ibn Ezra noted that the reference to the Persian king Cyrus in Isa 41:25 seems to indicate that its author not only knew of this king ruling two hundred years after the time of Isaiah, but could describe him to a contemporary audience as one "foretold from the start." Over the last two hundred years, scholars have used these and other observations to distinguish between the words of the eighth-century prophet Isaiah in the book of Isaiah and layer upon layer of prophecies by later writers now in the book as well.

This research has helped scholars see both the complexity and the grandeur of the book of Isaiah. On the one hand, scholars now believe that most sayings actually from "Isaiah ben Amoz" can be found in *parts* of Isaiah 1–11 and 28–32, with most of the rest of the book (and all of Isaiah 36–66) coming from later authors. On the other hand, scholars also have an ever increasing appreciation of the insight and artistry of the entire 66-chapter book, later portions included. Certainly later communities of faith have found inspiration in Isaiah as a whole. Virtually all of the later prophecy in Isaiah 40–66 appears in the cycle of readings used in Jewish synagogues, and the same visions of comfort and restoration have been central to Christianity from the outset. There will be occasion to return to both the design and the interpretation of these portions of the book of Isaiah in Chapters 6 and 7 of this *Introduction*.

For now it is important to recognize that this is another place where modern presuppositions about authorship and "inspiration" can mislead us in reading the Bible. Often modern interpreters assume that the *real* inspiration can only lie with an original author, a prophet in this case, while all later materials must be corruptions of the original, pure message. What emerges, however, from a look at the book of Isaiah and its history of interpretation, is that Isaiah – the eighth-century prophet – provided a dynamic and complex vision that was only the start of a much bigger process. Ultimately, the power of his vision *increased* as later authors, addressing quite different times, expanded on and adapted it so that it would speak to those times. The result was a grand book of 66 chapters, the first of the three books of the **"major prophets"** (Isaiah, Jeremiah, and Ezekiel).

Let us turn now to take a closer look at the eighth-century vision of Isaiah ben Amoz. Much of this vision is focused on Yahweh's message amidst threats related to the Assyrian onslaught. The first such major threat was the attempt by Syria and Israel in 735 BCE to force Ahaz of Judah into joining an anti-Assyrian alliance by laying siege to Jerusalem (the Syro-Ephraimite war). The book of Kings describes Ahaz as responding to the siege by asking for help from Assyria (2 Kgs 16:5–9). As we can see in Isaiah 7–8, Isaiah saw this request by King Ahaz as a fatal failure to trust in Yahweh's protection of Zion. In Isa 7:1–9 Isaiah assures Ahaz that the coalition against Judah will not stand and that Ahaz should "not be afraid." Ahaz in 7:10–17 rejects Isaiah's offer of a sign from Yahweh, and Isaiah announces that the result of this rejection will be an imminent attack by the king of Assyria. Finally, Isa 8:1–8 continues these themes, proclaiming disaster on the attackers from Israel and Syria (8:1–4), but also on the people of Judah for refusing to trust in God's protection of Zion (="the flowing waters of [Jerusalem's spring] Shiloah," 8:6). Each of these stories features a child with a Hebrew name that signifies the core of Isaiah's message: "a remnant shall return" (7:3), "God with us" (7:14), and "speedy comes the booty" (8:1). In light of the rejection of his message, Isaiah tells in 8:10–18 of Yahweh's command to "seal" his prophetic "teaching" in his "students" (8:16), so that these students can serve as a sign for future generations of "Yahweh who dwells in Zion" (8:18). Perhaps some of these students were

Isaiah's own, strangely named children, since literate fathers often taught their own children. In this case, Isaiah is passing on to his children a "teaching" and a "witness" that his own generation would not hear. We probably have this process to thank for the initial preservation of Isaiah's words and the beginnings of the book.

The story of Isaiah's commission in Isaiah 6 reflects his experience of rejection during the time of Ahaz. Many readers are well familiar with the beginning of this text, where Isaiah actually sees Yahweh's terrifying presence in the Jerusalem temple, surrounded by "seraphim" (see Figure 4.7 for more on these) – an Egyptian symbol. Awed by the spectacle, he proclaims a lament, "woe upon me, for I am a man of unclean lips in a people of unclean lips, looking onto the king of kings, Yahweh of armies!" (6:5). One of the winged cobras then burns his lips with a fiery coal, saying that this has removed the prophet's sin and bloodguilt (6:6–7). The rest of the passage then describes how Isaiah's people are about to be subjected to a similar burning process, starting with the prophet's commission to deliver a message that will not be heard:

> "Keep listening, but do not comprehend.
>   Keep looking, but do not understand."
> Make the mind of this people senseless,
>   And stop up their ears,
>   And shut their eyes,
> Lest they see with their eyes,
>   And hear with their ears,
> And understand with their mind
>   And change their ways and be healed. (6:9–10)

Isaiah is understandably upset at receiving this commission and asks "how long?" The answer is that Judah is about to be laid waste – again a probable reference to Assyrian attacks. Only after successive invasions is there any sign of hope. It is a "stump," which can regrow (6:13a).

Isaiah 6 and the "Call Narrative"

Many scholars would call Isaiah 6 a **"prophetic call narrative**." Such a narrative is a story, told in the first person by the prophet ("I," "me"), where he tells of how he was authorized by God to be a prophet and deliver God's message. Other examples are Jer 1:4–10 and Ezekiel 1–3.

Here are the typical parts of a prophetic call narrative, with illustrations from Isaiah 6:

1	A divine appearance	1–4
2	An introductory word by God	5–7
3	The call of the prophet (or leader)	8–10
4	An objection from the prophet	11a
5	A divine reassurance/answer	11b–13
6	A sign reinforcing the answer	[not present]

These prophetic call narratives stand toward the outset of a prophetic book (Jeremiah and Ezekiel) or collection in a prophetic book (the Isaiah memoir in Isaiah 6–8) and emphasize God's authorization of the message in that book. They are as different as the books that they authorize, and some scholars dispute the application of the term "call narrative" to some of these texts (particularly since the word "call" has its home in later Christian theology). Sometimes these texts lack one or another part of the typical form. Nevertheletss, they share with each other the idea that the prophet's message arose not with him, but with God. The prophet was but a messenger, as signified by the Hebrew word for prophet, *nabi*.

Isaiah 6 was probably written as an introduction to his memoir, insisting on God's role in authorizing his prophecy during the Syro-Ephraimite war even though it was rejected. As this text became part of the larger book of Isaiah, it came to authorize the book as a whole.

Other call narratives: an exercise

Judg 6:11–24 and Exod 3:1–4:17 are call narratives for other figures, Gideon and Moses. Compare these texts with Isa 6:1–13. What is similar and what is different about the form of these texts? What is similar or different about the role they play in the biblical books where they occur?

We see this image of the "stump" used elsewhere in Isaiah to communicate that there is hope on the other side of apparent absolute destruction: for an apparently dead stump can have a shoot spring forth from it (see Job 14:8–9). At the end of Isaiah 10, Isaiah describes Yahweh as coming through the whole area, cutting down the tallest trees and chopping off their branches (Isa 10:33–4). Since "trees" were an image for royal dynasties, many understand this to be Isaiah's prediction that Yahweh is about to send the Assyrian army through the area, "cutting off" all of the royal dynasties and thus terminating the monarchies of Judah, Israel, and their neighbors. Yet Isaiah sees a future on the other side of this awful event. Though the Davidic dynasty in Jerusalem might seem like a completely dead stump, Isaiah proclaims that a "shoot shall spring forth from the stump of Jesse [David's father]" (Isa 11:1). This "shoot" will be an ideal king:

> With social solidarity he will judge the poor,
> And he will rule the oppressed fairly.
> He will strike the earth with the rod of his mouth,
> And he will kill the wicked with the breath of his lips. (Isa 11:4)

Figure 4.7 Judean seals from the time of Isaiah and Micah, showing strong Egyptian influence. Note especially the winged cobras, which probably were the referent for the "seraphim" mentioned in Isaiah 6.

Although later Christian interpreters came to see this text as relating to Jesus, it originally stood as an ancient prophecy that a new king would arise over Judah who would fulfill all the promises of royal theology: a king who judges justly and successfully defends his people. The passage then turns to a grand vision of peace centered in Zion:

> The wolf will sojourn with the lamb,
>> The leopard will lie down with the calf ...
> They will not hurt or destroy
>> in all my holy mountain,
> For the earth shall be as full of the knowledge of Yahweh
>> As waters cover the sea. (Isa 11:6a and 9)

This whole complex of texts (Isa 10:33–11:9) beautifully displays Isaiah's affirmation of the royal and Zion theology that was so important to Judah, even as he proclaims an awesome, forest-felling destruction of its current leadership. His words, both in Isaiah 6 and in Isa 10:33–11:9, helped explain why Judah had undergone such suffering, even as they also offered images of hope that Yahweh eventually would restore Zion and its kingship.

The uniqueness of Isaiah's message is nicely illustrated through comparing Isaiah's words about Zion in Isa 1:21–6 with Micah's proclamation that Zion will be "plowed as a field" (Micah 3:9–12; see pp. 124–5 below, "Contrasting Prophetic Visions of Zion's Future" for a side-by-side comparison with Isa 1:21–26). Where Micah presents God as utterly rejecting Zion (/Jerusalem) as having been built "with blood" (3:10), Isaiah's God sounds more like Hosea's, in agony over how his city – envisioned as female – has been corrupted by violent, corrupt leaders:

> How she has become a promiscuous woman,
>> The city that once was faithful!
> She that was full of justice,
>> Social solidarity made its home in her,
>> And now murderers! (Isa 1:21)

To be sure, Isaiah does resemble Micah in his understanding of Jerusalem's ills. He, like Micah, criticizes a loss of "justice" (Isa 1:21; see Micah 3:9) caused by its leaders' robbery (1:23, "companions of thieves"; see Micah 2:2), taking of bribes, and perversion of due process owed to the most vulnerable people (Isa 1:23; see Micah 3:11). Yet Isaiah does *not* proclaim a final end to Jerusalem as a result of these misdeeds by its leaders. Instead, in an echo of Isaiah's own burning purification process (Isa 6:6–7), Isaiah announces that God is about to purify Jerusalem as metal alloy is purified in a hot forge (Isa 1:25). This image of a refining fire is Isaiah's way of announcing grand hope for Zion on the other side of painful judgment:

> I will restore your judges as at the first,
>> And your counselors as at the beginning.
> Then you will be called "city of social solidarity"
>> "The faithful settlement." (Isa 1:26)

Again, Isaiah contrasts here with Micah. Where Isaiah affirms that Yahweh dwells in Zion and will defend and restore it (Isa 8:18), Micah directly attacks its leadership for saying "Isn't Yahweh in our midst? No disaster will come on us!" (Micah 3:11). It is even possible that Micah had prophets such as Isaiah in mind when he blamed Jerusalem's future destruction on those who would affirm Zion theology in this way (Micah 3:12).

Apparently Isaiah's message evolved decades later when he prophesied during the time of King Hezekiah, son of Ahaz. This was the time, described in 2 Kings 18–20//Isaiah 36–9 (and 2 Chronicles 29–32), when Hezekiah joined an anti-Assyrian coalition and barely escaped destruction when the Assyrian army of Sennacherib laid siege to Jerusalem (only to withdraw). The narratives about this event found in 2 Kings and Isaiah depict Hezekiah as a positive contrast to his father Ahaz and Isaiah as more affirming of this later king. Where Ahaz refused the sign offered by Isaiah and failed to trust in Yahweh's care for Zion (Isaiah 7–8), Hezekiah actually consulted with Isaiah, and – as a result – the city was rescued (2 Kgs 18–19//Isaiah 36–7; compare with 2 Chronicles 32). The oracles found in Isaiah 28–31, however, show that Isaiah was more critical in this time than these narratives indicate. He repeatedly announces judgment on leaders like Hezekiah who go to Egypt to form anti-Assyrian alliances (30:1–5; also 28:14–22) and rely on military strength for salvation (30:15–16). Yet again, Isaiah seems to have experienced rejection, with people telling him to shut up or preach more comfortable words (30:10–11). This is why, he says, God commanded him to write these prophecies down, preserving them in scroll form as a witness against the people of Hezekiah's time (30:8).

The Use and Reuse of Biblical Traditions

All this suggests that one major impetus for the initial *writing* of prophecies such as those of Isaiah was the experience of rejection. None of the prophets discussed in this chapter seems to have been a major success in his own time. Yet their words were preserved for a later time by their closest students and/or associates. Moreover, as the words of Isaiah and other prophets (e.g. Hosea, Amos, Micah) appeared to come true over time, the significance of their written prophecies grew. For example, what started as Isaiah's counter-wisdom to the false wisdom of Jerusalem's leaders (see Isa 29:14; 31:1–2) was treasured by later Judeans and expanded in subsequent centuries. Eventually, the smaller groups of sayings seen in Isaiah 1–11, 28–32, and elsewhere grew into the 66-chapter book we now have.

This highlights the multi-layered quality of interpretation of such biblical texts. If the significance of these writings had been exhausted in the time of Amos and Isaiah, we probably would not be reading them now. We have these books because later communities found their sayings so helpful that they copied and expanded them. Moreover, this process of rereading and creative reworking continued in Jewish and Christian communities even after the texts of these prophetic books were fixed. For example, later readers reinterpreted predictions of the imminent arrival of a just Judean monarch (e.g. Micah 5:2–4; Isa 11:1–5) as predictions of a royal messiah who would overcome Rome or some successive oppressive empire. These and other prophecies have retained a lasting significance because problems of injustice and imperial rule did not cease after the Assyrian onslaught in the eighth century.

FOCUS
TEXT

Contrasting Prophetic Visions of Zion's Future

We conclude with a brief focus on contrasts between the different ways that Isaiah and Micah related to Zion theology and viewed the ultimate future of Jerusalem/Zion. Consider first the summary of Zion theology seen in Psalm 46:

> God is our refuge and strength,
>> a very present help in trouble.
> Therefore we will not fear though the earth should change,
>> though the mountains shake in the heart of the sea;
> though its waters roar and foam,
>> though the mountains tremble with its tumult.
> There is a river whose streams make glad the city of God,
>> the holy habitation of the Most High.
> God is in the midst of her, she shall not be moved;
>> God will help it when the morning dawns.
> The nations rage, the kingdoms totter;
>> God utters God's voice, the earth melts.
> Yahweh of armies is with us;
>> The god of Jacob is our refuge. (NRSV adapted)

As we saw in Chapter 3, these kinds of beliefs long preceded prophets like Isaiah and Micah. They were part of the theology that supported the Davidic monarchy with its capital in Jerusalem. In the midst of the Assyrian crisis, Isaiah and Micah present contrasting understandings of the ongoing relevance of such Zion theology. Compare and contrast the following:

Micah 3:9–12	Isaiah 1:21–6
Hear this, you heads of the house of Jacob and rulers of the house of Israel,	How she has become a promiscuous woman, The city that once was faithful!

who abhor justice
    and pervert all equity
	She that was full of justice,
	    Social solidarity made its home in her,

who build Zion with blood and Jerusalem with wrong.	And now murderers!

Its leaders administer justice for bribes,
    Her priests give rulings for a fee,
	Your silver has turned to dross,
	    Your wine is watered down.

And her prophets predict the future for pay.	Your princes are rebels, Accomplices of thieves.

And then they rely on Yahweh, saying,
"Isn't Yahweh in our midst?
    No disaster will come on us!"
	All of them greedy for gifts
	    and pursuing bribes,

Micah 3:9–12	Isaiah 1:21–6
	They show no justice to the orphan, and the widows' lawsuit never reaches them.
	Therefore, [oracle of] the Lord Yahweh of armies, the Mighty One of Israel, "I shall get satisfaction from my enemies, I shall avenge myself on my foes.
Therefore, because of you Zion shall be plowed as a field, Jerusalem shall become a heap of ruins and the mountain of the house, a wooded height.	I shall turn my hand against you, I shall purge your dross as though with lye, I shall remove your alloy.
	And I shall restore your judges as at first, Your counselors as at the beginning,
	After which you will be called 'City of Social Solidarity" 'Faithful City'."

The passage in Micah 3:9–12 is an important summation of Micah's prophecy, probably concluding an early collection of his sayings (Micah 4–7 contains material from later times and figures). Notice Micah's critique not only of Zion theology, but of those who trust in such Zion theology. How might Micah have felt about prophecies like that from his contemporary, Isaiah (in the right-hand column)? Meanwhile, note that Isaiah's prophecy is not a mere repetition of Zion theology as seen in Psalm 46. What are both specific similarities and specific differences between Isaiah's message and the affirmations in Psalm 46?

This example provides a specific illustration of how two biblical figures, even prophesying at the same time and place, can have significant differences in perspective. Building on this, use the chapter review questions below to reinforce your sense of the differences between the messages of these eighth-century prophets.

CHAPTER FOUR REVIEW

1 Know the meaning and significance of the following terms discussed in this chapter:
   - Assyria
   - book of the Twelve Prophets
   - chiasm
   - major prophets
   - minor prophets
   - prophetic call narrative
   - Syro-Ephraimite war

2 Name one or two clues that point to the specifically northern origins of early Jacob narratives in Genesis 25–35, standing as a response to claims for Jerusalem seen in Zion theology.

What clues point to similar northern Israelite origins for the Joseph novella across much of Genesis 37–50 or for early traditions about Moses?

3 How did Amos and Hosea relate in different ways to the ancient Israelite idea of election?

4 How do the eighth-century prophecies from Micah and Isaiah respond differently to Zion theology? (See the focus text section of this chapter to help with this question.)

5 Which chapters in the books of Isaiah and Micah have the largest amounts of material from the eighth-century prophets, and which

parts of each book are made up virtually exclusively of texts added by later authors?

6 What differences do you see between the views of these four eighth-century prophets on what is wrong with Israel and/or Jerusalem? What are their main differences in their views of Jerusalem's future?

RESOURCES FOR FURTHER STUDY

General Works on Prophecy and All of the Prophets

Heschel, Abraham. *The Prophets*. 2 volumes. New York: Harper & Row, 1962.

Koch, Klaus. *The Prophets*. 2 volumes. Philadelphia, PA: Fortress, 1983.

Commentaries on Multiple Minor Prophets

Birch, Bruce. *Hosea, Joel and Amos*. Louisville, KY: Westminster John Knox, 1997.

Sweeney, Marvin. *The Twelve Prophets*. 1 volume. *Hosea, Joel, Amos, Obadiah, Jonah*. Collegeville, MN: Liturgical, 2000–1.

Isaiah 1–39

Blenkinsopp, Joseph. *Isaiah: A New Translation and Commentary*, part 1. New York: Doubleday, 2000.

Childs, Brevard. *The Book of Isaiah: A Commentary*. Louisville, KY: Westminster Press, 2001.

Clements, R. E. *Isaiah 1–39*. Grand Rapids, MI: Eerdmans, 1980.

Tull, Patricia. *Isaiah 1–39*. Macon, GA: Smyth & Helwys, 2010.

Torah and Other Texts Written in the Wake of the Assyrian Empire

5

Chapter Outline

Chapter Overview

Chapter 4 featured prophecies responding to Assyrian attack in the eighth century, while this one focuses on texts formed in the wake of the collapse of Assyrian domination in the late seventh century (600s). Foremost among these is the first text to be known as a "Torah of Moses." This first "Torah," however, is not Genesis–Deuteronomy, but rather an earlier, seventh-century edition of the book of Deuteronomy. In this chapter of the textbook we will see how Deuteronomy shows the impact of Assyrian oppression even after the Assyrians had lost control of Judah. The same is true of the books that follow Deuteronomy – Joshua, Judges, 1–2 Samuel, and 1–2 Kings. Each of these books promotes the values of Deuteronomy in different ways, reframing earlier traditions about Israel's history in light of those values. Finally, the prophetic books of Nahum, Zephaniah, and Jeremiah provide a different

A Contemporary Introduction to the Bible: Sacred Texts and Imperial Contexts, Second Edition.
Colleen M. Conway and David M. Carr.
© 2021 Colleen M. Conway and David M. Carr. Published 2021 by John Wiley & Sons Ltd.

perspective on the late seventh century, celebrating Assyria's decline and pronouncing God's judgment on the politics and worship of Judah. By the end of this chapter you should see multiple ways in which the central tenets of the Bible and later Judaism – such as the emphasis on law and the importance of worship of God alone – were formed as part of Judah's "hybrid" response to Assyrian oppression and attempt to build a God-centered community, purified of foreign influence, that would not have to undergo another such experience.

Religious and Textual Reform Amidst the Downfall of Assyria

READING

Nahum 3; Zephaniah 1; and 2 Kings 21–3.

> Your shepherds are asleep [dead],
>> Oh, king of Assyria;
>> Your nobles slumber.
> Your people are scattered on the mountains,
>> With no one to gather them.
> There is no easing of your [Nineveh's] pain,
>> your wound is fatal
> All who hear the report of you,
>> Clap their hands in celebration.
> For who has escaped
>> your continual cruelty?
> (Nahum 3:18–19 NRSV modified)

The oracle quoted above concludes a seventh-century book of prophecy, the book of Nahum. Where eighth-century prophets like Hosea or Micah proclaimed the oncoming attack by Assyria, this seventh-century prophet proclaims that Assyria itself has been laid low. Decades of cruelty have come to an end. The Assyrian armies have withdrawn from Judah and the surrounding countries. And the capital of Assyria, Nineveh itself, was to fall in 612 BCE, marking the end of Assyria's imperial ambitions. The book of Nahum celebrates this, proclaiming that Yahweh was the one who brought Assyria down.

Basics on the Book of Nahum

I	Hymn: Yahweh, destroyer of oppressors	1	**Outline: proclama-**
II	Taunt song: destruction of Nineveh	2–3	**tion of the end of Assyrian Nineveh**

Though the poem in Nahum 2–3 celebrates the downfall of a specific imperial **Themes** city, Nineveh, the poem at the outset makes this book into a more general celebration of Yahweh's ability to destroy imperial oppressors and restore the oppressed. For the later revisers of this book, the destruction of Nineveh was but one demonstration of Yahweh's power to destroy oppressive empires.

This does not mean that everything was fine in Judah. Another seventh-century prophet, Zephaniah, proclaims Yahweh's irreversible judgment, a "Day of Yahweh," against Judah and Jerusalem for the kinds of cultic practices that Hosea criticized: worship of Baal and heavenly objects, swearing by the god of Ammon (Milkom), and failure to seek Yahweh (Zeph 1:4–6). And indeed, archaeological evidence shows that the seventh century was a time when diverse worship practices flourished in Judah, particularly under the 40-year reign of Manasseh, Hezekiah's son (697–642 BCE). In response, Zephaniah proclaims that Yahweh is about to destroy the officials and royalty who promote such impure worship. Echoing the anti-foreign sentiment we also see in Nahum, Zephaniah says that "the officials and king's sons who wear foreign clothes" are about to bear the brunt of Yahweh's judgment. Where others might think of the "Day of Yahweh" as a time when Yahweh comes to rescue the people, Zephaniah 1:7–2:2 – echoing Amos (Amos 5:18–20) – proclaims that this "Day of Yahweh" will be a time of great punishment and sorrow.

Basics on the Book of Zephaniah

I	Announcement: "Day of Yahweh" against Judah	1:2–18	**Outline: judgment**
II	Exhortation to repentance	2:1–3:20	**and exhortation to Jerusalem**
	A Call for repentance amidst judgment of nations	2:1–3:8	
	B Reason for repentance: impending restoration	3:9–20	

This book provides another example of how an earlier prophet's words of **Seventh-century** judgment (e.g. Zeph 1:2–18) now introduce words of hope written at a later **judgment and** time for later Judeans (e.g. 3:9–20). Thus expanded, the book had a message **later words of** for generations long after the time of Zephaniah. It taught the need for peo- **hope** ple in God's holy city, Jerusalem, to repent in light of Yahweh's judgment of other empires.

As long as Manasseh was in power, the religious and political status quo in Judah continued. With his death and the assassination of his son shortly afterwards, however, the people of Judah saw an opportunity. Rather than letting the usual pattern of royal succession continue, the "people of the land" anointed Manasseh's 8-year-old grandson, Josiah, as king of Judah (2 Kgs 21:19–25). This young king would rule for over thirty years (640–609 BCE) and eventually would implement Hosea's (and Zephaniah's) call for religious purity as part of a broader program of national revival in the wake of Assyria's fall. Establishment of religious devotion was one way that Josiah and others believed they could revive the glory of David's kingdom and avoid ever having to experience the kind of foreign oppression they had suffered for decades under Assyria.

The book of 2 Kings tells how, in the eighteenth year of his reign, Josiah funded a renovation of the Temple. At some point in the process the priests told him that "the book of the Torah" had been found there (2 Kgs 22:3–10). When it was read to him, Josiah realized his nation faced curses for disobeying the Torah, and he immediately sent to have its authenticity verified by a prophet, named Huldah. She prophesied that the words of the book were true, but that King Josiah would die in peace (2 Kgs 22:14–20). Josiah then had the book read to the elders and the rest of the people, and he led the people in making a "covenant" to follow all the words of the book of the Torah that had just been found (2 Kgs 23:1–3). This then started a process that is often described as "**Josiah's reform**" (623 BCE). Josiah commanded the priests to remove the statue of the goddess Asherah from the Temple in Jerusalem along with all elements related to Baal and all deities other than Yahweh (2 Kgs 23:4, 6–7). He also destroyed all the sanctuaries ("high places") outside Jerusalem and removed their priests (2 Kgs 23:5, 8–14). In an apparent move to claim lands associated with David and Solomon's kingdom (see Map 5.1), he even desecrated the ancient royal altar at Bethel (2 Kgs 23:15). Finally, he commanded a national Passover in which people from his broader kingdom were to come on pilgrimage to the Temple in Jerusalem (2 Kgs 23:21–3). Such a Passover had not been celebrated "from the days of the judges who judged Israel through to the days of the kings of Israel and Judah" (2 Kgs 23:22).

This final note indicates that many elements of Josiah's reform were new. Where the Jerusalem Temple had once been the home of worship of various deities alongside Yahweh, now Josiah dedicated it to worship of Yahweh and Yahweh alone. Where the people of Judah and Israel had worshipped in local sanctuaries since the time of the judges, Josiah destroyed those sanctuaries and had them worship in Jerusalem. And where Passover previously had been a local festival celebrated by clans in their villages, Josiah required all now to come to Jerusalem, the capital city, in a national pilgrimage festival. Contemporary scholars see an element of political centralization in these moves of religious reform, with Josiah aiming to restore David's Jerusalem-centered kingdom spanning north and south and achieve independence from the Assyrian empire. Nevertheless, the biblical text itself focuses on another rationale for his actions: 2 Kgs 23:24 asserts that all of Josiah's actions were done to implement "the words of the Torah that Hilkiah, the priest, found in the house of Yahweh."

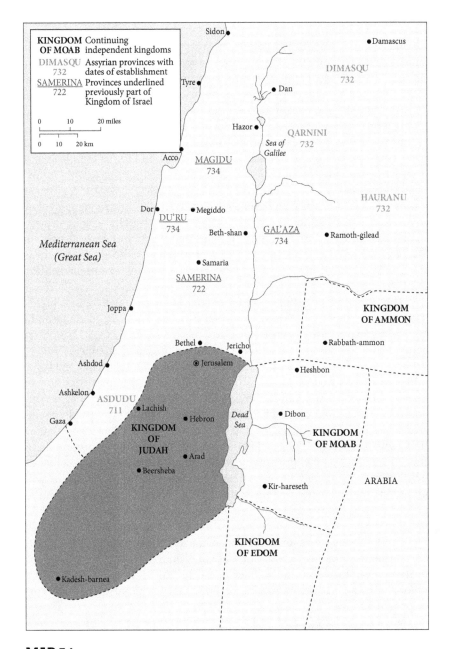

MAP 5.1

The Judean kingdom after the fall of the north. Redrawn from Norman Gottwald, *The Hebrew Bible: A Socio-Literary Introduction*. Minneapolis: Fortress, 1985, page 291.

Indeed, scholars have long seen links between Josiah's reform and a book of "Torah" found in the Hebrew Bible. In 1805, the German scholar Wilhelm De Wette noticed that these elements of Josiah's reform are rooted in central emphases of the book of Deuteronomy. The laws in Deuteronomy start with a regulation to destroy all non-Yahwistic worship items and local sanctuaries and worship Yahweh in only one place (Deuteronomy 12). This sounds like an authorization for the temple purification and sanctuary destruction that Josiah implemented. Deuteronomy also includes laws for festivals that require all to come to the central worship place (Deuteronomy 16). This sounds like the background for Josiah's Passover. Deuteronomy concludes with curses that will come upon a people that does not follow its stipulations (Deut 28:15–68). This sounds like the curses that Josiah feared would come upon his people for not obeying the Torah found in the temple (2 Kgs 22:13). Throughout, the book of Deuteronomy refers to itself as the "Torah" or the "scroll of the Torah" and so on (Deut 1:5; 31:9–12, 24–6; etc.), much as 2 Kings refers to the scroll reported by the priest Hilkiah and implemented by Josiah as "the scroll of the Torah" (2 Kgs 22:8, 10, 13, 16; 23:2–3; etc.). In sum, the biblical story of Josiah's reform implies that the "scroll of the Torah" in Deuteronomy – with its instructions for centralized worship and Passover – is the "Torah" that 2 Kings 22–3 describes Josiah as reading and implementing in his reform.

This narrative in 2 Kings, like other texts to be discussed here, is highly shaped by the theology of its authors. Nevertheless, we have good reason to believe that parts of the description of Josiah's reform in 2 Kings 22–3 reflect actual historical changes that took place during the late monarchy of Judah. Prior to this point, we have tax documents from ancient Samaria and some other early texts that include a proportion of personal names that feature deity names other than Yahweh (e.g. Abibaal "Baal is my father"). After this point, the names found in caches of late Judean letters show virtually exclusive devotion to Yahweh. Archaeologists have found a number of sanctuaries that were used for sacrifice outside Jerusalem from the time before Josiah. In the time of Josiah and afterwards, however, the evidence for such sanctuaries diminishes considerably. Finally, there is a massive shift in the diversity of art around the end of the seventh century. In previous chapters we saw examples of female figurines and images, animals, etc. from earlier periods in Israel and Judah's history. Now our archaeological finds – some pictured in Figure 5.1 – are heavy on text and light on images. The few images that appear are an isolated human or plant. Thus, not only does the Bible testify to a purification and reform, but the archaeological record confirms that this was a time of significant transformation in how Judeans represented and worshipped their God.

What might have caused such a transformation in the religious and political life of ancient Judah? The first thing to affirm is that this reform was built on older roots. For example, the emphasis on pure worship of Yahweh alone and elimination of Baal worship is a major focus in Hosea's prophecy in the northern kingdom of the eighth century, discussed in Chapter 4. There we also saw signs that Deuteronomy itself, like Hosea, may have originated as an early northern tradition. Judging from this and similar emphases on cultic purity in narratives about the northern prophets, Elijah and Elisha (1 Kings 17–2 Kings 10), it appears that some groups in the Israelite heartland in the north had already strongly advocated pure worship of Yahweh. Moreover,

FIGURE 5.1
Seals and other images from the late seventh century. They well illustrate the decline in use of images in Judah and the rise in importance of texts.

these views may have found expression in an earlier, pre-Josianic version of Deuteronomy, one that later found its way into Judah to be discovered in Josiah's time.

Transfers of such northern texts to the south were not uncommon. Late in the eighth century, the northern kingdom was destroyed and the kingdom of Judah became the sole place for the preservation of the values and texts of these groups advocating pure worship of Yahweh. As we have seen, Hezekiah was the king in the south then and instituted some cultic centralization and purification while attempting independence from Assyria as well (see 2 Kgs 18:4 and the later descriptions in 2 Chronicles 29–31). This religious reform by Hezekiah is not explained in the biblical narratives, but may have been motivated by Hezekiah's wish to avoid the mistakes of the northern kingdom as identified by Hosea and other northern traditions. Decades later his religious changes were reversed by his successor, Manasseh (2 Kgs 21:3–7//2 Chr 33:3–7), but they were not forgotten. Indeed, Josiah's reform can be seen as a reinstatement of ancient northern emphases on cultic purity and centralization that had already been introduced to Judah, preliminarily, by Josiah's great-grandfather, Hezekiah.

Even as we recognize the precursors to Josiah's reforms, there are also important new elements. First, the biblical reports are more clear in Josiah's case than in Hezekiah's about how Josiah extended his reforms to encompass some parts of the former northern kingdom – e.g. Bethel – that were closest to Judah (2 Kgs 23:15–20//2 Chr 34:6–7; compare with 2 Kgs 18:4//2 Chr 31:1 on Hezekiah). By the time of Josiah's reform the Assyrian empire had collapsed. This left Josiah room to put his own stamp on the worship of Yahweh in Jerusalem and even extend his power over areas once controlled by northern Israel, such as Bethel, a town about ten miles north of Jerusalem that had once been the site of Israel's main royal temple. Another mark of Josiah's aspirations may be his institution of a Passover celebration where all came to Jerusalem. Indeed, this is the last major act reported of Josiah (2 Kgs 23:21–3).

This unified celebration of Passover represents one of several ways that Josiah's reign conforms to the regulations of Deuteronomy. Whereas the earlier Covenant Code allowed for Passover to be celebrated at multiple sanctuaries (Exod 23:14–18), the festival calendar in Deuteronomy 16 has Moses instructing Israel to celebrate Passover at just one place, "the place that God will choose" (16:16). So also, the preceding report of Josiah's desecration of the former sanctuary at Bethel (2 Kgs 23:15–20) conforms to the regulations in Deuteronomy 12 about the need to worship Yahweh in one and only one place. Finally, there is an overall parallel between the regulations of Deuteronomy and the above-discussed purifying transformation that apparently took place under Josiah.

All this suggests a final way in which Josiah's reform was distinguished from Hezekiah's: it was connected to a text, in this case a pre-Josiah text sounding much like Deuteronomy (scholars sometimes refer to this pre-Josiah lawbook as "Ur-Deuteronomy"). To be sure, there are signs that some kind of reform was already under way before the "scroll of the Torah of Yahweh" was brought to light. Chronicles suggests that Josiah's purification and centralization preceded the discovery of the scroll (2 Chronicles 34), and even 2 Kings implies that temple renovations were already under way when Josiah was informed about it (2 Kgs 22:3–10). Yet the biblical tradition suggests that this book played an important role in Josiah's reign. This does not necessarily mean that everyone agreed immediately on the authenticity of the book that Josiah put at the center of his reform. Rather, he seems to have felt a need to have the book authenticated (2 Kgs 22:14–20//2 Chr 34:22–8), indicating some doubts about its origins (note also a possible critique of this "Torah" in Jer 8:8–9, a potential seventh-century text discussed below). Nevertheless, whatever the origins of the "scroll" announced by the priest, Hilkiah, it appears to have come to play a pivotal role in Josiah's inauguration of a new era in Judah's monarchy.

The present book of Deuteronomy, however, is not the same as the "Ur-Deuteronomy" that preceded Josiah's reform. That earlier Torah book was a more legally focused collection, a lawbook. Yet as that book came to be the center of Josiah's reform, it was supplemented with new elements such as the historical review at its outset (Deuteronomy 1–3) and concluding elements aimed at reinforcing obedience (e.g. Deuteronomy 27–30) that turned the book into a covenant with God. These and other parts of Deuteronomy reflect Judah's experience of oppression by the Assyrians and then their later trauma of exile in Babylonia. We turn now to take a look at this complex mix of lawbook and supplements added in light of later oppression.

The Deuteronomic Torah of Moses and the Phenomenon of Hybridity

Deuteronomy 1–3, 6–7, 12, and 17.

READING

The book of Deuteronomy reveals a remarkable blend of ancient Israelite law and radical adaptation. To start, the book appears to have ancient roots. Not only does it show signs of northern origins (discussed previously), but many of its laws are revisions of older laws seen in the "Covenant Code" of Exod 20:22–23:33. For example, the altar law in Deuteronomy 12 emphasizes the importance of one altar, while its parallel in Exod 20:24–5 provides instructions for building altars around the land. Similarly, the law about festivals in Deuteronomy 16 parallels the rules about them in Exod 23:14–17, making sure that they are celebrated in only one place. In this way and many others the book of Deuteronomy builds on and revises older legal teachings in Israel, as well as a variety of wisdom teachings in Proverbs (such as Prov 22:28 in Deut 19:14).

Basics on the Book of Deuteronomy (and the Ten Commandments)

I	Introduction of Yahweh's acts, Ten Commandments, and exhortations	Deut 1:1–11:32	**Outline: farewell teaching of vassal treaty with Yahweh**
II	Central rules of the treaty with Yahweh (organized by the order of the Ten Commandments)	12:1–26:19	
III	Means of remembrance and enforcement of the Treaty with Yahweh	27:1–31:29	
IV	Moses's farewell	31:30–34:12	

Late pre-exile and exile: Deuteronomy is a combination of an earlier, pre-exilic **Date(s)** Deuteronomic lawbook and later, exilic additions to that lawbook. The Deuteronomic lawbook probably includes yet earlier northern materials, but these are impossible to identify precisely.

The Ten Commandments in Deut 5:6–21 (seen in slightly different form in Exod **The Ten** 20:1–17) are classic teaching materials, short and easily memorized by using **Commandments** your fingers. Their form is similar to the "instruction" form found in Proverbs **and Deuteronomy** and other teachings. Like such instructions, the Ten Commandments are difficult to date. They almost certainly do not derive from Moses, but do represent many of Israel's deepest shared values.

The importance of these commandments in the book of Deuteronomy is reflected in the fact that the topics at the center of Deuteronomy (Deuteronomy 12–26) follow about the same order as the topics of the Ten Commandments found in Deuteronomy 5. In this sense, the Ten Commandments form the core of the Mosaic "teaching" given in Deuteronomy.

That said, Deuteronomy is an example of another, quite remarkable form of revision of a foreign textual form, one originating from Judah's oppressor, Assyria. During the century that Assyria dominated Israel and Judah, it subjugated many nations through a "vassal treaty" form and a related "loyalty oath" insuring the orderly succession of Assyrian rulers. These were like political contracts, in which the subjugated people were required to pronounce curses on themselves if they did not show proper devotion, termed "love" in these treaties, toward their vassal lord, the Assyrian king and his designated successor. Deuteronomy resembles the Assyrian treaties in emphasizing the requirement of allegiance – "love" – that Israel is to offer, but now Israel must offer allegiance to *Yahweh* "with all [its/your] heart, life strength, and might" (Deut 6:4–6). The laws of Deuteronomy include prohibitions of treason against Yahweh (Deuteronomy 13) that resemble Assyrian prohibitions of treason against the chosen successor of the Assyrian king. Finally, parts of the curses in Deuteronomy 28 are almost exact replicas of curses found at the end of Assyrian loyalty oaths imposed across their empire in the late eighth century. Thus, in the wake of Assyrian oppression, it appears that the authors of the book of Deuteronomy envisioned Israel as in a treaty-like relationship with Yahweh, their God. This was what "covenant" (Hebrew *berit*) with Yahweh meant to them. It was a formal relationship, sealed by blessings and curses. Its core was a requirement of exclusive allegiance to a lord. Yet the authors of Deuteronomy made a revolutionary shift vis-à-vis the vassal treaties and loyalty oaths that they knew: where before Judah had to be exclusively obedient to the Assyrian king, now they were to be exclusively faithful to Yahweh. Where before the Assyrian king was jealous and would tolerate no rivals, now Yahweh is depicted as jealous and intolerant of any rival gods. Before the people feared the invasion of the massive Assyrian army if they were disobedient. Now they faced direct divine punishment, the "curses of the treaty covenant" (Deut 29:20), if they failed to be faithful to the words of Deuteronomy. Thus when Josiah read some form of Deuteronomy to the people and led them in a covenant ceremony based on it (2 Kgs 23:1–3//2 Chr 34:29–31), he was moving them from one vassal relationship to another. Previously they had known subjugation to Assyria. Now Josiah was leading them – by means of an early written edition of Deuteronomy – into a treaty with Yahweh.

We will never know the precise manner in which some yet older form of Deuteronomy was shaped in light of such experiences of Assyrian oppression, but scholars do know analogies to this overall process. In particular, postcolonial theorists have uncovered many examples of writers, artists, and others who appropriate the cultural forms of their former oppressors in the process of trying to develop their own, *post*colonial expressions. For example, even after India achieved independence from Britain in 1947, Indian writers developed a rich tradition of distinctively Indian novels in English. In doing so, they adopted their colonial oppressor's language and an originally non-Indian cultural form, the novel. Yet they used these tools to build a distinctively Indian literature. This is but one example of the way that peoples who must redefine themselves in the wake of oppression often find it helpful to revise and even invert the cultural forms of their former oppressors. Postcolonial theorists refer to this process of adaptation and inversion of oppressors' cultural forms as "**hybridity**." This concept will come up again in this *Introduction* because it is useful in understanding how many biblical texts were formed in a complex response to the cultural forms of Israel's oppressors.

Overview: The Covenant Code and Deuteronomy

The laws below cover similar topics, but read a few and see how they treat these topics differently! Though Deuteronomy covers topics not found in the Covenant Code (Exod 20:22–23:33), most topics in the Covenant Code are covered in Deuteronomy. Deuteronomy is thought to be the later of the two. In particular, it makes changes in the Covenant Code laws so that they are consistent with the idea that there should be only one central sanctuary.

Law about altars	Exod 20:22–6	Deut 12:13–28
Slave release laws	Exod 21:1–11	Deut 15:12–18
Cities of asylum	Exod 21:12–14	Deut 19:1–13
Kidnapping	Exod 21:16	Deut 24:7
Consequences of sex with a virgin	Exod 22:16–17	Deut 22:28–9
Penalty for unlawful religious practices	Exod 22:18	Deut 18:9–14
Penalty for sacrifice to other gods	Exod 22:20	Deut 17:2–7
Prohibition of charging interest	Exod 22:25	Deut 23:19–20
Requirement to return a cloak taken as collateral	Exod 22:26–7	Deut 24:10–13
Requirement of first-born sons and livestock	Exod 22:29–30	Deut 15:19–23
Legal justice rules	Exod 23:2–8	Deut 16:18–20
Returning livestock	Exod 23:4–5	Deut 22:1–4
Prohibition of oppressing foreign workers	Exod 23:9	Deut 24:17–18
Sabbath year rules	Exod 23:10–11	Deut 15:1–11
Sabbath command	Exod 23:12	Deut 5:12–15
Pilgrimage festivals	Exod 23:14–17	Deut 16:1–17
Requirement to bring first fruits	Exod 23:19a	Deut 26:1–10
Not boiling a calf in its mother's milk	Exod 23:19b	Deut 14:21b

For now, it is important to recognize that Deuteronomy, this hybrid vassal treaty with God, presents itself as the most important "teaching" Israel could ever have. It bears the label of "Torah," which is the Hebrew equivalent of "teaching," and the book names numerous ways in which the people of Israel are to insure that this Torah/teaching is foremost on their hearts and minds.

They are to memorize this Torah's words (Deut 6:6; 11:18), recite them constantly to their children (Deut 6:7; 11:19), bind copies of Torah commands on the entryways of their houses and on their bodies (Deut 6:8–9; 11:20), make sure that the king reads and obeys this Torah/teaching constantly (Deut 17:18–20), and carefully copy the Torah and read it aloud to the entire community (Deut 31:11–13). As the Assyrian vassal treaty used some of the same means to instill absolute loyalty to the king of Assyria, so also Deuteronomy uses a yet fuller array of these strategies to insure memorization of this Torah/teaching and loyalty to Yahweh alone.

MORE ON METHOD: POSTCOLONIAL CRITICISM

The term "**postcolonial criticism**" embraces a wide range of approaches that look at how texts and their interpretations are interrelated with structures of colonial domination. Within biblical studies it has taken two main forms.

First, many scholars have taken categories developed in earlier postcolonial studies of contemporary literature and used those categories to illuminate the production of ancient biblical literature in relation to imperial domination. This chapter's discussion of Deuteronomy as an example of "hybridity" would be an example of this approach.

Second, other scholars have looked at how the Bible itself has been used as a tool for colonial domination.

For more on this approach, see R. S. Sugirtharajah, *Exploring Postcolonial Biblical Criticism: History, Method, Practice* (Chichester: Wiley, 2011).

Basics on the Book of Joshua

Outline: the conquest and settlement of the promised land	I	Exodus-like, holy war conquest	1–12
	II	Distribution of the land	13–22
	III	Joshua's covenantal farewell	23–4

Date Late pre-exilic (especially Joshua 1–12) and exilic/post-exilic (13–24).

Theme Though the book of Joshua starts with an apparent total conquest of the land (Josh 11:23) in fulfillment of Yahweh's command (Deuteronomy 7), chapters 13–22 hint that the conquest was *incomplete* (Josh 13:1–7; 15:63; 16:10; 17:12–13) and show a diversity in the makeup of the people that threatens to split them by the end (Joshua 22). This, then, is the context for Joshua's exhortations to the people in Joshua 23 and 24, where he urges them to avoid the worship practices of the foreign peoples among them (Josh 23:5–13; 24:14–15). Instead, they should, like Joshua, be devoted to Yahweh and the book of the Torah (Josh 23:6; 24:26; compare Josh 1:7–8). This narrative depiction shows every sign of reflecting the religious challenges of Josiah's and later times, rather than being an accurate depiction of tribal religion. After all, the religion of ancient Israel grew out of Canaanite religion and resembled it in many respects (see Chapter 2). It was only in the wake of Assyrian oppression and Josiah's reform that Israelites saw a need to purify their religion of all foreign influence and thus resist what was now seen as foreign, "Canaanite" elements.

Joshua is Moses's appointed successor in Deuteronomy (Deuteronomy 31), and he is presented in the book of Joshua as a second Moses. Like Moses, he presides over the people crossing water "on dry ground" (Joshua 3–4; compare Exodus 14), and he celebrates a Passover preceded by a circumcision of the new generation of males who were born in the wilderness (Joshua 5; compare Exodus 12). In these and other ways, Joshua is presented as the last semi-Mosaic leader before things fall apart during the time of the judges.

More information: Joshua and Moses

Historical Texts Infused with the Theology and Values of Deuteronomy

Joshua 1–2, 11; 23–4; Judges 1–2; 1 Samuel 12; 1 Kings 8; 2 Kings 17, 22–3. Review readings from Judges–2 Kings done for earlier chapters.

READING

Though Deuteronomy currently stands as the fifth and final book of the Pentateuch/Torah, it actually has as much or more in common with the books that follow it. These are historical narratives that retell and reframe Israel's history from land conquest to the end of kingship in Judah: Joshua, Judges, 1–2 Samuel, and 1–2 Kings. As we will see, the term "historical" here needs to be understood properly, because these books are not "history" in the modern sense of the word. Instead, they are highly theological presentations of different periods of Israel's life in the land, from the tribal period to exile.

The Books of the Former and Latter Prophets

The books of Joshua, Judges, 1–2 Samuel, and 1–2 Kings are sometimes termed "**the books of the former prophets**" in Jewish tradition. This contrasts them with "**the books of the latter prophets**," which contain oracles and stories connected to prophetic figures (e.g. Isaiah, Amos, Hosea, Micah). As we already saw, these "books of the latter prophets" (e.g. Isaiah, Amos, Hosea) are not wholly written by the figures with which they are associated, but instead contain a mix of material by those prophets and later texts. In the case of the "books of the former prophets" none of the material originates from a prophetic figure. Instead, they are originally anonymous narratives about Israel's history that only became associated in later tradition with some famous figures (e.g. Joshua, Samuel). Despite this, it is useful to know which books each of these terms ("former prophets" and "latter prophets") refers to.

Your challenge in this chapter is to learn to spot signs of that theological slant in these books of the "former prophets" (Joshua to 2 Kings). In particular, note the ways that each one connects to ideas in the book of Deuteronomy. For example, the book of Joshua opens with an exhortation for its readers to meditate on the Torah teaching in Deuteronomy (Josh 1:7–8) and the conclusion of 2 Kings includes the above-discussed scene where Josiah makes a covenant based on a book resembling Deuteronomy (2 Kgs 23:24). Moreover, throughout these books we find the repetition of common themes that promote the values seen in Deuteronomy. These include (among other themes) the importance of faithfulness to Yahweh alone, the belief that Yahweh will punish unfaithfulness, the importance of pure worship and sacrifice in only one place, and hostility toward foreigners and/or foreign influence. These are stipulations of the vassal covenant with Yahweh that is presented in Deuteronomy. Because these and other ideas are so characteristic of Deuteronomy, scholars often term these books **Deuteronomistic**. Moreover, they apply this adjective, "Deuteronomistic," to particular verses or chapters that have been shaped in light of these values.

Basics on the Book of Judges

Outline: decline of order/ obedience in the time of judges	I	Prologue: incomplete conquest and overview of disobedience after Joshua	1:1–3:6
	II	Specifics on spiraling chaos:	3:7–21:25
		A Worsening judges: Othniel to Samson	3:7–16:31
		B People on their own with no king	17:1–21:25

Date	Pre-exilic and exilic/post-exilic.

Theme	Though Judges includes older traditions, they have been radically adapted to fit a theological framework that expresses the values of Deuteronomy. The shape of this framework is given in a narrative overview (Judg 2:11–22) that follows the death of Joshua (Josh 2:6–10). We hear in this text of a recurring cycle of punishment and rescue that is repeated in many of the following chapters:

1   Israel disobeys Yahweh and his commands.

2   Yahweh lets them be conquered by a foreign people.

3   They cry out and Yahweh sends a judge to deliver them.

4   The judge dies, and the people start disobeying again.

The stories in Judg 3:7–16:31 roughly follow this framework, but they also diverge in minor ways, ways that show a spiraling decline of order and obedience in Israel. For example, the judges seen in the book progress from unblemished figures, such as Othniel and Deborah, to less impressive leaders, such as Jephthah and Samson. The final chapters, Judges 17–21, then show how bad things get when the people are without a king and "do what is right in their own eyes" (Judg 17:6; 21:25).

The books of the former prophets (Joshua, Judges, 1–2 Samuel, 1–2 Kings) promote Deuteronomistic values in diverse ways. The stress in Joshua is on Israel's successful completion of the holy war ordered by Moses in Deuteronomy 7, and Joshua concludes with a renewed covenant commitment on the part of Israel (Josh 24). Judges likewise stresses the importance of obedience to Yahweh, but its series of cycles (of disobedience, oppression, and rescue) depicts ways that Israel repeatedly failed to be sufficiently devoted to Yahweh and ultimately descended into social disorder. 1–2 Samuel depict Yahweh's reluctant establishment of kingship in response to the people's ungrateful request for a royal leader in place of Yahweh. Finally, 1–2 Kings evaluate various kings by the standard of the Deuteronomic strictures of centralization and purification, including a mixed evaluation of Solomon as both positive (1 Kings 3–10) and negative (1 Kings 11).

Learning to Recognize Deuteronomistic Theology and Influence in Biblical Texts

EXERCISE

Pick some of the texts assigned above from Deuteronomy, Joshua, Judges, 1–2 Samuel, and 1–2 Kings, and make a list of the chapters and verses in those texts where you see the following themes (from Deuteronomy) appear, such as those listed at the outset of this discussion: (1) the importance of faithfulness to the LORD (Yahweh) alone; (2) the belief that Yahweh will punish unfaithfulness; (3) the importance of pure worship and sacrifice in only one place; and/or (4) hostility toward foreigners and/or foreign influence. These sorts of themes are among the elements that scholars use to identify the addition of **Deuteronomistic** theology and values to earlier traditions.

With this background, we encourage you to try the above exercise, where you can see for yourself how certain passages in these books are particularly saturated with Deuteronomistic language and values. One key skill in reading these books from an academic perspective is learning to recognize the distinctive language and thought of such Deuteronomistic passages and see how they frame the passages around them.

Basics on the Books of 1–2 Samuel

Outline: the beginnings of the Davidic monarchy (1–2 Samuel)	I	Transitions to kingship	1 Samuel 1–31
		A Samuel: a judge who anointed kings	1 Samuel 1–8
		B Samuel to Saul: a failed king	1 Samuel 9–15
		C Saul to David: the dynastic founder	1 Samuel 16–31
	II	David's reign as Israel's first king	2 Samuel 1–24

Date   Late pre-exile and exile, with some early pre-exilic sources.

Theme   This work spread over two scrolls (1 and 2 Samuel) presents an ambivalent picture of the origins of the monarchy. The reign of David is presented as an improvement on that of Saul. Nevertheless, in episodes such as the affair with Bathsheba and murder of her husband (2 Samuel 11–12), David proves to have flaws of his own. Deuteronomistic speeches at points such as 1 Samuel 12 and 2 Samuel 7 present the move to the Davidic monarchy as a negative development, but one that Yahweh accepted. Such Deuteronomistic speeches reflect the much lower monarchal expectations of scribes looking back at three centuries of Davidic rule.

Of course, these historical books incorporate earlier sources. The book of Joshua frames older stories of local military victories with new descriptions of total destruction of all Canaanites in the land (Joshua 11–12), certifying that Israel had taken the land just as Yahweh commanded it in Deuteronomy (Deuteronomy 7). The book of Judges radically adapts older texts about the tribes of Israel – such as the song of Deborah – so that they now fit into a cyclical pattern of the people forgetting to be faithful to Yahweh, Yahweh letting them fall into oppression, the people crying out, and Yahweh rescuing them. The books of Samuel contain large blocks of probable older compositions, such as an "ark narrative" (1 Sam 4:1–7:1; 2 Sam 6) and a "succession narrative" (2 Samuel 9–20 along with 1 Kings 1–2) that may have been written much earlier. To these and other traditions the authors of Samuel added their own perspective on the monarchy in 1 Samuel 12 and also in parts of the oracle to David in 2 Samuel 7:1–16. Finally, one finds a similar combination of old and new in the books of Kings. Here the authors cite earlier books such as the "Acts of Solomon" (1 Kgs 11:41), the "Annals of the Kings of Israel" (1 Kgs 14:19; 15:31; etc.) and the "Annals of the Kings of Judah" (1 Kgs 14:29; 15:7, 23; etc.). Yet they put their own stamp on the whole, particularly through inserting major theological speeches at important junctures. These include the dedication of the Temple (1 Kings 8), the theological rationale for the destruction of the northern kingdom (2 Kings 17), and Josiah's reform and attempt to reunite the north and south in a kingdom centered on Jerusalem (2 Kings 22–3). As you saw in the exercise that opened this section, these and other speeches express central values seen in the book of Deuteronomy. Such close links to and dependence on Deuteronomy are what lead scholars to call these materials **"Deuteronomistic."**

Basics on the Books of 1–2 Kings

I	Solomon's rule: devotion and sin	1 Kings 1–11	**Outline: obedience and sin in the history of the monarchies**
II	Divided monarchy: northern sin and southern obedience and sin	1 Kings 12–2 Kings 17	
III	Decline of Judah: Hezekiah to exile	2 Kings 18–24	

Pre-exilic edition and exilic/post-exilic redaction.   **Date**

The books of Kings were divided for space reasons across two scrolls, 1 and 2   **Theme**
Kings, but they tell one story of the rise and fall of the monarchy of Israel, from
Solomon to the exile. The story starts with Solomon's building of the Temple in
Jerusalem (1 Kings 6–8), which becomes the one place that Israel is allowed to
sacrifice, according to the law in Deuteronomy (Deut 12:13–28). The narrative
goes on, however, to describe Solomon's fall toward disobedience (1 Kings 11),
which is quickly followed by the revolt of the northern tribes and their building
of their own altars outside Jerusalem (1 Kings 12).

From then on, each king of Israel and Judah is measured by his faithfulness to
the commands in Deuteronomy to worship Yahweh alone and to sacrifice at
only one place. The destruction of the Israelite monarchy is explained by the
failure of Israel and its kings to follow these rules (2 Kings 17). Despite some
ideal leaders, such as Hezekiah and Josiah, most kings in Judah likewise fail.
From the perspective of Kings, the final result of such disobedience of Deuteronomic laws is the destruction of Jerusalem and the exile (2 Kings 24).

Stepping back, one can perceive a certain broader narrative arc in this part
of the Bible, one extending from Moses's farewell speech in Deuteronomy to
Josiah's rediscovery of the law and implementation of it (2 Kings 22–23) followed by Israel's exile from the land because of the great disobedience of
Josiah's father, Manasseh (2 Kgs 23:26–7; 24:3). These kinds of patterns have
led many scholars to speak of an overall **Deuteronomistic History**. This
hypothesized history began with Deuteronomy and its review of earlier events
in Deuteronomy 1–3. It then continued with the story of Israel's life in the land,
from Joshua through Judges and the books of 1–2 Samuel and 1–2 Kings. Some
theorize that a pre-exilic edition of this Deuteronomistic History originated in
Josiah's time, extending from a modified form of his lawbook now found in
Deuteronomy to Josiah's implementation of that book in his reform (see the
above textbox on 1–2 Kings). Others hold that this Deuteronomistic History
came together for the first time during the Babylonian exile with which it now
concludes. And still others question the whole idea of a Deuteronomistic
History, focusing instead on the diverse ways that these books draw on and
promote Deuteronomistic values.

With this background, we can and should view much of Deuteronomy
through 2 Kings as written in the wake of decades of oppression by Assyria and
(later) Babylonia. Like Deuteronomy discussed above, the historical books that
follow it exemplify the phenomenon of hybridity. For example, the law-ori-
ented history of kingship now in Samuel–Kings resembles the kind of

ideological, pro-royal history writing used in the Assyrian empire to instill pro-royal sympathies in leadership near and far. Yet there are differences between those Mesopotamian histories and the Deuteronomistic books in the Bible. Rather than ensuring loyalty to a human king, books like 1–2 Kings were aimed at ensuring complete and exclusive loyalty to the Israelite God, Yahweh. They embodied the values of Josiah's reform, reframing earlier historical traditions through inserting speeches and other texts that echo the language and ideas of the book of Deuteronomy.

Such reframing of history is analogous to the kind of retelling of individual stories that many people do on the other side of a major crisis. A person may tell their own life story one way for a long time, and then something happens – divorce, a near-death experience, struggle with addiction, or another crisis – that makes them realize that some things that they thought were important were not, and other things that they had ignored were very, very important. In light of this experience, that person will tell their life story differently.

Building on this analogy, books like Joshua, 1–2 Samuel, or 1–2 Kings can be viewed as ancient Judah's equivalent to this sort of retelling of a personal story. Judah was on the other side of the crisis of Assyrian oppression, and the retelling of its story was aimed at gaining and maintaining freedom from oppression by foreign powers. Like someone retelling their own personal story, this retelling of Israel's story incorporates earlier elements, such as the Succession Narrative or older lists of kings and their years of rule. But the retelling as a whole is now reframed in light of the experience of liberation from Assyria. It is a retelling of the people's history that is completely reoriented toward their new chance to achieve permanent freedom through obedience to Yahweh's Torah.

Each of the Deuteronomistic historical books now reflects central themes of that Torah, from hostility to foreign influence to valuing of pure and centralized worship of Yahweh alone. Much like the memorizing of the Torah in Deuteronomy, this retelling of the people's story in Joshua through 2 Kings was aimed at reshaping the communal soul of Israel. In contrast to the kinds of texts that may have circulated in the time of Judah and Israel's earlier kings, such historical books represented a new form of post-traumatic cultural memory, one aimed at replacing its predecessors. They re-presented memories of Israel's life in the land through a prism of covenantal theology influenced by Assyrian treaty language and the experience of Assyrian oppression.

The Conquest and Ancient Holy War

The books of Deuteronomy and Joshua describe Israel as conquering all of Canaan and destroying *all* of its inhabitants (Deuteronomy 7; Joshua 1–11). This is a description of an ancient "holy war" (Hebrew *herem*); that is, a sacred war engaged in not for the purposes of gaining economic profit or wives, but at divine command. Biblical rules for the conduct of such sacred wars are found particularly in Deuteronomy 20. One gruesome mark of the "not-for-profit" character of such a war was the destruction of all living beings, human and animal, of the conquered people.

We see this idea outside Israel as well. One example is found in the ninth-century inscription of King Mesha of Moab. He describes a holy war commanded by his god, Chemosh, against a town in Israel called Nebo.

> Chemosh said to me, "Go, take Nebo from Israel." So I went at night and fought against it from dawn until noon. I seized it and killed all its inhabitants—seven thousand men, youths, women, girls, and even pregnant women. For I had dedicated them [the verb here is related to *herem*] to Chemosh.

One key difference between this inscription and the biblical book of Joshua is that the Mesha text is reporting on a recent killing of people that actually happened. In contrast, Joshua (along with Deuteronomy) draws on the concept of "holy war" to imaginatively depict a conquest centuries before that probably never happened in this way.

All this can give us a new perspective on some of the most troubling aspects of these books, such as the report of a divine command to eliminate all foreigners in the land (Deuteronomy 7) and the description in Joshua of the Israelites' fulfillment of that command, killing all Canaanites (Josh 10:40–42; 11:16–23). For many people, these are some of the most disturbing texts in the Bible, and they have been used in destructive ways to justify the killing or displacement of Native Americans and others.

Yet as we read these texts in Joshua, we should realize that they are not historically factual reports of the Israelites' total conquest of the land (as noted previously, the Bible itself contains traditions to the contrary). Rather, these narratives were designed to help the people who were suffering under imperial domination believe in a God who could help them succeed in a battle against all odds. Much like other Deuteronomistic historical narratives, the conquest account in Joshua was written with the idea that Judah's past oppression was caused by its failure to obey Yahweh's Torah and eliminate foreign influence. Writing from this perspective, the authors of Joshua crafted a narrative that could empower later Judeans to eliminate every trace of foreign influence that might cause them to fall back into oppression. Like many disempowered peoples, these authors wanted a God who could fight and fight successfully on their behalf. Of course, contemporary readers who interpret these texts from a position of privilege should recognize their dangers, but should also note how differently such warlike texts can be perceived by people fighting for liberation against more powerful foes.

Jeremiah's Prophecy of Judgment on Zion

Jeremiah is the second **major prophet**. The book focused on him is a bridge between the time of Josiah's reform and the catastrophic end of Judah: the destruction of Jerusalem, end of the monarchy, and exile of Judah's leaders to Babylonia. Jeremiah's earliest prophecy comes from the time of Josiah and his reforms. His prophecy continued with a critique of Josiah's successors. He has a few prophecies directed at Judeans, who were among the first to be forced into Babylonian exile. And these prophecies were shaped and reshaped by exiles and others after the time of Jeremiah, who believed that his words had important lessons for later generations.

READING

Jeremiah 1:1–3:5; 7:1–15 (compare with Jeremiah 26); 20:7–18; 28 and 36.

In the early part of his career Jeremiah shared Josiah's focus on the importance of pure worship of Yahweh, and some have found affirmations by Jeremiah of Josiah's program of reunification of north and south in passages such as Jer 3:19–23. Yet there is a tantalizing hint in a judgment speech in Jer 8:4–13 that Jeremiah rejected the authenticity of the Deuteronomic Torah that came to stand at the center of Josiah's reform:

> How can you say, "we are wise,
>> And we have the Torah of Yahweh,"
> When, in fact, it has been made into a lie
>> by the false pen of the scribes? (Jer 8:8)

This text suggests that the Torah of Moses – perhaps some form of Deuteronomy – is the product of contemporary authors, "scribes." It does not represent a truly ancient word. Though Jeremiah recognized Josiah as a king of justice in comparison with his son, Jehoiakim (Jer 22:15–16), in this central respect – the recognition of the authority of a form of Deuteronomy – the Jeremiah seen in Jer 8:8 is skeptical of a crucial part of Josiah's reform.

While Jeremiah may have supported parts of Josiah's program, his relationship with Josiah's successors was resolutely bad. A particularly large number of his prophecies are associated with the time of Jehoiakim, who was appointed king over Judah by the Egyptians on their way back from their fight with Babylonia (2 Kgs 23:34–5). Early during Jehoiakim's reign, Jeremiah delivered a sermon against the Jerusalem Temple that is described twice in the book of Jeremiah, once in Jer 7:1–15 and again in Jeremiah 26. Both versions of this "Temple sermon" feature a frontal attack on Zion theology, especially the idea that Jerusalem and its Temple were invulnerable. To those who continually affirm "this is the temple of Yahweh, the temple of Yahweh, the temple of Yahweh," Jeremiah proclaims that Yahweh will make it a heap of ruins, much like the ruins of the ancient tribal sanctuary at Shiloh, where the ark of the covenant once was (Jer 7:14//26:6). Such a claim was virtual blasphemy to the people of the time, since the belief in Zion's invulnerability had been reinforced all the more in the wake of the Assyrian king Sennacherib's withdrawal from besieging Jerusalem during the time of Hezekiah. According to Jeremiah

26, the people were ready to kill Jeremiah for speaking such words. Nevertheless, some recalled that Micah had earlier proclaimed that "Zion shall be plowed as a field" (Jer 26:18; see Micah 3:12). Ultimately, Jeremiah was protected by Ahikam, the son of Josiah's former scribe, Shaphan (Jer 26:24).

Another biographical narrative, Jeremiah 36, preserves a fascinating picture of the delivery and writing of Jeremiah's prophecy. It describes how Jeremiah was commissioned by God in Jehoiakim's fourth year to write a scroll containing all of his oracles up to that point in hopes that Judah might hear it and repent (36:1–3). Nevertheless, when the scroll was read to Jehoiakim, he was not pleased with its contents. As each part of the scroll was read, the king cut it off and threw it into the fire. After this, Jeremiah received a divine commission to write "another scroll." So Baruch, Jeremiah's scribe, produced a new scroll with the words of the original one, along with "many words like them" (Jer 36:27–32). Many scholars believe that much of what is now chapters 1–25 of the book of Jeremiah contains the remnants of that new scroll (see Jer 25:13). Earlier we saw how Isaiah's memoir was compiled a century before Jeremiah in response to the rejection of his prophecy by his contemporaries (Isa 6:1–8:16). Now this rewriting and expansion of Jeremiah's burnt scroll (Jer 36:27–32) stands as an additional example of how the rejection of a prophet's oral prophecies led to them being written down and even (in this case) expanded.

Yet Jeremiah, partly because of his long career, appears to have experienced more than his share of rejection. Chapters 26–45 of Jeremiah contain biographical narratives that chronicle Jeremiah's difficult experiences, starting with his brush with execution after the Temple sermon (Jeremiah 26; cf. Jer 7:1–15), and continuing with episodes such as his battle with Hananiah over falsely hopeful prophecy (Jeremiah 28), the burning of his scroll (Jeremiah 36), his imprisonment during the Babylonian siege of Jerusalem as a possible traitor (Jeremiah 37), his being dumped in a cistern to die by opponents (Jeremiah 38), and finally his being carried off into Egypt by rebels against Babylonian rule (Jeremiah 43). Though these narratives about him postdate the prophet, they probably reflect his increasing isolation as he prophesied judgment throughout Judah's long slide from dreams of glory under Josiah to total destruction by the Babylonians.

The difficulty of Jeremiah's career is also reflected in a set of laments in the book where Jeremiah protests to God about the unfair job that God has given him. For example, in the lament assigned for this section, Jer 20:7–18, the prophet describes being "taken advantage of" by God, who has required him to proclaim a harsh message that leads to his own rejection:

> O Yahweh you have seduced me, and I let myself be seduced.
>> You have overpowered me and won.
> I'm a laughingstock all day,
>> Everyone makes fun of me.
> For every time I speak, I cry an alarm.
>> I call out, "Violence and ruin."
> For the word of Yahweh has become for me
>> A cause of embarrassment and criticism all the time. (Jer 20:7–8)

Jeremiah goes on to say that he has no choice, because every time he tries to stop speaking God's message, the word becomes "like a burning fire raging in my bones; I cannot keep holding it in" (Jer 20:9). The lament continues and even reaches a fairly hopeful point, where Jeremiah envisions his eventual restoration and praises Yahweh for it (20:11–13), but then we hear another lament, perhaps originally a separate text, where he curses the day he was born and those who announced his birth (20:14–18). These and other laments chronicle the fact that Jeremiah's work was difficult and did not reach a happy ending (see also Jer 11:18–20; 12:1–6; 15:10–21; 17:14–18; 18:18–23).

Though Jeremiah's prophecy was rejected in his own time, his written words became important to later generations of Judeans. His prophecies of disaster appeared in a different light in the wake of the destruction of Jerusalem, removal of the monarchy, and exile of thousands of Judeans to Babylonia. Apparently, Jeremiah's scribe, Baruch, wrote down some of his prophecies, and later authors added biographical accounts about Jeremiah and expanded the book of Jeremiah with numerous additional prophecies, often in the form of prose rather than poetry.

Ultimately, it was writers during the time of exile who put together these diverse materials (poetic prophecy, narratives, and prose prophecies) into a collection much like the one we have now. These exilic authors, working well after the time of Jeremiah, were heavily influenced by the language and ideas of the book of Deuteronomy. That is why so many passages in Jeremiah, such as the version of the Temple sermon found in Jeremiah 7, sound so much like the Deuteronomic Torah. Ironically, though Jeremiah himself appears to have rejected that Torah (Jer 8:8–9), these post-Jeremiah texts quote him as announcing Yahweh's judgment on those who reject God's "Torah" (e.g. Jer 26:4). Such associations with Deuteronomy have led scholars to speak of a "Deuteronomistic redaction" throughout the book (with "redaction" = "editing"). This exilic redaction starts with the description of Jeremiah's call in Jer 1:4–10 (compare with Isaiah 6 and Ezekiel 1–3) and includes many other texts across the rest of the book. We even see the incorporation into the book of Jeremiah (Jer 39:1–10; 40:7–41:18; 52:1–34) of texts also seen in the books of Kings (2 Kgs 24:18–25:30). In sum, when we look at the book of Jeremiah, much of it reflects the words of his scribe, Baruch, and these exilic Deuteronomistic authors rather than the words of Jeremiah himself.

As in the case of Isaiah, we should not judge that such later parts of the book of Jeremiah are of little worth. On the contrary, some of the most important texts for Jewish and Christian communities have been ones that scholars have identified as coming from these later "Deuteronomistic" redactors. For example, Jer 31:31–4 speaks of a "new covenant" that Yahweh is about to make with the house of Israel and the house of Judah. Unlike the covenant of the exodus, Yahweh will put this covenant inside the people, writing it "on their hearts." The prose form of the text and its language mark it as a probable later addition to this part of Jeremiah. Nevertheless, later communities were powerfully affected by its vision of God willing to go to any lengths to make sure the people would be able to obey the covenant that they could not follow before. For example, the Jewish community at Qumran who collected the Dead Sea Scrolls saw themselves as a community of the "new covenant" mentioned in

Jeremiah. Just a century or two later, the expression "new covenant" came to play a very important role in the early Jesus movement as well (see Luke 22:20; 1 Cor 11:25; 2 Cor 3:1–18). Indeed, later Christians applied a derivative of this term, "New Testament," to the scriptures associated with their movement, and they labeled the Jewish scriptures with the corresponding term "Old Testament." In sum, Jer 31:31–4, a probable post-Jeremiah vision of God's salvation, has played a major role in defining multiple movements in Judaism.

Basics on the Book of Jeremiah

I	First scroll: oracles against Judah (and Israel)	1–25	**Outline (of the Jewish [Masoretic] form) of Jeremiah: Judah's judgment in broader context**
II	Biography: Jeremiah's call for submission and hope	26–45	
III	Oracles against foreign nations	46–51	
IV	Historical appendix (adapted from 2 Kings 24:18–25:30)	52	

The book of Jeremiah aims to make sense of the destruction of Jerusalem (described in the historical appendix, Jer 52) through looking back at Jeremiah's once unpopular prophecy of judgment and call for submission to the Babylonian empire. In addition, it contains words of judgment on other nations and – particularly in the "book of consolation" in Jeremiah 30–31– words of hope for Judah. **Themes**

Scholars actually have manuscripts of a version of Jeremiah different from *and earlier than* the version translated in most bibles. These ancient manuscripts – both old Hebrew manuscripts found near the Dead Sea (at Qumran) and the ancient Greek translation (Septuagint) of Jeremiah – reflect a version of Jeremiah that was about one-eighth shorter than the standard Hebrew (Masoretic) edition of Jeremiah that has been transmitted in Jewish communities. This earlier (and differently organized) version lacked many phrases and even whole passages (such as Jer 33:14–26 and 39:4–13) that were added by later scribes. We have similar manuscript documentation of earlier versions of the books of Exodus, Joshua, Ezekiel, and Proverbs, among others. **Documentation of the growth of the book of Jeremiah**

Deuteronomy 6:4–9

FOCUS TEXT

Having completed an overview, let us turn now to a specific text that exemplifies many of the central dynamics of seventh-century biblical literature, Deut 6:4–9. Many scholars have seen in this text a possible beginning of an early form of Deuteronomy, before later authors added the review of history in Deuteronomy 1–3, the teaching in Deuteronomy 4, and the Ten Commandments in Deuteronomy 5. Whether or not Deut 6:4–9 started an early form of the book, it certainly sums up many of its major themes, along with themes that play a major role in other Deuteronomistic literature, such as Joshua through 2 Kings and the present (post-Jeremiah) form of the book of Jeremiah.

The first sentence is marked off in the Hebrew of the Masoretic text tradition by unusually large final letters at the end of its first and last words. Such letters are often used elsewhere in the Bible to mark the outset of a biblical book (examples are found in Genesis, Proverbs, Chronicles) or an important point in a biblical book. Here they mark the beginning of what is known in Judaism as the "Shema," named after the first Hebrew word in the verse: *shema* – "Hear!" The rest of the sentence can be translated in two ways. One could translate it, "Hear, oh Israel, Yahweh is our God, Yahweh alone." This translation emphasizes that Israel should have one and only one God. The other, equally correct translation (in terms of the Hebrew) is, "Hear, oh Israel, that Yahweh, our God, is one Yahweh." We know from earlier inscriptions that earlier Judeans and Israelites worshipped different forms of Yahweh, "Yahweh from Teman" or "Yahweh from Samaria." According to this translation of Deut 6:4, such local manifestations of Yahweh are false. The Yahweh who belongs to Israel is one and only one deity. This would reinforce Josiah's push to centralize and standardize worship of Yahweh. Both translations link with other traditions in Deuteronomy and Deuteronomistic historical books like 1–2 Kings. Perhaps part of the power of this verse was its capacity to express both meanings.

The next verse expresses a core commandment in Deuteronomy and beyond. The people are to "love" God with all that they are and have. The list is often translated as "all your heart, soul and might" (NRSV) or the like, but these English words are a pale reflection of the Hebrew. The first word in the series, *lebab*, is not just the "heart," but also the "mind." For ancient Israel and other ancient Near Eastern peoples, the "heart" and "mind" were connected, not distinct as they so often are in Western culture. The second word that is often translated as "soul," Hebrew *nephesh*, actually refers to the vital life strength that infuses an entire person. It is the power that distinguishes a living person from a corpse, that powers desire, thought, will, and movement. Deut 6:4 calls on all Israel to devote that entire life strength to love of Yahweh. Finally, the word often translated as "might," Hebrew *meod*, refers to power or strength. Most often it appears in the Bible as an adverb, meaning "very." It may serve a similar function in this series in Deut 6:5, emphasizing how very much Israel must "love Yahweh, your God," with all Israel's heart/mind and life strength.

This call to love connects to other texts, both inside and outside the Bible. One of the places in the Bible where we see a similar description of someone "loving" another with their "life strength" (*nephesh*) is the Song of Songs. Several times the woman in the Song of Songs describes her lover as the one whom her "life strength loves" (Song 1:7; 3:1–4). Whether or not one believes that some form of the Song of Songs predates Deuteronomy, the author of this text in Deuteronomy probably expanded on this more general expression for a lover found in ancient love poetry. Where such ancient love poetry spoke of one's love as the one whom one's "life strength" loved, the author of this text speaks of love with one's "whole heart/mind, life strength, and power." Furthermore, similar to Hosea (which also shows possible links to ancient love poetry), this expanded description of love is focused on the people's love of Yahweh, rather than on one human's love for another.

We see this expanded version of the description of love in one other major historical narrative – the description of Josiah at what would have been the conclusion of a Josianic edition of the books of Kings:

Before Josiah there was no king like him who turned to Yahweh with all his heart/mind, all his life strength, and all his power, in accordance with the Torah of Moses, and after him there was never another like him. (2 Kgs 23:25)

This is the highest praise given any king in any part of the books of 1–2 Kings. It marks Josiah as the superlative example of a king who followed the law of the king seen in Deut 17:14–20, which specifies that the king must study and follow the "Torah" as he leads his people in faithfulness. Later authors added material after this text to explain why the exile still happened despite Josiah's virtues (2 Kgs 23:26–7), but that does not appear to be in view here. Nor does Josiah's strange and seemingly pointless death at the hands of the Egyptians fit with the preceding materials about him (2 Kgs 23:29–30). Rather, this final evaluation of Josiah's reign in 2 Kgs 23:25 concludes a narrative arc that began with the call to "love" in Deut 6:4–5.

This call to "love" in Deut 6:5 also connects, however, to yet another discourse, and that is the Assyrian requirement that vassal kings and their people "love" the Assyrian king. In this case, the "love" required was far from the sort of passionate love envisioned in love poetry like the Song of Songs. Rather, the "love" – Akkadian *ramu* – required in Assyrian treaties was faithful obedience to the Assyrian king: paying tribute, not joining alliances with other nations against Assyria, reporting traitors and extraditing them to Assyria, etc. As a hybrid response to this experience of Assyrian domination, Deuteronomy 6:5 and other Deuteronomistic texts reflect this dimension of "love" as well. But now Israel is to show faithful obedience to Yahweh and Yahweh alone.

The people must not follow other gods (//alliances), and they must report and try prophets who encourage betrayal of Yahweh (//traitors). Thus the "love" envisioned in Deuteronomy is not a passionate or romantic emotion that one feels at one time and might not feel at another. It is a basic attitude of loyalty and devotion to one far more powerful than one's self; in this case, to Yahweh, the god of Israel. Deut 6:5 represents a basic reorientation of such loyalty and devotion from the Assyrian king to Yahweh in the wake of the collapse of the Assyrian empire.

The rest of the passage, Deut 6:6–9, aims to reinforce that reorientation through making sure that the people internalize the commands of Yahweh that are expressed in the Torah. Wisdom texts, such as the adaptation of the Instruction of Amenemope in Prov 22:17–18 (also Prov 3:3 and 7:3), urged the student to memorize the sayings of the teacher and recite them – "establish them firmly on your lips." The Torah of Moses in Deuteronomy represents a new form of "wisdom," which likewise should be memorized – "put on your heart/mind" (Deut 6:6) – and recited constantly in the presence of one's children, sitting at home, going on one's way, lying down, and getting up (Deut 6:7). This constant repetition of the words of the Torah is not just aimed at reinforcing the loyalty of adult Israelites, but is also intended to teach children the Torah as well, almost like a language that they hear spoken by parents at home. As if this were not enough, the words of Yahweh's commandments are also supposed to be worn on the bodies of Israelites and inscribed on their doorways and gates. Every aspect of their lives is to reflect Yahweh's commands, particularly the call to honor one and only one God, Yahweh, and love Yahweh with all one's heart/mind, life strength, and power (Deut 6:4–5).

Over the long haul, these injunctions appear to have been effective, since this passage ended up being one of the most important texts in both Judaism and Christianity. A version of this command – "you shall love Yahweh, your God, with all your heart, your soul and your mind/energy" – is named as the greatest commandment of all by Jesus in the Christian Gospel of Mark and later parallels to it in Matthew and Luke (Mark 12:28–9//Matt 22:34–7; Luke 10:25–7). This corresponds to the honoring of this command in Judaism as one of the holiest of all. Jews are expected to recite this command and then others in Deut 11:13–21 (more on love and memorization) and Num 15:37–41 (on wearing fringes) twice a day, when rising and when going to bed. The great Jewish rabbi Akiba is reputed to have died at the hands of the Romans with the words of the Shema on his lips, and Jewish martyrs in later centuries have followed his example, reciting Deut 6:4 and the following verses while dying during medieval riots associated with the crusades, in the Spanish inquisition, and in Nazi gas chambers. Ironically and tragically, many of these Jewish martyrs have died at Christian hands while reciting what Christians recognized as the "greatest commandment." Deut 6:4–5 has been important in both traditions, but that has not prevented centuries of deplorable Christian persecution of Jews.

New Scriptures in the Twilight of Judean Monarchy

Other chapters in this book have included an imaginary overview of the sorts of texts (and some traditions) that were in circulation at a given time in ancient Israel and Judah. Here we conclude with a picture of two different groups of texts that probably were prominent in different groups in late seventh-century Judah. On the one hand, many in ancient Judah continued to study older sorts of texts: proverbs and wisdom instructions, royal and other sorts of psalms, love poetry, creation and flood myths, along with assorted traditions with strong northern connections, such as an earlier form of the story of Jacob and Joseph now found in Genesis 25–50. On the other hand, the book of Deuteronomy laid claim to be a new kind of "wisdom." Some, such as Jeremiah, seem to have been skeptical of Deuteronomy's claims to be true Torah wisdom (Jer 8:8–9), and our historical evidence suggests that kings after Josiah did not take the Deuteronomic Torah very seriously. Nevertheless, the book of Deuteronomy lays claim to be a potential replacement of older forms of teaching, and the following Deuteronomistic historical books retell the people's history from that perspective. Though Deuteronomy echoes older wisdom texts, it calls on the people to devote all their time to memorizing Moses's Torah teaching (Deut 6:6–9). There is little room in Deuteronomy or the history that follows it for competing claims or texts.

With Josiah's death, many probably dismissed the claims of Deuteronomy and related historical books, but at least one family appears to have continued to treasure and expand those writings: the family of Shaphan. Shaphan was Josiah's scribe, and he is described as very involved in the process leading to the introduction of the Deuteronomic Torah to the king and the people (2 Kgs 22:3–10) and the verification of it through the prophet Huldah (2 Kgs 22:14–20). Shaphan may have been involved in the revision of the Deuteronomic Torah at the time of Josiah and the Deuteronomistic reframing of other historical traditions to bolster Josiah's reform. Furthermore, his family played a particular role in later Judean history. His son, Ahikam, sheltered Jeremiah when people wanted to kill him after his Temple sermon (Jer 26:24), and Shaphan's grandson was the first one to hear Jeremiah's scroll of oracles and make sure it was passed on to officials in the palace (Jer 36:10–13). By this point, the family of Shaphan no longer seems to have been part of the Judean inner circle. Yet one of their members, a grandson of Shaphan's named Gedaliah, is put in power by the Babylonians after the last king is removed (2 Kgs 25:22), and he gives a message of cooperation with Babylonia that sounds somewhat like Jeremiah's prophecy (2 Kgs 25:23–4//Jer 40:7–12). Gedaliah was soon killed (2 Kgs 25:25//Jer 41:1–3), but his family is the most likely group to have cherished and protected the texts discussed in this chapter. In the twilight of the Judean monarchy, when others may have dismissed texts like Deuteronomy or Jeremiah, they revised and expanded upon both.

Thus the late seventh century is a time when major traditions in the Bible were introduced, but all these texts still had a journey to make before becoming the biblical texts they now are. They do not seem to have been broadly recognized as important until total disaster struck Jerusalem, with the destruction of the Temple and the monarchy. Moreover, Jeremiah along with Deuteronomy and the Deuteronomistic historical books were revised in light of this catastrophe, so that those historical books, for example, now extend up to the first part of exile in Babylonia. In the next chapter we will look at the impact of this catastrophe across a broader stretch of biblical traditions. This chapter, however, has traced the introduction in the late seventh century of major building blocks of the future "Torah" and "prophets."

CHAPTER FIVE REVIEW

1 Know the meaning and significance of the following terms discussed in this chapter:

- books of the former prophets
- Deuteronomistic
- Deuteronomistic History
- Josiah's reform
- major prophet
- postcolonial criticism
- hybridity

2 In a few sentences summarize the important role played by Josiah's reform in shaping books like Deuteronomy and introducing important changes in Israelite religion. In addition, note a couple of textual and archaeological clues that have led scholars to perceive the importance of Josiah's reform.

3 What is a vassal treaty and what are its major parts? How is the book of Deuteronomy similar to and yet different from a vassal treaty?

4 What is postcolonial criticism and what are two different ways in which biblical scholars draw on it? What is an example of the use of postcolonial criticism to analyze Deuteronomy and the Deuteronomistic History?

5 What is the ancient concept of "holy war"? How does this concept function in the books of Deuteronomy and Joshua?

6 When did Jeremiah prophesy? How is this time distinguished from the periods in which the book of Jeremiah was formed?

7 (Focus text: Deut 6:4–9) Compare the language and ideas of Deut 6:4–9 with the passages assigned above from Joshua, Judges, 1–2 Samuel, and 1–2 Kings. Where do you see echoes of Deut 6:4–9 in these passages? Look also for places where these passages have a different emphasis from Deut 6:4–9. Given this comparison what do you think about the idea that these books were once united as one long "Deuteronomistic History" that started with Deuteronomy (featuring the Shema in Deut 6:4–9) and extended through these books to the end of 2 Kings? Does it seem plausible? Why or why not?

RESOURCES FOR FURTHER STUDY

Broader discussion of Deuteronomistic historical books

Nelson, Richard D. *The Historical Books*. Nashville, TN: Abingdon, 1998.

Deuteronomy

Miller, Patrick. *Deuteronomy*. Louisville, KY: John Knox Press, 1990.

Tigay, Jeffrey. *Deuteronomy*. Philadelphia, PA: Jewish Publication Society, 1996.

Joshua and Judges

See "Resources for Further Study" in Chapter 2.

1 and 2 Samuel

Wijk-Bos, Johanna. *The Road to Kingship: 1–2 Samuel*. Grand Rapids, MI: Eerdmans, 2020.

1 and 2 Kings

Nelson, Richard. *First and Second Kings*. Atlanta, GA: John Knox Press, 1987.

Sweeney, Marvin. *1–2 Kings*. Louisville, KY: Westminster John Knox, 2007.

Zephaniah, Habakkuk, Nahum, and Other Prophets

O'Brien, Julia M. *Nahum, Habakkuk, Zephaniah, Haggai, Zechariah, Malachi*. Nashville, TN: Abingdon, 2004.

Jeremiah

Clements, R. E. *Jeremiah*. Atlanta, GA: John Knox Press, 1988.

Stulman, Louis. *Jeremiah*. Nashville, TN: Abingdon, 2005.

Bible for Exiles: Promise and Story in the Neo-Babylonian Empire

6

Chapter Outline

Chapter Overview

The Hebrew scriptures were shaped by exiles and their children, and this means that the experience of exile is the central point of biblical history, the period around which all others are oriented. Josiah's reform is a crucial turning point in the pre-exilic period, but already that formulation – "pre-exilic" – shows that the period of the exile is more important still for biblical study. Most discussions of the history of the Hebrew Bible revolve around three periods: the pre-exilic, exilic, and post-exilic, thus adopting the perspective of the exiles (and their descendants) who shaped the Bible. The "post-exilic" period, as we will see in Chapter 7, is defined particularly by those who returned from exile to Judah. Yet for most others whose families had left Judah, there was no return from "exile" to life in the land, and many Jews have lived away from the land of Judah ever since the exile. Thus the exile of waves of Judeans, first in 597 and then in 586 (and yet another in 582), introduced a new era in the history of the Israelite people and development of the Bible. From this point onward, they had no

A Contemporary Introduction to the Bible: Sacred Texts and Imperial Contexts, Second Edition.
Colleen M. Conway and David M. Carr.
© 2021 Colleen M. Conway and David M. Carr. Published 2021 by John Wiley & Sons Ltd.

nation-state. In the wake of the exile and destruction of Jerusalem, those scriptures were now scriptures for exiles and returnees living in a land dominated by others. The link between texts and a city-state monarchy was broken. After exile, the Israelites' scriptures were never the same.

This chapter explores the many ways in which the exile shaped the Hebrew Bible we now have. After discussing the exile and general ways that it changed the community, we will look at several texts that are explicitly linked to the exilic experience: laments over the destruction of Jerusalem, the response to exile in the book of Ezekiel and chapters 40–55 of Isaiah ("Second Isaiah"), and the addition – in the exilic period – of some new texts to the Deuteronomy, Jeremiah, and other biblical texts. These exilic texts and additions to texts provide clues to the increasing importance of Israel's pre-land traditions during the exile and the emphasis in many exilic traditions on Yahweh's promise and ability to work with the people no matter how sinful.

The balance of the chapter then shows how our present Pentateuch is an interweaving of two main source documents that reflect these exilic themes of promise: an L Source created by lay scribes and leaders, and a slightly later P (Priestly) Source created by priests. In many ways, it is best to think of both of these sources, L and P, as expressions in narrative form of the exilic promise addressed to despairing exiles that we see in the later prophecies of Ezekiel and Second Isaiah. Though the L and P narratives purport to be about ancient figures such as Abraham and Moses (and build on earlier traditions about them), they are stories and laws *reshaped* to address the questions and concerns of exiles. The challenge of this chapter is to see how the concerns of the exiles in Babylonia not only are reflected in clearly exilic laments and prophecies, but are also subtly reflected in biblical stories about characters (e.g. Abraham, Sarah, Moses) from a much earlier point in Israelite history. Though these characters were certainly known before, the Judean exiles focused ever more on stories about them, since these figures, like them, contended with the doubts and dangers of living in a land that was not their own.

The Neo-Babylonian Destruction of Jerusalem and Exile

READING

2 Kgs 23:29–25:30.

Exilic laments: Ps 137; Lamentations 1; and Isa 63:7–64:12.

EXERCISE

Before reading this section, read the "exilic laments" listed above and then write down five words that these texts from the exile evoke for you.

Despite high hopes during the time of Josiah, the kingdom of Judah never achieved an extended period of independence, nor was its control over the north firm for any length of time. Instead, Josiah was killed in 609 in a confrontation with the Egyptian Pharaoh Necho as Necho was traveling through Israel on his way to assist Assyria in trying to contain a rising military power in Mesopotamia.

That power was the emergent "Neo-Babylonian" state (distinguished from the "Old Babylonian" empire of the early second millennium), a state ruled by a group of Aramean people called "Chaldeans." Thus began a period of Judah and its kings struggling under the shadow of Neo-Babylonian domination. Though the Egyptian Necho appointed one of Josiah's sons, Jehoiakim, as Josiah's successor, Jehoiakim quickly became a Babylonian vassal. A few years later, he sought to get out from under Babylonian domination with Egypt's help, but the Babylonian army eventually came and laid siege to Jerusalem. In an attempt to avert the wrath of the Babylonians, the people of Jerusalem apparently killed Jehoiakim and replaced him with his son, Jehoiachin, but the Babylonians still took young Jehoiachin and several thousand elite Judeans into exile (in 597), the first of several waves of forced resettlement of Judeans in the Babylonian empire. In place of Jehoiachin, the Babylonians appointed as king his uncle, Zedekiah, a son of Josiah. As a Babylonian appointee, Zedekiah was a weak ruler who was not recognized as king by many of his countrypeople. After about ten years he, like his brother Jehoiakim, tried to get free of Babylonia by joining an anti-Babylonian coalition of nations.

This rebellion by Zedekiah was the final straw for the Babylonians. Nebuchadnezzar marched on Jerusalem in 586 BCE and breached the walls (see Figure 6.1). He destroyed the Temple that Judah had thought was invulnerable, took yet more of Judah's elite into exile (though fewer than in 597), and installed Gedaliah, the grandson of Shaphan, Josiah's scribe, as governor in Mizpah, a town a few miles northwest of Jerusalem. Our last historical records point to the collapse of power structures in the land. In Judah things went from very bad to worse. Gedaliah was assassinated, his assassins fled to Ammon before Gedaliah's forces, and Gedaliah's forces fled to Egypt out of fear of Babylonian reprisals, forcing Jeremiah to come with them (2 Kgs 25:25–6// Jeremiah 41–2). The last we hear of life in Judah, the Babylonians had attacked again and taken a third wave of Judeans into exile in 582 BCE (Jer 52:30; see Map 6.1).

Meanwhile, life went on in Babylonia for the thousands of upper-class Judeans who had been forcibly resettled there. The books of Kings (and Jeremiah) end with a brief account of how the king, Jehoiachin, was taken out of prison during his thirty-seventh year of exile in Babylonia, given a place at the Babylonian king's table, and given rations (2 Kgs 25:27–30; appropriated in Jer 52:31–4; cf. Ezek 1:2). This narrative is confirmed by a Babylonian list of rations given to Jehoiachin. It shows the sliver of hope that such exiles found in the elevation of their king. Nevertheless, we never hear of Jehoiachin again, and Davidic kings never regained power. The sun had gone down on the Jerusalem monarchy. The people's future now lay in a life without their own king over them.

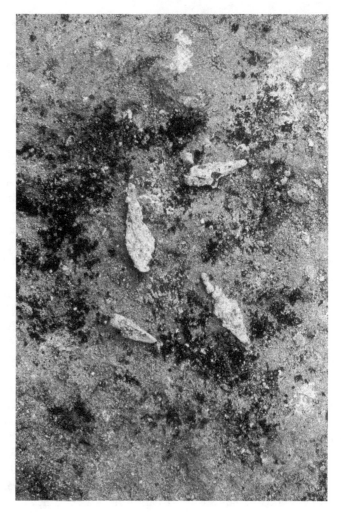

FIGURE 6.1
Ashes and arrowheads left from the Babylonian attack on Jerusalem.

With no monarchy left to sponsor the writing of any history, we are in the dark about other specific events during the Babylonian exile. Biblical texts only provide indirect information about what life was like in exile. Certainly it was no picnic. The exiles were forcibly resettled into abandoned areas of central Babylonia where they worked and tried to form a viable communal life hundreds of miles from their homeland. Though the exiles were allowed to settle together and were not all enslaved, exilic texts refer to Babylonian domination as a "yoke" (Ezek 34:27; Isa 47:6; also Jer 30:8) and Babylonia, along with its capital city Babylon, became a symbol of arch-evil throughout the rest of biblical tradition. Multiple traditions suggest that some exiles were in chains (Jer 40:1; see also Nah 3:10), and exilic texts in Isaiah speak of Jerusalem's time of "forced labor" (Isa 40:2), of being confined in prison (Isa 42:7; 49:9) and robbed (Isa 42:22). Meanwhile, one of Nebuchadnezzar's inscriptions boasts of how he

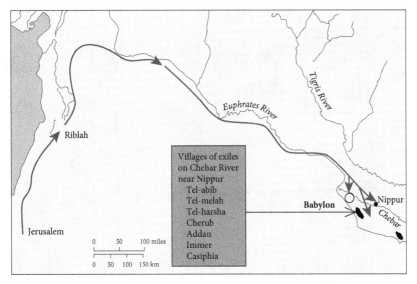

MAP 6.1
The journey to Babylonia. Redrawn from Yohanan Aharoni and Michael Avi-Yonah (eds.),
The Macmillan Bible Atlas (revised edition). New York: Macmillan, 1977, map 163.

forced people from Judah and elsewhere to rebuild the temple in Babylonia
(see box on p. 160). Babylonia had become their new Egypt (see Figure 6.2).

Laments and prophetic quotes from this period give a sense of the inner
experience of this exile. Psalm 137 speaks of weeping by the rivers of Babylonia
where the captors of the Judeans mockingly asked them to "sing one of the
songs of Zion." The exiles sing of how they will keep Jerusalem in their memory, though they are far from home.

> If I forget you, O Jerusalem,
> let my right hand wither!
> Let my tongue cling to the roof of my mouth,
> if I do not remember you,
> if I do not set Jerusalem
> above my highest joy. (Ps 137:5–6 NRSV)

Lamentations 1 is an alphabet of suffering, where each stanza begins with
a different letter of the Hebrew alphabet. After an initial lament over Zion, she
cries forth her suffering herself:

> My crimes have been bound into a yoke,
> my misdeeds braided together by [God's] hand.
> They lie on my neck,
> They sap my strength.
> The Lord has given me into the hands of
> Those I cannot overcome. (Lam 1:14)

FIGURE 6.2
Reproduction of part of the magnificent temple of Ishtar located in the heart of the empire of Babylonia.

FORCED LABOR FOR EXILES UNDER NEBUCHADNEZZAR

This is an excerpt from a building inscription by Nebuchadnezzar II about his use of peoples from across his empire to build "Etemenanki," the grand temple for Marduk in the heart of Babylonia:

> the whole of the races, peoples from far places, whom Marduk, my Lord, delivered to me, I put them to work on the building of Etemenanki. I imposed on them the brick basket. (Translation: D. Smith-Christopher, "The Politics of Ezra: Sociological Indicators of Postexilic Judaean Society." P. 79 of Philip Davies, ed., *Second Temple Studies, I*, JSOTSup 117. Sheffield: Sheffield Academic Press, 1991)

Echoing pre-exilic prophets like Hosea and Jeremiah, this Zion figure says, "I called out to my lovers, but they betrayed me. My priests and elders died in the city while seeking food to survive" (Lam 1:19). Meanwhile, in a lament found in Isa 63:7–64:12 (64:11 in some translations), the ancient Judeans cry out to God, "your holy cities have become a wasteland, Zion has become a desert, Jerusalem a heap of ruins" (64:10) and assert to Yahweh, their "father" (64:8), that he has made them "stray from your paths and turn our hearts from fearing you" (64:7). Such laments are part of an ancient literary tradition in Israel of honest crying out to God, even accusing God of being responsible for the people's shortcomings. These laments will be discussed in Chapter 7. For now, it is important to recognize that this type of text, particularly the communal lament, voiced the exiles' mixed feelings of guilt, sadness, fear, and rage as they lived for decades under Neo-Babylonian oppression.

Basics on the Book of Lamentations

I	Four alphabet poems detailing the suffering of Jerusalem and its people	1–4	**Outline: five-part (=Torah) cry for restoration of Jerusalem**
II	Final communal plea for restoration	5	

Other ancient Near Eastern cultures had written and taught laments over the destruction of great cities. These chapters in Lamentations were composed to commemorate the destruction of Jerusalem in 586, particularly on the holiday remembering this event, the Ninth of Av. Over time, however, these poems in Lamentations have come to serve as a cry over Jewish suffering of many kinds, from the destruction of the Second Temple to the genocide of Jews under Hitler and other suffering up to today. **Theme and purpose**

The dynamics of exile can be illuminated through **social-scientific analysis** of the Bible; that is, analysis that draws on contemporary sociological and anthropological studies to provide a more nuanced picture of ancient Israel. For example, Daniel Smith-Christopher's book, *Religion of the Landless* (see this chapter's "Resources for Further Study"), draws on ethnographic studies of contemporary groups who have experienced displacement from their homelands to try to reconstruct what the experience of Babylonian exile might have been like. He finds that separation from one's homeland inevitably involves major changes for the displaced group. Continuity is not the norm. Transformation is.

In addition, Smith-Christopher found that displaced communities change in similar ways, reflecting the comparable challenges that many such diaspora communities face. Because they must now live as a minority in a majority culture, family and clan traditions often become more important, while other traditions connected with their old life either disappear or are transformed. For example, Judean traditions about the king's blessing may have been adapted in exile so that they now applied to an ancient ancestor's blessing or God's blessing of a foreign deliverer. Meanwhile, in place of the now defunct royal bureaucracy, the sole means of organization of Judean exiles were family units, "houses of the father," which were ruled by a group of "elders." These elders, along with the remnants of the priesthood, were the leaders in the exiled Judean community.

New practices became important for the Judeans who were in Babylonia, practices that preserved communal identity in a hostile cultural environment. It appears that circumcision (which was not practiced by Babylonians) and Sabbath observance grew in importance. Furthermore, exiles like them had to struggle against the tendency to assimilate into the broader culture, particularly through intermarriage. In the face of this, these exiles, like many contemporary communities in diaspora, sought ways to discourage their children from marrying foreigners. This is but one major way in which peoples in exile, both ancient and contemporary, change in order to survive culturally and build identity.

The violence of the exiles' departure may have been yet another factor leading to the transformation of their traditions. Though it is possible that Judean exiles took some scrolls of ancient texts with them into Babylonia, it is also quite likely that many did not have a chance to pack much up while Jerusalem burned and the Temple – often a storage place for ancient scrolls – was destroyed. Yet the literate elite who went into exile had memorized ancient texts as part of their education. The Deuteronomic Torah, Proverbs, Song of Songs, and other texts were "written on the tablet of their hearts," as Proverbs would put it (Prov 3:3; 7:3). Once in Babylonia, these people could call on their detailed memories of these texts as they produced new copies of them – copies that often reflected the new challenges and hopes of life in exile.

MORE ON METHOD: TRAUMA STUDIES AND THE BIBLE

Earlier chapters in this introduction on the history of Israel and Judah under Neo-Assyrian imperialism have already applied the term "trauma" to their experiences – including the destruction of Israel in the north and the almost century-long Assyrian domination of Judah in the south. Key themes of prophetic and Deuteronomistic theology were forged amidst such overwhelming experiences of communal defeat, humiliation, and suffering. The exile in Babylonia, however, appears to have been Judah's clearest and most profound experience of what would be described today as "trauma" in a communal form. According to one contemporary definition of trauma (by Cathy Caruth), "trauma is the confrontation with an event that, in its unexpectedness or horror, cannot be placed within schemes of prior knowledge." Another leading theorist, Judith Herman, characterizes traumatic events as those that "overwhelm the ordinary systems of care that give people a sense of control, connection and meaning."

The exile in Babylonia appears to have been just such an event for the inhabitants of Jerusalem, and their texts manifest symptoms often seen in trauma. For example, like many traumatized individuals and communities, the exiles do not seem to have been able to speak much about their experience. Instead, there is a gap in communal memory. Biblical history reaches from creation to the exile at the end of 2 Kings, has a blank, and does not pick up again until the conclusion of the Babylonian exile with a Persian king's edict that Judah could return (Ezra 1:1–4//2 Chr 36:22–23). We even see a major gap among the named prophets in the Bible, with a series of prophets extending up to the edge of the exile (Jeremiah, Ezekiel), a gap of more than half a century, and then a series of post-exilic prophets (e.g. Haggai, Zechariah, Malachi). This does not mean that the exiles in Babylonia did not write anything. They just did not write much directly about themselves. (The main exceptions are a brief note in 2 Kgs 25:27–30 and some songs of lament like Psalm 137. The legends about exile in Daniel are dated to much later centuries.)

As we will see in this chapter and the next, biblical texts dated to the exile reflect numerous symptoms seen frequently in traumatized communities. These include a tendency toward self-blame for the community's suffering, growth of us/them thinking that defines an in-group against outsiders, rage at foreign "others" who are perceived to be responsible for the catastrophe, and an increased communal focus on identities and stories about ancient times before the displacement. This latter tendency is particularly evident in the increasing focus on stories of pre-land ancestors (Abraham, Moses) that is seen during the exile. We will see this focus both in this chapter and in the next chapter's discussion of Pentateuchal texts that were shaped amidst trauma.

For more on this approach, see David Carr, *Holy Resilience: The Bible's Traumatic Origins* (New Haven: Yale University Press, 2014).

The Exilic Editions of Biblical Books

Review Deut 30:1–10 (cf. Deut 30:11–20);

Read 2 Kgs 21:2–16; 23:26–8; 25.

READING

One example of such preservation and change of ancient textual traditions is revision and extension of Deuteronomy and related Deuteronomistic historical books. In Chapter 5 we noted that an early, Josianic edition of Kings (or a broader Deuteronomistic history) may only have reached as far as the description of Josiah's reign. There, we hear that Josiah surpassed all other kings in fulfilling the greatest command in Deuteronomy (seen in Deut 6:5) by turning to Yahweh "with all his heart/mind, all his life strength, and all his power, in accordance with the Torah of Moses" (2 Kgs 23:25). This enthusiastic endorsement of Josiah caps a narration in 2 Kings 22–3 of how he showed this loyalty to Yahwh through his reform. Later authors, however, were confronted with a difficult quandary. According to Deuteronomistic theology, Josiah should have been rewarded with long life, and the people who he led in his reform should have enjoyed lasting security. In fact, however, Josiah was killed in an unexplained encounter with Pharaoh Necho (2 Kgs 23:29), and Judah was soon destroyed by the Babylonian empire (2 Kgs 25).

Exilic scribes had to explain why this happened, and we see this explanation immediately after the positive comments about Josiah's righteousness in 2 Kgs 23:25: "there was no king before Josiah who was like him, turning to Yahweh with all his heart, his life breath, and his strength ... and there was never one after him." The exilic extenders of this history go on to say:

> Yet, the Lord did not turn back from his great anger against Judah and all the awful things that Manasseh [Josiah's predecessor] had done to anger God. The Lord said, "As I banished Israel from my presence, so will I also banish Judah, and I will reject this city that I chose, Jerusalem, and the house where I said my name would live." (2 Kgs 23:26–7)

This is how one group of exiles, those extending the books of 1–2 Kings into the exile, explained the destruction of the supposedly invulnerable city, Jerusalem, and its sanctuary. The reason they gave was that Manasseh's sin was so grievous that Josiah's virtue could not overcome it. One generation's guilt meant that another generation had to suffer. A proverb quoted by Ezekiel's audience puts it vividly: "the fathers have eaten sour grapes and the children's teeth are set on edge" (Ezek 18:2). As we will see, Ezekiel rejects this idea that a later generation must pay for the sins of their parents. Nevertheless, this passage from 2 Kgs 23:26–7 is a biblical affirmation of this concept. It asserts that later generations of Judah had to suffer the destruction of Judah and Jerusalem because of the sins of Manasseh. Sour grapes indeed.

This is only one example of a range of places where exilic authors seem to have added material to earlier biblical books, much of it influenced to a greater or lesser degree by Deuteronomistic ideology. For example, Chapter 4 of this *Introduction* included discussion of how the book of Micah (especially Chapters 4–5) contains prophecies of hope for Jerusalem/Zion that probably were written to encourage exiles. The promise appended to the end of the book of Amos, Amos 9:11–15, is another place where exiles appear to have added a word of hope to earlier words of judgment. The book of Jeremiah was thoroughly revised during the exile through the addition of passages such as God's promise of a new covenant written on the heart (Jer 31:31–4) that was discussed in Chapter 5. We see our first close analogies to this idea of God actually changing the heart of God's people in the next prophet to be discussed, Ezekiel.

Ezekiel's Move from Judgment to Promise with the Fall of Jerusalem

READING

Ezekiel 1–3, 8–11, 16, 36–7.

Ezekiel is the only prophet in the Hebrew Bible whose prophecy can be dated with certainty to the exilic period. He was a priest who went into exile in Babylonia with King Jehoiachin and thousands of other exiles in 597. There he lived in a Jewish settlement, Tel-abib, located just a few miles from the ancient Sumerian center of learning at Nippur. Though Zedekiah ruled in Jerusalem from 597 until its destruction in 586, all of Ezekiel's prophecies are dated by the years of Jehoiachin's exile. Apparently his career began six years before Jerusalem was destroyed and then continued another fourteen years after Jerusalem's destruction (see Ezek 1:2; 40:1). Many divide Ezekiel's book into two major parts, corresponding to the two major periods of his prophecy. Ezekiel 1–32 features oracles of judgment dated to the period before Jerusalem's destruction. These judgments by Ezekiel are roughly contemporary with the last phase of Jeremiah's prophecy but are delivered in Babylonia to Judean exiles there. Then the tone shifts: once Jerusalem is destroyed and the exiles are in despair about their future with God, Ezekiel develops vivid images of hope, and these are stressed in chapters 33–48 of the book.

Like the other books of major prophets, the book of Ezekiel prominently features a story of his commissioning by God, in Ezekiel 1–3. Nevertheless, this commissioning is different in ways that mark the uniqueness of Ezekiel's prophecy. It begins, like Isaiah's, with a vision of God and God's attendants (1:4–28), but Ezekiel's vision is more elaborate: with four strange creatures (1:4–14), each associated with a chariot wheel (1:15–25), and a brilliant blue throne overhead on which God is seated, "an appearance of the likeness of the glory of the LORD" (1:28). Moreover, Ezekiel, unlike Isaiah, sees God outside the temple (1:2–28; 3:22–3), and the imagery of the wheels in his call narrative anticipates his later "Temple vision," where he sees God leave the Temple and go into exile (Ezekiel 8–11). This focus on God's presence outside the temple in both Ezekiel 1–3 and 8–11 is the first mark of the radically new, exilic context of Ezekiel's prophecy.

The message that Ezekiel is commissioned to speak, however, sounds like an extreme version of the message seen in Amos, Isaiah, and other prophets of judgment. God tells him to speak to God's people of "rebels," whether they listen or not (2:1–7). Indeed, God predicts that they will not listen, but will reject his message (3:4–9). Nevertheless, like a sentinel on a watchtower who sees an approaching army, Ezekiel must sound the alarm about God's oncoming judgment and let the people make the decision about whether to respond. Otherwise, the blood of his people will be on his hands (Ezek 3:16–21).

When other prophets faced rejection of their prophecy, they had their oracles written down for other generations (e.g.: Isa 8:11–18; 30:8–14; Jeremiah 36), and this element of writing is yet more prominent in Ezekiel's call narrative. God offers him a scroll with words of doom written on it and tells Ezekiel to eat it. Ezekiel does eat it, an act signifying his obedient memorization of all that God has told him to prophesy (Ezek 2:8–3:3). Yet the scroll has not lost its purpose. Rather, this narrative implies that its words of doom were included in the book now found in the Hebrew Bible. Though his own generation did not listen, the writing down of his prophecy allowed it to endure and teach future generations.

One central element of Ezekiel's teaching was his proclamation that each generation stood on its own before God: a disobedient generation would be punished for its sins, but if the children of people in that generation were righteous, they would be rewarded. Not everyone agreed on this point. As we saw above, the exilic portions of the books of Kings blamed the suffering of Ezekiel's generation on the sins of an earlier one, especially the evil of Manasseh (2 Kgs 23:26–7). Ezekiel quotes people of his time saying "the fathers have eaten sour grapes, and the children's teeth are set on edge" (Ezek 18:2), but he decisively rejects that saying. On the contrary, he insists, the fathers will be punished or rewarded for their righteousness, and their children will stand or fall on the basis of their own righteousness as well (Ezek 18:3–24). Many who have read this chapter in the contemporary context of emphasis on the individual have seen here the first emergence in the Hebrew

Bible of individual responsibility, but this is mistaken. At issue in every example in the chapter is whether or not later generations must pay for the sins of their parents. The point is to get the exiles to stop saying how "unfair" God is for punishing them on the basis of an earlier generation's sins (18:25, 29). Instead, Ezekiel calls on them to repent of their own past crimes, get a "new heart and a new spirit," and live (Ezek 18:31–2).

Basics on the Book of Ezekiel

Outline: judgment and restoration of Jerusalem	I	Sentinel announcement of judgment	1:1–33:20
	II	Restoration of Jerusalem and Temple	33:21–48:35
Date	Early to late exile.		
Themes	The judgment and restoration theme is familiar from other prophets, but Ezekiel, a Zadokite priest, adds a different level of spectacle to his visions (e.g. Ezekiel 1–3 and 37) and a new emphasis on purity, and features a particular focus on the Temple (Ezekiel 9–11) and its restoration (Ezekiel 40–48).		
More information	Ezekiel is also known for his weird symbolic actions, such as lying on his side for more than a year (Ezek 4:4–8) or not mourning the death of his wife (Ezek 24:15–27). Some in the past have explained these and other aspects of his prophecy as the result of a mental imbalance in Ezekiel. Nevertheless, such attempts to psychologically analyze the prophet on the basis of literature linked to him are extremely risky. Moreover, these approaches miss the emphasis throughout the book on the idea that Ezekiel's words and actions, however unusual, were a message from God for the exiles and later generations.		

Ultimately Ezekiel, like other prophetic books, ends with hope, not judgment. After a series of oracles against foreign nations (Ezekiel 25–32), the book returns to a review of major themes from the first part of the book (33:1–20) before moving to prophecies dated to the destruction of the Jerusalem Temple (33:21) or later (40:1). Some of these are words of judgment, such as Ezekiel's oracle against people still in the land who claim Abraham as their ancestor (Ezek 33:23–9) or his condemnation of Judah and Israel's past kings, their "shepherds," for selfishness and injustice (Ezek 34:1–10). Yet these oracles of judgment introduce words of hope to exiles, promising that God will be their shepherd and rescue them from exile and resettle them under a new Davidic king (Ezek 34:11–31). Where Ezekiel prophesied against the mountains of the land in the first part of the book (Ezekiel 6), he offers them hope in this latter part (Ezekiel 36). Where he watched the glory of God leave the temple before (Ezek 11:22–5), he now sees it returning (Ezek 43:1–6). In one of the most powerful visions of all, he imagines Israel as a valley full of "dry bones," bones that symbolize exiles who are convinced that they are completely finished and hope is lost (Ezek 37:11). God calls on Ezekiel to prophesy to this valley of dry bones, this exiled people, and watch their miraculous resurrection (37:12–14).

The restoration imagined in Ezekiel does not depend on the people finding a way to change themselves. Rather, in this part of the book, Ezekiel reiterates promises given earlier that God will give the people a new heart and new spirit so that they can obey God's laws (Ezek 36:26–7; 37:14; cf. 11:14–21). Though the exiles might despair that God would ever have anything more to do with them after all that they had done wrong, Ezekiel reassures them that God will do all this "for the sake of [God's] holy name" (Ezek 36:22–3, 32). This idea of "holy name" refers to God's reputation. According to Ezekiel, God's reputation among the nations had suffered when they watched God's chosen people removed from their land (Ezek 36:20–21). Yet God promises to redeem God's own name, God's reputation, through bringing the Israelites back and settling them in the land so that the nations can see this too (36:28–36). In this way, Ezekiel describes a restoration that does not depend on any goodness in the exiles themselves. God's promises of restoration depend on God's wish to look good in front of the nations, not on the people suddenly changing their ways.

The Divine Council

The people of Israel and surrounding countries believed their god had a royal court of divine beings, a "divine council." Just as human kings had counselors and courtiers, so also the divine king had his. We see reflections of this idea of the divine council across the whole Hebrew Bible: Psalm 89:7 refers to Yahweh's "council of the holy ones."

Isaiah 6:8, 40:1, and 40:3 feature commands addressed to an unspecified heavenly group. God debates with a group about whether Job is altruistic in Job 1–2. We may even see a pale reflection of this idea in Genesis where God decides to make humanity "as *our* image" (Gen 1:26) and later fears that humans will be "like *us*" (Gen 3:22 and 11:7).

Hope for Exiles in Second Isaiah (also called "Deutero-Isaiah")

Isaiah 40, 48–9, and 52:13–53:12

READING

Very similar themes appear in the other major prophet that is associated with the exile: the anonymous prophet that wrote chapters 40–55 of the book of Isaiah. Chapter 4 of this *Introduction* mentioned biblical scholarship that has identified this section of Isaiah as coming from a later period of Judah's history than the time of the original Isaiah. Here we examine how these chapters addressed the fears and hopes of exiles a few decades after the time of Ezekiel. By this point in the exile, this "**Second Isaiah**" (or **Deutero-Isaiah**) can proclaim that the LORD has anointed the Persian king Cyrus as God's shepherd, that is, God's king (Isa 44:28–45:1). We know from other historical documents that this Cyrus would eventually bring down the Neo-Babylonian empire in 539 BCE.

This exilic portion of Isaiah opens with a commissioning scene in the **divine council** (Isa 40:1–8) that echoes the scene where the earlier prophet, eighth-century Isaiah, was commissioned (6:1–13). The Hebrew of both texts, Isa 6:1–13 and 40:1–8, indicates that God speaks with a *plural* group, probably members of God's divine council, in the process of deciding who will take God's message to God's people (Isa 6:8; 40:1–5). In Isa 6:8 God asks a group of people, "whom shall I send on our behalf?" while Isa 40:1–2 calls a group to go and tell God's people that the exile, the "time of forced labor," is over:

> Comfort my people, comfort them,
> > Says your God.
> Speak tenderly to the heart of Jerusalem,
> > And call out to her.
> That her time of forced labor is now over,
> > That her bloodguilt has been paid for,
> That she has received from Yahweh
> > double for all her sins. (Isa 40:1–2)

Isaiah 6, the call narrative for Isaiah of the eighth century, stressed his confrontation with his and his people's "bloodguilt" (Isa 6:5). In contrast, this later exilic text emphasizes God's forgiveness. Isaiah 6 described Yahweh's "glory" as filling the whole earth (Isa 6:3), but this exilic text in Isa 40:5 now has the whole earth actually *seeing* Yahweh's "glory" (Isa 40:3–5). Just as Ezekiel had pictured God's reputation being restored through the nations' witnessing God's rescue of God's people (Ezek 36:28–36), so this exilic "Second Isaiah" imagines God's glory being revealed to the whole world in the exiles' departure from Babylonia (Isa 40:3–5).

God's announcement of Jerusalem's liberation is followed by the prophet's call and his objection to the call (40:6), an exchange similar to ones in the call narratives for Isaiah (Isa 6:5) and Jeremiah (Jer 1:6). In this case, however, the exilic prophet is worried about despairing exiles, who wither "like grass" when "the breath of Yahweh blows upon it" (40:6–7). He knows that he must address a discouraged people who have heard many false hopes. Yet a divine presence answers his doubts, first by acknowledging their partial truth, "Yes, the grass withers, and the flower fades," then adding the reassurance that "the word of our God endures forever" (40:8). Though the exiles may feel weak and hopeless, God's word of hope and restoration persists and will prevail.

Basics on Second Isaiah/Deutero-Isaiah

| I | Exhortation for exiles to join a second exodus (out of Babylonia) | 40–48 | **Outline** |
| II | Announcement of hope and return to Jerusalem | 49–55 | |

Late exile.   **Date**

This part of Isaiah focuses on giving hope to the hopeless. Though possibly **Themes**
written as a separate prophetic collection, it now links in interesting ways with
earlier parts of Isaiah (e.g. Isaiah 40:1–9//Isaiah 6). It is also the part of Isaiah that
contains the famous "servant songs" (Isa 42:1–4; 49:1–6; 50:4–11; 52:13–53:12) that
have been the subject of much religious and scholarly debate.

The rest of Isaiah 40–55 is divided into two main parts: Isaiah 40–48 and 49–55. The first part, Isaiah 40–48, is a passionate call for the exiles to embrace God's plan to take them out of Babylonia. Central to this call is the prophet's reassurance that their God, who might have seemed defeated by other gods in the destruction of Jerusalem, is powerful enough to liberate them. Here "Second Isaiah" invokes creation traditions to affirm that the god who created the world can bring them out of Babylonia (Isa 40:12–27). He reminds the exiles of God's care for their ancestors, both Abraham and Jacob and the people of the exodus generation (41:8–9; 44:1–2; also 51:1–2).

It is in the context of these arguments for Yahweh's power that Second Isaiah makes a monotheistic claim that is new in Israelite religion: he asserts that there is no other god anywhere but Yahweh. All other gods are false idols, worthless pieces of wood and metal (40:18–20; 41:7; 44:9–20). In this way Second Isaiah reassures the exiles that other nations' gods offer no contest whatsoever for the creator-liberator God of Israel. We have not seen this sort of argument for the non-existence of any other gods in Israelite traditions clearly datable to earlier periods. In Hosea and Deuteronomy we saw calls for Israel not to worship any other gods, yet those calls did not include the assumption that such gods did not exist. Yet here, in the context of Second Isaiah's reassurances to exiles, the prophet argues for just this point of view. Later traditions will take such **monotheism** for granted.

Isaiah 40–48, the first half of Second Isaiah, concludes with an argument from prophecy, an argument that only works if it was directly addressed to exiles and not to an earlier audience. God reminds the exiles of earlier prophecies that have come true, "former things" declared through the prophets. Through seeing the past fulfillment of these prophecies, this text insists, God's "stubborn" people should now be able to trust God's announcement of "new things" (Isa 48:4–6), including God's plans to destroy the sixth-century Neo-Babylonian empire (48:14). Even though it is theoretically possible that an eighth-century prophet, Isaiah, could have accurately predicted the demise of the Babylonian empire, he would not have addressed his eighth-century audience as if his prophecies about Judah lay in the past. Nor would Isaiah of the eighth century have called on his audience, still in Judah, to "go out from Babylonia, flee from Chaldea, declare with loud shouts ... 'God has freed God's servant, Jacob'" (Isa 48:20). These are words addressed by an unknown exilic prophet to a later audience of Judeans exiled in Babylonia, an audience longing to go home.

The second major section of Second Isaiah, Isaiah 49–55, focuses on the task of resettling and restoring Jerusalem. Like 40–48, these chapters start with a commissioning (49:1–6; cf. 40:1–8). This time, God commissions a "**servant**" who is to gather the exiled Israelites back to the LORD and reveal God's glory to the end of the earth (49:5–6). The identity of the "servant" in this and other passages in Second Isaiah has puzzled readers for centuries (see other "**servant songs**" in Isa 42:1–8; 50:4–9; 52:13–53:12 that likewise focus on a distinctive "servant"). In most of Isaiah 40–48, God addresses the whole people of Israel/Jacob as God's servant (Isa 41:8–9; 43:10; 44:1; 48:20). In other cases (e.g. Isa 52:13–53:12), however, the "servant/suffering servant" seems to be separate from the people, serving them (e.g. 49:5–6). Early Christ followers insisted that the servant of these passages was Jesus Christ. It is highly doubtful, however, that an exilic Judean prophet originally understood himself to be prophesying Jesus Christ. Instead, scholars of the Bible usually conclude that the "servant" in Second Isaiah was either a now unknown individual in the community of the exiles or stood for the community of Israel as a whole. There are grounds for both positions in Isaiah 40–55.

The servant passage in Isa 49:1–6 is followed by a speech where God addresses Jerusalem, personified once again as a woman. Echoing the book of Lamentations, she cries out that "the LORD has abandoned me, my Lord has forgotten me" (Isa 49:14; compare Lam 5:20). God then answers this lament with a remarkable use of parental imagery:

> Can a woman forget her nursing child,
> > Or her compassion for the child of her womb?
> Even if these ones forget,
> > I will never forget you. (Isa 49:15)

The exilic prophet uses mothers as the ultimate example of compassion and then says that God embodies such compassion and more toward the exiles.

Thus begins a series of speeches in Isaiah 49–55 that alternate between speeches of comfort to female Zion (50:1–3; 51:1–52:12; 54:1–17) and speeches by or about God's "servant" (50:4–11; 52:13–53:12). The climax of the songs about the servant is Isa 52:13–53:12, a poem about the shaming and exaltation of a "servant" who has borne the sicknesses of others. The corresponding climax of the songs about female Zion is Isaiah 54, a picture of God's eternal remarriage to Zion after abandoning her "for a brief moment" (54:7). This latter poem is a sharp contrast to Ezekiel's use of marriage imagery earlier in the exile to stress the people's wrongdoing and punishment (Ezekiel 16 and 23). The prophet in Isaiah 54 downplays any past troubles and uses the marriage metaphor to stress God's abiding love for God's beloved city.

The final chapter of Isaiah 40–55 features several distinctive promises to exiles in Babylonia. Where once the Davidic monarchy was promised an eternal covenant (2 Sam 7:12–16; 23:5; Pss 89:3–4, 20–21), now – in the wake of the destruction of the monarchy – God promises an eternal, Davidic covenant with the people themselves (55:3). Echoing the earlier affirmation that "the word of our God endures forever" (40:8), this concluding chapter affirms that God's word "will not return to [God] empty" (55:11). As a result, the exiles should "go out in joy and be led back in peace," watching the mountains and hills break forth in song to greet them on their way home (55:12–13). These extravagant promises, made on the eve of the destruction of the Babylonian empire, were on the minds of many exiles when they returned home with high hopes.

From Promise in the Prophets to Promise in Two Pentateuchal Sources: L and P

In this chapter we have seen a turn toward promise in the two main exilic prophets: Ezekiel and Second Isaiah. In Ezekiel, we could see a contrast between a primary focus on judgment before Jerusalem was destroyed and a primary focus on promise after Jerusalem was gone and the Judean exiles in Babylonia were despairing. In Second Isaiah we see a much more sustained focus on promise addressed to Judeans much later in the exile process. These promises were addressed to the despair and disorientation that we see in the exilic laments read at the outset of the chapter. The Zion that Judah thought was invulnerable was destroyed. Its leadership was scattered, its monarchy out of power. Many exiles seem to have doubted whether Yahweh would still care about them anymore, sinful as they were. The exiles needed powerful words of promise to maintain hope. The later prophecy of Ezekiel and the entire prophecy of Second Isaiah gave them such words of promise. These words acknowledged that Judah had not done Yahweh's will, but it assured them that Yahweh would liberate them anyway, for the sake of Yahweh's honor and to reveal Yahweh's power.

We turn now to another place where exiles found words of promise and hope: the narratives now found in the Pentateuch (Genesis–Deuteronomy). As we will see, these stories were not always together as they are now. Instead, during the exile there were two written stories about early Israel – a Priestly Source (P) created by priests and a slightly earlier, non-Priestly Source created by lay scribes (non-P or L, see below on "L"). Though both sources built on earlier materials, those materials were connected to each other and reshaped in light of the exile. In particular, both the lay and priestly scribal authors added an emphasis on God's promise to Israel's ancestors, a promise with some resemblance to promises seen in prophets such as Ezekiel and Second Isaiah. This promise, however, was expressed differently. Where Ezekiel and Second Isaiah spoke the promise in words of prophecy addressed directly to Judeans, the non-Priestly and the Priestly narratives spoke words of promise to exiles by telling stories of God's promises to their ancestors. Through revising and combining older traditions about Israel's life before the land, the authors of these

Pentateuchal sources reassured exiles who had been separated from their land. They implied that Yahweh would redeem them, just as Yahweh had redeemed their ancestors.

Traditions That Moses Wrote the Pentateuch

It can be a bit of a shock to learn that the Pentateuch was created out of earlier sources, especially since both Jewish and Christian traditions came to claim Moses as the author of the Pentateuch. This idea, however, is not biblical. Prose narrative texts like the Pentateuch were typically anonymous in the ancient Near East. This seems to be the case with the Pentateuch as well, which is not attributed to any author in ancient manuscripts. At the most, we see references in Deuteronomy to a "Torah" teaching that Moses gave to Israel just before the people entered the land (e.g. Deut 1:5; 31:9), but these references are focused on Moses's speeches in that book.

We do not see something like the idea of Mosaic authorship of the whole Pentateuch until post-biblical times, when Jews interacted with a more author-focused Greco-Roman culture. During this period, we start to see Jewish writers, such as Josephus and Philo, speak of Moses writing the Pentateuch. We also see mention – within a variety of early Jewish writings of the time (including the New Testament) – of the entire Pentateuch as "the Law of Moses" (the Greek word for law, *nomos*, here taking the place of the Hebrew word for teaching, *Torah*). The tradition developed further from there, with subsequent rabbinic interpretations working to explain how the Pentateuch, even including the report of Moses's death and burial (Deut 34:5–8), might all have been written by Moses himself.

Promise-Centered Storytelling in the Lay Pentateuchal Source (L)

READING   **Genesis 12–16, 18–22; Exod 19:2–24:14 and 32:1–34:35.**

We start with what will be termed here the "**L**" source. Most scholars term this material "non-Priestly" (focusing on the agreed-upon distinction of it from P), but this designation only says what this material is *not*. The label "L" corresponds to "P" and signals some things that we can affirm about the non-Priestly material of the Pentateuch. To begin, the L non-Priestly material appears to have been composed by lay scribes (perhaps [former] royal scribes) and features the "elders" as the main leadership group of the generation who lived during the time of Moses. These lay scribes added multiple layers of later expansions to the earlier compositions that they connected to each other. Sometimes these L layers are mere extensions of earlier stories (see the textbox below on the story of Jacob at Bethel). Some other L materials might be longer narratives, such as the non-P Abraham story as a whole (and yet later L additions to it, like Genesis 15). Either way, the designation "L" says three things about the non-Priestly materials: it indicates that these materials were reshaped by supplementary layers, the fact that these layers were written by lay scribes, and the dating of these layers to relatively later periods of Israel's history, especially the Babylonian exile.

The non-Priestly materials of the Pentateuch include texts like the following: the older non-Priestly primeval history (Gen 2:1–4:26; 6:1–4; a flood story starting with 6:5–8; 7:1–5, 10, 12 and concluding with Gen 8:20–2; 9:18–27), a story about Abraham (Genesis 12–16, 18–22), a revised form of the northern Jacob and Joseph compositions (most of Genesis 25–50), and a transformed version of older stories about Moses leading Israel out of Egypt to the wilderness. If you want to imagine this source, try to picture a text up through Numbers that included stories such as the non-P primeval history, and most stories about Abraham and other ancestors (e.g. Genesis 12–16, 18–22) along with parts of the Moses story (some of Exodus 1–34; Numbers 11–24), but did not have stories such as the Priestly creation story (Gen 1:1–2:3), the genealogy in Genesis 5, the covenant of circumcision in Genesis 17, etc. We have no separate manuscript of these non-Priestly materials, but scholars have agreed on their basic identification for over one hundred and fifty years.

This idea can be a challenge to grasp at first: the idea that biblical stories set in a much earlier time (e.g. in the primeval period or time of Abraham, Moses) are a combination of textual layers from long after that time – both earlier compositions (e.g. the northern Jacob and Joseph compositions) and later (L) layers. Previous chapters of this textbook have discussed some of the older non-Priestly materials about creation and flood (Chapter 3) and writings about Jacob, Joseph, and Moses-exodus (Chapter 4). The key idea in this chapter is the following: all of the non-P texts, whether older ones from the pre-exilic period or exilic additions to those compositions, have been processed through the filter of the experience of exile, being connected to each other and expanded upon by L(ay) scribes. Seeing this traumatic background can help us read them better.

We focus here on the L (re)shaping of the Abraham story as a promise-focused bridge between an earlier non-Priestly primeval history (see Chapter 3) and earlier compositions about Jacob and Joseph (see Chapter 4). The figure of Abraham seems to have become a particularly important figure during the exile. Consider, for example, Second Isaiah, where the prophet calls on Judean exiles to look to Abraham for a picture of the kind of divine restoration that they would soon experience:

> Consider the rock from which you were cut,
> the quarry from which you were dug.
> Look to Abraham your father
> and Sarah who bore you.

He was but one person when I called him,
  but I blessed him and made him numerous.
Yahweh will comfort Zion,
  will bring comfort to her ruins;
he will turn her desert into an Eden
  and her wastelands into the garden of Yahweh.
Joy and gladness will be found in her,
  thanksgiving and the sound of song. (Isa 51:1–3)

The non-P stories about Abraham in Genesis, though built on earlier traditions about him, can be seen as providing a narrative form of the comfort that
Second Isaiah offered exiles. This comfort starts with the following text where
Yahweh commissions Abraham to depart from his homeland and promises to
multiply, bless, and protect him:

Go now from your country, your kindred, and your father's house to the land
that I will show you. And I will make you a great nation, bless you, and make
your name great. Be a blessing! I will bless those who bless you, and I will curse
anyone who treats you lightly. And all clans of the ground will bless themselves
by you. (Gen 12:1–3)

This promise text is the linchpin connecting the non-P primeval history to the
following ancestral materials. Its focus on blessing to Abraham stands as a contrast to the curses that occurred across multiple parts of the primeval history
(e.g. Gen 3:17–19; 4:11–12; 5:29; 9:25).

The following non-P narratives then tell of Abraham and Sarah's journey
to the promised land, reception of Yahweh's promise of that land to them (Gen
12:7), and of God's initial fulfillment of promises of protection and blessing as
Abraham and Sarah lived among foreigners. In reading these dramatic stories,
it is easy to get caught up in the narrative and overlook how much these stories
mirror the experience of later Judeans. For the narratives about Abraham and
Sarah do not just tell of Yahweh's promises to vulnerable, landless ancestors of
Israel. They also vividly depict the struggle of those ancestors to trust and
believe in those promises. Immediately after Yahweh's promise of protection in
Gen 12:2–3 (see the discussion of this text at the end of the chapter), the story
then tells of Abraham's attempt to protect himself in Pharaoh's court by passing Sarah off as his sister (Gen 12:10–20). Moreover, the broader narrative puts
the future of the promise in doubt, since it starts with a note about Sarah's
infertility (Gen 11:30) and it is thus unclear who will be Abraham's heir.
Abraham and Sarah work to solve this problem themselves by having Abraham
impregnate Hagar, Sarah's female slave, but she and her son end up receiving
promises of their own (Gen 16:10–12; see also 21:13, 18). In the end, Abraham
and Sarah do succeed in having a child together, Isaac (Gen 18, 21), but Yahweh
then tests Abraham by commanding him to offer Isaac as a burnt offering (Gen
22). This awful command for Abraham to sacrifice the son who represents his
future echoes Yahweh's initial command for him to leave his family of the past:

Initial command for Abraham to leave his family of the past	Concluding command for Abraham to sacrifice his family of the future through Isaac
Go now from your country, your kindred, and your father's house to the land that I will show you. (Gen 12:1)	Take your son, your only one, whom you love, Isaac, and go to the land of Moriah, and offer him as a burnt offering on a mountain that I will show you. (Gen 22:2)

The narrative builds up suspense by slowing down as Abraham prepares to slit Isaac's throat (22:7–10). Yet just before Abraham kills Isaac, a messenger of Yahweh stays his hand, proclaiming that Abraham has proven to be one who fears God by being prepared to offer up his only son (Gen 22:11–12).

On one level, this is simply a powerful story about human characters that almost anyone in any time could relate to. This helps explain why it has been read and reread in Jewish, Christian, and Muslim contexts. On another level, this story depicts Abraham facing a dire threat to his future that was analogous to that faced by later Judeans under imperial domination. We cannot be sure exactly where an ancient Abraham tradition stops and later reshaping of the story begins. Nevertheless, we can say that non-P stories like these about Abraham are saturated with themes particularly characteristic of later Judean texts. Whatever their earlier background, they have been reshaped into an account of "Abraham your father, Sarah who bore you" (see Second Isaiah) that could encourage and instruct later Israelites facing imperial trauma.

Traumatized individuals and groups often tend toward self-blame – trying to find a reason for their suffering in something that they did wrong to cause it. This also seems to have been the case for Judeans in exile. They felt Yahweh's anger at them, and many wondered if Yahweh could still live with them after their misdeeds (in their view) had caused the destruction of the Temple and exile into Babylonia. As a result, both Ezekiel and Second Isaiah had to reassure the exiles, who doubted that Yahweh would redeem them, *despite their past and present shortcomings*. Similar themes run through the Lay Source version of the stories of the patriarchs. Like the exiles whom Ezekiel and Second Isaiah addressed, so also the Abraham character in Genesis – the ancestral model of an exile in the L Source – doubts God's promise of protection and lies about Sarah being his wife (Gen 12:10–20; 20:1–18). He also shows doubts concerning God's promise of a son by arranging to have a son through Hagar (Genesis 16). Later on, as a result of the addition of the promise theme to the older Jacob narrative (see the Special Topics Box on the next page), the stories about Jacob in L now depict him as receiving the promise (Gen 28:13–15) despite having cheated his brother and tricking his father (earlier trickster narratives in Genesis 25, 27). Yahweh's promise apparently does not depend on the absolute virtue of its recipients.

The Story of Jacob at Bethel as an Example of the Addition of Promise to an Older Story

Many scholars now think that the speech in which God gives Abraham's promise to Jacob in Gen 28:13–14 was added secondarily into a story about Jacob at Bethel that focused on Yahweh's promise of protection to Jacob as he fled his homeland (Gen 28:15, 20–22). At least part of the material in **boldface** probably was added to an original story about the "gate of heaven" at Bethel. Try reading the story without the boldface elements. How is it different?

> Jacob came upon a place and spent the night there because the sun was going down. He took a stone and placed his head on it, and lay down in that place. He dreamed, and, look!, a stairway was founded on the earth with its top in heaven. And, behold, divine messengers were going up and down it.
>
> And, look!, Yahweh was standing on it and said, **"I am Yahweh, the god of Abraham, your father and the god of Isaac. The land on which you are lying I will give to you and your children. Your descendants will be as numerous as the dust of the earth, and they will spread out to the west, east, north and south. All clans of the earth shall bless themselves by you and your descendants. [Gen 28:13–14]** Look! I will be with you. I will protect you continually as you go onward and return you to this place. Indeed, I will not abandon you until I have done what I have said to you."
>
> And Jacob woke up from his sleep and said, "Look, Yahweh is in this place, and I did not know it." And he was afraid and said, "how awesome this place is! It is nothing other than the house of God and the gate of heaven." He called that place Bethel [Hebrew: "house of God/El"]. It had formerly been called Luz.
>
> And Jacob made a vow, "If God is with me, protecting me on this way on which I am going, giving me bread to eat and clothes to wear, and I return in peace to the house of my father, Yahweh will be my God and this stone which I have set as a pillar will be a house of God and I will offer a tithe to you of all that you give me." (Gen 28:12–22)

Before the addition of the Abraham-promise theme, the older Jacob Bethel story (in regular type) was addressed to Israelites of the north. It connected the northern kingdom's royal sanctuary at Bethel, "the house of God and gate of heaven," with Jacob, the hero of the Israelites. Now, with the addition of the Abrahamic promise, the revised story connects this Jacob to the promise of land and blessing to Abraham (Gen 12:2–3, 7), assuring later Israelites of God's promise ultimately to them.

The L Source story of Yahweh's covenant with Israel at Sinai (Exodus 19–24, 32–4) provides the clearest illustration of this theme of Yahweh's steadfast love of a disobedient Israel. It stresses Yahweh's forgiveness of Israel even in the wake of Israel's building of the golden calf. This is not an easy forgiveness. The making of the golden calf in Exod 32:1–6 is depicted in the L text as an awful act, one that, point by point, reverses the covenant that Israel just made with Yahweh (Exodus 19–24). Where Yahweh had just led Israel out of Egypt (Exod 19:4), the people now think Moses did (Exod 32:1); where Yahweh specifically prohibited making "gods of gold and silver" (Exod 20:22–3), the people now feel the need to make a golden calf to lead them in the wilderness (Exod 32:1); and where the previous covenant with Yahweh was sealed with a feast, "whole offerings" and "shared offerings" (Exod 24:5), the very same things seal the new covenant that the Israelites, including Aaron, make with the golden calf (Exod 32:5–6). Faced with this golden calf anti-covenant, Yahweh of this L story is ready to destroy all of the Israelite people and start all over with Moses (Exod 32:7–10). It is only after Moses reminds Yahweh of the promises to the patriarchs and pleads with Yahweh to think about how the Egyptians would perceive such destruction (Exod 32:11–13) that Yahweh changes his mind (Exod 32:14). Punishment still comes. Moses recruits the Levites – who up until this point in the story are just another tribe – and their first act is to kill every Israelite that their sword can reach (Exod 32:26–9). In addition, Yahweh brings a plague on the people (Exod 32:35). Nevertheless, Yahweh eventually comes back to dwell amidst Israel via the "tent of meeting" (Exod 33:7–17), and makes a new covenant with Israel (Exodus 34).

Thus, like the more hopeful prophecies in Ezekiel and Second Isaiah, the L Source stresses Yahweh's ability to work with his people *no matter what they do*. To be sure, the L Source stories and exilic prophecies insist that God gets angry about disobedience and imposes consequences. Nevertheless, as in Ezekiel, Yahweh's ultimate promise to the people does not depend on their virtue. Yahweh saves Israel for the sake of his reputation ("name") and/or his promise to their ancestors (Exod 32:11–13). On this basis, the exiles can trust that Yahweh will lead them out of Babylonian bondage and back into their homeland, despite the fact that they have not always lived up to Yahweh's expectations for them, do not do so, and will not do so.

Basics on the non-P (L) Source
Outline: Yahweh's promise-based, unbreakable covenant

I	Gift of ancestral promise-covenant in the wake of repeated primeval problems	Genesis*
	A Problems with creation and post-flood	Genesis 1–11* (non-P parts)
	B Gift of promise to Abraham and heirs	Genesis 12–50* (non-P parts)
II	Creation + preservation of Moses-led, covenant people	Parts of Exodus*, Numbers*

Outline: Yahweh's promise-based, unbreakable covenant

* Here and elsewhere, an asterisk indicates that *some parts* of the textual ranges contain relevant (P) texts.

Exile (building on earlier, pre-exilic compositions). **Date**

If we focus on the later L materials within the non-Priestly layer and not probable pre-exilic compositions that the L layers expanded upon, the emphasis seems to be on the gift of Yahweh's covenant despite any shortcomings in the recipients. We see this as early as Yahweh's gift and transmission of the covenant to Abraham, Isaac, and Jacob despite their misdeeds and occasional lack of trust. Then, in the Moses story, Yahweh perseveres in giving a covenant to Israel despite their making of the golden calf (Exodus 32) and lack of trust in the promise of conquest (Num 14:11–25), largely on the basis of the earlier promises to the patriarchs. **Themes**

MORE INFORMATION: THE GAP BETWEEN ANCESTORS AND MOSES

Scholars note that the non-Priestly texts in the Pentateuch, aside from a few exceptions such as Genesis 15 or Exodus 32, do not explicitly link the time of the ancestors in Genesis with the time of Moses. This is an indicator to many that writings about the ancestors were not linked with those about Moses until a very late time. Before this time, the stories about Jacob–Joseph, and possibly even those about Abraham and Isaac, stood separately from the Moses story. They were an alternative account of how Israel became related to Yahweh and came into the land.

Thus the exilic (L) link of the primeval, ancestral, and Moses traditions with each other was important. It took what were once competing traditions and put one (the ancestral traditions) before the other (the Moses traditions).

J (the "Yahwistic Source"), E (the "Elohistic Source"), and the Documentary Hypothesis

Throughout the twentieth century, most bible specialists believed that the material discussed here as non-P comprised two, long sources from the early pre-exilic period: a **J Source** composed in Judah around the time of Solomon and an **E Source** composed in (northern) Israel sometime in the eighth century. The J Source or **Yahwistic Source** was so called because it frequently used the divine name "Yahweh," which, in the German language of those who pioneered this theory, is spelled with an initial "J." The E Source or **Elohistic Source** was so called because it more frequently preferred the divine name "Elohim," which means "god" in Hebrew. For example, earlier scholars maintained that the bulk of Genesis 12–16 and 18–19 came from the hypothesized J Source (note the predominance of "LORD" = Yahweh), while parallel stories about Abraham found in Genesis 20–2 were from E (note the predominance of "God" in these chapters).

Problems for the older hypothesis

A number of scholars still find this idea of J and E persuasive. Nevertheless, many specialists in the study of the Pentateuch (including these authors) have abandoned this approach, for multiple reasons. The first problem for the idea of early J and E sources has to do with identifying them in the first place. The non-P material

lacks widespread indictors that it was created out of interwoven, parallel sources. For example, we do not see the sorts of extensive doublets and contrasting perspective that allowed scholars to achieve such consensus in distinguishing a Priestly layer from the non-P materials. As a result, aside from the Abraham story and a few other texts, scholars have had a lot of trouble gaining consensus on what might have been the contents of J and E.

The second problem has to do with the early dating often assigned to these hypothesized "J" and "E." If such large, tenth- and ninth-century Pentateuchal sources had existed, it is hard to know why we see so few references to the three patriarchs and God's promise to them before the book of Deuteronomy (mostly seventh century and later) and Ezekiel (sixth century). Hosea, for example, is an early prophet from the north who seems to refer to the Jacob story (Hos 12:3–5, 13) along with the Moses-exodus tradition (e.g. Hos 12:14). But there is no sign that Hosea is familiar with Abraham and the idea of a promise to him, Isaac, and Jacob. Instead, it seems that the demonstrably early material in early prophetic books (e.g. Hosea, Amos, eighth-century Isaiah, Micah 1–3) knows nothing of the broader promise theme that unites the non-P parts of the Pentateuch, while we do see this theme more and more frequently in Deuteronomy, Ezekiel, and Second Isaiah (Isaiah 40–55).

Terminology

Scholars who build on this older approach would call the non-Priestly texts under discussion here "JE," a term for the combination of the hypothesized J and E documents. Those specialists who no longer find the J and E hypothesis plausible refer more neutrally to the same group of texts with the term used in this textbook, "non-P" (for non-Priestly). Back when the great majority of scholars thought that P and the book of Deuteronomy (considered as source D of the Pentateuch) were preceded by early J and E sources, this theory was termed the "**Documentary Hypothesis**," and all students were taught that the Pentateuch had four sources – J, E, D, and P. Now J and E have dropped from that scholarly consensus and only **D** and **P** remain as agreed-upon, identifiable sources from the older hypothesis. That is the position adopted in this textbook.

For contrasting arguments for a revival of the Documentary Hypothesis in new ("Neo-Documentarian") form see Joel Baden, *The Composition of the Pentateuch: Renewing the Documentary Hypothesis* (New Haven: Yale University Press, 2012).

An Alternative Vision for Exiles in the Priestly Pentateuchal Source (P)

Gen 1:1–2:3,17:1–27; Exodus 6:2–8 and skim Exodus 25–31 and 35–40.

READING

Not everyone in the exile, however, would have appreciated the depiction of Israel's early history in the non-P/L Source. Alongside the lay elders, there was another prominent group of exilic leaders – the priests – and they do not come off well in the L Source, especially in the L Source story of the covenant at Sinai. In general, many lower-ranking priests traced their ancestry back to Jacob's son Levi, and the leading priests of the exile and post-exile traced their descent to a particular Levite, Aaron. The non-P (L) Sinai story does not positively portray either Aaron or the descendants of Levi as a group. In it Aaron helps the people make the golden calf (Exod 32:1–6) and later challenges the authority of Moses (Numbers 12). Moreover, the non-P Sinai narrative depicts the Levitical priesthood as being founded in blood, with their first act being to kill as many of their fellow Israelites as their swords could reach (Exod 32:25–29). In sum, the pre-P (L) Sinai narrative depicted the priesthood, particularly the priests claiming descent from Aaron (see, e.g., Ezra 7:1–5), as founded in idolatry and the shedding of Israelites' blood – hardly the kind of picture the priests would want to paint of themselves.

These and other concerns prompted the leading Aaronide priests in exile to formulate their own story of Israel's history before it had taken possession of the land, a story aimed at replacing the pre-P/L version of events with one more favorable to the priests and their concerns. Although the present Pentateuch now has texts from this **P Source** or **Priestly Source** intertwined with the L Source, P probably stood separately from L when it was originally composed in the exilic period. There are too many repeated narrations of events in L and P for one of them to have been created as a supplement to the other, and there are several instances where the original point of a Priestly text is only clear when it is read separately from its Lay Source counterpart. Consider, for example, the divergent accounts in L and P of the reasons for Jacob's departure from Canaan. The L Source version of this story is the old trickster tale about Jacob stealing his father's blessing and fleeing Esau's murderous wrath (Gen 27:1–45). The (later) P version of these events aimed to provide a different reason: Esau had married foreign wives (Gen 26:34–5), those wives had been awful to Rebekah (Gen 27:46), and so Isaac blessed Jacob (on purpose!) and sent him homeward to get a proper wife (Gen 28:1–6). Though they are now separated from one another by the older trickster story (Gen 27:1–45), the P texts that give this alternative explanation connect well together (Gen 26:34–5; 27:46–28:6). They probably originally stood apart from the trickster story in Gen 27:1–45 and were designed to replace it.

Thus, we can learn something about this exilic Priestly Source when we read it as a separate document. When the P Source was separate from the L/non-P materials, it chronicled God's involvement with the world in three major stages: (1) creation, (2) the flood and following covenant with Noah, and (3) the covenant with Abraham and eventual creation at Sinai of Israel out of the heirs to Abraham's promise. The first stage, found in Gen 1:1–2:3 along with most of Genesis 5, is God's creation of an orderly and peaceful universe, a cosmos crowned by God's creation of godlike humans to rule earth's other creatures (Gen 1:26–31). The second stage, found in Priestly texts scattered across Genesis 6–9 (such as 6:9–22 and 9:1–17), describes God's actions after this creation was violated by violence: God's destruction of almost all life through a flood, God's rescue of Noah's family and other animals, and God's making of a covenant with Noah and the rest of life not to bring such a flood again. The third and most important stage in P is God's creation of the holy community of Israel. This starts with God's making of a special covenant of circumcision with Abraham (Genesis 17), a covenant in which God gives Abraham and his heirs a version of the creation blessing given in Genesis 1 (Gen 17:6–8; compare Gen 1:27–8). Other Priestly texts in Genesis show the passing of this blessing on to Jacob (not Esau; Gen 26:34–5; 27:46–28:5; 35:9–15) and trace the genealogies of Abraham's offspring (Gen 25:7–18; 35:22–6; 36:1–43). Jacob in the P Source next goes to Egypt, where his descendants multiply into the people of Israel (Exod 1:1–7) and are oppressed by Pharaoh (Exod 1:13–14; 2:23–5). God then calls Moses and Aaron – in Priestly texts – to lead Israel out of Egypt through plagues and the dividing of the Red Sea (Exod 6:2–7:13; etc.). This prepares for the Priestly story of events and instructions given at Mount Sinai (most of Exodus 25 through Numbers 10). There God works through Moses to build a wilderness sanctuary, a "tabernacle," in which God can dwell (Exod 24:15–31:17; 35:1–40:33) and then instructs Israel (through Moses) on how it can become a holy community gathered round the tabernacle (Leviticus and Num

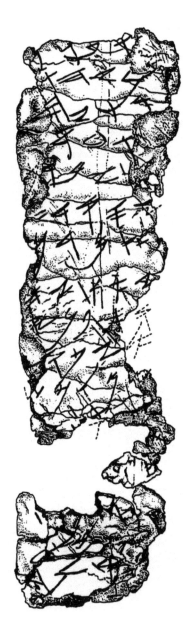

FIGURE 6.3
Silver amulet, possibly dating to a period around the fall of Jerusalem. It contains a version of
the priestly blessing found in Num 6:24–6.

1:1–10:10). The other main narratives that were part of P focus on God's confir-
mation of Moses's and Aaron's leadership of this new, holy community.

This mass of Priestly material contains some of the oldest texts in the
Pentateuch. One Priestly text, the priestly blessing in Num 6:24–6, has been
found on an ancient silver amulet, our earliest copy of a text now in the Bible
(see Figure 6.3), and scholars have found signs that other P laws and even some

narratives may date from before the exile. Nevertheless, the overall sweep of the Priestly narrative shows several signs of being shaped in the exilic or early post-exilic periods:

Basics on the P Source

Outline	I	Expanded genealogy: creation and promise	
		A Elohim: creation–re-creation	Gen 1:1–2:3; 5:1–9:28*; 11:10–26
		B El-Shaddai: the Abrahamic covenant	Gen 11:27–50:26*
	II	Yahweh: Moses + Aaron-led pilgrimage to the land	Exodus 1–19*
		A Pilgrimage to Sinai	
		B Sinai indwelling and instruction	Exodus 20– Numbers 10*
		C Pilgrimage from Sinai to the land	Numbers 11–36*

Date   Exile into post-exile (with short pre-exilic sources).

Themes: shifts in the divine name   As indicated in the outline above, some of the shifts in the Priestly Source correspond to shifts in the divine designation that it uses for God. In the primeval period God is known as *Elohim* (Hebrew for "God") and makes with Noah and all life a covenant that is marked by a rainbow. During the ancestral period God appears to Abraham as *El-Shaddai* (Hebrew for "God Almighty") and makes a covenant with him that is marked with circumcision and passed on by Abraham's heirs, Isaac and Jacob. In the final period, God appears to Moses and the rest of Israel as Yahweh (see the P version of Moses's call in Exod 6:2–8). The centerpoint of this period is Israel's stay at Sinai, where the tabernacle is built, the priesthood of Aaron and his sons is established, and Yahweh's glory comes down to dwell amidst Israel.

More information: P as "redaction" or separate "source"?   The bulk of past and present scholars believes that a shorter form of this Priestly narrative once existed as a separate source, independent of the non-P texts with which it is now combined. Others, however, believe that the Priestly texts of the Pentateuch were written from the outset as an expansion of the non-P texts and never existed separately. This alternative perspective – P as "redaction" – can make a difference in how one understands the structure and themes of the first Priestly Pentateuch. It becomes another priestly layer (or set of Priestly layers) beyond the "L" layers that were discussed above.

For your purposes, it is not crucial to resolve this issue one way or the other. To some extent, the Priestly source itself seems to have had some layers, much like non-P. Texts emphasizing the holiness of all Israel in Leviticus 17–26, for example, are now seen by many scholars to be part of a distinctive "Holiness" layer of Priestly material found across different parts of the Pentateuch. At the same time, the previously mentioned doublets of P and non-P stories suggest that some early form of a P source – one with its own narratives of creation, flood, Moses, etc. – originally existed separate from the non-P narratives that it parallels.

- Where Deuteronomy and other Deuteronomistic historical books *argue* for the idea that sacrifice to Yahweh can only happen in one place, the Priestly narratives appear to presuppose this. P does not describe any sacrifice by Noah or the patriarchs before the establishment of the tabernacle at Mount Sinai.
- The P narrative focuses before Sinai on practices that could be carried out in exile and were particularly important then, such as circumcision (Genesis 17), an ancient form of Passover celebration that was celebrated at home (Exod 12:1–20), and Sabbath (Exodus 16).
- Consistent with tendencies of exilic communities to focus on communal boundaries, the P document includes a prominent emphasis on the importance of ethnic purity and the problems with intermarriage, an emphasis seen particularly clearly in the story of Isaac's rejection of Esau because of intermarriage and his sending of Jacob to Haran to get a proper wife (Gen 26:34–5; 27:46–28:9).
- The P document as a whole leads up to the story of God's creation of the wilderness tabernacle with the priests of Aaron at its head. This points to an exilic time when the monarchy is no longer a living institution, and its accoutrements (e.g. a crown; Exod 28:36–8) are assumed by the priests.

Basics on the Book of Leviticus

I	Establishment of the tabernacle cult	1–10	**Outline**
	A Instructions for sacrifices	1–7	
	B Establishment of priesthood subject to instructions	8–10	
II	Establishment of holy people	11–26	
	A Purity rules	11–15	
	B Holiness Code	16–26	

Exilic to early post-exilic (building on pre-exilic sources).   **Date**

Leviticus now stands at the center of the Pentateuch, and it represents the **Themes** center of Priestly teaching. Though the book starts with specific instructions for priestly sacrifice (Leviticus 1–7), it concludes with rules for creating a holy, priest-like people (Leviticus 16–26, sometimes termed the "Holiness Code"). Many eating and purity rules, once meant only for priests, are extended in Leviticus to the whole people of Israel. These cultic rules are not seen as a burden in the book or difficult to follow. Instead, they are an affirmation of the special, particularly holy character of Yahweh's beloved people.

The language and concerns of this Priestly document are closest to exilic texts like Ezekiel and Second Isaiah. Like Second Isaiah, the author of the P story encourages exiles to return to the land, in this case through emphasizing God's power in the exodus, the importance of the land in the promise (see Exod 6:2–8), and God's punishment of those who lack enough belief to embrace God's promise and return (Num 13:32; 14:36–7). In these ways and others, the narratives of P show the impact of the Babylonian exile, along with hopes of return, on the Priestly understanding of Israel's history before the conquest. Though the authors of this P document drew freely on pre-exilic texts of various kinds, the whole that they put together is a distinctively exilic story for exiles about ancient Israel before the people had a land.

These exilic emphases show up already at the outset of the P source in the creation account with which it opens (Gen 1:1–2:3). The whole structure of this account is oriented around a seven-day scheme that climaxes in God's observance of the Sabbath (Gen 2:1–3). We see a similar emphasis on the Sabbath in Ezekiel (Ezek 20:12–24; 22:8, 26; 23:38). In addition, the text transfers royal traits to non-royal figures, much as in Second Isaiah. In this case, the text builds on ancient ideas in Egyptian and Mesopotamian royal theology that the king was made as the image of God; he was made to serve as the deity's representative among humans, ruling them (see the More on Method textbox on "History of Religions" below). The description of the creation of humanity in Gen 1:26–7 takes these ideas and applies them to humanity in general, both men and women. Indeed, many translations overlook the fact that the Hebrew of this passage explicitly connects the creation of humanity as God's image with their destiny to rule creation. God's speech to the divine council (note the plural address) makes this clear, "Let us make humanity as our image, similar to our likeness *so that* they may rule the fish of the sea, the birds of the heavens, the cattle and all the earth, and all the creatures creeping on the earth" (Gen 1:26, emphasis added)" (Gen 1:26).

MORE ON METHOD: INSIGHTS FROM HISTORY OF RELIGIONS

Often we can learn more about the ancient images, metaphors, and ideas in the Bible through looking at other ancient religious ideas and practices studied as part of what is sometimes termed "**history of religions**." An example is the tantalizing reference to humans being made "as the image of God" in Gen 1:26–7.

The king as the image of god in the ancient Near East
Texts in both Mesopotamia and Egypt depict the king as an image of god, representing that god on earth much as a divine statue would. For example, one Mesopotamian letter to the king says:

> The father of the king, amy lord, was the image of [the god] Bel, and the king, my lord, is likewise the image of Bel.

Similarly, an Egyptian text has the god Amun proclaim about the king:

> You are my beloved son, who came forth out of my love, my image that I set on earth. I let you rule the land in peace.

How this might inform a reading of Gen 1:26–7
These royal ideas are applied to all of humanity in Gen 1:26–7, both the idea of humans being made as divine images and the idea of this divine image being a mark of their authority to rule others.

MORE ON METHOD: ECOLOGICAL BIBLICAL CRITICISM

Ecological biblical criticism (also known as ecological hermeneutics) is a set of approaches that analyze the biblical text and interpretations of it in relation to present ecological crises. In an influential 1967 article in *Science* magazine ("The Historical Roots of Our Ecologic Crisis"), Lynn White Jr. argued that texts like Genesis 1 (with its description of humans as divine images) had helped form "the most anthropocentric religion the world has seen" and thus were among the roots of the ecological crisis. A number of biblical scholars responded to White by arguing that Genesis 1 actually depicts a human responsibility to rule *and care* for creation. Nevertheless, such arguments have been undermined by the lack of any emphasis in Genesis 1 on the need for human care for creation and by the presence of elements in Genesis 1 – such as its uncritical affirmation of human population growth (Gen 1:28) – that are ecologically problematic. In more recent years, biblical scholars have looked at a broader range of biblical texts and interpretations of them. Moreover, though the bulk of ecological interpretations of the Bible have attempted to provide earth-affirming rereadings of biblical texts, some scholars also recognize ways that the Bible – shaped for a quite different time – can sometimes be a problematic resource for addressing current environmental challenges.

One good source for more of an overview of past readings of the Bible in relation to ecology and proposals of some new rereadings is Hilary Marlow, *Biblical Prophets and Contemporary Environmental Ethics: Re-reading Amos, Hosea, and First Isaiah* (New York: Oxford University Press, 2009).

History and Fiction

By this point many readers may be wondering, "But what about what actually happened with Abraham or at Sinai? Does all this just mean that the exiles made all these stories up?" To this, the answer is both "no" and "yes." The answer is "no," because ancient peoples, including ancient Israel, almost always built new stories out of older ones. Especially with respect to stories about people (rather than gods), ancient authors almost always started with a tradition – whether oral or written – about a given person and then built on that tradition. They did not "make them all up." Yet there is also a sense in which the answer to the question is "yes." Ancient authors did make up certain things. Unlike many contemporary historians, these ancient authors felt free to embellish, modify, and extend the traditions given to them. In light of their experience of imperial trauma, for example, Judean authors found new, promise-centered ways to tell stories about Jacob and Moses, ways that would never have occurred to them before. They saw these stories through the lens of their community's need for resilience and the insights into themselves and God that they were learning in exile. As a result, they retold, extended, and connected these stories in light of these trauma-forged truths, in light of what they believed "must have happened."

Now we no longer can untangle later "truths" learned in exile or other periods from the kinds of "historical truth" about Israel's early history that contemporary readers often want to know. Through using both data from archaeology and analysis of non-biblical literature, we can affirm that the traditions in the Pentateuch probably have some kind of historical core. Later storytellers would not have made up characters such as Abraham and Sarah. Certainly, exiles would not have created a deliverer figure like Moses with an Egyptian name and foreign wives. Nevertheless, it appears that the stories as we have them now, including almost all their dialogue and other details, reflect their being written (or reshaped) in later periods of Israel's history. As a result, they are more useful as sources for the "truths" learned by Israelites in these later periods than in reconstructing historical "truths" about the times of Abraham and/or Moses. We might wish we knew exactly what Sarah said to God or Moses said to Pharaoh, but the biblical texts about them are not good sources for this. They *can* tell us, however, what later Israelites had to say to each other about their identity as a people and God's intentions toward them.

Consider this in relation to a concrete example: the non-P/L story of covenant at Sinai discussed above (Exodus 19–24, 32–4). Contemporary readers of this story could argue endlessly about whether or not it actually happened. Yet in the end, such arguments miss the larger point of the story. The story that we now have is addressed to Israel of the "thousandth" generation, long after Sinai, an Israel who wonders – as in the laments discussed above – whether God will be eternally angry for past disobedience or will turn and save God's people. The answer given in this story is a decisive affirmation of God's intent to save the people no matter what. This text, with its "yes" to God's mercy, has been absolutely central to Jewish worship and thought, and this affirmation of God's unconditional relationship with Israel can be read by Christians as an anticipation of God's broader unconditional grace toward the world as seen through Jesus Christ. Ultimately, such "truths" about God in Judaism and Christianity are much more central to the ongoing significance of the Bible than specific historical "truths" that could be affirmed or uncovered using modern historical methods. Moreover, these important ideas in ancient biblical texts can be missed if the debates about them all focus on whether or not the events described in them actually happened.

FOCUS TEXT

Gen 12:1–3

We conclude by taking a brief look at God's first speech to Abraham, still called "Abram" at this point, in Gen 12:1–3. This text, which was discussed above as a linchpin in the L layer of non-P Genesis, has two main parts: Yahweh's command to Abram to "go now from your country, your kindred, and your father's house to the land that I will show you" (Gen 12:1), and the following promises that Yahweh will make Abram into "a great nation," make his "name great," and grant him abundant blessing (Gen 12:2–3). These promises echo a more ancient prayer for kings, seen in Ps 72:17, that the king be blessed, have his "name" (reputation) endure forever, and be so fortunate that others "bless themselves by him." This means that the king will be such a paradigm of good luck that others wish on themselves the kind of blessing that the king enjoys (for example, "may God make me as blessed and fortunate as King David of Israel"). Now, in the climactic promise in Gen 12:3, Abram is promised that he, like such kings, will be such an example of blessing that all "clans of the earth" will look to him and bless themselves by him, so that people in other nations might say something like, "may God bless me like Abram and more so."

This promise is echoed in various forms throughout other parts of Genesis (Gen 22:15–18; 26:2–5; 28:13–15), yet Christians and Jews disagree in a basic way on how to interpret the final part about Abram's blessing and other nations: "all the clans of the earth shall ..." Many Jews follow the lead of Rashi, one of the greatest Jewish commentators on the Bible, who followed a translation much like that given above: that all clans of the earth shall "bless themselves by" Abram; that is, wish on themselves a blessing as good as the one he has. Understood this way, the rest of the Pentateuch following Gen 12:1–3 is a story of God's (partial) fulfillment of the special promises of blessing on Abraham and his offspring, especially God's blessing and protection of God's chosen people, Israel. In contrast, many Christians follow the lead of Paul in understanding this text as a promise to Abram that "all the gentiles shall be blessed through you" (Gal 3:8), that blessing will flow through Abram – by way of Jesus Christ – to the other nations of the earth. Understood this way, the rest of the Pentateuch following Gen 12:1–3 is focused not on God's blessing and protection of Israel per se, but on the way the people of Israel, Abram's offspring, are a medium of blessing for the other nations of the earth. Thus these two options for translating the promise in Gen 12:3, both of which are possible in Hebrew, lead to very different understandings of the whole Pentateuch. Rashi's reading remains closest to the emphasis on the people of Israel in the rest of the Hebrew Torah. Paul's reading – reflected in many contemporary translations of Gen 12:3 – reinterprets Abraham's promise in the context of a broader Christian Bible that includes Jesus Christ.

Turning to historical interpretation, Gen 12:1–3 looks quite different depending on whether one thinks it was written by Solomon's scribes or by exilic authors. Some would see Gen 12:1–3 as part of an early continuation of the non-Priestly primeval history, a continuation written to support and endorse Solomon's kingdom. Read this way, God's promises of greatness and blessing to Abram in Gen 12:1–3 anticipate the time when Israel will "become a great nation" under Solomon, and Solomon will enjoy an immense reputation and fabled blessing. If this is correct, Gen 12:1–3 and the rest of the extended J/Yahwistic document thus provide divine sanction to Solomon's mini-empire. This has led some, such as Walter Brueggemann in his influential book, *The Prophetic Imagination* (Minneapolis: Fortress, 2001), to criticize texts such as Gen 12:1–3 because they see them as J texts endorsing an oppressive empire.

Things look quite different, however, if one understands Gen 12:1–3 and other promise texts to be words of hope to despairing exiles in the wake of the destruction of Jerusalem and loss of the monarchy. Put in this context, Gen 12:1–3 is a story where a non-royal figure, Abram, receives promises that were once given to kings. We have seen similar exilic gifts of royal promises to other figures in Second Isaiah – to the Persian Cyrus in Isa 44:28–45:1 and to the people in Isa 55:3. Yet the author of Gen 12:1–3 and surrounding texts tells the Abram/Abraham story in a special way, so that Abraham almost sounds like an exile living long before the Babylonian exile. He is made into someone to whom the exiles can relate. Like them, he lives in Mesopotamia, "Ur of the Chaldees" (Gen 11:28), and, like them, he has been called to go and live as a stranger in a land he does not know (Gen 12:1). In light of this, the promises to Abram become promises of hope to the exiles, much like the prophecies of hope to exiles that we saw in the exilic portions of Isaiah (40–55), Jeremiah, and Ezekiel. Where the exiles longed for a restoration of their nation, they hear in Gen 12:2 that their ancestor Abram, also an exile, was promised that he would "become a great nation." Where we know that the exiles felt "cursed" because of their exile, this text asserts the opposite: they will be so blessed that they will become an example of blessing to other peoples on earth (Gen 12:3). Moreover, there is an additional promise in Gen 12:2–3 that relates specifically to the vulnerability that exiles faced when living as a minority in a larger culture. God reassures Abram of God's protection. God will bless those who bless him, and God will curse those who so much as "treat [him] lightly" (Gen 12:3). Exiles would have heard this as a promise that God will provide similar protection to them, as Abraham's children, while living in Babylonia.

Conclusions on (Exilic) Trauma and the Bible

In sum, the Bible may not directly describe the exile in Babylonia, but it profoundly reflects the Judeans' experience of forced dislocation. Knowing this background is crucial for understanding the background of laments like Psalm 137 and prophecies like Ezekiel and Second Isaiah. But it also helps us understand how Judah ended up focusing its initial and most important (Torah) texts on landless ancestors (e.g. Abraham and Sarah) and wandering in the wilderness, texts that resonated with their trauma.

This chapter has included extra treatment of sources and theories of Pentateuchal formation because that information is relevant for connecting Torah (Pentateuch) to trauma. It makes a big difference whether you read Gen 12:1–3 and related texts as endorsing Solomon's (proto)monarchy or as reassuring exiles who had been crushed by the Neo-Babylonian empire. This book has followed recent scholarship that dates Gen 12:1–3 and other L promise texts to times of imperial oppression, especially the exile of Judeans to Babylonia. Yet whatever the original date of the P and non-P/L texts, it was during later periods, when Judeans needed words of hope, that these writings about God's promises to Abraham's children and God's formation of Israel in the wilderness moved to the center of the Hebrew Bible. In particular, it was during the exile of Judeans to Babylonia that stories of Israel's history *before* conquest and monarchy started to become the literary foundation on which everything else in the Bible was based.

Up through the exile, however, this literary foundation, this "Torah of Moses," was split. On the one hand, there were the non-P/L stories of Genesis and Moses-exodus. On the other hand, there was a P source paralleling numerous parts of its non-P counterpart. The L narrative features the "elders," a major group of lay leaders in the exilic and post-exilic periods. The P narrative features the Aaronide priests, a priestly group that first achieves dominance in the late exile and post-exilic periods. These groups, and their texts, remained separate throughout the exile. There was no unifying political structure in this period to bring them together; the monarchy was gone. We will not see conditions for unifying these L and P stories until the Persians sponsor the rebuilding of a community of returnee exiles in Jerusalem. We turn next to that important event.

CHAPTER SIX REVIEW

1 Know the meaning and significance of the following terms discussed in this chapter:
- divine council
- E (or Elohistic) Source
- history of religions
- ecological criticism
- J (or Yahwistic) Source
- L (or Lay) Source
- monotheism
- non-Priestly or non-P
- P (or Priestly) Source
- Second Isaiah (also be able to recognize and define "Deutero-Isaiah" as the same thing)
- servant (in Second Isaiah)
- servant songs
- social-scientific analysis

2 What insights can we gain into the experience of ancient Judeans in exile from survey of contemporary social-scientific studies of people living outside their homelands? What dynamics intensified the impact of the exile on Judean culture and identity?

3 Where do the exilic edition of the books of Kings (its ending) and the book of Ezekiel disagree? Why was this important in this period?

4 What are four symptoms of trauma that are reflected in biblical traditions from the exile?

5 What practices and beliefs became especially prominent in the exile (especially in P)?

6 What sorts of "history" are best discussed in relation to the Pentateuch? How?

7 (Focus text: Gen 12:1–3) How do the promises to Abraham in Gen 12:1–3 compare to the wishes for the Davidic king in a royal psalm like Psalm 72 (especially its conclusion in 72:15–19)? How might such a story about Abraham be heard differently in a time of exile than in a time when there still was a Davidic monarch? What does the story "do" for the audience in each case?

RESOURCES FOR FURTHER STUDY

Sociology of Exile

Smith-Christopher, Daniel L. *Religion of the Landless: The Social Context of Babylonian Exile.* Bloomington, IN: Meyer-Stone Books, 1989.

Ezekiel

Bowen, Nancy. *Ezekiel.* Nashville, TN: Abingdon, 2010.

Joyce, Paul. *Ezekiel: A Commentary.* New York and London: T&T Clark, 2009.

Second Isaiah

Blenkinsopp, Joseph. *Isaiah 40–55: A New Translation with Introduction and Commentary.* New York: Doubleday, 2002.

More on the Formation of the Pentateuch

Carr, David. *Reading the Fractures of Genesis.* Louisville, KY: Westminster John Knox Press, 1996.

Genesis

(See also p. 94 for commentaries on the first Part of Genesis)

Brueggemann, Walter. *Genesis.* Interpretation. Atlanta, GA: John Knox Press, 1982.

Sarna, N. M. *Genesis.* Philadelphia, PA: Jewish Publication Society, 1989.

Exodus

Meyers, Carol. *Exodus.* New York: Cambridge University Press, 2005.

Sarna, Nahum. *Exodus.* Philadelphia, PA: Jewish Publication Society, 1991.

Leviticus

Balentine, Samuel E. *Leviticus.* Louisville, KY: Westminster John Knox Press, 2011.

Gerstenberger, Erhard S. *Leviticus.* Louisville, KY: Westminster John Knox Press, 1996.

Levine, Baruch A. *Leviticus.* Philadelphia, PA: JPS Publication, 2003.

Numbers

Olson, Dennis. *Numbers.* Louisville, KY: Westminster John Knox Press, 1996.

Wenham, Gordon J. *Numbers.* Sheffield: Sheffield Academic Press, 1997.

Persian Empire and the Emergence of a Temple-Centered Jewish Community

7

Chapter Overview

This chapter traces how central parts of the Hebrew Bible subtly reflect a *positive* relationship between Judeans and the Persian empire inaugurated by Cyrus. We will see how the Persians played a supportive role at several stages in the restoration of Judah, allowing many exiles to return and helping establish a Temple-centered community of returnees in Jerusalem (see Figure 7.1). In significant ways, the present Hebrew Bible, and especially the Torah/Pentateuch, is a collection of Hebrew texts made by former exiles sponsored by the Persian government. This helps explain why so many biblical texts sharply criticize the Assyrian and Babylonian empires but adopt a generally positive tone the few times they mention Persia.

The other major theme of the chapter, however, is diverse perspectives during this period on who was included in this rebuilt community. We will see how some returned exiles, especially Ezra, felt it important to purify the community so that it would never have to undergo exile again. Building on lessons

A Contemporary Introduction to the Bible: Sacred Texts and Imperial Contexts, Second Edition.
Colleen M. Conway and David M. Carr.
© 2021 Colleen M. Conway and David M. Carr. Published 2021 by John Wiley & Sons Ltd.

FIGURE 7.1
Relief from the Persian capital of Persepolis. It depicts the many subjects of the Persian empire, dressed in the distinctive dress of each country, bearing tribute to the Persian king. The image well illustrates ways that the Persian empire cultivated the support of diverse cultures for its far-flung empire.

they felt they had learned during exile, these leaders required Judean men to divorce foreign wives and expel them and their children. Meanwhile, other texts, such as chapters 56–66 of Isaiah and the books of Ruth and Jonah, provide an alternative accent on God's mercy toward foreigners and on ways foreigners who were attached to Yahweh (such as Ruth) could be crucially important for the people of Yahweh. Thus, even as the community was uniting around Temple and Torah in this Persian period, we once again encounter multiple biblical voices from a given time speaking quite different words.

History: The Persian-Sponsored Building of a Temple- and Torah-Centered Judaism

READING

Zechariah 1 and 4; Haggai 1:1–2:9, the Nehemiah memoir (e.g. Neh 1–3) and other narratives about return and rebuilding (Ezra 1–9 and Neh 8; recommended); Isaiah 56:1–8 (part of the Persian-period material in Isaiah). Recommended: Jonah, Ruth, and Job 1–5, 38–42.

EXERCISE

Using the parallel below, compare and contrast the Persian king Cyrus's edict about his anointing by the Babylonian gods (Marduk, Bel, and Nabu) with Ezra 1:1–4.

Cyrus cylinder	Ezra 1:1–4
"I am Cyrus, king of the world, great king, mighty king, king of Babylonia, king of the land of Sumer and Akkad, king of the four quarters, son of Cambyses … whose rule Bel and Nabu cherish, whose kingship they desire for their hearts' pleasures. … I did not allow any to terrorize the land of Sumer and Akkad.	1:2 Thus says King Cyrus of Persia:
I kept in view the needs of Babylonia and all its sanctuaries to promote their well being. The citizens of Babylonia … I lifted their unbecoming yoke …	
At my deeds Marduk, the great Lord, rejoiced, and to me, Cyrus, the king who worshipped, and to Cambyses, my son, the offspring of my loins, and to all my troops he graciously gave his blessing, and in good spirit before him we glorified exceedingly his high divinity.	"Yahweh, the God of heaven, has given me
All the kings who sat in the throne rooms, throughout the four quarters, from the Upper to the Lower Sea, those who dwelt in … all the kings of the West Country who dwelt in tents, brought me their heavy tribute and kissed my feet in Babylonia.	all the kingdoms of the earth,
From … to the cities of Ashur and Susa, Agade, Eshnuna, the cities of Zamban, Meurnu, Der, as far as the region of the land of Gutium, the holy cities beyond the Tigris whose sanctuaries had been in ruins over a long period, the gods whose abode is in the midst of them I returned to the places and housed them in lasting abodes.	and he has commanded me to build a house for him in Jerusalem which is in Judah.
I (also) gathered together all their inhabitants and restored to them their dwellings.	1:3 Any of you who are from his people – may his God be with him! – are now allowed to go to Jerusalem in Judah, and rebuild the house of Yahweh, the God of Israel
The Gods of Sumer and Akkad whom Nabonidus had, to the anger of the Lord of the Gods, brought into Babylonia, I, at the bidding of Marduk, the great Lord, made to dwell in peace in their habitations, delightful abodes." (Translation: ANET 316)	he is the God who is in Jerusalem; 1:4 and let all who remain, wherever they live, be supported by the people of their place with silver and gold, with goods and with animals, besides freewill offerings for the house of God in Jerusalem."

The **Cyrus cylinder** quoted above (see also Figure 7.2) marks another major shift of empires in the Near Eastern world. The Persian king, Cyrus, had just conquered Babylonia without a fight, aided in part by disgruntled priests in Babylonia who violently disagreed with the religious policies of Nabonidus, the last king of Babylonia. Nabonidus had elevated the status of the moon god, Sin, over that of traditional Babylonian gods, and he had removed the divine

FIGURE 7.2
The Cyrus cylinder.

statues of those gods from their sanctuaries across Babylonia. In the Cyrus cylinder, Cyrus uses the Akkadian language and the form of an Akkadian inscription to describe how the Babylonian gods chose him to be king over Babylonia and restore the divine statues to their proper places. Apparently, Cyrus's self-promotion was at least partially successful. A Babylonian priest wrote another text around the same time, called "The Verse account of Nabonidus," that chronicles the religious crimes of Nabonidus, praises Cyrus's restoration of Babylonia's sanctuaries, and concludes by saying that the people of Babylonia now have "a joyful heart" and rejoice "to look upon Cyrus as king."

Though Cyrus never mentions Judah in his cylinder, we know from the Bible that the Judean exiles also celebrated this shift in power. Even before Cyrus had conquered Babylonia, Second Isaiah had seen him on the horizon and quoted Yahweh as anointing Cyrus to subdue nations and rebuild Jerusalem (Isa 44:28–45:1). Furthermore, similar texts at the end of the books of Chronicles (2 Chr 36:22–3) and beginning of Ezra (Ezra 1:1–4) give a Judean version of Cyrus's proclamation, this time proclaiming that Yahweh has given him rule over all the earth and appointed him to rebuild Jerusalem. Since there is no Persian copy of such an inscription, we do not know if something like this was issued by the Persian government or whether it was created by Judean scribes on analogy with inscriptions like the Cyrus cylinder. In either case, these texts from Second Isaiah and the beginning of Ezra show an important development among the exiles. Where they hated Babylonia, many fully supported the Persian empire and endorsed the idea that the Persian king, Cyrus, had been appointed by God to save and restore them.

Our main source for the history of Judah in this period, Ezra–Nehemiah, appears to be another example of the combination of earlier materials. One block of materials appears to have been a Nehemiah memoir, a first person account by the lay leader, Nehemiah, of how he rebuilt Jerusalem and provided for the Levites (Neh 1:1–7:4; parts of Nehemiah 13 and possibly 12). Another block of materials tells the story of the rebuilding of the temple and prominently features the priestly scribe, Ezra. Within the present form of the book, Ezra arrives and starts his work earlier than Nehemiah (Ezra 7–10), but he does not conclude his work, a work that included a grand reading of the Torah of Moses, until after Nehemiah has built his wall (Neh 8–10). That is the order of the book of Ezra–Nehemiah, but it is likely that the historical figure of Ezra actually followed that of Nehemiah. The two figures almost never overlap, and multiple early Jewish sources know their stories separately. So what might explain their present placement in Ezra–Nehemiah? Many scholars have concluded that this arrangement was produced through a misunderstanding by a much later author who confused the order of the two figures, not knowing that there were two different Persian kings named "Artaxerxes." He mistakenly placed Nehemiah, who arrived and rebuilt Jerusalem's walls in the twentieth year of Artaxerxes *the first* (Neh 2:1; 445 BCE), *after* Ezra, who found those walls rebuilt and probably arrived in the seventh year of Artaxerxes *the second* (Ezra 7:7; 397 BCE).

Basics on the Book of Haggai

			Outline:
I	Oracles around the start of Temple rebuilding		**blessing + new**
	A Prophetic-inspired beginning of rebuilding (including promise of blessing for rebuilding 1:2–11)	1:1–14	**rulership after Temple**
	B Encouragement: Zerubbabel's future riches	2:1–9	**rebuilding**
II	Oracles following up on start of rebuilding		
	A Renewed promise of blessing	2:10–19	
	B Encouragement: Zerubbabel's future rule	2:20–23	

Fifth century BCE (400s, building on prophecies from 520 BCE). **Date**

In his original setting, Haggai promised his discouraged post-exilic community **Themes** that investing now in rebuilding the Temple would yield returns of agricultural plenty and political independence under Zerubbabel. Amidst the turmoil of Darius's seizure of the throne of Persia in 522 BCE, Haggai may have hoped that Zerubbabel, a descendant of David, would re-establish the Davidic monarchy (2:23). Though this did not happen and the rebuilt Temple was later destroyed by the Romans (70 CE), the book of Haggai still preserves Jewish hope for renewal and restoration on the other side of another Temple rebuilding.

Alongside the materials collected in Ezra–Nehemiah, we also have the words of several prophets dated to this time as sources for learning about the period of the post-exilic restoration of the Jerusalem community. These include Haggai, Zechariah (particularly Zechariah 1–8), and post-exilic portions of Isaiah such as "Third Isaiah" in Isaiah 56–66 (see the Focus text discussion at the end of this chapter). Using these sources, scholars have identified four main stages of the restoration, each of which seems to have featured some sort of Persian support: the return of some exiles to Judah, Zerubbabel and Joshua's rebuilding of the Jerusalem Temple, Nehemiah's rebuilding of the walls of Jerusalem, and Ezra's elevation of the Torah of Moses to the center of a

Jerusalem community who had just expelled foreign wives and their children. The following paragraphs discuss each stage in turn before briefly considering the situation of Judeans still living abroad in Egypt and Mesopotamia.

Basics on the Book of Zechariah

Outline: from Temple restoration to Yahweh's rule	I Zechariah's visions surrounding Temple rebuilding	1–8
	II Later visions of Yahweh's establishment of rule	9–14
Date	Fifth century BCE (400s) for a form of Zechariah 1–8 (earlier oracles). Fourth century BCE (300s) for whole book (note Greeks in Zech 9:13).	
Themes	The book of Zechariah is a combination of an earlier book surrounding eight visions attributed to Zechariah (Zechariah 1–8) and so-called "Deutero-Zechariah" (Zechariah 9–11) and "Trito-Zechariah" (Zechariah 12–14). The earlier book, like Haggai, was associated with Temple rebuilding and the future rule of Zerubbabel and Joshua. Zechariah 9–14, however, lacks the superscriptions and dates of the earlier chapters that link them to Zechariah and the Temple-building process. Divided into two "oracles" (9–11 and 12–14), this latter part of the book envisions Yahweh's dramatic punishment of all Judah's enemies and the lifting up of Jerusalem to be the center of the world.	

The biblical account of Cyrus's decree gives permission to exiles to "go up to Jerusalem which is in Judah and build the house of Yahweh, god of Israel, the god who is in Jerusalem" (Ezra 1:3). This introduces the first of a series of returns of exiles from Babylonia to Jerusalem. The first wave, probably a tiny fraction of the exiles, returned under the leadership of Sheshbazzar, possibly a son of the exiled king Jehoiachin, shortly after Cyrus's defeat of the Babylonians in 539 BCE. The book of Ezra asserts that Cyrus even gave Sheshbazzar the Temple implements stolen by the Babylonians so that he could take them back to Jerusalem (Ezra 1:7–11), and Sheshbazzar is reported to have rebuilt the foundation of the Temple (Ezra 5:16). A few years later, around 520 BCE, one of Jehoiachin's grandsons, Zerubbabel, led another group of exiles back to Jerusalem. Still other exiles appear to have returned to Jerusalem under Ezra one hundred and twenty years later (397 BCE; Ezra 7:1–7). In sum, not all exiles came back to Jerusalem, and those who did return came back in several waves. Many, if not most, exiles probably did not want to leave Babylonia. Some, such as Sheshbazzar and Zerubbabel, had assimilated enough to Babylonian culture to have Babylonian names, and we know from later documents of a Jewish family in Babylonia (in the Murashu archive) that some exiles remained there in subsequent centuries. This means that the expression "post-exilic period" is only accurate in indicating the end of *forced* exile, since many Judeans never stopped living away from their homeland.

In addition to allowing some Judeans to return to Judah, the Persians played a major role in the **rebuilding of the Jerusalem Temple** that had been destroyed by the Babylonians. This rebuilding, a centerpiece of Cyrus's decree in Ezra 1:1–4, happened in at least two stages. The first, mentioned above, was Cyrus's giving of the Temple vessels to Sheshbazzar and Sheshbazzar's delivery of these vessels to Jerusalem and laying of the foundations for this **Second Temple** there. This probably occurred shortly after Cyrus's victory over Babylonia, around 538 BCE. The second stage of the temple rebuilding work was not completed, however, until about twenty years later, from 520 to 515 BCE. By this point, Cyrus had died (in 530), his son Cambyses had reigned for eight years (530–522), and Darius, a more distant member of the royal family, had seized power in the wake of Cambyses's death. Darius gained support among peoples of his empire by reversing the harsh policies of Cambyses and rebuilding temples and priesthoods, especially in Egypt (which Cambyses had conquered and subdued). The rebuilding of the Temple in Jerusalem early in Darius's reign was probably part of this broader project. Yet an important shift in Judean leadership seems to have occurred sometime before the Jerusalem Temple was finished. Its rebuilding had begun under both the Davidic leadership of Zerubbabel and the priestly leadership of Joshua. Indeed, certain prophecies by Haggai (2:20–3) and Zechariah (the "branch" in 3:6–10; 4:6–10; 6:9–14) indicate that some hoped that Zerubbabel would re-establish the monarchy in Jerusalem, working alongside Joshua. Yet we hear no more of Zerubbabel in traditions after the Temple was completed. No one knows why. From that point forward the Davidic monarchy was completely finished, and the time of Temple-centered Judaism had begun, the time of the Second Temple (515 BCE–70 CE).

The next major step in the restoration that we know much about is Nehemiah's rebuilding of the walls of Jerusalem seventy years later in 445 BCE. According to his memoir, Nehemiah was a cupbearer in the court of Artaxerxes, probably Artaxerxes I, who reigned from 464 to 423 BCE. Having heard reports of the dilapidated state of Jerusalem, Nehemiah convinced Artaxerxes to send him back to Jerusalem to rebuild the city (Neh 1:1–2:8). There he organized the Judean community to rebuild Jerusalem's walls, despite the opposition of neighboring peoples and internal dissenters (Neh 2:17–6:19). His role was that of Persian-appointed "governor" of Judah (Neh 5:14–19), a lay leader alongside the cultic leadership of the priests. His biggest achievement was the re-establishment of Jerusalem as a walled city, an independent political entity (see Map 7.1). Sometime later, perhaps in a second term as governor, Nehemiah may have taken additional measures, such as the purging of the Jerusalem temple of foreign priests (see Neh 12–13). If so, this was an anticipation of more major purges that were to happen under Ezra.

Ezra took this purging to a new level as part of a more general program of centering Judaism on observance of the Torah of Moses. Like Nehemiah, Ezra was an exiled Judean who was also a highly placed Persian official – some sort of secretary in the Persian court. According to Ezra 7, he was commissioned by king Artaxerxes to bring offerings to the Jerusalem Temple and evaluate the extent to which people in the province were obeying "the law of god and the law of the king" (Ezra 7:26). There has been endless debate about

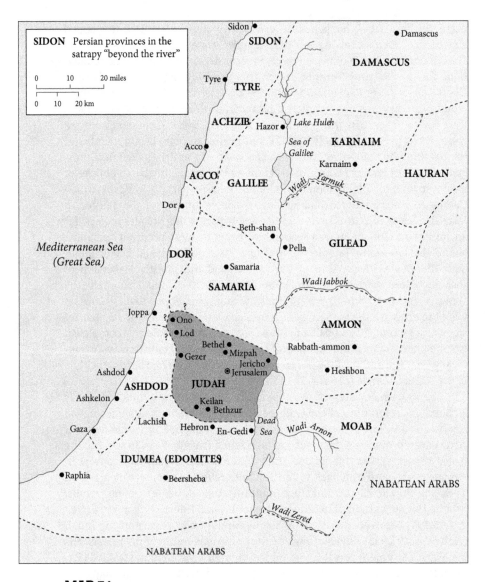

MAP 7.1

Judah as a province of the Persian empire. Redrawn from Norman Gottwald, *The Hebrew Bible: A Socio-Literary Introduction*. Minneapolis: Fortress, 1985, page 406.

what each of these laws contained, and whether some kind of "Persian governmental authorization" of the law was involved. Whatever one decides on these issues, the subsequent narrative of the reading of the "Torah of Moses" in Nehemiah 8 makes clear that something like the present Pentateuch is understood in this narrative to be "the law of god." Nevertheless, on his way to publicly reading and enforcing this holy law, Ezra comes to learn that earlier returnee Judean men have intermarried with foreign women and thus

– in his mind – put at risk the whole project of the restoration of the people (Ezra 9:1–3). Many exiles such as Ezra perceived intermarriage with foreigners as a primary reason why Judah had gone into exile in the first place. Seeing this intermarriage among the returnee exiles, Ezra cries out to God:

> God has not forsaken us in our slavery, but has extended to us his steadfast love before the kings of Persia, to give us new life to set up the house of our God, to repair its ruins, and to give us a wall in Judea and Jerusalem.
>
> And now, our God, what shall we say after this? For we have forsaken your commandments, which you commanded by your servants the prophets, saying, … do not give your daughters to their sons, neither take their daughters for your sons, and never seek their peace or prosperity, so that you may be strong and eat the good of the land and leave it for an inheritance to your children forever. (Ezra 9:9–12 NRSV)

Ezra sees the whole Persian-sponsored process of the rebuilding of Jerusalem put into question by intermarriage of returnee Judean men with "foreign women," this latter group actually including a mix of non-Israelite women *and also* Judean women from families who had not gone into exile. In response, Ezra urges all the men of Judah to divorce their foreign wives and expel them along with their children. This description of divorce of foreign wives (and expulsion of their children) is among the most difficult events for students to understand in the history of Israel. This seems to many to be a damaging and excessive way of preventing foreign influence. Within this context it may be helpful to remember three things. First, the documents that report such divorces are far removed from the events they describe and may not be reliable historical records of those events. Second, insofar as such a divorce of foreign wives occurred, it was part of the returning community's attempt to avoid the mistakes of foreign influence that they believed caused the exile. Third, there are other biblical texts, likely dating from around the Persian period, that offer a different perspective on the role and significance of foreigners in relation to Judah/Israel. For example, the positive picture of Assyrians in the book of Jonah, the account in the book of Ruth of how David had a Moabite grandmother, or the inclusive vision of Israel in what is called "Third Isaiah" (Isaiah 56–66; see especially Isa 56:1–8) all suggest more affirming perspectives on the role of foreigners in Israel (see the following page for a Special Topics Box on "Alternative Perspectives on Foreigners").

Within the Ezra narrative, the divorce of foreign wives is the prelude to Ezra's climactic reading of the "Torah of Moses" before all of Judah (Neh 8), a Torah that seems (at least in this narrative) to be much like the present Pentateuch, with P and non-P source materials combined into a single whole. This enactment of the "Torah of Moses" by Ezra is a major step in the formation of a Torah-centered Judaism. After this, virtually all groups in Judaism, whatever else they may disagree about, agree on at least one thing: the importance of the Torah of Moses.

Basics on the Book of Isaiah

The above outline builds on scholars' observations of an inclusio in Isaiah, where themes appearing together in the exhortation to repentance in Isa 1:1–31 reappear in the paired divine speeches to the disobedient and obedient in 65:1–66:24. In addition, several parts of the first half of the book, Isaiah 1–33, parallel portions of the second half, Isaiah 34–66:

Isaiah 1–33 (plan for Yahweh's rule from Zion)	Isaiah 34–66 (initial realization of plan)
Introduction: call to hear (Isaiah 1)	Call to hear revenge and restoration (Isa 34–5)
Commission of eighth-century Isaiah (Isaiah 6)	
Isaiah–Ahaz materials (Isaiah 7–8)	Isaiah–Hezekiah narratives (Isaiah 36–9)
	Commission of exilic prophet (40:1–11)
Anti-nations/Babylonia (Isaiah 13–27)	Oracle against Babylonia (Isaiah 47)
Oracles focused on Zion (Isaiah 28–32)	Oracles on Zion's restoration (49–66)

These and other patterns also bind the book together into a complex unity. It is a chorale of prophetic voices from different centuries, joining in witness to Yahweh, "the holy one of Israel," and his plans for Zion and the nations around it.

Date   Fifth century BCE (400s, building on earlier materials).

Themes   See the discussions of the eighth-century prophet, Isaiah, in Chapter 4 and of Second Isaiah in Chapter 6.

Alternative Perspectives on Foreigners

History may be written by the winners, but, in the case of post-exilic Judah, prophets and others got a chance to write a rejoinder. Indeed, several texts in the Hebrew Bible appear to respond to the hostility toward foreigners found in post-exilic traditions such as the Ezra stories. Sometimes the response to the issue takes the form of a narrative, as in the story of God's grace toward Assyrians in the book of Jonah, Naomi's evolving attitude toward her Moabite daughter-in-law in the book of Ruth, or the story of an Edomite's unjust suffering in the book of Job. Sometimes, however, the response takes the form of direct prophetic engagement, as in the call in Isaiah 56:3 that the foreigner should not say "Yahweh will separate me from his people," an apparent response to post-exilic efforts to purify Israel through expelling foreigners. Though it is not certain that each of these texts dates from the post-exilic period, they address concerns about foreigners and foreign influence that became prominent in that time.

Much of the significance of all these changes can be seen when comparing Jerusalem of Ezra's time with the situation around the time of Ezra in Elephantine, a Jewish colony of mercenaries (soldiers for hire) settled in the southern Nile area of Egypt. This colony had its own temple, dating from before the rebuilding of the Jerusalem Temple. The members of the community did correspond with leaders in Jerusalem and Samaria about various cultic matters, such as the celebration of Passover and rebuilding of their local temple, but they do not seem to have known the Torah of Moses advocated by Ezra, or to have followed the more stringent rules against foreign religions seen in the book of Deuteronomy. Only after many years did communities like this either die out or conform to the Torah-centered form of Judaism that arose in Jerusalem. Documents such as the Elephantine archives give us a small taste of the broad diversity of Jewish religion and life in the Persian period, which supplements the biblical accounts given by Jewish returnees to Jerusalem.

Significant Dates: The Persian-Sponsored Restoration of Judah

Cyrus's defeat of Babylonia	539 BCE
Wave 1 of returnees to Judah with Sheshbazzar (laying Temple foundation)	~538 BCE (or later)
Another wave of returnees with Zerubbabel	520 BCE
(Completion of) Rebuilding of Second Temple under Zerubbabel	520–515 BCE
Nehemiah's return and governorships	445–425 BCE
Rebuilding wall, purification of priesthood	
Another wave of returnees with Ezra	397 BCE
Divorce of foreign wives	
(Combination of L + P?) Elevation of Torah	

The Final Formation of the Torah

Gen 1:1–3:24; 26:34–28:7; skim Exodus 19–40.

READING

The major literary event of this period was the completion of the Torah and its elevation to the center of post-exilic Judaism. This was a work as much or more about combining older texts as it was about the writing of new ones.

Building on earlier traditions, Judeans in exile had already written larger stories of Israel's early history in P and non-P sources (non-P here including Deuteronomy and various L revisions connecting and revising earlier materials). These histories were separate from one another and cherished by the two major leadership groups in the exile and afterwards: the priesthood descending from Aaron (celebrated in P) and the elders (featured in non-P/L). Yet at some point an author combined these sources into one, producing a Pentateuch much like the one we have now. The process of Persian governmental authorization mentioned above may have played some role in this, since it would not have helped someone like Ezra to have the Persians authenticate *two* competing local narratives, L and P. Nevertheless, it would be a mistake to see this joining of traditions as a purely political process. Rather, whatever occasion prompted this creation of the combined Lay and Priestly Torah, there is evidence of considerable theological-literary genius in its execution.

One example of this is the combination of the P and non-P primeval narratives so that both human possibilities and human limitations are more fully expressed. Genesis starts with the Priestly narrative of creation, where God crowns the cosmos with the creation of humans "as our own image and likeness" (Gen 1:26–7), blesses humanity, and says that the whole creation is "very good." In our present Pentateuch this is now balanced by the Garden of Eden story (Gen 2:4–3:24; non-Priestly). Placed after the P creation story (Gen 1:1–2:3), this earlier non-P text now tells us more about the sixth "day" on which God created animal and human life (Gen 2:4; cf. 1:24–31). The Eden story ends with curses (Gen 3:14, 17–19) and stresses all of the problems that come from humans' eating the fruit of knowledge and seeking to be "like God" (Gen 3:1–19). In contrast to the P creation story, in which God made humans godlike from the beginning, in this non-P story God is concerned about humans becoming ever more godlike and expels them from the garden so that they will not gain divine immortality (Gen 3:23–4). So goes the beginning of the combined creation and flood story, a story that balances affirmation of human godlikeness (Gen 1:26–7; 5:1–3; P) with stress on God's care to preserve the divine–human boundary (Gen 6:1–4; 11:1–9; non-P). In this way and others, the P and non-P perspectives are put in a creative tension that is more theologically evocative than either one alone would have been.

Basics on the Book of Genesis

Outline: the transmission of the Abrahamic promise to Jacob as an answer to the problems of creation

I	Story of creation and re-creation of humanity	1–11:26
II	Yahweh's response: promise to ancestors	11:27–50:26
	A Abraham (and Lot)	11:27–25:11
	B The next generation: non-heir and heir	25:12–35:39
	1 Genealogy of Ishmael, the non-heir	25:12–18
	2 Stories of Isaac's family, the heir	25:19–35:29
	C The next generation: non-heir and heir	36:1–50:26
	1 Genealogy of Esau, the non-heir	36:1–37:1
	2 Stories of Jacob's family, the heir	37:2–50:26

Note: though the preceding outline focuses on men who inherit or do not inherit the promise, it is women such as Sarah and Rebekah who play a prominent role in determining who inherits the promise (Isaac, Jacob) and who does not.

Post-exilic (building on earlier sources). **Date**

Genesis is a grand synthesis of Priestly and non-Priestly Lay texts. The introduc- **Themes**
tion and structure of Genesis come from the Priestly Source. The book starts
with the Priestly vision of creation in Genesis 1:1–2:3, and the rest of the book is
punctuated with Priestly genealogical headings that now structure the whole
(Gen 2:4; 5:1; 6:9; 10:1; 11:10, 27; 25:12, 19; 36:1; 37:2). Much of the substance of Genesis, however, is non-Priestly, detailing Yahweh's struggles to interact with fal-
lible humans, from the early primeval account of Adam and Eve (Gen 2:4–3:24)
to the (originally northern) story of Joseph and his brothers (Genesis 37–50).
The result of this combination is a book that presents both Yahweh's power to
produce order and his struggles to effect his designs with humanity in general
and Abraham's family in particular.

We see a similarly majestic combination of sources in the Sinai narrative, where the combined P and non-P (L) narrative describes God's overcoming of the divine–human boundary that was so carefully protected in the primeval history. As we saw in Chapter 6, the separate P and non-P sources described events at Sinai quite differently. The non-P (L) Sinai story stressed God's forgiveness in the face of Israel's building of the golden calf, an act of idolatry that signaled the ultimate rejection of the covenant God had just made with them to make them a kingdom of priests (Exod 19:1–24:11; 32:1–34:35). The "elders" stand at the center of this lay-oriented, non-P narrative (Exod 19:7; 24:1, 9), and God only appoints a special priesthood, the Levites, as a measure to punish the disobedient Israelites (Exod 32:26–8). In contrast, the Priestly story says nothing about any disobedience and focuses instead on God's founding of a wilderness sanctuary run by an Aaronide priesthood (Exod 24:15–31:18; 35:1–40:38; Leviticus; Num 1:1–10:10). The emphasis in P is on the creation of a holy people with a sanctuary and proper priesthood to atone for the people's sins.

Basics on the Book of Exodus

(See M. Smith, *The Pilgrimage Pattern in Exodus*, Sheffield: Sheffield Academic Press, 1997.)

I	From Egypt		**Outline: pilgrimage of Moses and of Israel from Egypt to Sinai**
	A Oppression and journey of Moses to Midian	1:1–2:25	
	B Two calls and two confrontations	3:1–15:21	
II	To Sinai		
	A Provision on wilderness journey to Sinai	15:22–18:27	
	B Two covenants and two sets of tablets	19:1–40:38	

Post-exilic (building on earlier sources). **Date**

Many think of the book of Exodus solely in terms of its initial story of Israel's **Themes**
escape from slavery in Egypt. But the climax of the book is Israel's entry into

service to a new lord, Yahweh, as a cultic community centered on the wilderness tabernacle (Exodus 19–40). Thus Exodus is not just a story of getting away. Instead, it is a pilgrimage from painful service to Pharaoh to life-giving service to Yahweh. This exodus journey by Israel now occurs across the Jewish liturgical year, starting at Passover (Exod 12:2, 39–42), with arrival at Sinai at the feast of weeks (Exod 19:1) and building of the tabernacle at the New Year (Exod 40:2, 17).

More information: whose exodus?   Jon Levenson has criticized some liberationist Christians, such as George Pixley, for their claim that the people of Israel was not the actual historical group to leave Egypt in the exodus. Instead, according to Pixley, the actual exodus group was an impoverished group of slaves that would only later join "Israel." For Levenson, this approach is one more example of an all-too-familiar Christian tendency to try to separate the Hebrew Bible from the Jewish people. He argues that the present, canonical form of the book of Exodus emphasizes the idea that Yahweh rescued Israel not because it was poor, but because it was special to Yahweh. Moreover, this exodus did not mean a rejection of slavery in general, but of Israel's slavery to Pharaoh rather than Yahweh. The *Bible's* story of exodus is *Israel*-centered, not a general endorsement of liberation of the poor.

In response, Pixley and others question whether Christians must focus only on the final form of a book like Exodus. They argue that their historical reconstruction should be evaluated on its historical merits, rather than on its theological implications. For these perspectives, see Alice Ogden Bellis and Joel Kaminsky (eds.), *Jews, Christians, and the Theology of the Hebrew Scriptures* (Atlanta: Society of Biblical Literature, 2000).

Basics on the Book of Numbers

(For basics on Leviticus, see box on p. 183.)

Outline

I	Dissolution of the exodus generation		1–25
	A	Preparations for departure from Sinai	1:1–10:10
	B	Disobedience, death in the wake of Sinai	10:11–25:18
II	Beginning of the conquest generation		26–36

Date   Post-exilic (building on earlier sources).

Themes   Priestly material again provides the introduction (1:1–10:28) and general structure, with the overall book moving from the Priestly counting of the exodus generation (Numbers 1–4) to another Priestly counting of the next generation after their parents have died in the wilderness (Numbers 26). In between, we have P and non-P stories about rebellion against the authority of Moses and Aaron (11–12, 16–17), the failed expedition to spy out the land (13–14), and a final catastrophic rebellion at Baal Peor (25). These stories help explain the destruction of this exodus generation before their children can enter the land. In the post-exilic period, this form of the book would have mirrored the experience of most Judean families displaced to Babylonia, in which the vast majority of parents who went into exile did not survive to take their children back to the promised land.

More information: the book of Numbers in context   The focus of Numbers on the transition between generations provides a context for the book of Deuteronomy that follows. Read after Numbers, Deuteronomy is the story of Moses's review of history and law for a generation that did not experience all these events themselves.

When these two narratives were combined, the Priestly emphasis on the sanctuary for atonement became part of God's answer to the people's sin that was emphasized in the non-P (L) narrative. Thus our present combined (L and P) story in Exodus has two simultaneous scenes follow the non-P story of Yahweh's covenant with the people of Israel (Exod 19:1–24:14). On the mountain (here P material), God gives Moses instructions for creating the sanctuary through which the people can atone for their sin (Exod 24:15–31:18). At the very same time, down below (non-P material), the people build the golden calf and thus prove their desperate need for such a means of atonement (Exod 32:1–6). In the rest of the combined Sinai account, the Priestly story of the building of the tabernacle sanctuary (Exod 35:1–40:38) becomes the crowning moment of the non-Priestly story of Yahweh's gradual forgiveness of Israel and willingness to make a new covenant with them (Exod 32:7–34:35). The non-P text describes God's new covenant with God's "stiff-necked" people (Exod 34:1–28; non-P/L) before the P text tells of how Moses led that people in building a tabernacle sanctuary through which they could atone for their sins (35:1–40:33; P).

This event is a high point of the present Pentateuch, and we see this through parallels between the conclusion of the Priestly creation narrative (Gen 1:1–2:3) and the conclusion of the Priestly tabernacle narrative (Exod 39:42–40:33).

Creation of the cosmos	Construction of the tabernacle
Gen 1:31	*Exod 39:43*
God saw all which God had done and indeed it was very good (Gen 1:31a)	And Moses saw all the work and indeed it was done just as YHWH had commanded (Exod 39:43a)
And the heavens and earth were finished (2:1)	And all the work on the tabernacle of the tent of meeting was finished (39:32a)
And God finished on the seventh day God's work (2:2a)	And Moses finished the work (40:33b)
And God blessed the seventh day (2:3a)	And Moses blessed them (39:43b)

These parallels are between parts of the Priestly narrative, but the completion of the tabernacle means yet more in the combined P and non-P (L) narrative we now have. The story of God coming down to the tabernacle follows non-Priestly stories in Genesis about how God once worked to preserve the divine–human boundary, expelling humans from the garden (Gen 3:22–4), limiting their lifespan after they intermarried with divine beings (6:1–4), and ending their attempt to build a tower up toward heaven in Babel (11:1–9). Within this broader stretch, the Priestly description of the descent of God's glory to dwell in Israel is a crossing of the divine–human boundary described in the non-Priestly primeval narratives. Indeed, it stands as the climax of earlier, non-Priestly promises that God would "be with" the patriarchs and their descendants (Gen 26:3; 28:15; 46:4; Exod 4:12).

Though later authors and editors made some additional changes to the Pentateuch, this combination of P and non-P (L) narratives was the most significant stage in the formation of the Pentateuch. It was a daring move, taking a non-Priestly, lay-oriented narrative and combining it with a Priestly narrative that was originally designed to replace it. Turning back to the example of the P and non-P stories of Jacob's gaining his father's blessing (discussed in the previous chapter), we see that parts of the P story are placed before (26:34–5; P) and after (27:46–28:7; P) the non-Priestly trickster story they were meant to replace (27:1–45, early Jacob story). As a result, the P materials provide a new context for Jacob and Rebekah's deceitful actions. In the combined text now in Genesis, Esau marries foreign wives (Gen 26:34–5; P), which provides some justification for Jacob's theft of his father's blessing (Gen 27:1–45; non-P), which in turn provides a context for Isaac's repeated blessing of Jacob and sending him abroad to get a proper wife (Gen 28:1–5; P). Thus, at this place and others, the post-exilic author who combined P and non-P balanced the perspectives of both sources without hiding or homogenizing the contrasts. Enough traces of his work were left that scholars could achieve consensus on the basic contents of the P and non-P sources despite the fact that we have no separate manuscript of either.

The Book of Psalms as a Torah-Centered Collection of More Ancient Psalms

Though the book of Psalms probably contains some of the earliest texts in the Hebrew Bible, its present form shows the rising importance of the Pentateuchal Torah in the Persian and later periods. *As a whole*, the book of Psalms (also known as the **Psalter**) is a collection oriented toward Torah instruction. It opens with a psalm encouraging its readers to "meditate" day and night on the "Torah of Yahweh" (Psalm 1), and its longest psalm is a praise of God's Torah that is one hundred and seventy-six verses long, organized into alphabetic stanzas (Psalm 119). The book of Psalms is divided into five parts by a set of similar calls to praise found at Pss 41:13; 72:18–19; 89:52; 106:48; and a concluding psalm of praise in Psalm 150. The focus on praise in these sections helps explain the name of the book of Psalms in Hebrew, *tehillim* – (book of) praises. At the same time, the fivefold division of the book of Psalms (Psalms 3–41, 42–72, 73–89, 90–106, 107–50) mirrors the fivefold division of the Pentateuch (Pentateuch is Greek for "five scrolls"). The focus of the present, five-part book of Psalms is on praises that are grounded in and flow from meditation on and study of God's Torah.

This focus on Pentateuchal Torah did not always exist in the book of Psalms. Rather, scholars have found clues in the psalm superscriptions that the Psalter is made up of yet older collections of psalms, such as a series of psalms used in pilgrimages (Psalms 120–134) or an "Elohistic" collection of psalms in 42–83 that predominantly uses "Elohim" for God and occasionally duplicates psalms found elsewhere (such as Psalm 53//Psalm 14). Often various psalms reflect the sorts of textual forms used in ancient Israelite worship, such as hymns of praise (e.g. Psalm 8), "laments" praying for help (e.g. Psalm 22), and thanksgivings for God's provision of such help (e.g. Psalm 32). "Form critics" (see the More on Method Box on "Form Criticism and Genre" on p. 208) have uncovered these echoes through comparing the forms of such biblical psalms with each other and some ancient Near Eastern worship texts. Through this kind of research we can appreciate how the book of Psalms encapsulates within itself the broader history of the formation of the Hebrew Bible, from the writing of early worship texts that often echoed traditions seen in non-Israelite empires (see Chapter 3) up through the increasing focus on the Pentateuchal Torah characteristic of the Persian and later periods of Israelite history.

Pss 8 and 104 (hymns of praise), 22 (a lament psalm), 32 (a thanksgiving song). Read and compare Pss 41:13; 72:18–19; 89:52; 106:48; 150.

READING

Basics on the Book of Psalms: Part 2

(For "Basics on the Book of Psalms: Part 1," see Basics Box on p. 73.)

I Torah and king introduction	1–2	**Outline: Torah-centered praise of Yahweh's kingship**
II Five-part collection	3–145	
A Book 1: concludes with individual praise associated with King David	3–41	
B Book 2: concluding in prayer for king	42–72	
C Book 3: concluding with lament about destruction of the Judean monarchy (Psalm 89)	73–89	
D Book 4: moving toward exile (Psalm 106) and stressing Yahweh's kingship (Pss 93, 95–9)	90–106	
E Book 5: moving toward restoration	107–45	
III Fivefold concluding praise of Yahweh	146–50	

Post-exilic (building on earlier sources).   **Date**

In addition to the Torah focus mentioned in the main text, scholars have observed ways that the complex collection of psalms now reflects Israel's journey through history, from monarchy to exile and then post-exilic restoration. As indicated in the outline, the concluding psalms in the first four books show a movement from focus on the king (Psalms 3–41) and his role vis-à-vis the people (Psalms 42–72), to the collapse of the monarchy (Psalms 73–89) and rise of Yahweh's kingship in exile (Psalms 90–106). This prepares for the final book, which starts with a psalm focusing on return from exile (Psalms 107–145).   **Themes**

Several psalm scrolls found among the Dead Sea Scrolls at Qumran contain collections of Psalms that are quite different from the Masoretic edition of Psalms that is used in Jewish tradition and surveyed above. The divergences are particularly striking after Psalm 89. This suggests to some scholars that Psalms 1–89 (books 1–3 of the Psalter) may have reached their form earlier, while the following Psalms (90–150) may have been organized later into the form we now see them in.   **More information: another edition of the book of Psalms**

MORE ON METHOD: FORM CRITICISM AND GENRE

Biblical **form criticism** looks at the characteristics, intention, and social setting of typical categories of psalms, that is, it looks at **genres** in biblical texts. For example, the **lament psalm** is a genre characterized by some or all of the following elements: complaint, plea for help, vow, statement of trust in God's help, and thanksgiving for God's help. One typical intention of such psalms is to gain God's help in a desperate situation. The original social setting for the lament psalm was worship, whether at home, at a local sanctuary, or at the Jerusalem Temple.

Form criticism has achieved many of its greatest results in the study of psalm genres and their social settings, but there have been form-critical studies of many other genres in the Bible as well. Some genres already discussed in this textbook include proverbs and instructions (Chapter 3) and prophetic call narratives (Chapter 4).

As study of form criticism has progressed, scholars have seen more and more complexity, both in the genres and in their links to particular social settings. Many biblical texts are a mix of genres. Moreover, genres can be inverted, as in Amos's use of the lament form to pronounce doom on the nation of Israel. Finally, some genres, such as the Hebrew short story, may be linked to a set of cultural conventions rather than a particular social setting like worship.

For more, see Marvin Sweeney, "Form Criticism." Pp. 58–89 in S. McKenzie and S. Haynes (eds.), *To Each Its Own Meaning* (Louisville, KY: Westminster John Knox Press, 1999).

Contemporary readers of psalms can now work with them on multiple levels, depending on their interests and their community. Study of the psalms in relation to their original historical contexts has illuminated their diverse types and possible settings in worship, their roots in older pre-Israelite traditions, and their rich imagery (among other topics). Yet, as in the case of biblical prophets whose words were preserved for later generations, the book of Psalms has survived because the texts in it have transcended their original contexts. Many psalms probably originated in some form during the time of Solomon's first Temple, but that Temple was destroyed and these older psalms (along with newer ones) came down to us as part of a post-exilic, Torah-centered collection. Now, thousands of years later, the book of Psalms is used more consistently in Jewish and Christian worship than almost any other biblical book. Each community places the psalms in a different context. Jews use psalms in a cycle of Torah-oriented worship, while Christians often reread psalms as Christological prophecies. The use and reuse of these ancient, evocative texts, a process already begun in the formation of the book itself, continues even today.

Isa 56:1–8

Isa 56:1–8 opens a collection of post-exilic prophecies in Isaiah 56–66, prophecies that immediately follow Second Isaiah's words of "comfort" to exiles in 40–55. Second Isaiah had promised that Yahweh would soon bring his salvation and deliverance. This "Third Isaiah" asserts that the fulfillment of these promises requires a prior act by the people themselves: that they "bring about justice and act with social solidarity" (Isa 56:1). The post-exilic prophet adds that only those who "observe the Sabbath" and "keep away from evil" will be "happy" (56:2). These two verses sum up Third Isaiah's addition of moral conditions to the promises of Second Isaiah.

Nevertheless, the balance of the passage goes on to address a particular moral concern of the post-exilic community: the status of foreigners and people considered to be cultically impure. A passage in Deuteronomy insists that neither eunuchs (men whose testicles have been removed) nor Ammonites and Moabites (foreign peoples neighboring Judah) should be allowed to enter the worshipping community of Yahweh (Deut 23:1, 3). In Isa 56:3–8, Yahweh addresses the matter of eunuchs and foreigners who are being excluded from the Temple on this basis, despite their observing the Sabbath and keeping Yahweh's covenant:

> Let not a foreigner say,
>> who has joined himself to Yahweh,
> "Yahweh will surely separate me
>> from his people,"
> And let not a eunuch say,
>> "I am a dried up tree." (56:3)

To these people, the prophet gives a direct word from Yahweh that contradicts the law in Deuteronomy:

> For thus says Yahweh,
> To the eunuchs who keep my Sabbaths,
>> who have chosen that which I desire,
>> And hold fast to my covenant,
> I will give them a monument and name in my house and my walls
>> better than sons or daughters ...
> And to the foreigners joined to Yahweh,
>> to serve him and love the name of Yahweh ...
>> and to be servants of God
> I will bring them into my holy mountain,
>> And help them celebrate in my house of prayer;
> Their burnt offerings and sacrifices
>> will be pleasing on my altar.
> For my house shall be called a house of prayer
>> for all peoples. (56:4–7*)

Thus the prophet offers a direct quotation from Yahweh that contradicts a part of the Mosaic Torah. As we have seen, the Mosaic Torah was ever more prominent in the post-exilic period, and there was an increasing concern to avoid a future exile by "separating" from foreign peoples, as in Nehemiah's and Ezra's initiatives against intermarriage with foreign women. In this case, the focus is not on intermarriage but on foreigners (and eunuchs) who are faithful to Yahweh but find themselves excluded, on the basis of the Mosaic Torah, from the Temple because of their foreign status. Yahweh in this passage contradicts that Torah, assuring them that all who keep his Sabbaths and hold fast to the covenant are welcome in his house.

The basis for this radical contradiction of Mosaic Torah is the message of Second Isaiah. There the exilic prophet described Yahweh as appointing a "servant" for a task that went beyond just bringing Judeans back from exile in Babylonia:

> It is too light a thing that you should be my servant,
>   To establish the tribes of Jacob
> And bring back the survivors of Israel.
>   I will make you a light to the nations,
> To be my salvation
>   to the end of the earth. (49:6)

In this passage in Third Isaiah, a post-exilic prophet echoes this message, saying:

> Thus says the Lord, Yahweh,
>   Who gathers the scattered of Israel,
> I soon will gather yet others to them,
>   Besides those already gathered. (56:8)

By this point the prophet can look back on an in-gathering of exiles that has already occurred. Both he and the rest of his post-exilic audience know Yahweh now as a God who has proven true to promises to bring back the exiles. Building on this and on Second Isaiah's message, he extends this idea to foreigners, saying that Second Isaiah's message about being a "light to the nations" also holds. Yahweh is about a larger project of in-gathering, one that means that foreigners joined to Yahweh, Yahweh's "servants" (56:6), will have a full place in worship at Yahweh's mountain. This proclamation of including foreigners is later echoed toward the very end of (Third) Isaiah with a prophecy that some foreigners will even become priests and Levites (66:18–23).

These prophecies stand in sharp contrast to the application in the Ezra traditions of messages from the Pentateuch and Second Isaiah. Ezra seems to have modeled his procession from Babylonia to Judah on the exodus from Egypt, departing on the first day of the year (Ezra 7:9; cf. Exod 12:2) and then making sure that his caravan corresponded to Moses's in having Levitical priests and 12 lay leaders (Ezra 8:1–20). Yet he also seems to have understood this second exodus in terms taken from Second Isaiah, praying, for example, that Yahweh would "make [their] way straight" on the way home to Judah (Ezra 8:21; see Isa 40:3). Ezra soon finds out that the people already in Judah have failed to "separate themselves" from foreign peoples, intermarrying with them (Ezra 9:1), and he moves to expel foreign wives as a precondition for leading the people in devoting themselves to the Torah of Moses (Ezra 9–10; Neh 8).

Third Isaiah is not focused on exactly the same issues, but still represents a sharp contrast to Ezra. Ezra aimed for "separation" from foreign peoples (Ezra 9:1–3; 10:11), while Third Isaiah proclaimed Yahweh's reassurance to foreigners who were concerned – perhaps on the basis of initiatives like Ezra's – that "Yahweh will surely separate me from his people" (56:3). Ezra focused on Second Isaiah's message that Yahweh would bring the exiles home in a second exodus. Third Isaiah added an emphasis on the other half of Second Isaiah's message: that this homecoming of exiles was part of a broader plan in which Yahweh's servant would be a light to "the nations." Ezra's narrative climaxes with the reading of the Torah and the people's rededication of themselves to it (Neh 8). Third Isaiah contradicts a part of that Torah that excludes foreigners and eunuchs from God's temple (Deut 23:1, 3), quoting Yahweh as saying, "my house shall be a house of prayer for all peoples" (56:7). Thus Third Isaiah stands alongside other traditions mentioned above, such as Ruth and Jonah, as an important witness to the ongoing diversity of perspectives in Persian-period Judah. Seeing the period purely through the lens of the Ezra and Nehemiah narratives misses an important part of the picture.

Concluding Reflections on Scriptures in and After the Exile

Ultimately, the Pentateuchal Torah, in combined P and non-P (L) form, became the scriptural foundation of later Judaism. Other holy texts were increasingly understood in light of this Torah. Not only were ancient collections of psalms organized into a Torah-centered whole, but shorter prophetic books such as Hosea and Zechariah were combined into a collection of twelve books that concludes with a passage that urges constant memory of the "Torah of my servant Moses" (Mal 4:4). And readers of other prophetic texts would have seen this combined P/non-P Torah in other references to God's "Torah" in Isaiah, Jeremiah, and Ezekiel.

In these and other ways, the Torah that first started to emerge under Josiah and was affirmed – in P and non-P forms – in the exile became ever more central in the post-exilic Persian period. But this process took time. Some early post-exilic texts, such as Third Isaiah (Isaiah 56–66) and Job, do not yet reflect the dominance of the Mosaic Torah that we see later. The community of Judah evolved significantly from the initial returns of exiles under Davidic descendants (Sheshbazzar, Zerubbabel) to its consolidation around Torah under Ezra the priest. Only toward the end of this period do we see the clear outlines of a Temple- and Torah-centered Judaism that would persist for several centuries of Hellenistic rule. Next we shall turn to look at that chapter in the history of the people and development of the Bible.

CHAPTER SEVEN REVIEW

1 Know the meaning and significance of the following terms discussed in this chapter:
- Cyrus cylinder (know similarities to and differences from Ezra 1:1–4)
- form criticism
- genre
- lament psalm
- Psalter
- rebuilding of the Jerusalem Temple (know the date and circumstances)
- Second Temple

2 Why is the Bible's depiction of the Persians so different from its depiction of the Assyrians and Babylonians?

3 Know the four major stages in the post-exilic rebuilding of the Judean community:
- several waves of return;
- rebuilding of the Temple;
- rebuilding of the wall around Jerusalem;
- centering on the Torah.
  Be able to summarize the Persian role in each of these stages.

4 What is a way that the documents from the post-exilic Jewish colony at Elephantine are significant?

5 What difference does it make to know that Genesis 1–3 is a combination of P and earlier (non-P) creation stories? What do we learn through realizing that Exodus 19–40 is probably the combination of very different L and P accounts of Sinai?

6 How does the book of Psalms reflect its origins in the Persian period? How does it reflect yet earlier origins?

7 (Focus text: Isa 56:1–8 contrasted with the figure and book of Ezra) The expulsion of foreign wives is one of the most difficult events for contemporary readers to understand. Are there circumstances in which you can imagine supporting a community's wish to ensure that their children only marry other members of that community, thus agreeing with a perspective akin to that of Ezra? Or are there circumstances where you can imagine a community legitimately needing to protect its identity in other ways? Conversely, in what kinds of circumstances can such tendencies be particularly dangerous, thus supporting a perspective more like that in Isaiah 56:1–8 (or Jonah or Ruth)?

RESOURCES FOR FURTHER STUDY

Genesis and Exodus (see pp. 94 and 190 for commentaries on these books)

Haggai and Zechariah 1–8
O'Brien, Julia M. *Nahum, Habakkuk, Zephaniah, Haggai, Zechariah, Malachi*. Nashville, TN: Abingdon, 2004.

Sweeney, Marvin. *The Twelve Prophets*, vol. 2. *Micah, Nahum, Habakkuk, Zephaniah, Haggai, Zechariah, Malachi*. Collegeville, MN: Liturgical, 2000–1.

Ezra, Nehemiah, and Esther
Blenkinsopp, Joseph. *Ezra–Nehemiah: A Commentary*. Philadelphia, PA: Westminster Press, 1988.

Clines, David. *Ezra, Nehemiah, Esther*. Grand Rapids, MI: Eerdmans, 1984.

Psalms
Brown, William. *Seeing the Psalms: A Theology of Metaphor*. Louisville, KY: Westminster John Knox Press, 2002.

Brueggemann, Walter. *Praying the Psalms* (revised edition). Winona, MN: St. Mary's, 1993.

Holladay, William. *The Psalms Through Three Thousand Years: Prayerbook of a Cloud of Witnesses*. Minneapolis, MN: Fortress, 1993. (History of interpretation of Psalms.)

Mays, James L. *Psalms*. Louisville, KY: Westminster John Knox Press, 1994.

Jonah

Trible, Phyllis. *Rhetorical Criticism: Context, Method, and the Book of Jonah*. Minneapolis, MN: Fortress, 1994.

Ruth

Fewell, Danna Nolan, and Gunn, David Miller. *Compromising Redemption: Relating Characters in the Book of Ruth*. Philadelphia, PA: Westminster John Knox Press, 1990.

Kates, Gail Twersky, and Reimer, Judith, eds. *Reading Ruth*. New York: Ballantine Books, 1994. Excellent collection of contemporary interpretations by Jewish women.

Job

Janzen, J. Gerald. *Job*. Atlanta, GA: John Knox Press, 1985.

Newsom, Carol. "Joh." Pp. 319–637 of vol. 4 of the *New Interpreters Bible*. Nashville, TN: Abingdon, 1996.

Isaiah 56–66 (See also the End of Chapter 6 for Commentaries on Isaiah 40–66)

Blenkinsopp, Joseph. *Isaiah 56–66: A New Translation with Introduction and Commentary*. New York: Doubleday, 2005.

Hellenistic Empires and the Formation of the Hebrew Bible

8

Chapter Overview

It is hard to come up with a sharper contrast in the experience of empire than that between the Judeans' experience of Persian support and their later near annihilation by the Hellenistic (Greek) king Antiochus Epiphanes IV. Though Hellenistic rule was not a serious problem in the first 157 years after Alexander the Great's conquest of the area (in 332 BCE), a major confrontation occurred in Judah in 174 BCE when Hellenizers sought to take control of Jerusalem and turn it into a Greek city. This led to an attempt to eradicate Judaism by the Hellenistic king, Antiochus IV, a successful rebellion led by a family of provincial priests, the Hasmoneans, and their establishment of a priest-ruled kingdom in Jerusalem that lasted eighty years.

A Contemporary Introduction to the Bible: Sacred Texts and Imperial Contexts, Second Edition. Colleen M. Conway and David M. Carr.
© 2021 Colleen M. Conway and David M. Carr. Published 2021 by John Wiley & Sons Ltd.

This chapter examines writings composed before and after this confrontation. Some writings composed earlier in the Hellenistic period, such as the Ben Sira/Sirach or some apocalypses now in Enoch, were included in the Old Testament collections of the Roman Catholic and/or Orthodox churches, but excluded from the Jewish Tanakh (and, as a result, the later Protestant Old Testament). Some later writings composed during or after the Hellenistic confrontation, such as the book of Daniel, were included in the Jewish Tanakh (as well as the Old Testament of all churches). Toward its conclusion, this chapter explores the important question of when Jewish communities started to define which texts were included in Hebrew scripture and how the later Jewish Tanakh and Christian Old Testament(s) developed.

Judaism and Hellenism Before the Hellenizing Crisis

Though early Hellenistic rule was not benign, it was not antagonistic toward the religion and culture of peoples such as the Judeans. From the time of Alexander's conquest (332 BCE) up to initial efforts to Hellenize Jerusalem (174 BCE), Judah was ruled by a succession of Hellenistic rulers without major incident. After Alexander's death in 323 BCE, his kingdom was split among his generals, including Ptolemy in Egypt and Seleucus in Mesopotamia. Judah was ruled first from Egypt by heirs of Ptolemy (323–198 BCE). Then, after a series of major battles, the Seleucids (heirs of Seleucus) took over in 198 BCE and ruled Judah for much of the following half-century. Things were difficult as the two Hellenistic empires struggled for control of the area, but there is no evidence (prior to the ruler Antiochus IV: more on him below) that either the Ptolemaic or the Seleucid rulers interfered with the religion of those they ruled or otherwise tried to Hellenize them. Nevertheless, Greek cities and people who had Greek education received privileges in these kingdoms, while those lacking Greek culture sometimes faced prejudice. For example, a non-Greek camel driver complains in an inscription that he was treated poorly because "I am a barbarian" and "I do not know how to behave like a Greek." An Egyptian priest complains in another inscription that a person whom he is suing "despises me because I am an Egyptian." Within Hellenistic cultures, Greek-educated children of Greek parents were at the top of the social pyramid, followed by Greek-educated children of non-Greek parents. Those who lacked any Greek education were disadvantaged even if they – like the Egyptian priest mentioned above – had extensive education in local, non-Greek texts, such as Egyptian classics or Hebrew books.

READING

Enoch 6–11 (the "Book of the Watchers"; see Wiley.com)Sirach/Ben Sira 1:1–10; 24:1–34; 44–50.

This meant that societies under Hellenistic rule had a growing cultural divide. On the one side stood Greek culture, the knowledge of which gave students access to government positions and/or business contacts across the Greek world. On the other side stood the cultures and native texts of peoples in Judah, Egypt, and Mesopotamia. The knowledge of ancient Near Eastern texts was less and less important in the broader Hellenistic culture but was still valued in temple–priestly circles. Therefore, within Judah, the Temple and various priesthoods connected to it became the primary place where people still learned and wrote texts in Hebrew. Otherwise, priests found themselves and their knowledge of ancient texts increasingly marginalized. In earlier times, knowledge of ancient Hebrew texts gave a person privileges in the Hebrew monarchy or Persian empire, but things were different under Hellenism. Now primary political and economic power belonged increasingly to those who could claim on some level to be "Greek."

Judeans and others dealt with this divide in different ways. Some priestly groups in both Egypt and Judah wrote esoteric visionary texts, called "**apocalypses**" after the Greek word for "uncovering." Some of these texts featured detailed tours of heaven ("heavenly apocalypses"), while others reviewed past history and then predicted divine intervention to remove Hellenistic rulers and restore native leaders ("historical apocalypses"). These apocalypses reflected both the broad scholarship of their priestly authors and their alienation from the surrounding Greek-dominated culture. The book of (first) Enoch, revered as scripture in the Ethiopic church, contains some of Judaism's oldest visionary texts, such as the calendar-focused "Book of the Luminaries" (now in parts of Enoch 72–82) and the "Book of the Watchers" (in Enoch 6–11), which told an expanded version of the story of divine human marriages seen in Gen 6:1–4. Jewish groups like the Qumran community (see textbox below on the Dead Sea Scrolls) appear to have revered books like Enoch as much or more than some other books later included in the Hebrew Bible. The early Jesus movement also valued the Enoch traditions. Indeed, a verse from Enoch is cited as authoritative in the New Testament book of Jude (Jude 14–15; referring to Enoch 1:9).

The meaning of these often obscure visionary texts is unclear initially to most readers. On one level, they elaborate on biblical narratives and feature many unfamiliar characters and scenes, battles between angels and the like. Yet on another level, these apocalypses in Enoch are coded descriptions of battles between Hellenistic rulers (Enoch 6–11) or crises in the Jerusalem priesthood (Enoch 12–16) and God's plan to intervene and set things right. These texts speak to concerns that were present in the third century BCE about Hellenistic domination and the corruption of the Temple, but they claim as their author an ancient, pre-Hellenistic sage, Enoch (see Gen 5:21–4). Such attribution of a later text to an ancient author, termed "**pseudepigraphy**," was particularly common in the Hellenistic age, when ancient authorship determined whether or not a given text would be studied in schools. In this case, however, Hellenistic-style pseudepigraphy was used by Jewish authors to provide extra authority to their predictions of liberation from Hellenistic kings and corrupt leaders.

FIGURE 8.1
Copy of the Hebrew book of Ben Sira found near the Dead Sea.

The book of **Ben Sira** (also known as **Sirach**, its Greek name), originally written in Hebrew by Joshua ben Sira around 200–180 BCE, shows a different way to respond to the divide between local and Hellenistic culture (see Figure 8.1). In a possible critique of esoteric apocalypses such as those in Enoch, Ben Sira discourages speculation about heavenly realms (3:21–4) and rejects dreams as generally misleading (34:1–8). Instead, he writes a wisdom instruction to fit (both) the Torah focus and the Hellenistic tenor of his present time. Like older instructions in Proverbs, Ben Sira directly addresses his students, encouraging them to live prudently and put wisdom above other values. Like more recent works from the exile and post-exile, Ben Sira portrays the Torah as the ultimate wisdom, now going so far as to identify the Torah of Moses with the female personified wisdom seen in Proverbs and elsewhere (Ben Sira 24; see Proverbs 8).

Yet Ben Sira also shows influence from Hellenistic culture. At various points, his sayings resemble Greek sayings by the sixth-century BCE Greek poet Theognis that were commonly used early in the process of Greek education. Moreover, the Torah takes on a role in Ben Sira that is similar to that of Homer's epics in Greek education. It, like Homer, is the foundation and end point of the rest of the process of education and study. Finally, the book of Ben Sira concludes with a set of praises that have much in common with the Hellenistic genre of *encomium* (work of praise): a praise of "great fathers" that is divided between figures in the Pentateuch (Ben Sira 44–5) and figures found in all of the rest of the Hebrew Bible (46–49), followed by an extended praise of the high priest in Ben Sira's own time, Simon (50:1–21).

Many scholars rightly have seen in this "praise of great fathers" evidence that virtually all of the books in the Hebrew Bible were known and revered by

Ben Sira's time (200–180 BCE). Nevertheless, other parts of the book of Ben Sira show that its author was not yet working with an idea of a closed collection of scriptural books. His own description of what a scribe studies includes "the law of the most high" (probably the Torah), wisdom of the ancients, prophecies, sayings of the famous, parables, and proverbs (Sir 39:1–3), as well as foreign wisdom (39:4). The book of Ben Sira, explicitly written in the late second century by a sage of that time, aims to be a new addition to that broader scribal curriculum.

Ben Sira is just one example of a book written in a local language (Hebrew) that reflects Greek learning. But Jews also wrote Greek works and translated into Greek works that originally were in Hebrew. Sometime in the third century the Pentateuch was translated into Greek, and other Hebrew books (including Ben Sira) were translated later on. This group of early Greek translations of Hebrew scriptures is usually referred to with the term "Septuagint." New works written by Judeans in Greek often drew deeply on models and values seen in the Greek literature that they had learned. Some of these are found in the deuterocanonical books of the Roman Catholic and other churches, books such as 2 Maccabees, Judith, and the Wisdom of Solomon. For example, the Wisdom of Solomon is a work in Greek that draws deeply and broadly on Stoicism and other parts of Greek philosophy in the process of retelling the story of Solomon's search for wisdom.

When we look across the full range of Jewish texts of this time, it becomes clear that all parts of Judaism were deeply affected by Hellenism and Hellenistic culture, even when they opposed elements of that culture. The apocalypses undergird their messages with Hellenistic-style pseudepigraphy. Ben Sira writes in Hebrew, but draws on sayings, ideas, and forms from Greek education. And the author of the Wisdom of Solomon draws on multiple strands of Greek philosophy in its depictions of wisdom. As a result, there is no clear distinction between "Hellenistic Judaism" and other forms, since all of Judaism was touched by Hellenistic culture and ideas. The main distinction that does appear is between forms of Hellenistic Judaism that were neutral or positive about Hellenism and forms of Hellenistic Judaism that were opposed to it. This distinction emerges particularly in the crisis around the attempt to Hellenize Jerusalem, to which we turn next.

The Emergence of "Judaism"

This Hellenistic period is the time when we can start to talk about the emergence of a "Jewish" identity in addition to and distinct from a "Judean" identity. The word "Jew" comes from the Greek word for Judean, *Ioudaios*. Though it encompassed Judeans living in Judah, it also embraced the ever expanding number of Jews living permanently outside Judah. Such Jews still had deep ties to Judah, but they were best known for their distinctive religion and set of practices.

The Crisis Over Hellenizing Jerusalem and the Book of Daniel

READING

Narratives about the Maccabean crisis: 2 Maccabees 4–8. Apocalyptic writing: Daniel 7.

The Seleucids under Antiochus III were initially quite friendly to Jews and Judaism. When Antiochus III took control of Judah from the Ptolemies in 198 BCE, he affirmed more ancient Persian policies toward Judah. He gave tax relief to the city and money for the Temple, and affirmed by royal decree the right of Jews to live "according to [their] ancestral laws." Later on, however, he suffered defeat by the Romans and started to pay heavy tribute to them. He died in the process of trying to raid one of the temples in his kingdom for money, and a similar attempt apparently was made during the reign of his successor, Seleucus IV (see 2 Maccabees 3). By the time Antiochus Epiphanes IV seized the throne from Seleucus IV in 175 BCE, the kingdom had been humiliated by the Romans, and Antiochus needed money to pay them a large annual tribute. At this point, Judah was one of the few Seleucid territories remaining on the Western Mediterranean.

It was under these circumstances that Antiochus IV started to sell the high priesthood in Jerusalem to the highest bidder, a significant move, since the high priest of Jerusalem's Temple functioned at this time as the local ruler and tax collector for the region. First, Jason, who was a brother of the existing high priest, paid money to Antiochus on the occasion of the latter's accession to the throne for two privileges: (1) the office of high priest and (2) the right to turn Jerusalem into a Greek city, complete with its own gymnasium within sight of the temple (174 BCE). Three years later, another leading figure, Menelaus, outbid Jason, took over the high priesthood, and forced Jason to flee (171 BCE). Menelaus's rule proved highly unpopular, however, and the Seleucids had to intervene twice to restore him to power. The second time, fed up with revolts, Antiochus IV enacted harsh measures aimed at crushing any trace of Jewish culture (in 167 BCE). He imposed the death penalty on Jews for continuing to follow Torah laws such as eating regulations and circumcision, and he set up an altar to Zeus Olympius over the altar to Yahweh in the Jerusalem Temple. What had started as a mild attempt by Jason and other Jerusalemites to gain Greek privileges for Jerusalem and its citizens had turned into a life-and-death struggle for the continuance of Torah observance.

Basics on the Book of Daniel

Several chapters of Daniel are in Aramaic (2–7), others in Hebrew (1, 8–12). **Language**

The Aramaic legends in Daniel 4–6 probably go back, in some form, to the late **Date** Persian or early Hellenistic period, while the other stories in Daniel 1–6 largely date to the later Hellenistic period before the crisis over Hellenization. The book as a whole, including the visionary chapters in Daniel 7–12, dates from just before 164 BCE and reflects the crisis of that time.

The Greek translation of Daniel preserves yet other traditions about Daniel and **More information** other figures (e.g. Susanna in Daniel 13). In addition, an Aramaic story about Nabonidus was found in the Dead Sea Scrolls at Qumran and represents a different form of the tradition seen in Daniel 4.

The visions in Daniel 7–12 were written to give Judeans hope in this crisis. Like the apocalyptic visions in Enoch, these chapters of Daniel are attributed to an earlier figure, this time the exilic figure of Daniel who is featured in the tales of Daniel 1–2, 4–6. Moreover, like other historical apocalypses, these visions in Daniel give a coded overview of past history before predicting God's intervention to make things right. We can see an example of this in the vision of four beasts coming out of the sea in Daniel 7. These four beasts correspond to four major world empires leading up to the time of Antiochus IV: the Babylonians who destroyed the Jerusalem temple (7:4), the Medes who dominated lands east of Babylonia (7:5), the Persians (7:6), and the Greeks, particularly the 10 rulers – "horns" – of the Seleucid dynasty (7:7), from which a "little horn," Antiochus IV, sprouts (7:8).

After surveying these four empires, the vision moves to the future, predicting the destruction of the fourth, Greek beast and God's gift of eternal dominion to a mysterious "one like a son of man" (7:9–14). Many Christians have read this text in light of gospel accounts where Jesus refers to himself as the "son of man," and have understood Daniel 7 as a prediction of the coming of Jesus. Nevertheless, the details of the text, especially the "interpretation" given to Daniel in 7:15–27, indicate that this chapter was originally intended to give hope to Torah-observant Jews under threat from Antiochus. Antiochus is the one who attempted to end sacrifice and forbid Torah observance, to "change the sacred times and the law" (7:25). In his vision, Daniel is told that God will destroy the kingdom of Antiochus and grant eternal rule to those who have remained faithful to the Torah, "the holy ones of the most High" (7:27).

Things did not work out exactly as this or other visions in Daniel 7–12 predicted, but these visions have continued to give hope to generations of Jews and Christians. Jews have read the text as a prediction of God's establishment of God's rule with the future arrival of the messiah. Christians have read it as a prediction of God's transformation of the world with the second coming of Jesus Christ. In each case, people have found numerous ways to coordinate the obscure symbols of Daniel 7–12 with groups and events of their own time. At their best, such interpretations have given much-needed hope to communities facing oppressors as bad as or worse than Antiochus IV. At their worst, these reinterpretations of Daniel have encouraged people to withdraw from the world and wait for God's imminent intervention on their behalf. Certainly it would be a mistake for any community to suppose that their own understanding of the visions in

Daniel is the one and only true way to unlock the code of the book. The persistently strange imagery of the book resists this kind of certainty and is part of what has allowed Daniel to be revered and reinterpreted by communities long after the time of the Hellenistic crisis.

A Hellenistic Period Kingdom of Israel: The Hasmonean Revolt and Monarchy

Ultimately, Antiochus IV was unsuccessful, though not in the ways envisioned in Daniel 7–12. Members of a marginal priestly family in rural Judah, the **Hasmoneans** or **Maccabees**, launched a guerilla war against the Seleucids. They started by destroying pagan altars, killing Jewish collaborators with the Seleucids, and forcibly circumcising males who had been left uncircumcised under Seleucid order. Their effort culminated with the recapture of Jerusalem and purification of the Temple (164 BCE). (Note: **Hanukkah** is the Jewish holiday celebrating this triumph and the purification of the Temple.) In addition, the Hasmoneans were able to negotiate an end to the edict of Antiochus IV against Judaism. Jews were free to observe Torah regulations again, and we hear no more of any attempts to reverse this policy.

Significant Dates in the Rise of the Hasmonean Kingdom

Antiochus IV seizes power over Seleucid empire	175 BCE
Jason buys high priesthood and initiates Hellenizing	174 BCE
Menelaus purchases priesthood	171 BCE
Unpopular rule, uprisings	
Harsh measures by Antiochus IV to eradicate Judaism	167 BCE
Beginning of Maccabean rebellion under Hasmoneans	
Purification/rededication of Temple	164 BCE
End of harsh edicts against Judaism	
Independent Hasmonean rule	142–63 BCE
Beginning of Roman rule of Palestine	63 BCE

All this did not, however, mean an end to Greek domination. Though Antiochus IV died around this time, the Seleucids soon regained control over Judah, killing the leader of the Hasmonean family, Judas Maccabeus ("the hammer"), in battle and forcing the other Hasmoneans and their supporters to flee. Around 152 BCE, however, the Hasmoneans played their cards right in a power struggle over the Seleucid throne, choosing to back the winner of that struggle, Demetrius. In return, Demetrius appointed the Hasmonean Jonathan as high priest and thus ruler of the province of Judah. When Jonathan was murdered about a decade later, his brother Simon declared independence from the Seleucid empire (142 BCE). By then the Seleucids did not have the power to bring Judah back under their control.

Thus Judah was free of direct foreign rule for the first time in hundreds of years. For approximately seven decades (142–63 BCE), the Hasmoneans controlled Jerusalem and the high priesthood. Moreover, they gradually expanded their realm to include not only the old heartland of Judah and Israel but also areas that had few Jews and had not been dominated by Jerusalem for centuries: the Phoenician coastland, Edom and the rest of the Transjordan, and Galilee (see Map 8.1 on p. 225). At the beginning of their activity the Hasmoneans fought for Jewish rights to observe the Torah. Now as rulers, they expelled gentiles from some of the areas they conquered, converted others, and imposed (male) circumcision on their subject populations. Their passion for ancient ways is seen in their promotion of the Torah, their advocacy for the Hebrew language in a now Aramaic-speaking populace, and their use of ancient Hebrew script on the new coins that they minted. The book of 1 Maccabees was originally written in Hebrew to celebrate and support the Hasmonean kingdom. It presents the Hasmoneans as true heirs of the Israelite judges, proponents of the Hebrew heritage, and righteous opponents of the forces of Hellenism.

Nevertheless, the Hasmonean rulers were also influenced in multiple ways by the Hellenistic culture they purported to oppose. The whole practice of issuing coins was a Greek one, and the Hasmonean coins with ancient Hebrew letters also featured images and symbols drawn from older Greek coins of the Ptolemies and Seleucids. In this way, coins, such as the one pictured in Figure 8.2, vividly illustrate the kind of cultural hybridity we have seen at other points in Israelite history: the blending of self-determination with elements drawn from the culture of the past oppressor. We see similar hybridity in other cultural products of the Hasmonean period. The Hasmoneans built palaces with Greek columns and friezes but were careful to equip them with baths to preserve ritual purity. Jewish burial tombs from this time are virtually identical with their Greek-pagan counterparts in other countries except for their avoidance of pictorial representation, in obedience to dictates found in Deuteronomy (Deut 4:15–19). The book of 2 Maccabees celebrates heroes who fought for the Torah, using Hellenistic modes of history writing and imitating Greek models of heroic martyrs. In these and other ways the Hasmoneans developed a hybrid culture that promoted anti-Hellenism while adapting Hellenistic features.

The Book of Judith (as an example of a Hasmonean text)

The **book of Judith** tells a tale of how a Judean female deliverer, Judith, saves her people from a threat posed by an Assyrian general, Holofernes. In a plot reminiscent of the story of Jael and Sisera (Judg 4:17–24; 5:24–7), Judith seductively lures Holofernes into being alone with her in his tent, cuts off his head, and then orders a successful attack on Holofernes's massive army. Though there are signs that the book may be based on an older set of traditions from the Persian period, multiple historical anachronisms mark it as unhistorical, and the story has been updated so that "Judith's" victory anticipates the victory of Judas and other Hasmoneans over Antiochus IV. It and other histories related to the Hasmonean period (e.g. 1, 2, 3, and 4 Maccabees) did not end up being included in the Jewish Tanakh (and thus also not the Protestant Bible). Nevertheless, they were included in early Christian Bibles and are part of many present Christian Old Testaments.

FIGURE 8.2
Coin from the time of the Hasmoneans, combining the Greek practice of coinage (with an image!) with an inscription on the other side in archaic Hebrew lettering.

Writings about life in the diaspora: Esther, Daniel 3.

READING

The Hellenistic Period as the Setting for Other Hebrew Bible Texts

The Hebrew Bible contains several books that were probably written sometime during this Hellenistic period. We have already discussed the visions of Daniel, which show clear signs of having been written sometime during the Hellenistic crisis of 169–164 BCE. But other books of the Bible were also either written or modified in the years after Alexander conquered the area. In addition, some of the tales about Daniel and other Judeans in the Persian court (e.g. Daniel 4–6) probably originate in the late Persian or early Hellenistic period. Most scholars would date the book of Esther to a similar time. And the books of Chronicles and Ezra–Nehemiah, though containing earlier materials, likewise show multiple signs of a Hellenistic period dating.

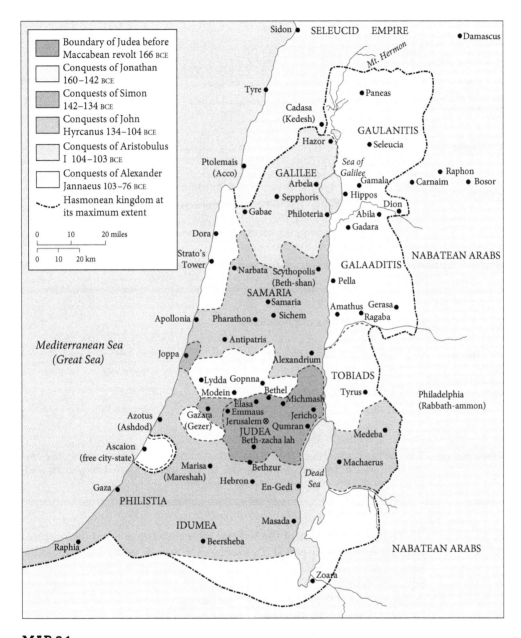

MAP 8.1
The expanding kingdom of the Hasmoneans. Redrawn from Norman Gottwald, *The Hebrew Bible: A Socio-Literary Introduction*. Minneapolis: Fortress, 1985, page 407.

Basics on the Book of Esther

Outline: story of victory behind the holiday of Purim	I	Esther's rise and saving of her people	1–8
	II	Revenge of Jews and beginning of Purim	9–10

Date   Third century BCE (200s).

More information   The book of Esther in Hebrew is distinguished by its lack of mention of God or traditional piety. The Greek translations of Esther include additions that solve this problem by inserting prayers, references to God, etc. These more pious forms of Esther were preserved in the Christian church.

     Meanwhile, Esther has become the central reading within Judaism for the raucous holiday of Purim. This holiday, which happens in late February or early March, features dressing up, candy, gifts for the poor, and audience response during the reading of the Esther scroll.

Basics on the Books of Chronicles

Outline: Temple and priest-centered history of Judah's kings	I	Genealogy: Adam to exile	1 Chr 1–9
	II	Reign of David	1 Chr 10–29
	III	Reign of Solomon	2 Chr 1–9
	IV	Judean kingship until exile	2 Chr 10–36

Date   Fourth century BCE (300s).

More information   Though isolated parts of Chronicles preserve unique historical sources, the vast majority of its differences from Samuel–Kings represent late divergences added in light of Persian or later historical realities.

Overall, many parts of the Hebrew Bible probably reached their present form in the Hellenistic period. This seems to be the case with books such as the Song of Songs and Ecclesiastes, both of which feature late forms of Hebrew typical of Hellenistic period texts. Though earlier in this textbook we suggested that some part of these books may have been written during the early monarchy (see Chapter 3), they were certainly modified later. For example, a Hellenistic period scribe appears to have added the following orthodox conclusion to the book of Ecclesiastes:

> The conclusion of the matter, all which was heard: fear God and keep God's commandments. This is the duty of every person. For God will bring every deed to judgment, even every secret thing, whether good or bad. (Eccl 12:13–14)

This conclusion shows ideas of Torah obedience and final judgment that are common in the Hellenistic period. They contrast strongly with the skepticism of most of the rest of Ecclesiastes, such as "Do not be too righteous and do not be too wise, for why should you be ruined?" (Eccl 7:16). In this way and many others, the present Hebrew Bible/Old Testament, in Ecclesiastes and many other books, is an intricate blend of old and new.

Basics on the Books of Ezra–Nehemiah

I	Return and rebuilding of Temple	Ezra 1–6	**Outline: the cultic and political establishment of Torah-centered Judean community**
II	Torah + Temple-centered community		
	A Preparations		
	1 Ezra's commission and divorce of foreign wives	Ezra 7–10	
	2 Nehemiah's building of politically independent Jerusalem	Nehemiah 1–7	
	B Ezra and Nehemiah's creation of Torah-centered community	Nehemiah 8–13	

Ezra 4:8–6:18 and 7:12–26 are in Aramaic, while the rest is in Hebrew. **Language**

The present form of the book may date as late as the mid-second century (160–150s BCE). **Date**

The bulk of the book is probably earlier, particularly the sources for Ezra (Ezra 7–10; Neh 8) and Nehemiah (Neh 1:1–7:4; 13:10–14, 30b–31) that were discussed in Chapter 7. **More information**

Daniel 10–12

FOCUS TEXT

The report of a vision in Daniel 10–12 is one of the best examples of a text that is presented as old, but is manifestly new. At the outset we hear that the exilic figure Daniel received this vision in "the third year of king Cyrus of Persia" (Dan 10:1). Nevertheless, the following two chapters make clear that the author knew world history up to the time of the Hellenistic crisis, but not events afterward. The vision starts with an angelic figure, perhaps Gabriel, appearing to Daniel and anticipating future events in the Hellenistic and Persian periods: the defeat of the Persian empire by Alexander ("the warrior king" in 11:3), the division of his kingdom among his four generals (11:4), various specific events in the history of the Ptolemies of Egypt ("the king[s] of the south," 11:5–12), the conquest of Judah and Egypt by the Seleucid Antiochus III (11:13–16), the attempt to rob the Jerusalem Temple under his successor, Seleucus IV (11:20), the rise and initial conquests of Antiochus IV (11:21–8), and his profaning of the Temple and persecution of observant Jews (11:29–39). At this point, however, the text diverges from history, inaccurately predicting further conquests by Antiochus IV (11:40–5) and the time when the Temple would be purified and rededicated (12:11–12). Clearly this vision was written after the onset of the Hellenistic crisis in 169 BCE but before its end and the death of Antiochus IV.

This text is particularly important, however, because it concludes with a vision of resurrection that is unique in the Hebrew Bible. Elsewhere, the Hebrew Bible has little place for an idea of afterlife. There is no belief in heaven and hell. Instead, all who died were thought to go to a shadowy existence in "Sheol" that involved neither reward nor punishment. As Proverbs indicates, the main hope for virtuous reward was prosperity in this life, along with children and a good name to continue after death (e.g. Prov 10:4, 7, 27–8; 12:28). This perspective, however, did not provide much comfort amidst a situation like the Hellenistic crisis. There people (and their children) were being killed for staying faithful to the Torah. This text in Daniel promises that this is not the end for them. Instead, those that have been faithful – that is, "the wise ones" – will be resurrected after the death of Antiochus IV and "shine like the brightness of heaven." Meanwhile, those of their persecutors who have died will also be resurrected, but to shame and continual punishment (Dan 12:1–3).

The Greeks had long believed in some kind of individual afterlife (e.g. the kingdom of Hades), but this Hebrew idea of collective afterlife in Daniel now empowered resistance to Greek oppression. It gave people hope to resist Antiochus IV even if opposition to his decree would cost them their lives. Here again we can see how the cultural traditions of the oppressor could be used by the oppressed to enable resistance. Moreover, this idea of afterlife has continued to empower resistance by people facing difficult odds. The belief in a reward during God's final judgment has helped generations of Jews and Christians remain faithful even when facing powerful oppressors capable of killing them.

Two centuries later, these kinds of beliefs in God's (coming) transformation of the world would be common among the Jews of the first century, among whom Jesus and his followers should be numbered. By then a new powerful empire, that of the Romans, had taken control of Judah. Soon Judah was hammered by crises at least as severe as, if not more so than, the Hellenistic crisis of the second century BCE. Within this context, visions such as Daniel 10–12 gave Jews hope that death at the hands of the Romans was not the final chapter in their lives. Though it might seem to them as if the political powers of evil were triumphing, texts such as Daniel reassured them that God soon would intervene, destroy evil empires, and resurrect the faithful ones to everlasting glory.

The Dead Sea Scrolls

Starting in 1946, local Bedouin and then archaeologists began to find extremely old Jewish texts that had been stored in caves in the desert hills on the northwest shore of the Dead Sea. The very dry climate and isolation of the area meant that hundreds of these scrolls had been at least partially preserved over thousands of years. They were collected and stored by a community that appears to have had a base in the ruins known as *Khirbet Qumran.* This Qumran community wrote and stored a wide variety of texts, including some written within and for their community, texts now in the Bible, and yet other Jewish texts. The discovery and study of these Dead Sea Scrolls has provided priceless insight into the final formation of biblical texts and the diversity of Jewish literature in the Second Temple period. Thanks to them, we now have increased insight into the different forms of Judaism that existed in the centuries up to and including Jesus. The texts also show how the ancient Jewish community at Qumran, like the early Jesus movement, read and revered a broader range of books than those included in the Jewish Tanakh and Christian Old Testament(s).

For more information, see James C. VanderKam, *The Dead Sea Scrolls Today*. 2nd revised edition. Grand Rapids: Eerdmans, 2010. For images and information about the scrolls, see also https://www.deadseascrolls.org.il.

The Formation of the Jewish Tanakh and Christian Old Testament(s)

Thanks to the discovery of the Dead Sea Scrolls and other developments (see the above textbox on the Dead Sea Scrolls), we now know that there was no authoritative set of Hebrew scriptures up through the period of the Second Temple. To be sure, most Jews shared a reverence for the Torah of Moses (=Pentateuch) and saw themselves as related in some way to the land of Israel and the temple there. Nevertheless, otherwise there was a great variety in Judaism of the period, and this was reflected in a variety of ways that Hellenistic- and Hasmonean-period Jews related to older texts. Certain groups that were closely related to a temple – such as the Sadducees (linked to the Jerusalem Temple) or the Samaritans (linked to a northern temple at Gerizim) – seem to have focused particularly on the Torah/Pentateuch as an authoritative reference text. Many other Jewish groups, like the Jesus movement or the community based at Qumran (see the above textbox on the Dead Sea Scrolls), affirmed the authority of "The Torah and Prophets," with "prophets" here relating to a broad array of books considered to be prophetically inspired, both books like Isaiah that were put in the later "Prophets" category of the Tanakh and other books like Enoch that were not included in the later Tanakh at all.

It is not clear exactly when Jews began determining exactly what books were included in a more formal set of scriptures and which were left out. There is a chance that the Hasmoneans might have begun this process. The Hasmonean kings, who built a reputation for themselves as defenders of Judaism against Hellenism, had the power and the motivation to establish a standardized set of Jewish texts that then could compete with the similarly standardized set of Greek texts valued in the Hellenistic world (e.g. Homer and the classical authors).

Nevertheless, if the Hasmoneans did attempt such a standardization of Hebrew scripture, that standardization was not recognized by a number of Jewish groups. The above-mentioned Jewish community based at Qumran revered a wide range of texts extending beyond the later Jewish Tanakh, and the same was true for the early Jesus movement. Indeed, we do not start to see potential references to the particular set of books that now constitute the Jewish Tanakh until well *after* the Hellenistic period, such as in a listing of "Torah and allied documents" by the first-century CE Jewish historian Josephus (*Against Apion* 1:38–41), a listing that comes close to the contents of the later Jewish Tanakh.

If this evidence seems confusing to you, it should clarify why scholars profoundly disagree on these questions. There is no royal pronouncement, no meeting of leaders, no identifiable time that one can point to and say "this is when and why the books in the Bible were included and others were left out."

All we can know is that later Jewish and Christian communities each ended up with slightly different versions of these scriptures. Rabbinic writings like the Babylonian Talmud (from the sixth century CE) contain lists of twenty-four books in a three-part Jewish Bible, the Tanakh (Torah, Prophets, Writings). Meanwhile, Christian church councils of the third and fourth centuries produce various lists of books in their "Old Testament." As noted in this textbook's prologue, these latter books of the Christian Old Testament(s) overlap with those in the Jewish Tanakh, but they also include other books like Ben Sira, Judith, etc. During the Protestant reform of the 1500s, however, Martin Luther and other Protestant leaders decided to conform the contents of their Old Testament to books found in the rabbinic Tanakh. As a result, Christian Old Testaments now vary in contents. The Protestant Bible has the fewest books (parallel in contents to the Jewish Tanakh), while Roman Catholic and various Orthodox Christian Bibles have an Old Testament that includes additional books, often termed "deuterocanonical."

Conclusion

This chapter has focused on biblical texts written (or revised) during the Hellenistic period, but we must remember again that these texts transcended their original historical contexts. The tales of Daniel 1–6 and Esther gave hope to Jewish exiles of later centuries. The book of Ben Sira provided a new fusion of Torah wisdom with Greek learning. The visions of Enoch and Daniel 7–12 reassured Jews and Christians facing persecution. The histories in Chronicles and Ezra–Nehemiah communicated a vision of Temple- and Torah-centered Judaism to later generations, and narratives like Judith celebrated the triumph of underdogs over imperial aggressors. Overall, the Hellenistic and Hasmonean periods were a fruitful time of cultural cross-fertilization and Jewish literary productivity in Hebrew, Aramaic, and Greek.

In addition, as we have seen, the Hebrew Bible as a whole, the "Torah and Prophets," underwent transformations as it became the foundation of two religious movements: Judaism and Christianity. An increasingly Torah-focused Judaism developed the three-part Tanakh, and these older Hebrew scriptures were studied alongside a newer set of rabbinic legal traditions. Christianity gradually separated from its Jewish roots, but it continued to recognize the books of its Jewish heritage as scripture. Yet now Christians arranged those books of Jewish scripture into an "Old Testament" that led into a "New Testament" of specifically Christian books. People of these times valued what was old, so this labeling of Hebrew scriptures as "Old Testament" reflected an ongoing reverence for these texts. Yet the naming of specifically Christian scriptures as "New Testament" also showed an emphasis within Christianity on the special importance – both in theology and in worship – of Christian writings such as the gospels and Pauline letters. We turn now to take a closer look at these texts and their contexts.

CHAPTER EIGHT REVIEW

1 Know the meaning and significance of the following terms discussed in this chapter:
- apocalypse
- Ben Sira/Sirach
- Hanukkah
- Hasmoneans
- Maccabees
- pseudepigraphy

2 What major empires are reflected in the coded visions of Daniel 7 and 10–12? How is the Persian empire viewed in these visions in comparison with the Nehemiah memoir and Ezra narrative?

3 How was the Hasmonean kingdom different from the ancient Davidic monarchy?

4 How is the phenomenon of hybridity reflected in the works of the Hasmoneans? How might it be reflected in the final formation of the Hebrew Bible?

5 What are other major candidates in the Hebrew Bible to be writings from the Hellenistic period?

6 (Focus text: Daniel 10–12) Drawing on this chapter's discussion of the book of Daniel and of Daniel 10–12 in particular, try writing a brief historical apocalypse that would empower a contemporary oppressed group. Use Daniel 10–12 as your overall model, but make up your own imagery and connect your apocalypse to recent history and contemporary crises. Try to incorporate the kinds of features (pseudepigraphy, historical review, and projection of divine triumph) that are seen in texts such as Daniel 10–12, but attribute the apocalypse to a major authoritative figure of the more recent past. Have a friend read and try to decode it. What is similar and different about your twenty-first-century apocalypse and the one found in Daniel 10–12?

RESOURCES FOR FURTHER STUDY

Jewish Writings from the Hellenistic and Early Roman Periods

Nickelsburg, George. *Jewish Literature Between the Bible and the Mishnah* (revised edition). Minneapolis, MN: Fortress, 2005.

Daniel

Newsom, Carol. *Daniel*. Louisville, KY: Westminster John Knox, 2014.

Chronicles

Japhet, Sara. *1 and 2 Chronicles*. Louisville, KY: Westminster John Knox, 1993.

Esther

Beal, Timothy. *The Book of Hiding: Gender, Ethnicity, Annihilation, and Esther*. London: Routledge, 1997.

Berlin, Adele. *Esther*. Philadelphia, PA: Jewish Publication Society, 2001.

The Formation of the Jewish Tanakh and Christian Old Testament(s)

McDonald, Lee Martin. *Origin of the Bible: A Guide for the Perplexed*. New York: Continuum, 2011.

Prologue to the Study of the New Testament

The second half of this textbook turns to the study of a collection of writings known as the New Testament. This English title comes from the Latin translation (*novum testamentum*) of the early Greek designation "New Covenant" (*kainē diathēkē*). There are 27 "books" in the New Testament. They are listed in the chart below in canonical rather than chronological order.

The New Testament Canon

The four gospels

Matthew	Luke
Mark	John

Acts of the Apostles

Pauline Letters (also known as Pauline "Epistles")

Romans	1 Thessalonians
1 Corinthians	2 Thessalonians
2 Corinthians	1 Timothy
Galatians	2 Timothy
Ephesians	Titus
Philippians	Philemon
Colossians	

General Letters (or General Epistles)

Hebrews	1 John
James	2 John
1 Peter	3 John
2 Peter	Jude

Revelation to John

A Contemporary Introduction to the Bible: Sacred Texts and Imperial Contexts, Second Edition.
Colleen M. Conway and David M. Carr.
© 2021 Colleen M. Conway and David M. Carr. Published 2021 by John Wiley & Sons Ltd.

The four gospels narrate stories about the words and deeds of Jesus of Nazareth and his conflict with authorities in Jerusalem. Each gospel concludes with an account of his trial and crucifixion by Roman authorities followed by references to or stories about his resurrection from death. The Acts of the Apostles is an account of the growing Jesus movement after the death of Jesus. It was written by the same author as the Gospel of Luke and in that sense should be read as a second volume to that gospel. The earliest New Testament writings are the letters written by the apostle Paul. He was not a disciple while Jesus was alive but became a leading figure in the spread of the Jesus movement about two decades later. While there are thirteen letters attributed to Paul, as we will see, not all of them were written by him. Finally, we have a group of diverse writings some of which are attributed to important figures like Peter or James. The New Testament canon concludes with the Revelation to John, an apocalyptic text directed toward Christ-followers living in the cities of Asia Minor.

In this introductory textbook we focus on the gospels, Acts, and some of the Pauline epistles. Chapter 15 provides a brief study of three other writings (Revelation, Hebrews, and 1 Peter).

Before we turn to the study of the New Testament, we should keep in mind several important points. On the one hand, we will see that the New Testament differs in important ways from the writings of the Hebrew Bible/ Old Testament. The writings focus mainly on Jesus and his followers and were written across a shorter time span. On the other hand, we will see many connections with the history of Israel and the writings that we have studied in the first half of the book. The "Torah and Prophets" were scriptures for the New Testament authors and they frequently turn to them to interpret the person and work of Jesus.

In addition, we should keep in mind that the New Testament was written in the context of ongoing development and diversity in Jewish thinking and writing. We already saw evidence of this diversity in the previous chapter in texts such as Enoch, Ben Sira, and the Wisdom of Solomon. These are just some of the Jewish writings from the Second Temple period. Others offer continued reflection and speculation on ideas such as God's final judgment, the resurrection from the dead, the afterlife, and a coming messiah. These Jewish writings had a strong influence on the New Testament authors, even though they may be less familiar to us. Meanwhile, there is also a large body of Greek and Roman literature that is part of the literary context of the New Testament. While there is not space to study this literature in detail, in the coming chapters we will note where Greek or Roman ideas and literary forms are reflected in New Testament writings.

Finally, we need to explain some terminology that we will use in the rest of this book. You probably already noticed our use of the terms "Christ-followers" and "Jesus movement" rather than "Christians" and "Christianity" when discussing the early followers of Jesus and the emerging church. We use these terms because during the first and early second century CE, the period when most of the texts of the New Testament were written, the term Christian was not regularly used for people who believed in Jesus as God's messiah. In fact, the term "Christian" appears only three times in the New

Testament – twice in Acts (11:28 and 26:28) and once in 1 Peter (4:16). When the apostle Paul addresses the people to whom he writes, he uses terms like "holy ones" (often translated as "saints") or "brothers" (sometimes translated more inclusively as "brothers and sisters" or "believers"). Meanwhile, the term "Christianity" never appears in the New Testament because it did not yet exist as an organized religious tradition, distinct from Judaism. Even in Acts, where the word Christian does make two appearances, the character Paul says he is a follower of "the Way" (Acts 24:14).

Another problem with using the term Christian, apart from its rare appearance in the New Testament is that for 21st century readers, the word evokes a set of associations that would be completely anachronistic to the 1st century CE. Even when the word does appear in ancient texts, it would not mean what it does today. Twenty-first century Christianity is the product of two thousand years of history and ever-changing traditions. Indeed, one could argue that what we now have is "Christianities," given the wide variety of Christian belief and practices that exist in the contemporary world.

We encounter similar translation problems with the word "church" in the New Testament. Most people who hear the word church may well think first of a building where Christians gather, or a specific religious institution (as in church vs. synagogue or mosque). Yet, the Greek word behind the English translation "church" is *ekklesia* which did not refer to a building, nor a specific type of religious institution. In ancient Greece, *ekklesia* referred to a public assembly, typically a political one. In the first century CE, the word could be used as a designation for both civic assemblies and non-civic associations in both Jewish and Greco-Roman contexts. In fact, *ekklesia* could refer to Jewish synagogue communities. In this textbook, I typically use the word assembly, or sometimes Christ-group instead of "church" in order to avoid anachronistic images of steepled buildings, or groups of Christians as opposed to Jews.

It is likely that terms like Christ-followers or Jesus movement will seem odd and unfamiliar to you. Likewise, it may feel uncomfortable not to read about Paul's "churches." These translation choices are not meant to take away from the value of the New Testament writings as scripture for Christian churches today. Rather, they are designed to help us remember that at the earliest stages of this movement, being a Christ-follower did not mean one was not Jewish, let alone *against* Judaism. Throughout the book, we will keep at the forefront of our study the fact that the New Testament writings represent just the very beginning of a centuries-long process of 1) the development and establishment of rituals and doctrines that would come to define normative Christianity 2) the eventual separation of Christianity from Judaism.

Here is one last important point about terminology used in the coming chapters. We will use terms such as the historical Jesus, the Markan Jesus, the Matthean Jesus, the Lukan Jesus, and the Johannine Jesus. These are common ways of distinguishing between the different representations of Jesus in the four canonical gospels. They are used to reinforce two points. The first is that the person who lived and died in the first century, referred to as the historical Jesus, is not identical to the different presentations of Jesus that are evident in the gospels. This leads to the second point. Each of the four canonical gospels offers a picture of Jesus that is in keeping with the author's view of the significance of this figure for Christ-followers. Each gospel writer develops themes linked to his particular understanding of Jesus. So, a term like the "Markan" Jesus is used to refer to the Jesus who is portrayed in the Gospel of Mark, compared to, say, the "Johannine" Jesus who is depicted in the Gospel of John. You may think this is one and the same Jesus, with only some minor difference in details about how he is portrayed. One of the goals of our study of the gospels will be to show how these differences matter for appreciating the unique visions of each of the gospel writers. Another goal for our study of the gospels will be to see how the gospel writers told a story about Jesus in light of their historical, social, and political contexts. Finally, we will often use the term "audience" rather than readers to refer to the ancient groups for whom these writings were intended. This is because it was still the case that most people in the first-century CE Mediterranean world could not read or write. Even if they could, they would not own copies of New Testament manuscripts to read on their own. The New Testament writings were intended for use in assemblies of Christ-followers where most would listen to them as they were read out loud. With these ideas in mind, we turn now to study of the New Testament.

RESOURCES FOR FURTHER STUDY

Burridge, Richard A. *What Are the Gospels? A Comparison with Graeco-Roman Biography* (twenty-fifth anniversary edition). Waco, TX: Baylor University Press, 2018.

Henze, Matthias. *Mind the Gap: How the Jewish Writings between the Old and New Testament Help Us Understand Jesus*. Minneapolis, MN: Fortress, 2017.

The Jesus Movement in the Context of the Roman Empire

9

Chapter Overview

In this chapter we come to the last of the imperial powers that influenced the formation of the Christian Bible – Rome. We begin with a "tour" of ancient Jerusalem as it looked under Roman rule during the time that Jesus would have traveled there. It may come as a surprise to discover the extent of both Greek and Roman influences evident in Jerusalem by the first century CE. Next the chapter will explore the oral stage of the Jesus traditions that eventually led to the formation of the New Testament writings, especially the gospels. Just as we began with oral traditions in our study of the Old Testament, here we must consider the role that oral traditions about Jesus played in the growth of the New Testament. The chapter concludes with a discussion of what we can know about the person that generated the growth of these traditions, a figure that biblical scholars refer to as the "historical Jesus." Students often have trouble understanding what is different about the historical Jesus compared to the Jesus they have heard about their whole lives. In this chapter, we explain this difference while exploring the problems and questions associated with the study of the historical Jesus. We conclude with suggestions about what we can know about the historical Jesus. But first, we take another imaginary journey, this time to Jerusalem during the time of Jesus, sometime around 20–30 CE.

A Contemporary Introduction to the Bible: Sacred Texts and Imperial Contexts, Second Edition.
Colleen M. Conway and David M. Carr.
© 2021 Colleen M. Conway and David M. Carr. Published 2021 by John Wiley & Sons Ltd.

Imagining the Jerusalem That Jesus Knew

Chapter 3 took you to the tenth-century BCE Jerusalem of David and Solomon. In this chapter, we will travel to this famous city as it stood some thousand years later. This was a Jerusalem transformed under the expansive building projects of King Herod. Imagine that you are a traveler arriving in Jerusalem, as Jesus did, during the time of the Passover festival. Approaching the city, you would be able to see the massive Temple mount, that is, the foundation for the Temple itself with its surrounding walls and fortified corners (see Figures 9.1 and 9.2). As you make your way up on the wide stone staircase to the Temple, you pass under impressive archways. You might take a stroll on Solomon's porch (Figure 9.3), the beautifully colonnaded walkway on the east side of the Temple. If you were a worldly traveler, this stately hall atop the outer walls of the Temple mount might bring back memories of your travels in Greece. In fact, the one hundred and eighty-two Corinthian columns were designed to imitate the best of Greek architecture. The size of the Temple plaza itself would have rivaled any of the finest open civic esplanades in the Roman empire (see Figure 9.4). Adjacent to the Temple mount you would see the refurbished Antonia fortress, named after Herod's patron the Roman general Marc Antony. Finally, gazing out from the height of the Temple mount, you could look across the city of Jerusalem and see the Greek-styled amphitheater for the performance of Greek and Roman plays, the hippodrome for chariot races, and the elaborate palace of King Herod with its three enormous fortified towers.

To understand the cultural context of the New Testament writings, one must understand why Jerusalem in the first century CE looked like this. How

FIGURE 9.1
Excavation of outer stairway and arches of the Jerusalem Temple.

FIGURE 9.2
Model of the Second Temple of Jerusalem, built on the site of Solomon's Temple c. 520 BCE and expanded under Herod in 1 BCE.

was it that Jerusalem came to be ruled by a king appointed by the Romans who built up Jerusalem to resemble a Greek city? In other words, one must understand Jerusalem and Palestine more broadly in its first-century CE context.

FIGURE 9.3
Model of first-century CE Jerusalem. The Antonia fortress is on the right of the Temple mount.

FIGURE 9.4

The Forum of Augustus in Rome. Compare the colonnaded porticos to those on the Jerusalem Temple mount.

Rome Comes to Jerusalem

By the second century BCE, the Roman Republic had taken control of much of the area that is present-day Europe and was pressing eastward. Meanwhile, despite the successful Maccabean revolt against Antiochus IV, Judea did not transition smoothly into independent rule. Instead, the power vacuum left after the revolts was filled with ongoing disputes about who should hold the high priesthood. It was during this time that distinct groups within Judaism began to take shape, such as the Pharisees, the Sadducees, and the Essenes. More will be said about these different groups in later chapters. The important point here is that these tensions hastened Rome's entry into Jerusalem, in the person of the Roman general Pompey.

In 63 BCE, Judea was embroiled in a civil war between two Hasmonean brothers, Hyrcanus and Aristobulus. At various points in this struggle for power, both brothers sent embassies to Pompey, the Roman general who was then stationed in Syria. Pompey responded by moving his army into Jerusalem to take direct control of the region. Unlike the much earlier invasions by Assyria or Babylon, when the Roman empire seized control of Judea, there was no massive destruction of Jerusalem or its Temple. Nor was there a major deportation of the residents. Instead, Pompey inflicted minimal damage on Jerusalem, ordered the Jewish priests to properly purify the temple after his military advance, and reinstated one of the brothers, Hyrcanus, as high priest.

These actions were in keeping with the way that Rome expanded and maintained its empire. The Roman army could not depend on military rule across its vast empire – the army was simply not big enough. Instead, the typical Roman practice was to choose local leaders to rule on their behalf.

These **client kings** or procurators, as they were sometimes titled, were typically the elite men of the local communities who stood to benefit from demonstrating their loyalty to Rome. One such local elite man was Herod the Great, who, after carefully working his way into Roman favor, was designated as king of Judea by the Roman Senate in 37 BCE.

Herod, whose reign lasted more than forty years, is a prime illustration of the cultural complexity that existed in Palestine during this time. Herod was from Idumea, a region south of Judea whose inhabitants had been forced to convert to Judaism when the Hasmoneans expanded their kingdom (see Chapter 8). Given this, local Judeans remained skeptical of Herod's Jewish identity. For his part, Herod understood the need to gain favor both from his Jewish constituents and from his Roman patrons. He therefore began an extensive building program in Jerusalem and throughout Palestine. The people of Jerusalem could hardly object to the massive renovation and expansion of the Jerusalem Temple that he funded, nor the construction of roads or aqueducts that improved the infrastructure of Palestine. Herod's Roman patrons would likely be impressed with the colossal size and grandeur of his building projects that competed with the best of Greek architecture elsewhere in the empire.

Indeed, in a paradoxical way, to become Roman during this time was also to become Greek, particularly in the eastern provinces. The first-century Roman poet, Horace, explained the phenomenon this way: "Greece, the captive, made her savage victor [Rome] captive." In other words, although Rome conquered Greece, it was enamored by Greek culture. This is why historians often refer to this time as the **Greco-Roman period**. Culturally speaking, large swaths of the Roman empire were heavily influenced by an increasing interest in all things Greek. For example, the Roman cities that were either newly built or reconstituted across the Roman empire closely resembled the Hellenistic urban centers established by Alexander the Great. So, too, the Jewish King Herod built cities in Palestine complete with Greek-styled theaters, agoras, and gymnasiums. If David and Solomon looked to Egyptian and Mesopotamian as models for their own emerging kingdom, Herod looked to the Greek-influenced Roman cities as a model for his renovated Jerusalem.

Thus when Jesus was born in the town of Nazareth in the region of Galilee, he was born into a region that was inhabited predominantly by Jews, ruled by the Romans, and close to cities infused with Greek culture. When he traveled up to Jerusalem to the Temple, it would have been to the grand Temple expanded by Herod. A decade or so after Jesus's death, when the apostle Paul began his missionary journeys, he traveled to cities with Greek-speaking inhabitants. Decades later, when the gospel writers wrote their accounts of Jesus's life and death, they wrote in Greek for a largely Greek-speaking audience. But none of this Greek influence lessened the fact that politically, all of the regions that concern the New Testament writers were ruled by the Romans. Their accounts of Jesus and their experiences of being Jesus-followers were influenced by their life under Roman occupation. As we turn to examine the earliest traditions about Jesus, we will need to keep in mind this complex cultural and political mix.

The Earliest Jesus Traditions

EXERCISE

Read 1 Corinthians 15:3–8 and compare it to the empty tomb and resurrection stories in the four canonical gospels (Mark 16:1–8; Matt 28:1–10; 16–20; Luke 24:1–53; John 20:1–29). How do the gospel accounts compare to each other and to the tradition that Paul says he received? Make a list of similarities and differences.

In the same way that ancient Israelites formed a community identity around shared cultural memories, so too the early followers of Jesus formed a group identity around shared cultural memories of Jesus. We need to be flexible in our sense of what the term "memories" designates in this context, because human memory is a quite fluid phenomenon. Community memories of Jesus could certainly include accounts from some immediate followers of Jesus about what he did or said. But such "memories" about Jesus could also include stories about him that helped to define the community even though the events that the stories relate did not actually happen. While we have discussed cultural memory earlier in the textbook another example of this idea may help at this point. Most school children in the United States are taught the story of a six-year-old George Washington cutting his father's cherry tree with a new hatchet. When he was confronted by his father, young George supposedly admitted to the act, telling his father, "I cannot tell a lie." We now know that none of this happened – an American minister and Washington biographer made up the story. Nevertheless, the "memory" has been transmitted in the United States for centuries (including through the ritual baking of cherry pies on President's Day). The story is transmitted as part of a national nostalgia that reinforces a "truth" about the first president of the United States, namely that he was a person of integrity. In a similar way, the cultural memories of Jesus transmitted to future generations by early Christ-followers conveyed their central truth claims about Jesus.

You can see this process of oral transmission reflected in the apostle Paul's description of what he had "received" about the resurrection of Jesus, an account that he then "delivered" to the Corinthians (1 Cor 15:3). Although he writes about this process in his letter, his use of the words "received" and "delivered" indicate an oral communication of tradition. Here it is important to know that when Paul was writing his letters, none of the canonical gospels had been written. Also, as you could see from comparing the passages in the exercise above, the apostle Paul's resurrection tradition does not match any of the later gospel accounts of the empty tomb and resurrection stories. Moreover, the gospels themselves vary in their accounts of who went to the tomb and what they saw there, not to mention their differing resurrection stories.

It would be a mistake to assume that there was *one* original and correct account that was later distorted. The children's game of "telephone" does *not* offer a parallel to explain the existence of different stories of the empty tomb and Jesus's resurrection appearances. Instead, the evidence suggests that a variety of traditions about Jesus's death, burial, and resurrection circulated orally among the earliest followers of Jesus. We cannot determine exactly how, when, and under what conditions these stories about Jesus began to take shape. To be sure, there is a core element that we see in all of the traditions – that Jesus died, was buried, and was raised from the tomb. But the details of who was at the tomb, what was said, and what happened afterward differ. These parts of the empty tomb tradition were told differently by different tellers, or perhaps by the gospel writers themselves.

One example of what we can learn from a close reading of the different empty tomb stories concerns the depiction of women in the tradition. In Paul's account, no women at all are mentioned. (Note that in the Greek text, 1 Cor 15:6 states that "he appeared to more than five hundred *brothers* ....") Meanwhile, various combinations of women at the empty tomb are described in the four gospel accounts. Notably, in the Gospel of Luke, the author takes special care to claim that the male apostles did not believe the women's account of the empty tomb (Lk 24:10–11). The variations in details about the women at the tomb suggest that in the earliest stages of the Jesus movement the role of women was a contested topic. The argument about women's participation is not explicitly spelled out but rather is reflected in different "memories" regarding the testimony and authority of women in the Jesus movement. From a feminist historian's perspective, these conflicting accounts suggest that women did indeed play a prominent role in the early movement.

Paul's account in 1 Corinthians 15 provides evidence for the early circulation of resurrection traditions about Jesus. This seems to be the main tradition that Paul received when he became part of the Jesus movement, since his letters say very little about the teaching and ministry of Jesus. Nevertheless, the early stages of oral traditions about Jesus must also have included stories about his teaching and healing ministry. Indeed, the depictions of Jesus in the gospels suggest that he had a memorable style of oral communication. The gospel writers portray Jesus teaching in **parables**; that is, by means of short narratives, or comparative language. They also include various **pronouncements** of Jesus. These are short, direct sayings often designed to defeat opponents in a verbal sparring match. Note, for example, the short, memorable pronouncement addressing the Pharisees' complaint that Jesus and his disciples are working on the Sabbath: "the Sabbath was made for the sake of humankind, not humankind for the Sabbath" (Mark 2:27).

The difficulty in appreciating the oral quality of the historical Jesus's ministry is that it has been preserved only in written form. By their very nature, written accounts typically mask the flexibility, fluidity, and repetitiveness that characterize oral communication. For example, reading the account of Jesus's "Sermon on the Mount" (Matt 5–7), one would understandably get the impression that there was one occasion on which Jesus stood on a mountain and preached this very sermon. As we will see in Chapter 12, it is far more likely that Matthew's sermon is a literary creation that reflects the sort of teaching that Jesus did on several occasions in several different places. Similarly, we should imagine Jesus repeating parables and pronouncements on a variety of occasions during his ministry. When he did so, the details likely varied, even as the basic outline of his teachings might have remained the same. The transmission of such sayings of Jesus comprise an early stage in the formation of the written text of the gospels.

Not long after the death of Jesus, his followers not only transmitted his teachings, they also began to tell stories *about* Jesus. These, too, would have been repeated on different occasions in different places. As stories about Jesus began to spread, there would have been demand for additional stories about him. New believers may have wanted to hear more about the circumstances of his birth, or what he was like as a boy. Although such details may not have been available to the storytellers, there were plenty of cultural models on which they could develop their own versions of Jesus's early days. Stories of "great men" typically included tales of divine omens regarding their birth and their precociousness as children. In addition to wanting to fill out the story of Jesus's life, early Christ-followers likely adapted or even created traditions about Jesus to address new circumstances in their communal life. While we might be surprised at the idea of these followers "making up" stories about Jesus, this is because we do not live in an oral culture. Rather than focusing on whether these oral traditions about Jesus are "true" (where "truth" is unhelpfully equated with historical veracity), we should think in terms of what fundamental convictions or "truths" about Jesus these storytellers wanted to convey by means of their stories.

The Infancy Gospel of Thomas: the Boy Jesus and His Superpowers

Among the canonical gospels, only the Gospel of Luke mentions Jesus as a young boy and then only in one episode (Lk 2:41–51). One entertaining non-canonical gospel, known as the Infancy Gospel of Thomas, addresses that gap. The gospel, likely written sometime in the second century CE, fills in details about the precocious boy Jesus creating mischief with his divine superpowers. So, for instance, a five-year-old Jesus makes birds out of clay, brings them to life, and has them fly away. On another occasion, when a boy accidentally bumps into him, Jesus strikes the boy dead with his words. Such behavior earns a scolding and ear-pulling from his father, Joseph. The episodes in the gospel take Jesus from age five to twelve, where after many impulsive and arrogant displays of his power, Jesus eventually becomes obedient to his parents and grows in wisdom (echoing Luke 2:51). Overall, this imaginative account of the boy Jesus reads rather like an ancient coming-of-age superhero story. The Infancy Gospel of Thomas shows how Jesus traditions continued to develop even after the canonical gospels were written. It illustrates the sort of invention and development of tradition that is evident also in the canonical gospels.

FIGURE 9.5
This parchment illustration from around 1340 CE shows a scene from the Infancy Gospel of Thomas where Jesus brings clay birds to life.

Searching for the Historical Jesus: Problems and Proposals

The discussion of the fluid and variable nature of oral traditions about Jesus may have left you wondering about what we can know for certain about Jesus. If so, you are not alone. For centuries, some New Testament scholars have been on a "quest for the **historical Jesus**" (so called after the title of Albert Schweitzer's famous 1906 book, *The Quest of the Historical Jesus*). If you are used to considering the gospels as eye-witness reporting of what Jesus said and did, it may be difficult to understand the concept of a "historical Jesus" as a figure distinct from the presentations of Jesus in the New Testament. But based on evidence such as the differing empty tomb stories, we have seen that the gospels are something other than eyewitness accounts.

This becomes even clearer when we consider questions of dating and authorship of the gospel. The earliest of the canonical gospels, the Gospel of Mark, was likely written around 70 CE. This means that there was a forty-year gap between the death of Jesus and the first written gospel. The other three gospels were written at an even greater distance from the living Jesus. Such a time gap adds to the difficulty of considering the gospel narratives as reliable historical records. Moreover, all four of the canonical gospels were originally anonymous. Only in the second century CE, when the four gospels were circulated as a collection, did scribes add titles to the top of the manuscripts. These superscriptions uniformly asserted that the gospels were "according to" (in Greek *kata*) Matthew, Mark, Luke, and John respectively. This is also the time that traditions begin to appear about these four figures, claiming that they were either original apostles of Jesus (Matthew and John) or close associates of other well-known apostles (Mark of Peter and Luke of Paul). Despite these attributions, most scholars do not think any of these people were the original gospel writers. None of the gospels is written in a style that suggests the author was present at the events that are being narrated. Nor is it likely that the disciples of Jesus were able to write, especially not in Greek, the language in which the gospels were written. So we are left with the reality that the New Testament gospels were written by anonymous Christ-followers decades after the events that they relate. (In the rest of this book, we will refer to the gospels using the traditional names associated with each one, even though we recognize that the gospel writers are unknown.) These authors, whoever they were, believed Jesus to be the long-awaited Jewish **messiah** (Hebrew, "anointed one") and Son of God, and their writings were intended to demonstrate the meaning and truth of this faith claim. This means that while the gospels do provide a textual picture of Jesus that grew out of the faith and cultural memory of believers, they do not offer easy access to the historical Jesus.

Still, despite the difficulties, the centuries-long interest in finding the "real" Jesus behind the gospels continues to this day. After all, Jesus was, in fact, a person in history, and it is not unreasonable to expect some traditions about Jesus to be grounded in historical events. This assumption lies behind the so-called "quest for the historical Jesus." In fact, there have been several such quests. The first one began in the eighteenth century when many authors produced biographical "Lives of Jesus." This quest abruptly ended with Schweitzer's book mentioned above. After carefully reviewing these eighteenth-century attempts to write a life of Jesus, Schweitzer convincingly concluded that:

> each successive epoch of theology found its own thoughts in Jesus; that was, indeed, the only way in which it could make Him live. But it was not only each epoch that found its reflection in Jesus; each individual created Him in accordance with his own character. There is no historical task which so reveals a man's true self as the writing of a Life of Jesus.

Anyone attempting to construct a historically accurate figure of Jesus should be aware of Schweitzer's insight: people in search of a historical Jesus are likely to "find" a Jesus that suits their needs and beliefs. It is all too tempting to see the Jesus of history just as we would want him to be, rather than what the evidence might suggest. On this point, too, Schweitzer had something to say. He argued that if we succeed in finding the actual historical Jesus, "[he] will be to our time a stranger and an enigma." By this Schweitzer meant that we must take seriously the temporal, social, and cultural gap between our world and the

More on the Historical Jesus Search

Read and study the way each of the four canonical gospels describes the baptism of Jesus (Mark 1:9–11; Matt 3:13–17; Luke 3:21–2; John 1:29–34). What details are the same? What differences do you notice? Note also the context for each of these scenes. What comes before and after the baptism in each gospel?

In the nineteenth and twentieth centuries, scholars developed criteria to assess the historical reliability of a given gospel tradition about Jesus. Recently, scholars have rightly challenged the usefulness of this supposedly scientific set of criteria for evaluating the historical accuracy of Jesus traditions in the gospels. Still, some of these principles remain useful. For example, the "criterion of embarrassment" posits that a group would not invent a story that did not match their own confessions of belief about Jesus. So, for example, the story of Jesus's baptism by John was unlikely to have developed later in the community for at least two reasons. First, the act of being baptized by John suggests that Jesus was a disciple of John, which is not an idea that would likely develop from early Christ-followers. Second, John's baptism was for the forgiveness of sins (Mk 1:4), but the later developing traditions about Jesus claimed that he was without sin (2 Cor 5:21; Heb 4:15; 1 Peter 2:22). These sorts of tensions suggest that Jesus *was* baptized by John. This historical fact was remembered, and the gospel writers worked in various ways to explain or downplay this "embarrassing" detail in Jesus's actual life. Mark's gospel opens with the baptism scene but makes sure to have John predict that there is one coming who is more powerful than he is (Mk 1:7). The Gospel of Matthew deals with the same problem by featuring a conversation in which John objects to the idea of baptizing Jesus, suggesting that Jesus should be the one baptizing him (Matt 3:13–15). What about the Gospels of Luke and John? How do they deal with the question of Jesus's baptism?

world of Jesus. If the historical Jesus we imagine seems at home in the twenty-first century, chances are we do not have an accurate historical construction. Instead, our picture of Jesus may reflect our own dreams and ideals.

As part of his work, Schweitzer offered his own theory about the historical Jesus. He argued that a "thoroughgoing eschatology" motivated Jesus. **Eschatology** means "study of the last things." Schweitzer highlighted the eschatological themes in Jesus's teaching, demonstrating that like many other first-century Jews, the historical Jesus expected the imminent arrival of the reign of God. According to Schweitzer, Jesus's final pilgrimage to Jerusalem was intended to help usher in God's divine kingdom. In more recent years, scholars such as E. P. Sanders, Bart Ehrman, and Paula Fredriksen have followed Schweitzer in showing how the teaching and actions of the historical Jesus align with the role of an eschatological or, more precisely, an **apocalyptic** prophet. By using the term "apocalyptic," these scholars suggest that Jesus had an expectation of God's direct intervention in human affairs – an idea that we have already seen introduced in the book of Daniel. **Apocalypticism** indicates a belief that divine intervention will inaugurate a glorious new age for those who have remained faithful and just. At the same time, God will punish the evil powers that have been in control of the world.

Eschatology versus Apocalypticism

While these two terms are sometimes used interchangeably, for biblical scholarship there is a difference in their meaning. "Eschatology" is a general term that refers to ideas related to the end times. "Apocalypticism," however, refers to a specific worldview that expects God's cosmic intervention to set right the injustice of the world.

As you saw in Chapter 8, the term "apocalypse" literally means "uncovering," and historical apocalypses purport to reveal special knowledge about God's impending intervention. Recall, however, that not all apocalypses are of the historical type. The heavenly apocalypses described in Chapter 8 may have little to do with the end times.

As we will see in the chapters that follow, apocalypticism runs through much of the New Testament writings, beginning with the letters of Paul. And, as we have already seen, Jesus most likely started as a follower of John the Baptist, who proclaimed an apocalyptic message of preparation for the coming judgment of God. According to the Gospel of Mark, Jesus's own preaching focused on the coming of the reign of God, and many of his parables were about the coming kingdom. This supports the idea that Jesus was one of many apocalyptic Jewish thinkers living in the first century CE.

In addition to recognizing the apocalyptic worldview of Jesus, any historical construction of Jesus must consider the fact that Jesus was crucified by the Romans. The Romans would not have crucified Jesus unless his words or activities were perceived as a threat to the Roman civic order. Of course, the gospel narratives do portray Jesus in conflict with Jewish leaders in Jerusalem. But it was not the typical practice of Roman rulers to execute someone over intellectual and/or religious disagreements with their contemporaries. We may not ever know the precise nature of the historical Jesus's disputes with local Jewish leaders, but we know for certain that his activities gained the attention of the Roman authorities in Jerusalem.

One clue as to why this occurred may lie in the report provided by all of the gospels that Jesus was crucified under the charge that he called himself "king of the Jews." The title appears in various accounts of Jesus's trial before Pilate (Mark 15:2; John 18:33) and is also in accounts of an inscription that was hung on the cross with Jesus (Matt 27:37; Luke 23:38; John 19:19–21). "King of the Jews" is not a title that Jesus's own followers seem to have used. In may be that John's gospel deliberately avoids the title (see John 1:49 where Jesus is called "the king of Israel"). In any case, if this was the charge that was brought to the Roman authorities, it may have been the reason for his death at the hands of the Romans. Roman authorities would have viewed such a claim as treason against the emperor and thus cause for execution.

Apart from this charge, the Gospel of Mark suggests that Jesus's actions in the Temple were a decisive factor leading to his arrest and crucifixion (Mark 11:18; see also Luke 19:47). If Jesus did engage in this act of protest, he would not have been alone in his critique of Temple leadership and practices. We have already learned about disputes among different Jewish groups during the Maccabean period. There is additional evidence from the first century CE for ongoing disputes about the Temple. For instance, the writings discovered in the desert caves at Qumran suggest that a Jewish group had retreated to the Judean desert in protest over the Temple leadership. The group, which many scholars identify as the Essenes, rejected the authority of "the wicked priest" and lived under the leadership of a figure described as the "teacher of righteousness." Several of these writings suggest that the group was waiting for the restoration of the proper family to the Temple priesthood. Given this general time of unrest, it is thus quite conceivable that the historical Jesus also engaged in a critique of the Temple leaders and their practices. Perhaps he predicted the Temple's destruction (see Mark 14:58), and symbolically enacted this destruction by causing a disturbance in the Temple precincts. As we saw in our study of the prophets, this sort of symbolic enactment was common in the prophetic tradition. Moreover, a civil disruption like this would have triggered a strong reaction from the Roman authorities.

FIGURE 9.6
There are no descriptions of the physical appearance of Jesus in the New Testament. Given his Mediterranean ethnicity, we can be sure he was not the blue-eyed, fair-skinned man seen in countless European paintings. Joan Taylor argues that this wall painting of Moses from a third-century synagogue (Dura Europos) may be the closest we can come to picturing the historical Jesus because it shows how a Jewish sage was imagined in the Greco-Roman world. See her discussion at https://www.bbc.com/news/magazine-35120965.

In the end, we can only speculate about the historical realities that lie behind the narratives of Jesus as we find them in the gospels and other New Testament writings. The discussion in the coming chapters will focus more on the different depictions of Jesus that come to us from the New Testament texts. This is the Jesus known by early Christ-followers living in the midst of the Roman empire. It is this Jesus that lived on in the social memory of adherents of the Jesus movement and was transmitted in oral and written form for later generations.

CHAPTER NINE REVIEW

1 Know the meaning and significance of the following terms discussed in this chapter:
   - apocalyptic
   - apocalypticism
   - client kings
   - cultural memory
   - eschatology
   - Greco-Roman period
   - historical Jesus
   - messiah
   - parables
   - pronouncements

2 Explain why historians refer to the period in which the New Testament was written as "the Greco-Roman" period.

3 Describe the earliest stages of traditions about Jesus.

4 Why is it difficult to know much for certain about the historical Jesus? Why do some scholars think it is likely that Jesus had an apocalyptic worldview?

5 Students are often troubled to learn that some of the gospel stories of Jesus may not have happened just as they are reported. The question that seems to follow is, "Are the stories true?" Can you think of more examples of stories that communicate something that you think to be "true" even if the events related in the story did not really happen? What does this suggest about using historicity as the ultimate measure of "truth"?

RESOURCES FOR FURTHER STUDY

Carter, Warren. *Seven Events that Shaped the New Testament World*. Grand Rapids, MI: Baker Academic, 2013.

Carter, Warren. *The Roman Empire and the New Testament: An Essential Guide*. Nashville, TN: Abingdon Press, 2006.

Kelber, Werner. *The Oral and the Written Gospel: The Hermeneutics of Speaking and Writing in the Synoptic Tradition, Mark, Paul, and Q* (2nd edition). Bloomington and Indianapolis, IN: Indiana University Press, 1997.

Kelber, Werner H., and Byrskog, Samuel, eds. *Jesus in Memory: Traditions in Oral and Scribal Perspectives*. Waco, TX: Baylor University Press, 2009.

Historical Jesus Studies

Bond, Helen K. *The Historical Jesus: A Guide for the Perplexed*. London and New York: T & T Clark, 2012.

Charlesworth, James H. *The Historical Jesus: An Essential Guide*. Nashville, TN: Abingdon Press, 2008.

Ehrman, Bart D. *Jesus before the Gospels: How the Earliest Christians Remembered, Changed, and Invented Their Stories of the Savior*. New York: HarperOne, 2016.

Schweitzer, Albert. The Quest for the Historical Jesus. Minneapolis, MN: Augsburg Fortress, 2001. A republished English translation from the 1901 original.

Simpson, Benjamin I. *Recent Research on the Historical Jesus*. Sheffield: Sheffield Phoenix Press, 2014.

Paul and His Letters in the Roman Colonial Context

10

Chapter Outline

Chapter Overview

This chapter will introduce you to the apostle Paul and to a group of letters that are attributed to him. While we have looked at the ways that imperial forces have helped to shape the biblical text, here we can explore how these same forces shaped an individual. Paul provides a rare occasion in the academic study of the Bible where we can actually identify an author and the timeframe of his writings. Because Paul wrote letters, rather than a narrative, we can also learn something about his understanding of the world and his work. Learning more about how Paul viewed the world will help us understand the Pauline letters better.

Studying these letters also provides an opportunity to explore the urban settings in which the Jesus movement took root and spread. Paul's letters provide evidence for how this movement grew beyond a small group of Jewish Christ-followers to attract non-Jewish people living across the Roman empire. Paul and other New Testament writers refer to these non-Jewish

A Contemporary Introduction to the Bible: Sacred Texts and Imperial Contexts, Second Edition.
Colleen M. Conway and David M. Carr.
© 2021 Colleen M. Conway and David M. Carr. Published 2021 by John Wiley & Sons Ltd.

people with the Greek word *ethne*. In English, this term is translated as either "gentiles" or "nations" depending on the context. This chapter will show how Paul understood his God-given mission to be one of convincing gentiles to worship the God of Israel and to believe in Jesus Christ as God's messiah. We examine Paul's letters in light of this mission, focusing especially on how he dealt with the implications of the inclusion of gentile Christ-followers in what was a Jewish movement. Our focus will be on issues related to Paul's gentile mission as they occur in three of his major letters: Galatians, 1 Corinthians, and Romans. In the last part of the chapter, we discuss some letters that are attributed to Paul, but whose authorship is disputed by many scholars.

Paul's Travels and Letter Collection

Imagine that you discover a collection of letters written by someone who lived two thousand years ago. The letters are written to communities in several different cities, or in some cases to individuals. While the letters share common themes, they address different issues. Moreover, the tone of the letters ranges from joyous to angry. Your task is to learn as much as you can about who wrote the letters, why they were written, and what they were intended to communicate to their recipients. These are central questions in the academic study of Paul and his letters.

It may seem unusual to begin the study of the New Testament with this letter collection, since the gospels and the Acts of the Apostles appear before Paul's letters in the New Testament canon. But, in fact, Paul's letters were written between ten and twenty years before the first canonical gospel was written. This means that Paul was writing to quite recently formed assemblies of Christ-followers. Neither they, nor he, could have read any of the gospels nor any of the New Testament as we have it now. It did not yet exist! Beginning our study with Paul gives us a glimpse of the real-life issues that concerned these communities as they began to define themselves as a distinct group in the midst of the Roman empire.

We begin with a brief look at the cities in which Paul concentrated his missionary efforts. By the first half of the first century CE, Rome had conquered vast amounts of land, reaching the peak of its power in the early second century (see Map 10.1). This expansion was made possible by military strength, but also by the impressive system of roads that Rome developed, maintained, and protected. These roads are one concrete example of Roman imperial influence on the formation of the New Testament. The same roads that transported Roman armies also enabled the spread of the Jesus movement. For example, if you were a co-worker of Paul, you would have traveled on the major Roman thoroughfare called the Via Egnatia (Egnation Way), named after Gnaeus Egnatius the Roman governor who ordered it built (see Figure 10.1). This road connected a series of Roman colonies, one of which was Philippi. This small Greek city was named after its founder, Philip of

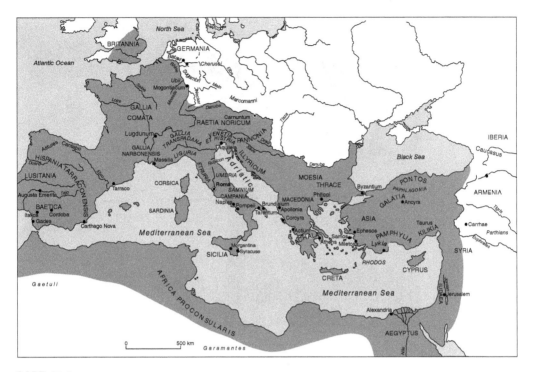

MAP 10.1
The Roman Empire in the 1st century CE.

Macedon, the father of Alexander the Great. Arriving there with Paul, you would have entered a city that had been colonized by Rome for more than one hundred years and settled by Roman war veterans and their descendants. Latin inscriptions would mark the civic buildings and imperial statues, visually depicting the power of Rome. Nevertheless, the majority of the inhabitants would be Greek speaking.

If you continued westward on the Via Egnatia you would come to Thessalonica, a major trading hub between Europe and Asia, located at the crossroads where the east–west Via Egnatia intersecting with the north–south road connecting the Danube River (in the north) with the Aegean Sea (in the south). In Paul's time, Thessalonica was the capital city of Macedonia, a Roman province. It had a cosmopolitan population, but remained a culturally Greek city under Roman rule, with Greek inscriptions outnumbering Latin ones.

Another major city on Paul's missionary route was Corinth, located to the south (see Map 10.2). Like Philippi, Corinth had been reconstituted as a Roman colony and thus had a strong Latin presence. Like Thessalonica, it served as the capital of a Roman province, Achaia, which included southern Greece. Given its control of two harbors, Corinth was a major center of trade. In Paul's time, the city would have been bustling with life and a diverse group of inhabitants (see Figure 10.2).

FIGURE 10.1
Remains of the Via Egnatia, Rome's primary artery to the east. Paul would have traveled along this road to Philippi and Thessalonica.

All of these cities would have elements common to the Greco-Roman cities of this period such as large amphitheaters, temples devoted to various deities, an agora or outdoor assembly place, a gymnasium, and a colonnade leading to important buildings such as the forum for civic affairs.

Moreover, these cities would convey the power of Rome in a variety of ways. Statues of the emperor would proclaim him as the bringer of peace and savior of the people. Inscriptions on public pillars would celebrate military achievements, or honor imperial officials. One famous example is the Priene inscription discovered in modern-day Turkey. Dating from 9 BCE, the Greek inscription marks the institution of a new calendar "for good luck and salvation" based on the birthday of Augustus. The decree announces the reign of the emperor as "the beginning of the good news for the world" and describes the emperor as "a savior, who brought an end to war and established peace." (See "The Priene Calendar Inscription," p. 333.) Other marble reliefs depicted the important priestly role of the emperor as one who mediated between the people and the gods, thus ensuring divine favor toward the empire (see Figure 10.3).

These are the urban settings in which Paul worked. His letters were addressed to people who were immersed in diverse urban populations that had long been under the reign of Rome. The issues that concerned them in their new religious identity often grew out of their urban environment. But what about the Paul? What more can we know about the man who traveled thousands of miles across the empire to preach about Jesus in these Greco-Roman cities?

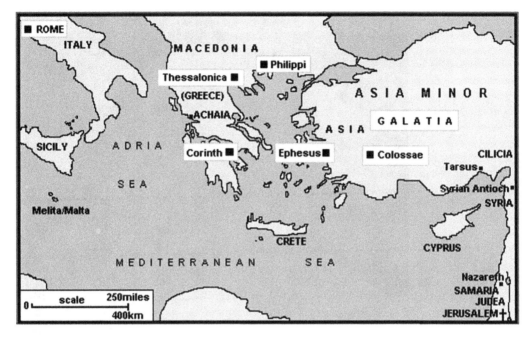

MAP 10.2
Map of cities addressed in the Pauline letters. Note that Galatia is a region rather than a city.
Map by Gordan Smith courtesy of http://www.ccel.org/bible/phillips/JBPhillips.htm.

FIGURE 10.2
Doorways of shops in ancient Corinth.

FIGURE 10.3
Statue of Augustus showing him wearing the veil of the *pontifex maximus* ("greatest priest").
The *pontifex maximus* was the highest priestly position in the Roman state religion.

Who Was Paul?

READING

Gal 1–2; Phil 3:1–11: Rom 9:1–5. Focus on what these passages suggest about Paul's self-perception.

Paul represents the sort of person that imperialism and its aftermath tend to produce: one shaped by multiple and sometimes competing cultural influences. Paul
claims for himself a strong Jewish identity: he is a "Hebrew of Hebrews," circumcised on the eighth day, a Pharisee who is blameless in matters of the law (Phil
3:5–6, see also 2 Cor 11:22). He speaks of the Israelites as his own people, his kin
according to the flesh (Rom 9:3–4). He asserts that he was more advanced than
his peers in the traditions of the ancestors (Gal 1:14). This suggests he had an
education based on the Torah and the oral traditions of the Pharisees. At the
same time, Paul was thoroughly Hellenized. He is able to write well in Greek,
with a style that could only have been learned through a Greek-based education.

He knows the proper Greco-Roman letter form and builds arguments following the conventions of Greco-Roman rhetoric. In this way, Paul is a hybrid product of a mix of cultural influences: his Jewish ethnic identity, the Hellenistic empire that introduced the standard of a Greek education across the Mediterranean, and the Roman empire that reinforced the importance of this education for successful Roman citizens.

The Structure of Paul's Letters

You know well how to properly begin and end different types of written communication, whether a formal letter of application, an email to your professor, or a brief text to your friend. So too Paul uses first-century cultural conventions of written communication, with some modifications. Greco-Roman letters typically adopted the following structure:

- salutation (identification of letter writer and the addressee[s])
- health wish or blessing
- body of letter (using standard rhetorical conventions depending on the purpose of the letter)
- greetings to particular people associated with the addressee(s)
- closing

Paul follows this same basic form with two changes. Rather than the health wish, he typically substitutes a thanksgiving section in which he praises the community for their acceptance of and work on behalf of the gospel (see, for example, 1 Thess 1:2–10; Phil 1:3–11). Similarly, instead of standard words of closing, Paul ends his letters with a blessing (for example, 1 Thess 5:28; Phil 4:23). In the body of his letters, Paul follows convention by using patterns of argumentation that he likely learned as a youth. Such patterns include deliberative rhetoric (persuading his audience to take a particular course), judicial rhetoric (defending his actions), or epideictic rhetoric (praise and blame of others).

Was Paul a Roman citizen? Possibly. But the fact that we are not certain raises the question about sources for learning about Paul. In his letters, Paul never mentions that he is a Roman citizen. This claim comes from the Acts of the Apostles, a text written by another author. Using Acts as a secondary source for understanding the historical Paul is complicated because the picture of Paul in Acts does not always match Paul's own account of his work. For example, in the book of Acts, the character Paul reports five trips to Jerusalem, including one immediately following his time in Damascus (for references to five trips see Acts 9:26; 12:25; 15:4; 18:22; 19:21, 21:17). But in Paul's own letter to the Galatians he emphasizes that he did *not* go to Jerusalem until three years after his time in Damascus (Gal 1:15–19). Indeed, one gets the impression from Paul's letters that Paul visited Jerusalem only twice and was planning on one more visit before heading west to Spain (Rom 15:23–6). Differences like these mean that we must use Acts with caution as a source for learning about the historical Paul. For this reason, most scholars focus on the letters of Paul as the primary source for learning about him.

But here we encounter another difficulty. Although thirteen letters in the New Testament are attributed to Paul, there are good reasons to doubt that Paul wrote all of them. Most scholars agree that seven of the thirteen Pauline letters are "authentic," meaning that they were written by Paul. These **undisputed letters** share a common writing style and set of vocabulary. The undisputed letters all seem to fit within a span of about ten years beginning around 49–50 CE. The remaining six letters are "**disputed**." This means that scholars have raised serious questions about whether Paul wrote them. We will discuss these letters later in this chapter.

Undisputed Pauline letters	Disputed Pauline letters
Romans	Ephesians
1 Corinthians	Colossians
2 Corinthians	2 Thessalonians
Galatians	1 Timothy
Philippians	2 Timothy
1 Thessalonians	Titus
Philemon	

In this chapter, we draw on the undisputed letters for our understanding of Paul, even while recognizing that Paul himself might consciously shape his self-presentation in certain ways to meet his aims. When he writes about himself, he is communicating what he wants others to know about him. Nevertheless, such statements give us insight into what Paul thinks is important about his work. In the next two sections, we focus on two major aspects of his identity and worldview that are key to interpreting his letters.

Apostle to the Gentiles

First, Paul perceives himself as an **apostle** (from the Greek verb *apostellein*, to send) to the gentiles. He is one who has been called and sent by God to non-Jewish people, or as he sometimes puts it, to the "uncircumcised." In the opening chapters of Galatians, Paul expresses his understanding of his God-given mission to the gentiles most clearly. He claims that God set him apart before his birth ("from my mother's womb") and called him to "bring the good news of [his son] to the gentiles" (Gal 1:15–16). He describes a meeting with early leaders of the Jesus movement in Jerusalem where they all agree that he should continue his mission to the gentiles, while Peter goes to the "circumcised," that is, the Jewish people (Gal 2:1–10). Paul's letter to the Romans conveys similar ideas. There, too, he writes of being called by God, and set apart for the gospel in order to bring about obedience of faith among all the gentiles (Rom 1:1–6; see also 1 Cor 1:1). In what is probably his earliest surviving letter, 1 Thessalonians, Paul indicates the success of his work. He praises the group's faith in God, describing how they turned from idols to serve a "living and true God" (1 Thess 1:9). Examples like these show how Paul saw himself as an apostle to the gentiles.

Paul's Apocalyptic Worldview

The second major aspect to keep in mind in our reading of Paul's letters concerns his apocalyptic worldview. When Paul writes semi-personally about his revelatory experience, he writes in terms of a heavenly journey. Using the third person, Paul describes "knowing a man" who experienced "visions and revelations from the Lord," and was transported to the "third heaven," to hear things that "no mortal is permitted to speak" (2 Cor 12:2–4). His account recalls descriptions of heavenly journeys in Jewish apocalyptic literature.

As we saw in the last chapter, by Paul's time in the first century CE, the **apocalyptic worldview**, first reflected in the literary apocalypses of the third and second centuries BCE (see Chapter 8), had gained in popularity among many Jewish communities. These writings shared the view that the world was currently in the grip of evil forces, but that God would intervene in a decisive, cosmic way, to punish the evildoers and reward the righteous. The primary idea was not that the world would come to a catastrophic end, but that the suffering of God's faithful people would end as God ushered in a glorious new age of peace and justice. This literature was meant to give hope to those who felt persecuted, and to give meaning to their present suffering. The popularity of this apocalyptic worldview among Jewish people in the first century CE is not coincidental. A perspective that emerged in the Hellenistic period appealed also to those living several centuries later under Roman domination.

Like other Jewish apocalyptic thinkers, Paul thought that the world in which he lived was ruled by evil powers that God would defeat. But his experience of the risen Christ led him to reshape this worldview in a distinct way. For Paul (along with other early Christ-followers), God's defeat of these evil forces was no longer a future event. Rather, he thought that God *already* had intervened decisively in the world through the death and resurrection of Jesus. So, for example, Paul writes of how Jesus "gave himself" to set believers free from the present evil age (Gal 1:4). The cross, for Paul, was step one of God's cosmic intervention.

But this modified apocalyptic view presented a problem. If God intervened in the world through the death and resurrection of Christ, where was the promised glorious new age? Paul regularly acknowledges that he and other Christ-followers were still suffering (see, for example, 2 Cor 1:3–7). Paul deals with this reality by speaking of Christ's resurrection as the "first fruits" of God's saving work in the world (1 Cor 15:20–3). Believers, according to Paul, must wait for the return of Christ that will signal the full completion of God's saving act. This second coming of Christ (in Greek *parousia*, meaning "presence") will also bring God's final judgment against the "ungodly."

Note that there is an important connection between these two major aspects of Paul's identity: Paul's mission to the gentiles is directly connected to his apocalyptic anticipation of God's coming judgment. For Paul, gentiles who become Christ-followers become righteous before God. So, for example, he praises the Thessalonians who "turned toward God, away from false gods, to serve a living and true God and to wait for his son from heaven whom he raised from the dead – Jesus, the one who delivers us from the coming wrath" (1 Thess 1:9–10, see also Rom 1:18). Similarly, Paul refers to the Corinthians as waiting for the revealing (Greek, *apokalypsis*) of Jesus Christ. Paul further reassures them that God will strengthen them "to the end," so that they will be found blameless on "the day of our Lord Jesus," that is, on the day of judgment (1 Cor 1:7–8).

But there is a second, less obvious connection between Paul's work among the gentiles and his end-time expectations. Paul's Jewish apocalyptic perspective included an understanding that God's ultimate triumph would include the bringing in of the nations (that is, the gentiles) under God's reign. This was not a new idea within Judaism. The book of Isaiah ends with a vision of all nations/gentiles who had not yet heard of Yahweh now declaring his glory and worshipping him (Isaiah 66:19, 23). 1 Enoch, a popular Second Temple text, also features the bringing in of the gentiles. Paul likely fit into this stream of Jewish tradition. He viewed his gentile mission as contributing to God's salvific plan. Moreover, Paul's success in persuading his gentile audiences "to serve a living and true God" (1 Thess 1:9) likely reinforced this belief.

Finally, Paul expected that the second coming of Christ would happen during his lifetime. We see this in his reassurances to the Thessalonians, who apparently were worried about the fate of those among them who had died before Jesus returned. Paul writes that those who have died will not be forgotten:

> For this we say to you with the word of the Lord, that we who are living, who are left until the Lord's coming, will definitely not go before those who have died. Because the Lord himself, with a shout of command, with an archangel's voice and the sound of God's trumpet, will come down from heaven, and the dead in Christ will rise first. Then we who are living and who are left, will be carried off together with them in the clouds to meet the Lord in the air. And so we will be with the Lord always. (1 Thess 4:15–17)

Paul's expectation of this imminent and cosmic event affects the way he teaches his communities to live. He sees no point in changing one's position or status in life since soon everything will be changed. Thus Paul exhorts his readers to "each live in the way that the Lord assigned, each as God called" (1 Cor 7:17). According to Paul, this is his command "in all the assemblies." The rule, according to Paul, applies to the Jews and gentiles, or as he puts it, the "circumcised" and "uncircumcised," slaves and freed persons (though see the discussion in "Paul and Slavery"), married and unmarried, and virgins. All should stay as they are "in view of the present crisis" (1 Cor 7:26). In other words, according to Paul, one's personal status will soon be irrelevant because "the time is short" and "the form of this world is passing away" (1 Cor 7:29, 31).

Paul and Slavery

One troubling aspect of Paul's letters is that he nowhere condemns the practice of slavery. He may come closest in 1 Corinthians 7:21, though scholars have long debated the meaning of this verse. The NRSV's translation implies that Paul is exhorting slaves in the Corinthian community *not* to seek freedom. Alternate translations suggest the opposite. Consider J. Albert Harrill's translation of the verse: "You were called as slave. Don't worry about it. But if you can indeed become free, use instead freedom." (See "Revisiting the Problem of 1 Corinthains 7:21" *Biblical Research* 65 (2020) 77-94, page 82). Even this translation does not mean necessarily that Paul was against the institution of slavery, only that he recognizes that freedom is preferable. Meanwhile, the Deutero-Pauline letters explicitly exhort slaves to obey their masters with sincere hearts (Col 3:22; Eph 6:5). Added to the ambiguity is Paul's letter to Philemon. Many read this letter as addressing a situation in which Paul is sending a runaway slave named Onesimus, back to his owner, Philemon. In this reading, the purpose of the letter is to urge Philemon to receive Onesimus without penalty. Philemon is to welcome him "no longer as a slave, but more than a slave, as a beloved brother" (16). But Paul's letter is so filled with innuendo that it is difficult to know his intent with any certainty. The letter's ambiguity is further reflected in the fact that in the pre-civil war southern United States, Paul's letters, including Philemon, were used both to justify slavery and to teach slaves that it was their Christian duty to obey their masters. Meanwhile, northern abolitionists drew on Philemon to argue that Paul supported an end to slavery. From our twenty-first-century perspective, it is easy to see that slavery was and is a violation of the basic rights of every human being. Still, the example of these diverse pro- and anti-slavery uses of Paul reminds us to look carefully at how the Bible is interpreted to support competing positions in other more contemporary cultural debates.

To summarize so far: to understand Paul means to be attuned to his complex identity as a self-described Jewish Pharisee, immersed in the Greco-Roman culture, and convinced that God had called him to be an apostle to the gentiles. It also means understanding his thoroughgoing belief that the world would soon undergo a radical change in which God, through the return of Jesus Christ, would come to judge the evildoers and reward the righteous. These fundamental aspects of Paul's identity and context explain much of what we find in his letters. The fact that he could write in Greek, travel between urban centers of the Roman empire, and communicate through letters with communities of Christ-followers is the result of the Hellenizing influence of Alexander from centuries earlier and the extensive transportation system built under Roman rule. The energy that Paul brought to his mission to the gentiles is a direct result of his Jewish apocalyptic understanding of how God is working in the world through Jesus Christ.

Three Undisputed Letters of Paul: Galatians, 1 Corinthians, and Romans

While it is not possible to discuss all of Paul's letters in depth in the space of this chapter, we will explore three of them briefly. Our aim will be to show how Paul approached three different situations based on his fundamental conviction that God had sent him to the gentiles to bring about their *pistis* in relation to the God of Israel. This Greek word, *pistis*, is typically translated as "belief" or "faith," which in its ancient context designated not so much a belief in God's existence (as it often connotes in the modern sense) but something more like "trusting in" or "having confidence in." This newfound trust, Paul urges, should result in obedience to God. This is evident in Romans where Paul describes the purpose of his work as bringing about "the obedience of faith among all the gentiles" (Rom 1:5). Our discussion of these letters will also provide an opportunity to see communities of Christ-followers under construction, as they sort out what their new life means in relation to one another and their broader Roman imperial context.

Paul's Letter to the Galatians

Galatians.

READING

Galatia was not a city like Corinth or Thessalonica, but a Roman province. Paul apparently traveled throughout this region and sent his letter to the "assemblies of Galatia" (Gal 1:1).

From the beginning of his letter, Paul appears especially agitated about the situation in Galatia. He omits altogether the thanksgiving section that typically opens his letters. Instead, Paul admonishes the Galatians for "deserting" him and calls curses down on those who are confusing and perverting the gospel of Christ (1:6–9). And with this, Paul is just getting warmed up! Later in the letter he calls the Galatians ignorant (3:1) and wishes that those who are leading them astray would separate themselves, or perhaps more sarcastically, castrate themselves (5:12). In short, the letter to the Galatians presents a striking example of the passion and vigor with which Paul could argue his point and defend his position against opposing views.

The issue that so disturbs Paul concerns circumcision. There are some in Galatia who have urged gentile Christ-followers to become circumcised. We do not have more details about this group. Paul refers to them only as "those of the circumcision" (Gal 2:12). We know only that the "circumcision faction," as the NRSV translates the Greek phrase, thought it necessary that gentiles must be circumcised in light of their new allegiance to the God of Israel. For modern readers, it is difficult to understand *why* Paul feels so vehemently opposed to circumcision for the gentiles, only *that* he is. His passionate objections seem more assertions than argument: "if you are circumcised, Christ will not benefit you" (5:2). Or, as Paul graphically puts it, for the gentiles to be circumcised would be to cut themselves off from Christ (5:4). Nevertheless, there is a logic behind his objection to gentile circumcision, as we will see below.

Basics on Galatians

I	Salutation and invocation of curse	1:1–10	**Outline: defining identity in Christ for the gentiles**
II	Body of the letter: the problem of circumcision for the gentiles	1:11–6:10	
	A Establishment of Paul's authority	1:11–2:14	
	B Argument against circumcision	2:15–4:31	
	C Instructions for a life of freedom in Christ	5:1–6:10	
III	Closing	6:11–18	

The letter to the Galatians was likely written in the mid-50s CE. Who Paul meant by his address to the "Galatians" is not clear, since Galatia was a large Roman province in Asia Minor. The letter may have been intended for cities in the southern part of the province (Antioch, Iconium, Lystra, Derbe), inhabited by a Hellenized population, or for the northern part of the province, home to ethnic Galatians (descendants of the Gauls who invaded the territory in the third century BCE).

Date and audience

The Question of Circumcision

The question of whether circumcision was required for gentiles who were interested in the Jewish traditions was not limited to early Christ-followers. According to the Jewish historian Josephus, a Jewish merchant named Ananias persuaded the Mesopotamian king Izates to "worship god according to the Jewish religion." Izates then assumes that he also needs to be circumcised to fully practice Judaism. Ananias assures him otherwise, arguing that the king could worship God without being circumcised. God would forgive the omission, Ananias claims, because were Izates to be circumcised his subjects might reject him due to his fondness of foreign rites. When a second Jewish teacher, Eleazar from Galilee, comes to the palace and finds the king reading the Torah, he offers an opposing opinion. Eleazar, who has a reputation for being "skillful in the learning of his country," argues that it was not enough to read the law, the king must also practice it. "How long will you continue uncircumcised?" he asks Izates. "But if you have not yet read the law about circumcision, and do not know how great impiety you are guilty of by neglecting it, read it now." At this, the king sends for a surgeon, and does "what he was commanded to do" (Josephus, *Antiquities* 20.3–4). The story related by Josephus illustrates both the possibility that there were missionizing efforts toward gentiles on the part of some Jews (represented by Ananias) and disagreements about whether circumcision was necessary for gentiles who worshiped the God of Israel.

First, we should note that Paul refers to the Jewish Torah to make the case that the law regarding circumcision does not apply to the gentiles. Given this, it cannot be the law itself that is an issue for Paul, in spite of a long history of interpreting his letters in just that way (see textbox "Changing Perspectives on Paul"). Indeed, Paul makes his method explicit, "Tell me, you who desire to be subject to the law, will you not listen to the law? (Gal 4:21). The point that Paul makes through his reading of the law (which in this case is Genesis) is that the gentiles in Galatia are descendants of Abraham, the father of Judaism, not by way of adherence to the law, but through the spirit (*pneuma*) given through Christ.

Paul uses the example of Abraham to argue that the inclusion of the gentiles as part of the ancestor's descendants was already anticipated in the scriptures:

> Just as Abraham "had faith in God, and it counted as righteousness for him" [Gen 15:6], so, you know, those who have faith are the sons of Abraham. And the scriptures, foreseeing that God would justify the gentiles on the basis of faith, announced the good news to Abraham in advance, saying, "All the gentiles shall be blessed in you" [Gen 12:3]. For this reason, those who have faith are blessed with Abraham who had faith. (Gal 3:6–9)

As noted, Paul's example of Abraham's faith and God's response comes from Gen 15. What is significant for Paul is that God's announcements to Abraham occur before the covenant of circumcision that is described in Genesis 17:10–14. In other words, Paul is arguing that Abraham entered into a relationship with God *before* he was circumcised.

Having established this, Paul makes an interesting move. Using a typical Jewish method of interpretation, he pays special attention to grammatical form, noting that God made promises to Abraham and to his "offspring" (Gal 3:16). Since the Greek word *sperma* (seed, or offspring) is singular rather than plural, Paul argues that it must refer to one person only, namely Christ. This is a good illustration of the way Paul and other Christ-followers reread the Hebrew scriptural traditions in ways that linked these traditions to their own setting and experiences. In this case, Paul connects Abraham to Christ so that the promises that God made to Abraham extend through his "offspring," Jesus. However, Paul must still make the crucial link between Christ and the gentiles. He does this through baptismal imagery. Now that the gentiles have "clothed themselves" with Christ and "belong" to Christ, they are also heirs to Abraham, and thus children of God (Gal 3:29). Paul has reread the Genesis text to show that the baptized gentile Christ-followers are fully included in the promises of God without being circumcised. Here, a key point to see is that the divine promises to Abraham are still centrally important to Paul, so important that he must show how the gentiles are now included in that heritage.

What Paul does not explain in a clear way for the modern reader is the reason for his strong opposition to circumcision for gentile Christ-followers. Nevertheless, we can be certain of a few facts. One is that Paul did "preach circumcision" at an earlier time, by his own admission (Gal 5:11). A second is that Paul nowhere advocates the end of circumcision on the eighth day for Jewish baby boys. Indeed, he sees his own eighth-day circumcision as a reason for confidence (Phil 3:5). Together, these observations suggest that before his revelatory vision, Paul may have held a position similar to his current opponents, namely that if one was male and aimed to be obedient to the God of Israel, one must be circumcised. This is the position represented by Eleazar in the story that Josephus relates (see textbox "The Question of Circumcision"). Paul's new position is that not only is circumcision unnecessary for gentiles, it would actually be detrimental. It will cut them off from Christ, tying them to the whole law of Judaism. This, Paul seems to think, would be disastrous because gentiles *cannot* fully obey that law, starting with the requirement to be circumcised on the eighth day after birth (Genesis 17:12.). Finally, if one reads Paul in light of his understanding of the impending end times, part of his objection to circumcision of gentile males could be that such gentiles must *remain* gentiles in their transformation through Christ in order to represent the "coming in" of the gentiles. We will return to this point in our discussion of Romans 9–11.

Toward the end of the letter to the Galatians, Paul instructs the gentiles on how they are to "live by the spirit" (Gal 5:16). He introduces these instructions by drawing on a tradition made famous by a Jewish teacher named Hillel, and known also from a gospel saying of Jesus – that the whole law can be fulfilled with one saying: "You shall love your neighbor as yourself" (Gal 5:14, see Lev 19:18). Paul then follows with lists of vices and virtues that resemble similar lists commonly used in ethical instructions by Roman moral philosophers. In this way, we once again can see Paul reflecting his own life context. He is an educated Hellenistic Jewish man living in the Roman world.

Changing Perspectives on Paul

The critical interpretation of the letters of Paul has moved through multiple stages. For the sake of simplicity, we will distinguish between the "old perspective," the "new perspective," and the newest **"Paul within Judaism"** perspective. The old perspective was deeply influenced by Martin Luther and other Protestant reformers in two ways. First, these reformers anachronistically projected their critique of the medieval Roman Catholic Church onto Second Temple Judaism. For instance, one of Luther's objections to Roman Catholicism was that it was "legalistic" insofar as one had to earn one's salvation by doing good. Luther took his critique of the Roman Catholic church to his reading of Paul, and argued that Paul rejected Judaism as a "legalistic" religion compared to the Christian religion of grace. The second way that Luther

influenced interpreters of Paul was made clear by a scholar named Krister Stendahl. In a highly influential article titled "Paul and the Introspective Conscience of the West," Stendahl showed how Luther and generations of scholars after him mistakenly imagined Paul as a person with a developed sense of the Western individual ego. They did not see him as the ancient Mediterranean Hellenistic Jew that he was. Luther turned Paul into a Christian with a troubled conscience, a man concerned with personal salvation (like Luther was!). But Stendahl showed how Paul was not focused on the salvation of *individuals* but of *groups* (Jews and gentiles). Stendahl also made an important basic observation that while Paul writes of his *call* to apostleship (1 Cor 1:1; Gal 1:15), he never refers to *conversion*. He does not exchange his Jewishness for a different religion called Christianity. Thus began what came to be called the "**New Perspective on Paul**," which attempted to read Paul through the lens of his Jewish identity. Still, while this was an important step forward in understanding Paul, the New Perspective has its own limitations. In this view, Paul becomes an advocate of a new universal idea of salvation (Jews and gentiles) over against a too exclusive notion of God's salvation in his own tradition. In the New Perspective, Paul remains a critic of Judaism, as he was in the old perspective.

More recently scholars like Matthew Thiessen and Paula Fredriksen have offered an even "newer" perspective on Paul, one that maintains an interpretation of Paul *within* Judaism rather than *against* it (on this formulation, see Matthew Thiessen, *Paul and the Gentile Problem* [New York: Oxford University Press, 2016, page 169]). This perspective maintains that not only was Paul unequivocally Jewish, he followed his fellow Jews in understanding his Jewishness to be grounded in genealogical descent. (Note, for example, his use of the phrase "my kin according to the flesh," Rom 9:3). According to the Paul *within* Judaism perspective, Paul would not have thought it possible for "Gentile sinners" (see Gal 2:15) to become Abraham's descendants without a *physical* change. Paul's unprecedented idea is that such a material change is possible for uncircumcised gentiles through the bodily reception of Christ's spirit (in Greek, *pneuma*). In its ancient Greco-Roman context *pneuma* was understood as a fine, ethereal substance. A gentile who received this substance, the *pneuma* of Christ, would undergo a substantive bodily change that made it possible to be "an heir to Abraham." Thiessen uses a modern medical analogy to explain this idea: "... to Paul's mind gentile circumcision is mere cosmetic surgery compared to the holistic remedy of gene therapy that the infusion of Christ's pneuma into gentile flesh provides" (15). If this seems strange to us in our twenty-first-century setting, this might be a sign that we are on the right track in understanding Paul within his first-century Hellenistic Jewish context!

The First Letter to the Corinthians

The situation that Paul faced in Corinth was quite different to that in Galatia. Whereas Paul had to remind the Galatians of their freedom from the law (that is, from circumcision), in the case of the Corinthians he feels the need to instruct and sometimes admonish them about their conduct.

READING   1 Corinthians 1–10.

EXERCISE   Make a list of the different issues that Paul addresses in these chapters that are causing tensions in the community. Note how Paul responds to each of these issues. What issues seem foreign to our current context? What issues are still relevant?

Paul's correspondence with the Corinthian community provides a fascinating glimpse of his process of working with newly converted gentiles. Several letters passed between Paul and this group, and it is likely that fragments of these have been combined in the two letters that we now have in the New Testament. In what we know as "first" Corinthians, Paul refers to a letter that he had already written to them (1 Cor 5:9) and also indicates that he is responding to a letter that they wrote to him (1 Cor 7:1). In what we label "second" Corinthians, Paul mentions yet another letter that he wrote out of distress and "with many tears" (2 Cor 2:3–4, 7:8). Some argue that this "tearful letter" is 2 Corinthians 10–12 because these chapters take on a particularly anguished tone. In any case, the references to this ongoing correspondence suggest that Paul's relationship with this group was a rocky one, culminating in a challenge to his leadership, which seems to have been resolved in his favor (2 Cor 7:9).

Basics on 1 Corinthians

I	Salutation and thanksgiving	1:1–9	**Outline:** negotiating life as new Christ-followers
II	Body of the letter: conflicts in Corinth	1:10–16:12	
	A Divisions and Paul's authority	1:10–4:20	
	B Issues of sexuality and marriage	5:1–7:39	
	C Eating food sacrificed to idols	8–10	
	D Problems with rituals and worship	11–14	
	E Disagreements over resurrection	15:1–58	
III	Concluding matters and greetings	16:1–21	

Paul started the Corinthian community in 50/51–2 CE. This letter, which is not actually Paul's first letter to the Corinthians (see 1 Cor 5:9), was probably written about 55 or 56 CE. The evidence from the letter suggests that Paul was writing to a diverse group, no doubt reflecting the cosmopolitan nature of the city itself. **Date and audience**

The opening of the letter points to factions in Corinth, seemingly based on allegiance to different leaders (1 Cor 1:12–13). But there are clues in the letters suggesting that tensions around social status may also have been an issue. Addressing the Corinthians, Paul claims "not many of you were wise by human standards, not many of you were powerful, not many of you were of noble birth" (1:26). In other words, not many, but some, *were* of a higher social standing than others in the group. Later in the letter, he admonishes some in the group who are apparently eating a full meal in the context of the Lord's supper, while others go hungry (11:21–2). Again, Paul's description suggests a difference in socio-economic class among members of the group. Some had enough food for a good meal, while others had none.

Conflicting opinions are also evident about basic life issues such as sexuality, lawsuits, married life, diet, and ritual practices. For example, with regard to sexuality, at least some in the assembly adopted a lifestyle of self-denial, arguing that "it is good for a man not to touch a woman" (1 Cor 7:1). Others in the group were not so inclined, as is clear from Paul's sharp criticism of their sexual practices (5:1–2; 6:16). Some Corinthians insisted that there was nothing wrong with eating food that had been sacrificed in pagan temples, while Paul felt the practice was potentially problematic (1 Cor 8–10). Some in the assembly appeared to elevate certain ritual practices above others, while Paul resists privileging one "gift" over another (1 Cor 12–14).

From Paul's perspective, there is a general attitude of arrogance that underlies many of these issues. Indeed, the theme of arrogance shows up several times in 1 Corinthians (1 Cor 4:6–8; 4:18–19; 5:2; 8:1). It may be that the Corinthians understood themselves to have achieved a higher status in their new life in Christ that gave them certain liberties. Perhaps when Paul brought his apocalyptic message to them (God has already intervened through Jesus Christ to bring about salvation for the gentiles), they did not fully grasp the second part (Christ will return for a day of judgment). Thus, on the matter of sexuality, some among the Corinthians apparently thought that what they did with their bodies was irrelevant, given their newly achieved superior spiritual existence. Such claims by the Corinthians that "all things are possible for me" and "food is for the stomach and the stomach is for food" (1 Cor 6:12–13) are indirect ways of saying that sex is meant for the body. Paul rejects this argument about sexuality, insisting that what the Corinthians do with their bodies *is* directly relevant to their spiritual state. In fact, since Paul understands the Holy Spirit to dwell within the believer, he considers the body to be a temple for the Spirit (1 Cor 6:19).

Another issue that shows up in this community concerns food. Chapters 8–10 of 1 Corinthians address the issue of eating meat that was sacrificed to Greco-Roman deities. The issue here is not just one of diet or religious practice, but also one of basic social relations. To flourish and have important contacts in an urban center such as Corinth, one needed to be a member of a **voluntary association**, perhaps a trade guild, or a cult devoted to a Roman god or goddess. A prominent part of such associations was gathering for meals, which often included meat that had been offered to a deity. Paul's converts had to decide whether it was acceptable to eat such food. Their decision had implications for their participation in the broader culture of their city. The Corinthians' position on this issue again reflects their self-confidence: "We all have knowledge," they argue (1 Cor 8:1). This "knowledge" is apparently what Paul taught them about their former religious practices and their newly adopted ones, namely, "there is no idol in the world," and that "there is no God except one" (1 Cor 8:4). In other words, if there are no other real gods besides the one true God, then the sacrificial nature of the food offered in Greek or Roman temples is insignificant. The Corinthians suggest that there is no harm in eating the meat, or presumably in participating in the social events connected to the meal. As they argue, "Food will not make us present to God. We will not lose an advantage if we do not eat, nor gain one if we do" (1 Cor 8:8). Paul, however, remains critical. While he agrees with their position in principle, he is concerned about what it might mean in practice. It may cause some who are less certain of their new trust in only one god to return to the idea of sacrificing to many gods (1 Cor 8:10).

In sum, in dealing with the members of the Corinthian community, Paul addresses a range of questions related to daily life for these newly converted gentiles: what they do with their bodies, what they eat, who they can associate with, whether they should get married, whether they should have sex, and so on. He also had to instruct them on ritual practices – how to worship, how women should wear their hair when they pray and prophesy, and how to celebrate the Lord's supper. While addressing this range of issues, Paul pushes back against expressions of freedom or confidence that he sees as immoral and/or destructive to the community he is trying to build. "See that this liberty of yours," he argues, "does not cause the weak to stumble" (1 Cor 8:9).

The Letter to the Romans

Romans 1–4, 9–11.

READING

Try to follow the course of Paul's argument in these sections of Romans. What issues are involved? How does he describe God's relationship with the Jews? How do the gentiles fit into God's plan for salvation?

EXERCISE

Paul's letter to the Romans provides the fullest account of his understanding of the gospel. He writes to the Romans in preparation for his pending journey to Rome (1:10–11; 15:23). Although Paul has never visited the Roman community of Christ-followers, he seeks their support as he moves his mission further westward to Spain (1:13; 15:24). Thus his letter serves, in part, as an introduction of his gospel for the gentile Christ-followers in Rome (see Romans 1:5–6). Especially the first eight chapters seem to serve this purpose. Here Paul returns to the themes of his letter to the Galatians: being in relationship with God based on faith, the example of Abraham as one faithful to God, the issue of the law in relation to the gentiles, and the significance of life in the spirit. Chapter 9 signals a shift in tone where Paul writes personally about the anguish he feels regarding the unbelief of "Israelites" whom, as we have seen, he describes as his own people "according to the flesh" (Rom 9:3). Here he has in mind those in the Jewish community who have not become Christ-followers. His understanding of why this has occurred comes to a dramatic climax in chapters 9–11, which will be the focus text for this chapter.

RECONSTITUTION DU FORUM ROMAIN VU DE LA MAISON DES VESTALES

FIGURE 10.4
Artist's reconstruction of ancient Rome, depicting the emperor's palace in the background and the Roman Forum, the main center of the city. One should imagine other major Greco-Roman cities as similarly majestic, though on a smaller scale.

Basics on Romans

Outline:	I	Salutation and thanksgiving	1:1–15
Paul's letter of introduction to the Romans	II	Body of the letter: Paul's gospel	1:16–15:13
		A God's impartiality to Jews and gentiles	1:16–4:25
		B The role of Christ, sin, law, and spirit	5–8
		C The problem of Israel and the place of the gentiles	9–11
		D Instructions for life as a community of believers	12–14
	III	Concluding matters with extended greetings	15:14–16:27

Date and audience

This is the last of the letters of Paul, written toward the end of the 50s CE. It is also written to an assembly that he did not found and had not yet visited. Thus the purpose of the letter is, in part, an introduction of his gospel to a group who had not yet heard him preach. The letter suggests that its intended audience was a mixed association of Jews and gentiles, perhaps living in some tension, given Paul's concerns that gentiles "not boast" over the Jews (Rom 11:17–21).

In some ways, Paul's view of God that is expressed in Romans is an extension of developments seen earlier in Second and Third Isaiah (Isaiah 40–55 and Isaiah 56–66). Recall how during and after the exilic period, after extensive engagements with foreign nations, the exiles in Babylon reconceived their local God of Israel in much broader terms – as the only "real" creator God who controls the cosmos. As we saw in Chapter 7, Third Isaiah depicts a creator God who welcomes foreigners who observe the Sabbath and keep the covenant (Isa 56:6–7). Paul takes this position further, arguing that trust in God and the reception of the spirit of Christ makes possible the inclusion of gentiles as heirs to God's promises (Rom 8:12–17). Again, what is required of the gentiles is sharing the same faith in God that Abraham had (Rom 4:1–25).

Juxtaposed with this argument about the importance of faith are the seemingly contradictory statements about the place of the Jewish law. These tensions are especially apparent in Romans. On the one hand, Paul writes in his letter to the Galatians that those who adhere to the law are under a curse (Gal 3:10). In Romans 4:15, he writes that the law brings wrath. Statements such as these have reinforced interpretations of Paul as against the Jewish law. But Paul also states that "doers of the law will be justified" (Rom 2:13) and "the law is holy, and the commandment is holy, just, and good" (Rom 7:12). Here again, we need to remember Paul's audience. From Paul's perspective the negative comments about the function of the law *pertain to gentiles*. That is, when he writes of the law bringing judgment (or wrath) he has in mind how the law works in relation to non-Jews. Paul, like other Jewish thinkers of his time, saw the law as something that privileged Jews and judged gentiles. Paul agrees with his fellow Jews that the law brings a curse to anyone who does not obey it, including gentiles who *cannot* obey crucial parts of the law (Gal 3:10). But what Paul also believes is that God's cosmic transformation brought about through Christ has answered this dilemma for the gentiles. God's gift of the Spirit through Christ means that no one can now condemn the gentile followers of Christ. They are counted among "God's elect" (Rom 8:33–4)! Paul ends the first part of the letter on a high point celebrating the unbreakable relationship between God and God's people (Rom 8:38–39).

Following this exaltation, chapter 9 marks a stark shift in tone. However much Paul affirms the elect status of Christ-following gentiles, Paul also does not dismiss the long tradition of God's election of Torah-observant Israel that is at the heart of Israelite and Jewish tradition. On the one hand, he insists on God's impartiality (2:11). On the other hand, he asks, "Then what is the special advantage of the Jew? Or what is the usefulness of circumcision?" His answer is, "much in every way" (3:1–2). And in chapters 9–11, Paul takes up at length the question of his Jewish kin who have not become Christ-followers.

The Problem of Israel and the Place of the Gentiles (Romans 9–11)

FOCUS TEXT

In Romans 9–11 Paul writes in a poignant and personal way, revealing his deep theological convictions about God's work with both Jews and gentiles. These chapters are arguably the climax of the whole letter as they address the fundamental question of how God works to bring about salvation for all people. To reach his grand conclusion in chapter 11, Paul engages in creative rereadings of Hebrew scriptures. In this way, Romans 9–11 provide more evidence of the way Paul and other early Christ-followers freely reinterpreted their scriptural traditions in light of their belief in Jesus as the messiah.

Romans 9 opens with an intensely personal expression of Paul's feelings. The preceding section of his letter concluded with soaring words of praise (8:38–9). But as chapter 9 begins, Paul abruptly changes tone and speaks of his great sorrow and unceasing anguish on behalf of his own people. Affirming their status before God, he claims, "They are Israelites, and to them belong the adoption, the glory, the covenants, the lawgiving, the rituals, and the promises; to them belong the ancestors, and from them is the Christ according to the flesh" (9:4–5). These Israelites, according to Paul, are "his kin according to the flesh," and he goes so far as to wish that he himself would be cut off from Christ for their sake (9:3). The double mention of "according to the flesh" in these verses demonstrates how Paul has in mind an actual material connection to his fellow Jews. This fleshly, physical connection also matters for Paul in terms of their place in God's plan of salvation.

As Paul considers his fellow Jews who have not recognized Jesus as God's messiah, he is troubled by two things: (1) their lack of belief in Jesus as the messiah and (2) what their rejection of this claim says about God's broader plans. If God promised to be the God of Israel, and if these Israelites rejected the messiah sent from God while the gentiles did not, did God somehow make a mistake? Paul already anticipated this second problem in chapter 3. There, while listing the advantages of the Jewish people, he raised the question, "What if some do not believe? Will their unbelief put an end to the faithfulness of God?" (Rom 3:3). Chapters 9–11 are Paul's answer to this question. Using a series of different arguments, Paul insists that God's promises and justice remain steadfast. As he asserts early in the argument, "... it is not as if the word of God had failed" (9:6).

To make this point, Paul draws on the Hebrew scriptures. In 9:6–13, his argument is based on the concept of election. The idea that God chooses his people, which was so central in books such as Deuteronomy and Hosea, now becomes the key to Paul's explanation of why some Jews believe that Jesus is God's messiah and some do not. Paul points out that the promise did not go to *all* of Abraham's children (9:7), but only to one genealogical line of descendants. According to Paul, this idea of election applies also to God's mercy. God has mercy on whomever God chooses and hardens the heart of whomever God chooses (9:15). In other words, Paul explains the lack of belief of some of God's people by claiming that God has hardened their hearts (9:18).

Next Paul anticipates objections to this argument. You may already have thought of these yourself. If God is choosing mercy for some and not for others, how can anyone be blamed for a lack of faith? And how can it be fair for God to choose some and not others? In responding to such objections, Paul alludes to the traditions of Job (Job 9:12) and Isaiah (Isa 29:16; 45:9), both of which point to the inappropriateness of a mere person questioning the creator God. While this may not be a satisfying answer, Paul is not ultimately worried about questions of fairness or even about an individual's standing before God. He is not thinking about *individual* salvation at all, but rather of the place of Jews and gentiles in God's plan. That this is on his mind is clear as Paul continues his reading of the prophets. With a creative "misreading" of the prophet Hosea, Paul finds scriptural expression of the eschatological inclusion of the gentiles in two modified quotations from the prophet:

> I will call "not my people," "my people" and "not beloved," "beloved." And in the place where it was said to them. "You are not my people," there they will be called "sons of the living God." (Rom 9:25–6; see Hos 1:10; 2:23)

In Hosea, these words refer to the estranged people of Israel with whom God restores a relationship. But Paul reinterprets Hosea's words to apply to God's inclusion of the gentiles.

Before reaching his conclusion, Paul turns to the prophet Isaiah to introduce yet another explanation of what God is up to. He draws on Isaiah's concept of a "remnant" among Israel that God will save (Rom 9:27; cf. Isa 10:21–2). In the eighth-century BCE context Isaiah's "remnant" referred to Israelites who would survive Assyrian attacks and live to see the restoration of a unified Israel. Paul draws on the remnant idea to explain why only a small number of Jewish people have expressed belief in Jesus as the messiah. This argument, though, does not ultimately satisfy Paul. He is not content with only a remnant of his people being saved. We see what troubles him as he reaches the high point of his argument in chapter 11. Paul begins with a direct question: "I ask then, has God rejected his people?" He quickly and firmly rejects the idea, using himself as an example – he is an Israelite and God has not rejected him! (11:1). Paul then takes another tack, suggesting that the role of the Jewish "stumblers" (those who do not yet trust in Christ) bears on the fate of the gentiles (11:11–12). It is God's initial hardening of some Jews that has allowed salvation to come to the gentiles. The conclusion that Paul arrives at in chapter 11 is that God is working with *both* groups in ways that will bring about salvation to all of *Israel* (11:26).

It is important to see that Paul concludes this discussion with a direct address to gentiles, not Jews. He warns them not to become proud or feel superior because they are Christ-followers while some Jews are not. As gentiles, they are but a wild olive branch that, because of God's kindness, has been grafted on to the rich root that is Israel (Rom 11:17–20).

By reading Romans 9–11 as an address to gentiles about God's faithfulness to both them and to Paul's "kin according to the flesh", we see that he can no more condemn his people than he can give up on his belief in Christ. The centuries of scholarship that have read Paul's letter to the Romans as an expression of Paul's anti-legalism or anti-Judaism failed to take this climactic portion of Romans into adequate account. Of course, one can point to weaknesses in Paul's argument. He is struggling to make sense out of his current reality, one that he does not fully understand. He describes the unbelief of many of his fellow Jews as "a mystery" and points to the inscrutable nature of God's ways (11:25, 33). In the end, what Paul reveals in Romans 9–11 is his firm conviction that the promises of God that were extended to Israel in the past remain steadfast, "for the gifts and the calling of God are irrevocable" (11:29).

The Disputed Letters

So far in our discussion of Paul, we have focused on three of the undisputed epistles (1 Corinthians, Galatians, and Romans). But the Pauline letter collection also includes letters attributed to Paul that likely were not written by him. Three of these letters – 2 Thessalonians, Colossians, and Ephesians – are typically referred to as **Deutero-Pauline** ("secondary to Paul") because they differ from the undisputed letters in style, vocabulary, and basic ideas. For instance, 2 Thessalonians sounds much like 1 Thessalonians on the surface, but its view of the end times, its **eschatology**, is quite different. In 1 Thessalonians, Paul expects "the day of the Lord" to come during his lifetime. The community is to be vigilant because Jesus could return at any moment (1 Thess 4:15, 5:1–7). But in 2 Thessalonians, the author assures the readers that the day of the Lord will not come until other events take place (2 Thess 2:1–12). Note, too, how the author of 2 Thessalonians prefaces his discussion with a warning that the audience should not be deceived by a letter "as though from us" (2:2). Calling attention to the possibility of **pseudonymous** writers (those writing under a false name) was actually a common practice that pseudonymous writers during this period used to give their own letters the appearance of being authentic. These aspects of the letter have led many scholars to conclude that 2 Thessalonians was not written by Paul, but by an author during the latter half of the first century.

Two other Deutero-Pauline letters, Ephesians and Colossians, have a writing style that is quite different from what we find in the undisputed epistles. The sentence structure is more complex than the writing in the undisputed letters and the vocabulary also differs. Also, the letters appear to reflect a later stage of development than is reflected in the undisputed letters. For instance, whereas Paul speaks about Christ as the foundation for the community in 1 Corinthians (1 Cor 3:11), the letter to the Ephesians adds another layer of authority so that "household of God" is built upon the foundation of the apostles and the prophets, with Christ as the cornerstone (Eph 2:20). The ideas about Christ also reflect more development. The author of Colossians describes Christ as "the image of the individual God, the firstborn of creation," who "is before all things, and in him all things hold together" (Col 1:15–16). This is a more cosmic conception of Christ than one finds in the undisputed Pauline letters.

Ephesians and Colossians are also distinctive in their inclusion of **household codes**; that is, instructions for proper conduct of various members of the household (Col 3:18–4:1; Eph 5:21–6:9). The codes urge all members of the household – husbands, wives, children, and slaves – to maintain their proper positions in the household hierarchy. Such codes are not unique to these letters; they appear frequently in Greco-Roman moral philosophy. What is significant here is that the author of the epistles calls for behavior that is aligned with the cultural values of the Roman empire. It may be that, by the time these potentially post-Pauline letters were written, Christ-followers were increasingly recognized as a distinct group. In response, the authors of these letters advocated traditional family structures that matched the values of the broader Greco-Roman culture. At a time when new cultic practices were regarded with suspicion, embracing traditional cultural values would make the early communities of Christ-followers less threatening to others.

The last three of the disputed epistles, 1 and 2 Timothy and Titus, are often referred to as the **Pastoral Epistles** because they offer instructions regarding pastoral duties. Whereas there is considerable debate regarding the Pauline authorship of 2 Thessalonians, Colossians, and Ephesians, virtually all critical biblical scholars agree that the pastoral letters were not written by Paul. 1 Timothy assumes a level of organization in the assemblies that did not exist when Paul was forming his groups of Christ-followers. It lists proper qualifications for bishops and deacons in a way that suggests these are established leadership positions in the communities (1 Tim 3:1–13; see also Titus 1:7). Paul's undisputed letters, written during the formative stages of thcsc communities, show no knowledge of such leadership positions because they did not exist yet.

The position regarding women that is reflected in the Pastoral Epistles also differs from Paul's attitude toward women in the undisputed epistles. While Paul certainly was a person of his time in holding hierarchical views of men and women, there is ample evidence that he perceived women to be co-workers and leaders in the Jesus movement. For example, in his long list of greetings at the end of the letter to the Romans, nine greetings are directed toward women, with several receiving high praise from Paul. Prisca is referred to as a co-worker of Paul's who risked her life for him (Rom 16:3). Tryphena and Tryphosa are workers in the Lord, and Mary and Persis both worked hard (Rom 16:6, 12–13). Junia is outstanding among the apostles (Rom 16:7). Such greetings show that Paul recognized and welcomed the participation of these women. In his letter to the Corinthians, Paul gives further evidence of his acceptance of the active role of women: receiving reports from "Chloe's people" (1 Cor 1:11), accepting that women pray and prophesy (in spite of his concern about their hair covering) (1 Cor 11:5), and recognizing the advantages of a life of celibacy for women in a culture that emphasized marriage and child-bearing (1 Cor 7:34).

Compared to this evidence from Paul's own letters, the Pastoral Epistles are narrow in their perception of women's roles in the assemblies of Christ-followers. Rather than promoting celibacy, the "Paul" behind these letters claims that women will be saved through childbearing (1 Tim 2:15). Rather than recognizing the contributions of women to the work of the Jesus movement, these letters portray women as "silly," and "overwhelmed by their sins and all kinds of desires" (2 Tim 3:6). In the Pastoral Epistles no woman is permitted to teach or have authority over a man, "she is to keep silent" (1 Tim 2:12). To bolster the point, the author evokes the story of Adam and Eve, contributing to a long and distorted history of interpretation that places the blame for human transgression on Eve alone (1 Tim 2:13–14; cf.1 Cor 5:12). Such extensive departure from the undisputed epistles suggests that this author has taken on a decidedly more restrictive approach to women than Paul himself did. Overall, the evidence suggests that the Pastoral Epistles were written by a second-century author, who wrote in Paul's name to bolster the authority of the letters.

Conclusion: From Letters to Scripture

At some point in the early second century, Paul's letters were published together as a collection. Paul himself might have gathered some of his letters together for publication, since letter writers frequently had their secretaries make copies of their own letters before the original was sent. Later, followers of Paul added to the collection until all thirteen of the letters that are now in the New Testament were published together. Once they were published as a whole, the "occasional" nature of the letters began to recede from view. That is to say, readers did not focus on the circumstances of why Paul wrote what he did to Christ-followers in different cities. Instead, interpretations of the letter collection focused more generally on Paul's theology and Christology. From an academic perspective, we do well to continue to explore Paul's letters written at a particular time and addressing particular issues. Understanding Paul's perspective before it was made to conform to the questions and concerns of the later church helps us understand this highly influential and formative figure better. Attending to the historical circumstances of the letters also provides fascinating insights into the early years of a movement that would eventually grow into a world religion. Finally, reading Paul within Judaism, as we have attempted to do here, helps avoid harmful interpretations that anachronistically turn the Jewish Christ-follower, Paul, into a Christian who converted from and then opposed Judaism.

CHAPTER TEN REVIEW

1. Know the meaning and significance of the following terms used in this chapter:
   - apocalyptic worldview
   - apostle
   - Deutero-Pauline
   - eschatology
   - household codes
   - the "New Perspective on Paul"
   - Paul within Judaism
   - Pastoral Epistles
   - pseudonymous
   - undisputed and disputed letters
   - voluntary association
2. In what way did the interests of the Roman empire contribute to Paul's missionary efforts?
3. What aspects of Paul's identity are important to understand for interpreting his letters?
4. What was the major issue confronting Paul in his work with the community in Galatia? How did he respond to this issue?
5. What issues were at stake in Paul's correspondence with the Corinthians?
6. In what ways do you think Paul's own hybrid identity affected his understanding of the relationship of Jews and gentiles in the letter to the Romans?
7. (Focus text: Rom 9–11) What is the theological question that Paul addresses in these chapters? What are some ways he tries to answer it? Do you find his argument (or parts of it) convincing? Explain.
8. On what basis do some scholars dispute the authorship of some of the Pauline letters? For example, what is distinctive about the Pastoral Epistles compared to the undisputed letters?

RESOURCES FOR FURTHER STUDY

Elliott, Neil, and Reasoner, Mark, eds. *Documents and Images for the Study of Paul.* Minneapolis, MN: Fortress Press, 2011.

Fredriksen, Paula. *Paul: The Pagan's Apostle.* New Haven, CT: Yale University Press, 2017.

Harrill, James Albert. *Paul the Apostle: His Life and Legacy in Their Roman Context.* New York: Cambridge University Press, 2012.

Marchal, Joseph A., ed. *Studying Paul's Letters: Contemporary Perspectives and Methods.* Minneapolis, MN: Fortress Press, 2012.

Porter, Stanley E. *The Apostle Paul: His Life, Thought, and Letters.* Grand Rapids, MI: Eerdmans, 2016.

Stendahl, Krister. *Paul among Jews and Gentiles and Other Essays.* Philadelphia, PA: Fortress, 1976.

Thiessen, Matthew. *Paul and the Gentile Problem.* New York: Oxford University Press, 2016.

Twomey, Jay. *The Pastoral Epistles Through the Centuries.* Chichester and Malden, MA: Wiley-Blackwell, 2009.

Zetterholm, Magnus. *Approaches to Paul: A Student's Guide to Recent Scholarship.* Minneapolis, MN: Fortress, 2009.

The Gospel of Mark: Suffering and Trauma Under Imperial Rule

11

Chapter Outline

Chapter Overview

This chapter begins with an overview of a watershed event in the history of Judaism and emerging Christianity: the Jewish War and the destruction of the Jerusalem Temple by Rome. All of the gospel writers have this traumatic event in mind as they relate their stories of Jesus. In this chapter, we first explore evidence that the Gospel of Mark is the earliest of the canonical gospels. Sometimes students assume that this means that it is also the most historically accurate of the canonical gospels. But that is not necessarily the case. We will see how this gospel, like all of the New Testament gospels, tells a story of Jesus that speaks to the historical context of the gospel. In this case, the major themes of the Gospel of Mark fit well with the time of suffering connected to the Jewish War and the destruction of the Jerusalem Temple. We will see how the Gospel of Mark tells the story of a messiah who must be rejected, suffer, and die. At the same time, it depicts his closest followers, the disciples, having difficulty understanding or accepting this idea. By the end of this chapter, you will see how these themes work together to address Christ-followers during a situation of instability and crisis.

A Contemporary Introduction to the Bible: Sacred Texts and Imperial Contexts, Second Edition. Colleen M. Conway and David M. Carr.
© 2021 Colleen M. Conway and David M. Carr. Published 2021 by John Wiley & Sons Ltd.

The Jewish War (66–70 CE)

As we saw in Chapter 9, toward the end of the first century BCE, Herod engaged in a massive building program designed to gain favor from his subjects and from his Roman benefactors. A tour of Jerusalem during this time would have offered much to impress the traveler. But a traveler to Jerusalem decades later would have encountered a very different sight. Instead of gazing on the architectural achievements of Herod, after 70 CE the traveler would have found broken city walls, the Jerusalem Temple looted and ravaged by fire, and much of the city destroyed by war. All of this would have been the result of the **Jewish War** – the Jewish revolt against Rome that began in 66 CE, an event that changed the history of the Jewish people forever.

As you may recall, the end of Jewish independent rule came with the invasion of Palestine by the Roman general Pompey in 63 BCE. By 6 CE, Judea and the surrounding regions were reorganized by Rome into a larger Roman province. This change to provincial status meant that Rome now had direct rule over the region through "prefects" or governors that were appointed by the Roman Senate. These prefects, including Pontius Pilate of the gospels, were notorious both for their incompetence and their brutality. Living under such inept rulers led to increasing unrest among the local Jewish community, culminating in an armed revolt against Rome in 66 CE.

The Jewish rebels had some initial success, managing to occupy the Temple and even mint their own silver coins in the first year of the revolt (see Figure 11.1). But by 70 CE, the Roman army had Jerusalem in the grip of what would become a protracted siege. According to the Jewish historian Josephus, this was a time of great suffering for the inhabitants of Jerusalem. He writes of widespread starvation in Jerusalem during this time and deadly struggles for

FIGURE 11.1
Silver shekel minted about 67 CE during the Jewish revolt. The inscription in archaic Hebrew recalls the Zion theology of the ancient past, stating "Jerusalem the Holy".

FIGURE 11.2
Pillaging of the Jerusalem Temple depicted on the Arch of Titus, which still stands in Rome, commemorating Titus's triumph over the Jewish revolt.

FIGURE 11.3
"Judaea Capta" coin minted in Rome to commemorate victory over the Jewish rebels. The seated woman represents conquered Judea. Depicting a defeated opponent as a woman was a common means of humiliation in the Roman world.

remained. Those who left the city in search of food were captured by the Romans and crucified outside the city walls. Of these, Josephus states, "so great was their number, that space could not be found for the crosses nor crosses for the bodies" (*Jewish War* 5.451). Eventually, in an effort led by the Roman general Titus, the Roman army breached the walls of Jerusalem, destroying most of the city, including plundering and burning down the Temple (Figure 11.2). For the Jewish people, this was a devastating end to the rebellion against Roman imperial rule. With the city and Temple destroyed and large numbers of the population either dead or scattered to other regions, it may well have seemed like the end to the Jewish people altogether (see Figure 11.3).

READING

Mark 13. Pay attention to details that match the circumstances of the Jewish War.

Pointers to the Dating and Context of the Gospel of Mark

Although it is unlikely that the Gospel of Mark was written in Jerusalem, there are indications that the tragic events that occurred in the city from 66 to 70 CE helped shape this author's story of Jesus. From your reading of Mark 13, the links between this chapter and the Jewish War with Rome should be evident. The Markan Jesus's description of increased suffering through war, famine, and betrayal in Mark 13 matches the experience of those besieged within the walls of Jerusalem. (Recall that the term "Markan Jesus" is used to distinguish this gospel's presentation of Jesus from the historical Jesus and from the depiction of Jesus in other gospels.) These historical connections suggest a date for the Gospel of Mark to sometime close to 70 CE. Notice especially the reference to "the desolating sacrilege set up where it ought not to be" (Mark 13:14). This is an allusion to Dan 11:31, which evokes an earlier violation of the Temple by a foreign presence, the Seleucid king Antiochus IV (see Chapter 8). Notably, the narrative is interrupted at this point by a direct address to the reader ("let the reader understand"). In other words, the audience of the gospel is supposed to interpret the allusion in light of events occurring in their own time.

Basics on the Gospel of Mark

Outline: Mark's story of Jesus as the suffering messiah			
	I	Rising popularity of Jesus and rising conflict with authorities	1:1–8:21
	II	Transition: passion predictions and instructions about the demands of discipleship	8:22–10:52
	III	Predictions fulfilled: the suffering messiah	11:1–16:8

There is no certainty about who wrote the gospel or where it was written. **Location and** Church tradition has associated the gospel with Peter, claiming that Mark was **audience** Peter's "interpreter" and suggesting that Peter related these stories to Mark while he was in Rome. Many have questioned this traditional association, finding little evidence in the gospel that it is narrated from Peter's point of view. Some have theorized that the gospel was written somewhere closer to Jerusalem, perhaps in northern Galilee or Syria. At points, the narrative seems to assume a lack of familiarity with Jewish customs (7:3–4), leading some to argue that the author had primarily a gentile audience in mind, or was himself a gentile Christ-follower.

The reference to Daniel also highlights the apocalyptic flavor of Mark 13. Indeed, scholars often refer to this chapter as Mark's "little apocalypse". Its presence is another indication of the influence of Jewish apocalypticism on the Jesus movement. Along with the reference to increased suffering comes the expectation of divine intervention that will reward the faithful who have endured (Mark 13:13). The description of suffering includes not only war and famine, but also persecution from synagogue and governmental authorities, and hatred because of Jesus's name (Mark 13:9, 13). There is no evidence of widespread persecution of Christ-followers as early as 70 CE, but we do have reports of isolated incidents. The best-known of these is the report by the first-century CE Roman historian Tacitus of Nero's persecution in Rome of a group called Christians (in Latin, *chrestianos*) by the populace. According to this account, Nero used the Christians as a scapegoat for a devastating fire that swept through Rome in 64 CE (see textbox p. 366). The references to persecution in the Gospel of Mark may allude to this event, or more generally to increased tensions toward the Christ-followers as their growing numbers drew more attention from local authorities.

Markan Priority

Scholars use the phrase **Markan priority** to refer to the consensus opinion that the Gospel of Mark, the shortest of the four canonical gospels, was written before the other canonical gospels. Readers of the gospels did not always think this was the case. Until the nineteenth century, the Gospel of Matthew was thought to be the earliest gospel, while the Gospel of Mark was viewed as an abbreviated version of Matthew. But this theory requires an explanation for why the author of Mark would omit significant sections of the Gospel of Matthew. For example, the Gospel of Mark does not have any stories about Jesus's birth and resurrection. It begins with the story of Jesus's baptism as an adult and concludes without any scenes featuring the resurrected Jesus. Although one could imagine a writer who knew the Gospel of Matthew or Luke deciding to compose a shorter story of Jesus, it is harder to explain why such a writer would conclude that accounts of Jesus's birth and resurrection should be left out of his narrative. Observations like these have led scholars to posit that Mark was written before the other gospels. The author seems to have collected oral traditions about Jesus – stories about what he did and said – and combined them into an extended written narrative. Some scholars argue that the author built on an early written account of Jesus's suffering and death, a **passion narrative**, by adding stories about Jesus's ministry. That may be true, but we do not have any certain evidence of a pre-Markan passion narrative. For now, it is enough to understand the idea of Markan priority: the idea that the Gospel of Mark, itself written decades after Jesus's death, appears to be the earliest of the biblical gospels. The theory of Markan priority is a first step in answering the question of how the canonical gospels are related, a question we discuss in more detail in the next chapter.

With this evidence for the dating and context of Mark in mind, we turn to the story itself. The Markan narrative has two parts with a transition section that links them together. The first part of the gospel (Mark 1:1–8:21) tells a story of Jesus's miracle-working ministry, resulting in his increasing popularity among the crowds. This growing popularity among the people is juxtaposed with accounts of growing conflict with the Jerusalem authorities. The transition section (Mark 8:22–10:52) features Jesus traveling to Jerusalem from the northern region of Caesarea Philippi. On the way, the Markan Jesus tries to prepare his disciples for his coming trial and crucifixion and instruct them in the ways of discipleship. For their part, the disciples continue a pattern of misunderstanding Jesus that is already evident in the first section. The transition section also prepares the gospel audience for a shift from the miracle-working Jesus of the first section to the stark picture of the suffering messiah featured in the second part of the gospel. This second part of the book (Mark 11:1–16:8) focuses on Jesus's final days in Jerusalem, during which his predictions of his suffering and death are fulfilled.

Rising Popularity of Jesus and Rising Conflict with the Authorities (Mark 1:1–8:21)

Mark 1–4, 8:1–21.

READING

Pay attention to what the Markan Jesus says and does in these chapters. How do the crowds respond to Jesus in the opening chapters? Where do you see signs of conflict between Jesus and the authorities? What are the conflicts about?

EXERCISE

Chapters 1–8 of the gospel tell the story of the rapidly rising popularity of Jesus juxtaposed with the increasing conflict between Jesus and the Jewish authorities. The first words of the Markan Jesus take the form of a proclamation: "The time is fulfilled, and the kingdom of God has come near, repent and believe in the good news" (Mark 1:15). The first chapter of the gospel then depicts Jesus in the full range of activities that will make up his ministry in the rest of the narrative: calling disciples (Mark 1:16–20), teaching (Mark 1:21–2), casting out demons (Mark 1:23–6, 32–4, 39), and healing the sick (Mark 1:29–34, 40–2). Jesus seems to move quickly through these activities, especially because of the frequent use of the Greek word *euthus*, "immediately." This word occurs so often in this chapter, and in the first half of the gospel more generally, that English translations typically find different ways to render the term to avoid repetitiveness (see, for example, 1.10, 12, 18, 20, 21, 23, 28, 29, 30, 42, 43; also 2:8, 12; 3:6; 4:5; 4:15, etc.). The repetition of the word may indicate the author's limited Greek skills. Even so, the frequent references to Jesus acting "immediately" gives an impression of fast-paced activity that corresponds to Jesus's rapidly increasing fame. One reason given for Jesus's appeal is that he speaks with authority or power (Greek *exousia*), in contrast to the scribes (Mark 1:22, 27). By the end of the chapter, the Markan Jesus is so popular that, as the narrator reports, "he was no longer able to go into a town openly ... and people came to him from all directions" (Mark 1:45).

Mark 2 introduces the other dynamic at work in the first section of the gospel: the increasing hostility on the part of the authorities toward Jesus. The story of the paralytic (Mark 2:1–12) begins as a healing story that again highlights the popularity of Jesus. The only way to get near to Jesus is by lowering the paralytic down through the thatched roof of the house that Jesus is in (Mark 2:3–4). But the healing story soon hints at the conflict to come as the "scribes from Jerusalem" appear on the scene. The Jerusalem scribes are portrayed as "questioning in their hearts" and accusing Jesus of blasphemy (Mark 2:6–7). By chapter 3, the two themes of popularity and opposition are closely linked. After Jesus performs another healing, this time on the Sabbath, the Pharisees conspire with the Herodians about how to destroy him (Mark 3:6). Meanwhile, the very next scene shows the Markan Jesus so overwhelmed by crowds from all over Palestine that he must get into a boat on the lake to avoid being crushed (Mark 3:7–8). The juxtaposition of these two themes in the early part of the gospel produces an image of the fervent expectations around this miracle-working healer on the one hand, and the lurking and dangerous threat from his opponents on the other.

Here it is worth pausing over the identity of Jesus's opponents in this gospel. They are typically identified as the chief priests, scribes and Pharisees (for example Mark 2:6; 3:22; 7:1; 8:31; 10:33; 11:27). Past scholarship has often assumed that these figures represented religious authorities on the written and **oral Torah** of Judaism whom Jesus challenged in the interest of a more spiritual and humane interpretation of tradition. In the next chapter, we will return to the question of who the Pharisees actually were compared to the gospel portrayals of this group. Here we focus on the often-unrecognized political dimension behind the depiction of the Markan Jesus's opponents. As discussed in Chapter 9 of this *Introduction*, Roman imperial structures of authority operated primarily through local elite men. Even Rome's military strength was not large enough to keep its vast empire under control. Instead, Roman commanders enlisted the support of local leaders who stood to benefit from cooperating with Rome. This was certainly true of the chief priests. It is also how the Jerusalem scribes would have functioned toward the end of the Second Temple period. The scribes would have either worked in the Temple or been employed in the government administration. In either case, they would have been perceived as working closely with Roman authorities.

While the gospel narrative assumes the importance of the scribes for interpreting scriptural traditions (Mark 9:11; 12:32–3), it also portrays the Markan Jesus warning his followers about them. He describes them as men who love public recognition and prestige but are vicious toward the disadvantaged (Mark 12:38). Note also that these opponents are repeatedly described as coming from Jerusalem, the seat of Roman power for Judea. Given that, it is intriguing that in Mark's gospel, Jesus's ministry begins in Galilee, the place where the Jewish revolt against Rome began. Moreover, it ends with an exhortation for the disciples to return to Galilee to find the risen Jesus (Mark 16:7). In this gospel, then, Jerusalem is the origin of Jesus's opposition and also the place where he is crucified. In contrast, Galilee, the region where the revolt against Rome began, is the point of origin for Jesus and the place where he will appear to his disciples after he has been raised from the dead. A critique of Jerusalem and its leaders will be evident throughout the gospel. Note that this critique pertains to more than religious matters. The gospel also offers a political critique of the way these leaders cooperated with Rome to maintain their local authority.

An Exorcism of Rome?

An allusion to Roman power (and its imagined demise) is found in the story of the demon-possessed man in Gerasene (Mark 5:1–20). In the story, Jesus arrives by boat in "the region of the Gerasenes" and encounters a demon-possessed man living among the tombs. Unlike other exorcism stories in the gospel, in this one Jesus demands to know the name of the demon. The response, "My name is Legion," is the first clue that this exorcism may be more than a healing story (5:9). "Legion" is the term for a Roman cohort of soldiers. Caesar's tenth legion, which took part in the Jewish War and was then stationed in Jerusalem, had an image of a boar on its standards. In the story, the demon named Legion begs to be permitted to enter a herd of pigs, which then runs into the sea and drowns (5:12-13). The story contains other military terms as well. For example, the Greek term for "herd," which refers to the group of pigs, is a term that was used to refer to military recruits. Two verbs used in the story, *epetrepsen* (he permitted) and *hormesen* (they charged), are both typically used in a military context. These are subtle allusions and not every scholar is convinced that the author had Rome in mind. To be sure, the story serves equally well as an example of Jesus's battle with Satan at the ushering in of God's reign on earth. But for the ancient readers, these two interpretations would not be mutually exclusive.

Another theme that emerges quite early in the gospel concerns the identity of Jesus. In several places, the Markan Jesus makes clear that he wants to keep his identity hidden from others. Scholars have labeled this aspect of the Gospel of Mark "the messianic secret." Although the most striking examples of this theme will occur in the transition section (Mark 8:22–10:52), this secrecy motif is already evident in some of the early healing and exorcism stories in Mark 1–7. For example, the Markan Jesus urges those he has healed not to speak to anyone about it (Mark 1:43–4; 5:43; 7:36, see also 8:26). Similarly, Jesus silences the demons "because they knew him" (Mark 1:34; 3:11–12). We will return to this puzzling aspect of the gospel in the next section.

Related to the theme of Jesus's identity is the characterization of the disciples as followers who repeatedly misunderstand Jesus and his teaching. The first indication of the disciples' lack of comprehension appears in Mark 4. There Jesus answers a question about why he teaches in parables:

> To you has been given the mystery of the kingdom of God, but for the ones on the outside, everything comes in parables; in order that "seeing, they may see but not perceive, and hearing, they may indeed hear, but not understand; so that they may never turn and be forgiven." (Mark 4:11–12)

Contemporary readers are often surprised by this passage. They do not expect Jesus to say that he teaches in parables so that outsiders are kept on the outside, with no chance of forgiveness. Given this explanation, it is even more startling when the Markan Jesus asks the disciples: "Do you not understand this parable? Then how will you understand all the parables?" (Mark 4:13). Does this mean the disciples are on the outside?! It may be reassuring that the Markan Jesus goes on to explain the parable to them (Mark 4:14–20). Indeed, the narrator later reinforces the point that Jesus "privately explained everything to his own disciples" (Mark 4:34). Still, they do not seem to benefit from these explanations. Instead, the narrative soon turns again to the disciples' lack of understanding and also the claim that their "hearts were hardened" (Mark 6:52). You may remember seeing this phrase in Exodus where God hardens the Egyptian Pharaoh's heart (Exod 4:21; 7:3, 13; 8:15; 9:12). In a later scene the Markan Jesus associates the disciples' hardened hearts with the same words that he used to describe those on the "outside" in chapter 4:

> And he ordered them, saying, "Look! Watch out for the yeast of the Pharisees and the yeast of Herod." They discussed it together, saying, "We have no bread." And perceiving it, Jesus said to them, "Why are you discussing that you have no bread? Do you not yet perceive or comprehend? Have your hearts been hardened? Having eyes, do you not see? Having ears, do you not hear?" (Mark 8:15–18; cf. 4:12)

This scene ends with a final question from Jesus lingering in the air, unanswered: "Do you still not understand?" (Mark 8:21). By this point in the narrative, the ancient gospel audience themselves may not have understood what the Markan Jesus expected the disciples to "see" and "hear." They may have felt confused about what they were supposed to understand as Christ-followers. But tapping into this sense of confusion may be part of the point. Given the traumatic destruction of the Second Temple and the loss of the war against Rome, Christ-followers may have felt uncertain about the movement they had joined. Perhaps their initial trust in Jesus as God's messiah had included a hope for the restoration of Israel and its release from Roman occupation. Instead of experiencing such a release, the events of 70 CE demonstrated the unyielding power of Rome. The devastating results of the Jewish revolt against Rome likely raised questions for some about whether Jesus was actually the longed-for messiah.

Teaching and More Misunderstanding on the Way (Mark 8:22–10:52)

READING

Mark 8:22–10:52.

EXERCISE

What are some general themes of Jesus's teaching in this section? What does he teach about himself? What does he teach about discipleship? How do the disciples respond?

The central section of the gospel responds to such confusion. From 8:22 to 10:52, the Markan Jesus travels with his disciples from the northern city of Caesarea Philippi southward to Jerusalem (see Map 11.1). At this point, the rapid pace of narrative slows down and the focus shifts to Jesus's instructions to his disciples. To that end, narrative reports several conversations between Jesus and his disciples that occur "on the way." This phrase indicates both their journey together to Jesus's deadly confrontation with the authorities and the way of discipleship that Jesus teaches. The section continues themes that emerged in the first part of the gospel regarding Jesus's identity and mission, and the portrayal of the disciples. In fact, the question of the Markan Jesus's identity and the repeated misunderstandings of the disciples become even more accentuated.

Note first how the author creatively frames this part of the gospel with two healing stories. The first healing story, Mark 8:22–6, is unusual because Jesus must try twice to successfully heal the blind man. After the first attempt, the man reports that he has limited vision: "I see people, but I see them as trees that are walking" (Mark 8:24). Only after Jesus's second try can the man see clearly (Mark 8:25). The story's location in the narrative suggests its symbolic significance. It comes just after Jesus's sharp questioning of the disciples' lack of understanding and just before an extended section of instruction. The disciples are like the blind man – it will take a determined effort on Jesus's part to help them see clearly. Indeed, coming at the beginning of the teaching section, the story suggests that understanding Jesus may be a gradual and initially difficult process not just for the disciples but also for the audience of the gospel. Then at the end of the teaching section, a second healing takes place. This time a blind beggar from the roadside calls to Jesus asking to see again (Mark 10:47–8). Jesus tells him that his faith has healed him, and significantly, the man who can now "see" immediately follows Jesus "on the way." In other words, at the end of the transition section, the narrative provides an example of a new disciple with newly acquired vision.

What are the disciples (and the gospel audience) supposed to understand as a result of the Markan Jesus's instructions? The teaching section communicates two related ideas: the experience of suffering that awaits Jesus in Jerusalem and what it will take to be Jesus's disciple. A distinctive pattern across chapters 8–10 encourages the gospel audience to define their own discipleship in light of the suffering, death, and resurrection of Jesus. Three times the Markan Jesus predicts what is to happen to him when he arrives in Jerusalem (Mark 8:31; 9:31; 10:33–4). Each time these **passion predictions** ("passion" is from the Latin *passus*, "to suffer") are followed by some type of misunderstanding on the part of the disciples. In the first instance, Peter rebukes Jesus (a verb used elsewhere only for Jesus's "rebuking" of the demons). Jesus rebukes Peter in return, exclaiming, "Get behind me, Satan! You are not thinking of the things of God, but of the things of humans" (Mark 8:33). The implication is that Peter is not willing to hear of Jesus's suffering and death, something that Jesus describes as the "things of God." The second passion prediction is followed by a report of an argument among the disciples about who among them is the greatest (Mark 9:33–4). The third prediction is followed by a request from James and John that they be given seats of honor beside Jesus "in his glory" (Mark 10:35–7). In each case, the disciples' response to Jesus's description of his suffering and death involves misguided ideas, concerns of greatness, and glory on the part of the disciples. All three times, the disciples' misunderstanding provides Jesus with an opportunity to instruct them in the ways of discipleship. Each time, in different ways, Jesus informs his companions that to follow him means to put aside greatness in favor of suffering and service. Followers of Jesus are to deny themselves, take up their crosses, be last of all, and slaves of all (Mark 8:34–5; 9:35; 10:42–5).

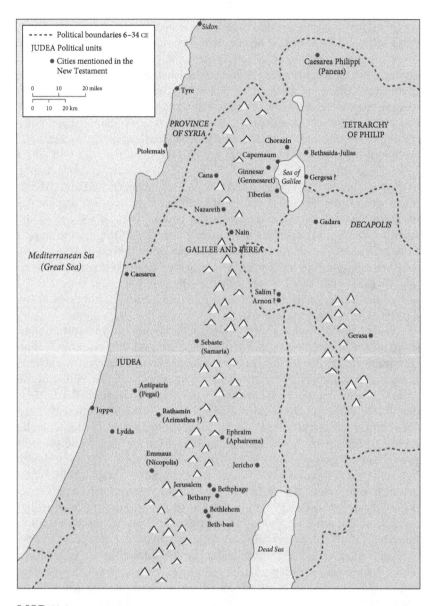

MAP 11.1

Palestine in the first century CE. Redrawn from Bart Ehrman, *The New Testament: A Historical Introduction to the Early Christian Writings* (3rd edition). Oxford: Oxford University Press, 2004, page 73.

Finally, this central section includes two significant passages regarding the secrecy motif in the gospel. The first passage relates a climactic moment in the Markan narrative where Jesus asks his disciples, "Who do you say that I am?" (Mark 8:27). Peter responds to Jesus's question about his identity with the statement, "You are the Christ" (Mark 8:29). (The Greek word *christos* means anointed one, translating the Hebrew word messiah.) This is the first time in the gospel that anyone has attributed this title to the Markan Jesus, and his response is emphatic: they are not to tell anyone about him (Mark 8:30). Jesus's command to secrecy at this point is why scholars have named the secrecy motif the "messianic secret." The second important passage related to the messianic secret occurs in Mark 9. Jesus takes Peter, James, and John with him up a mountain, where they see him transformed, wearing dazzling white clothes and talking with Moses and Elijah. A voice from a cloud pronounces, "This is my son the beloved. Listen to him" (9:7). The words recall God's designation of his "son" as his anointed king in Psalm 2. After this extraordinary experience, the Markan Jesus once again warns the disciples "not to tell anyone about what they had seen until after the Son of Man had risen from the dead" (Mark 9:9). This verse may be the most significant clue to the meaning of the secrecy theme. It suggests that before moving too quickly to a glorified image of Jesus, one must first understand that as God's anointed one, Jesus will suffer and die.

MORE ON THE MESSIANIC SECRET

The **messianic secret** emerged as a scholarly puzzle with the 1901 publication of William Wrede's book of the same title. Wrede noticed a number of elements in Mark's narrative that contributed to a theme of secrecy around Jesus's messianic identity: Jesus's silencing of the "unclean spirit" (1:25), his commands to tell no one about his healings (1:43–44; 3:11–12; 5:43), and his order to the disciples "not to tell anyone about him" (8:30). Although Wrede identified and linked these various aspects of the text, there is much that remains unclear about the secrecy motif. One debate concerns its origins. Most scholars do not think that Jesus himself actually gave commands to others to keep silent about his identity. So where did this theme in the Gospel of Mark come from? Wrede suggested that the tradition developed in early stories about Jesus as a way of explaining why people did not recognize Jesus as the messiah during his lifetime. Perhaps more likely is the idea that the author of the Gospel of Mark added this theme himself. Nevertheless, it is still difficult to explain why the Markan Jesus is so inconsistent in his commands to secrecy and silence (see, for example, Mark 5:19–20). Sometimes the point seems to be that the secret *cannot* be kept despite Jesus's commands to silence (for example, 1:40–5). To date, no single explanation has been offered that accounts for all the elements of the gospel that have been grouped under the idea of the messianic secret.

As mentioned above, the teaching section concludes with a healing story that suggests that Jesus's instructions will contribute to the formation of new disciples with new understanding. In truth, as the story continues, those closest to Jesus do not exhibit such clear vision. There is still betrayal and denial to come. Nevertheless, Mark 8:22–10:52, framed as it is by stories of people gaining their sight, seems designed to help open the eyes of the gospel audience to the idea of a suffering messiah. The conclusion to the gospel then puts the image of such a messiah directly before them.

Jesus the "Son of Man"

Throughout the gospel, the Markan Jesus refers to himself with the phrase "the son of man" (e.g. 2:10, 28; 8:31, 38; 9:12, 31; 10:33, 45; 13:26). The title is particularly intriguing since it appears only in sayings *of* Jesus, never in sayings *about* Jesus. Given this fact, some scholars think that the historical Jesus used the phrase in reference to himself, in contrast to titles that Christ-followers attributed to Jesus after his death. What the "son of man" means remains a point of debate. In some cases, the phrase can simply indicate "human" or "self." For example, "son of man" appears throughout Ezekiel, where it is used by God as a reference to the prophet. Here the NRSV translates the phrase as "mortal one" (see Ezek 2:1ff). Other texts, such as 1 Enoch, use "son of man" to refer to an apocalyptic judge. This also seems to be the meaning in Dan 7:13, which refers to the "son of man" coming with the clouds of heaven ("like a human being" in the NRSV). If the historical Jesus had this apocalyptic idea in mind, it reinforces the idea that he viewed his work though the framework of Jewish apocalypticism.

The Suffering Messiah (Mark 11:1–16:8)

The last section of the gospel is traditionally called the passion narrative because it relates the story of Jesus's suffering. It is the earliest surviving written narrative about Jesus's trial and crucifixion. As mentioned earlier, because these chapters present a sustained narrative as compared to the episodic quality of the first section of the gospel, some have hypothesized that the author used an already written account of the passion as a source. Whether the source was written or oral, the author was relying on traditional interpretations of the last days of Jesus in writing his account. A close reading of the Markan passion narrative shows how thoroughly the story was shaped by texts from the Jewish scriptures, especially passages from the prophets and the psalms. Early believers reread the scriptures in light of their experience of Jesus and then told the story of his death in light of their new scriptural interpretations. We see the fruits of this interpretative process in the passion narrative. We can also see the familiar Markan themes in this final section of the gospel: the conflict with the Jerusalem authorities, the disciples' failure to understand Jesus, and especially the idea of the suffering messiah.

The link between the passion narrative and the Hebrew prophetic tradition is already present in Jesus's "triumphal" entry into Jerusalem on a colt secured by his disciples (Mark 11:1–10). The procession appears to be an enactment of the following text from Zechariah:

> Rejoice greatly, O daughter Zion! Proclaim, O daughter Jerusalem! See, your king comes to you. He is just and one who saves, showing clemency and mounted on a donkey, that is, on a new colt. He will cut off the chariot from Ephraim and the horse from Jerusalem; and the bow shall be destroyed, and he shall command peace to the nations. He will rule from sea to sea, and from the river to the ends of the earth. (Zech 9.9–10)

In Zechariah, the oracle concerns God's defeat of Israel's enemies, followed by a royal procession of the victorious king into the capital city, Jerusalem. In the gospel, the crowd prepares a royal processional way for Jesus, welcoming him as a king. Their words of acclamation come from Ps 118:25–6. "Hosanna! Blessed is the one coming in the name of the Lord! Blessed is the coming kingdom of our father David! Hosanna in the highest!" (Mark 11:9–10). With these words, the gospel shows the crowd symbolically welcoming Jesus into Jerusalem as the anointed king, God's messiah, who will bring peace to the city. Given this, the Markan Jesus's entry into the Jerusalem Temple is anti-climactic. He goes in, looks around, and then leaves because, as the text explains, it was already late (Mark 11:11). Even after the long trip to Jerusalem, Jesus and his disciples do not stay in the city but go back to the village of Bethany to spend the night. Perhaps this is a way that the author distances Jesus from Jerusalem and the Temple – he will not even stay inside the city walls. This idea is confirmed by Jesus's actions in the Temple on the following day.

Mark 11:12–21 is an example of Markan **intercalation** (see "Intercalation or the Markan 'Sandwich'"). In this seemingly odd account, the Markan Jesus curses a fruitless fig tree because he is hungry, even though it is not the season for figs (11:13). He then enters the Temple again, this time causing a massive disturbance, overturning tables and driving out those who are buying and selling animals for Temple sacrifices. By way of explanation, the Markan Jesus cites a passage from Isaiah: "Is it not written, 'My house will be called a house of prayer for all the nations?' But you have made it a cave of bandits" (Mark 11:17; see Isa 56:7). The implication is that the Temple is infested with corrupt practices and Jesus's actions are a protest against this corruption. After the Markan Jesus leaves the Temple, the fig tree is once again the focus, as the disciples notice that it has completely withered to its roots (11:20). On the surface, the combination of fig tree and Temple makes little sense. Why would Jesus curse a tree for not having fruit when it is not the season for fruit? And what does a fig tree have to do with Temple corruption? As with the entry into Jerusalem, the key to understanding this scene is found in the prophetic literature. Earlier in our study, we saw how the eighth-century prophets linked corruption with the downfall of Israel and Judah. Now the same type of prophetic critique is introduced at a time when Jerusalem is suffering through the aftermath of a war with a dominant foreign power. In this case, Hos 9:10–16 appears to be the backdrop for Jesus's actions. In the Hosea passage, Israel is first identified as "the first fruit on the fig tree, in its first season" (Hos 9:10). As the text continues, it describes Israel's corruption and the resulting judgment from God: "Because of the evilness of their deeds, I will throw them out of my house" (Hos 9:15). The oracle in Hosea closes with a description of the stricken Israel: "the root is dried out. It will no longer bear fruit" (Hos 9:16). The Gospel of Mark features the same pattern as the book of Hosea to express judgment against corruption – a fig tree with reference to its season, an expulsion from God's house/Temple, and a reference to a barren fruit tree. By evoking the figure of the corrupted and rejected fig tree/people in Hosea, the gospel writer suggests that Jesus's confrontation with the Temple authorities is in keeping with earlier prophetic expressions of God's judgment.

Intercalation or the Markan "Sandwich"

Historically, biblical scholars have debated whether the author of Mark simply strung a series of stories about Jesus together or gave attention to narrative structure. Those who argue that the author intentionally structured a literary work point to places in the gospel where one story is framed by another story. Scholars have called this literary device **intercalation**, or more descriptively, Mark's "sandwich" structure. The fig tree/Temple episode is one example of Markan intercalation, but there are others. Mark 5:22–43 relates two healing stories – a request for healing for a synagogue leader's daughter frames the account of a lone woman's surreptitious seeking of Jesus's healing power. In this case, the intercalation increases narrative tension because the diversion created by Jesus's encounter with the woman allows enough narrative time to pass for the leader's daughter to die. Other examples of the sandwich structure include Mark 3:21–35; 6:7–30; 14:53–72. Read these and consider how the interwoven stories comment on each other.

Other details of the passion narrative are also influenced by the Jewish scriptures, especially Isaiah and the Psalms. For instance, the Markan Jesus's silence during much of his trial recalls the servant songs of Isaiah (Mark 14:61; 15:4–5; cf. Isa 53:7). Similarly, details drawn from Psalms 69 and 22 are used to fill out the description of Jesus's suffering. Just as Ps 69:4 speaks of false accusations, the writer describes the opponents of Jesus bearing false witness against him (Mark 14:56). The detail of bystanders giving Jesus sour wine (Mark 15:36) echoes the description of the psalmist being given vinegar to drink (Ps 69:21). The reference to soldiers casting lots for Jesus's clothes (Mark 15:24) recalls the psalmist's experience in Psalm 22 (Ps 22:18), and the bystanders' mockery of Jesus (Mark 15:31–2) is like the mockery of the psalmist by others (Ps 22:7–8). Finally, the Markan Jesus quotes Psalm 22 directly at the moment of his death (Mark 15:34), a point to which we will return.

A Glimpse of Life under Roman Occupation

One Markan conflict story is especially revealing in light of the reality of Roman occupation and the difficulties it posed for local residents of Judea. In this case, the Pharisees and Herodians come to trap Jesus with a question concerning the Roman tax. "Is it lawful to pay taxes to the emperor, or is it not?" (Mark 12:14). The tax in question was first imposed on the region when it became a province of Rome in 6 CE. At that time, resistance to the tax was mounted by a certain Judas (not the disciple of Jesus), who called on others to refuse payment of the tax (see Josephus, *Jewish War* 2.8.1 §117–18). Some sixty years later, during the time of the revolt, the issue of paying tribute to Rome was again a pressing question. One point of this conflict story in the gospel is to show the rhetorical cleverness of the Markan Jesus as he bests his opponents. But the story also illustrates life under Roman occupation. The question of paying tribute to Caesar is another iteration of the centuries-long dilemma of Israel's paying tribute to a foreign nation when doing so was understood as paying tribute to a foreign god. The telling of this story around 70 CE would no doubt tap into the deep pain of a conquered people and the pressing question of whether one should resist paying tribute to the emperor.

In addition to linking with scripture in these ways, the story of the Markan Jesus's arrest, trial, and crucifixion is shaped by themes introduced earlier in the gospel. Indeed, the two themes from the first part of the gospel – the growing popularity of Jesus and his increasingly deadly opposition – move toward a climax. We saw earlier how Jesus is enthusiastically welcomed by crowds into the city of Jerusalem. But this kingly procession is followed by a series of conflict stories between Jesus and the Jerusalem authorities and their attempts to "trap him in what he said" (Mark 12:13). The relationship between the two themes is further evident in the dilemma expressed by Jesus's opposition: "The chief priests and the scribes were looking for a way to arrest Jesus by stealth and kill him; for they said, 'Not during the festival, or there may be a riot among the people'" (Mark 14:1–2).

What gives way, in the gospel story, is Jesus's popularity. As the narrative counts down days until the Passover (and Jesus's crucifixion), the adoring crowd that flocked to Jesus in Galilee, as well as the many who laid cloaks on the ground as he entered Jerusalem, fade from view. Instead, the last thing we hear from the crowd is its clamoring for Jesus's crucifixion (Mark 15:11–14).

Even worse, the Markan Jesus's own disciples fail him miserably in his time of need, continuing the theme of the disciples' misunderstanding and failure that emerged in the first half of the narrative. As Jesus approaches his death, he predicts the impending betrayal of one of his disciples (Mark 14:18–21), the abandonment of all of them (Mark 14:27), and the denial of Peter (Mark 14:30). Despite the disciples' protests about these predictions, all of them come to fruition (Mark 14:44–5, 50, 66–72). None of his followers or family is present in his final hour. The women followers are closest, but even they watch from far away (Mark 15:40). Most telling, however, are the Markan Jesus's final words, a quote from Psalm 22: "My God, my God, why have you abandoned me?" (Mark 15:34). There is no answer to the question.

Mark's Enigmatic Ending

Another puzzling aspect of the gospel concerns its closing scene. The Gospel of Mark has no stories of Jesus's appearance after his resurrection from the dead. Instead, Mark 16:1–8 relates the story of the empty tomb. To be sure, this story is intended to convey to the reader that Jesus "has been raised," as the young man in white reports to the women. What is surprising is the women's response to his words. Although they are asked to go and tell the others to meet the risen Jesus in Galilee, the narrator reports that the women say nothing to anyone, for they are terrified (Mark 16:8). At this point, according to the oldest surviving manuscripts, the gospel ends.

Therein lies the problem. Why would a gospel writer end his story with the failure of devoted, yet terrified women? The scribal activity around the gospel's ending suggests that at least some early Christ-followers were troubled by this abrupt ending. There were two different endings added to the gospel by later scribes. One, the "shorter ending," has the women fulfilling the command, then concludes with language unfamiliar to the Gospel of Mark about Jesus's "sacred and imperishable proclamation of eternal salvation." In a longer addition, a scribe added a series of resurrection appearances, some of which are found in other canonical gospels. But these two added endings to the gospel only reinforce the problem of the original ending. Some scholars note that ancient manuscripts often suffered damage and argue that a more complete ending of Mark was lost when some of the original manuscript broke off. Others, however, think that this is precisely how the author intended the gospel to end. These interpreters focus on the potential impact of the ending on the audience. Perhaps the fear of the women matches the audience's own fear in a time of political turmoil. The ending may be a way of empathizing with this emotion. Or, the silent women may act as literary foils for the audience, presenting a negative example of discipleship that the audience can surpass if they boldly spread the gospel to others. The narrative form of the gospel allows for multiple interpretations. The end of the gospel is truly open-ended.

FOCUS TEXT

Mark 12:1–12

We conclude with a close look at the parable of the vineyard in Mark 12:1–12, which conveys several of the themes that we have seen in the gospel. In fact, Mary Ann Tolbert in *Sowing the Gospel* has called this parable a "plot synopsis" for the gospel. The context for the parable is a challenge to the Markan Jesus's authority in which the chief priests, scribes, and elders ask him directly, "By what authority are you doing these things? Who gave you this authority to do them?" (Mark 11:28). Jesus first responds with a question concerning the authority of John the Baptist that the Jerusalem leaders are at a loss to answer (Mark 11:29–33). He then tells the parable.

The parable begins with an allusion to Isa 5:1–7, another parable of judgment. However, as we will see, the focus of God's wrath is different in the

Markan parable. Both texts begin with careful preparation of a vineyard. In Isaiah 5, the vineyard allegorically represents Israel and Judah, which despite God's care, yielded wild grapes instead of cultivated ones. That is, the two kingdoms produced corruption instead of justice, thus incurring God's judgment. The image of Israel and Judah as a vineyard grown/gone wrong is also used by Jeremiah (2:21), Ezekiel (19:10–14), and Hosea (10:1). In Mark 12, however, the problem is not with the vineyard itself. Instead, the critique is directed toward the tenants who are charged with caring for the vineyard. The tenants kill the many slaves who are sent to collect produce from them. In the Markan parable, these "slaves" likely represent the line of prophets who have been sent by God and rejected. The tension of the parable rises as the vineyard owner decides to send his "beloved son," assuming that the tenants would not dare to kill him. The "beloved son" is an obvious reference to Jesus (see Mark 1:11; 9:7). The tenants do not hesitate to kill the beloved son so that they will gain the inheritance. So, too, in the Gospel of Mark, the Jerusalem authorities plan for the death of Jesus. In this way, the parable of the vineyard serves as a prediction of Jesus's death as well as an indictment of the authorities who seek to kill him. Notably, the parable elicits sympathy for the vineyard owner, the one who wields power, rather than for the tenant workers who rebel against his authority. Indeed, in this version of the parable, the audience is intended to approve of the punitive actions of the vineyard owner, who "will come and destroy the tenants and give the vineyard to others" (Mark 12:9 NRSV).

This reappropriation of the Isaiah text and the prophetic image of the vineyard works on multiple levels in the political and religious context of the late 1st century CE, In Isaiah's vineyard story, it is God (through Assyria) who brings destruction upon Israel, the vineyard. In the Markan parable, the vineyard owner/God is coming to destroy not the vineyard itself, but the tenants of the vineyard, who in the larger context of the gospel are understood to be the elite Jewish leadership. What happened historically, of course, is that Rome brought destruction on Jerusalem, decimating its leaders and devastating what was once the center of power in the region. In this way, the gospel alludes to Rome as the agent of God's wrath that carries out God's judgment against the elite men (the chief priests, scribes, and elders) responsible for the death of Jesus. Indeed, the parable suggests that the destruction of Jerusalem and the Temple, and the resulting loss of authority for the priests and scribes associated with the Temple, is God's just punishment for their unjust behavior. The parable goes on to suggest that, as part of this divine intervention, the vineyard will be given to others.

Past interpretations of the parable, influenced by supersessionist interpretations of Christianity, saw these "others" as the gentile church of emerging Christianity. In this misreading of the parable, Judaism was destroyed, and God's people were now the gentile Christian church. However, as we have seen, it is not Israel/the vineyard that is destroyed in Mark's version, but the leaders/tenants. The "others" to whom the vineyard will be given in the parable represent the new, faithful Christ-followers who will replace the corrupt leaders (who were in power, in part, because of collaboration with Rome). One possible reading of the Markan parable, then, is that God is working in mysterious ways, using Rome to destroy the Temple because it was the source of economic exploitation, corrupted by authorities who cooperated with Rome. The parable suggests that the temple's destruction made possible the emergence of a new leadership of a renewed Israel, a community that will be a place of prayer for all the nations (Mark 11:17). Here we should note the mixed portrayal of Rome in the gospel. It is both an oppressive enemy, and in this case, a destructive agent of God. This is another example of the ambivalent attitude that often results between the colonizer and the colonized. Rome is the ever-present dominant power, whether seen as a political oppressor or a deliverer of divine justice against other, more localized opponents.

The parable concludes with a scripture citation, this time by way of direct quotation. The Markan Jesus asks, "Have you not read this scripture: 'The stone that the builders rejected has become the cornerstone; this was the Lord's doing, and it is amazing in our eyes'?" (Mark 12:10–11; see Ps 118:22–3). The link between Jesus and various "stone sayings" appears to be an early and well-established tradition (see Rom 9:32–3; Eph 2.20; Acts 4:11; 1 Pet 2:4–8). The gospel writer draws on the stone tradition here to shift the focus from judgment of Jesus's opponents to vindication of God's "beloved son." Thus the parable tells the whole story of God's work in Jesus Christ: the sending of the son, his rejection and crucifixion, and eventually – with this stone saying – the resurrection by which he will become the cornerstone of the new community of Christ-followers.

Finally, note that in this case, "those outside" have no difficulty understanding that the parable is told against them (Mark 12:12). This parable differs, then, from the earlier explanation about why Jesus teaches in parables. The opponents of Jesus *do* hear and understand this parable. So, too, perhaps the ancient audience is meant to understand that in spite of the present dismal circumstances, God is still working in the world, in the midst of Roman occupation and perhaps even *through* Roman occupation, to restore the people of God.

CHAPTER ELEVEN REVIEW

1. Know the meaning and significance of the following terms:
   - intercalation
   - Jewish War
   - Markan Jesus
   - Markan priority
   - messianic secret
   - passion narrative
   - passion prediction
2. Why do scholars typically date the Gospel of Mark to around 70 CE?
3. What are some possible reasons why the author portrayed the disciples as repeatedly misunderstanding Jesus?
4. How does the presentation of Jesus in the Gospel of Mark fit with the historical circumstances at the time the gospel was written?
5. (Focus Text: Mark 12:1–12) What is the difference between Isaiah's use of the vineyard imagery and the use of the vineyard in the Markan parable? How does our understanding of the parable's meaning change if we read it with an awareness of Rome's destruction of the Second Temple and Jerusalem?

RESOURCES FOR FURTHER STUDY

Beavis, Mary Ann. *Mark*. Grand Rapids, MI: Baker Academic, 2011.

Black, C. Clifton. *Mark*. Nashville, TN: Abingdon Press, 2011.

Carter, Warren. *Mark*. Collegeville, MN: Liturgical Press, 2019.

Collins, Adela Yarbro. *Mark: A Commentary*. Philadelphia, PA: Fortress, 2007.

Leander, Hans. *Discourses of Empire: The Gospel of Mark from a Postcolonial Perspective*. Atlanta, GA: Society of Biblical Literature, 2013.

The Gospel of Matthew: Defining Community in the Wake of Destruction

12

Chapter Overview

The gospel writers all compose their stories of Jesus on the other side of the destruction of the Jerusalem Temple by the Romans. Whereas the Gospel of Mark reflects the suffering, fear, and uncertainty in the immediate aftermath of this event, the Gospel of Matthew addresses the early stages of community rebuilding and redefinition a decade or more later. This was a time when the Jewish people were once more facing questions of survival. A foreign imperial power had again destroyed one of the central symbols of their religious and cultural identity. This is the historical context in which the Gospel of Matthew encourages Christ-followers to maintain their connection to the other central symbol of first-century CE Judaism – the Torah. This chapter will show how the gospel links Jesus to the Torah in multiple ways. It connects Jesus to the figure of Moses, who in Jewish

A Contemporary Introduction to the Bible: Sacred Texts and Imperial Contexts, Second Edition.
Colleen M. Conway and David M. Carr.
© 2021 Colleen M. Conway and David M. Carr. Published 2021 by John Wiley & Sons Ltd.

tradition received the Torah from Yahweh on Mount Sinai. Like Moses, the Matthean Jesus teaches his followers the importance of Torah obedience. The gospel also encourages group solidarity among the assembly of Christ-followers by vilifying perceived opponents such as the Pharisees. We will explore all of these dynamics of the gospel in this chapter. However, before we begin our study of the gospel, it is important first to understand the relationship between the canonical gospels. We began this discussion with the theory of Markan priority in the last chapter. Now we build on that idea by discussing what scholars call the synoptic problem. Understanding this problem and its proposed solution is crucial to interpreting this story of the Matthean Jesus.

EXERCISE

Using either your Bible or a gospel parallels compare the following passages. Here is a useful site to use for comparing the gospels: http://sites.utoronto.ca/religion/synopsis

- Healing of the Paralytic: Mark 2:12; Matt 9:1–8; Luke 5:17–26
- Stilling of the Storm: Mark 4:35–41; Matt 8:23–7; Luke 8:22–5
- A House Divided: 3:23–30; Matt 12:25–37: Luke 11:17–23

Now do a comparison of the birth stories and resurrection accounts in the gospels of Matthew and Luke: Matt 1–2 with Luke 1–2 and Matt 28 with Luke 24. (Remember that the Gospel of Mark does not have a birth story or resurrection accounts.) Write a few paragraphs describing what you observed from these comparisons. For now, our interest is not in the meaning of the gospel stories. Instead, focus on what you notice from closely comparing the content of these passages. What questions do you have as a result of doing this side-by-side reading of the gospels?

The Synoptic Problem

If you did the exercise above, you no doubt noticed that the gospels of Matthew, Mark, and Luke are very similar in many places. In fact, some of the stories or sayings they share have nearly identical wording. It is also the case that the individual stories in these three gospels often follow the same sequence. These gospels are so closely related that one *can* do this type of comparison – one can "see" (optic) them "together" (syn). That is why these three gospels are known as the **synoptic gospels**. The Gospel of John is not so easily compared. Many of the scenes in John are unique among the gospels. For this reason, it is not counted as a synoptic gospel.

As we saw in the last chapter, the Gospel of Mark is widely considered to be the earliest canonical gospel. How, then, do the other canonical gospels relate to this earliest one? Did the other gospel writers know about the Gospel of Mark? If so, did they have a copy of it? Did they build on the Gospel of Mark to write their own gospels? These are the types of questions that define what scholars call the **synoptic problem**. Understanding the consensus solution to this problem is foundational to the academic study of the gospels. Scholars who study the synoptic problem do a close comparison of the gospels similar to the exercise above.

Because the gospels of Matthew and Luke parallel the Gospel of Mark in many places, most scholars think that the authors of Matthew and Luke used this earlier gospel as a source for their own. At the same time, evidence like the differing birth and resurrection accounts in Matthew and Luke suggest that their authors did not know of each other's work. Instead, it appears that each author had a copy of the Gospel of Mark that they incorporated in their own gospel to different extents. The author of Matthew used about ninety percent of Mark, whereas the author of Luke used about half of it. They also edit what they incorporate from the Gospel of Mark differently to suit their own thematic purposes. We will see how this works in our discussion of each of these two gospels.

So far so good. We know of one source for the gospels of Matthew and Luke. But knowing this does not explain all of what we see when doing a close comparison of the gospels. Another fact that emerges is that Matthew and Luke share many sayings of Jesus that are *not* in the Gospel of Mark. The famous teaching of Jesus known as the "beatitudes" or "blessings" is an example of this type of shared material (compare Matt 5:3–12 with Luke 6:20–3). What is striking about this material is that in many cases the authors use identical wording. This would be surprising if they were recording material that they had heard. Instead, scholars posit that the two authors had access to another written source that was a collection of Jesus's sayings. This hypothetical source is commonly referred to as **Q**, an abbreviation of the German word for source, *Quelle*.

Putting these two ideas together, we arrive at what is known as the **two-source hypothesis** (or two-source theory; see Figure 12.1). The theory provides a convincing solution to the synoptic problem: the authors of Matthew and Luke each independently incorporated parts of the Gospel of Mark and parts of the Q sayings source into their narratives. In both cases the authors also revised and expanded their sources to shape their own stories of Jesus. We can easily study how they adapted the Gospel of Mark. It is harder to know how they worked with the hypothetical Q source since we, of course, do not have a copy of the posited source.

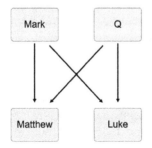

FIGURE 12.1
Two-source hypothesis.

More About the Q Document

The theory that a now lost collection of Jesus's sayings was used as a source for the gospels has been the scholarly consensus for around one hundred years. Evidence that Q was a written rather than oral source comes from the fact that much of the material shared between Matthew and Luke uses almost identical wording, and is often presented in similar order, something unlikely to be the case if the sayings had been transmitted orally. Also, the fact that these sayings shared between Matthew and Luke are identical sayings in *Greek* is significant. Jesus's native tongue would have been Aramaic, making it hard to account for identical Greek renderings of his sayings unless they were written down. In addition, the discovery of the Gospel of Thomas in 1945 lent more evidence to the theory. The Gospel of Thomas, found in Egypt along with a collection of other early Christian writings, is a list of sayings of Jesus. While it is not Q, the existence of such a separate written collection of sayings supports the idea that such collections existed in the early days of the Jesus movement. Some scholars have posited detailed reconstructions of the hypothetical Q document, but others are skeptical that such a project is possible. Finally, a minority of scholars doubt the existence of Q and instead support a theory known as the Farrer hypothesis. This theory posits that the author of Luke used both Mark and Matthew as sources.

One last piece of the solution to the synoptic problem remains. Passages such as the birth narratives and resurrection accounts show us that the gospels of Matthew and Luke also contain stories and sayings of Jesus that are unique to each of these gospels. Scholars have designated this type of material "Special M" and "Special L" passages.

As we will see, knowing about this proposed solution to the question of the relationship between the gospels can be enormously helpful in uncovering the individual interests of each writing. If we give close attention to how the gospel writers edited their sources while also attending to what is emphasized in each of the gospels' special material, we can learn much about their views of the significance of Jesus and what it means to be a Christ-follower.

By now, you may be thinking that the process by which the gospels were produced was far more complex than you imagined. You may have assumed that Matthew, Mark, Luke, and John were disciples of Jesus who simply wrote accounts of what they heard and saw as followers of Jesus. It turns out that each of the gospels was written anonymously. Rather than being eyewitness accounts, the gospels are a blend of oral and written traditions about Jesus with the creative additions of the gospel writers. Two of the gospels used an earlier one as a basis for writing their own account. All four of the gospel writers shaped their stories of Jesus to match their understandings of the meaning and significance of Jesus in their own social and historical contexts.

While these have been basic ideas in gospel studies for more than a century, students encountering them for the first time still often wonder about which gospel is the most historically accurate. Or, after learning that these gospels were *not* written by eyewitnesses, they wonder how we can truly know what Jesus did and said. As we saw in Chapter 9, these are questions about the historical Jesus. Not only are these questions difficult (if not impossible) to answer, they are not central to our task here. Our goal is to understand and appreciate the differing canonical stories of Jesus in their historical contexts. The gospels give us access to the early Christ-followers' convictions about Jesus. Further, they show us what each gospel writer wanted to convey about the figure of Jesus. We have already seen how Mark's gospel presents an image of Jesus as the suffering messiah. Now we turn to the Matthean Jesus and his teaching on Torah obedience.

The Structure of the Gospel of Matthew

The first indication of Matthew's own creative reshaping of Mark's gospel is in the different way he structures his gospel compared to Mark. A comparison with one scene in the Gospel of Mark illustrates the point. The opening chapter of Mark's gospel says that Jesus "went into the synagogue and was teaching" (Mark 1:21). The response from the crowd is astonishment because "he taught them as one having authority and not as the scribes" (Mark 1:22). We hear *how* Jesus teaches but not *what* he teaches. The Gospel of Matthew uses this same saying from Mark, but with a major difference: Matthew's version of the saying comes in Matt 7:28–9, standing as a conclusion to three full chapters telling us what Jesus taught (Matt 5–7). This extensive collection of teachings is the first of five sections of the gospel that contain sayings of Jesus. In between these collections of sayings, called "discourse" sections, one finds the story about Jesus, the narrative sections. The result is a gospel that alternates between teaching by Jesus and stories about Jesus. Each of the discourse sections is marked by a concluding formula such as "when Jesus had finished saying these things" (Matt 7:28; 11:1; 13:53; 19:1; 26:1). This alternating structure (see the chart below) contributes to the image of the Matthean Jesus as a teacher and guide for Christ-followers in the late first century CE.

Basics on the Gospel of Matthew

The following illustrates the five-part alternation of narrative and discourse. The narrative sections are often a loose collection of traditions about Jesus, while the discourse material collects sayings of similar types.

Outline: Matthew's reshaping of the story of Jesus

Location and author

We have no certainty about where Matthew was written. However, there is good evidence for locating its origin in Antioch of Syria. Matthew is cited frequently in the letters of Ignatius, bishop of Antioch in the second century. Another early Christian text that was used in Syria, the Didache, also makes frequent use of the Gospel of Matthew. In Matt 4:24, the author adds a reference to his Markan source, stating that Jesus's fame "spread throughout all of Syria."

Although the gospel was written anonymously, church tradition associated it with Matthew. This is a way of linking the gospel to a disciple of Jesus, but it is unclear why this association would be with Matthew in particular. Perhaps someone with the name of Matthew had prominence in the early communities that read this gospel. In any case, the interest in portraying Jesus in relation to the Jewish Torah and tradition and the ambivalent references to gentiles (e.g., Matt 5:47; 6:7, 32; 10:5) suggest a Jewish author.

The emphasis on Jesus's role as teacher contributes to the sense that the gospel writer is concerned with group formation and identity. To this end, the Gospel of Matthew is the only canonical gospel that uses the Greek word *ekklesia*. As we saw in the prologue to our study of the New Testament, *ekklesia* means "assembly," but English translations typically translate it as "church." The word occurs first in the Matthean version of the scene between Jesus and his disciples at Caesarea Philippi. Here is a place where one can learn from studying how the author of Matthew modified one of his sources, the Gospel of Mark. Comparing Matthew 16:13–30 with the parallel scene in Mark 8:27–30 shows how the author of Matthew expanded Mark's version. Matthew's expanded account features Peter as the "rock" on which Jesus will build his *ekklesia* (Matt 16:17–19). In this way, the author calls attention to Peter as the foundation of a newly formed group of Christ-followers. A second reference to the *ekklesia* is found in 18:15–17. In this case, the Matthean Jesus instructs his followers how to intervene in the case of a "brother" who sins. The instructions offer a policy for handling disputes that could result in exclusion from the group. Such policies are another way of reinforcing group identity and boundaries.

Recall that in Chapter 7, we considered issues of community rebuilding and self-definition during the post-exilic period. Two key events in the lives of the returning exiles were the rebuilding of the Jerusalem Temple and the establishment of the Torah of Moses as central to Judaism. Now, some five hundred years later, with the Jerusalem Temple destroyed, what remained intact was the centrality of the Torah. In the years following the Second Temple's destruction, Jewish leaders would turn with renewed vigor toward focused study of the Torah as a way of defining and sustaining the post-Temple Jewish community. Indeed, the forms of Judaism that have survived to this day trace their origins to the Jewish leadership that gathered the Jewish people around the study of the Torah during this time. This is the context to keep in mind as we explore the focus on Jesus, Moses, Torah, and "righteousness" in this chapter.

The Matthean Jesus and Moses

Review Matthew chapters 1–2. Pay attention to where you see allusions to Moses.

READING

As noted earlier, the story of Jesus's birth told in Matthew 1–2 is found only in this gospel. The narrative opens with a genealogy that reveals the author's interest in linking Jesus to King David and Abraham, two key figures for Judaism in the first century CE (see Matt 1:1). Once this lineage for Jesus is established, the gospel moves to the story of his conception and birth. In Matthew's gospel an angel appears to Joseph in a dream explaining why he should follow through on his impending marriage to Mary despite her surprising pregnancy. In a statement that proves to be programmatic for the gospel narrative, the angel predicts that "She will bear a son, and you are to name him Jesus, for he will save his people from their sins" (Matt 1:21). The Matthean Jesus's teaching in the rest of the gospel suggests that a significant part of this saving activity includes advocating a life of righteousness through Torah obedience. Following this important statement, the narrator uses the first of many **fulfillment citations**. These citations are a literary device used by the author to show how the events of

Jesus's life were predicted in the Israelite prophetic tradition (see also Matt 2:15, 17, 23; 4:14; 5:17; 8:17; 12:17, etc.). The first fulfillment citation is especially significant because it helps to frame the entire gospel with the idea of God's presence through the Matthean Jesus. It reads as follows:

> All this came about in order to fulfill what had been said by the Lord through the prophet: "Look, the virgin shall conceive and bear a son, and they shall name him Emmanuel," which means, "God is with us." (Matt 1:22–3)

At the opening of the gospel, the audience hears the phrase "God with us" as a prophetic fulfillment connected to the birth of Jesus. The closing frame is found in the very last verse of the gospel, where the resurrected Jesus pronounces "And remember, I am with you always, to the end of the age" (Matt 28:20). Such literary devices remind us of the creative activity that went into the gospel composition.

Gender and Matthew's Genealogy (Matt 1:1–17)

As is typical for biblical genealogies, the Matthean genealogy of Jesus traces his patrilineal line. Untypically, in the midst of this line of fathers, four women are mentioned – Tamar, Rahab, Ruth, and the wife of Uriah (that is, Bathsheba). Many have puzzled over why these four women are mentioned. Some interpreters point to their marginal status, noting how each of these figures was understood to be sexually suspect and/or foreigners. The point may be to put Mary in the same line of tradition as these women with whom God worked in unconventional ways. Some feminist readers of the gospel suggest that the women's presence in the genealogy *subverts* the patrilineal tradition. These interpreters note especially the conclusion of the genealogy where

Joseph is not described as "begetting" Jesus, as is customary in the Hebrew tradition. Instead, the genealogy describes Joseph as the husband of Mary, "of whom Jesus was born" (Matt 1:16). The point in this shift may be that according to the Matthean birth narrative Joseph was not literally the father of Jesus. Whatever the reason for including these women, a major point of the genealogy is nevertheless to place Jesus within a line of honorable masculine ancestry that links him both to the founding father of Judaism and to the royal Davidic line precisely through Joseph. So even though it is the Holy Spirit and not Joseph who is responsible for the conception of Jesus (Matt 1:18–20), the genealogy functions to connect Jesus to Joseph's ancestral line.

The Matthean birth narrative goes on to associate Jesus with the Torah in a creative way. The story of Jesus's birth includes several details intended to link Jesus to the figure of Moses. Recall that in the opening chapter of Exodus, Pharaoh ordered the slaughter of all the sons born to Hebrew women (Exod 1:15–16). Similarly, in Matthew's birth story, Herod orders the killing of all the children less than two years of age in order to eliminate the threat that Jesus poses to him (Matt 2:16). Reinforcing the allusion to Exodus, the gospel narrative describes Joseph's fleeing by night to Egypt to save his family from Herod (Matt 2:13–14). There is even a motif of trickery as Herod realizes that the three eastern astrologers (Greek, *magoi*) have failed to report back to him as instructed, much like the Hebrew midwives ignored the instructions of Pharaoh in Exodus (Matt 2:1–16). The Gospel of Matthew thus tells the story of Jesus in ways that recall the story of Moses, who by the first century CE had gained high prominence in the Jewish tradition as prophet and lawgiver.

We can also consider the story from another angle. We can read it from the perspective of life in the Roman empire for the Jewish people, especially after the destruction of the Second Temple. The Herod who is depicted in the birth story is Herod the Great, that is, the same client king of Rome described in Chapter 9 of this *Introduction*. While we have no evidence that Herod ordered a mass murder of young children, the brutality of the act captures the nature of his reign. In fact, Herod did have several of his own children executed during his rule. In any case, the story of the infant Jesus's escape from a murderous ruler associates the Matthean Jesus with Moses and also signals resistance to representatives of Roman imperial power. Note also how closely the Jewish leaders are linked with Herod at this point in this story. Frightened by news of the birth of "the king of the Jews," the client king assembles the chief priest and scribes to ask about expectations regarding the birthplace of the messiah, which the Jewish leaders readily supply (Matt 2:3–6). With this detail, the gospel depicts the local Jewish elite cooperating with Roman authority.

The Matthean Jesus, Righteousness, and Torah Obedience

Review Matthew chapters 5–7. Compare Matthew's version of Jesus's blessings with Luke's version (Matt 5:3–12 compare to Luke 6:20–6)

READING

In Matthew 5–7, the Matthean Jesus delivers what is known as the **Sermon on the Mount**. Much of this material comes from the Q source as a comparison with Luke 6:20-25 demonstrates. Chapters 5–7 also make up the first of the five discourse sections in Matthew. More like a series of teachings than a sermon, the section conveys themes that are important to the gospel writer. First, the Matthean Jesus ascends a mountain to offer his instructions (compare the Lukan Jesus's location on a "level place," Lk 6:17). Since much of this discourse concerns interpretation of the law, the author likely is again recalling the figure of Moses, who went up Mount Sinai to receive the commandments from God (Exod 19:20). Another important difference in the Matthean blessing compared to Luke's version occurs at 5:6, where Jesus says: "Blessed are those who hunger and thirst for righteousness, for they will be filled" (see Luke 6:21). The Matthean Jesus also blesses those who "are persecuted because of righteousness" (Matt 5:10). Most strikingly, he informs his audience, "... unless your righteousness exceeds that of the scribes and Pharisees, you will never enter the kingdom of heaven" (5:20 NRSV).

This is not the first time that the idea of "righteousness" occurs in the gospel. The Greek word behind the idea, *dikaios*, has a range of meanings that include being just, fair, or doing what God requires. Some form of the word shows up over twenty-five times in the Matthean narrative. Joseph, for example, is described as a "righteous man" who wants to avoid publicly humiliating Mary (Matt 1:19). The idea of righteousness is present also at the inauguration of Jesus's ministry. When John the Baptist resists the idea of baptizing Jesus, Jesus responds, "Let it be for now; for it is fitting for us to fulfill all righteousness" (Matt 3:15). Later in the narrative, the Matthean Jesus urges his listeners not to worry about food or clothing but to "seek first for the kingdom of God and its righteousness" (Matt 6:33).

Such repetition shows that the idea is important to the author, but how does one know if one is being "righteous"? What does it mean to do the will of God, according to this author? For a Jewish person living in the first century CE, the answer would be clear – being righteous required obedience to God's law. Obeying God's law would be the same thing as doing the will of God. This is what the author suggests in several places in the gospel. In another important statement from this same discourse, the Matthean Jesus asserts:

> Do not assume that I have come to destroy the law or the prophets; I have come not to destroy but to fulfill. For truly I tell you, until heaven and earth pass away, not one letter, not one stroke of a letter, will pass away from the law until all things take place. (Matt 5:17–18)

Also revealing is the saying that comes toward the end of the first teaching section:

> Not all who say to me, "Lord, Lord," will enter the kingdom of heaven, but the one who does the will of my Father in heaven. Many will say to me on that day, "Lord, Lord, did we not prophesy in your name, and cast out demons in your name, and do many deeds of power in your name?" Then I will declare to them, I never recognized you, depart from me, workers of lawlessness. (7:21–3 modified from NRSV)

In the first saying, the fulfillment of the entire law (not its destruction) is linked to eschatological events. In the second saying, the Matthean Jesus contrasts doers of the will of God with those who are doers of *anomia* – a Greek word that literally means "no-law." For this author, doing powerful acts in the name of Jesus is not enough if one is not also practicing obedience to Torah. One can see this idea expressed more positively in the following example. Note the subtle changes that the author of Matthew makes to his source, the Gospel of Mark:

Gospel of Mark (10:17–19)	Gospel of Matthew (19:16–18)
And as he was setting out on his journey, a man ran up and knelt before him, and asked him, "<u>Good Teacher, what must I do</u> to inherit eternal life?" And Jesus said to him, "<u>Why do you call me good? No one is good but God alone.</u> <u>You know the commandments.</u>	And behold, one came up to him, saying, "<u>Teacher, what good thing must I do</u> to have eternal life?" And he said to him, "<u>Why do you ask me about 'the good'?</u> One only is good. <u>If you want to enter life, keep the commandments.</u>"

Here the author purposely rewords the story from Mark so that use of the word "good" becomes a question of *doing* good. In response, the Matthean Jesus clearly states that entering "life" requires keeping the commandments. Contemporary readers might understand this statement to refer to the well-known "Ten Commandments," especially since Jesus goes on to list a few of them in this passage. However, in the context of first-century CE Judaism, the author would have in mind the whole of the Torah. We know this from the earlier claim that not the smallest bit of the law would pass away before "all things take place." This idea is reinforced further when the Matthean Jesus warns, "whoever loosens one of the least of these commandments, and teaches others to do the same, will be called least in the kingdom of heaven; but whoever does them and teaches them will be called great in the kingdom of heaven" (5:19 modified from NRSV).

Taken together, these passages suggest that the gospel writer defines being "righteous" as being Torah obedient and insists that such obedience is required for entry into God's kingdom. To be sure, this is not the only requirement. According to the narrative, one must be a follower who trusts, or has faith, in Jesus. And, one must be baptized, as the Matthean Jesus declares at the end of the narrative (28:19). But also included in the final words of the Matthean Jesus to his disciples are instructions for them to teach those baptized "to obey everything that I have commanded you" (28:19–20). One who has read the gospel knows what the Matthean Jesus has commanded. Overall, in the Sermon on the Mount, he teaches about the law with a goal of being "perfect" or "complete" in keeping it (5:48). Much of the instruction in Matt 5 is an example of what later rabbis would refer to as "forming a hedge around the law." The idea is that additional requirements are put in place to make certain one does not violate the Torah commandments. Here is the first of a series of this form of teaching:

> You have heard that it was said to those of ancient times, "You shall not murder"; and "whoever murders shall be liable to judgment." But I say to you that if you are angry with a brother or sister, you will be liable to judgment; and if you insult a brother or sister, you will be liable to the council; and if you say, "You fool," you will be liable to the hell of fire. (Matt 5:21–2, NRSV)

Note the underlying logic of this teaching. One who does not even get angry or insult a "brother" is certainly not going to kill him. In this way, one can be sure to keep the Torah commandment. This same pattern of instruction continues in Matthew 5:27, 31, 33, 38, 43. In each case, the Matthean Jesus extends the commandment, thereby offering a way for the righteousness of his followers to "exceed that of the scribes and Pharisees" as he says it should (Matt 5:20). We will discuss the Pharisees later in this chapter. For now, we turn to still another way this gospel writer associates Jesus with the Torah.

The Matthean Jesus, Wisdom, and Torah

Before the Gospel of Matthew was written, early traditions about Jesus associated him with the figure of personified Wisdom found in Jewish Wisdom literature. For example, a Q saying features Jesus defending himself against his opponents by asserting, "Wisdom is justified by her deeds" (Matt 11:19; Luke 7:35). In the Gospel of Matthew, this association of Jesus with personified Wisdom is further developed. Compare these sayings spoken by Wisdom in the second-century BCE book of Sirach (on Sirach, see Chapter 8) and by the Matthean Jesus:

Come to me, those who desire me, and be filled from my harvest. (Sirach 24:19)	Come to me, all those who are weary and burdened, and I will give you rest. Take my yoke upon you, and learn from me; for I am lenient and humble in heart, and you will find rest for your souls. For my yoke is easy to bear, and my burden is light. (Matt 11:28–30)
Put your neck under the yoke, and let your soul welcome instruction; it is close by to find. (Sirach 51:26)	

Reading these passages together, it is clear that the Matthean Jesus is speaking Wisdom's words. While we do not find an exact quotation from Sirach, the sayings are very similar. So much so that an audience familiar with the Wisdom tradition would certainly associate Jesus with God's Wisdom. Even more significant to our discussion is another statement about Wisdom found in Sirach. Following a speech by personified Wisdom, the author claims "all these things are the book of the covenant of the most High God, which is the law that Moses commanded us" (Sirach 24:23). In other words, according to the author of Sirach, God's Wisdom and God's Torah are the same thing! This idea continued into the first century CE, so that when the Matthean Jesus speaks in the words of personified Wisdom, he speaks also as personified Torah.

Thus the Gospel of Matthew links Jesus with the Torah in multiple ways – teaching about Torah, advocating obedience to Torah, and in a sense embodying Wisdom/Torah. The Matthean Jesus expresses this last association most clearly in Matt 18:20, when he claims, "... where two or three are gathered in my name, I am there among them." A very similar tradition is found in the Jewish Mishnah, a collection of early rabbinic teachings. There the rabbis claim that when the words of Torah pass between two who are studying, "the Presence is with them" (*Abot* 3.2). In Jewish tradition, "the Presence" (Hebrew *shekinah*) is God's presence. Thus, like this rabbinic teaching about Torah study, the Matthean Jesus teaches his followers that gathering "in his name" will be a means to experience his divine presence. Given all that we have already seen, this does not mean Jesus *replaces* Torah for this author. It is more the case that he understands that being a follower of Jesus offers a way of being Torah obedient, that is, "doing the will of the Father" (Matt 7:21).

Matthew's Apocalyptic Vision and the Kingdom of Heaven

Read Matthew 13, 18, 22, 25. Focus on the different ways that Jesus describes the kingdom of heaven and who can gain entry to it.

Another distinctive element of the Gospel of Matthew relates to Jesus's instructions about the coming kingdom of God, most often referred to as the "kingdom of heaven" in this gospel. All the synoptic gospels contain at least some kingdom parables, where Jesus uses a short saying or story to describe an aspect about the impending reign of God. Unique to Matthew, however, is a recurring theme of judgment connected to the kingdom, described in different ways as a sorting out of the "righteous" from the "lawless" ones. For example, two parables that occur only in Matthew refer to separating weeds from wheat at harvest time (Matt 13:37–40) and sorting good fish from bad out of a full fishing net (Matt 13:47–8). As we saw with the apostle Paul, judgment language is a standard element of Jewish apocalypticism. While Paul warned his gentile audience of the "wrath" that was coming (1 Thess 1:10; Rom 1:18), the author of Matthew conveys the idea of God's judgment even more graphically. The Matthean Jesus speaks of burning in fiery furnaces along with weeping and gnashing of teeth for the "lawless" ones (13:41–3; 49–50). Meanwhile, in sharp contrast, he declares that "the righteous will shine forth like the sun in the kingdom of their Father" (Matt 13:41–3). This reference to "shining" recalls the apocalyptic imagery in the book of Daniel. There the author uses similar language to promise that the "wise" and "those who lead others to righteousness" will shine like stars forever (Dan 12: 3).

The harsh language of punishment is not reserved only for those outside of the Jesus movement. Chapter 18 features a disturbing parable that tells of an angry master handing over his slave to be tortured because he had not shown mercy to a fellow slave. Matthew's Jesus concludes by threatening, "So will my heavenly father do to you, if you each do not forgive your brother from your hearts" (Matt 18:35). While the Matthean Jesus assures the gospel audience that the merciful will receive mercy (Matt 5:7), he also makes clear that the unforgiving will be harshly punished.

We should take special notice of this depiction of God in a New Testament writing because it complicates a popular Christian tendency to distinguish the "wrathful" God of the Old Testament from the "loving" God of the New Testament. Such a distinction does not match the diverse ways that the deity is portrayed across both parts of the Christian canon. On the one hand, in this Matthean parable and in some other places in the New Testament, we find depictions of a harsh and punishing God. On the other hand, we have seen places in the Hebrew Bible such as Exodus 34, where God describes Godself as merciful, gracious, slow to anger, loving, faithful, and forgiving. These divine traits are also regularly cited in the Psalms (for example, Psalms 86, 103, 145). The point is that all of the biblical depictions of God were shaped by biblical authors for different purposes in a time and place long distant from us. The task of critical biblical scholars is to consider the function that varying depictions of the deity may have served in the social and historical contexts in which they were formed.

For instance, the theme of divine judgment is common to both prophetic and apocalyptic genres. And historically both types of writing often took shape during times of collective trauma. That the author of Matthew draws heavily on both prophetic and apocalyptic texts may be the result of the collective

FIGURE 12.2
Roman coin indicating the ruling power of Augustus, as
he subdues the earth under his foot.

trauma still reverberating through Jewish communities in the decade after the
destruction of the Jerusalem Temple. The Jewish experience of Roman domination in the first century CE shared much with earlier times of trauma for
Israel and Judah. While we may find the language of burning hellfire, gnashing
of teeth, and eternal punishment problematic, it may have had a positive function for people who knew the ability of Rome to punish with fire and destruction. Biblical apocalypticism anticipates a day of reckoning that will bring
God's justice to bear on unjust regimes. So, too, in the Gospel of Matthew, an
apocalyptic vision of a coming kingdom of God would instill hope. Those suffering under Roman-appointed authorities could imagine that God would
intervene on their behalf.

Finally, we should consider the theme of the kingdom of God in the gospel
in light of Roman claims about imperial rule. The Latin word *imperium* conveys the notion of absolute power. From Rome's perspective, the emperor had
all authority over the whole earth. We see this idea in the words of a famous
Roman poet named Ovid:

> Jupiter controls the heights of heaven and the kingdom of the triformed universe;
> But the earth is under Augustus's sway. Each is both sire and ruler. (*Metamorphoses*
> 15:858–60)

Images of the emperor on Roman coins also included exaggerated claims
of earthly authority (Figure 12.2). Given these assertions of Roman power, two
scenes toward the end of the Gospel of Matthew are notable for their implicit

challenges to Roman claims of *imperium*. The first case involves details added to the crucifixion scene from the Gospel of Mark. Only the Gospel of Matthew describes the temple curtain being torn in two, the earth shaking, tombs opening, and bodies being resurrected (Matt 27:51–3). The gospel writer uses these signs to mark Jesus's death as literally an earthshaking and life-giving event. These signs indicate divine intervention and suggest that the demonstration of Roman power in putting Jesus to death is far superseded by the cosmic power of God that brings the dead to life. In the second scene, this divine power is extended to the resurrected Jesus when he appears to his disciples and proclaims: "All authority in heaven and on earth has been given to me" (Matt 28:18). Again, in the Roman imperial context, such a claim places Jesus far above the Roman emperor and puts him on a par with the gods. In these ways, the gospel ends with indications of a subversive resistance to claims of Roman imperial power.

The Matthean Polemic Against the Pharisees

Matthew 23, 26–8.

READING

Far more blatant than the places where the gospel writer may be subtly resisting Roman claims to power are the many outright critiques of Jewish authorities. They are designated as the Pharisees, Sadducees, chief priests, and scribes. The gospel regularly depicts the chief priests and Pharisees attempting to entrap Jesus (Matt 22:15–46) and plotting to put him to death (Matt 21:46; 26:3–5, 14–15; 27:1). Meanwhile, the Matthean Jesus engages in rhetorical attacks against the Jewish leaders. The most extensive of these occurs in chapter 23, where the author draws on Q material to include a series of "woes" against the scribes and the Pharisees. This chapter presents a caricatured image of the "hypocritical" scribes and Pharisees. The Matthean Jesus builds a picture of his opponents as men who concern themselves with outward appearances (Matt 23:27–8) and legal regulations (Matt 23:23, 25), but are actually greedy and self-indulgent (Matt 23:25). The Pharisees are accused of caring nothing about justice, mercy, or faith (Matt 23:23). Far from affirming that the kingdom of heaven is accessible to the poor in spirit (Matt 5:3), these leaders – according to Matthew – "shut the kingdom of heaven in front of people and do not permit them to go in" (Matt 23:13). The series of woes ends in judgment and condemnation, not just for the scribes and Pharisees but for "all of this generation" (Matt 23:36).

Who Were the Pharisees?

The earliest references to the Pharisees suggest that they began as a political party during the Maccabean period (167–63 BCE). They aligned themselves with certain Jewish leaders, and opposed others. During Herod's reign they counseled the people to accept him as their leader, according to the Jewish historian Josephus. He portrays them as having "the complete confidence of the masses" over against the Sadducees, who were supported by "the people of highest standing," or the aristocracy (Josephus, *Antiquities*, 13.13.5 §401). The political influence of the Pharisees is last attested in the early stages of the Jewish revolt against Rome of 66–70 CE, when the they joined the "principal citizens" in opposing the Jewish revolutions, speaking out against starting a war against Rome that they could not win.

Our sources are limited in describing the beliefs and practices of the Pharisees except for the following: in contrast to the Sadducees, the Pharisees followed the "traditions of the ancestors," an oral tradition that rabbinic tradition claims was given to Moses at Sinai, along with the written law. They believed in a resurrection from the dead (again in contrast to the Sadducees). Perhaps most significantly, they thought that the same purity regulations that were practiced by the priests should be extended to the common people, presumably so that the people could stand in the same relationship to God as did the priests. This may also be why they were called "Pharisees," a word that means "one who is separated." They encouraged ritual practices that would distinguish or "separate" the Jewish people from sources of ritual impurity such as gentiles. Again, as noted above, the Pharisees were apparently very popular. As part of his description of the group, Josephus claims "they are able greatly to persuade the body of the people; and whatever [the people] do in terms of divine worship, prayers, and sacrifices, they perform them according to [the Pharisees'] direction;" (*Antiquities* 18.1.3) Josephus writes his history well after the destruction of the Temple, and by then the Pharisees had secured their place as the dominant group among the Jews. Precisely such popularity would elicit strong polemical rhetoric from a competing group.

Most problematically, the gospel lays the blame for Jesus's crucifixion on the Jewish people themselves, rather than on the Romans. Only in this gospel does the Roman governor, Pilate, absolve himself of Jesus's death. He washes his hands before the crowd, stating, "I am innocent of this man's blood; see to it yourselves." To this all the people respond, "His blood be on us and our children!" (Matt 27:25). Because the gospel was written after the destruction of the temple, a statement like this encourages the audience to interpret the traumatic events of 70 CE as divine punishment. That is, it suggests that the next generation of those who put Jesus to death was punished with Roman violence. Recall that Mark's gospel features a similar theme, but it implies that God's judgment was restricted to the Jewish leaders, the "tenants" of the vineyard. In contrast, Matthew's gospel seems to blame *all* of the Jewish people for the death of Jesus and the destruction of Jerusalem.

From a twenty-first-century perspective we might wonder how a gospel so concerned to associate Jesus with the Torah of Moses and the lineage of Abraham and David could so harshly condemn the Jewish people and their leaders. But our own experiences may help us understand the sort of polemic we find in the Gospel of Matthew. Members of different political parties of one nation often use judgmental rhetoric against one another. Christian groups who hold different positions on social issues may direct inflammatory language toward one another. Especially when opposing groups share a common identity, say Americans or Christians, they often define themselves ever more sharply against those whose positions they oppose. In the ancient world as in the contemporary one, group cohesion is often formed and reinforced through polemical rhetoric against other groups. The Gospel of Matthew reflects a historical situation in which a group of Jewish Christ-followers was defining itself differently than other Jewish groups in the period after the Temple's destruction. Written by a Jewish Christ-follower, the gospel depicts Jesus attacking the Pharisees as hypocritical, not because they necessarily *were* hypocritical but because they held different views about how to be faithful Torah-observant Jews. These in-group tensions existed to some degree before the conflict with Rome. They likely increased in the aftermath of the catastrophic end to the Jewish revolt.

On this point, postcolonial criticism brings useful insight to understanding the gospel. It highlights the ways that colonization and imperial power create internal tensions within, and rivalries between, indigenous groups. Unable to confront the actual source of their oppression, these groups often turn against one another to express their frustrations. In the Gospel of Matthew, we find only implicit and infrequent critique of an all-encompassing Roman authority, but frequent and explicit attacks against local Jewish authorities. We will never know how the Jesus movement might have developed in relation to other expressions of Judaism apart from the events of 70 CE and without the pressures of living under Roman domination. Indeed, such pressures may well have contributed to the growing popularity of the movement. What we know for certain is that after the destruction of the Temple, surviving Jewish communities – both the followers of Jesus and those aligned with emerging rabbinic Judaism – contended between themselves over issues of identity and belief.

Matt 25:31–46

FOCUS TEXT

The focus text for this chapter is a parable that occurs only in the Gospel of Matthew. The parable illustrates God's judgment of human conduct based on doing acts of charity. This is a familiar theme in the Hebrew scriptures. Proverbs 14:31 and 19:17 assert that caring for the poor honors God and will be rewarded. Deuteronomy 15:7–10 instructs the Israelites to give willingly to the needy, with the assurance that God will bless their efforts. The call to feed and clothe the needy and give hospitality to the traveler also occurs in the prophets

(Ezek 18:7, 16; Isa 58:7) and in Job (31:32). In short, the Matthean parable draws on a well-known scriptural theme of caring for those in need.

The placement of the passage indicates the importance of this theme for the author. The parable concludes the final section of Jesus's teaching before the passion narrative begins in chapter 26. The passage opens with familiar apocalyptic imagery – the Son of Man coming in glory with his angels (see also Mark 8:38). In Matthew's gospel this image is used to introduce a vivid scene of divine judgment. Here the Son of Man sits on his throne as "the nations" or "the gentiles" (Greek *ethne*) come before him (Matt 25:31–2). This image of the Son of Man executing judgment from a heavenly throne is unique to Matthew's gospel. In Mark 14:62, the Son of Man is seated at the "right hand of the ruling power." But in Matthew's text the Son of Man *himself* executes judgment from his own throne. More than an apocalyptic figure ushering in the reign of God, he assumes the role of ruling authority and heavenly judge. The author may have been familiar with such a figure from Dan 7:13, which describes a "Son of Man" who is given "dominion and glory and kingship." Perhaps for this reason, the image of the Son of Man shifts from that of a shepherd separating sheep and goats (Matt 25:32–3) to that of "king" (Matt 25:34). This image of the resurrected Jesus as king links with the earlier association between Jesus and kingship in the gospel (Matt 13:41; 20:21). The image of Jesus as king also anticipates the conclusion to the gospel, where, as we have seen, the resurrected Jesus announces that he has been given "all authority on heaven and on earth" (Matt 28:18).

As the parable continues, the king invites those on his right to "inherit the kingdom" on the basis of their acts of mercy – providing food, drink, and clothing to those in need, caring for the sick, providing hospitality to strangers, and visiting the imprisoned (Matt 25:35–40). Such actions recall the gospel's earlier emphasis on righteousness and mercy (Matt 5:7). Meanwhile, the unmerciful are condemned to eternal punishment (Matt 18:8). Given what we have already seen in the Gospel, we should not be surprised to find that those who showed mercy are referred to as "the righteous" (Matt 25:37). Significantly, the righteous are not even aware of when they cared for the king. The passage suggests that it is not enough to be motivated to serve someone of higher rank (perhaps hoping to gain from doing so). Instead, the reward comes to those who extend care apart from concerns of rank or status, attending "to one of the least significant of these brothers of mine" (Matt 25:40). If the righteous are rewarded for their care of these members, we can anticipate the plight of the "goats." They also are unaware of their lack of care for the "Lord," but then, they had not cared for even one of the least significant (Matt 25:41–6).

While all of this might seem straightforward, there are ambiguities in the parable that have lent themselves to shifting interpretations. First, since the Greek word *ethne* can be translated as either "the nations" or "the gentiles," readers have offered different interpretations regarding who is included in the judgment scene. Similarly, the identity of "these least significant brothers" is vague. Does the passage refer to the needy in general? Or are the "needy" only those who are Christ-followers? Christian interpreters in the third century CE tended to interpret the parable as referring *only* to the

Christian community. They understood both the "least of these" and the "nations" who provided for them to be Christians. These ancient interpreters thought the parable was meant to motivate Christians to do acts of mercy for other needy Christians.

By the eighteenth century, different cultural conditions elicited a different reading of the passage. At this time, Christian groups were becoming more involved in foreign missionary work as part of the Western colonization of Africa and India. In this context, "the nations" were interpreted as a reference to all non-Christians while the "least of these" was interpreted as Christians. Defining the groups in this way meant that all non-Christians would be judged based on their treatment of Christians. Such a reading could have offered comfort to missionaries who felt oppressed and persecuted, suggesting that those who mistreated them would ultimately be punished.

At the same time, movement into these so-called "foreign" lands led to a growing recognition of the existence of a very large number of non-Christians who remained non-Christian. An interpretation of the parable that allowed non-Christians to receive rewards based on their charity toward Christians made room for the salvation of non-Christians. To be sure, many people today, including Christians, would be troubled by the idea that the parable referred only to a final judgment of non-Christians, especially when that judgment was based only on the charitable treatment of Christians! But in the world of eighteenth-century missionaries, this interpretation of the parable introduced the possibility of heavenly salvation apart from conversion to Christianity.

Beginning in the early church and continuing through the twentieth century, one can also find a more disturbing and persistent interpretation of the passage, in which the "goats" are assumed to be the Jews that did not accept Christ. Such a reading is problematic on several counts. First, there is nothing in the passage to identify the goats as the Jewish people. Second, this interpretation ignores the Jewish orientation of the gospel. Third, this reading ignores the basic intent of the passage. The parable says nothing about doctrinal belief or confessions of faith as conditions for judgment but focuses only on acts of mercy, which as we have seen was a thoroughly Jewish idea.

Along this line, the twentieth century brought yet another interpretation of the tradition, far more universal than most earlier readings. In this case, "the nations" are understood as *all* peoples coming under judgment, and "the least of these" as *anyone* that is in need, regardless of their religious convictions. This reading has been important for those who lift up God's concern for the poor as a central theological conviction. The interpretation emphasizes the undogmatic aspects of the passage and promotes the idea of a "practical" Christianity that is grounded in acts of love toward other human beings. It links with an earlier saying of the Matthean Jesus: "Not all who say to me 'Lord, Lord' will enter the kingdom of heaven, but the one who does the will of my father in heaven" (Matt 7:21 modified from NRSV).

Given these diverse interpretations, what can we say about the author's original intent? If we look to the broader themes of the gospel, we may find some clues. This is a gospel with a strong missionary emphasis – the Matthean Jesus sends out his disciples "like sheep in the midst of wolves" (Matt 10:16). They are to expect persecution and betrayal (Matt 10:21–3), and those who welcome the disciples and provide hospitality will be rewarded (Matt 10:40). The Matthean Jesus's last instructions to the disciples reinforce this missionary emphasis as they are told to go and "make disciples of all nations" (*ethne*). Note that this is the same word used to refer to the group that is called before the throne in Matt 25:32. Moreover, the reference in this passage to treatment of "the least of these *brothers* of mine" suggests a reference to those within the Jesus movement, rather than needy persons in general. Perhaps the gospel writer is acknowledging that the traveling missionaries of the Jesus movement do not rank very highly in the broader Roman culture and may not be well received as they travel from town to town. In this sense, the passage would serve to encourage hospitality to these traveling missionaries among other believers.

These multiple readings of Matt 25:31–46 remind us that the textual nature of Jesus and his teachings in the New Testament are open to shifting interpretations. Because readers bring their own experiences to the text, they regularly interpret the teachings of Jesus in ways that fit their own setting. This is not necessarily a problem. It is the way humans make meaning out of their engagement with stories. Nevertheless, the ongoing practice of reinterpretation does not mean that any interpretation is acceptable. We now have the benefit of looking back and assessing how this Matthean parable was used in different settings and we can identify interpretations that are problematic and harmful. For example, we should reject anti-Semitic interpretations of the passage that assert that Jesus condemned all Jewish people. We can reject readings that elevate the treatment of needy Christians alone as the criterion for heavenly reward. Indeed, in our current cultural context, even if we understand the original missionary focus of the text, we may now choose to emphasize a more universal interpretation, one that recognizes the value of all people and the necessity of caring for anyone in need regardless of their religious affiliation.

CHAPTER TWELVE REVIEW

1 Know the meaning and significance of the following terms:
   - two-source hypothesis
   - fulfillment citations
   - Sermon on the Mount
2 What sources did the author of Matthew's gospel use for writing his story of Jesus?
3 How does the structure of the Gospel of Matthew differ from the structure of the Gospel of Mark?
4 What effect does this different structure in the Gospel of Matthew have on the presentation of Jesus?

5 How and why does the Gospel of Matthew relate Jesus to the Torah?
6 How does the theme of God's judgment relate to the gospel's historical and cultural setting?
7 (Focus text: Matt 25:31–46) Discuss how the different interpretations of the parable relate to their cultural settings. How might you read the parable in ways that link directly to your own setting? Do you find the Matthean theme of divine judgment problematic or useful? Explain.

RESOURCES FOR FURTHER STUDY

Aland, Kurt. *Synopsis of the Four Gospels.* United Bible Societies, 1985.

Allison, Jr., Dale C., ed. *Matthew: A Shorter Commentary.* London and New York: T&T Clark International, 2004.

Blanton IV, Thomas R. "Saved by Obedience: Matthew 1:21 in Light of Jesus' Teaching on the Torah," *Journal of Biblical Literature*, Vol. 132:2 (2013), pp. 393–413.

Boxall, Ian. *Discovering Matthew: Content, Interpretation, Reception.* Grand Rapids, MI: Eerdmans, 2015.

Kampen, John. *Matthew within Sectarian Judaism.* New Haven, CT: Yale University Press, 2019.

Powell, Mark Alan. *Methods for Matthew.* Cambridge and New York: Cambridge University Press, 2009.

Pregeant, Russell. *Matthew.* St. Louis, MO: Chalice Press, 2004.

Luke–Acts: Legitimizing the Jesus Movement in the Midst of Empire

13

Chapter Outline

Chapter Overview

If your name was Theophilus and you lived toward the end of the first century CE, you might be the esteemed patron of a major, two-volume account of the life of Jesus and the growth of the Jesus movement. Both the Gospel of Luke and the Acts of the Apostles begin with prologues in which the author writes directly to a certain "most excellent" Theophilus (see Luke 1:1–4; Acts 1:1–5). Because of this, and because of the many thematic links between these two works, we can see that the same author wrote both the Gospel of Luke and Acts. In this chapter we will focus on the links between the two volumes (typically referred to as Luke–Acts) and the story that they tell about Jesus and his earliest followers. Even though in the New Testament the two books are now separated by the Gospel of John, reading them together as a two-volume work shows how the author wove common themes through his story of Jesus and the spread of the "Way" (the author's name for the Jesus movement). Part of this story involves linking Jesus and his followers to the history of Israel. Connecting the Jesus movement

A Contemporary Introduction to the Bible: Sacred Texts and Imperial Contexts, Second Edition. Colleen M. Conway and David M. Carr.
© 2021 Colleen M. Conway and David M. Carr. Published 2021 by John Wiley & Sons Ltd.

to God's past promises to Israel enables the author to assert one of his main theological claims: that Jesus and his followers are instrumental to God's plan for salvation of Jews and gentiles. The author is also concerned with legitimizing the Jesus movement in the context of the Roman empire. To that end, this chapter shows how the Lukan Jesus and his followers are depicted with traits that were respected by the educated elite of the Roman empire. Overall, the author writes to validate and affirm the significance of the Jesus movement in the late first century CE. We begin with a look at the prologues of the Gospel of Luke and Acts, which not only provide evidence of the common authorship of these two works but also tell us a bit about the author.

The Lukan Prologues

READING

Luke 1:1–4; Acts 1:1–5.

EXERCISE

Based on your reading of Luke 1:1–4, why do you think the author is writing the gospel? How does he portray his task? What does he imply about the sources that we know that he used? Why do you think the author mentions "most excellent Theophilus" in both Luke and Acts?

We do not know who wrote Luke–Acts, but the openings of both books offer some intriguing details about the author and how he viewed his work. First, the prologues are similar to prologues found in ancient history writing. Ancient Greek history writers like Herodotus and Thucydides began their works with prologues, as did history writers more contemporaneous to Luke–Acts, like Josephus. Perhaps the author of the Lukan prologues imitated this literary convention of history writing with the hope that it would elevate the status of his two-volume work. That would fit with the addresses in both prologues to "most excellent Theophilus," which create the impression that the author is writing on behalf of a wealthy patron. It is possible that Theophilus was a wealthy convert to the Jesus movement who commissioned the author to write the two-volume work. It is also possible that the use of this name is a literary device. Because Theophilus means "friend of God" or "God-lover," the figure may be intended as a stand-in for believers in general. In either case, the effect of the address to Theophilus is the same; it situates the author and his work in a setting of relatively high social status.

As we will see, the narrative of Luke–Acts does the same thing with Jesus and the apostles.

The prologue of the first volume, the Gospel of Luke, tells us yet more about the author and how he conceived of his work. His observation that "many have tried to write orderly accounts," implies that their efforts have not been entirely successful. Whom does the gospel writer mean with his reference to "many" and what written accounts does he know of? It is a tantalizing verse that leaves us wondering about the number of sources known by the author. Is he referring to the Gospel of Mark and the sayings source known as Q? Or were there other accounts of the life of Jesus that have been long lost to us? Notice also that the author makes clear that he is *not* an eyewitness but is using accounts that have been handed down by eyewitnesses to produce his own orderly narrative.

Beyond highlighting the links between the volumes and the author's literary skill, the prologues raise the question of genre. How should we classify this two-volume work within its ancient literary context? Because the prologues imitate the style of ancient history writing and because there is a second volume that tells of the growth and spread of the Jesus movement after his lifetime, we could consider Luke–Acts as a sort of history writing. But what sort? How does this type of history writing compare to our own ideas of how historians work?

These important questions are worthy of more discussion than we can give them here. But we can at least say that ancient history writing was different than most of our contemporary understandings of history. Much like ancient orators, ancient Greek and Roman history writers were concerned to shape model citizens for the city-state or empire. Their goal was to write a persuasive narrative of events to convey a sweeping historical idea. To that end, ancient historians constructed dialogues between historical figures and created speeches by prominent men based on what they thought these people must have said in a given situation. By communicating what they thought must have happened, ancient historians shape their accounts to match their interpretation of past events. Of course, modern historians do this also to a certain extent. But contemporary historians base their construction of past events on archival research of historical records, which might, for example, include actual recordings of speeches. This is an important difference. If we call Luke–Acts history, we need to keep before us this type of ancient Greek and Roman history writing. The author of Luke–Acts writes a history, insofar as he writes what he thinks must have happened based on his understanding of the significance of Jesus and the earliest believers. Like other ancient history writers, he creates speeches for his characters who convey the author's idea of how Jesus and his movement fit into the history of Israel. In so doing, he helped to shape how later generations would understand the growth of Christianity. In the next section, we trace the different ways that the author of Luke–Acts linked the Jesus movement to his view of God's plan of salvation to Jews and gentiles.

Basics on Books of Luke–Acts

Outline: Luke's story of Jesus and the expanding "Way"

I	Luke: from Galilee to Jerusalem	
	Prologue: introduction to the two volumes	1:1–4
	A Birth narrative and preparation for ministry	1:5–4:13
	B Jesus's ministry in Galilee	4:14–9:50
	C Journey to Jerusalem	9:51–19:27
	D Entry to Jerusalem and teaching in the Temple	19:28–21:38
	E Passion, resurrection, and ascension in Jerusalem	22:1–24:53
II	Acts: From Jerusalem to Rome	
	Prologue: introduction to the second volume	1:1–5
	A Apostolic mission in Jerusalem	1:6–7:60
	B Spread of mission beyond Jerusalem	8:1–12:25
	1 Spread of the mission in Palestine and Paul's call	8:1–9:43
	2 Initial mission to the gentiles as far as Antioch	10:1–12:25
	C Paul's journeys	13:1–28:31
	1 The mission from Antioch to Asia Minor and Greece	13:1–19:20
	2 The journey, by way of Jerusalem, to Rome	19:21–28:31

Date and authorship

The author of Luke was traditionally identified as a physician and traveling companion of Paul, likely based on the passages in Acts that use the first person plural (Acts 16:10–17; 20:5–15; 21:1–18; 27:1–28:16). This alone is not compelling evidence, however, since other ancient travel narratives also switch to the first person plural, seemingly for dramatic effect. Moreover, much of what is narrated about Paul in Acts does not cohere with what Paul himself claims in his letters. For one thing, there is no mention at all of Paul's letter writing in the book of Acts. In Chapter 9 of this textbook, we noted the difference regarding the number of times Paul travels to Jerusalem between Acts and Paul's own account. Another difference between the Acts narrative and Paul's letters concerns the outcome of the meeting at Jerusalem. Acts reports an agreement that gentile Christ-followers would be required to follow Jewish dietary regulations (Acts 15:19–20). Paul mentions no such agreement in his account of this meeting. Instead, Paul reports that he was asked only to collect donations for the poor in Jerusalem (Gal 2:10). Differences like these between the Acts narrative and Paul's own letters make it unlikely the author of Luke–Acts traveled with Paul. We can speculate about the interests and motivation of the author as we study the narrative, but his identity is unknown. There is also little evidence to help us identify the date or location of the composition of Luke–Acts. Since the author used the Gospel of Mark as a source for his gospel but does not seem to know of the Gospel of Matthew, we can guess that it was written sometime around 80–85 CE. The second volume, Acts, need not have been written at the same time and could have been composed one or even two decades later.

The Lukan Jesus in Continuity with Israel's Past

Luke 1–4, 24. Pay attention to ways that these narratives evoke ideas from Israel's past and note their focus on the Temple and Jerusalem.

READING

Throughout Luke–Acts, the author links the Lukan Jesus and his followers to the history of Israel. Immediately after the prologue, the narrative begins to "sound" like the Hebrew scriptures. This occurs both in terms of the writing style and in the content of the stories. In the first case, even though the author is writing in Greek, he uses grammatical structures and phrases that are more like what one would expect to see in Hebrew. In terms of content, the story begins with a description of the righteous priest Zechariah and his wife Elizabeth, who both live blamelessly "according to the commandments and ordinances of the Lord" (Lk 1:6). The mention of Elizabeth's infertility recalls this common theme from the ancestor stories of Genesis as does Zechariah's assumption that the couple is too old to conceive a child (Lk 1:18, compare Gen 18:11–12). The author also has his characters "speak" in a scriptural way in the birth narrative. Mary's song of praise (1:46–55) sounds like Hannah's song from 1 Sam 2:1–10. Moreover, both Mary and Zechariah speak of the blessings and mercy of God on Israel, and God's promise to the ancestors (1:55, 72–5). In this way, the story of the Lukan Jesus's birth is scripturally situated in the context of God's ongoing relationship to Israel.

An early focus on Jerusalem and the Temple creates another important connection between Jesus and Israel in Luke–Acts. Only this gospel relates scenes from Jesus's infancy and childhood that feature his connection with the Temple. The first of these scenes occurs when the family brings Jesus to the Temple to offer the required sacrifice for a first-born male (2:22–32). The second occurs when Jesus is twelve years old and the family travels to Jerusalem for Passover. As Jesus's parents travel home, they discover he has gone missing. He is found back in Jerusalem, sitting with teachers in the Temple, displaying his precocious learning abilities (2:41–51). These early connections between Jesus and the Temple foreshadow the importance that Jerusalem and the Temple will have later in the narrative.

The gospel also connects the Lukan Jesus with the traditions of ancient Israel by casting him in the role of the rejected prophet. The Lukan Jesus's first public teaching occurs in a synagogue and features him reading from a scroll of the prophet Isaiah. Following the reading he announces to those in the synagogue that "no prophet is accepted in his hometown" (Luke 4:24). His statement foreshadows the conclusion of the episode, where Jesus's listeners violently reject him (Luke 4:16–30). We will discuss this important scene in more detail as the focus text for this chapter. The theme of Jesus as rejected prophet continues in the gospel with the author's use of a lament over Jerusalem from the Q sayings source, "the city that kills the prophets and stones those who are sent to it" (Luke 13:34). In the Gospel of Matthew, this

Q saying occurs in the context of woes against the Pharisees and refers to a list of past prophets that have been killed (Matt 23:34–7). In Gospel of Luke, the saying occurs after some Pharisees warn Jesus about Herod's plans to kill him (Luke 13:31). Not only does this difference illustrate the author's more favorable depiction of the Pharisees compared to Matthew's, it also suggests that Jesus is one of the prophets that the people of Jerusalem will kill. The last chapter of the gospel underlines this point. Describing Jesus after this death, two of his followers say he was "a prophet strong in work and speech" who was handed over to be killed by their chief priests and rulers (Luke 24:19).

The Jesus Movement in Continuity with Israel's Past

Acts 1:1–7:60, 10.

READING

The book of Acts builds on the idea of continuity with Israel using many of the themes we have seen in the Gospel. First, just as the Lukan Jesus is shown in connection with Jerusalem and the Temple, so are the apostles. In fact, the focus on Jerusalem creates a bridge between the two volumes. At the end of the gospel, the Lukan Jesus instructs the disciples to stay in the city of Jerusalem to wait for "power from on high" (Luke 24:49–51). The last verse of the gospel depicts the disciples as "continually before he ascends into heaven in the Temple blessing God" (Luke 24:53). Then, at the beginning of Acts, this same ascension scene is described a second time, reminding the audience of where the action left off at the end of the first volume. The order from Jesus is reported again: the disciples are not to leave Jerusalem (Acts 1:4). Note that in the retelling in Acts, the author adds an additional exchange between the disciples and risen Jesus. The disciples ask a pointedly political question, "Lord, is it in this time that you will restore the kingdom of Israel?" (Acts 1:6). The response from Jesus discourages speculation about the timing of a political liberation and turns attention instead to the spread of the Jesus movement beginning from Jerusalem. The Lukan Jesus informs the disciples: "But you will receive power when the Holy Spirit has come upon you, and you will be my witnesses in Jerusalem and all of Judea and Samaria and as far as the end of the earth" (Acts 1:8). Immediately following this re-narrated ascension scene, the apostles return to Jerusalem (Acts 1:12). Their association with the temple continues even after they receive the Spirit as the narrator reports that the apostles were in the Temple "day by day" (Acts 2:46). Later, when they are imprisoned by Temple authorities, an angel rescues them and commands them to "Go, and stand in the Temple, speaking to the people all the words about this life" (Acts 5:20). Despite ongoing conflict with the Jewish authorities, "every day in the Temple they did not stop teaching and proclaiming about Jesus Christ" (Acts 5:42).

Acts also continues the theme of Jerusalem's rejected prophets, especially through the depiction of the character Stephen. In Acts 7, the author portrays the apostle Stephen giving a long speech that puts Jesus in the line of Israel's rejected prophets. He first relates the way that Moses was rejected by the people. He then states, "this is the Moses who said to the Israelites, 'God will raise up a prophet for you from your own people as he raised me up'" (Acts 7:35–41). Finally, Stephen criticizes his audience, the Jewish council, and other onlookers, claiming that by killing Jesus, they have done just what their ancestors did to prophets before him (Acts 7:51–53). The scene concludes with Stephen himself becoming an example of a rejected prophet when his hearers stone him to death (Acts 7:58–60).

One more way that this author emphasizes the connection to the history of Israel in Acts is with his depiction of the apostle Paul. Throughout the narrative, the apostle is shown to be closely connected to Jerusalem, the Temple, and Jewish rituals. As discussed in chapter nine, according to Acts, Paul's travels included five trips to Jerusalem (Acts 9:26; 11:2; 15:2; 18:22; 21:17). Even more striking is that the Paul of Acts has his gentile companion Timothy circumcised (compare Gal 2:3). The "Acts Paul" also takes care to demonstrate his adherence to Jewish rituals. In Acts 21:17-26, Paul is called on to address rumors that he is teaching Jewish Christ-followers to forsake the Jewish law. He does so by undergoing ritual purification so that he can enter the Temple with men who have taken a nazirite vow (see Numbers 6:1-21). Paul also pays the expenses related to the completion of the men's vows. Note also that a brief statement earlier in Acts suggests Paul himself had taken a nazirite vow (18:10). Finally, in the Acts narrative, Paul reports that he was praying in the Temple when he saw a vision of Jesus, who told him that he would send Paul "far away to the gentiles" (Luke 22:17–21). In this way, the book of Acts roots Paul's divinely sanctioned mission to the gentiles to his presence in the Jerusalem Temple. (Here we might note that the depiction of Paul in Acts as Torah obedient is likely more accurate than later interpretations which see Paul as converting from Judaism to Christianity. See "Perspectives on Paul," p. 265–6.)

Why is the author so intent on reinforcing the continuity between the traditions of Israel and the Jesus movement? There are likely several reasons. First, by showing Jesus's connection with the long-established traditions of Judaism and with the Jerusalem Temple (a well-known cultic center), the author may have intended to alleviate suspicions about the Jesus movement. By the first century CE, the Roman empire was engaged in a program of restoring Roman cultural values, including honoring the traditional Roman deities. Indeed, one of Caesar Augustus's major programs was to restore Roman temples and reinvigorate traditional Roman rites. This came at a time when many people were attracted to non-Roman deities such as Isis (a goddess figure originating in Egypt) or to the cult of Mithras (a Persian-inspired tradition). Both of these cults required personal initiation rites and promised benefits to the individual who devoted himself or herself to the deity. In this context, Christ-followers might also be viewed with suspicion if Jesus were understood as another new god from the East, one who required a rite of initiation (baptism) and promised devotees special benefits. Showing how the Jesus movement was a continuation of Judaism addressed such potential misperceptions.

Another reason for showing Jesus and his followers in continuity with Israel's past could be the author's own attraction to Judaism, especially if the author was a gentile Christ-follower. As we saw from Josephus's story of King Izates, there were gentiles who were interested in the Jewish tradition (see textbox on "The Question of Circumcision" on p. *). Indeed, as mentioned in on p. *, it is likely that the first gentile converts to the Jesus movement were those who were attracted to Judaism and already listening to the Septuagint in local synagogues. The author of Acts features one such gentile at a key point in the narrative. Cornelius is described as a Roman centurion of the Italian cohort who "revered God with his entire household" and "prayed all the time" to God (Acts 10:2). Keep in mind that "God" here means the God of the people of Israel in contrast to the Roman gods. Perhaps the author of Luke–Acts came from a similar "God-revering" background. If so, he would have interpreted Jesus through Jewish expectations of a coming messiah that he learned about in the context of a synagogue community.

Salvation to the Gentiles in Luke–Acts

The story of Cornelius links to another important emphasis in Luke–Acts, that God's plan of salvation includes non-Jews. This idea of inclusion of the gentiles appears early in the gospel. For instance, when the devout Simeon sees the infant Jesus in the Jerusalem Temple, he praises God saying: "My eyes have seen your salvation which you prepared in the presence of all people, a light for revelation to the gentiles and glory for your people Israel" (2:30–2). Notice also that the genealogy in the gospel traces the lineage of Jesus all the way back to Adam, a figure representing all of humanity (Luke 3:38, compare the genealogy in Matthew 1 that begins with David and Abraham). The theme of gentile inclusion appears also at the end of Luke's gospel in a way that forecasts its appearance in Acts. There the risen Jesus declares that the "repentance and forgiveness of sins must be preached to all gentiles" (Greek *ethne* = nations and/or gentiles, Luke 24:47).

This preparation for the inclusion of the gentiles comes to a climax in the story in Acts 10. The chapter depicts the Jewish Christ-follower Peter and the God-revering gentile Cornelius coming together on account of divinely inspired visions (Acts 10:3–33). At this point, the character Peter explains his new understanding that "God is not partial, but in every nation, anyone who reveres him and acts justly is pleasing to him" (Acts 10:34–5). Peter then preaches to those with Cornelius in Caesarea, just as he earlier preached to the Jews in Jerusalem, with similar results – the Spirit falls upon all who hear the word (Acts 10:34–44; compare Acts 2:14–48). At this, the narrator reports that the "circumcised believers" with Peter were "astonished that the gift of the Holy Spirit had been poured out also on the gentiles" (Acts 10:44–5 modified from NRSV). When Peter returns to Jerusalem, he faces criticism by "the circumcised" (that is, the Jewish Christ-followers) for his association with gentiles. He retells the events that led him to Cornelius "step by step" so that the gospel audience hears about the episode a second time (Acts 11:1–18). This repetition shows how important this Cornelius episode is to the author. On hearing Peter's narration, his critics withdraw their objections and offer the final words of the scene: "Then even to the gentiles, God has given the repentance leading to life" (Acts 11:18, compare Luke 24:47).

The theme of gentile inclusion is accompanied by the contrasting theme that some Jews would reject Jesus. For example, Simeon follows his prediction of God's salvation with the statement that Jesus is appointed "for the falling and rising of many in Israel" (Luke 2:34). In this context, the prediction means that some Jews will come to believe in Jesus as God's messiah, and some will not. The theme that some Jews rejected the idea of following Jesus is foregrounded especially in the portrayal of Paul's mission in Acts. Repeatedly, when Paul's preaching results in dissent among some synagogue members, he turns his attention to the gentiles (see, for example, Acts 13:42–51; 14:1–7; 17:1–15; 19:8–9; 28:17–28).

Noting these literary motifs helps to remind us that the author of Luke–Acts is composing a narrative, not recording events exactly as they unfolded. For example, we know that Paul understood himself to be sent by God to the gentiles from the outset of his ministry, not as a result of being turned away in Jewish synagogues (review Galatians 2, especially 7–10). The author of Luke–Acts presents a version of "history" that makes sense for him in light of his understanding of Jesus and of the emerging community of Christ-followers, a group including both Jews and gentiles. This movement had to account for the fact that not all of the Jewish community had joined them. Not all were convinced by the Christ-followers' insistence that Jesus was the long-awaited messiah. Thus the author of Luke–Acts tells a story that shares some similarities with Paul's argument in Romans 9–11. The rejection of Paul's preaching by some occurs in the context of God's larger plan for the salvation of Israel and the gentiles. In fact, in Acts, the geographical expansion of the Jesus movement is predicated on the persecution and resulting scattering of Christ-followers from their base in Jerusalem (Acts 8:1). The narrative suggests that the dispersion does not occur randomly, but as part of God's plan. The events related in Acts 1–8 correspond to the Lukan Jesus's declaration, "... you will be my witnesses in Jerusalem and all of Judea and Samaria and as far as the end of the earth" (Acts 1:8).

Possessions and the Poor: A Lukan Puzzle

In the opening chapter of the Gospel of Luke, Mary's song (1:46–56) describes a God of reversal, one who exalts the lowly and brings down the rich and powerful. Soon after, the Lukan Jesus suggests that he has been chosen to "announce good news to the poor and release to the prisoner" (Luke 4:18), and the Lukan version of the beatitudes reads simply "Blessed are the poor" rather than "Blessed are the poor in spirit" as in Matthew's version (Luke 6:20; compare Matt 5:3). Several parables that are unique to Luke highlight God's care for the poor and castigation of the rich (Luke 12:16–21; 16:19–31). The rich young man is told that he must sell all that he has and distribute the money to the poor to inherit eternal life (Luke 18:22).

What is puzzling is that this focus on reversal of status and concern for the poor is not sustained through the two volumes. In fact, we find mixed messages. For example, one character in the gospel, Zacchaeus is a rich tax collector who is granted salvation because he pledges to give *half* of his possessions to the poor (Luke 19:1–9). Moreover, while Acts 4:32–7 describes the Jerusalem Christ-followers as a group with no private ownership of possessions, they do not sell their possessions to give the money to the poor. Rather, proceeds from private possessions are distributed among the community on the basis of need. A couple who violates this process by holding some private money in reserve is struck down dead (Acts 5:1–11). After this scene, the theme of possessions disappears altogether from the rest of the book of Acts. In fact, the word for "poor" never occurs in Acts. The author also seems interested in appealing to the status-conscious members of his audience, por-traying the followers of Jesus as civilized men who are comfortable associating with men of high status. In sum, there is no consistent message about possessions that is woven all the way through the two books of Luke–Acts. We are left with a puzzle over what the author intended.

Although scholars have proposed a range of different solutions to this interpretive puzzle, there is to date no scholarly consensus regarding the poor and possessions in Luke–Acts. What do you think the author wanted to say? One thing is clear, Christian readers in poor communities have found the Lukan Jesus's proclamation, "Blessed are the poor" to be a powerful scriptural affirmation of God's special care for them. In fact, the gospel's message about God's liberation of the poor and oppressed has played a central role in liberation theology. Originating in poor communities in Latin America, liberation theology promotes the idea that God has a "preferential option for the poor." According to Peruvian theologian, Gustavo Gutierrez, the originator of this expression, God's preferential option for the poor means that God stands on the side of the poor. Moreover, Gutierrez argues, God calls the church to be engaged in actions with and on behalf of the poor, especially actions directed toward ending unjust social structures.

Situating the Jesus Movement in the Roman Empire

READING

Review Luke 1–3 and read Acts 21–8.

In addition to connecting the story of Jesus with the past history of Israel and God's plan for salvation, the author of Luke–Acts also links Jesus with the politics and culture of the Roman empire. This occurs in several ways ranging from regular mention of Roman rulers to depicting the Lukan Jesus and the apostles in Acts demonstrating the traits of admirable Roman men. This section explores how and why the author often presents Jesus and his earliest followers in line with the cultural values of Rome.

On a basic level, the author takes care to place the birth and ministry of Jesus in the context of Roman ruling authority. For example, in this gospel, Joseph and Mary must travel to Bethlehem because of a decree of the emperor Augustus, an event that the narrative portrays as taking place when Quirinius was governor of Syria (2:1–2). Neither of these claims is historically accurate – there is no record of such a decree from Augustus outside of this gospel, and Quirinius was not the governor of Syria at the time of Jesus's birth. But these elements only underscore that the aim of the gospel is not historical accuracy even if that is an interest of modern readers. The narrative aims to tell the story of Jesus against a backdrop of powerful Roman figures. We find a similar tendency when the gospel prefaces the inauguration of John's baptizing activity with a list of no fewer than five Roman rulers and two high priests (Luke 3:1–2). This interest in placing the early Jesus movement in the context of Roman rule is further reinforced in Acts, where Paul is repeatedly called before Roman authorities to make his case (Acts 18:12–13; 24–6). The Paul of Acts even demands a trial before the emperor's tribunal, resulting in a journey to Rome where the narrative concludes (though with no account of a trial) (Acts 25:10–12; 28:30). These multiple links between Jesus, his early followers, and Roman imperial authorities were likely meant to impress upon the reader the importance and significance of the movement growing across the empire.

Another way that the author situates the story of Jesus in the Roman empire is by using language typically reserved for the emperor to describe the importance of Jesus. For example, twice in the birth narrative the title "savior" is used to describe Jesus; once in Zechariah's song (Luke 1:69) and once in the angel's announcement to the shepherds (Luke 2:11). In Acts, Peter and the apostles refer to Jesus as ruler and savior (Acts 5:31) and later Paul also says that Jesus is a savior brought by God (Acts 13:23). The use of this title no doubt seems unsurprising now. Perhaps more surprising would be the fact that the title savior is rarely used in the gospels, or in the undisputed letters of Paul. Apart from these four instances in Luke–Acts, it only appears once in the Gospel of John (John 4:22) and only at Philippians 3:20 in the undisputed letters. The fact is that for a first- or second-century CE audience, to call Jesus a "savior" would bring to mind the Roman emperor, since this title *was* applied to him in imperial inscriptions (see the "Priene Calendar Inscription" below). Similarly, Zechariah's prediction that Jesus would direct "people toward the way of peace" (1:79) would have resonated with one of the fundamental claims of Rome – that the empire brought peace to a war-torn world. Luke–Acts counters this Roman claim with the idea that it is Jesus, not the emperor, who is the savior and bringer of peace.

The Priene Calendar Inscription

The following inscription, dating from 9 BCE, was found in ancient Priene, located in modern-day Turkey. It marks the institution of a new calendar "for good luck and salvation" based on the birthday of Augustus. The inscription illustrates the rhetoric typically used to describe the emperor. When similar claims were made about Jesus by early Christ-followers, this type of imperial rhetoric would be the most immediate frame of reference. Note also the idea of Augustus as a gift from Providence who is deeply invested in humankind.

It seemed good to the Greeks of Asia, in the opinion of the high priest Apollonius of Menophilus Azanitus: "Since Providence, which has ordered all things and is deeply interested in our life, has set in most perfect order by giving us Augustus, whom for the benefit of humankind she has filled with virtue, as if for us and for those after us she bestowed a savior, who brought an end to war and established peace ... and since he, Caesar, by his appearance (excelled even our anticipations), surpassing all previous benefactors, and not even leaving to posterity any hope of surpassing what he has done, and since the birthday of the god Augustus was the beginning of the good tidings for the world that came by reason of him which Asia resolved in Smyrna ..."

Just as the birth narratives draw on imperial rhetoric to present Jesus as a powerful savior, so also the ascension scenes at the end of the gospel (Luke 24:50–2) and at the beginning of Acts (Acts 1:6–11) make a connection with Jesus and Roman imperial status. In these two scenes, the Lukan Jesus gives final words of instructions to his disciples and is then "lifted up" into heaven. Again, an ancient Greco-Roman audience would associate this elevation scene with one even more familiar to them – that of imperial deification. Beginning with the death of Julius Caesar, the Roman Senate began a tradition of honoring a deceased emperor with divine status. The deification of Caesar Augustus in 14 CE was celebrated across the empire and commemorated with coins, temple dedications, and the establishment of priesthoods and cult rituals. This means that for a first-century CE audience, the ascension scenes in the gospel and Acts would be a way of making explicit Jesus's divine status and authority. The Lukan Jesus's ascension (which occurs without the vote of the Roman senate!) would call to mind and potentially challenge the most powerful position in the known world, the Roman emperor (see Figures 13.1 and 13.2). At one point in Acts, the opponents of Christ-followers in Thessalonica articulate this challenge to imperial authority. The Christ group is accused of "turning the world upside down" and "acting contrary to the decrees of the emperor, saying that there is another king named Jesus" (Acts 17:6–7).

The fact that Jesus was executed by the Roman empire complicates this imitation of imperial authority. Far from a display of power, the crucifixion of Jesus would appear to many as the utterly shameful death of a convicted

FIGURE 13.1
Base of an honorific column in Rome showing the deification of a second-century CE emperor and his wife.

criminal. The Lukan narrative deals with this problem by stressing the innocence of Jesus. In the Lukan trial scene, Pilate explicitly states that he can find no reason to charge Jesus with a crime (Luke 23:4, 14, 22). Only Luke's account includes a separate trial before Herod, governor of Galilee (Luke 23:8–16), who also does not charge him with a crime (Luke 23:15). Most striking is the way the author adapts the Roman centurion's statement at the death of Jesus. In the Markan version, the centurion at the cross declares, "Truly, this man was a son of God" (Mark 15:39). The author of Luke here edits his source and has the centurion declare, "Truly, this man was innocent" (Luke 23:47). Such a claim of innocence would be meant to reassure believers that Jesus was an honorable figure despite the way he died.

The narrative of Luke–Acts goes still further in making the case that Jesus and his followers have qualities that define them as highly respectable members of society – indeed, as civilized men who exhibit the traits of other elite men in the culture. We have already seen how the prologues to Luke and Acts signal to the reader that the work itself should be viewed on a par with literary Greek and Roman histories. The author extends this idea to his characters, showing them in ways that highlight their intellect and education. For instance, the story of a precocious Jesus learning from the rabbis in the Temple demonstrates his keen mind (Luke 2:46–7). Moreover, only this gospel explicitly presents Jesus as literate. He begins his public ministry by reading from a scroll in a synagogue (Luke 4:16). Later, the Jewish authorities marvel at the frank and bold public speech (*parresia*) of Peter and John, whom they know to be illiterate and common. Their bold speech enables others to recognize Peter and John as disciples of Jesus. The ability to speak confidently was regarded as a high skill in the Greco-Roman culture, so it is no coincidence that the author calls attention to it.

Another important quality for a Roman man was *pietas*. While this Latin word is often translated as piety, it means something closer to duty

FIGURE 13.2

Book cover dating to the fifth century CE and depicting the heavenly ascent of an emperor. That such images could still be found in the Christian empire of the fifth century illustrates how deeply the idea of a divine emperor was embedded in Roman culture.

or loyalty to the gods, as well as loyalty to one's family and country. The first-century BCE poet Vergil regularly described Aeneas, the hero of his epic poem about the founding of Rome, as "*pius Aeneas*," that is, as dutiful or "pious" Aeneas. So too Luke–Acts illustrates the "piety" (loyalty, duty) of Jesus and the apostles. The connection to the Jerusalem Temple that we have already discussed is one way to feature such piety. From a Greco-Roman perspective, a close association with the Temple would indicate the apostles' *pietas* and thereby their high standing. Later in the narrative, the quality of *pietas* is illustrated by the way Jesus and his followers engage in frequent prayer (see, for example, Luke 3:21; 5:16; 6:12; 9:18; Acts 1:14; 2:42; 4:31; 6:4; 7:59; 10:30; 11:5).

One more fundamental trait in the Greco-Roman culture was moderation or self-control (Greek, *sophrosune*). This quality of character was especially associated with being a respectable man. Many of the practical philosophers at this time provided instructions on how to live a "manly" life of virtue that included control over the passions – anger, lust, and so on. Notably, Luke–Acts suggests that being a Christ-follower can help one achieve such manly self-control. This is most evident in Paul's speech to Agrippa, where he contrasts his early life with his life as a follower of Jesus. He describes how earlier he persecuted "many of the saints" and was "furiously enraged at them, pursuing them to other cities" (Acts 26:11). The Paul of Acts paints a picture of a man out of control, and thus "unmanly" in the Roman culture. At the end of his speech, the Roman governor Festus asserts that Paul is highly educated and that so much learning is making him insane (Acts 26:24). The first claim bolsters the status of Paul. The second claim Paul denies by pointing out that he is speaking with "truth and moderation" (*sophrosune*) (Acts 26:25). In other words, Paul argues that he formerly was a man out of control, but now that he is a Christ-follower, he speaks truthfully and with the self-control that was so highly esteemed in the culture. In sum, the story of the early Christ-followers in Luke–Acts suggests that joining "the Way" would actually help one attain a life of virtue, and thus be seen as a manly and respectable member of society. The Lukan Jesus and his followers are presented as self-controlled, educated, and pious – in short, as civilized men.

Thus, in Luke–Acts we see the sort of hybrid response to imperial rule that we have seen earlier in this textbook. The use of imperial titles for Jesus is a way of imitating Rome to make a claim about the surpassing power of Jesus. At the same time, the suggestion that becoming a Christ-follower helped one achieve a life of virtue and therefore a higher social status shows the ready adoption of common cultural values of the Greco-Roman elite.

The Holy Spirit in Luke–Acts

Just prior to the Lukan Jesus's heavenly ascent, he gives instructions that provide a clue as to how the author understood the connection between Israel's past, the present reality of Jesus's crucifixion and resurrection, and the future growth of the "Way":

> Then he said to them, "These are my words that I spoke to you while I was with you, that it was necessary that all the scriptures concerning me in the law of Moses, the prophets and the psalms be fulfilled." Then he opened their minds to understand the scriptures. And he said to them, "Thus it is written, that the Christ will suffer and be raised from the dead on the third day, and repentance for forgiveness of sins is to be proclaimed in his name to all nations, starting with Jerusalem. You are witnesses of these things. Look, I am sending the promise of my Father on you. So you are to stay in the city until you have been clothed with power from on high." (Luke 24:44–9, modified from NRSV)

Three key ideas appear in these closing words of the risen Jesus in Luke: the notion of the fulfillment of the Hebrew scriptures, the proclamation of repentance and forgiveness, and the importance of the Holy Spirit, here expressed as "power from on high" (Luke 24:49). All three of these themes serve to connect Israel's past to the present Jesus movement.

We have seen the fulfillment theme before, especially in the Gospel of Matthew. But the author of Luke–Acts does something new with this theme. Because this is a two-volume work, the author extends the idea of fulfillment of the Hebrew scriptures to the fulfillment of the Lukan Jesus's words. Thus not only is it written "that the Christ is to suffer and to rise from the dead on the third day," but also – and this is the particularly Lukan theme – "repentance and forgiveness of sins is to be proclaimed in his name to all the nations starting from Jerusalem" (Luke 24:47). This is precisely what the apostles do as the narrative continues in Acts, beginning with Peter's speech (Acts 2:38–9). From there, the apostles take the message of repentance to the Jews (Acts 3:19; 5:30–1), and also to the gentiles (Acts 11:18; 17:30–1). In this way, they fulfill the Lukan Jesus's command.

According to the narrative, this mission will take place by means of "power from on high," that is, the Holy Spirit (24:49). The figure of the Holy Spirit takes a leading role from the very beginning of the gospel. The opening chapter relates parallel stories of Elizabeth and Mary conceiving and giving birth to John and Jesus. In both stories, the Holy Spirit drives the events. An angelic announcement foretells that John will be filled with the Holy Spirit even before his birth, and both Elizabeth and Mary are reported to be filled with the Spirit (Luke 1:35; 1:41). In Mary's case, it is the Holy Spirit that is responsible for her conception. Zechariah and Simeon are also Spirit-filled, causing them to prophesy about John (Luke 1:67–79) and Jesus (Luke 2:27–32) respectively.

The prominence of the Holy Spirit continues in the depiction of the Lukan Jesus. To be sure, the Spirit descends on Jesus in all the gospels, but only in Luke's gospel do we find repeated references to Jesus being filled with the Holy

Spirit. For instance, Jesus is "full of the Holy Spirit" as he is led by the Spirit into the wilderness to be tempted (Luke 4:1–2). He then begins his Galilean ministry, "with the power of the spirit" (Luke 4:14). Only in the Gospel of Luke does Jesus speak of handing over his spirit to God at the time of his death (Luke 23:46). Finally, only in Luke's gospel does the resurrected Jesus instruct the disciples to stay in Jerusalem to wait for the Holy Spirit (Luke 24:49).

As we have already seen, in Acts, the promise that the followers of Jesus will receive the Holy Spirit is repeated two more times (Acts 1:5, 8), and is then fulfilled during the Jewish spring harvest festival known as Shauvot (or Pentecost in Greek) (Acts 2:1–9). To explain what has occurred, Peter's speech begins with a long quote from the Hebrew prophet Joel. The opening lines predict the reception of God's spirit:

> "And it will be in the last days," says God
> "that I will pour out my Spirit on all flesh,
> and your sons will prophesy and your daughters,
> and your young men will see visions,
> and your old men will dream dreams.
> Even on my male slaves and female slaves,
> I will pour out my Spirit in those days, and they will prophesy." (Acts 2:17–18)

Including this quotation has the effect of making the gift of the Spirit something that was predicted long ago in Israel's past. The author of Luke–Acts inserts the phrase "in the last days" before the quotation from Joel, giving an eschatological interpretation to the prophecy.

As the story continues, the apostles, like Jesus before them, preach and teach as they are "filled with the Holy Spirit" (see, for example, Acts 4:8; 4:31; 6:3; 7:55; 13:9). The Holy Spirit is so prominent in Acts, it seems to take on the role of a character, speaking to other characters (Acts 8:29; 11:12; 13:2; 16:6) and even moving them from place to place (Acts 8:39; 13:4). In some cases, the apostles are forbidden by the Spirit to travel to certain places (Acts 16:6–7). The author uses the figure of the Holy Spirit throughout the gospel and Acts to illustrate God's continuing presence in the past history of Israel and the present growth of the Jesus movement.

MORE ON METHOD: AFRICAN AMERICAN BIBLICAL INTERPRETATION IN THE NEW TESTAMENT

As with the study of the Hebrew Bible/Old Testament, African American biblical interpretation has produced important insights for the study of the New Testament. What follows are two examples of African American interpretations of the figure of the Ethiopian eunuch in Acts 8.

Clarice J. Martin analyzes the perceptions of Ethiopians in Greek and Roman literature, including the thematizing of Ethiopian dark skin color. She argues that the author of Luke–Acts uses the Ethiopian eunuch to represent the exotic foreigner whose baptism demonstrates that the gospel has indeed reached the "end of the earth" (see Acts 1:8). (See Clarice J. Martin, "A

Chamberlain's Journey and the Challenge of Interpretation for Liberation," *Semeia* 47, 105–35, 1989).

Demetrius Williams sees the figure of the Ethiopian eunuch demonstrating the limitations of the supposedly universalizing promise of salvation of the Joel quotation in Acts. While the Joel prophecy suggests that the Spirit will enable *anyone* to prophesy, in the book of Acts the characters who prophesy are only certain Jewish and gentile men. The Spirit is *not* poured out, Williams observes, on the Ethiopian eunuch at his baptism. Williams also shows how, despite such limitations in the narrative, African American women have read the Joel prophecy in Acts as a scriptural warrant for their full inclusion in church leadership. (See Demetrius K. Williams, "Upon All Flesh: Acts 2, African Americans, and Intersectional Realities," pp. 289–310 in Randal Bailey et al. *They Were All Together in One Place: Toward Minority Biblical Criticism*. Atlanta: SBL, 2009. Other essays in this volume include Asian-American, Cuban, and Latinx approaches to the Bible. See also Brian K. Blount, gen. ed., *True to Our Native Land: An African American New Testament Commentary*. Minneapolis: Fortress, 2007.)

Jesus's Sermon in Nazareth (Luke 4:14–30)

FOCUS TEXT

The story of the beginning of Jesus's work in Luke 4:14–30 is a programmatic text for the Gospel of Luke and also points ahead to the narrative of Acts. The author builds on a tradition of Jesus's rejection in his hometown to convey several central ideas in the two-volume work. While the Gospel of Mark has a very short story about Jesus's rejection in his hometown (Mark 6:1–6), the author of Luke both expands the story and moves it earlier in his narrative. In Luke's version of the story, Jesus returns to Galilee after the temptation in the wilderness. He is "filled with the power of the Spirit" and quickly gains recognition and praise as he teaches in the synagogues (Luke 4:14–15). It is not until he comes to his hometown that the content of his teaching is reported. The scene unfolds in two parts. In the first part, Luke 4:16–22, Jesus's words gain high praise from his hometown audience. In the second part, Luke 4:23–30, events turn in a radically different direction.

As noted earlier, only this gospel writer portrays Jesus as reading from a scroll (4:16). This detail may seem unremarkable to us, but in the ancient world it would have been an indicator of Jesus's literacy, and thus his status as an educated man. Beyond the fact *that* Jesus reads, however, is *what* he reads:

> The Spirit of the Lord is upon me, because he has anointed me to bring good news to the poor. He has sent me to proclaim release to the captives and recovery of sight to the blind, to let the oppressed go free, to proclaim the year of the Lord's favor. (4:18–19 NRSV)

The Lukan Jesus reads a text from Isaiah that coincides with several major themes of the gospel: the identification of Jesus with the prophets of Israel, the role of the Holy Spirit, and the Lukan Jesus's attention to the poor and oppressed. All these themes were introduced in the birth narrative, and this opening statement of Jesus reaffirms their importance to the gospel. The story builds tension as Jesus rolls the scroll back up, hands it to the synagogue attendant, and then sits down to comment on the scripture. The Lukan Jesus's announcement that the scripture has been fulfilled in their hearing brings words of praise from the synagogue members (Luke 4:21–2). Here is another indication that this author has a story to tell that differs from his source, the Gospel of Mark. In the Markan version people question Jesus's origins in a way that criticizes his presumptuousness. "From where is he getting these things? … Isn't this the carpenter, the son of Mary, and the brother of James and Joses and Judah and Simon? And aren't his sisters here with us? And they were offended by him" (Mark 6:2–3). In the Gospel of Luke, this line of questioning is changed into words of praise: "And all were impressed with him and amazed at the gracious words that came from his mouth, saying, 'Isn't this Joseph's son?'" (Luke 4:22). They are proud of the hometown boy.

At this point, the scene shifts in tone. The author juxtaposes two different proverbs. With the first one, "physician heal yourself," the Lukan Jesus anticipates the skepticism of the crowd and their demand for proof of his wonders. With the second proverb, he predicts their rejection of him: "No prophet is acceptable in his hometown" (Luke 4:23–4). Again, the author gets this second saying from the Gospel of Mark (Mark 6:4) but puts it to a different purpose. In Mark, the saying is a fitting conclusion to the offense the crowd has already shown. In Luke's version, the people have only praised Jesus to this point. The rejection will not occur until another expansion of the scene introduces a particularly Lukan theme. The story thus continues with the Lukan Jesus offering a series of examples about how God worked (or not) with ancient Israel in the time of earlier prophets – Elisha and Elijah. The evocation of these prophets is another example of linking Jesus with the prophetic tradition of Israel. But the reference to the prophets does more than that. By the time the Lukan Jesus has finished his discussion of Elisha and Elijah, just as he predicted, the synagogue members decide he is not acceptable in his hometown. They become so enraged with his words that they try to throw him off a cliff (4:28–9).

What has caused this sudden change in mood? The examples that the Lukan Jesus provides are both cases when God helped non-Israelites rather than an Israelite in a time of need – the widow in Sidon and Naaman the Syrian. With these examples, the gospel continues the theme already introduced in the birth narrative that God will save both Israel and the gentiles. Luke 4 thus stands as a programmatic passage that introduces a major theological claim of Luke–Acts: God's saving acts include both Jews and gentiles. The reaction of the crowd anticipates the narrative pattern discussed earlier in this chapter: the rejection of Jesus (and followers of Jesus) by the synagogue community. Although Luke–Acts has a more open attitude in general toward the Jewish community (many repent and believe in Jesus), as we have seen, the author also links the spread of the Jesus movement across the Roman empire with rejection from the synagogue.

The theme of salvation extending to the gentiles is so important that Luke–Acts concludes on this theme. As Paul is under house arrest in Rome, he meets with the local Jewish leaders and tries to convince them about

Jesus "both from the law of Moses and the prophets" (Acts 28:23). As has been the case throughout the book, some are convinced but others refuse to believe. In response, Paul quotes an extended passage from the prophet Isaiah that begins:

> Go to this people and say,
> "You will indeed listen, but never understand,
> and you will look, but will never perceive." (Acts 28:26 NRSV)

Other New Testament writings use this passage from Isaiah to explain why Jesus spoke in parables (cf. Mark 4:12; Matt 13:14–15), or why some did not believe in Jesus (John 12:40; and recall the ideas in Romans 9–11). In Acts, the Isaiah quotation is used as a final statement of support of the mission to the gentiles. The last words of Paul in the book are: "Let it be known to you then that this salvation of God has been sent to the gentiles; they will listen" (28:28 NRSV). The combination of the Isaiah quotation with Paul's final words encourages a contrast between the gentiles who listen and some Jews who listen but "never understand." Thus although the Gospel of Luke opens with a proclamation of God bringing light to Israel and to the gentiles (Luke 2:30–2), Acts closes with an emphasis on Jewish rejection in contrast to the gentiles. Perhaps the author offers an overall tragic story of the history of Israel (this is the argument of Robert Tannehill, see "Resources for Further Study"). Or perhaps, in the author's view, the end of his literary work is not the end of the salvation history that he is narrating. Note that the author does not offer a final word on Israel. Nor does he portray Paul in a final encounter with Rome. Instead, Acts concludes with Paul under house arrest but "welcoming all" who came to him and preaching the Kingdom of God. In the end, the author leaves the narrative of Luke–Acts open-ended.

CHAPTER THIRTEEN REVIEW

1 What are the different ways that the author of Luke–Acts connects Jesus to the story of Israel in the Jewish scriptures? List as many as you can.

2 How and why does Luke–Acts situate the Jesus movement in relationship to the Roman empire and Roman values?

3 What are some character traits that were valued by elite men in Roman culture? How and why does Luke–Acts stress ways that Jesus and his followers exemplify these characteristics?

4 How does the author of Luke–Acts emphasize the role of the Holy Spirit? What importance does the Spirit have in the Jesus movement according to this work?

5 (Focus text: Luke 4:14–30) How does the story of Jesus's sermon at Nazareth in Luke 4:14–30 illustrate central themes of Luke–Acts, such as associations with Israel's past history, the aim of universal salvation, and Jesus's status vis-à-vis Roman masculinity? Why do you think the author of Luke–Acts portrays Jesus as preaching "good news to the poor" at the beginning of his ministry? What do you think it meant in his context? How might contemporary readers understand in a twenty-first-century context?

RESOURCES FOR FURTHER STUDY

Green, Joel. *Methods for Luke*. Cambridge and New York: Cambridge University Press, 2010.

Grimshaw, James P., ed. *Luke–Acts*. Texts@Contexts Series. London and New York: Bloomsbury T&T Clark, 2019.

Parsons, Mikeal C. *Luke: Storyteller, Interpreter, Evangelist*. Peabody, MA: Hendrickson, 2007.

Shillington, V. George. *An Introduction to the Study of Luke–Acts* (2nd edition). London: T&T Clark, 2015.

Tannehill, Robert C. *The Narrative Unity of Luke–Acts: A Literary Interpretation. Foundations and Facets.* Philadelphia, PA: Fortress, 1986–90. A dated, but detailed discussion of the thematic links between the two volumes.

The Gospel of John and the Johannine Letters: Turning Inward as a Strategy for Life in the Empire

14

Chapter Outline

Chapter Overview

With the Gospel of John, we enter a different narrative world to that of the synoptic gospels. In this world, there is little talk of the kingdom of God, no talk at all of miracles, but plenty of talk of signs, the hour, glory, and Jesus as one who was sent into the world by the Father. There are also significant chronological differences between the synoptic gospels and the Gospel of John, as well as different characters and events. And, far from urging secrecy about his identity, the Johannine Jesus speaks in bold, self-descriptive, "I am" statements. These distinctive features of the Gospel of John have intrigued readers for centuries. Scholars have long debated the origins and composition of the gospel and how it relates to the synoptic tradition. Already in the second century CE, a bishop known as Clement of Alexandria tried to explain why the gospel differed to such a degree from the others. Clement famously argued that because John knew that the other gospels had "set out the outward facts" about Jesus, he composed a "spiritual gospel." While this suggestion likely helped the Gospel of John secure a place in the canon alongside the synoptic gospels, it also led to misconceptions. On the one hand, there is no shortage of spirituality in the synoptic

A Contemporary Introduction to the Bible: Sacred Texts and Imperial Contexts, Second Edition.
Colleen M. Conway and David M. Carr.
© 2021 Colleen M. Conway and David M. Carr. Published 2021 by John Wiley & Sons Ltd.

gospels. On the other hand, some elements of the Gospel of John may be more "factual" than the synoptic traditions (within the limits of our ability to know "facts" from this time).

Rather than labeling John as more "spiritual" and rather than arguing that the gospel writer wants to show Jesus's divinity (another common claim for this gospel), the focus in this chapter will be on highlighting the distinctive elements of the Gospel of John, especially its unique depiction of Jesus. We will also examine the way the language of the gospel is more inwardly focused than the synoptic gospels. It seems designed to draw boundaries and create a sense of belonging by focusing on the idea of alienation from "the world." Toward that end, the gospel paints an oppositional world of light and dark, above and below, from God and not from God, belief, and unbelief. The dualistic language is used to make emphatically clear that the Johannine Jesus is *not* of the world. He is described as one sent by God into the world to draw "his own" to him and give them power to become children of God. One especially troubling aspect of the gospel is its negative characterization of "the Jews." We will discuss possible reasons for this antagonistic language and the implications of its presence in the Christian canon.

Who Is the Johannine Jesus?

READING

John 1–5.

EXERCISE

As you read the opening chapters of John, keep track of the different claims that are made about the identity of Jesus, including the different titles that are attributed to him. Note also how the Johannine Jesus describes who he is, where he has come from, and for what purpose. What overall impression do you have of the Johannine Jesus in these opening chapters compared to the different synoptic versions of Jesus?

The Johannine Prologue: Jesus as Pre-existent Logos Made Flesh

The question of the identity of the Johannine Jesus is the central question running through the Gospel of John. The opening lines already begin to address this question in striking fashion with a focus on Jesus's origins.

Recall how the gospels of Matthew and Luke use genealogies to trace Jesus's family line back to Abraham (Matthew 1:1) and Adam (Luke 3:38). The Gospel of John traces the origin of Jesus even earlier. It opens with a poetic prologue that takes the audience back to a time before the created world: "In the beginning was the *logos* and the *logos* was with God and the *logos* was God" (John 1:1). Typically, the Greek term *logos* is translated as "word," which readers understand as "word of God." This is one possible meaning of the term *logos*, but this translation alone does not fully capture the Greek word's multi-faceted meaning. In ancient Greek and Roman philosophy, *logos* often refers to the universal rational principle that gives order to the entire cosmos. In John, reference to the *logos* being involved in the creation of "all things" shares a similar cosmic scope. In the writings of Philo, a first-century Jewish philosopher, *logos* refers to God's wisdom and this meaning is certainly part of *logos* in the Gospel of John. We have seen the association between Jesus and personified Wisdom in the Gospel of Matthew. So also in John, the author uses *logos* to associate Jesus with the figure of divine wisdom. Like personified Wisdom in Proverbs 8, this *logos* is active in creation *with* God, bringing life and light into being (John 1:3–4). Most striking is the gospel's assertion that this pre-existent divine *logos* became flesh in Jesus (John 1:14). This idea of a divine being becoming embodied as a human, seen in a number of religious traditions, is referred to as **incarnation**. The Johannine Prologue links the figure of personified Wisdom with the incarnate *logos* (that is, the Johannine Jesus). The same association continues later in the gospel as the chart on the following page shows.

The last two verses of the prologue, 1:17–18, compare Moses and Jesus. Again, you may recall that the Gospel of Matthew links Jesus to Moses and the law to emphasize the importance of Torah obedience. In the Gospel of John, it is more the case that Moses is put in contrast with Jesus. The gospel distinguishes between Moses as a mediator of the law and the Johannine Jesus who mediates "grace and truth." This already hints at tensions regarding the authoritative position of Jesus compared to Moses. The statement that "no one has seen God" except the only begotten God/son (ancient copies of the gospel differ at this point) heightens the tension. The statement contradicts the scriptural tradition of Moses speaking with God "face to face" as a friend (Exodus 33:11). Such bold assertions about Jesus vis-à-vis Moses, as well as an early statement that not all of Jesus's "own" accepted him (John 1:11), foreshadow debates in the narrative about the identity of the Johannine Jesus.

Overall, the prologue functions as a sort of overture to the rest of the gospel. The theme of the light coming into the world, the rejection and acceptance of Jesus, the focus on belief, all will recur across the narrative. At the same time, the term *logos* never occurs again in reference to the Johannine Jesus. Once the *logos* becomes flesh, the Johannine Jesus himself, as well as the characters that he encounters, will do the work of defining who he is. The point of this opening claim about Jesus's divine origin is to assist the audience in interpreting statements by and about Jesus that occur in the rest of the gospel.

Personified Wisdom in Jewish scriptures (translations are modified from the NRSV)	Jesus as Wisdom in the Gospel of John
Sirach 24:9 Before the ages, in the beginning, he created me, and for all the ages I shall not cease to be.	**John 1:1** In the beginning was the Logos, and the Logos was with God and the Logos was God. It was in the beginning with God.
Sirach 24:7–8 Among all these I searched for rest, and looked to see in whose territory I might pitch a tent. Then the Creator of all instructed me and my Creator chose the place for my tent. He said, "Pitch your tent in Jacob, make Israel your inheritance."	**John 1:14** And the Word became flesh and pitched a tent among us and we beheld its glory…
Sirach 24:17–22 I am like a vine sprouting grace, my blossoms bear the glorious fruit of glory and riches. Come to me, you who desire me, and take your fill of my fruits, for memories of me are sweeter than honey, inheriting me is sweeter than the honeycomb. They who eat me will hunger for more, they who drink me will thirst for more. No one who obeys me will ever have to blush, no one who acts as I dictate will ever sin.	**John 15:1–2** I am the true vine and my father is the gardener. All branches that do not bear fruit, he removes. All that bear fruit, he prunes so they bear more fruit. **John 6:34–5** "Sir," they said, "give us that bread always." Jesus answered them: I am the bread of life. No one who comes to me will ever hunger; no one who believes in me will ever thirst.
1 Enoch 42 (modified from Robert Henry Charles's 1913 translation) Wisdom found no place where she might dwell; Then a dwelling-place was assigned her in the heavens. Wisdom went forth to make her dwelling among the children of humans, and found no dwelling-place: Wisdom returned to her place and took her seat among the angels.	**John 1:11** He came to what was his own, and his own people did not accept him. **John 13:1** … Jesus knew that his hour had come to depart from this world and go to the Father.

Basics on Gospel of John

The gospel has two main sections. The first part focuses on the signs of Jesus and concerns his time in the world. A clear break is indicated at 13:1, where the narrator reports that Jesus knew that his hour had come to depart from the world and return to the Father. John 11 and 12 serve as a transition to the second section. These two chapters narrate the last of Jesus's signs (11:1–44) and foreshadow his death and glorification (11:45–12:8; 12:27–36). The second part of the gospel then focuses on Jesus's "hour," that is, his death and resurrection. Together the two parts of the gospel trace the journey of the Johannine Jesus coming into the world and then departing to return to his origin with God.

I	Signs of the Johannine Jesus	1–12
	A Prologue: the *logos* coming into the world	1:1–18
	B Belief and unbelief in response to the signs	1:19–11:44
	C Transition: the final sign and foreshadowing of the hour	11:45–12:50
II	Jesus's departure from the world	13–20
	A Farewell meal with the disciples	13
	B Farewell discourse and prayer	14–17
	C The hour of glorification	18–20
III	Epilogue: Jesus's last meeting with his disciples	21

Outline: the sojourn of the incarnate *logos* in the world

The question of authorship of the gospel attracts even more scholarly attention than that of the authorship of the synoptic gospels. This is due to the intriguing figure of the "beloved disciple" (13:23; 19:26; 20:2; 21:7, 20) whom some have supposed to be the author. Although this disciple is never named in the gospel, scholars have offered dozens of theories about his or her identity from the resurrected Lazarus to Mary Magdalene. Such attempts are speculative at best. In terms of identifying the author they are also misguided. There is no compelling evidence that this figure is intended to represent the author. Meanwhile, church tradition says that a disciple of Jesus, John the son of Zebedee, wrote the gospel in his old age in Ephesus. Again, because the gospel was written anonymously, this remains tradition rather than fact.

Date and authorship

There are indications that the Gospel of John went through several editorial revisions before it reached its current form. The clearest evidence of this is at John 20:30–1, which sounds like a conclusion to the gospel. However, after this seeming conclusion, the gospel continues with chapter 21, which appears to be an epilogue that was added to the gospel. The chapter resolves issues of Peter's status after his denial of Jesus (21:15–19) as well as rumors about the beloved disciple (21:20–3). Another possible addition to an earlier version of the gospel are chapters 15–17, Jesus's farewell words to his disciples. Note the way chapter 14 concludes with Jesus saying, "Rise, let us be on our way," but then Jesus continues speaking for three more chapters. Some scholars argue that what modern readers see as breaks in the text resemble similar literary patterns found in ancient Greek drama. Apart from theories of composition, most scholars think the gospel in its present form is the latest of the canonical gospels, probably undergoing a final editing sometime between 95 and 125 CE, or perhaps even later in the second century (Figure 14.1).

The Johannine Jesus as God's Divine Agent in the World

Following the prologue, the story gets under way. Like the Gospel of Mark, the Gospel of John has no birth narrative. Jesus enters the narrative first mostly by way of others' descriptions of him. He appears to draw followers

FIGURE 14.1

This famous papyrus fragment, Rylands Library P52, contains seven lines from John 18:31–3 on the front and lines from 18:37–8 on the back. The precise date of the fragment is unknown but most scholars date it to the first half of the second century CE.

to him simply by walking around. Moreover, those who encounter the Johannine Jesus generate an impressive list of titles for him. Just in the first chapter, the Johannine Jesus is called the lamb of God, rabbi, messiah, one written about in the law and prophets, son of Joseph from Nazareth, Son of God, king of Israel, and Son of Man. Apart from "lamb of God," we have already seen most of these titles in the synoptic gospels. What is different in the Gospel of John is that these traditional titles become far less prominent in the rest of the gospel.

Much more frequently, the gospel depicts the Johannine Jesus as "the one sent" by God or "from above" (for example, 3:34; 5:38; 6:29, 44, 57; 7:16, 28–9; 10:36; 11:42). He is also called the one coming into the world (1:9; 11:27). Likewise, both the Johannine Jesus and the narrator frequently refer to God as the one who sent him. In fact, this type of reference to God occurs more than two dozen times! (See, for example, 3:17; 4:34; 5:23–4; 5:37; 6:38–9; 7:16; 8:42; 9:34; 11:45; 12:49, and so on.) In effect, the Johannine Jesus is represented as a divine agent of God, sent into the world to follow God's commands. Indeed, this is how the Johannine Jesus describes his presence in the world. He claims that he can do nothing on his own but seeks only to do the will of the one who sent him. Likewise, he claims that his words are not his own, but he speaks as he has been instructed (5:19, 30; 8:28; 14:10). As a divine agent, the Johannine Jesus has been given "works" to complete by the Father (5:36). His teaching is not his own, but the teaching of the one who sent him (7:16). He does as the Father has commanded (14:31).

This also suggests that the Johannine Jesus functions in a subordinate role to the Father. Indeed, he says just this when he tells his disciples, "the Father is greater than I" (14:28). Paradoxically, however, because the Johannine Jesus is so intimately associated with God, he can also say "I am in the Father and the Father is in me" and "the Father and I are one" (10:30; 17:22). He claims that those who know him also know the Father (14:7), and those who honor him also honor the Father (5:22–3). This paradoxical relationship recalls the opening lines of the gospel, where the *logos* is said to be both *with* God *and* God (1:1).

If the Johannine Jesus is an agent sent from God, "one coming into the world," he is also one who anticipates departing from the world and returning to the Father (13:1, 14:28; 16:5). Because he is not of this world, but "from above" (8:23), his death can be spoken of figuratively as a "lifting up" (3:14; 8:28; 12:32) or even a glorification (12:23, 27–8; 13:31; 17:1). Again, note how different this depiction of Jesus is from, for example, the Markan Jesus. In Mark 14:36, an anguished Jesus prays in a place called Gethsemane to "have the hour pass from him." In contrast, almost as if commenting on this

Gethsemane tradition, the Johannine Jesus states, "Now my soul is troubled. And what should I say, 'Father, save me from this hour?' On the contrary, I have come for this hour" (John 12:27). This decisive statement shows how in the Gospel of John, the crucifixion is not depicted as a sacrificial death for others. Rather, it signals Jesus's departure from the world back to his divine origins. It is the ultimate sign of his glory, which in turn, reflects the glory of God (John 17:4–5).

The "I Am" Sayings in the Gospel of John

The gospel writer regularly presents Jesus talking with other characters, though these conversations often feature lengthy monologues from Jesus. This is another way that the Johannine Jesus differs from what we have seen in the synoptic gospels. Recall how the Markan Jesus commanded those he healed, as well as his own disciples, to say nothing to anyone about his identity. In sharp contrast, the Johannine Jesus speaks openly about his identity throughout the narrative. The gospel writer even calls attention to this point as the Johannine Jesus tells the high priest, "I have said nothing in secret" (John 18:20, also 7:25).

This open speech involves the use of the Greek phrase *ego eimi* ("I am"). The Johannine Jesus uses this phrase across the narrative, both when he speaks with other characters and in longer discourses about himself. The phrase is often used metaphorically. For example, the Johannine Jesus describes himself as the bread of life (6:35, 48), the living bread that comes down from heaven (6:51), the light of the world (8:12), the gate for the sheep (10:7), the good shepherd (10:11), the resurrection and life (11:25), the way, truth, and life (14:16), and the true vine (15:1). Such self-descriptive statements are unique to the Gospel of John. They offer a rich array of images alongside the traditional titles applied to Jesus, like those in chapter 1. For this gospel writer, it seems that the identity of Jesus cannot be expressed fully with traditional titles like messiah or king. He uses these metaphorical "I am" statements to symbolically evoke the life-giving significance of the Johannine Jesus.

In some instances, the *ego eimi* ("I am") phrase stands on its own. In English translations, these occasions are typically rendered "I am he" (John 8:24, 28, 58; 13:19; 18:6, 8). While grammatically correct, this translation dilutes the intended force of the phrase. In the Septuagint, especially in the oracles of Isaiah, this unmodified "I am" connotes divine, self-revelatory speech. So, for example, in the Greek Septuagint version of Isaiah 43:10, God declares that God's witnesses are to "know and believe and understand that I am" (*ego eimi*). This is perhaps an echo of Exodus 3:14, when Moses asks God to reveal his name and God responds, "I am (*ego eimi*) the one who is" (see also Isaiah 43:25). In the Gospel of John, Jesus's use of "I am" by itself carries a similar weight – it is revelatory language. This is most clear in the arrest scene. When the soldiers report that they are looking for Jesus of Nazareth, the Johannine Jesus replies, "I am." The author obviously intends to convey a more significant idea than Jesus simply identifying himself for arrest. We can tell this is the case first, because the phrase is repeated and second, because the soldiers react by stepping back and falling to the ground! (John 18:6). This is not an action one would expect from those coming out to arrest a man. It *is* a reaction that makes sense if the point is to show that these words are revelatory. The "I am" statement in the arrest scene is meant to reinforce the divine quality of Jesus for the gospel audience. To this end, note how Jesus's statement does not play a crucial role in the plot. In fact, after the dramatic reaction of the soldiers, the story proceeds as if they had not just fallen to the ground! Here is another place that shows how the gospel writers are doing more than simply narrating a story about Jesus; they are shaping their stories to communicate their understanding of Jesus to their audiences.

Knowing and Believing in the Johannine Jesus

John 9 and 11. Pay attention to the questions and responses between different characters or character groups in these two chapters.

The focus on who Jesus is and where he comes from in the Gospel of John serves another central theme in the gospel. Those who encounter the Johannine Jesus are called on to recognize who he is and to believe in him. This aspect of the narrative works at two levels – inside and outside of the story world. Inside the story world, the characters of the gospel are confronted with the question of knowing and believing in Jesus. Some form of the verb *pisteuo* (to believe or to trust) occurs 98 times in the Gospel of John. Compare this to the Gospel of Mark, where the verb occurs just eleven times (and even less in Matthew and Luke). The blind man healed by the Johannine Jesus is asked by him, "Do you believe?" (John 9:35–8). Martha, too, is asked whether she believes in Jesus as "the resurrection and the life" (11:25–6).

There are places where the words of the Johannine Jesus seem more directed toward the gospel audience *outside* the story world than at characters *in* the story. Notice, for example, how the conversation with Nicodemus blends into a more general speech about belief in the Son of God (John 3:11–21). Perhaps the Johannine Jesus is still speaking to Nicodemus at 3:15 but starting at 3:16 the third person references to the Son and the Father suggest that these are now the narrator's words. Another example occurs in chapter 12 where Jesus has departed and gone into hiding (12:36), and soon after "cries out" and then summarizes his teaching about belief in him and in "the Father" (12:44–50). This blurring between story and audience means that those hearing the gospel face the same challenge. Both are confronted with the question of belief in Jesus. Indeed, at the end of the gospel, the audience is told explicitly that these things were written so that "you all may believe that Jesus is the Christ, the Son of God" (John 20:30–1).

One major way that characters in the gospel come to belief is by seeing "signs" performed by Jesus. Here, too, the Gospel of John differs from the synoptic gospels. The Markan Jesus performs miracles (*dunameis*) to indicate that the kingdom of God is near. The Johannine Jesus's signs (*semeia*) point to his divine identity. They "reveal his glory" (John 2:11). In some cases, the Johannine Jesus's signs become occasions for further conversation about who he is. The two primary examples are the story of the healing of the blind man (John 9:1–7) and the raising of Lazarus (John 11:38–44). In both of these accounts, the healing event is narrated in just a few verses. Both of these healing scenes are part of longer narratives that help the audience see a deeper meaning in Jesus's actions. The healing of the man born blind, for instance, becomes an occasion to contrast the "blindness" of the Pharisees with the sight of the formerly blind man. The Pharisees are unable to recognize the Johannine Jesus as one sent from God. In contrast, the once blind man gradually sees who Jesus is. He moves from calling Jesus a man (9:11), to a prophet (9:17), to one who is from God (9:33), to a direct confession of belief in and worship of Jesus (9:38–9). Similarly, the raising of Lazarus precedes a discussion between Jesus and Martha that prepares the reader to understand the raising of Lazarus as an indication that Jesus is "the resurrection and the life" (11:25). The conversation also elicits Martha's full confession of faith before the sign even occurs (11:25–7).

MORE ON METHOD: GENDER CRITICISM AND MASCULINITY STUDIES

Gender criticism grew out of feminist criticism, expanding the focus from considerations of women and the Bible to an examination of how a culture "constructs" gender by defining what is "normal" or "recognizable" for different gender identities. For the study of the New Testament, gender criticism includes analyzing evidence from the first-century Greco-Roman culture to understand how that ancient culture defined what it meant to be a man or woman. Whereas early feminist studies focused on the roles of women in the gospel, gender critical approaches compare how both female and male characters are depicted in the gospel in relation to each other and to the Johannine Jesus. (See, for example, Colleen M. Conway, *Men and Women in the Fourth Gospel: Gender and Johannine Characterization.* Atlanta: SBL Press, 1999.)

> **Critical masculinity studies** of the Bible analyze social and literary constructions of masculinities. New Testament masculinity studies often compare depictions of New Testament characters to first-century CE Greco-Roman ideas about being "manly." Here is one brief example of what we learn from this approach. As we learned in Chapter 13, many Greek and Roman writers emphasize self-control as a primary measure of one's manliness. This idea of self-control extended to control over one's own body. Having one's body violated by another was seen as emasculating. Seen through the lens of critical masculinity studies, when the Johannine Jesus claims that "no one takes" his life from him, and that he has the power to lay it down and take it up (John 10:18), it is a way for the author to depict the Johannine Jesus as asserting a manly self-control over his own body. Having this assertion made before the crucifixion is a way of encouraging the ancient audience to view the Johannine Jesus's death as a voluntary and thus honorable death rather than a shameful, emasculating death. (See "Resources for Further Study" at the end of the chapter for examples of New Testament masculinity studies.)

These two examples illustrate a main theme in the gospel, that belief in the Johannine Jesus is the criterion for eternal life and salvation (3:16–18). This may seem unremarkable until we recall that not all the gospel writers make this point. For example, the Gospel of Matthew has a different emphasis. There, as we have seen, one enters the kingdom of heaven because one is Torah obedient, doing the will of God, and (or through) following Christ. But as the Gospel of John unfolds, characters are portrayed in terms of their recognition and belief in Jesus as one sent by God. In fact, the gospel prologue prepares us for this theme. Already in the first chapter, the gospel contrasts the world "who did not know him" and his own "who did not accept him" with those who "received him" and "believed in his name" (1:10–12). The rest of this chapter will explore how the gospel develops the contrast between these groups in relation to the Johannine Jesus.

Opposition from the World

READING

John 14–17. Pay attention to the depiction of "the world" in these chapters in relation to Jesus and his disciples.

A pronouncement that comes early in the gospel is that the Johannine Jesus was sent by God to save the world (John 3:16–17). This conclusion is also reached by the Samaritans who declare that Jesus is "truly, the savior of the world!" (4:42). Despite these claims, the rest of the gospel suggests that "the world" is decidedly hostile toward the Johannine Jesus and his followers. This theme of hostility from the world is conveyed most strongly in the farewell discourse, the name that scholars give to the Johannine Jesus's parting words to his disciples in chapters 14–16. In this discourse, the Johannine Jesus acknowledges to his followers that the world hates him, and therefore may hate them also (15:18). He explains how he will reveal himself to his followers but not to the world (14:22–3), and he asserts that in the world his followers have affliction, or more literally "pressure" (16:33). The Johannine Jesus has chosen his followers out of the world and instead of loving the world, he loves "his own who were in the world" (13:1). Together this language creates a sense of alienation on the one hand and group cohesion on the other. Note, for example, that the Johannine Jesus commands his disciples to "love one another" (13:34). This is quite different from Jesus's command in Matthew and Luke to love one's enemies (Matt 5:44//Luke 6:27). The Johannine command focuses on relations between Christ-followers who do not belong to the world, but rather have been "chosen out of the world" (John 15:19).

The Johannine Jesus also speaks of an ongoing struggle with "the ruler of this world." Earlier in the gospel he claims that this ruler will be driven out (12:31). In the farewell discourse, Jesus tells his disciples that he will no longer be able to speak with the disciples because the ruler of the world is coming (14:30). Nevertheless, the Johannine Jesus asserts also that this "ruler" has no control of him (14:30), and that the ruler has been condemned (16:11). Indeed, the Johannine Jesus proclaims that he has conquered the world (16:33). What should we make of these references to the "ruler of this world"? It is likely that the author had the figure of Satan in mind, although this designation explicitly appears only once in the gospel at 13:27. But it is also true that for the ancient audience, the Roman emperor was quite visibly "the ruler of this world." In either case, the audience is urged to believe that (appearances notwithstanding) the Johannine Jesus has gained a victory over the present earthly authority and therefore conquered the world. Maintaining such a belief would be both a catharsis and a challenge in a world in which the Romans exerted their power at will in the lands they occupied.

Some scholars interpret the gospel's polemical language regarding the world as an indication of **Johannine sectarianism**. This is a technical term that comes from the sociological study of religious groups. It describes a type of group that has withdrawn from the broader culture and defines itself in opposition to it. When applied to the Gospel of John, the term sectarianism involves a historical claim that there existed a distinct Johannine community that defined itself not only against those who did not believe in Jesus, but also against other Christ-followers. As we will see below, the Johannine Letters may support the idea of Johannine sectarianism. However, not all agree that the gospel's polemical language provides evidence of sectarianism. There is no evidence outside of the Johannine literature for the existence of a separate "Johannine" community of Christ-followers that distinguished itself from other Christ-followers. It could be that the language of being "hated" by the world and not being "of the world" is a rhetorical strategy designed to *foster* a group identity rather than a reflection of an actual group. (See textbox: "Was there a Johannine Community?") One might feel comforted by descriptions of mutual love between those who believe. Similarly, expressions of unity could create a sense of belonging. Finally, for those living under foreign rule, a narrative depicting a powerful divine figure who claimed to have conquered the world and its evil ruler would have a powerful appeal.

The Johannine Jesus promises another means of comfort in his parting words. He says that he will send a **Paraclete** after his departure. This Greek word literally means "one who is called beside to help" and is variously translated as comforter, advocate, intercessor, and counselor. This full range of meanings is lost when one chooses one English word over another. In addition to being a comforter or advocate, the Paraclete will testify on behalf of the Johannine Jesus (15:26; 16:8). Presumably, this means the advocate will defend the gospel's claims about the identity of Jesus as God's divine representative who was sent into the world. Finally, the Paraclete will guide and instruct the believers (16:13–14) and remind them of Jesus's words (14:26). Because the Gospel of John itself guides, instructs and reminds later believers of Jesus's words, the author may be suggesting that the Paraclete has been active in its composition.

The Problem of "the Jews" in the Gospel of John

READING

John 6, 8–9. Pay attention to the gospel's portrayal of "the Jews" in these chapters, especially the language used by the Johannine Jesus in his exchanges with this group.

In addition to a general opposition from the world, the Johannine Jesus encounters opposition from a group identified as "the Jews" (*hoi Iudaioi*). We have already seen the negative portrayal of scribes, Pharisees, and chief priests in the synoptic traditions, but only in the Gospel of John do we find frequent use of the general phrase "the Jews" to refer to opponents of Jesus. From the beginning of the gospel, this group persecutes Jesus (5:16), seeks to kill him (5:18; 7:1, 25), complains about him (6:41), claims that he is demon-possessed (8:48, 52), tries to stone him (10:31), and insists over Pilate's protests that Jesus must die (19:7). During the trial of Jesus, the narrative aligns the "Jews" with the Roman emperor. They hint to Pilate that releasing Jesus would be treasonous, and they openly claim that they have no king but Caesar (19:12, 15). "The

Jews" cause fear in others in this gospel. The parents of the formerly blind man will not speak to the authorities about Jesus because they are afraid that they will be expelled from the synagogue (9:22). This fear is reiterated later in the gospel when some of the leaders keep their belief in Jesus a secret, again because of the fear of expulsion (12:42).

The gospel's portrayal of "the Jews" as hostile opponents of Jesus is reinforced by the negative rhetoric directed at the Jews by the Johannine Jesus. The Jews are from "below" and are "of this world" (8:23). He wonders why he bothers speaking with them and has much to condemn about them (8:25–6). Most troubling, the Johannine Jesus denies their claim that they are children of Abraham (a foundational truth claim for Jewish identity) and insists instead that their father is the devil, "a murderer from the beginning" and "the father of lies" (8:44). In his farewell discourse, the Johannine Jesus prepares his followers for expulsion from the synagogue and death at the hands of his opponents (16:2).

The Gospel of John also offers a paradoxical picture of Jesus in relation to Jewish ritual practices. On the one hand, the story of the Johannine Jesus unfolds in relation to the Jewish Sabbath and festivals (John 2:13; 5:1, 9–10; 7:2, 22–3; 14; 12:1). On the other hand, the rhetoric of the gospel frequently distances Jesus and his followers from Jewish traditions in general. In speaking to "the Jews," the Johannine Jesus refers to "your law" (8:17; 10:34; 18:31), as if it is not also his law. Recall that the Matthean Jesus insisted that he came to *fulfill* the law. How different is this gospel's depiction of Jesus's attitude toward "the Jews" and "their" law! We see a similar distancing from the Jewish traditions in the gospel references to "the festival of the Jews" or "the "Passover of the Jews" (John 2:13; 5:1; 6:4; 11:55). It is as though the gospel's author and audience no longer viewed these festivals as their own.

Understanding who is intended by the use of the term "the Jews" and the reasons for this strongly negative portrayal has been one of the most important yet vexing problems of recent scholarship on the Gospel of John. The issue became particularly pressing in the aftermath of World War II, when the Nazi genocide perpetrated on European Jews became more widely acknowledged. Many Christians began to examine Christian complicity, not only in this horrific event, but also in contributing more generally to the long history of anti-Semitism. One part of this process has been reconsidering the portrayal of the Jews and Judaism in biblical texts like the Gospel of John.

A first step is to view the gospel in its late first-century CE context, the setting of the gospel's composition, rather than as an accurate account of the time of Jesus. Here is a place where it is particularly important to maintain a distinction between the historical Jesus and the textual Jesus. Indeed, there is widespread agreement among biblical critics that the historical Jesus would not have distanced himself from the Jewish tradition in the way he is described as doing in this gospel. That said, even shifting the interpretive focus to the time of the gospel's composition can be a problem. Indeed, one prominent theory posits that the Gospel of John reflects a time when Jewish Christians were being driven out of their local synagogues because of their belief in Jesus. According to this theory, the Johannine Jesus's strong invectives against the Jews actually represent the Johannine community's reaction to being persecuted by local synagogue leaders. (See textbox "Was there a Johannine Community.") The problem with this interpretation is that the gospel is still perceived as an accurate account of Jewish misdeeds, if not in Jesus's time (Jews killing Jesus), then in the time of the gospel writer (Jews persecuting early Christians). From here it is a short step to viewing the victimized church as superior to the persecuting synagogue (see Figure 14.2).

This dominant theory about the Gospel of John and the Jewish persecution of early Christians has serious limitations. A major problem is that the gospel reflects a one-sided view of this heated conflict in which Jesus's opponents are cast in the worst possible light. It is more likely that the animosity flowed both ways. Anyone who has ever had a bitter argument with a once-close friend should be wary of taking the depiction of "the Jews" in the Gospel of John at face value, whether in the time of Jesus, or in the late first/early second century CE. Unfortunately, the historical details of this ancient argument are lost to us. Some evidence suggests that in the second century the worry for some Christian writers was that people were *returning* to the synagogue, not being *driven from* it. If this worry was present when the gospel was written, it would explain the gospel's strong emphasis on belief in Jesus. The gospel's depiction of Christ-confessors being rejected by the synagogue may have been a rhetorical way of discouraging a return to the synagogue. Another possibility may be that in the author's local setting the assembly of Christ-followers had already separated from the synagogue. If this is the case, the depiction of Jesus and "the Jews" in John's gospel may serve an explanatory role. It would explain how their current

FIGURE 14.2
Medieval Christian image of the church preferred over the synagogue. The angel under Christ's arm on the left ushers in the church, while the angel under Christ's arm on the right violently drives out the synagogue, who is blindfolded and has lost her crown.

division came to be (not necessarily accurately), projecting their own tensions back into the life of Jesus. It would not be the first time that we have seen traditional stories (in this case, the story of Jesus) retold to provide a meaningful foundation for a later community.

Was There a Johannine Community?

Beginning in the mid-twentieth century, scholarship on the Gospel and Letters of John has been dominated by the idea of a Johannine community and its relationship with the synagogue. In North America, the work of J. Louis Martyn has been enormously influential in the development of what we could call the "synagogue expulsion" theory (*History and Theology in the Fourth Gospel.* New York: Harper & Row, 1968). Martyn famously described the Gospel of John as a "two-level drama." He meant that on the surface level, the gospel tells the story of Jesus. But on a second, deeper level, it tells the history of a distinct group of Christ-followers living decades after the time of Jesus. A crucial part of this group's history, according to Martyn's two-level reading, was that the group was expelled from a synagogue community (John 9:22 and 12:42). A later stage of this history supposedly involved a split within the community, based on a verse in 1 John that says, "they went out from us" (1 John 2:19).

Other scholars have challenged this type of "mirror reading" where the interpreter assumes that one can read accurately a detailed community history through a narrative about Jesus. Scholars such as Adele Reinhartz have focused instead on the rhetorical strategies of the gospel. For instance, Reinhartz does not assume that the gospel's references to synagogue expulsion reflect historical events. Rather, she considers how the expulsion passages along with the gospel's anti-Jewish language might *shape* a group identity. In this reading, the language of the gospel works to discourage Christ-followers from participating in the Jewish synagogue community (the rhetoric of disaffiliation) and to promote ongoing relationships with a distinct group of Christ-followers (the rhetoric of affiliation) (see Reinhartz in "Resources for Further Study").

Another line of scholarship suggests that none of the canonical gospels, John included, were written to address distinct audiences or groups of Christ-followers, as in a "Johannine community" or a "Matthean community" (see Richard Baukham, ed., *The Gospel for all Christians: Rethinking the Gospel Audiences.* Grand Rapids, MI: Eerdmans, 1998). The theory of a Johannine community will no doubt be an ongoing point of debate for Johannine scholarship.

Postcolonial criticism offers yet another way to understand the dynamics of the Gospel of John. As we saw in our study of the Gospel of Matthew, the destruction of Jerusalem by Rome opened the way for different Jewish movements to compete for power and the allegiance of the Jewish people. Our study of the Gospel of Mark suggested that the conflict of Jesus with the scribes and Pharisees from Jerusalem may reflect political as well as religious conflict between Christ-followers and collaborators with Rome. Both of these dynamics may be present in the Gospel of John. However, in this case, the gospel explicitly addresses the Judean leaders' *fear* of Rome and links that fear to their perception of Jesus:

> So the chief priests and the Pharisees gathered the council, and said, "What should we do? This man is doing many signs. If we allow him to go on like this, all will believe in him, and the Romans will come and destroy our place and our people." (11:47–8)

Here, the opponents of the Johannine Jesus view belief in him as a threat, not primarily to their religious beliefs, but to their safety and survival under Roman occupation. They see him as dangerous precisely because he may draw the unwelcome attention of Rome to their land. While we are intended to see the Jews and the Pharisees as the opponents of Jesus, a postcolonial reading can sympathize with these "chief priests and Pharisees" as they struggle to ward off imperial violence. Depicted as the leaders of the religious community, they are in fact powerless before the empire and can only hope to divert Roman attention from their nation by silencing Jesus and therefore the crowds he attracts. This expression of the tension of living under Roman occupation may be one historically accurate element of the narrative.

In an ironic way, the gospel writer uses this scene to put a fundamental claim about the significance of the death of Jesus into words voiced by the chief priest:

> "You don't understand that it is more to your advantage to have one man die for the sake of the people than to have the whole nation destroyed." He did not say this on his own, but being high priest that year he prophesied that Jesus was about to die for the sake of the nation, and not for the nation only, but so that the scattered children of God might be gathered into one. (11:50–2 modified from the NRSV)

With this assertion, the gospel writer hints still more at the trauma of a colonized people. After all, the gospel was written after the whole Jewish nation *had* been destroyed by Rome. While the gospel writer does not acknowledge that brutal reality directly, this tragic irony should not be lost on us as contemporary readers.

FOCUS TEXT

John 17

John 17 is a prayer that comes at the conclusion of the farewell discourse (John 14–16). There are a number of places in the gospel where the Johannine Jesus summarizes the message of the gospel (3:31–6; 5:19–24; 12:44–50), but only here does such a summary come in the form of a prayer. This artfully crafted passage has three sections: the Johannine Jesus prays for himself in 17:1–5; he prays for his disciples in 17:6–19; and he prays for future believers in 17:20–4, before a concluding statement in 17:25–6.

In the opening section, the prayer points to the temporal dimension of the incarnation: at the time of his departure, the Johannine Jesus takes the audience back to the prologue, recalling the glory he had as the pre-existent *logos* in the presence of God (17:5) and acknowledging that the "hour" has now arrived

(17:1). While this hour indicates his impending death, Jesus prays for glorification from the Father so that he may glorify God in turn. Jesus recalls the authority given to him by God over "all flesh" (17:2), but also the qualified nature of this authority. The Johannine Jesus may give eternal life only to those whom the Father has given him. Such language reminds the audience that Jesus does not act independently of God. It also explains why not all have believed in Jesus, an issue that we have seen trouble other New Testament writers, like Paul. Notably, the prayer includes a defining statement about eternal life: "This is eternal life; that they may know you, the only true God, and the one whom you sent, Jesus Christ" (17:3 modified from NRSV). This definition of eternal life connects with the central purpose of the gospel. In this sense, for the gospel writer, gaining eternal life is not something that happens when one dies. It does not mean, for example, "going to heaven." According to the Johannine Jesus, eternal life is a present reality available for those who recognize Jesus and God as presented in the gospel.

Scholars refer to this idea as **realized eschatology**. That is, the tradition of a future judgment and salvation available in the "last days" is here transformed into an already realized state of affairs in the life of a believer. We see indications of this realized eschatology earlier in the gospel where the Johannine Jesus paradoxically proclaims, "the hour is coming and is now here" (4:23; 5:25; 16:32). Indeed, he regularly teaches about the present possibility of eternal life (5:24; 6:47, 54; 10:28; 11:25–6) and the present reality of judgment (3:19; 5:22–4), both of which are linked to knowing and believing in Jesus and God.

In the second part of the prayer, the Johannine Jesus petitions God on behalf of his disciples who will remain in the world once he is gone (17:6–19). These disciples are described as the ones whom God gave to Jesus "from out of the world" (17:6). They are counted among those who have recognized the Johannine Jesus. They know that he came from God and was sent by him (17:8). The Johannine Jesus prays for the same unity for them that he shares with the Father (17:11). Meanwhile, he also reinforces their sense of alienation from the world; the world hates them because they do not belong to it (17:14). In this way, the prayer contributes to the inward turn of this gospel. It helps to construct a group identity that draws strength through its perception of victimization and alienation vis-à-vis the world. Note that the Johannine Jesus asks that God protect his followers from the "evil one" (17:15). Primarily this designates a supernatural evil power, "Satan," but, as noted earlier, from the audience's perspective such a reference could also include the earthly authorities in whom this evil is manifest – the Roman emperor, as well as local governing authorities.

Finally, the prayer reaches forward to the future to address believers who were not immediate disciples of Jesus but "will believe because of their word" (17:20–4). This may include the audience of the gospel, as well as other future believers. The hope for unity or "oneness" extends to these future believers as well. However, the prayer's reference to future believers lacks the urgency or imminent apocalyptic expectations we read in the letters of Paul. The concluding section of the prayer reiterates the theme of unity and mutual love. By becoming "completely one," believers will be a witness to the world; they show that Jesus was sent by God and that they are loved by God (17:22–3). Finally, the prayer returns to the place where the gospel began as the Johannine Jesus reiterates ideas from the gospel prologue. He highlights the eternal relationship between the Father and the Son, whom God loved "before the foundation of the world" (17:24 see 1:1). Though the world does not know God (17:25; see 1:10), Jesus's role is to make him known (17:26 see 1:18). In the prologue, those who believe in Jesus, become God's children (1:12-13). In Jesus's final words of the prayer, those to whom Jesus has made God known are infused with the love of God and the abiding presence of Jesus (17:26 see 1:12-13).

The Johannine Letters

READING

1, 2, and 3 John. What similarities to you see between the Johannine Letters and the Gospel of John?

The texts of 1, 2, and 3 John, although quite different from one another, are commonly grouped together as the Johannine Letters. This is the case even though 1 John is not actually a letter, and none of the texts indicates the name of its author. Nevertheless, the language of each of the texts is so similar to the language and dualistic worldview of the Gospel of John that they seem connected to the gospel in some way. Perhaps they were written by the same person who revised the original gospel, or simply by someone familiar with the language and traditions of the gospel.

The longest of these three texts, 1 John, most closely reflects the ideas of the Gospel of John. In fact, the opening verse recalls the opening verse of the gospel, with its reference to what was in "the beginning" (1 John 1:1; see John 1:1). Likewise, the opening section of the letter contains the dualistic language of the gospel. The world of 1 John is characterized by light versus dark, love versus hate, obedience versus disobedience, children of God versus children of the devil (1 John 1:5–7; 2:9–10; 3:10). The "Paraclete" is also mentioned, identified as Jesus Christ (1 John 2:1). The letter shares the same animosity toward "the world" as we saw in the gospel (1 John 2:15–17; 3:13; 4:4–5), and it reiterates the commandment that the letter's audience should believe in Jesus and love one another (1 John 3:23; 4:11). Such evidence points to some type of relationship between 1 John and the Gospel of John.

Many scholars have focused on 1 John 2:19 as a clue to understanding the occasion for the writing of this text. Here the author refers to a group "who went out from us, but were not from us." This verse, in addition to the repeated references to those who "hate their brothers" (1 John 3:15; 4:20; see also 2:11), suggests that a break occurred in the author's community. There are several places in 1 John that work to bolster the group solidarity of the audience over against those who left. The author refers to the coming of an "antichrist" and the presence of "many antichrists" just before he writes about those who left the group (1 John 2:18). Later, the author writes that "every spirit that confesses that Jesus Christ has come in the flesh is from God, and every spirit who does not confess Jesus is not from God" (1 John 4: 2-3 NRSV). The authority of the writer is reinforced with statements such as "the one who knows God, listens to us. The one who is not from God, does not listen to us" (1 John 4:6).

We cannot be certain about the chronological relationship between 1 John and the Gospel of John. The dominant theory has been that 1 John was written *after* the Gospel of John, reflecting a later stage in the life of a particular group of Christ-followers. This theory suggests that the controversy in 1 John was no longer with the synagogue but was internal to the community and involved differing ideas about Christ. But, as mentioned above, it may be that some of the community were returning to the synagogue, no longer confessing that Jesus is the messiah and Son of God. If this is the case, the controversy could have generated the type of animosity toward "the Jews" that is reflected in the gospel. The fact is that the author's references to those who left are vague, suggesting that they were not the main focus of his composition. Perhaps the most we can say is that 1 John is concerned to shape and strengthen the identity of a group of Christ-followers and he does so in ways that coincide with the worldview and language of the Gospel of John.

The brief letters of 2 and 3 John draw on the same language but apply it to different situations. For example, 2 John, written by "the elder" to an "excellent lady," uses the same language of truth and love versus deceivers and also references "the antichrist" (2 John 1:4-7). (Note that while the figure of "the antichrist" looms large in some Christian imaginations, the references in 1 and 2 John are the only places the term occurs in the New Testament.) 2 John also specifically discourages the recipient from offering hospitality to those who do not come with the "teaching of Christ" (2 John 1:10-11). Even more specific is 3 John. It refers to a conflict between the author and a certain Diotrephes who does not recognize the author's authority (3 John 1:9). These texts, together with 1 John, reflect an ongoing tradition that flowed out of a "Johannine" way of conceiving of Jesus, God, and the believers' role in relation to the world.

CHAPTER FOURTEEN REVIEW

1 Know the meaning and significance of the following terms:
   - gender criticism
   - incarnation (especially for the Gospel of John)
   - Johannine sectarianism
   - masculinity studies
   - Paraclete
   - realized eschatology

2 In the Gospel of Matthew, one must obey to enter the kingdom of heaven. What does one need to do according to the Gospel of John? How is this shown in the gospel?

3 What is the dominant theory about why the Gospel of John depicts Jews rejecting Jesus, and Jesus as hostile to "the Jews"? What are the problems with this theory, and what might be an alternative understanding of the background to this theme in John?

4 How might postcolonial theory inform our view of tensions between Jews and Jewish Christ-followers at the time the gospel was written?

5 (Focus text: John 17) How does Jesus's prayer in John 17 represent a shift from the expectation in some other New Testament texts (e.g. Paul) of the coming of the last days? How do you understand the gospel's definition of "eternal life"? How might the gospel's idea of eternal life appeal to people living in the late first or second century?

6 What similarities are there between the Johannine Letters and the Gospel of John?

RESOURCES FOR FURTHER STUDY

Brant, Jo-Ann. *John*. Grand Rapids, MI: Baker Academic, 2011.

Brown, Raymond Edward. *The Gospel according to John*. Vol. 29, 29A. The Anchor Bible. Garden City, NY: Doubleday, 1966 and 1970. A dated, but detailed critical study of the gospel.

Conway, Colleen M. *Behold the Man: Jesus and Greco-Roman Masculinity*. Oxford: Oxford University Press, 2008.

Conway, Colleen M. *John and the Johannine Letters*. Abingdon Press, 2017.

Lieu, Judith. *I, II, III John: A Commentary*. Louisville, KY: Westminster John Knox Press, 2008.

Reinhartz, Adele. *Cast Out of the Covenant: Jews and Anti-Judaism in the Gospel of John*. Lanham, MD: Lexington Books and Fortress Academic, 2018.

Following Christ in the Empire: Diverse Approaches in the New Testament

15

Chapter Overview

As we approach the end of this introduction to the Bible, this chapter compares how three different writers connected belief in Jesus as the messiah to daily life in the broader culture of the Roman empire. The Revelation to John, Hebrews, and 1 Peter represent three different literary genres, as well as three different responses to the experience of living under imperial rule as a Christ-follower.

We first discuss the Revelation to John, a text that expresses a resistant and hostile stance toward the empire. Even with its coded language, it is the most blatant of the New Testament writings in its attacks on Roman rule. We then turn to Hebrews, a writing that appears less concerned with Rome than it is with the relations of Christ-followers to the Jewish sacrificial cult. Still, the effects of imperial conquest are evident as the author of Hebrews draws on a Greek philosophical framework to talk about Jesus. Moreover, the emphasis in Hebrews on the alien status of believers suggests the author's unease with the current state of world affairs. The third text, 1 Peter, offers another form of

A Contemporary Introduction to the Bible: Sacred Texts and Imperial Contexts, Second Edition. Colleen M. Conway and David M. Carr.
© 2021 Colleen M. Conway and David M. Carr. Published 2021 by John Wiley & Sons Ltd.

accommodation to life in the empire. As in Hebrews, we find references to exile and alienation. But 1 Peter also offers guidance for Christ-followers who face difficult questions of accommodation versus resistance to Roman power.

The Revelation to John: Visions of "Conquering" Roman Power

Revelation 1–5, 12–21.

READING

The Greek word in the title of the last book in the New Testament book is *apokalypsis*. The actual title of the book is the "Apocalypse of John." In popular usage, this word has come to mean a frightening, catastrophic event. Some years ago, for instance, the US media named a big snowstorm "snowpocalypse." But as we now know, the Greek word means "uncovering." It signifies revealing something that is hidden. That is why in English the book is often called "Revelation to John." However, we should keep in mind that the "apocalypse" in the name of this book also designates a literary genre. We saw one biblical example of this genre in Daniel 7–12. There are many more examples of the genre from the Second Temple period that are not in the Bible. To begin our discussion of Revelation, we will focus on two questions: What is "apocalyptic" about the apocalypse of John? And what is the point of this apocalyptic book?

As you may recall from Chapter 7, the literary genre of apocalypse reveals divine wisdom to its audience and occurs in two general forms: heavenly apocalypses that feature tours of heaven by the seer and historical apocalypses that predict divine intervention against foreign rulers. Both of these literary types typically include the use of symbols, reference to numbers, animals, or strange beasts, and an angelic mediator who interprets the meaning of these things. The book of Revelation draws on all of these generic features. The book opens with John's vision of a flaming-eyed, white-haired, bronzed-footed "one like the Son of Man" who recites messages to be written to seven communities in cities around Asia Minor (Map 15.1). As the book continues, the seer offers the audience visions of God's heavenly throne room, cosmic battle scenes, and eventually the gruesome destruction of a so-called "whore of Babylon." Such scenes are what make the book an "apocalypse" in the literary sense.

As for the question of the book's purpose, it may not be what you have been led to think. Many modern appropriations of the Revelation to John, whether in film, websites, novels, or sermons, are designed to instill fear in the audience. And the book certainly contains plenty of frightening images: torturing locusts with scales and scorpions' tails (Rev 9:1–10), seven-headed dragons ready to devour a newborn child (Rev 12:1–17), and a multi-headed,

Basics on Revelation to John

Outline: John's vision of wrath and renewal

At one time, the "John" of Revelation was thought to be the author of both the Gospel and Letters of John, who was also thought to be the apostle John. Now few would identify the disciple John of the gospels as the author of any of these texts. In fact, scholars no longer think the same author wrote all of these texts. There is no reason to doubt that the author of Revelation was named John since this was a very common name. We should simply consider him to be a leader among the groups of Christ-followers who were living in the cities in Asia Minor that are addressed in Rev 2–3. He reports that he experienced the visions on the island of Patmos, located off the coast of Turkey (Rev 1:9). The date of composition is uncertain. Many have linked the writing to the imperial reign of Nero, given Tacitus's account of Nero's persecution of Christians. This would mean an early date in the 60s CE. Others have argued it was written during the reign of Domitian in the mid-90s CE. Both suggestions are based on efforts to connect the suffering described in the book to a state-sponsored, widespread persecution of Christians. Since most scholars are no longer convinced that such widespread persecution took place, dating the book to the reign of a particular emperor is more tenuous. The most we can say is that the book was written sometime in the second half of the first century CE.

Date and authorship

leopard-like beast rising from the sea (Rev 13:1–3), to name a few! But this popular use of the Book of Revelation to scare people is a long way from what the ancient writer had in mind for his audience. Consider the fact that the book offers repeated assurances of rewards to those in his audience who "conquer," provides dramatic visions of angelic worship (Revelation 4–5), and concludes with a promise of God who lives among humans and wipes away their tears (Rev 21:3–4). Such images demonstrate that in its ancient context, the work was not intended to frighten its readers. Its purpose was to provide hope and comfort, encouraging Christ-followers living under Roman rule.

Because we know that the Book of Revelation concerns cities of Asia Minor, we can be more specific about the experience of Roman rule in this region. First, most scholars now agree that there is no evidence for an official Roman policy of Christian persecution in the period when Revelation was written. Indeed, as we have seen throughout our discussion of the New Testament, for much of the first century CE there was little recognition of Christians as a group distinct from Jews.

However, following the Jewish revolt in 70 CE, Jewish people living throughout the empire (including Jewish Christ-followers) may have been the target of ongoing local hostilities. At a few points, there may also have been specific targeting of Christ-followers. As discussed in Chapter 11, according to the Roman historian Tacitus, Emperor Nero blamed the Christians in Rome for a catastrophic fire that destroyed large sections of Rome. Rumors of this accusation may have led to poor treatment of Christ-followers in their local communities.

Tacitus's Account of Nero's Persecution of Christians in Rome

The following quote from the Roman historian Tacitus is important as an early non-Christian reference to the crucifixion of Jesus and the origin of the Christians. Tacitus's statement that "the crowd called them Christians" suggests the term was a negative designation. This fits with its rare occurrences in the New Testament. As we have seen, "Christian" occurs only three times in the Bible (Acts 11:26; 26:28; 1 Peter 4:16), adding to the impression that it was originally a derogatory label that was eventually appropriated by Christ-followers.

But neither human help, nor imperial benevolence, nor all the modes of placating Heaven, could stifle scandal or dispel the belief that the fire had taken place by order. Therefore, to put an end to the rumor, Nero substituted as culprits, and punished with the utmost refinement of cruelty, a class of men, loathed for their vices, whom the crowd called Christians. Christus, the founder of the name, had undergone the death penalty in the reign of Tiberius, by sentence of the procurator Pontius Pilatus, and the pernicious superstition was checked for a moment, only to break out once more, not merely in Judea, the home of the disease, but in the capital itself, where all things horrible or shameful in the world collect and are celebrated. First, then, the confessed members of the sect were arrested; next, on their disclosures, vast numbers were convicted, not so much on the count of arson as for hatred of the human race. And derision accompanied their end; they were covered with wild beasts' skins and torn to death by dogs; or they were fastened on crosses, and, when daylight failed were burned to serve as lamps by night. Nero had offered his gardens for the spectacle, and gave an exhibition in his circus, mixing with the crowd in the habit of a charioteer, or mounted on his car. Hence, in spite of a guilt which had earned the most exemplary punishment, there arose a sentiment of pity, due to the impression that they were being sacrificed not for the welfare of the state but to the ferocity of a single man. (Tacitus, *Annals* 15.44, modified from the Loeb edition)

The Revelation to John expresses a sense of crisis in two main ways – through the messages written to seven communities in Asia Minor and through its detailed accounts of visions. We look first at the messages. Although written in coded language, they offer insight into the lived experience of Christ-followers in these cities, at least as far as the author perceived it. In the message to Pergamum, for instance, John refers to the community living where "Satan's throne" is (Rev 2:13). Pergamum was a provincial capital and home to the first emperor cult in Asia Minor, which was dedicated to Augustus. The city was also home to a monumental altar to Zeus built on a high acropolis. In both of these cultic settings, performing one's civic duty would have included offering sacrifices for the welfare of the city and empire. If the reference to "Satan's throne" refers to either of these places, it would signal the author's opposition to these civic expectations. In this same message, the author refers to a certain "faithful witness" named Antipas, "who was killed among you, where Satan lives" (2:13). We do not know anything more about this figure, except that the author's description implies that he was martyred for his confession of Christ.

Two other messages reveal tensions with local synagogues, again by way of references to Satan. According to the author, both Smyrna and Philadelphia have a "synagogue of Satan" and at least some of its members are "those who say they are Jews and are not" (2:9; 3:9). We do not know the details behind such language, but it is important to notice what the author is contesting. The author seems to oppose synagogue members who are not truly Jewish by his definition. This critique is yet another reminder that while the New Testament writings *do* depict a diversity within Judaism in the first century CE, they *do not* reflect a conflict of two different religions, as in Judaism vs. Christianity. At issue in the book of Revelation is whether Christ-followers can coexist comfortably with other Jews within the synagogue. Calling these synagogues in Smyrna and Philadelphia "synagogues of Satan" indicates the author's view that this coexistence is no longer possible.

Together the seven messages in Revelation 2–3 provide another example of the postcolonial concept of **hybridity**, where a subjected group adapts the cultural expressions of power of its oppressor (see also Chapter 5). In this case, the seven proclamations that open the book imitate the form of royal and

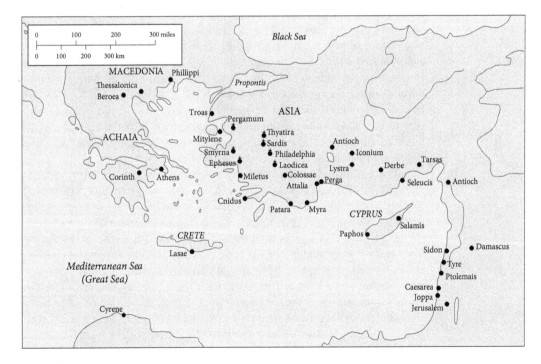

MAP 15.1
Cities of Revelation. Redrawn from Steven L. Harris, *Understanding the Bible* (6th edition). McGraw Hill, 2003, page 597.

imperial edicts. Such edicts were commonly used by imperial rulers for issuing instructions to local communities. Royal edicts began with a formal introduction of the authority issuing the edict, and then moved to a direct address to its recipients. This direct address was introduced with a recognizable formula, such as "The words of ...." In Revelation, this formula is the Greek phrase *tade legei*, "This is what he says ...." The main body of an imperial edict would express decisions made and sanctions given. The concluding section would reinforce the need for obedience. The seven proclamations in Revelation contain all of these elements. They begin by identifying the issuing authority in ways that emphasize Jesus's ruling power as the exalted Son of God. In each case, the authoritative voice of Jesus follows the phrase *tade legei*, translated in the NRSV as "these are the words." The address to each Christ group identifies the group's merits and shortcomings before concluding with promises of rewards or sanctions. Note that Jesus's authority is exerted on multiple fronts in these messages – against those in the group who are accused of false teaching (Rev 2:14; 20–3), against those in the synagogue who are deemed to be non-Jews (Rev 3:8–9), and against those in the group who are going astray (Rev 2:4–5, 14–15; 3:14–19). In sum, the opening chapters of Revelation imitate imperial authority by presenting Jesus as one having the status and authority to issue formal edicts with an expectation of obedience.

As is the case with other examples of cultural hybridity, this imitation comes with a twist. On the one hand, rewards are promised to those who "conquer," something that would be in keeping with Roman rewards for those who are victorious in battle (Rev 2:7, 11, 17, 26, 28; 3:5, 12, 21). On the other hand, what the author means by his use of "conquer" is sobering. Believers are victorious if they remain faithful to the point of death, perhaps like Antipas did (see, e.g., Rev 2:10–11). If they conquer in this way, they are assured that like Jesus, they will be rewarded with ruling power. They will hold authority over the nations, ruling them with a rod of iron (Rev 2:26–8; see also 12:11). They will be clothed in white robes (Rev 3:5) and given a seat with the risen Christ on his throne (Rev 3:21). Thus we find another indication of imperial imitation in the book of Revelation. The ultimate reward envisioned by those who feel oppressed by Rome is to become the one who rules over others.

As if to affirm that such a reward is possible, the text next transports the audience to a scene of heavenly worship in the throne room of God (Rev 4–5). The vision continues the project of imperial imitation, in this case mimicking scenes of Roman court ceremonials. For instance, the audience "watches" as the twenty-four elders show their submission to the one seated on the throne. They cast off their golden crowns before God, much like supplicants bowing before the Roman emperor. They sing acclamations to God and the Lamb echoing similar acclamations directed toward the emperor (Rev 4:10–11). The entire vision reinforces the idea that "the Lord God, the Almighty" (Rev 4:8) is the real ruler of the universe and rightful recipient of "glory, honor and power" (Rev 4:10–11). Honors are also given to the central figure in the heavenly throne room, the Lion/Lamb with seven horns and seven eyes (symbolic indications of strength and wisdom). He, too, is worthy "to receive power and wealth and wisdom and might and honor and glory and blessing" because of his self-sacrifice for people from every tribe and nation (Rev 5:12 NRSV). Overall, the scene asserts the ultimate ruling authority of God and the Lamb over the seeming authority of the emperor. It does this by offering a visual parallel to a court ceremony for the emperor, but one that surpasses in splendor and spectacle anything that could be found in Rome.

Having established who is actually ruling heaven and earth, Revelation goes on to display a cosmic conflict that occurs as the wrath of God and the Lamb is unleashed upon the earth and its inhabitants (Rev 6:15–17). The text's audience, along with the seer, John, "sees" gruesome scenes of war, death, and destruction that manifest God's final judgment over the unrepentant inhabitants of the earth. These judgments are deemed "true and just," as acts of divine vengeance on behalf of those righteous ones who were killed for the word of God and for their witness (Rev 6:9–10; see also 15:3; 16:5–7; 19:2).

More coded allusions to the struggle with Roman imperial power occur in the description of the two beasts (Rev 13:1–18). The first beast rises from the ocean much like the sea monsters symbolizing oppressive empires in prophetic texts (see Isa 51:9–11; Ezek 29:3–5; 32:2–6; Jer 51:34). In appearance, the first beast combines the features of the four beasts representing different empires in Dan 7:2–7. By combining these various biblical monsters into one beast, the author of Revelation implies that this beast/empire represents the worst of them all – the culmination of evil in the world. The question, "Who is like the beast and who is able to fight against it?" (Rev 13:4) might be exactly the question that someone living under Roman domination might ask. The claim that the beast has authority over "every tribe, people, language and nation" (Rev 13:7) would feel practically true to those who were subjected to Rome's power. A further clue to associating the beast with the Roman empire is the claim that "all the inhabitants of the earth will worship it" (Rev 13:8). This is a reference to the emperor cult, which was instituted to encourage allegiance to Roman rule.

The description of another beast in Rev 11 evokes the role of the elite class in the cities of Asia Minor. These affluent men controlled the political, religious, and economic affairs of their communities in close association with Rome. They held political offices, as well as priesthoods in prominent local cults. Such men worked on behalf of the "first beast" (Rome) and made others worship this same beast (through participation in the emperor cult, Rev 13:12). The description of the second beast also suggests that local leaders had the authority to kill those who do not "worship the first beast" (Rev 13:12). Alternatively, they could cut off the livelihood of resisters by denying them participation in the local economy (Rev 13:15–17). For Jews living in the empire, including Christ-followers, offering a sacrifice to the emperor posed serious problems because it was an offence to Jewish monotheism (see Figure 15.1). Yet, refusing to support the local emperor cult was refusing to perform a basic civic duty. The book of Revelation suggests that such refusal caused tensions on a local level that could turn violent.

The rest of the book of Revelation provides graphic descriptions of the coming defeat and punishment of Rome and Satan. The angel's call to worship "the one who made the heaven and the earth, the sea and the springs of water" (Rev 14:7 NRSV) is juxtaposed with a picture of eternal torment of those who

FIGURE 15.1

Fourth-century CE catacomb painting illustrating how early Christians viewed their own experience of the Roman empire through the lens of the biblical text. Though it depicts a scene from Dan 3:12–18 in which three men refuse to honor the image of the Babylonian king Nebuchadnezzar, the bust of the king looks like a Roman emperor and the officer demanding their veneration of the king is in Roman military attire.

worship the beast (Rev 14:9–11). Throughout these violent scenes, the task of the faithful believer is to endure (Rev 13:10; 14:12). The violence against Rome and Satan is carried out by others, whether by the angels of God pouring bowls of his wrath or locking up Satan in a bottomless pit (Rev 16:1–21; 20:1–3), or by the warrior rider striking down enemies with the sword of his mouth (Rev 19:11–18). There is no question about who will win these contests between God and his opponents. Instead, the main point of the visions is to show God's vengeance and punishment on his defeated enemies. The final scenes complete the fantasy of a fallen Rome and the defeated evil power of Satan. A new holy city of Jerusalem comes down from heaven to a new earth. The city is to be home to God so that God will live among the people (Rev 21:1–4). This is the hope offered to those living under the oppression of the empire.

FOCUS
TEXT

Revelation 17–18

Although we will discuss two other New Testament texts below, the focus text for this chapter is from Revelation, so we include it here. Revelation 17–18 expresses the most explicit anti-Roman sentiment in the entire New Testament. Up to this point, the author of Revelation has led the audience to visualize the wrath of God being exacted on Satan, the beast, the earth, and most of its inhabitants. In these chapters, the focus is on the city of Rome itself, personified as "the **whore of Babylon**" (Figure 15.2). The image of the "whore" is introduced in chapter 17. She wears royal colors, is adorned in jewels and gold, holds a golden cup "full of abominations," and sits on a bright red, seven-headed beast (Rev 17:1–6). On her forehead is the name "Babylon the great, mother of whores and of earth's abominations." Soon her identity is revealed. She is "the great city that rules over the kings of the earth" (Rev 17:18). In the author's time, this "whore of Babylon" could only have symbolized Rome. The author draws on Israel's past trauma with Babylon to symbolize the source of the present trauma for Christ-followers in Asia Minor. The figure of the prostitute is also familiar from Israel's scriptures. Prophets like Hosea and Ezekiel used a similar image as a way to critique their own people's waywardness. Here the "whore" is used in reference to the enemy city. The fact that the woman is "drunk with the blood of the saints and the blood of the witnesses to Jesus" (Rev 17:6) suggests the author is aware of instances of suffering at the hands of the Romans, perhaps under Nero. Revelation 17 concludes with a disturbing image of the destruction of the personified city. She will be stripped, eaten, and burned with fire (Rev 17:16). The gruesome description of her fate indicates the intense level of hostility directed toward Rome. It is also another troubling example of an ancient writer using violence against a female body to convey the judgment of God.

FIGURE 15.2
Revelation's figure of the "whore of Babylon" has captured the imaginations of artists for hundreds of years. This 1809 pen and watercolor was done by the artist and poet William Blake.

Revelation 18 opens with an angelic announcement of the city's demise: "Fallen, fallen is Babylon the great!" Thus begins a scene of destruction that reflects a deep anger against Rome and its exploitative practices that produced its great wealth. Much of the chapter is modeled on Ezekiel 27, which details the luxury and trading practices of the city of Tyre before predicting the day of its ruin. Likewise, Revelation 18 details the luxury of Rome and its eventual destruction. Its demise is considered to be a just punishment for its destruction of other nations: "render to her as she herself has rendered" (18:6). As we saw in the discussion of Revelation 13, the leaders of the Roman empire grew rich off the lands Rome conquered, as did those who cooperated with imperial expansion (see Rev 18:3). Notice the detailed list of the cargo sold to Rome by the "merchants of the earth," which concludes with a reference to trading in "human lives," that is, slaves (18:12–13). While the details of this chapter may seem exaggerated, it coincides with other accounts of how the Roman elite disenfranchised the lower classes. The poor were cut out of local governing assemblies and often denied citizenship. They were also subject to price gouging. The Roman writer Plutarch offers an account of bread riots in Asia Minor caused by the hoarding of grain and resulting price increases. Such conditions help explain the bitterness reflected in Revelation 18.

Finally, we should note that while the chapter refers to Rome's destruction as a past event, the concluding verses return to the future tense: "With sudden violence Babylon the great city will be thrown down" (18:21). In fact, throughout the book of Revelation, past, present, and future are intertwined. This enables the reader both to fantasize about the utter demise of Rome and to acknowledge that Rome's destruction remains in the future.

MORE ON METHOD: CULTURAL CRITICISM OF THE BIBLE

Cultural criticism is interested in the interactions between the Bible and popular culture. Cultural critics might focus on appropriations of the Bible in Hollywood films, popular novels, television, comic books, advertisements, clothing, jewelry, and so on. Or, they might focus on how the book has been read through the lens of a particular cultural context. Indeed, the possibilities for such a study are almost endless. Cultural criticism also examines the reverse process, that is, the way that popular culture influences the interpretation of the Bible.

The Revelation to John is a prime candidate for a cultural critical approach, given the endless popular fascination with end times. One might study the use of images from Revelation in artwork, such as the painting shown in Figure 15.2. Or one might study the popular fiction series such as *Left Behind* by Tim LaHaye and Jerry B. Jenkins, exploring what images and ideas from Revelation are used in the novels and to what end. One example of a cultural critical reading of the book of Revelation is Brian Blount's interpretation of Revelation through the lens of African American culture. Another is Timothy Beal's *The Book of Revelation: A Biography*. In Beal's book you will find, for example, a discussion of a prevalent Western cultural phobia known as *hexakosioihexekontahexaphobia* – fear of the number 666 (see Rev 13:17–18).

Hebrews: Platonic Perspectives on Christ

Hebrews 1:1–14; 4:14–10:39. Pay attention to the imagery used for Jesus in these passages.

READING

If the book of Revelation is the clearest biblical example of resistance to Rome, the biblical book of Hebrews seems the most removed from such concerns. At first glance, there is little to suggest that the author has anything in mind but Jesus's relation to Jewish tradition, in particular the Jewish sacrificial cult. Nevertheless, the text is a fascinating combination of cultural influences and thus another example of the type of hybrid text generated in an imperial context. The author combines neo-Platonic ideas with Jewish scriptural and cultic references in the service of his unique image of Jesus. Like other images of Jesus that we have seen in the New Testament, this one draws on cultural images of Roman imperial authority. But Hebrews also contains themes of alienation and marginalization, suggesting that this author recognized the difficulty of living under imperial authority. Indeed, even the interest in the Jewish sacrificial cult may be a result of the pressures of imperial occupation.

Hebrews first circulated with the collection of Pauline letters, although it nowhere purports to be by Paul. Even the earliest church writers did not think it was written by Paul. The second-century writer Origen asserted that "only God knows" who wrote it. Nor is Hebrews actually a letter. Aside from the concluding benediction and greetings (Heb 13:20–5), the text reads more like a homily. We can say for certain that the author of Hebrews was well educated. Compared to much of the rest of the New Testament, Hebrews uses a complex and sophisticated writing style.

The central image of the text is distinctive: the author presents Jesus as a high priest offering an atoning sacrifice for "the sins of the people" (Heb 2:17). In describing the Messiah/Christ as a high priest, the author is in keeping with other Second Temple writings that anticipate a priestly messiah. The prophet Zechariah, for example, speaks of a royal and a priestly messiah. But while there are references in other New Testament writings to the sacrificial nature of the death of Jesus (see, for example, Paul's sacrificial language in 1 Cor 5:7 and Rom 3:25), only in Hebrews is Jesus presented as the priest who carries out the sacrifice. Specifically, Jesus is depicted as a high priest according to the order of Melchizedek (Heb 5:10; 6:20; 7:1–3). If you have never heard of Melchizedek, there is good reason. The name occurs only twice in the Hebrew scriptures. It appears first in a brief account in Gen 14:18–20, where Melchizedek is described as both a king and a priest who blesses Abraham. The second reference is in Ps 110:4, where the Davidic king is called "a priest forever in the order of Melchizedek." For the author of Hebrews, this double identity of king and priest was important. Recall that a major role of the Roman emperor was that of high priest, *pontifex maximus*. In the same way the Roman emperor mediated with the gods on behalf of the people, so too the Jesus of Hebrews is a royal priest who intercedes for those who approach God (Heb 7:25). The author also points to the superiority of Jesus to earthly high priests, whether the Jewish high priest, or the Roman emperor in his role as high priest. In fact, this is another reason why the figure of Melchizedek is significant to the author. The author calls attention to what is missing from the brief mention of Melchizedek in Genesis: "no father, no mother, no genealogy" (Heb 7:3; Gen 14:17–20). For the author, this introduces a sense of timelessness to the figure, indeed, it explains the eternal nature of his priesthood. As he puts it, "neither having beginning of days nor having end of life, like the Son of God, he remains a priest forever" (Heb 7:3). So, too, according to the author of Hebrews, the priesthood of Jesus is permanent and eternal (Heb 7:23–4).

Basics on The Letter to the Hebrews

While this book has "letter" in its title, the only letter-like elements come in the last chapter, which contains exhortations and greetings. Otherwise, the book is more sermon-like in form.

Outline: a literary sermon

I	The superiority of Christ	1:1–4:13
II	Christ's high priesthood	4:14–10:18
III	Encouraging faithful endurance	10:19–13:33

Date and authorship

Much about Hebrews remains unclear to modern scholars: the author, date, place of composition are all difficult to determine with any certainty. The author is unknown and proposed dates for the book range from the 60s to the 90s CE. This range reflects a debate on whether the text was written before or after the destruction of the Temple in 70 CE. There is no explicit recognition of the Temple's demise, but the book's focus on the heavenly sanctuary and high priesthood of Jesus could be a response to its destruction. Similarly, the admission that "we have no enduring city" (Heb 13:14) suggests an awareness of Jerusalem's destruction. Given this, it seems most likely that the text was written post-70 CE. As for location, most scholars now think the text was directed toward the Christ-followers in Rome. There is one reference to location in Heb 13:24 ("those from Italy greet you"), which may indicate greetings from fellow Italians now living outside of Italy sending greetings to the the Christ group in Rome. The earliest text that quotes Hebrews, *1 Clement*, is a letter written by the Roman bishop Clement in the late first or early second century.

The description of the high priesthood of Jesus also points to the fundamentally Platonic worldview of the author of Hebrews. The Greek philosopher Plato (427–347 BCE) believed that the objects that made up the earthly material world were imperfect reflections of the true ideal (and immaterial) forms of these objects. In Platonic thought, for example, a physical chair is merely a copy of the eternal idea of a more real and perfect chair. This **Platonic theory of forms**, as well as other aspects of Plato's thought, continued to influence Christian writers until well into the fifth century CE. The early stages of this influence are evident in Hebrews, which uses the Platonic idea of forms to elevate Jesus above the Jewish temple cult. So, for example, the author claims that Levitical priests offer sacrifices in a sanctuary that is a "copy and shadow" of the heavenly one (Heb 8:5). As high priest, Jesus has entered not an earthly sanctuary, "a copy of the true one," but rather what is truly real, "heaven itself" (Heb 9:24). Even the law is but "a shadow of coming good things, and not the form itself of these things" (Heb 10:1). Again, the author uses this Platonic perspective to underscore the superiority of Jesus over various aspects of the Jewish cultic and legal traditions (see especially Heb 3:1–3; 7–9). In our study of the gospels, we saw how assertions of Jesus's superiority over Moses reflected inter-group competitions that were heightened, if not created, by dynamics of foreign rule. The fact that Hebrews uses a Greek-influenced framework to speak of Jesus's relation to the Jewish cult in a Roman-ruled empire reflects the long-term effects of imperial forces.

Finally, there may be a more direct link between the Platonic perspective of Hebrews and associations with imperial authority. In Heb 1:3, Jesus is described as an exact representation of God's real being. Here the author draws on a standard Greco-Roman political theory in which an ideal ruler is understood to embody reason and law, or, to use the Greek phrase, divine *logos*. To speak of the relationship between Jesus and God as one of "exact representation" highlights Jesus's own exact image of divine essence and authority. This is another example of how a New Testament author both lifts up Jesus while also subtly critiquing similar claims made about the Roman emperor. The fact that Jesus is an *exact* representation of God stands in contrast to the "shadows" and "copies." According to the author, these shadowy copies, unlike Jesus in relation to God, do *not* convey the true essence of their forms.

While most of Hebrews conveys the image of Jesus as high priest, there are also exhortations directed toward the audience. These sections reveal how the author views the position of Christ-followers the world. For example, in a list of faithful ancestors, the "great cloud of witnesses" (Heb 12:1), the author points to times when some lived as strangers and foreigners on the earth in search of a better homeland (11:13–14). The author contrasts the ancestral search for a homeland with the present one. Recalling the scene at Mount Sinai, he depicts it as a terrifying experience complete with a blazing fire, darkness, gloom, a windstorm, and a voice warning of death that the audience begs not to hear (12:18–20). In comparison, he offers a "better homeland" (11:16), which is not a place "that can be touched," but rather, the heavenly Mount Zion/Jerusalem (12:22). Like Jesus, who was executed outside the gates of Jerusalem, believers are to go "outside the camp," for they have no lasting city, but are looking for the city that is to come (Heb 13:14). In these ways, the author offers a subtle critique of past searches for a homeland and of present imperial rule. Neither in the past nor in the present has the people's lived experience been permanent or ideal. Rather, using a Platonic perspective of reality, the author suggests that the experience of earthly life in the empire only leaves them longing and searching for a better homeland.

1 Peter: Living as Aliens and Accommodating to the Empire

READING

1 Peter.

Our third and final example of the variety of New Testament responses to life in the empire is 1 Peter. Like Hebrews, 1 Peter uses a rhetoric of alienation, opening with an address to "aliens in the diaspora" (1:1). **Diaspora** is a transliteration of the Greek word for "scattering," and in a Jewish context it refers to Jewish people living as foreigners in regions outside of Palestine. Like Revelation, 1 Peter is directed toward Christ-followers scattered across Asia Minor. The regions listed in the first verse – Pontus, Galatia, Cappadocia, Asia, and Bithynia – are all Roman provinces in Asia Minor. Intended to circulate in this region, 1 Peter is an example of a "diaspora letter." It resembles other Jewish diaspora letters like Jer 29:4–23 and some Septuagint texts, such as Baruch (a letter associated with Jeremiah's scribe) and the epistle of Jeremiah. These diaspora letters often evoke themes of alienation and exhort those living in exile to conduct themselves in particular ways. Thus 1 Peter contains an exhortation to readers to live "in fear" during their time of alienation (1:17) and to conduct themselves honorably as "aliens and strangers" (2:11). Some scholars have argued that this language should be taken literally, and that the letter addresses actual communities of exiles living in Asia Minor. But given what we have already seen in texts like the Gospel of John and Hebrews, it is more likely that the language of exile and alienation is used metaphorically to describe the relationship between Christ-followers and the world. They are no longer at home in the world, but instead live as aliens in a foreign land.

A major theme of 1 Peter helps explain this feeling of alienation. Throughout the text, the author points to the experience of suffering on the part of the believers (1 Pet 1:6; 3:14; 4:12–19). There is no specific mention of physical suffering. Instead, the author suggests that the communities were experiencing the sort of local mistreatment that was discussed above. For example, the author refers to their being accused of doing evil (2:12). He urges them not to be afraid or intimidated (3:14) even if they are being slandered

(3:16) and insulted (4:14). Notably, the author also exhorts his audience not to be ashamed if they suffer "as a Christian" but to glorify God in this way (4:16). As we have seen, this is one of the rare occurrences of the term "Christian" in the New Testament. That the author associates the designation with the experience of suffering offers further illustration of the sense of fear and alienation that his intended audience may have been experiencing.

Basics on 1 Peter

I	Opening salutation and thanksgiving	1:1–12	**Outline: an elder's letter to the churches of Asia Minor**
II	Letter body: the identity and proper conduct of the people of God – accommodation and persistence	1:13–5:11	
III	Concluding greetings and wishes	5:11–12	

The text purports to be from "Peter, an apostle of Jesus Christ," but few scholars think that Peter was the author. A Galilean fisherman would not likely be able to read or write, let alone write with the sophisticated Greek style of 1 Peter. Moreover, there is nothing about the content of 1 Peter that suggests it was written by one of Jesus's first disciples. Rather, 1 Peter is an example of a **pseudonymous** early Christian writing (pseudonymous in Greek = "false name"). In the ancient world, authors would sometimes use the name of an esteemed figure in the tradition to enhance the authority of their writing. That is likely the case here. Most scholars think the text was written in Rome, probably sometime after 70 CE. **Date and authorship**

However, 1 Peter illustrates a different approach to the experience of alienation than what we saw in Revelation. Whereas the book of Revelation takes an openly hostile stance against Rome, 1 Peter urges its audience to keep closely to the standards of Roman society. They are to live honorably (1 Pet 2:12) and submit to all human authorities, whether to the emperor or to governors appointed by him (2:12–14). Indeed, they are to honor everyone, including the emperor, as the author takes special care to note (2:17). In strong contrast to Revelation, this may be an example of a biblical text that advocates participating in the emperor cult. Although many scholars have suggested that the author means to say, "Do anything to honor the emperor *but* offering sacrifice," there are no such qualifications in the text. On the contrary, the author's overall stance – that his readers should not give cause for gentiles to despise them – would suggest conformity even to the sacrificial emperor cult. Warren Carter has made a compelling case that what the author promotes is a *public* accommodation to the civic demands of life under imperial rule while *private* convictions to Christ are maintained. Note, for example, the author urging believers to revere Christ "in their hearts" (1 Pet 3:15). They are to do so while being zealous to "do good." This "doing good" likely refers to a general sense of civic good conduct, since no mistreatment will come to them if they conduct themselves in this way (1 Pet 3:13). Again, this is quite a contrast to Revelation, which encourages its audience to resist such conduct even if it means their death!

In addition to advocating "doing good," the author assumes that the community should embrace the same hierarchical relationships that shaped the social structure of the Greco-Roman world. Slaves should submit to the authority of their masters – "not only to those who are good and gentle but also to those who are perverse" (1 Pet 2:18). Wives should be submissive to their husbands (1 Pet 3:1). Husbands are to honor their wives, the "weaker female vessels" (1 Pet 3:7). The younger should submit to the elders (1 Pet 5:5). None of these exhortations would seem unusual for the readers of 1 Peter, and this is not the first time we have seen hierarchical relationships reinforced in a New Testament text. Similar **household codes** were used in the Deutero-Pauline letters (Col 3:18–4:1; Eph 5:21–6:9). Paul himself urged people to remain in whatever social position they were in when they became believers (1 Cor 7:17). In 1 Peter, the author draws on these standard codes of conduct to encourage cultural conformity among the community of believers.

In sum, amidst the identification of the intended audience as aliens and strangers in the world, the letter urges its readers to conduct themselves in ways that conform to the expectations of their society. It may well be that this was a deliberate strategy of accommodation, employed by the author to help Christ-followers avoid ongoing harassment by their neighbors and local authorities.

Conclusion: Three Different Relationships to the Roman Empire

This chapter has shown the diverse ways that certain authors outside of the gospels and Pauline traditions responded to the challenge of living as a follower of Jesus during the late first century in the Greco-Roman world. The Revelation to John, Hebrews, and 1 Peter all suggest that life in the empire was difficult at best, and a life of suffering at worst. However, each text presents a different approach to this reality. The apocalyptic text of Revelation takes a stance of hostile resistance toward Rome. It engages the audience in an extended fantasy in which they are invited to witness God's violent destruction of Rome. This vision of divine justice includes the ultimate promise of a restored Jerusalem where God will live among the people and wipe away their every tear. In contrast, Hebrews seems largely detached from the Roman political and economic sphere. It more directly engages the Jewish sacrificial cult, presenting an image of Jesus as a superior high priest and king. Nevertheless, even this image is a subtle way of pointing to Christ as superior also to the emperor. Likewise, the author's Platonic perspective allows him to highlight the perfection of Jesus, seated in the heavenly temple alongside God, in unspoken contrast to the imperfections of the present earthly Roman imperial rule. Finally, 1 Peter urges accommodation to Roman authority and culture, even while it recognizes the alienated position of its audience. In stark contrast to Revelation, it looks toward a way of peaceful existence in the world, one that enables believers to fit into their cultural surroundings, while still maintaining their commitment to Christ.

CHAPTER FIFTEEN REVIEW

1 Know the meaning and significance of the following terms:
- diaspora
- hybridity
- Platonic theory of forms
- whore of Babylon"

2 If Revelation was not designed primarily to inspire fear, what was it meant to do?

3 In what ways do the Revelation to John, Hebrews, and 1 Peter reflect distress in the audiences that they address? What was mostly likely the cause of this distress for early Christ-followers?

4 What is the difference between the apparent positions of Revelation and 1 Peter on the issue of honoring and sacrificing to the Roman emperor? How does this reflect the different ways that Revelation and 1 Peter respond to feelings of alienation in their audiences?

5 How does Hebrews, with its Platonic perspective, subtly critique the Roman empire?

6 Summarize in three sentences the different ways in which Revelation, Hebrews, and 1 Peter relate to their Roman imperial context.

RESOURCES FOR FURTHER STUDY

Barr, David L., ed. *Reading the Book of Revelation: A Resource for Students*. Atlanta, GA: Society of Biblical Literature, 2003.

Beal, Timothy K. *Revelation: A Biography*. Princeton, NJ: Princeton University Press, 2018.

Beavis, Mary Ann. *Hebrews*. Collegeville, MN: Liturgical Press, 2015.

Blount, Brian K. *Can I Get a Witness? Reading Revelation Through African American Culture*. Louisville, KY: Westminster John Knox Press, 2005.

Blount, Brian K. *Revelation: A Commentary*. Louisville, KY: Westminster John Knox Press, 2009.

Carey, Greg. *Apocalyptic Literature in the New Testament*. Nashville, TN: Abingdon, 2016.

Carter, Warren. "Going All the Way? Honoring the Emperor and Sacrificing Wives and Slaves in First Peter 2.13–3.6." Pp. 14–33 in A. J. Levine and Marianne Blickenstaff (eds.), *Feminist Companion to the Catholic Epistles and Hebrews*. London: T & T Clark, 2005.

Collins, Adela Yarbo. *Crisis and Catharsis: The Power of the Apocalypse*. Philadelphia, PA: Westminster Press, 1984.

Horrell, David G. *1 Peter*. New Testament Guides. London and New York: T & T Clark, 2008.

Kovacs, Judith, and Rowland, Christopher. *Revelation*. Blackwell Bible Commentaries. Oxford and Malden, MA: Blackwell, 2004.

Schüssler Fiorenza, Elisabeth. *1 Peter: Reading Against the Grain*. Sheffield: Sheffield Phoenix Press, 2015.

Epilogue: The Final Formation of the Jewish and Christian Bibles

While we have come to the end of our study of the Bible, we have not yet discussed the final formation of the Christian Bible, or the shaping of the Hebrew scriptures into the "Tanakh" used by Jewish communities. One of the most frequent questions about the Bible is why particular books were included, and others excluded. Was there a conscious decision to exclude certain books because of political reasons? Or was it a gradual process that was later ratified by church or rabbinic groups? Or something else? This epilogue addresses these questions.

Unfortunately, we do not have much direct evidence for the factors that led to the definition of what was included as scripture in the Jewish and Christian communities. What we can say is that most scholars think that the books in the Bible, including the books of the New Testament, were not originally written to be part of a separate "Bible." As we saw in the discussion of the origins of writing in early Israel, many early Israelite writings were probably meant to educate generations of students, serving as objects of study and memorization. Especially in a largely oral culture, such written works were seen as particularly old and holy, but they were not set apart from other texts. That is why prophets, royal historians, and others could keep producing new writings up into the Hellenistic period. This shows that there is a significant distinction between the production and circulation of a work for reading and education and the process of "canonization." It is one thing to produce a work and for it to become popular. It is another to establish a collection of such works as a "canon," and thus separate it from all other books.

As we saw in Chapter 8, we do not even have a clearly defined Jewish Bible in the Hellenistic period. Though there is a chance that Hasmonean monarchs may have promoted a defined collection of *Hebrew* "Torah and Prophets" to counter the similarly sharply defined Greek curriculum of pre-Hellenistic authors (Homer and others), such a collection – if it even was defined as such – was not recognized by other Jewish groups. The Jewish community at Qumran who collected the Dead Sea Scrolls worked with a broader collection of scriptures, as did early Jewish Christ-followers. For example, the New Testament letter of Jude cites the book of Enoch as if it were scripture (Jude 14–15). Not yet fully separated from Judaism, such early Christ-followers

A Contemporary Introduction to the Bible: Sacred Texts and Imperial Contexts, Second Edition.
Colleen M. Conway and David M. Carr.
© 2021 Colleen M. Conway and David M. Carr. Published 2021 by John Wiley & Sons Ltd.

worked with a collection of Jewish scriptures that included a variety of Jewish works not included in the narrower group of Hebrew "Torah and Prophets."

This was especially true as emerging Christianity became a largely Greek-speaking phenomenon. Indeed, quite early in the development of the church, Christ-followers were working with the Greek (Septuagint) versions of authoritative Jewish books (Genesis, Isaiah, etc.), as well as some works originally written in Greek (such as the Wisdom of Solomon). In sum, even if the Hasmoneans started to define something like a Hebrew Bible, there were still plenty of Jewish groups – including Christ-followers – who worked with a broader and more flexible idea of scripture that included other books.

The books now in the New Testament were written and collected in this environment. Early on, the four canonical gospels began circulating together. Similarly, the Pauline letters soon circulated as a collection. Other texts were slower to gain universal acceptance and were more popular in one area or another. Revelation, for instance, was popular in the Western churches, but came under critique from some of the Christian writers in the East. Conversely, the letter of Hebrews was more popular in the Eastern church, and only reached acceptance in the West at a later point. One second century Christian writing, the Shepherd of Hermas was considered as scripture in some circles, even though it was not ultimately included in the New Testament. Other works, such as an early form of the Gospel of Thomas, may have been in circulation as well. But there was no collection of writings known as the "New Testament" in this early stage of circulation.

So what, one may ask, led to the creation of the Jewish Tanakh (Torah, Prophets, and Writings) and the Christian Bible (Old and New Testaments)? How did these communities find consensus on what books to include? Why did they seek such definition?

We cannot be sure, but it seems that unity on these questions of scripture was connected to the consolidation and unification of Judaism on the one hand and Christianity on the other. Judaism achieved a new level of unity in the wake of the first Jewish revolt (discussed in Chapters 11 and 15) and a second revolt that occurred in 132–5 CE. These revolts provoked a devastating Roman response, including the total destruction of Jerusalem, the elimination of dissident groups such as that found at Qumran, and the decline of diverse Jewish communities across the Mediterranean. Within this context, rabbinic scholars connected to the Pharisaic movement succeeded in unifying Judaism around a growing body of oral legal tradition that was later written down (particularly the Mishnah and Talmud). We first see regular references to an authoritative collection of "Torah, Prophets, and Writings," a "Tanakh," in the writings of these scholars from the third and fourth centuries CE. To return to our theme of empire, this standardized three-part Tanakh, containing twenty-four books, thus emerges as a unifying point for Judaism in the wake of imperial, Roman destruction.

Meanwhile, Christianity underwent its own form of consolidation during the same early centuries of the common era. We know from the diverse writings collected at Nag Hammadi in Egypt and other sources that there were many different sorts of Christ groups in the first and second centuries CE, some of which produced texts that were not included in the New Testament. The first generations of Christ-followers seem to have valued oral traditions about Jesus passed down through recognized authorities over written documents that could be falsified. Rarely, the earliest Christian authors would mention written authoritative works of the "Apostles" alongside Jewish books of "Prophets."

This situation changed as Christianity grew and consolidated itself as a centralized religious movement that was separate from Judaism (see Map 16.1). The Jewish scriptures were still valued, but came to be defined as part of a separate "Old Testament." Certain writings that were especially valued in the church, used in the liturgy, and/or deemed to originate from one of the original apostles, came to be part of a "New Testament." In the third and fourth centuries theologians produced varying lists of what books were included in each part of the "Old" and "New Testament." Generally, theologians working in the Western Mediterranean included a broader range of books, while theologians working in the East had more restrictive lists.

By the end of the third century (200s) the church agreed on virtually all books to be included in the Old and New Testaments, but a new level of agreement came in the early fourth century when Constantine became the first Christian emperor of the broader Roman empire (Figure 16.1). At this point,

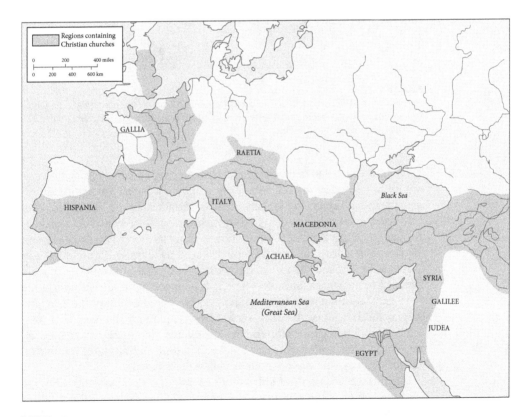

MAP 16.1

Spread of Christianity across the Mediterranean world by 300 CE. Redrawn from Bart Ehrman, *The New Testament: A Historical Introduction to the Early Christian Writings* (3rd edition). Oxford: Oxford University Press, 2004, page 43.

FIGURE 16.1

Bust of Constantine, who acceded to the throne in 306 and secured control of the whole Roman empire in 324 CE. He ended persecution of Christians and began to use imperial power to resolve inter-Christian disputes.

Christianity started to make the final transition from being a movement *under* empire to becoming the religion *of* the empire. Divisions among Christians were viewed as threats to the unity of the imperial realm. For this reason, over the following century, a series of ecumenical councils was convened to resolve disputed theological matters. Most of these councils focused on debates about the nature of Christ, but several councils (such as those at Hippo in 393 and Carthage in 397 and 418) produced authoritative lists of which books were included in the Christian Bible. These lists included more Jewish texts in the Old Testament than were found in the Tanakh of contemporary Judaism, and they included a range of books, such as Revelation and Hebrews, that were valued in different parts of the empire. Meanwhile, some early writings associated with Christ groups that were deemed heretical, and/or works whose connection to an apostle was not established, were excluded.

In this way the final definition of the Christian Bible was facilitated by the Christianization of the Roman empire, or one might say the imperialization of Christianity. Some forms of Christianity that developed outside the immediate orbit of the Roman empire, such as the Ethiopian, Armenian, and Syrian churches, went their own way in terms of canon and developed somewhat different lists of the contents of the Old and New Testaments. Nevertheless, by the third and fourth centuries the pattern was set. Judaism had a twenty-four-book, three-part Tanakh of books largely written in Hebrew. Christianity had a two-part Bible, consisting of an Old Testament (generally the Greek Septuagint) and a New Testament (see Figure 16.2). And just a couple of centuries later, we would see the emergence in Arabia of another important text, incorporating some Jewish and Christian traditions and somewhat modeled on their idea of scripture: the Muslim Qur'an of the prophet Mohammed.

Following the establishment of the Jewish and Christian canons, these scriptural collections have played central roles not just in the religious communities where they have their home, but in the cultural and political contexts connected to those communities. For example, from the eighteenth to the twentieth centuries, the teaching of the Christian Bible was a key element of European evangelization and colonization. Even now, debates about the Bible play a central role in disputes about the boundaries of the nation of Israel or

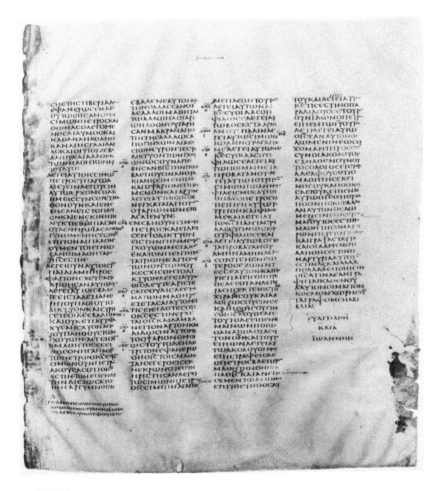

FIGURE 16.2
The Codex Sinaiticus. This Greek manuscript from the fourth century is one of the earliest complete copies of the entire Old and New Testaments.

US, UK, and European immigration policies. In these ways and many others, the rich range of texts now collected in the Old and New Testaments continue to play a major role in people's lives, both religious and not. Deeper knowledge of those texts helps one become a more informed participant in a world still dominated by empires and infused with these scriptures.

GLOSSARY

Each entry includes (in parentheses) reference to the first location where a term is discussed, whether Prologue or chapter number, along with other major location(s). **Boldface** indicates terms that occur elsewhere in this Glossary.

act-consequence (3) – see **moral act-consequence**.

African American interpretation (2, 13) – forms of critical biblical study whose questions grow out of the experiences of people of African descent. Such study critiques racist interpretations of the Bible, highlights the presence of African characters in the Bible, and/or critically analyzes the diverse ways that scripture has been used in African American religion and culture. See also **Afrocentric and womanist interpretation**.

Afrocentric interpretation (3) – forms of interpretation that foreground and celebrate the bodies and cultures of people of African descent. See also **Womanist** and **African American interpretation**.

apocalypse (8, 15) – a text commonly attested in the Hellenistic and later periods that describes a heavenly revelation to a human recipient, often a human recipient from Israel's distant past (e.g. Enoch, Levi, etc.; see **pseudepigraphy**). Such apocalypses appear in two main types, the heavenly apocalypse and the historical apocalypse, frequently show priestly connections, and feature much focus on esoteric knowledge.

apocalyptic (9) – predicting or describing the end of the current, unjust age and the arrival of a new age through God's direct intervention in history.

apocalypticism (9) – see **apocalyptic worldview**.

apocalyptic worldview (10) **or apocalypticism** (9) – a worldview, or social movement associated with the worldview, which emphasizes God's anticipated intervention in history, thus bringing the current, corrupt world order to an end. In this view, the unjust are punished, those who have suffered are rewarded, and a new, just world order is initiated.

apocrypha (Prologue) – Protestant term for **deuterocanonical books**, in this case designating books that are not viewed in the Protestant tradition as fully **canonical**.

apostle (10) – literally, "one who is sent" from the Greek verb *apostellein*, to send. Paul uses the term to describe his preaching ministry among the

A Contemporary Introduction to the Bible: Sacred Texts and Imperial Contexts, Second Edition. Colleen M. Conway and David M. Carr.
© 2021 Colleen M. Conway and David M. Carr. Published 2021 by John Wiley & Sons Ltd.

gentiles. In the synoptic gospels, Jesus's disciples are called apostles when he sends them out as messengers. See Matt 10:1–7, Mark 3:14, Luke 6:12–16.

Asherah (2) – the mother goddess of the Canaanite pantheon, consort of the chief god, **El.**

Assyria (4) – a Mesopotamian state based in what is now northern Iraq.

Baal (2) – a storm god in the Canaanite pantheon.

Babylonian exile (1, 6) – 586–538 BCE, a time when most of the elite living in Judah (especially Jerusalem) were forced to live outside the land in Babylonia (with many never having the chance to return).

beginning of the Roman period (1) – 63 BCE: the end of the **Hasmonean monarchy** and the beginning of rule of Palestine by rulers appointed by Rome.

Ben Sira (8) – a collection of instructional texts authored in the early second century BCE (c. 200–180 BCE). It is one example of a **deuterocanonical** book included (under its Greek name **Sirach**) in the **Old Testament** of the Roman Catholic and Orthodox churches, but excluded from the Jewish **Tanakh** and Protestant Old Testament.

book of the Twelve Prophets (4) – a book in the Jewish **Tanakh** that includes the twelve **minor prophets** (Hosea through Malachi).

books of the former prophets (5) – the historical books of Joshua, Judges, 1–2 Samuel, and 1–2 Kings.

books of the latter prophets (5) – the prophetic books of Isaiah, Jeremiah, Ezekiel, and the book of the Twelve Prophets.

canon and **canonical** (Prologue) – "canon" is a collection of books that are recognized as divinely inspired scripture by a given religious community. Such books are recognized as "canonical."

chiasm (4) – a circular literary form that moves through a set of themes to the center (e.g. A, B, C, D) and then goes through similar themes in reverse order after the center (e.g. D', C', B', A'). Major emphasis is often put on the texts that occur at the center of a chiasm.

client kings (9) – Roman-appointed local leaders who ruled the provinces of Rome for the emperor (considered their "patron"), allowing some level of independence for the province and extended influence by Rome.

conjectural emendation (Prologue) – a correction of the biblical text proposed by scholars that is not based on any **manuscript witness**.

couplet (3) – along with the less common **triplet**, a basic unit in Hebrew poetry, where the first line is paralleled, contrasted, or otherwise **seconded** by the climactic second line. Many translations identify the second line of a couplet by indenting the beginning of the line a few spaces.

Covenant Code (3) – a set of early laws embedded in Exod 20:22–23:33 that (apart from some late additions) seem to predate later regulations asserting the requirement to worship Yahweh in just one place (e.g. Deut 12; cf. 2 Kings 22–3). The parallels between the topics of these laws and large portions of the Code of Hammurabi are an indicator that some form of this collection may have been composed already in the early monarchal period, e.g. tenth or ninth century BCE.

critical masculinity studies (14) – with respect to the Bible, analysis of how biblical writings construct ideas about manliness and how these constructions relate to hierarchical systems of gender injustice.

cultural criticism (15) – when applied to the Bible, study of the many ways in which biblical texts are reflected or used in different cultural contexts. Often the focus is on the use and interpretation of the Bible in popular culture, a focus that distinguishes cultural criticism from **history of interpretation**.

cultural memory (2) – a common set of memories, taught to each generation and celebrated in common rituals, that helps define a group by its shared past.

Cyrus cylinder (7) – a proclamation by the Persian king Cyrus that he was appointed by the Babylonian gods to liberate the Babylonians and rebuild their temples. It shows many parallels to the Cyrus proclamation quoted in Ezra 1:1–4 that Yahweh had appointed him to rebuild the Temple and allow the Judeans to return home.

destruction of Jerusalem (1) – 586 BCE: a climactic event in the history of Judah, including the destruction of Solomon's Temple and the end of the holy city many thought to be invulnerable.

destruction of the Second Temple (1) – 70 CE: occurred in the wake of a Jewish revolt against Rome and – along with the total destruction of Jerusalem in 135 CE after another revolt – represented the end of the local Jewish temple state and the recentering of much Jewish life in the communities outside the land.

deuterocanonical books (Prologue) – books recognized as **canonical** by the Roman Catholic church, but not part of the Jewish **Tanakh** or Protestant **Old Testament**.

Deutero-Isaiah (6) – see **Second Isaiah**.

Deuteronomistic (5) – adjective describing biblical texts that feature terminology and/or theology similar to that permeating the book of Deuteronomy.

Deuteronomistic history (5) – a historical work that is hypothesized to have extended from Moses's speech to Israel on the edge of the land (Deuteronomy) through the books of Joshua, Judges, 1–2 Samuel, and 1–2 Kings to Judah's eventual exile from the land at the end of the books of Kings. Though incorporating potential earlier blocks of tradition (e.g. a possible early "Succession Narrative"), this broader history of Israel in the land is dominated by the later theology articulated most clearly in Deuteronomy.

Deutero-Pauline (10) – designation for the disputed Pauline epistles 2 Thessalonians, Ephesians, and Colossians. See **disputed letters** of Paul.

diaspora (15) – the "scattering" or dispersion of Jews throughout lands outside of Palestine, particularly during the **Babylonian exile** in the sixth century BCE and after the end of the **Jewish War** in 70 CE.

disputed letters (of Paul) (10) – Pauline letters whose authorship is disputed on the basis of difference in tone, language, or theological positions, or because the letter presupposes a stage in the institutional organization of the Jesus movement that likely postdated Paul. These letters include 2 Thessalonians, Colossians, Ephesians, 1 and 2 Timothy, and Titus.

divine council (6) – the idea that the divine world is organized on analogy with a human monarchal court, with a divine king, his consort, his officials, and other parts of his administration. This idea is reflected in many non-biblical texts as well as in the Bible itself.

Documentary Hypothesis (6) – a hypothesis that the Pentateuch was formed out of the combination of a limited number of earlier written sources. In its oldest and most commonly known form, this hypothesis held that the Pentateuch was formed from four source documents: **J**, **E**, **D**, and **P**, but many scholars now doubt whether extended, early **J** and **E** sources are identifiable or even existed. This leaves only **D** and **P** as agreed-upon earlier sources of the Pentateuch along with a block of non-Priestly material in the Pentateuch whose origins are debated.

dynamic equivalence translation (Prologue) – a translation that aims to produce a meaning-for-meaning translation of a (biblical) text, diverging from a word-for-word translation as necessary to produce a meaning more equivalent to the original language than a word-for-word translation would render.

E (6) – see **Elohistic Source**.

ecological biblical criticism (or ecological hermeneutics; 6) – diverse biblical approaches that share a focus on analysis of biblical texts in relation to ecology and current environmental challenges. Some approaches aim to provide more ecofriendly readings of biblical texts, while others focus on ways that biblical texts – written in a quite different time – can prove problematic resources for guiding present action.

ekklesia (12) – a common Greek word, meaning "assembly" or "gathering," that could be used for civic assemblies, Greco-Roman **voluntary associations** and synagogue groups. It is often translated as "church," its later meaning.

El (2) – the name of the head creator god of the Canaanite pantheon, husband of **Asherah**.

election theology (2) – a set of beliefs surrounding God's choosing of and special protection of a people, Israel. Distinguished from **Zion theology** by its focus on God's relationship to a people rather than a place (Jerusalem).

Elohistic source (6) – a *hypothesized* source of the **Pentateuch** (no separate copies have been found) that many scholars think is preserved in parts of Genesis 20–2 and other **non-Priestly** parts of the Pentateuch where the divine designation "Elohim" predominates (the **Priestly source** also uses Elohim for God in Genesis, but is seen as distinct from this Elohistic source). According to this hypothesis, this Elohistic source was composed in the north of Israel sometime in the late ninth or eighth century, thus coming from a later time and different place from the **Yahwistic source** (**J**). This textbook is one of a number of recent treatments that has discarded the idea that there is an identifiable **E** source in the Pentateuch, but there are still many references to this hypothesized source in past and some recent scholarship.

empire (2) – as analyzed in this textbook, a form of ancient social organization where a particular monarchal state dominated other states through amassed military power (often drawing on the resources of subject states), creation of interlocking economic networks, and propagandistic use of terror, or in the case of Rome, a rhetoric of peace and salvation.

eschatology (9 and 10) – an aspect of theology that is concerned with the end of the world, the end of humanity, or the end of the current order of the world.

feminist (biblical) criticism (1, 3 and 14) – applied to the Bible, a range of methods aimed at addressing women's inequality, including analyzing biblical depictions of women (or lack of these depictions), the use of feminine imagery in the Bible, and the effects of patriarchal interpretations of the Bible.

formal correspondence translation (Prologue) – a word-for-word translation of a (biblical) text.

form criticism (1, 7) – the study of different types of texts, **genres**, in the Bible along with their typical social settings and purposes.

former prophets (5) – see **books of the former prophets**.

fulfillment citations (12) – the repeated claim that aspects of Jesus's life story "happened in order to fulfill" or actualize the words of the **Torah** and the prophets. These citations constitute a distinctive emphasis in the Gospel of Matthew.

gender criticism (14) – applied to the Bible, the analysis of the ways gender categories function in biblical texts, not just in terms of male and female characters, but also with respect to gendered metaphors, images, and even sacrificial animals.

genre (7, 15) – a type of text, such as a **lament psalm** or **prophetic call narrative**, or an **apocalypse**.

Greco-Roman period (9) – with respect to the New Testament, the period beginning with the Roman invasion of Palestine in 63 BCE, characterized by the ongoing influence of Greek culture (including art, architecture, social organization, and values) in the broader Mediterranean world during a time of Roman rule.

H (6) – a designation either for the **Holiness Code** in Leviticus 17–26 or for a broader layer of material in the **Pentateuch** that is characterized by the central emphases of Leviticus 17–26 (e.g. the importance of Israel's holiness).

Hanukkah (8) – the Jewish holiday celebrating the rededication of the **Second Temple** by Judas Maccabeus in 164 BCE after it had been temporarily transformed by Antiochus Epiphanes IV into a temple to Zeus Olympius.

Hasmonean monarchy (1) – 142–63 BCE: the period of rule of members of the Hasmonean priestly family descended from Judas Maccabeus, who led a successful rebellion against the Hellenistic rule of Antiochus Epiphanes IV.

Hasmoneans (8, 9) – a provincial priestly family who led a revolt against Antiochus Epiphanes IV and eventually founded the **Hasmonean monarchy**.

Hebrew Bible (Prologue) – scriptures shared by Jews and Christians.

Hellenistic period (1, 8) – 332–167 BCE: a period when, following the conquest of the Persian empire by Alexander, Palestine was ruled by a succession of Greek kings based in Egypt (the Ptolemies), Anatolia (contemporary Turkey), or Mesopotamia (the Seleucids).

historical criticism (1) – a family of historical methods that analyzes how and where the biblical texts (and oral traditions in them) were composed.

historical Jesus (9) – the Jesus who is the person behind, but still separate from, the narratives about him in New Testament writings. Scholars have drawn conclusions about the historical Jesus by paying attention to the ways these texts contain overlapping and distinctive traditions about Jesus's life and teachings, and by applying the methods of **historical criticism** to these traditions.

history of (biblical) interpretation (1 and 3) – study of how biblical texts have been interpreted, especially in faith communities (e.g. Judaism, Christianity, Islam).

history of religions (6) – a term used in biblical scholarship to refer to the study of ideas and themes relating to gods and ritual in ancient Near Eastern cultures outside Israel so that we might better understand biblical religious ideas and practices.

Holiness Code (6) – a collection of laws in Leviticus 17–26 *hypothesized* to have once existed separately (no separate copies have been found) and characterized by a frequent focus on the need for the people of Israel to preserve its holiness. Many recent scholars now think that the language and themes predominant in Leviticus 17–26 are characteristic of a broader layer of **H** material spanning the rest of material in the **Pentateuch** assigned by others to **P**.

holy war (5) – a concept, shared by peoples surrounding Israel, of a war where all of the spoils of conquest – both people and property – are consecrated to the deity and destroyed.

honor (vs. shame) (13) – a cultural value in the ancient Mediterranean that emphasizes personal or family status and reputation in the community.

household codes (10) – in Colossians (3:18–4:1), Ephesians (5:21–6:9), Titus (2:1–10), and 1 Peter (2:18–3:7), specific codes of conduct for how members of households in the community (including husband, wife, children, and slaves) should behave toward one another. These instructions generally mirror common expectations of behavior in Greco-Roman households, which means a strict social hierarchy of the patriarch over wife, children, and slaves (in more or less descending order).

hybridity (5, 8, 13 and 15) – a concept drawn from postcolonial theory that designates the blending of self-determination with elements drawn from the culture of a past or current oppressor. Different from a mere blending of diverse cultural elements in identity, hybridity refers to the complex identity formed in the midst and wake of the experience of domination.

ideological criticism (1) – the analysis of ways that biblical texts can be, have been, and should be read in the midst of systemic structures of power. As such it overlaps with other methods (e.g. **history of [biblical] interpretation**), but with a particular accent on analysis of ideology and power.

incarnation (14) – within the study of the New Testament, the idea of God becoming human and fully embodied in the person of Jesus, signaled especially by the Johannine phrase "word made flesh" (John 1:14).

intercalation (11) – sometimes called a "sandwich" structure; a narrative technique regularly used in the Gospel of Mark, in which one story or episode is interrupted in the middle by another, complete episode, followed by the ending of the first one. The "inside" episode often offers an interpretation or complication of the story that enfolds it.

intertextuality (6) – a word used to refer to the myriad ways different texts can be related to each other. It can refer to conscious or unconscious ways that texts draw on the wording of earlier texts, but also to the ways that the readings of any text can be influenced by what the reader (or reading community) knows of other texts, whether texts dated before or after the text being read.

Israel (1) – two meanings: refers more narrowly to the tribal groups settled in the northern highlands of Canaan or more broadly to Judah (in the south) along with those northern groups.

Israelite (1) – a person who was part of ancient Israel, including Judean individuals who identified themselves as the true heirs of ancient Israel. Should be distinguished from Israelis, who are members of the modern state of Israel.

J (3 and 6) – the one-letter designation of the hypothesized **Yahwistic Source**. The prominent use of the divine "Yahweh" in the Yahwistic Source is only one indicator used to argue for the existence of the source, but it has led to the frequent designation of the source as "J" (the German letter for the "y" sound at the outset of Yahweh).

Jewish War (11) – the war between the Jews of Palestine and the Romans that began in 66 CE with an armed revolt by the Jews, and ended with the destruction of the **Second Temple** and the sack of Jerusalem in 70 CE.

Johannine sectarianism (14) – the idea, derived from the sociological study of religion, that the Gospel and Letters of John are products of a "sect," in this case a distinct group that perceived itself as the unique bearers of the truth about Jesus.

Josiah's reform (5) – approximately 623 BCE: a socio-religious reform that Josiah is said to have undertaken in the wake of the decline of Assyrian influence over the area (2 Kings 23; compare 2 Chronicles 34), eliminating sanctuaries outside Jerusalem and laying claim to some of the territories of the former northern kingdom.

Judith (book of) (8) – a deuterocanonical book that tells a story of how a female heroine, Judith, saved the people of Judah by seducing and killing a general of the Assyrian army, named Holofernes. The tale is unhistorical, likely crafted during the Hasmonean period to stress the ability of Judeans to repel powerful foreign enemies.

King James Version (Prologue) – an authorized translation of the Christian Bible completed under royal sponsorship by the Church of England in 1611.

L (6) – a term used in this textbook to designate a layer of late (especially exilic) **non-Priestly** Pentateuchal material written by lay scribes that reshapes earlier traditions about the primeval history, Israel's ancestors, and the Israelites under Moses. This layer adds promise, blessing and other themes to those traditions in order to address the concerns of later Judeans, especially during the Babylonian exile.

lament psalm (7) – a type of psalm that is a cry for God's help and typically includes most of the following elements: complaint, plea for help, vow, statement of trust in God's help, and thanksgiving for God's help. Though some refer to such lament psalms simply as "laments," the cry for help typical of a lament psalm is distinguished from a lament proper by the fact that it does not mourn something that is already finished (e.g. a death). Instead, it is a plea that things may get better. Because of this difference, some scholars prefer to call these lament psalms complaints or supplications.

literary criticism (1, 4) – the use of methods from modern study of literary texts (e.g. attention to plot, characterization, signification) to illuminate the poetic-narrative dynamics of biblical texts.

LXX (Prologue) – an abbreviation for **Septuagint**.

Maccabees (1 and 8) – another word for the **Hasmoneans**.

major prophets (4 and 5) – the three larger prophetic books: Isaiah, Jeremiah, and Ezekiel.

manuscript witness (Prologue) – an ancient copy of a biblical book or quotation of a biblical book (in the original language or translation).

Markan priority (10 and 11) – the theory that the Gospel of Mark was the first written of the synoptic gospels and was used as a source by the authors of Matthew and Luke.

Masoretic text (Prologue) – the authoritative version of the Hebrew text of the **Tanakh** or Hebrew Bible produced by Jewish scribes in the medieval period and used as the base text in most translations.

messiah (7) – a Hebrew word meaning "anointed one," which during the **Second Temple** period came to designate a hoped-for anointed king who would deliver Jews from domination and/or a hoped-for anointed priest to replace the priests in Jerusalem who were perceived by some to be corrupt.

messianic secret (11) – a recurring pattern in the Gospel of Mark in which Jesus urges secrecy about his miracles of healing or about his identity.

minor prophets (4) – twelve smaller prophetic books (Hosea, Joel, Amos, Obadiah, Jonah, Micah, Nahum, Habakkuk, Zephaniah, Haggai, Zechariah, and Malachi) that follow the three books of the **major prophets** (Isaiah, Jeremiah, Ezekiel) in the Jewish **Tanakh** and appear at the end of the Old Testament in the Christian Bible.

monarchal city-state (2) – a state based in a walled city (and often supported by other fortified settlements) and ruled by a hereditary monarchic dynasty. This ancient form of social organization allowed an amassing of military resources and wealth not possible for more decentralized tribal groups.

monotheism (6) – a term referring to the belief that there is only one god and that all other gods are false. This is to be distinguished from the idea, attested up through the late pre-exilic period, that a given people should worship only one god among the various gods that exist, an idea sometimes designated as "henotheism."

moral act-consequence (3) – the idea that the cosmos is morally coherent; that is, morally good actions eventually lead to good results for the doer(s), while morally bad actions lead to disaster.

MT (Prologue) – an abbreviation for the **Masoretic text**.

neighboring monarchies (1) – 930–722 BCE: a time when there were separate, related monarchies in the south (based in Jerusalem and ruled by descendants of David) and the north (ultimately based in Samaria and ruled by a variety of royal dynasties).

New Perspective on Paul (10) – an interpretive approach to the Pauline letters that focuses on Paul's concern for gentile inclusion in God's plan of salvation. The approach refutes earlier interpretations that caricatured ancient Judaism as legalistic religion in contrast to the Christianity as a religion of grace.

non-Priestly and non-P (6) – term used to refer to texts in the **Pentateuch** not assigned to P. It is used by scholars who no longer posit the existence of the early **J** and **E** sources.

Old Testament (Prologue, 8) – Christian term for the scriptures originating in ancient Israel. It and the Jewish **Tanakh** contain nearly identical books, but the order of the (Christian) Old Testament culminates in Malachi's prophecy of Elijah (leading into Matthew 3).

oral traditions (2, 9) – traditions important at every stage in the formation of the Bible, especially if one includes the oral aspects of written traditions, since even the latter often were memorized and performed. More specifically, we see some reflections in the written traditions of the Bible of exclusively oral traditions, and these reflections are the typical focus of biblical **tradition criticism**.

P (3 and 6) – see **Priestly Source**.

Palestine, Palestinian (1) – "Palestine" is a designation that the Romans came to use for a province including the land of Israel and much of Syria. The word "Palestinian" was used to characterize inhabitants of that province and continues to be used to refer to descendants of non-Jewish people who lived in the region prior to the establishment of the modern state of Israel.

parables (9) – brief, open-ended, comparative stories using metaphor that invite the listener to make conclusions about the nature of the comparison being offered. Jesus is depicted as speaking in parables in the **synoptic gospels**, often comparing the kingdom of God to everyday people, things, and events.

Paraclete (14) – the figure that Jesus describes in the **farewell discourse** of the Gospel of John, who Jesus promises he will send to comfort and guide his disciples after he departs. In 1 John 2:1, Jesus is described as a "paraclete."

passion narrative (11) – from *passus*, a Latin word for "suffering"; the story of Jesus's trial, suffering, and death in the canonical gospels. An independent passion narrative may have predated Mark's gospel.

passion predictions (11) – the instances in the gospels in which Jesus, referring to himself as the "son of Man," anticipates his own approaching suffering and death. Jesus does this three times in Mark, in keeping with Mark's preferred pattern of repeating important information in triplicate.

Pastoral Epistles (10) – 1 and 2 Timothy and Titus, called "pastorals" because they are addressed to particular leaders within communities of Christ-followers with instructions for those communities. The Pastoral Epistles were likely written in the second century CE. See **disputed letters** of Paul.

Paul within Judaism (10) – an interpretive approach to the Pauline letters that assumes Paul was a Torah observant, Jewish Christ-follower. Advocates of this approach argue that Paul's negative statements about the Jewish law pertain to gentiles, but not to Jews.

Pentateuch (Prologue, 3, 6, and 7) – the first five books of the Bible, namely Genesis, Exodus, Leviticus, Numbers, and Deuteronomy, otherwise known as the (written) **Torah**.

Persian period (1) – 538–332 BCE: a time of Persian rule of Judah, when the Persians are recorded in the Bible as helping the Judeans who returned to rebuild the Temple and walls of Jerusalem and establish the **Torah** as the authoritative law of the returnee community.

Platonic theory of forms (15) – Plato's theory that non-material abstract forms possess a higher form of reality than the material world of sense perception.

postcolonial criticism (1, 5, 14) – study that examines ways in which texts such as the Bible were formed in imperial contexts and/or how biblical texts later functioned in colonial or imperial contexts (e.g. missionary efforts).

post-exilic period (1) – from 538 BCE: the period following the forced exile to Babylonia, starting with the **Persian period**. Often the Persian period is the primary one meant when referring to the post-exilic period. Note: despite the term *post*-exilic, it is clear that many Judeans still lived outside the land after 538 BCE.

pre-state tribal period (1) – 1250–1000 BCE: a time when Israel lived in villages (joined loosely in larger tribal affiliations) in the hill country without any monarch over them.

Priestly Source (3 and 6) – a *hypothesized* source of the **Pentateuch** (no separate copies have been found), that most scholars agree contained texts such as the Genesis 1 creation story, genealogies such as Genesis 5, a strand of the flood narrative where no sacrifice happens (e.g. Gen 6:9–22 to 9:1–17), the covenant of circumcision with Abraham (Genesis 17), the second call of Moses (Exod 6:2–8), the whole section about Sinai (Exodus 19 to Num 10:10), and many other texts in Genesis–Numbers with similar language and themes (though not all focusing on priests). Though this layer contains much earlier traditions, most scholars agree that the broader Priestly Source was not composed until the **Babylonian exile** or early **post-exilic period**.

primeval narrative (3) – the stories of creation, flood, and other events concerning early humanity in general found in Genesis 1–11.

pronouncements (9) – short, direct sayings in the form of sharp responses to tricky questions posed by one's rhetorical opponent. The gospels feature Jesus offering such retorts to his opponents.

prophetic call narrative (4) – a story, usually told in the first person, where a prophetic figure tells of how he was authorized by God to be a prophet, usually including some or all of the following elements: an appearance of God, introductory words by God to the one to be called, call of the prophet, objection by the prophet that he is somehow unfit for the task, divine reassurance, and sign reinforcing the divine reassurance. Examples include Isaiah 6; Jer 1:4–10; and Ezekiel 1–3, though some scholars dispute whether some of these texts are proper "call narratives," and disagree about whether "call" (a term whose home is in later Christian theology) is appropriate for these ancient Hebrew narratives.

protomonarchy (1, 3) – early tenth century (900s) BCE: the time when David and Solomon ruled Israel from Jerusalem, beginning to develop the structures (standing army, fortified base) characteristic of an ancient city-state monarchy.

Psalter (7) – another word for the book of Psalms.

pseudepigraphy (8, 10) – attribution of a later text to a more ancient author. Such **pseudonymous** attribution was particularly common in the Greco-Roman period, when Judaism came into contact with a Hellenistic culture that was more focused on establishing ancient authorship of authoritative texts.

Q (9) – a *hypothesized* source (Q stands for *Quelle*, the German word for source). The term designates a set of sayings of Jesus found in Matthew and Luke, but not in Mark. Scholars have supposed that this shared material comes from an independent written source that the authors of Matthew and Luke incorporated into their gospels in different ways.

Qur'an (Prologue) – the holiest text in Islam, seen in that faith as the collected recitations by Muhammad, the prophet, of direct revelations from God. These recitations on ethical and theological matters sometimes refer to biblical traditions, often as filtered through early Jewish and/or Christian interpretation of those traditions.

realized eschatology (14) – the notion in the Gospel of John that the judgment and salvation of the last days is an already present reality for the believer. This is particularly seen in Jesus's words to the Samaritan woman, "The hour is coming and is now here" (John 4:23), as well as in the "I am" statements that emphasize Jesus's incarnational presence.

rebuilding of the Jerusalem Temple (7) – 515 BCE (completion), described in the Bible as done over a period of years with Persian sponsorship: this **Second Temple** represented an important center of leadership and social organization in **post-exilic period** Judah in the years after the destruction of the monarchy.

reception history (3) – designates the study of the variety of ways that texts are used over time, in both textual and other media (e.g. art, drama, film) as well as in various faith community and other contexts. It thus encompasses the range of both **history of interpretation** and **cultural criticism**.

redaction (3) – a form of ancient textual revision involving the expansion of an older text and/or the linking of different texts with each other. The word "redaction" can refer both to the process of such revision and to the material that is added.

redaction criticism (3) – the attempt to identify the ways in which the scribal authors or redactors of the present biblical books created those books through arrangement, transformation, and extension of earlier source materials. It is a form of **transmission history**.

royal psalms (3) – a set of psalms in the **Psalter** that focus on the king and God's special relationship to him. See **royal theology**.

royal theology (3) – a set of beliefs and images surrounding God's appointing of the king as ruler and high priest, God's equipping of the king with power, justice, and blessing, and God's granting the king anything he wishes, particularly military victory and long life.

seconding (3) – a term coined by James Kugel in *The Idea of Biblical Poetry* (New Haven: Yale University Press, 1981) for the multiple and complex ways that the final line of a **couplet** or **triplet** can build on the meaning of the initial lines of the given poetic unit. Many find this to be a more flexible and accurate designation for this phenomenon in Hebrew poetry than older and more commonly used terms such as "parallelism."

Second Isaiah (6) – alternatively **Deutero-Isaiah**: term used to refer to chapters 40–55 of the book of Isaiah, a section that shows many signs of being composed during the time of the **Babylonian exile** (with parts possibly even later). Few scholars today think that the author of these later chapters was named "Isaiah." The term "Second Isaiah" reflects the fact that this portion of the book of Isaiah was the first one to be distinguished from the words of the first "Isaiah," which are now to be found particularly in portions of Isaiah 1–11 and 28–32.

Second Temple (1, 7) – the Temple rebuilt under Persian sponsorship by 515 BCE and eventually destroyed by the Romans in 70 CE, a center for Judean leadership and social organization throughout the intervening period.

segmentary society (2) – a term designating the kind of decentralized, horizontal social framework that tribal Israel had prior to the onset of the monarchy.

Septuagint (Prologue) – an ancient set of translations of Jewish scriptural books into Greek.

Sermon on the Mount (12) – Jesus's mountaintop speech in Matthew 5–7, in which Jesus is presented as a figure like Moses, interpreting the **Torah** and giving instructions to his followers.

servant songs (6) – a set of texts in Isa 42:1–8; 49:1–6; 50:4–9; and 52:13–53:12 that focus on a "servant" figure. Some scholars have thought these servant songs might represent a separate literary layer in **Second Isaiah**.

Sirach (8) – see **Ben Sira**.

social-scientific analysis (6) – when applied to the Bible, analysis that draws on contemporary sociological and anthropological studies to provide a more nuanced picture of ancient Israel.

source criticism (3) – the attempt to reconstruct (now lost) written sources used by the authors of the present biblical texts. It is a type of **transmission history**.

Special L (12) – material that is found only in the Gospel of Luke.

Special M (12) – material that is found only in the Gospel of Matthew.

suffering servant (9) – the particular image of the **servant** in **Second Isaiah** found in Isa 52:13–53:12, an image that often has been interpreted by Christians to refer to the crucifixion and resurrection of Jesus Christ.

supersessionism (Prologue) – the idea that Christianity and the Christian church have superseded and thus replaced Judaism and the people of Israel.

synoptic gospels (9) – the gospels of Matthew, Mark, and Luke, which have a strong similarity in their story structures and content, as well as some instances of shared exact wording. "Synoptic" means to "see together."

synoptic problem (9) – the question of how to understand the similarities and differences between the **synoptic gospels** of Matthew, Mark, and Luke. See **two-source theory**.

Syro-Ephraimite war (4) – a war occurring around 735 BCE in which Syria and the northern kingdom of Israel laid siege to Jerusalem and thus attempted to force Judah, under King Ahaz, to join a coalition of local states resisting Assyrian rule (though Judah was not yet under Assyrian rule). Ahaz appealed for and received help from Assyria in repelling the Syrian–Israelite alliance, but became subject to Assyria in return for the aid.

Tanakh (Prologue) – the Jewish term for the Hebrew scriptures, referring to the three main parts of those scriptures: the **Torah**, Nevi'im (Hebrew for "prophets"), and **Ketuvim** (Hebrew for "writings"). The arrangement of the Jewish Tanakh culminates in Cyrus's promise to rebuild the Temple at the end of 2 Chronicles.

textual criticism (Prologue) – the collection and analysis of different manuscript readings, e.g. different readings in Hebrew manuscripts and early translations of Hebrew manuscripts of books in the Hebrew Bible.

Torah (Prologue) – the first five books of the Bible, namely Genesis, Exodus, Leviticus, Numbers, and Deuteronomy. Jews often distinguish between this "written Torah" and the "oral Torah" given to Moses, transmitted through the sages, and embodied in the Mishnah and other authoritative Jewish writings.

tradition criticism (1) – the attempt to recover, via the written texts of the Bible, the traditions that stand behind them, usually with a particular focus on the **oral traditions** reflected in the written texts.

tradition history (2) – a history of traditions that existed before and often alongside the written texts now in the Bible. Though such traditions can be written as well as oral, the term often refers primarily to the history of pre-biblical **oral traditions** reconstructed through **tradition criticism**.

transmission history (2) – an umbrella term for the study of the different processes leading up to the final composition of biblical books. It can include **tradition criticism**, **source criticism**, and **redaction criticism**.

trauma (6) – an overwhelming, haunting experience of disaster (or ongoing violence) so powerful in its impact that it cannot be directly encountered and influences an individual's or group's behavior and memory in indirect ways.

trauma studies and the Bible (6) – utilization of insights from psychological, sociological, and other studies of trauma to illuminate the development and ongoing use of the Bible amidst situations of **trauma**.

trickster (2) – a character whose ability to survive through trickery and even lawbreaking is celebrated in religion, literature, or another part of culture.

triplet (3) – along with the more common **couplet**, a basic unit of Hebrew poetry. In it, the first two lines set the stage for the climactic third line. Many translations identify the second and third lines of triplets by indenting the beginning of the second line a few spaces.

tsedeqah (3) – a Hebrew word often translated as "righteousness," but perhaps better rendered as "social responsibility," fulfilling one's obligations to others in society, particularly those most vulnerable.

two-source theory (9) – the theory that Matthew and Luke both drew directly from the Gospel of Mark and the sayings source **Q** to compose their accounts.

undisputed letters (10) – refers to the general scholarly agreement that Romans, 1 and 2 Corinthians, Galatians, Philippians, 1 Thessalonians, and Philemon were written by Paul himself. This conclusion is based on the letters' shared vocabulary, themes, and rhetorical style, as well as their assumed composition dates around the 50s CE.

village (2) – an unwalled settlement inhabited by a few clans (50–300 people total) living in pillared houses in various extended family units. Though this ancient form of social life is introduced in the discussion of pre-state Israel in Chapter 2, it was the most common way for people to live throughout the history of Israel.

voluntary associations (10) – a variety of social clubs, professional guilds, unions, and religious groups that developed in the Hellenistic age. These associations were the center of Mediterranean social life through the Greco-Roman period. The members of the associations met, often in the name of a god, over leisurely meals in which eating, drinking, singing, discussion, and storytelling all took place. In their ancient Mediterranean context, synagogue groups and Christ-followers both within and outside of synagogue contexts can be viewed as types of voluntary associations.

whore of Babylon (15) – female figure in the book of Revelation who personifies the corrupt city of Rome. Revelation 17–18 presents a vision of her violent destruction.

womanist interpretation (3) – builds on and foregrounds the experience, wisdom, and/or biblical interpretation of African American women. As such it is an example of interpretive method linking to the intersection of diverse social identities, in this case gender and race.

Yahweh (1) – the name of the god of Israel, often translated as "LORD" in English translations. This name came to be seen as especially holy in Jewish tradition.

Yahwistic Source (3 and 6) – a *hypothesized* early source of the **Pentateuch** (no copies have been found) that some scholars think starts with the Garden of Eden and materials about Abel and Cain (Gen 2:4b–4:26), continues with a version of the flood story parallel to **P** (e.g. Gen 6:1–4; 7:1–5 to 8:20–22), and goes on to include the story of Noah and his sons, and large portions of the Abraham story (the bulk of Genesis 12–13, 16–19) along with various **non-Priestly** portions of the rest of Genesis, Exodus, and Numbers where the divine name **Yahweh** is used (translated as "LORD" in most English translations). According to this hypothesis, this source was composed in the early monarchal south, probably sometime during the tenth century. *Within this textbook* the probability of the existence of this broader **J**/Yahwistic Source is denied.

Zion (3) – the name of a holy mountain on which the fortress and Temple of Jerusalem stood. It often comes to serve as a synonym for Jerusalem.

Zion psalms (3) – a set of psalms in the biblical **Psalter** that focus on **Zion**/Jerusalem and emphasize themes of **Zion theology**.

Zion theology (3) – a set of beliefs surrounding the idea that God lives in Jerusalem, holds Jerusalem to a high ethical standard, and will prevent Jerusalem from being destroyed by any enemy. Note: this is *not* "Zionist" theology.

INDEX

The letter b after a page reference indicates that the topic appears in a textbox. Page numbers in *italics* refer to illustrations.

Printed in the USA
CPSIA information can be obtained
at www.ICGtesting.com
LVHW081526151123
763634LV00008B/63

9 781119 637059